Harappan Civilization

A Contemporary Perspective

HARAPPAN CIVILIZATION
A Contemporary Perspective

Edited by
GREGORY L. POSSEHL

ARIS & PHILLIPS LTD — WARMINSTER — ENGLAND

In cooperation with
American Institute of Indian Studies

© American Institute of Indian Studies 1982. All rights reserved. No part of this publication may be reproduced, stored in a retrieval system, or transmitted in any form by any means without the prior written permission of the publishers.

British Library Cataloguing in Publication Data

Harappan civilization.
1. Indus civilization
I. Possehl, G.L.
934'.01   DS425

ISBN 0-85668-211-X

Originally published by Oxford & IBH Publishing Co., New Delhi in collaboration with American Institute of Indian Studies.

Published by ARIS & PHILLIPS LTD, Warminster, Wilts, England.
Printed in India by Raj Bandhu Industrial Co., Mayapuri, New Delhi.

Preface

The conference on which this book is based was made possible through the generosity of the government of India and the Archaeological Survey of India. It was held in Kashmir on 22–24 June, 1979. A grant from the Smithsonian Foreign Currency Program provided the funds to the American Institute of Indian Studies, Center for Art and Archaeology that enabled the conference delegates to visit Srinagar, a splendid site for any meeting. The Smithsonian also provided the funds which have made this publication possible. The persons who played key roles in making the conference possible are too numerous to mention individually, however the former Directors General of the Archaeological Survey, Dr. M.N. Deshpande and Dr. B.K. Thapar; Ms. Francine Berkowitz of the Smithsonian Institution and Dr. F.R. Asher, former Chairman of the Art and Archaeology Committee of the American Institute of Indian Studies must be recognized.

The staff of the American Institute of Indian Studies in New Delhi was unselfish in devoting its time and energy to making the conference, and this publication, a success. Mr. P.R. Mehendiratta, Director of the Institute was our constant, patient leader and without his energy and wisdom the venture could not have been the success it was. In New Delhi and Srinagar Mr. L.S. Suri and V. Ram Nambiar saw us through the traumas of living in an unfamiliar environment. Their efforts were largely concerned with matters of travel, accommodations and the duplication of papers—essential matters, the careful execution of which is essential for the peace of mind necessary for intellectual endeavors to succeed.

The editing of the conference papers was done in Philadelphia at the University of Pennsylvania. The excellent typists at the University Museum, Carolan Yarazower and Raymond Rorke, devoted many hours of their time to this book. Raymond Crow, my associate during the Summer of 1980, was unfailing in his devotion to the quality and accuracy of the bibliographies. His sharp eyes and keen mind have made a real contribution to this aspect of the publication. Many of the illustrations were photographically duplicated in the Museum's studio by William Clough and Fred Schoch. The quality of the end product is testimony to their superb skill. Thank you all.

Finally, I must thank the delegates to the seminar for their contributions to furthering our understanding of ancient Indian civilization.

GREGORY L. POSSEHL

Contents

Preface	v
Contributors and Participants	xi
Illustration Credits	xv
List of Abbreviations	xvi

Introduction

B.K. THAPAR: The Harappan Civilization: Some Reflections on Its Environments and Resources and Their Exploitation — 3

GREGORY L. POSSEHL: The Harappan Civilization: A Contemporary Perspective — 15

PART I: The Nature of Harappan Urbanization

1. VISHNU-MITTRE: The Harappan Civilization and the Need for a New Approach — 31
2. JIM G. SHAFFER: Harappan Culture: A Reconsideration — 41
3. S.P. GUPTA: The Late Harappan: A Study in Cultural Dynamics — 51
4. C.C. LAMBERG-KARLOVSKY: Sumer, Elam and the Indus: Three Urban Processes Equal One Structure? — 61
5. K.V. SOUNDARA RAJAN: Motivations for Early Indian Urbanization: An Examination — 69

PART II: Results of Recent Fieldwork

6. JEAN FRANÇOIS JARRIGE: Excavations at Mehrgarh: Their Significance for Understanding the Background of the Harappan Civilization — 79
7. M. RAFIQUE MUGHAL: Recent Archaeological Research in the Cholistan Desert — 85
8. GEORGE F. DALES: Mohenjodaro Miscellany: Some Unpublished, Forgotten, or Misinterpreted Features — 97
9. WALTER A. FAIRSERVIS, JR.: Allahdino: An Excavation of a Small Harappan Site — 107
10. R.S. BISHT: Excavations at Banawali: 1974–77 — 113
11. R.C. AGRAWALA and VIJAY KUMAR: Ganeshwar-Jodhpura Culture: New Traits in Indian Archaeology — 125

12. B.P. Sinha: Harappan Fallout (?) in the Mid-Gangetic Valley — 135
13. Y.D. Sharma: Harappan Complex on the Sutlej (India) — 141
14. R.N. Mehta: Some Rural Harappan Settlements in Gujarat — 167
15. S.A. Sali: The Harappans of Daimabad — 175
16. Jagat Pati Joshi and Madhu Bala: Manda: A Harappan Site in Jammu and Kashmir — 185
17. Y.M. Chitalwala: Harappan Settlements in the Kutch-Saurashtra Region: Patterns of Distribution and Routes of Communication — 197

PART III: Ecology, Technology and Trade

18. Vishnu-Mittre and R. Savithri: Food Economy of the Harappans — 205
19. D.P. Agrawal and R.K. Sood: Ecological Factors and the Harappan Civilization — 223
20. Bridget Allchin: Substitute Stones — 233
21. K.T.M. Hegde, R.V. Karanth and S.P. Sychanthavong: On the Composition and Technology of Harappan Microbeads — 239
22. Marcia Fentress: From Jhelum to Yamuna: City and Settlement in the Second and Third Millennium B.C. — 245
23. Shereen Ratnagar: The Location of Harappa — 261
24. Dilip K. Chakrabarti: 'Long Barrel-Cylinder' Beads and the Issue of Pre-Sargonic Contact between the Harappan Civilization and Mesopotamia — 265
25. Shashi Asthana: Harappan Trade in Metals and Minerals: A Regional Approach — 271

PART IV: Biological Anthropology

26. Kenneth A.R. Kennedy: Skulls, Aryans and Flowing Drains: The Interface of Archaeology and Skeletal Biology in the Study of the Harappan Civilization — 289
27. A.K. Sharma: The Harappan Cemetery at Kalibangan: A Study — 297
28. John R. Lukacs: Dental Disease, Dietary Patterns and Subsistence at Harappa and Mohenjodaro — 301

PART V: The Indus Script

29. Iravatham Mahadevan: Terminal Ideograms in the Indus Script — 311

PART VI: The Later Phases of the Harappan Tradition

30. A. Ghosh: Deurbanization of the Harappan Civilization — 321
31. F.R. Allchin: The Legacy of the Indus Civilization — 325
32. B.B. Lal: West was West and East was East, but When and How Did the Twain Meet? The Role of Bhagwanpura as a Bridge between Certain Stages of the Indus and Ganges Civilizations — 335
33. K.N. Dikshit: Hulas and the Late Harappan Complex in Western Uttar Pradesh — 339

34. S.R. Rao: New Light on the Post-Urban (Late Harappan) Phase of the Indus Civilization in India — 353
35. M.K. Dhavalikar: Daimabad Bronzes — 361
36. Robert Sharer: Did the Maya Collapse? A New World Perspective on the Demise of the Harappan Civilization — 367

PART VII: History of Research

37. Krishna Deva: Contributions of Aurel Stein and N.G. Majumdar to Research into the Harappan Civilization with Special Reference to Their Methodology — 387
38. B.M. Pande: History of Research on the Harappan Culture — 395
39. Gregory L. Possehl: Discovering Ancient India's Earliest Cities: The First Phase of Research — 405

PART VIII: Conclusion

40. Robert H. Dyson, Jr.: Paradigm Changes in the Study of the Indus Civilization — 417

Index — 429

Contributors and Participants

D.P. Agrawal
Physical Research Laboratory
Ahmedabad, Gujarat 380009

R.C. Agrawala
Former Director
Department of Archaeology and Museums
Ram Hiswar Garden
Jaipur, Rajasthan

Bridget Allchin
Center of South Asian Studies
Laundress Lane
Cambridge, England
CB2 1SD

F.R. Allchin
Faculty of Oriental Studies
Cambridge University
Sidgwick Avenue
Cambridge, England
CB3 9DA

Shashi Asthana
Keeper, Archaeology
National Museum
Janpath, New Delhi 110001

N.R. Bannerji
Former Director
National Museum
Janpath, New Delhi 110001

R.S. Bisht
Superintending Archaeologist
Archaeological Survey of India
Srinagar, Kashmir

Dilip K. Chakrabarti
Department of History
Delhi University
Delhi 110007

Y.M. Chitalwala
Superintending Archaeologist
Department of Archaeology
Western Circle
Jubilee Bagh
Rajkot, Gujarat

George F. Dales
Department of South and Southeast Asian Studies
University of California
Berkeley, CA 94720

S.B. Deo
Director
Deccan College
Pune, Maharashtra 411006

M.N. Deshpande
Former Director General
Archaeological Survey of India
c/o Nehru Centre
7th Floor, Sterling Centre
Dr. Annie Besant Road
Worli, Bombay 400018

Krishna Deva
American Institute of Indian Studies
Center for Art and Archaeology
Chief Court House
Ramnagar (Varanasi), U.P. 221008

M.K. Dhavalikar
Joint Director
Deccan College
Pune, Maharashtra 411006

K.N. Dikshit
Superintending Archaeologist
Archaeological Survey of India
Excavations Branch
Purana Qila, New Delhi 110011

Louis DuPree
American Universities Field Staff
Hanover, NH 03755

Robert H. Dyson, Jr.
Department of Anthropology
University Museum
University of Pennsylvania
Philadelphia, PA 19104

Walter A. Fairservis, Jr.
Department of Anthropology
American Museum of Natural History
Central Park West at 79th Street
New York, NY 10024

Marcia Fentress
Department of South and Southeast Asian Studies
University of California
Berkeley, CA 94720

A. Ghosh (Late)
Former Director General
Archaeological Survey of India
Bankuli
Gurgaon Road, New Delhi 110037

S.P. Gupta
Keeper, Central Asian Antiquities
National Museum
Janpath, New Delhi 110001

K.T.M. Hegde
Department of Archaeology and Ancient History
M.S. University of Baroda
Vadodara, Gujarat 390002

Jean-Francois Jarrige
Musee Guimet
6 Place d'Iena
Paris, France 75116

Jagat Pati Joshi
Director, Exploration
Archaeological Survey of India
Janpath, New Delhi 110001

R.V. Karanth
Department of Archaeology and Ancient History
M.S. University of Baroda
Vadodara, Gujarat 390002

Kenneth A.R. Kennedy
Department of Anthropology
Cornell University, Ithaca, NY 14853

Vijay Kumar
Superintendent
Department of Archaeology and Museums
Ram Hiswar Garden
Jaipur, Rajasthan

B.B. Lal
Director
Indian Institute of Advanced Study
Rashtra Pati Niwas
Simla

Carl C. Lamberg-Karlovsky
Department of Anthropology
Harvard University
Cambridge, MA 02138

John R. Lukacs
Department of Anthropology
University of Oregon
Eugene, OR 97403

Madhu Bala
Deputy Superintending Archaeologist
Archaeological Survey of India
Janpath, New Delhi 110001

Iravatham Mahadevan
Vaijayanti
112 Chambers Road
Nandanam
Madras, Tamil Nadu 600035

R.N. Mehta
Head of the Department of Archaeology and
    Ancient History
M.S. University of Baroda
Vadodara, Gujarat 390002

M. Rafique Mughal
Ministry of Education
P.O. Box 43
Bahrain, Arabian Gulf

B.M. Pande
Superintending Archaeologist
Archaeological Survey of India
Western Circle, Mahadev Bagh
Makar Pura, Vadodara

Gregory L. Possehl
Department of South Asia Regional Studies
University Museum
University of Pennsylvania
Philadelphia, PA 19104

Contributors and Participants

S.R. Rao
1233, 34th Cross, IV 'T' Block
Jayanagar, Bangalore 560011

Shereen Ratnagar
Center for Historical Studies
Jawaharlal Nehru University
New Delhi

S.A. Sali
Superintending Archaeologist
Archaeological Survey of India
Janpath, New Delhi 110001

R. Savithri
Birbal Sahni Institute of Palaeobotany
53, University Road
Lucknow, U.P. 226007

Jim G. Shaffer
Department of Anthropology
Case Western Reserve University
Cleveland, OH 44106

Robert Sharer
Department of Anthropology
University Museum
University of Pennsylvania
Philadelphia, PA 19104

A.K. Sharma
Deputy Superintending Archaeologist
Archaeological Survey of India
Pre-History Branch
Old High Court Building, Nagpur

Y.D. Sharma
Formerly Deputy Director General
Archaeological Survey of India
B-16, Kailash Colony
New Delhi

B.P. Sinha
Former Head of the Department of Ancient
    Indian History and Archaeology
Patna University
Patna, Bihar

R.K. Sood
Space Application Center
Ahmedabad, Gujarat 380053

K.V. Soundara Rajan
Additional Director General
Archaeological Survey of India
Janpath, New Delhi 110001

S.P. Sychanthavong
Department of Archaeology and Ancient History
M.S. University of Baroda
Vadodara, Gujarat 390002

B.K. Thapar
Former Director General
Archaeological Survey of India
Janpath, New Delhi 110001

Vishnu-Mittre
Birbal Sahni Institute of Palaeobotany
53, University Road
Lucknow, U.P. 226007

Illustration Credits

Most of the line drawings and photographs accompanying the papers in this book were supplied by each of the authors. The members of the Archaeological Survey of India drew upon the resources of that institution and most of their illustrations are by courtesy of the Archaeological Survey of India. Plate 11.12 is also courtesy of the Archaeological Survey. Plates 35.1, 35.3, 35.4 and 35.5 accompanying M.K. Dhavalikar's paper are courtesy of the National Geographic. Permission to reprint illustrations should be obtained by contacting individual contributors or the appropriate authority.

List of Abbreviations

DSW	Degenerate Siswal Wares
MASCA	Museum and Applied Science Center for Archaeology
NBPW	Northern Black Polished Ware
OCP	Ochre Colored Pottery
PGW	Painted Gray Ware
NBPW	Northern Black Polished Ware

INTRODUCTION

B.K. THAPAR

The Harappan Civilization: Some Reflections on Its Environments and Resources and Their Exploitation

HARAPPAN Culture is a field of study which has fascinated scholars and laymen alike for the past six decades. During this period, which has been marked by an advancement in science and technology, many revolutionary discoveries have been made, admittedly with some indispensable though volatile contributions. But, all have required a search for new interpretations of old evidence. It is fully well known that neither history nor any other human activity can be definitive as long as the human race continues to exist. Thus, new dimensions are being added to knowledge of the Harappan Civilization through fieldwork, conducted both in India and Pakistan and, if I may add, Afghanistan, Iran and the Turkmenian Republic of the U.S.S.R. This has resulted in a serious challenge to the old platitude concerning the homogeneity of this civilization. In fact, it might be said that one is now in a position to see the woods, thanks to the thinning of the trees.

The occurrence of a few sherds of Pre-Harappan type in the Neolithic levels at Burzahom only indicates an as yet isolated contact with the mid-Indus basin and not a cultural spread. Such a phenomenon provides the archaeologist a worthwhile basis for reflection, a reflection on *why* and *where*, and I have chosen for my paper, a germane theme, viz., the environment and resources of the Harappan Civilization.

GEOGRAPHICAL FEATURES

It is widely known that the earliest civilizations of the ancient world, such as the Mesopotamian and the Egyptian, were riverine in their environmental setting. However, the geographical factors relevant to the settlements in the Indus Valley are similar to those between the Mesopotamian lowlands and the Iranian highlands. The greater Indus Valley (Fig. 1) can be divided into two principal divisions: (1) the Baluchistan plateau with the western highlands, represented by Sind Kohistan, Kirthar, and Sulaiman ranges, and (2) the lower Indus Valley, represented by the western and eastern valley sections as well as the delta area. The Thar Desert on the eastern margin of the valley formed an effective barrier, isolating it from the rest of India. The western hill country on the other hand was not a barrier because of the numerous transverse lines of drainage through these mountain ranges which promoted communication from the valley to the Iranian Plateau. The most important of these are the Mula, Muskhat and Bolan Passes.

The Baluchistan Plateau and the Indo-Iranian borderlands, lie beyond this watershed. They had a different ecology, and this was the area that witnessed the early village-town settlements which formed the background for the evolution of cities along the Indus. The barely habitable dry plateau of Iran and Baluchistan drove the highlanders into the fertile valley of the Indus. This movement was possible because of the lower slopes of the Kirthar and Sulaiman ranges falling gently into the plains below.

The rugged and desolate character of the western highlands is accentuated by the extreme sparseness of its vegetation. In spite of the altitude (over 2000

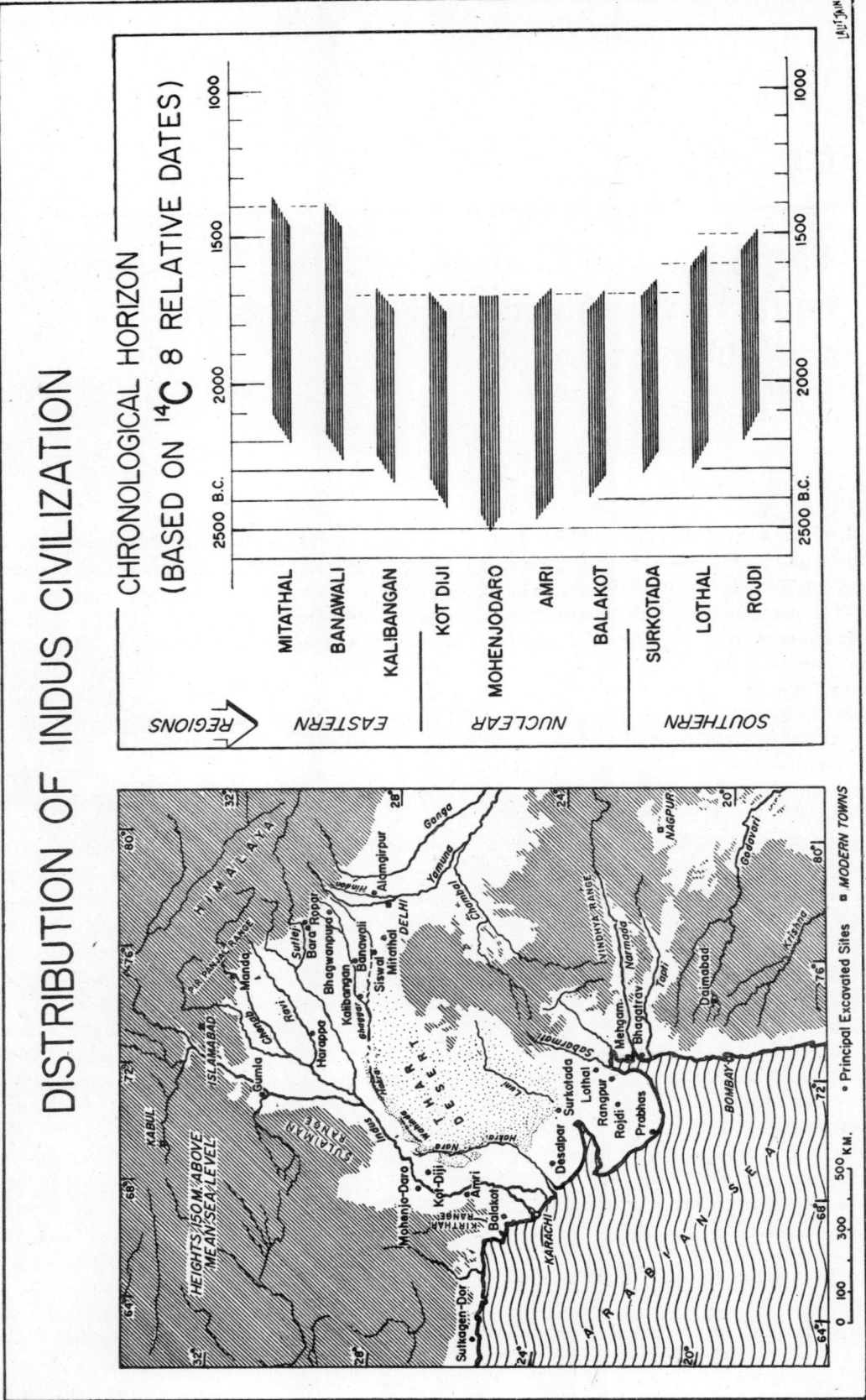

Fig. 1. Distribution of the Indus Civilization.

meters) rainfall is scanty. Nevertheless, it afforded excellent grazing to sheep and goats and to the wild ibex. A noteworthy feature of these hill ranges was the development of gravel slopes at the base of the hills, forming a piedmont zone between the western highlands and the alluvium in the east. The plain immediately adjoining these slopes in the northern sector across the lower reaches of the Bolan River and Nari and Chakar *nais* is known as Kachi. It is formed of alluvium deposited from the hills, quite distinct from that derived from the Indus from which it is separated by a flat desert of clay-like soil known as *pat*. An equally distinct tract, known as the plain of Las, extends about 90 kilometers northwards from the seacoast. It drains an area of considerable magnitude in Kohistan and is composed of alluvium deposited by the Porali, Hab, and Malir Rivers. Yet another potential agricultural area lay about Lake Manchar. This largest freshwater lake in India was the repository of water spilling from the flood-channels of the Indus, including the western Nara as well as the drainage of the hill country.

During periods of inundation, it covers an area of over 500 square kilometers but shrinks to a mere 36 square kilometers as a result of post-monsoonal drying. This periodically changing level of filling and emptying thus affords an excellent arable land for cultivation, especially for the *rabi* crop.

The Indus system, which primarily consists of two rivers, the Indus and the Hakra-Wahinda (modern eastern Nara) along with their tributaries, flows through Sind, Rajasthan, Punjab and Haryana. Both these rivers, especially the latter, have left marks of their old courses or channels (Figs. 2 and 3). These rivers have also been called the Mihran of Sind. The Indus Plain in Sind is a relatively narrow east-west strip about 200 kilometers wide contained by the Thar Desert on the east and the Kirthar Range on the west. The Kachi Plain and Lake Manchar are two distinct ecological regions which have had great influence on the settlement and subsistence pattern of the region.

In the Hakra system (represented by the Naiwal, Hakra, Wahinda and Sottar) which is now largely dried up, excepting the upper part (then represented by the Ghaggar, Sarasvati, Drishadvati) the middle and lower part (now converted into the Eastern Nara Canal), most conspicuous changes have taken place. Various theories have been advanced for this. Some scholars postulate that at one time the River Yamuna flowed westwards through a channel such as the Western Yamuna Canal or the Chautang (ancient Drishadvati) and fed the Hakra, while according to others the Sutlej followed on an independent course into the Hakra. In the alluvial tract of Bahawalpur the existence of several depressions and paleochannels, indicating dried-up river beds, seems to bear testimony to the link between the two rivers perhaps a flow of the flood waters from the Beas-Sutlej link when the latter flowed further south.

The Hakra branch of the great canal system, taking off from the Sutlej at the Sulemanki Weir, perhaps represented the ancient channel of the Sutlej, meeting the Ghaggar a little above Fort Abbas. The Sutlej, a snow-fed river, carried abundant water to the Hakra system through its channel. The added volume of its waters could reasonably be held to account for the much increased width of the Ghaggar-Hakra bed west of Fort Abbas and for the occurrence of ancient sites in a continuous line throughout the Bahawalpur region. The Ghaggar was fed entirely by the monsoons in the Siwaliks, and after its link with the Sutlej ceased, its diminished waters failed to sustain the settlements downstream. The Hakra was a degrading river with a well-cut bed in the alluvium and without a large delta which a river of this size would be expected to form. Although the chronology of stream movement still remains elusive, the observed shifts in the courses seemed to have resulted from "northering" and "westering" with the possibility of the capture of the Yamuna by the Gangetic system.

The Indus, on the contrary, is identified as an aggrading river. Traveling a long distance in the Himalayas, including the chains of Ladakh, it crosses the mountains of Kohistan and Hazara and finally debouches onto the Punjab plains below Darband. Thereafter it is met by tributaries, bringing the drainage of the Hindu Kush (Kabul River), the Sulaiman Range (Kurram, Tochi, Zhob, Gomal Rivers, etc.) and further downstream, at the *panchnad*, a little north of Mithankot, the accumulated waters of the Punjab rivers. The river does not flow directly north-south but makes a deep S-shaped curve, thus adding to its cultivable land. The contours in the northern tracts run almost north-west/south-east, those in the middle, nearly east-west and those in the south approximately north-east/south-west. Being fed both by snow and monsoons periodic flooding has been an important phenomenon of its regimen. The noteworthy features of the lower reaches of the river in the Sind region are: (1) its rushing flow through the

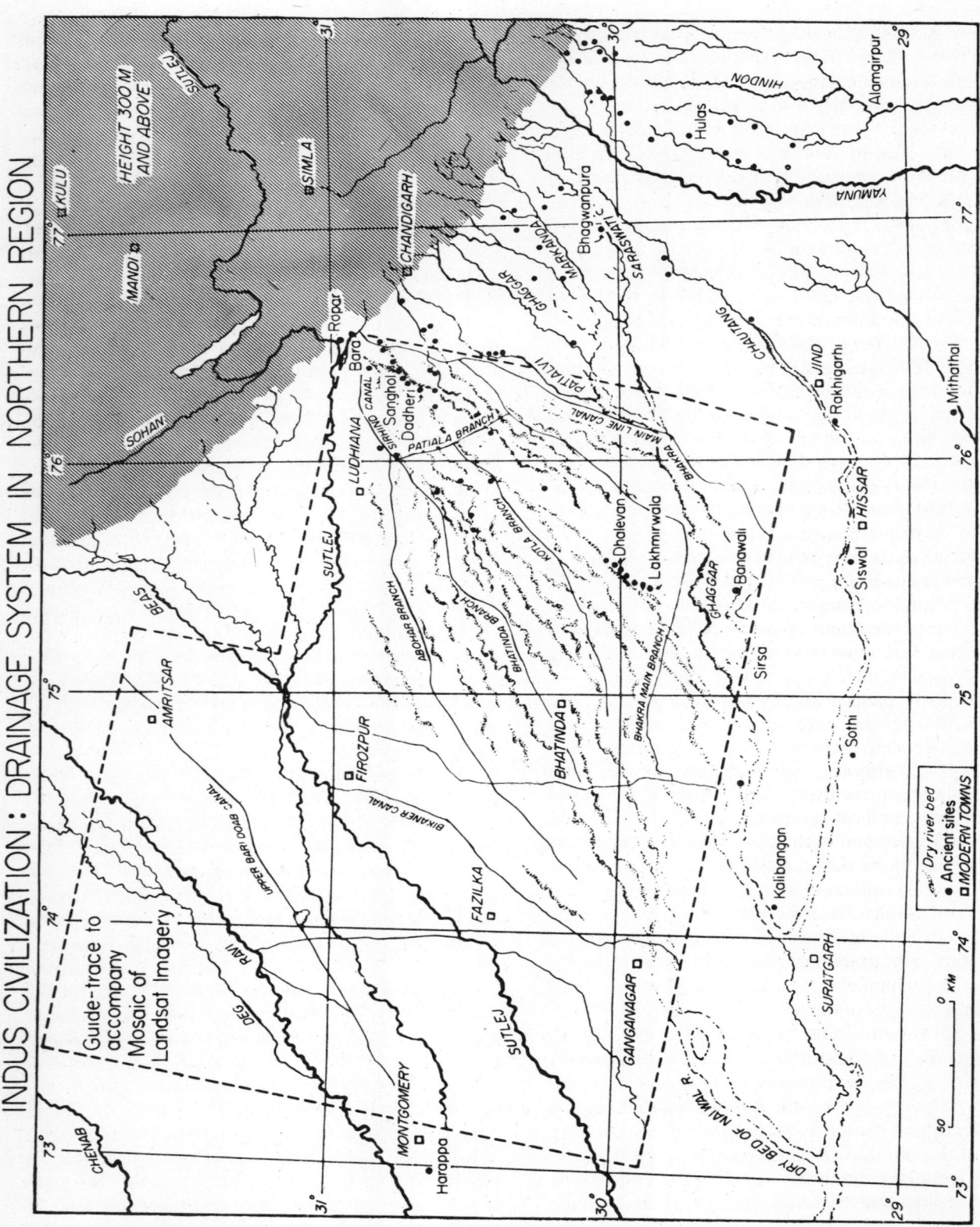

Fig. 2. Indus Civilization: Drainage system in northern region.

Bukkur gap between Sukkur and Rohri in the limestone rocks; (2) the overflow lake of Manchar and the various old channels through which it rushed during the flood season; (3) the curve around the rocky Kohistan defile near Kotri; and (4) the deltaic plain from Thatta south. With the rapid rate of aggradation, the Indus delta is thought to have extended nearly 80 kilometers during the last two millennia. The gradient of the river in the Sind region, 4.8 centimeters per kilometer, which, viewed against the fact that its bed is generally higher than the surrounding plain, and the fall of the country is nearly 13 centimeters per kilometer, makes it prone to periodic flooding. The flood plain sometimes extends to a width of 16 kilometers. This seems to result from two characteristics: (1) the insufficiency of its channel to carry large flood-discharge (ranging from 20 to 40 times than that of the fair weather); and (2) the vast quantity of silt suspended in the water. Excepting between Rohri and Sukkur, where it is confined to a narrow gorge between limestone hills, it has frequently shifted its course as is evident by the existence of abandoned courses, cut-off meanders and braiding channels. In its lower reaches it seems to have shifted nearly 160 kilometers to the west, and it no longer empties into the Rann of Kutch as it is reported to have done during the time of Alexander.

As against this, the rivers of the Punjab have broad alluvial plains with beds below the general level of the flood-plain, and are characterized by high ground between them which is unaffected by the floods. Furthermore, the Punjab is a multiriver system in sharp contrast to the one-river system of Sind. On the basis of landform studies, great changes have been observed in the courses of the Ravi, Beas and Sutlej. In the past the Ravi used to flow further south with its confluence with the Chenab and Jhelum a little below Multan. At one time the Beas also appears to have followed an independent course to the Indus without joining the Sutlej. The existence of this ancient channel is clearly visible in the mosaic of lands on imagery of the area. Due to the "westering" of this river it now joins the Sutlej at Harike.

In India, no Mature Harappan sites have so far been located in the present day valleys of either of these rivers, with the singular exception of Ropar, situated along the left bank of the Sutlej in the foothills of the Siwaliks. It is reasonable to argue, therefore, that the channels of both these rivers have long been erratic and that enduring permanent settlements were not attracted to these valleys during Harappan times. As regards Ropar, communication seems to have been through the Hakra-Ghaggar system, as indicated by the occurrence of a chain of Pre-Harappan and Harappan sites, located in the valleys of the various *chols* and *nais* like Sirhind Nadi, Markanda and Patialvi, all contributing to the Ghaggar system. Some of the Ambala streams even now flow from the Siwaliks close to the Sutlej gorge.

Another distinguishable difference between Sind (including Makran) and the Punjab is the rainfall: the former region receives markedly less annual rainfall (250 millimeters or less, reflective of warm, semiarid and arid conditions) than the latter (500 millimeters or more). However, the Indus in Sind, being snow-fed has two periods of inundation: one in March–April when the snows in the Himalayas melt and the other in August when the lower ranges of the mountains receive the southwestern monsoon. Both the snowfall and the rainfall are, however, variable. Nevertheless, they can provide for the raising of double crops, *kharif* (summer) and *rabi* (winter). Of the Punjab rivers, apart from the Sutlej, the remaining rivers are only partly snow-fed and largely fed by the monsoons; the Ambala streams like Ghaggar and Sarasvati were fed by monsoons in the Siwaliks and lower Himalayas.

In the southern region of the spread of the Indus Civilization (Fig. 4) the prominent rivers involved are the Luni, Banas, Sabarmati, Mahi, Narmada, Tapti and Godavari. These all have different geophysical features which result in small dissected plateaus and scarplands in Kutch and Kathiawad and flat alluvial plains and coastal lowlands and marshes in Gujarat.

The coast of Gujarat, with the exception of South Kathiawad, is generally characterized by tidal flats and saline wastes. The coast of the Gulf of Cambay is very irregular in its outline, projecting deeply inland, thus providing suitable sites for estuarine posts. Lothal is a typical example in this case. The coast from the head of Cambay to Bulsar is irregular in outline, broken by the estuaries of the Mahi, the Narmada, the Kim and the Tapti. The entire coast is marked by tidal flats and saline marshes, locally known as *kharlands*. The Gujarat plains, located between the marshy coastal zone and the plateau and the mountains of the region, are remarkably flat where most of the rivers descending from the highlands change into sluggish meandering streams. An interesting feature of the plateaus of Kathiawad is the occurrence of numerous dykes, sometimes as wide as 60 meters, which afforded raw material for many

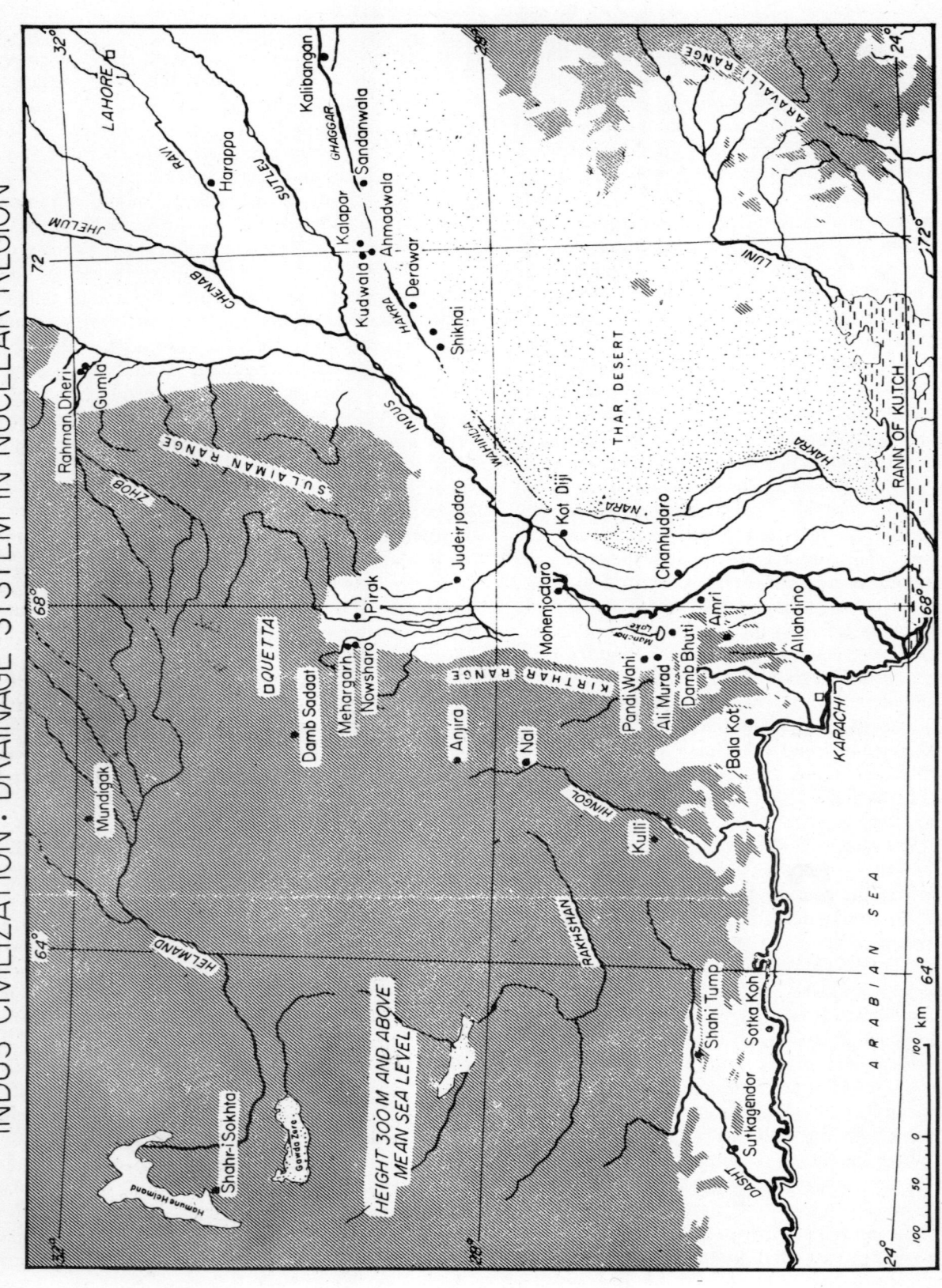

Fig. 3. Indus Civilization: Drainage system in nuclear region.

objects, including beads. The climate of the Kutch and Kathiawad regions varies from extreme aridity in the north to monsoonal conditions in the Cambay region.

The drainage networks of Kutch, Saurashtra (Kathiawad) and the rest of Gujarat are unrelated to one another. This partly explains the regional ramifications of the Indus Civilization in this region. In Kutch, the rivers (having a course hardly longer than 80 kilometers), flow both to the north and to the south from the central highland. They remain dry during the summer but present formidable barriers during floods. Drainage in Saurashtra has a radial pattern: rivers flow out from the central highlands in all directions. With no structural variation, the major rivers have developed a dendritic network. The drainage in the coastal areas is often impeded due to an inadequate gradient. The longest river is the Bahadar which flows westward and empties into the Arabian Sea 30 kilometers south of Porbandar. Rojadi, a Harappan site, is located in its valley. Of the rest of Gujarat, a few rivers like the Banas, Sarasvati and Rupen fall into the Little Rann, while the Sabarmati and Mahi, having their sources in the outliers of the Aravallis, and the Narmada and the Tapti, having catchment areas in different states, flow into the Gulf of Cambay. Both the Sabarmati and Mahi receive tributaries on their left banks, the Sabarmati-Mahi *doab* being essentially drained by the Sabarmati. The drainage pattern is reflective of low rainfall, permeable sandy and gravelly soils and an imperceptible gradient near the mouth. The most important rivers of Gujarat are, however, the Narmada and the Tapti. Of these, the Tapti drains the area of highest rainfall and has a higher economic potential. The lower Tapti Valley is very fertile and is covered with black cotton soil. This perhaps explains the flourishing of the Savalda and the so-called Late Harappan and other cognate Chalcolithic Cultures in this part of the valley.

The drainage of South Gujarat is characterized by parallel rivers (Narmada, Kim, Tapti, Purna, Ambika, Par), kept apart by well-defined interfluves. The mouths of these rivers are affected by tidal flow. The extension of the Harappan influence to the Godavari basin, as reflected by the finds at Daimabad, located on the Parvara in District Ahmednagar of Maharashtra, would thus be only overland through the Tapti Valley.

Paleoclimatic studies have indicated an environment little changed from that of the present day. In fact, the surviving specimens of wood do not support the theory that a moist forest flourished during the Harappan times. As is well known, most of the research on this subject has been done in Rajasthan and Gujarat; but very few pollen diagrams are available. The evidence for the Indus Civilization is largely an extrapolation of this evidence and as such has to be evaluated with caution. An onset of aridity in the eastern region of the Civilization around 1800 B.C. (without affecting the southern regions) has also been postulated as a possible cause for the weathering of the Indus Civilization. I need not discuss here at length the climatic pattern of the Indus Civilization, for detailed studies are available by Gurdip Singh, Vishnu-Mittre and S.K. Seth. Suffice it to mention that the pollen diagrams for the last 10,000 years portray only minor fluctuations within the prevailing dry or arid climate.

RESOURCES AND COMMUNICATION SYSTEM

Sind is devoid of useful minerals except salt, and thus metals of all sorts had to be imported from the hilly regions of Afghanistan, Baluchistan, Makran and Iran on the west and the Aravallis and other mountains in the east. Its chief asset is a rich alluvial soil which requires little tillage or manuring to yield at least one crop annually along with fodder.

Coming to resources and subsistence-related material like chert, sandstone, basalt, granite, slate, bitumen, lapis lazuli, jade, turquoise, copper and tin, it may be stated that some of these items involved long-distance trade through either simple or complex exchange systems. Beginning with copper, one finds that Oman has been mentioned as a source of this Indus metal, largely because of the presence of nickel as a trace element in the ore of the region and the high nickel content in Indus copper-bronze objects. Other copper sources indicated are the Garden Reg in the southern part of Afghan Seistan. Copper could have also been obtained from Khetri as revealed by the comparison of the trace impurity pattern between the Khetri copper mines and the Harappan artifacts. The find of a rich copper-using culture, ascribable to the end of the third millennium B.C., at Ganeshwar in District Sikar (Rajasthan), further supports the possibility of the exploitation of these mines in Rajasthan during the Harappan times. Interestingly enough, Ganeshwar is located in the Drishadvati (Ghaggar-Hakra-Wahinda) system and as such is connected

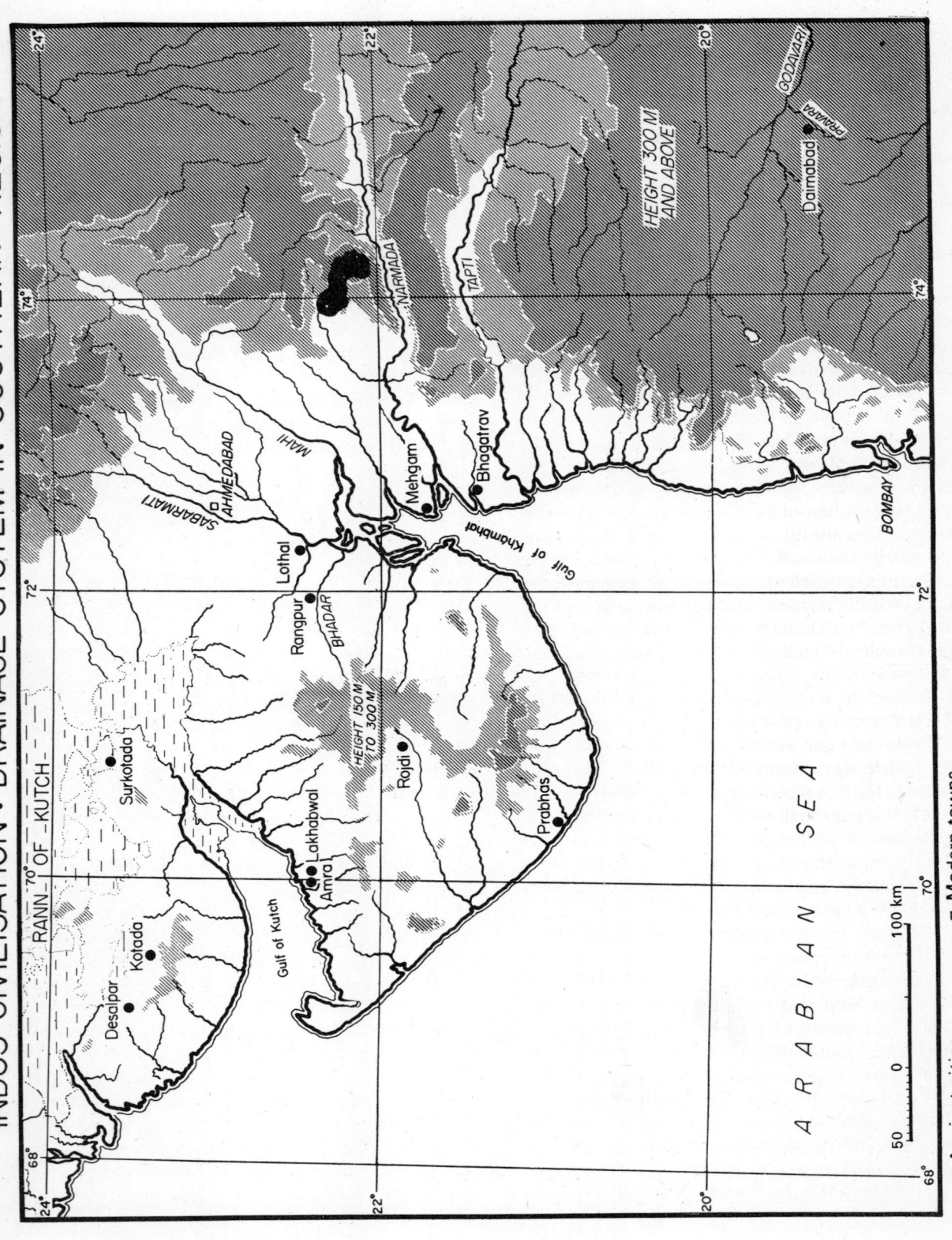

Fig. 4. Indus Civilization: Drainage system in southern region.

with other sites in the same system.

Tin is known to occur in Central Asia, particularly in Farghana, the eastern part of Kazakistan and in Iran. Tin ore deposits are also known to occur in many parts of India: particularly Rajasthan, Gujarat, Bihar and Karnataka. In the context of the present enquiry, one is perhaps concerned with the ore deposits in Rajasthan and Gujarat which may have been exploited during the Harappan times. In both regions these are found in the Aravalli hills: in districts Bhilwara and Udaipur in Rajasthan and in District Banas Kantha in Gujarat. This is particularly significant because of the occurrence of chalcopyrite deposits in the Aravallis. Lapis lazuli is known to occur in the Badakshan region of northeastern Afghanistan. The existence of Harappan pottery and a seal at Shortugai in the Oxus basin confirms the source of Indus lapis lazuli. Turquoise was probably obtained from Khorasan in northeastern Iran and jade from eastern Turkistan. Chert and flint were obtained from the outcrop near Rohri and Sukkur, while the other useful material for querns, mullers, etc., could be obtained from the highland areas. For Sind, the mineral-rich areas were to the west and the north in the hilly regions of Baluchistan and Afghanistan. For the Punjab they were to the northeast in the lower Himalayas including the Aravallis. Steatite, fine-grained yellow Jaisalmer stone and dark gray slate seemed to have come from Rajasthan. Construction timber like pine (*Pinus roxburghii*), deodar (*Cedrus deodar*) and elm (*Ulmus* sp. near *lancifolia*) were doubtlessly transported from the Himalayas. All these resources indicate the mechanism for trade and the routes through which exchange took place. The absence of settlements along a route may not necessarily imply that the route was not used.

Environment and terrain very often determine the lines of communication. The routes followed natural passes, the rivers and hill-streams, or *nais*. Internal communication between the Punjab, Rajasthan and Sind seems to have been largely via rivers, and between Sind and Gujarat, by both land and sea. Sind had access to a greater number of long-distance trade routes through Kirthar, Baluchistan, Kohistan, etc. There are various notches in the folds of the Sulaiman-Kirthar ranges which were utilized as trade routes in the past: the Gomal and Bolan Passes for Seistan and Turkistan across Kandahar and the Hari Rud; the Mula Pass for Central Persia; the Lak Phusi for Makran Baluchistan and Tiz-Lasbela across the Hab which the Arabs used in the eighth century. Besides, the complex folding of the Hindu Kush mountains also afforded some openings on the northwest. Punjab and Rajasthan's trade of greater complexity seems to have taken place via the Indus. This is an important factor to recognize while considering the circumstances for the collapse of the Indus Civilization. Some of the trade was carried out directly, while some was through a middle man.

ANALYSIS OF THE EVIDENCE

From the foregoing it is apparent that the Indus basin evidently provided a significant challenge which seems to have provoked a creative response for the growth and spread of the Harappan Civilization. In bringing the alluvium under cultivation the Indus people produced a surplus which indeed was small and reserved perhaps for use by the privileged minority, and in turn became the economic basis for the differentiation of classes. Human control of the alluvium must have been planned by leaders who had the imagination to work for returns, for they had calculated that the productivity of the alluvial silt would provide the establishment with means of living in comparative affluence, if not leisure. Linked to the emergence of Indus cities are increased levels of specialization of labor; the concept of trade, probably with a medium of exchange; innovations like writing, and that too of an individualistic kind; and the form of monumental architecture.

The settlement pattern during the Indus Civilization was conditioned by: (1) the behavior of the river affording an active and cover flood-plain; (2) navigability of the river, permitting transport for internal trade; (3) climate; (4) accessibility to natural resources and the location on trade routes, including those involving long distances. The expansion of this civilization is explained by the urge to seek out familiar environmental conditions and reach the limits of one ecological zone. The key pieces of land were those that afforded portage from the sea or from one navigable river to the other. Although the seaport stations did develop into urban complexes, their development was conditioned more by strategic location for trading than by the ecological factors. Sites like Manda, Ropar, Gumla, Rahman Dheri, Pandi Wahi, Ali Murad, Damb Bhuti, Hisham Dheri, Nowsharo, Allahdino, Sutkagendor and Lothal are examples of such a pattern. Manda and Ropar were nearest to the source of teak from the Himalayas; Gumla and Rahman Dheri were nearest to the mineral-rich areas; Pandi Wahi, Ali Murad and Damb Bhuti were in the Lake Manchar area; Judeirjodaro and Nowsharo were on the Kachi Plain; Allahdino was close enough to the traditional sea and overland routes; and Sutkagendor and Lothal were on coastal flats.

No sustained work has so far been done to substantiate or refute the central place theory in respect to the spatial spread of this civilization, excepting a rather presumptive suggestion that Mohenjodaro and Harappa represented provincial capitals respectively of the Sind and Punjab provinces of the civilization. In the light of the accruing evidence, this suggestion, however, does not seem to be valid. At the same time, it is seen that the central Indus system (covered by a rough triangle with Mohenjodaro, Kalibangan and Harappa as points) showed a greater concentration of large-sized sites and may thus be taken as the nuclear area of the civilization. We, however, do not as yet fully understand the relation which an Indus "city" maintained with village settlements. In fact no deterministic criterion, excepting perhaps size, exists to classify Indus sites into "cities" and "villages." It is widely known that the various items of cultural equipment of the civilization like pottery, chert weights and blades, copper-bronze objects, beads, terracotta cakes, toy cart-frames, bangles and animal figurines, faience objects, and above all the seals, are marked by an almost compelling standardization which makes it difficult to differentiate objects of the so-called "city" site from those of the village site. The difference is more in the scale or quantity than in quality. The only other apparent distinguishing feature of the city may perhaps be the planned layout and the concept of the citadel, including fortifications.

From the distribution pattern of the sites of the Pre-Harappan genre in the Subcontinent, it would appear that the limits of the ecological zones adopted by the Harappans in the Indus basin were already to a great extent known to their Pre-Harappan predecessors. This is evidenced by the occurrence of Pre-Harappan sites up to Gumla, Sarai Khola and Rahman Dheri in the Indus basin and a chain of Pre-Harappan sites including Sandhanawala, Chabbuwala Ther, Kudwala, Kalepar and Derawar along the ancient course of the Hakra. Then there are Kalibangan, Banawali, Dhalewan, Lakhmirwala, Gurnikalan and Balu in the Sarasvati Valley, and Siswal and Mitathal in the Drishadvati. The credit for responding to the challenge offered by the rivers of the Indus and Hakra system should, therefore, rightly be given to these people. The Harappans perhaps exploited the environments to their best advantage, favorably placed as they were in their organization and better technology.

As pointed out, environmental factors, including the behavior of the river, climate and accessibility of natural resources, were largely responsible for the growth into maturity and expansion of the Indus Civilization. Paradoxically, it is these very factors, in a multicausal framework, which became responsible for the weakening and ultimate collapse of the Indus Civilization. Long distance and internal trade in resource material was badly disturbed, affecting the distribution of raw materials and luxury goods, with the result that the settlements of the far-flung civilization became impoverished in cultural content. Shifts in drainage patterns occurred, resulting from extended pluviality in association with geomorphic changes, either through "westering" or through "northering." The Ghaggar-Hakra-Wahinda system disappeared due largely to the capture of the Yamuna by the Gangetic system. There was wholesale destruction of forests and intensive grazing in the Himalayan foothills. This led to erosion and to the wandering of the water channels due to the raising of their beds through the deposition of detritus. Tectonic disturbances, (1) made the Indus prone to frequent flooding, resulting in the ponding of some parts and consequent rise of the water table in the area, and (2) disrupted the Ghaggar-Nara flow channel, as is evident by the reverse gradient of the river near Manot, resulting in reduction in the supply of water. Eustatic phenomena (coastal uplifts or marine regressions) took place along the northern margin of the Arabian Sea with the result that, (1) some of the old ports, both on the Makran and Kutch-Kathiawad coasts, were left several kilometers inland, and lost their trading role, and (2) the water table receded on inland sites, leading to a decline in civic standards. In the context of environmental syndromes, it would be seen that the phenomena of eustasy, pluviality and aridity produced different reactions in the different physiographic regions, which would perhaps explain the survival and variability of the Indus Civilization in regions like Gujarat, Haryana, the Punjab and contiguous areas of Uttar Pradesh during the first half of the second millennium B.C.

BIBLIOGRAPHY

Agrawala, R.C., 1978
　Archaeological Discoveries at Ganeshwar. *Avagahana* 2 (1).

Allchin, B., A. Goudie and K.T.M. Hegde, 1978
　The Prehistory and Palaeogeography of the Great Indian Desert. London: Academic Press.

Chakrabarti, D.K., 1979a
　Size of Harappan Settlements. In *Essays in Indian Protohistory.* D.P. Agrawal and D.K. Chakrabarti, eds. Pp. 205-15. Delhi: B.R. Publishing Corp.

Chakrabarti, D.K., 1979b
　The Problem of Tin in Early India: A preliminary survey. *Man and Environment* 3: 61-74.

Dikshit, K.R., 1970
　Geography of Gujarat. New Delhi: National Book Trust.

Francfort, H.P. and M.H. Pottier, 1978
　Sondage Preliminaire sur L'Establissement Protohistorique Harappan et Post-Harappan du Shortugai (Afghanistan du N.E.). *Arts Asiatiques* 34: 29-86.

Hegde, K.T.M., 1978
　Sources of Ancient Tin in India. In *The Search for Ancient Tin.* T.A. Wertime and J.S. Olin, eds. Pp. 39-42. Washington D.C.: Smithsonian Institution.

Lambrick, H.T., 1964
　Sind: A general introduction. Hyderabad: Sindhi Adabi Board.

Lambrick, H.T., 1967
　The Indus Flood Plain and the 'Indus' Civilization. *Geographical Journal* 133 (4): 483-94.

Oldham, C.F., 1893
　The Sarasvati and the Lost River of the Indian Desert. *Journal of the Royal Asiatic Society, London,* New Series Vol. 25: 49-76.

Pithawala, Manek, 1959
　A Physical and Economic Geography of Sind. Karachi: Sindhi Adabi Board.

Raikes, Robert, 1965
　Physical Environment and Human Settlement in Prehistoric Times in the Near and Middle East: A hydrological approach. *East and West* 15 (3-4): 179-93.

Raikes, Robert, 1967
　Water, Weather and Prehistory. London: Humanities Press.

Roy Chowdhury, 1943
　The Saraswati. *Science and Culture* 8: 468-74.

Sarma, A.V.N., 1977
　Decline of Harappan Cultures: A relook. *East and West* 27 (1-4): 321-34.

Seth, S.K., 1978
　The Desiccation of the Thar Desert and its Environs During the Protohistorical and Historical Periods. In *The Environmental History of the Near and Middle East Since the Last Ice Age,* W.C. Brice, ed. Pp. 279-305. London: Academic Press.

Singh, G., 1971
　The Indus Valley Culture. *Archaeology and Physical Anthropology in Oceania* 6 (2): 177-89.

Singh, G. et al., 1974
　Late Quaternary History of Vegetation and Climate of the Rajasthan Desert, India. *Philosophical Transactions of the Royal Society, London: Biological Sciences.* 267: 491 ff.

Spate, O.H.K., 1967
　India and Pakistan: A general and regional geography. 2nd ed. London: Metheun.

Stein, Aurel, unpub.
　An Archaeological Tour Along the Ghaggar-Hakra River, 1940-42. Manuscript.

Vishnu-Mittre, 1974
　Plant Remains and Climate from the Late Harappan and Other Chalcolithic Cultures of India: A study in interrelationship. *Geophytology* 4 (1): 46-53.

Vishnu-Mittre, 1976
　Palaeoecology of the Rajasthan Desert During the Last 10,000 Years. *The Palaeobotanist* 25: 549-58.

Wheeler, Sir Mortimer, 1968
　The Indus Civilization. 3rd ed. Supplementary volume to the Cambridge History of India. Cambridge: The University Press.

GREGORY L. POSSEHL

The Harappan Civilization: A Contemporary Perspective

INTRODUCTION

THE most significant intellectual achievement of prehistoric archaeology in the twentieth century has been the emergence of a positivist approach to the past which eschews the impressionistic in favor of the rigor and intensity of systematic research. This has led to the development of explicit research designs which raise intuitive assumptions to a conscious level where they can be critically evaluated. The execution of these research designs has led to rigorous attention to sampling problems, intensive horizontal excavation, and a much-expanded definition of the data which apply to the human past. This is especially true of our awareness of the role which archaeobiological materials can play in understanding past human adaptations. Of equal, if not greater, importance is the realization that archaeological sites and settlement patterns are structures of past ways of life and can be read within their own context. In a real sense the study of the Harappan Civilization has come across this threshold separating the impressionistic from the explicit. There is certainly a vitality to the initiation of new research, if the number of reports on recent field work found in this volume are an indication.

SETTLEMENT PATTERNS

It is no surprise that most of the reports in this volume relate directly to the "mainline" Harappan theme. Dales' report on a little-known excavated area at Mohenjodaro, the so-called Moneer site, is typical in this regard. He even discusses the "downtown" area of the site. The point developed is an interesting, and important one: the notion that the whole lower town at Mohenjodaro can be reconstructed as a reproduction of the classic excavated areas, especially the DK sample, is not very precise, or useful. The Moneer site, although excavated under almost appalling conditions, would seem to be significantly at variance from the DK area in both architecture and some aspects of function. Drawing attention to this part of Mohenjodaro is significant in itself, and one is certain to know much more about it when Dr. Michael Jansen (1979) completes his detailed mapping of the site.

Harappa, the somewhat neglected giant, is an extraordinarily difficult city with which to deal. This is, in part, due to the fact that it was so thoroughly dismantled by railway builders in the nineteenth century. There are simply not very many areas of the site which appear to have a potential for rewarding excavation, but Harappa sits in a rather interesting isolation—a point noted in the papers by S. Ratnagar and M. Fentress in this volume, as well as one of my own (Possehl 1979a). The map (Fig. 1) shows that there are no Harappan sites in the Punjab to the west of Harappa, and it is not as though there has been an absence of exploration in the region. A point, again, covered by me earlier (Possehl 1979a). I am not suggesting that all of the exploration that needs to be done in this region has been completed. But there are many sites of the historic periods known in the area, and a number of competent people—Aurel Stein, A.H. Dani, M.R. Mughal, M.S. Vats to name a few—have worked here. They have been able to find a large number of sites, but none of them is Mature Harappan. There are even Early Harappan sites:

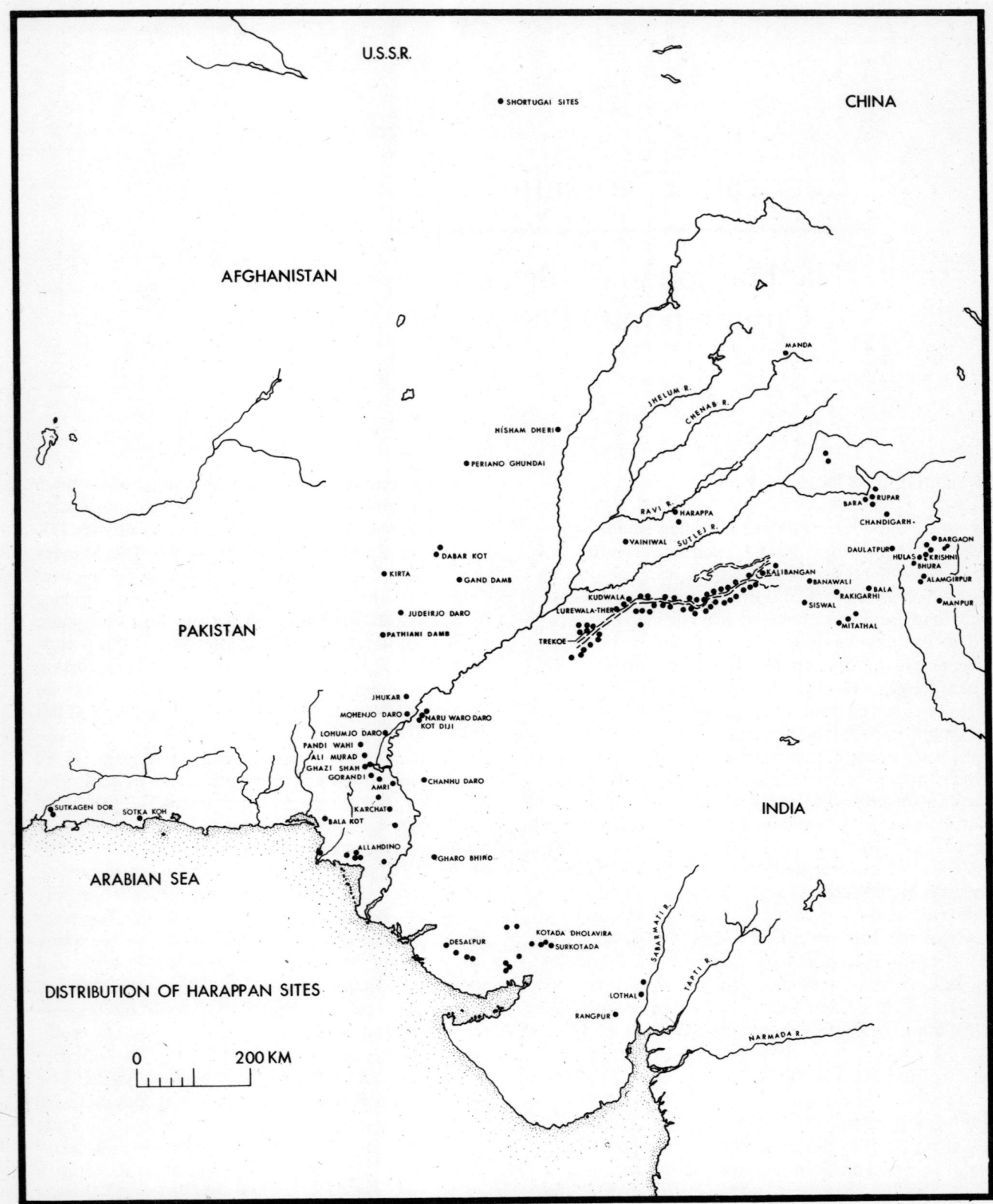

Fig. 1. Distribution of Harappan settlements.
Note: See the paper by M. Rafique Mughal in this volume for a detailed map of sites on the Ghaggar/Hakra and the contribution by M. Fentress for sites between the Sutlej and Yamuna.

Sarai Khola (Halim 1972a and 1972b) Jhang, Musa Khel, Tikrial, Leiah, and the glut of settlements discovered by A.H. Dani (1971) on the Gomal Plain. The work currently underway by the Peshawar/Cambridge team on sites of this period in the Bannu area can be mentioned as well. In other words, there is a large number of prehistoric sites in the region, but none is Harappan.

There can be little doubt that some form of sampling error is in part responsible for this situation. It seems reasonable to presume that there are at least a few Indus village farming communities in West Punjab. In fact, I think one can ascertain where they should be located. Harappa is found on a minor geomorphological anomaly within the entrenchment of the Ravi River. This feature is a finger of high ground which juts into the valley near the alluvium. The settlement was thus both close to cultivable land and more or less safe from floods. It seems reasonable to presume that other sites, predominantly dependent on agriculture for their livelihood, would be found in analogous situations: within the river entrenchment, but high enough to be safe from all but the most severe floods. That sites of this type will be found on the *bars* (high ground between the major rivers) of the Punjab is unlikely, based on both the empirical evidence so far available, as noted above, and from the fact that dry cropping has, historically, not been possible in the area.

Prior to the nineteenth century, when the British dug canals down the spines of the *bars*, and subsidiary channels to their peripheries, the Punjab was inhabited by a large number of what can conveniently be called cattle based, pastoral "tribes." The introduction of massive canals upset this subsistence regime and led to the settlement of these tribes in stable villages and the ascension of wet agriculture as the dominant subsistence form. Given the apparent absence of Harappan village farming communities in the *bars*, and my personal reluctance to imagine that this part of the Punjab was unpopulated during the Harappan times, I have suggested (1979a) that there may have been relatively large numbers of pastoralists in these areas during the prehistoric period as well—a testable proposition.

The area to the south and east of Harappa seems to fit into a much larger settlement context; a topic which will be discussed below. But for the moment one can say that the city is situated on some kind of "frontier," possibly one which separates two different modes of subsistence (and production?) *within* what one can only guess to have been the Harappan polity. S. Ratnagar pursues this approach in her paper and suggests that the city is best viewed as what geographers call a "gateway city." This is a notion which seems to be particularly useful in the examination of the Harappan Civilization (Possehl 1976; Possehl and Kennedy 1979). What emerges from Ratnagar's and Fentress' papers is that it is worthwhile to think of Harappa as a "commercial" center, deeply involved in the procurement of a wide range of materials from the Hindu Kush, Northern Baluchistan, perhaps even as far away as Afghanistan if the Shortugai sites are included. References to the vast resources known to be located in this northern mountainous rim of the Indus Valley can be found in Fentress (1976: 306-309).

It can only be assumed that the Harappans acquired this wide range of material to satisfy their own internal demand and for the networks of foreign trade in the third millennium. It is increasingly clear that a major component of this international commerce was via the Persian Gulf sea lanes (Ratnagar 1977) and that Meluhha can be identified in a generic way with the normative geography of the Harappan Civilization (Possehl 1979b: 153-54). The volume of individual shipments indicated in the Sumerian economic documents recounting this trade is considerable. For example, tons of copper. It is therefore no wonder that a place like Harappa grew and prospered in its own kind of central position. It was the center in the northern domain of Harappan economic geography. Figure 2 is instructive in graphically portraying the points I am making. Notice that the circle (325 kilometer radius) around Harappa completely fills the Punjab lowlands, and touches just the fringes of the Hindu Kush and Northwest Frontier. It is in that sense that I think one can consider Harappa as a centrally located place. It is not, however, central to the Indus settlement geography; at least of the village farming communities. The radius of 325 kilometers, of course, could be said to structure this, but the distance is not a completely arbitrary one. It was derived from the distance between Mohenjodaro and the Arabian Sea. The circles surrounding Mohenjodaro and Harappa on Fig. 3 have precisely the same radius, and, as it turns out, the distance from the seacoast to Mohenjodaro is half the distance between Mohenjodaro and Harappa. It also happens that the same diameter places Harappa in the center of the

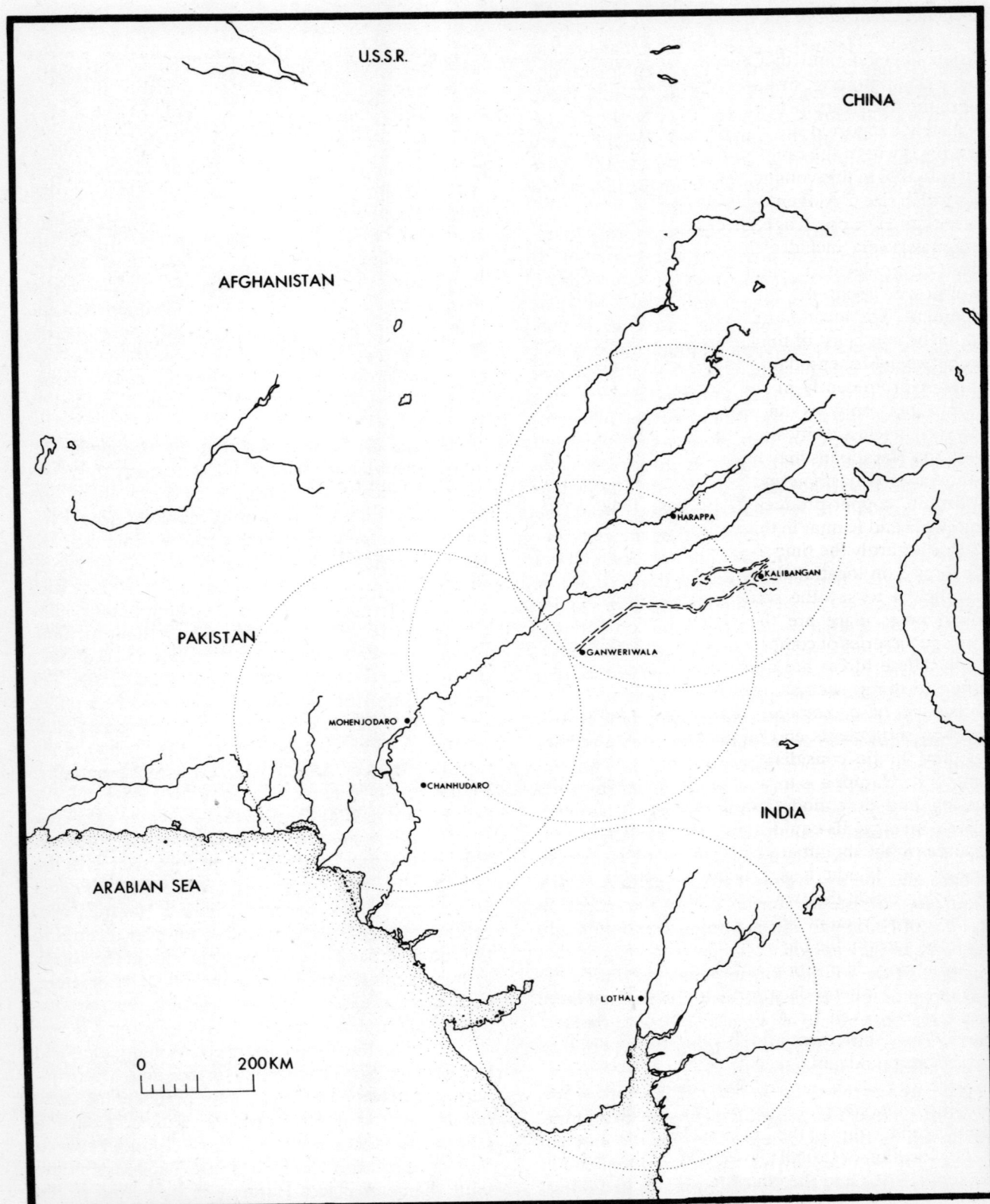

Fig. 2. Urban hinterlands of the Harappan Civilization.

Punjab lowlands and that the areas circumscribed have a slight intersection at the *panchnad*—the place where the five rivers form a single stream.

A newly reported site called Ganweriwala at 81.5 hectares is within the range of the Harappan cities as well (Mughal in this volume Fig. 7.1). It is essentially identical in size to Mohenjodaro (ca. 83 hectares) and larger than Harappa (ca. 65 hectares). City planning at Ganweriwala includes the normative Harappan design of an elevated "citadel" adjacent to a larger lower town, apparently the residential area of the settlement. The location of this third Harappan city just to the southeast of the *panchnad*, precisely midway between Mohenjodaro and Harappa would seem to figure prominently in the Harappan urban geography, not only as an intermediate settlement between the classic city sites, but as a place through which the Harappans may have been drawing on the resources of Rajasthan and possibly places like the important copper-producing site of Ganeshwar (Agrawala and Kumar in this volume).

This is hardly the time to deeply involve myself in an exercise on locational geography (Haggett 1976) so suffice it to say the settlement locations where growth takes place are those that best satisfy, or "average" a series of competing positive and negative forces. These forces are numerous, varied, and not limited to things such as: routes of communication, subsistence base, resource location, defense, surrounding settlements and populations, geomorphology and biotic considerations. As Dr. Ratnagar points out, Harappa is located at an important river crossing and at a node where several traditional routes converge. Its equidistant position vis-a-vis the resources in the mountains from the Sulaiman Range through the Hindu Kush is another factor which makes the notion that Harappa was deeply involved in the procurement of "exotic" materials an eminently reasonable one.

An analogous position can be developed for the location of Mohenjodaro, which, again noted by Ratnagar and even by Asthana, is not clearly surrounded by a settlement grid of village communities. It is, however, advantageously located near both the resources of Baluchistan and Rajasthan. At the same time the inhabitants could take advantage of the Indus-given fertility of the Larkana flood plain.

The location of Lothal (Possehl 1976, Possehl and Kennedy 1979), and the character of this extraordinarily interesting community, make it appear that it too was a procurement, "trading" center. This small, well-organized settlement was probably the least generalized of these three sites in terms of its function and there is little doubt that it was strategically placed, again on a frontier, in a position to gain Harappan access to the resources of southern Rajasthan, or the Deccan.

Returning to the major centers, Mohenjodaro, Harappa and Ganweriwala, one sees that the locations of the cities can be understood, at least in part, by thinking in terms of two principal, but opposed variables. The sites were in some form of interaction and this pull, basically a drive to minimize the "friction" or "work" caused by distance, was a force tending to pull the location of the centers together. On the other hand, the dispersed nature of the resources in which their inhabitants were interested—from the Hindu Kush through Rajasthan to the Deccan and the Aravallis through Baluchistan and the Northwest Frontier—drove the optimum position for the settlements away from one another. Lothal, the third settlement of interest in this regard, can now be seen as an outlier of Mohenjodaro—a settlement daughtered-off to capture the resources from a very specific terrain. This sense of Lothal is perfectly in keeping with the size and specialized character of the settlement. The site is not simply a miniature Mohenjodaro, or Harappa.

It may be wise at this time to offer something of a disclaimer. By pursuing these points having to do with trade, natural resources and the like I do not intend to imply that the Harappans were single-minded of purpose, or that every important, or even interesting, thing about these ancient peoples is somehow related to commerce/economics. There are many other things to be learned about the Harappan Civilization and some of them will be touched on later in this essay. But economics is interesting, too, and looking at the civilization in this way suggests that there is a basis for partitioning Harappan geography.

HARAPPAN DOMAINS

The internal structure of the Harappan Civilization has never been well understood. It is clear, however, that an area as large as the one inhabited by the Harappans, roughly the size of France, must have been differentiated into subunits, possibly as a nested hierarchy. The maps (Figs. 1 and 2) suggest an approach to uncovering the outlines of this structure.

That is, by taking the distribution of sites and noting the location of the presumably dominant cities and towns it may be possible to begin to sense something of the internal structure of the Harappan cultural landscape. Figure 3 is a first approximation of this organization.

It should be emphasized that these proposed units cannot be said to represent the Harappan equivalent of a "province" or "district" or any other formal political unit. In fact, they represent the blending of points of cleavage between major geographic features (e.g., the Kirthar Range, the Thar Desert and the Western Ghats), settlement clusters and the distribution of the largest of the Harappan centers.

Selecting an appropriate terminology for such units presents a problem since the usual run of words carries with it denotative and connotative suggestions of institutional configurations clearly not present in this rendering of Harappan geography. Terms such as state, province, district, and realm, plus many others, carry with them a distinct meaning relating to political geography, not justified in the present case. A word with a more neutral meaning is required to ensure that misconceptions are not developed and perpetuated. After some thought and search I have selected the term "domain" as an acceptable, not necessarily ideal, choice. One disadvantage to this term is that in one of its forms it carries a political meaning relating to sovereignty and the rule of a state. But, there are other sets of meanings which are different from this and which provide an acceptable usage for our purposes. These relate to a sphere of activity or influence without a specific institutional setting being involved, as in this or that domain of action or a city's domain as a hinterland. Granted, the term is not without its drawbacks if it is to be used to designate subdivisions of Harappan space, but it seems to me to be better than many of the alternatives that might be offered.

If the selection of the term to designate Harappan geography is difficult, naming the individual units is relatively easy. There seem to be two directions which one can take in this matter. The first is to designate each unit with a directional term (e.g. north, south, central, etc.). This tack is the safest, if dullest alternative. The second direction to take is to christen each unit with a recognizable geographic name, modern or ancient, a settlement or a region.

My preferences tend toward the second alternative since the terminology is significantly richer than the first, with one exception. The first domain, that to the east of Harappa in East Punjab, Haryana and western Uttar Pradesh does not seem to have a particularly appropriate modern or ancient regional name, and none of the major excavated sites seems to be appropriate. Kalibangan, unfortunately, is in a possible border area and could well be within the Bahawalpur Domain. Haryana is simply not broad enough in scope to be truly appropriate. Thus, "Eastern Domain" will have to suffice that area. My candidates for the other regions are as follows: Harappa Domain, Bahawalpur Domain, Mohenjodaro Domain, Gedrosia Domain, Lothal Domain.

Directional	*Geographical*
1. Eastern Domain	Haryana (Kalibangan) Domain
2. Northern Domain	Punjab (Harappa) Domain
3. Central Domain	Bahawalpur (Ganweriwala) Domain
4. Southern Domain	Sindh (Mohenjodaro) Domain
5. Western Domain	Gedrosia (Kulli/Harappan) Domain
6. Southeastern Domain	Gujarat (Lothal) Domain

THE BAHAWALPUR DOMAIN

One of the most significant discoveries relating to the Harappan Civilization is that made by M. Rafique Mughal in the fomer Bahawalpur state. His paper in this book outlines these finds in a preliminary way, as one awaits the full publication of his material in a forthcoming number of *Pakistan Archaeology*.

It can be said for the moment that Mughal's discoveries have isolated an area with a spectacular density of protohistoric settlements. Clearly, this was the, or one of the, centers of Harappan sedentarism. Figures 7.1 and 7.2 will give some impression of this. It is too early to fully understand the full significance of his work; however the Bahawalpur Domain now stands as a contrast to the openness of the remainder of the Harappan settlement grid, especially in West Punjab (Possehl 1979a).

CIVILIZATIONAL PROCESSES

Several papers in this volume address the issue of site distribution. While time and geography are different in most of these papers, several authors are concerned with an abstract problem about the nature of urban systems. For example, S.P. Gupta and C.C. Lamberg-Karlovsky both begin with observations of patterns and then develop these in a way which causes a new, interesting aspect of urbanism to emerge. If

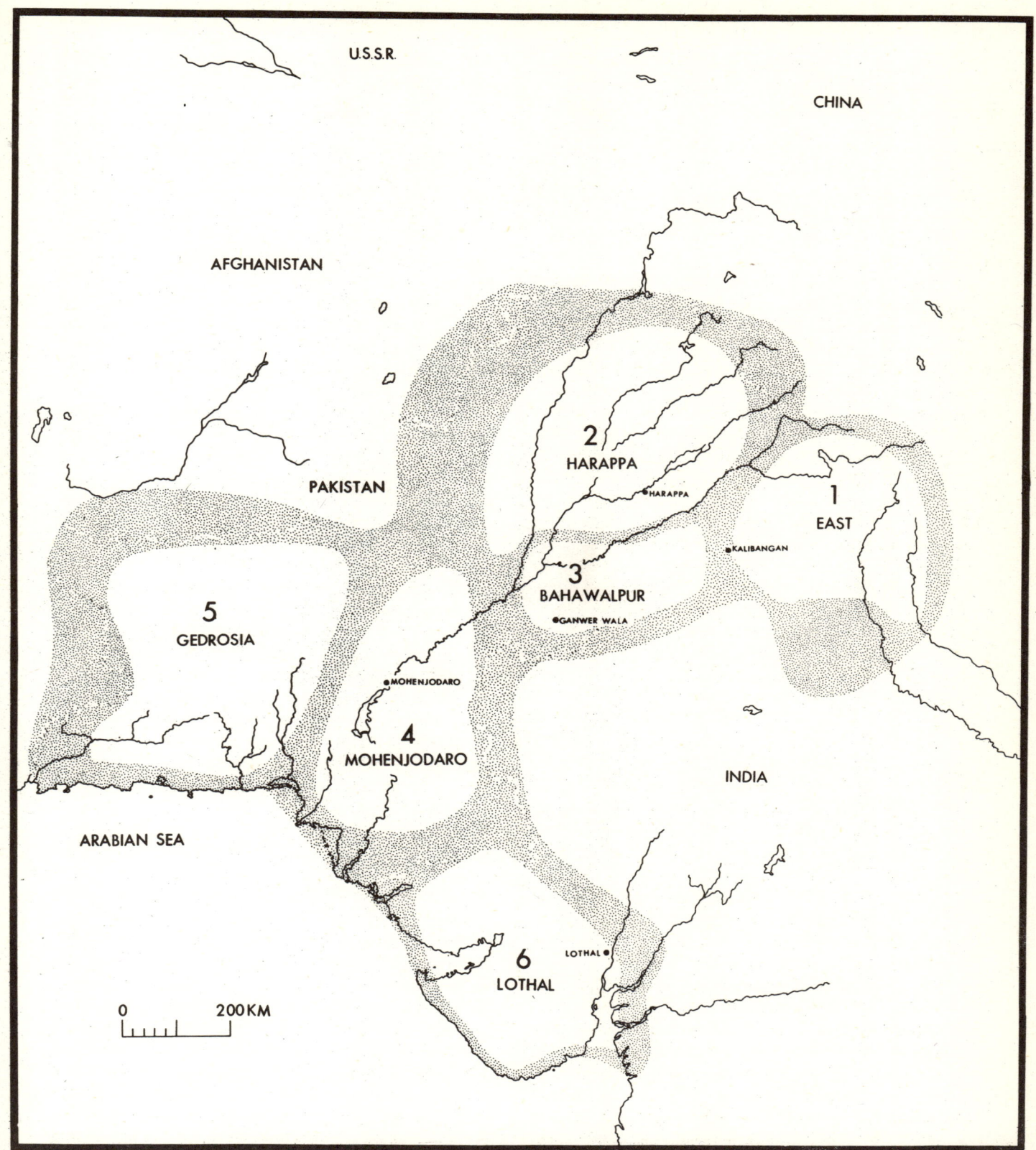

Fig. 3. Domains of the Harappan Civilization.
Note: The stippled areas between the individual domains are intended to indicate the area within which an actual border may have been located.

they cannot give a concise explanation for the material they discuss, at least they succeed in giving something new and interesting to think about.

This theme serves to sharpen something already quite apparent: the third millennium B.C. was an extraordinarily interesting period in the history of Asia between the valleys of the Tigris and Euphrates and the Great Indian Desert, extending as far north as Turkistan. There is an apparent vitality of interaction within this region and the formation of states, or something which is at least "state-like," within not only the traditionally accepted areas of Mesopotamia and the Indus but in Central Asia and Eastern Iran as well. The most visible archaeological sign of this convergence is in the form of trade goods, especially "esoteric" commodities such as lapis lazuli, metals, etched beads, stamp and cylinder seals, even elaborately carved chlorite vessels such as those from Tepe Yahya. The last half of this millennium, the apparent focus of Harappan urbanism, is a period of consolidation of a complex web of interrelationships which were begun, or at least intensified, during the earlier period. Just as I am struck by the possibility that Gupta and Lamberg-Karlovsky have something to say about the way civilizations "behave" at some level, so too am I compelled to think that the emergence of the Harappan Civilization cannot be divorced from this larger geographic context. The genesis of the Harappan Civilization is not separate from the processes attendant upon neighboring regions to the west. This is not to suggest that one is dealing with anything even vaguely resembling diffusion, or that, as Sir Mortimer Wheeler suggested, there was an *idea* of civilization in the air (Wheeler 1959: 104; 1968: 25). I have taken pains to thoroughly critique this elsewhere (Possehl in press) but an abridged position of this argument may not be out of place here.

One aspect of this position develops around the nature of urbanization and whether it is reasonable to believe that: (1) there ever was a sufficiently coherent ancient thought on urbanization for there to have been an *idea* of the phenomenon, and (2) if there had been such an idea that it was something which could have been inserted, or applied from one area (Mesopotamia) to another (the Indus). There is a great deal of anthropological, even contemporary developmental economics, literature which suggests that the second proposition is a naive one. The numerous failures which could be recounted in areas such as the twentieth century developmental projects (AID for example), unambiguously tell one that it is extremely difficult to transfer even rather well-defined technological features to "foreign" cultural spheres. How then can one imagine the development of an entire urban system on the same basis? The answer is, one cannot, and one is thus led to the inescapable conclusion that the Harappan Civilization is going to have to be understood on its own terms if it is to be understood at all. Its "own terms" includes not only the nature of its "interior structure" but social and cultural relationships with surrounding regions as well. The greater Indus Valley was, after all, not in a cultural vacuum in the third millennium and this context cannot be assumed to have been irrelevant to the history of Harappan urbanization. By raising this issue, however, there may be a temptation to begin to think in old fashioned (simplistic) diffusionist ways, with cultural traits and peoples wandering across various landscapes indiscriminately "influencing" whomever else happens to be around. Culture change just does not work this way. Even assuming that "diffusion" played some role in this culture history, and there is every reason to believe that it did, one must realize that the acceptance or rejection of any particular, or mass, of cultural traits is an independent operation of cause and effect, just as is the case for ontogenetic change. To understand the process of change in an holistic context, one must seek the basis on which this cause and effect operated and not fall back on weak concepts like "diffusion" or "influence." This point brings one close to another of the focal points addressed by a number of authors who have studied the Harappan Civilization: the issue of cultural affiliation.

CULTURAL AFFILIATION

Who were the Harappans? This frequently-asked question is at some level not uninteresting, but it contains a great amount of ambiguity and is probably not *central* to understanding the South Asian prehistoric record. The question is ambiguous because there is no sense that a level of abstraction is specified or even implied. Which aspect of "who-ness" is being addressed? Is it ethnicity, or a contribution to an historical tradition, or the people who made some distinctive or identifiable body of material culture? After all, an answer to the question could reasonably be stated as: The folk who built the places now called

Mohenjodaro and Harappa among others. But, I suspect that that is not the form an answer should take, at least for some. I suspect that the question really being addressed has something to do with affiliation and origins, with an implication of a search for ethnic connections. It may even be true that the question has to do with a search for the area(s) from which the Harappans might have migrated. Again, this is not an entirely unworthy problem; although most current thought on Harappan origins has concluded that a migration hypothesis for the genesis of the Mature Phase of the Harappan Civilization has little substance. Equally to the point is the fact that problems of this kind have proved impossible to solve given a purely archaeological context. Even with a substantial corpus of written historical material this problem can pose serious difficulties. I refer here to the Sumerian/Akkadian groups in ancient Mesopotamia and the immense difficulties scholars have had in dealing with that situation in all its complex reality in spite of the almost overwhelming corpus of texts. Thus, archaeological questions of this kind are best worked on within a theoretical/methodological context. Certainly these methods are not available today since it is obvious that correlations between ceramics and historical presumptions about ethnicity are an inconclusive test. There is simply an overwhelming mass of ethnographic and historical data which indicate that material culture does not correlate with ethnicity in spite of the fact that there are occasional instances where these paths do cross (see Gupta 1969 for an interesting example).

One of the domains of the Harappan Civilization about which much has been said with regard to cultural affiliation is that in the east: Punjab, Haryana and western Uttar Pradesh. The papers by Y.D. Sharma, K.K. Sinha, S.P. Gupta, R.S. Bisht, D.P. Agrawal and R.K. Sood as well as K.N. Dikshit deal with this domain.

THE EASTERN DOMAIN

One of the most interesting issues in the archaeology of the Harappan Civilization is concerned with the many sites of this cultural tradition which have been found in northwestern India: Punjab, Haryana, northern Rajasthan, western Uttar Pradesh, even Jammu and Kashmir. Some of these sites have been known for many years (e.g., Alamgirpur, Ropar, Bara and Kotla Nihang Khan) but recent work has led to the discovery of scores more. The maps provided with the papers by Y.D. Sharma, K.N. Dikshit and M. Fentress will give a fair indication of the scope of these discoveries. They may also be used in conjunction with Fig. 1.

There were early notices of Harappan sites in this region (Vats 1929–30) but the work substantively begins in the years immediately following partition, with the exploration of the Sarasvati by A. Ghosh (1952) the excavation of Ropar, Bara, even Hastinapura (IAR 1953–54; 1954–55a; 1954–55b; Lal 1955) as well as with the initiation of a number of other programs.

Four things were apparent by the mid to late fifties. First, the initial penetration of the region between the Sutlej and the Ganges by food-producing village farming communities was somehow connected to the Harappan cultural tradition. Second, evidence from sites such as Sothi, Kalibangan and Bara indicates that the first food producers arrived prior to the emergence of the Mature, Urban Harappan. The scope of this settlement process (migration?) was later expanded (Suraj Bhan 1973) with the discovery of the Siswal complex, and sites such as Manda (Joshi and Madhu Bala in this volume). Third, in addition to the Pre- or Early Harappan occupation, there was evidence for the Mature Phase of the civilization, as well as a phase which seems to have followed the Urban Period. The second and later phase was often referred to as "Late Harappan." Fourth, it was evident that during this time the region was culturally complex in the sense that it was one within which there were several different ceramic styles in variable association with one another. The evidence from Ropar, formerly Rupar, further complicated this situation by indicating that the Pre- or Early Harappan ceramics occurred in association with Mature Harappan pottery (Dikshit in press). This association has also been found at Manda (Joshi and Madhu Bala in this volume). Bara Ware is also a long-lived ceramic, with Early Harappan motifs carrying through the entire sequence. This situation of variable ceramic associations in both space and time led to terminological and conceptual problems, many of which have yet to be resolved. It would be presumptive for me to suggest that an immediate solution to these problems is at hand; however some clarification of the situation is possible, as is a focus of attention on particular issues.

This discussion will begin with a descriptive statement of this recalcitrant body of material which draws liberally on Sharma (1973, and in this volume), Shaffer (in press), Suraj Bhan (1973, 1975) and Dikshit (in this volume).

The Early Harappan, as defined by Mughal (1970) has been recovered from Kot Diji and northeast along the Sarasvati to Kalibangan and beyond. It has also been found in excavation at Siswal and Balu (Suraj Bhan and Shaffer 1978), the latter site is currently being investigated by Kurukshetra University. There are at least 16 other Early Harappan sites in southern Haryana and northern Rajasthan. An examination of this so-called "Siswal A" Early Harappan can leave little doubt of its clear relationship to Kalibangan I and hence to the larger Pre-Urban Harappan phenomenon. These sites, which generally line the now extinct waterways of the region, represent a continuation of the Early Harappan settlement of the Ghaggar/Hakra (Sarasvati) apparently testing the limits of the wheat/barley/sheep/goat/cattle subsistence constellation (Fairservis 1961). There are good reasons for us to suspect that direct migration, and the founding of pioneer settlements, played a substantial role in this process since the pattern of relationships and discontinuity in the settlement and subsistence regime are so clear (Haury 1958).

The reasons for this Early Harappan penetration of the region have yet to be understood. It can be said with some certainty, however, that they did not involve the direct exploitation of minerals or semiprecious stones since the area is devoid of such resources. Timber may have been a draw to the area, and research directed to determining the potentials of forest cover in this, and other places, would be appropriate. It is also possible that at least a portion of the region's attractiveness lay in its proximity to the mountains of Rajasthan. The eastern fringe of the Thar Desert was apparently densely inhabited by peoples with complex, subtle forms of adaptation not the least of which may have involved working the rich copper deposits of their territories (see Agrawala and Kumar in this volume). It is worth mentioning that the extraordinary richness of these sites is not highlighted by simply labeling them "microlithic." One knows that places like Bagor (Misra 1973), Jodhpura and Ganeshwar (Agrawala and Kumar in this volume) are just three of a number of third millennium settlements with substantial importance for understanding the early metals economy. Since it is clear that there was a relationship between this region, especially the Khetri belt, and the Urban Harappans there is some reason, admittedly speculative, to suggest that the relationship began in the Early Harappan times and that the extension of sites along the eastern tributaries of the Sarasvati were in part involved in it.

The suggestion that the inhabitants of these settlements were involved in the early metals economy should not be taken as a proposition removing them from the remainder of a diversified economy. They must have been, at some fundamental level, subsistence farmers and herders.

Early Harappan penetration of the area to the east of the Sutlej was followed by the emergence of the Urban Harappan. In this eastern border area the older ceramic tradition seems to have continued. The clear sense of things is that the center of change (if it is fair to suggest a core area within which culture change held chronological priorities over peripheral areas) was to the west of this region.[1] This has been discussed elsewhere in some detail (Mughal 1970, and in this volume; Fairservis 1967; Possehl in press) and while greater chronological and contextual control over this material would be desirable, it does seem that the Harappa/Ghaggar/Mohenjodaro axis is the region central to the emergence of urbanism in western South Asia. In this sense the Siswal A sites can be thought of as provincial in character, with all that implies in terms of change. This contention is something of a speculative leap, especially given the historical understanding of this part of India during the third millennium. But it does, as a model to be tested, help in understanding the complex interweaving of older traditions and newly emerged features during the period when the Urban Harappan was apparently very much a part of life in the western Subcontinent.

Early Harappan ceramics and/or small finds are associated with Mature Harappan materials at Ropar IA, Siswal B, Mitathal I, Balu II, Manda and elsewhere. An association between the Mature Harappan and the Bara "Culture," of which more will be said in a moment, has been identified at Ropar IB, Kotla Nihang, Sanghol, and a number of other places. These have caused no small amount of confusion, especially when assumptions concerning ceramic types and ethnic groups have been made, but there is good reason to think of these associations as a phenomenon characteristic of provincial regions, hinterlands, or "rural" areas as suggested by a number of contributors to this volume. As is frequently the case in such areas, older traditions tend to be preserved. Examples of this can be found in many settings from the contemporary United States to many parts of India. Thus, rather than one of these sites being reconstructed in terms of the cohabitation of Early (or Pre-) Harappans and Mature Harappans as separate communities, it might be profitable to think in terms of the variably paced rate of culture change in these areas and the preservation of older, deeper, aspects of a tradition. This occurs not only through the keeping of heirlooms, but in terms of the contemporary manufacture of new examples of materials with older styles. These may be, from the perspective of those who make and use them, a fully legitimate part of what they would call "their culture." This conservative tendency is adequately accounted for within the provincial context which this region seems to reflect during the late third and second millennium.

This is not to suggest that ancient Haryana, the Punjab and western Uttar Pradesh are places that cannot be understood within their own context, or that these areas were unimportant during Harappan times. Indeed, the region between the Sutlej and the Ganges to the north of the Sarasvati is interesting to us because of its distinctive qualities within the larger setting of the Harappan Civilization.

One of the most interesting aspects of the Eastern Domain during Harappan times is the way in which the ceramic inventories were stylistically expanded. There are at least two assemblages—those from Bara and Siswal—which seem to diverge sufficiently from the norms established for Early (Kot Diji/Sothi) and Mature Harappan pottery to be deserving of special nomenclature. These assemblages, and there are probably others which might be formulated, have a consistent association with more straightforward, recognizable Harappan wares in the region. Nonetheless, they are a divergent element to be considered, and one which seems to tell something about the region, and this is fully congruent with the earlier noted association between Early Harappan and Mature Harappan elements. That is, the evolution of the distinctive Siswal and Bara ceramic traditions are not so much the result of new peoples appearing on the scene, or even the emergence of new "cultures," but of the provincialism mentioned earlier. Such divergence from what is recognized as "main line" Harappan norms is a reflection of attenuated (intensity and/or frequency) interaction. Using a linguistic model, the universal process of culture change led peoples to different answers to the same questions, especially in the plastic ceramic medium. The clear relationship that the Bara Ware and Siswal materials have with the Early and Mature Harappan can be interpreted in terms of these three cultural norms having a common heritage and the differences are then a result of independent, local culture change in an area relatively removed from the region within which the development of the distinctive Harappan style was created. Again, I propose that it was the attenuation of interaction, in terms of frequency and/or intensity, which gave rise to this independence of development in the Eastern Domain of the Harappan Civilization.

Another of the problems which needs intensified, systematic investigation in the Eastern Domain is the transition from the Mature Harappan to the Post-Urban Phase. There are many sites where this has been observed, and from which a clear sense of continuity of occupation exists. But, there is a shift at this time in the material inventory that is very interesting since it involves those features which are most clearly Mature Harappan: loss of the writing system, abandonment of the weights, shifts in the ceramic corpus, changing architectural styles and the like.[2] This shift has been widely and reasonably taken to be generally coincident in time with the transition between the Urban and Post-Urban Phases of the Harappan tradition. In the Eastern Domain one of the fossil indicators of this shift has been the Ochre Colored Pottery (OCP) which was discovered at Hastinapura and named by B.B. Lal (1955). Since that time there have been a number of discussions of this ceramic as well as at least one conference (Sharma 1971-72). It was recognized at an early date that there were significant parallels between OCP and Harappan wares, especially in vessel forms. The stratigraphic position of the pottery, immediately preceding Painted Gray Ware (PGW) at Hastinapura, made this eminently reasonable. However, the softness of OCP made it difficult to deal with since it frequently came to archaeologists as not much more than amorphous lumps of pottery. It has been suggested that this quality is due to waterlogging, which may, in fact, be the case. But, it is also related to the technology used to produce this ceramic since some sherds from the same soil environment are not so affected.

It quickly became apparent to those following the discoveries in the *Doab*, Haryana and northern Rajasthan that the term OCP was being indiscriminately applied to a number of archaeological assemblages which appeared to be quite different. This situation created confusion conceptually and terminologically, which only served further to obscure even the basic outlines of Harappan Culture history in this domain. The publication of Suraj Bhan's (1975) report on the excavations at Mitathal and Siswal has, however, provided a new body of information and the following draws liberally on the perspective presented there (Suraj Bhan 1975: 83-86, 111-15).

Suraj Bhan has proposed two basic types of OCP (1975: 113). The first of these is confined to the northern *Doab* and can be characterized by the kind of material found at Ambkheri (IAR 1963-64: 56). This type of OCP can be derived from a Mitathal IIB (Post-Urban Phase) aspect of the Harappan tradition. The exact typological parallels to support this contention can be found in Suraj Bhan (1975: 85). The second OCP variant is found to the south of this in the central *Doab* and adjoining parts of Uttar Pradesh, Haryana and Rajasthan. This OCP is best illustrated by the wares found at Atranjikhera and Saipai. Suraj Bhan claims that there are certain typological similarities between Kalibangan II (Mature Harappan), the Siswal wares, and the Atranjikhera OCP. There is a further concentration of Siswal sites in lower Haryana neighboring the central *Doab*. The discovery of what Suraj Bhan has termed "Degenerate Siswal Wares" (DSW) (1975: 113) sites in southeastern Haryana can thus be interpreted as bridging the chronological and geographical gap once thought to separate the OCP from the Siswal complex (Suraj Bhan 1975: 113). But, one of the points to have emerged from the Srinagar conference is that the OCP/Late Harappan material is still a terminological and conceptual morass deserving of an airing in a separate meeting.

Such a conference might be used in part to test the veracity of several points which seem to apply to the Eastern Domain:

1) OCP is a ceramic whose physical properties are a product of waterlogging.

2) There are several varieties of OCP. Each variety has its own temporal and spatial distribution. At least one of these varieties of OCP is contemporary with the Urban Phase of the Harappan Civilization.

3) There is a continuity between what can be termed the Chalcolithic tradition of the Eastern Domain and later PGW/NBP occupations.

CONCLUSION

It is not unreasonable to propose that until issues such as those noted above are settled, and archaeologists reach some common ground on terminology, little progress will be made on understanding more fully the later phase of the Harappan tradition, in the east or elsewhere. The tools to accomplish this task are available today and they need only be applied to the materials in hand and still buried in ancient settlements. International cooperation is one way for problems such as this, and others mentioned earlier in this essay, to be addressed, since it would naturally bring to bear a variety of perspectives. Conferences such as that held in Srinagar might someday be seen as the beginning of such integrated archaeological research strategies.

NOTES

[1] This may be just the kind of generalization that J. Shaffer is cautioning against in his contribution to this volume.

[2] J. Shaffer (in press: 77) states: "There is no conclusive archaeological evidence to indicate that large 'urban' settlements disappear" during the Post-Urban Phase. This is a difficult statement to deal with because of the assumption implying a unique correlation between settlement size and a notion of "urbanization." Clearly large sites could be present in this area during the Post-Urban Phase but with a population that was organized along non-urban parameters. It is also conceivable that a sociocultural system of an urban type could be present at small sites during this time period. If the latter is the case, I would have to revise my (1977) terminology; something I am presently unwilling to do. Shaffer is correct in noting that there could be large sites in this area during the second half of the second millennium—say after 1800 B.C. But, it is a moot point since many, if not most, of the sites one would look to in this regard have many thousands of cubic meters of overburden covering the Harappan occupation. Determining the limits of these occupations may take many years, if not many lifetimes. Moreover site size might not be as important an indicator of urbanization as is frequently

believed. Other features, lying closer to the core of an urban form of sociocultural organization, are involved, as well, and may vary independently from settlement area, or population. Here one is talking about social classes, a state, craft and career specialization and the like. It is widely known that these parameters have been difficult to measure in the Harappan case. However, there are some features which seem to stand for them; writing, signs of long distance trade, unified systems of weights and measures, and evidence for occupational specialization. Therefore it is important to follow these "proxies" in peripheral regions such as the one under discussion since they seem to disappear, or be severely attenuated in evidence following the second millennium transformation of Harappan Culture. That is, while there may, or may not, have been large settlements in this region during the Post-Urban Phase one has a fairly good notion that the system of Harappan writing disappeared along with the weights and measures, and other proxied urban features. Thus, one is dealing with a non-urban form of organization for the "Late Harappan" sites in this area.

BIBLIOGRAPHY

Dani, Ahmad Hasan, 1971
  Excavations in the Gomal Valley. *Ancient Pakistan* 5:1-177.
Dikshit, K.N., in press
  A Critical Review of Pre-Harappan Cultures in the Indo-Pakistan Subcontinent. *Man and Environment.*
Fairservis, Walter A., 1961
  The Harappan Civilization—New evidence and more theory. *Novitates* 2055. New York: American Museum of Natural History.
Fairservis, Walter A., 1967
  The Origin, Character and Decline of an Early Civilization. *Novitates* 2302. New York: American Museum of Natural History.
Fentress, Marcia, 1976
  Resource Access, Exchange Systems and Regional Interaction in the Indus Valley: An investigation of archaeological variability at Harappa and Mohenjodaro. Unpublished Ph.D. dissertation, Department of Oriental Studies, University of Pennsylvania.
Ghosh, A., 1952
  The Rajputana Desert—Its archaeological aspect. *Bulletin of the National Institute of Sciences of India* 1: 37-42.
Gupta, S.P., 1969
  Sociology of Pottery: Chirag Dilli, a case study. In *Potteries in Ancient India*, B.P. Sinha, ed. Pp. 15-26. Patna: Department of Ancient Indian History and Archaeology.
Haggett, Peter, 1976
  Locational Analysis in Human Geography. 2nd ed. New York: St. Martins Press.

Halim, Muhammad Abdul, 1972a
  Excavation at Sarai Khola (Part 1). *Pakistan Archaeology* 7: 23-89.
Halim, Muhammad Abdul, 1972b
  Excavations at Sarai Khola (Part 2). *Pakistan Archaeology* 8: 1-112.
Haury, E.W., 1958
  Evidence at Point of Pines for a Prehistoric Migration from Northern Arizona. In *Migrations in New World Culture History*, R.H. Thompson, ed. Pp. 1-8. Tucson: University of Arizona Press.
Indian Archaeology: A review (IAR), 1953-54
  Rupar, District Ambala. Pp. 6-7. Delhi: Archaeological Survey of India.
Indian Archaeology: A review (IAR), 1954-55a
  Bara and Salaura, District Ambala. Pp. 9-11. Delhi: Archaeological Survey of India.
Indian Archaeology: A review (IAR), 1954-55b
  Rupar, District Ambala. P. 9. Delhi: Archaeological Survey of India.
Indian Archaeology: A review (IAR), 1963-64
  Excavation at Ambkheri, District Saharanpur. P. 56. Delhi: Archaeological Survey of India.
Jansen, Michael, 1979
  Architectural Problems of the Harappa Culture. In *South Asian Archaeology 1977,* Vol. 1. M. Taddei, ed. Pp. 405-31. Naples.
Lal, B.B., 1955
  Excavation at Hastinapura and Other Explorations in the Upper Ganga and Sutlej Basins, 1950-52: New light on the dark age between the end of the Harappa culture and the Early Historical Period. *Ancient India* 10-11: 5-151.

Misra, V.N., 1973
   Bagor: A late mesolithic settlement in north-west India. *World Archaeology* 5(1): 92-110.

Mughal, M. Rafique, 1970
   The early Harappan Period in the Greater Indus Valley and Northern Baluchistan. Ph.D. dissertation, Anthropology Department. University of Pennsylvania.

Possehl, Gregory L., 1976
   Lothal: A gateway settlement of the Harappan Civilization. In *Ecological Backgrounds of South Asian Prehistory*. K.A.R. Kennedy and G.L. Possehl, eds. Pp. 118-31. Occasional Papers and Theses of the South Asia Program of Cornell University 4. Ithaca: Cornell University.

Possehl, Gregory L., 1977
   The End of a State and the Continuity of a Tradition. In *Realm and Region in Traditional India*. R. Fox, ed. Pp. 234-54. Durham: Duke University Press.

Possehl, Gregory L., 1979a
   Pastoral Nomadism in the Indus Civilization: An hypothesis. In *South Asian Archaeology, 1977*, Vol. 1. M. Taddei, ed. Pp. 533-51, Naples.

Possehl, Gregory L., 1979b
   Ancient Cities of the Indus. Durham: Carolina Academic Press.

Possehl, Gregory L., in press
   Kulli: Trade and the Emergence of the Harappan Civilization. Durham: Carolina Academic Press.

Possehl, Gregory L. and Kenneth A.R. Kennedy, 1979
   Hunter-Gatherer/Agriculturalist Exchange in Prehistory: An Indian example. *Current Anthropology* (3): 592–93.

Ratnagar, Shereen, 1977
   Trading Contacts between India and Western Asia in the Third and Second Millennia B.C. Ph.D. dissertation, The Faculty of the Center for Historical Studies, Jawaharlal Nehru University, New Delhi.

Shaffer, Jim G., in press
   The Prehistoric Period in the Eastern Punjab: A preliminary assessment. In *Essays in Indian Archaeology*. Jerome Jacobson, ed. Delhi: American Institute of Indian Studies.

Sharma, Y.D., ed., 1971-72
   OCP and NBP: 1971, Proceedings of the Seminar held by the Indian Archaeological Society, on the 11th May, 1971, at the National Museum, New Delhi, on Ochre Coloured Ware and Northern Black Polished Ware. *Puratattva* 6: 1-100.

Sharma, Y.D., 1973
   Value of Common Painted Ceramic Designs from Different Sites as Guide to Chronology with Special Reference to Pottery from Bara (Punjab). In *Radiocarbon and Indian Archaeology*. D.P. Agrawal and A. Ghosh, eds. Pp. 222-31. Bombay: Tata Institute of Fundamental Research.

Suraj Bhan, 1973
   The Sequence and Spread of Prehistoric Cultures in the Upper Sarasvati Basin. In *Radiocarbon and Indian Archaeology*. D.P. Agrawal and A. Ghosh, eds. Pp. 252-63. Bombay: Tata Institute of Fundamental Research.

Suraj Bhan, 1975
   Excavations at Mitathal (1968) and Other Explorations in the Sutlej-Yamuna Divide. Kurukshetra: Kurukshetra University.

Suraj Bhan and Jim Shaffer, 1978
   New Discoveries in Northern Haryana. *Man and Environment* 2: 59–68.

Vats, M.S., 1929-30
   Kotla Nihang. *Annual Report of the Archaeological Survey of India 1929-30*. Delhi: Government of India: 131-32.

Wheeler, Sir Mortimer, 1959
   Early India and Pakistan: To Asoka. New York: Praeger.

Wheeler, Sir Mortimer, 1968
   The Indus Civilization. 3rd ed. Supplementary volume to the Cambridge History of India. Cambridge: The University Press.

PART I

THE NATURE OF HARAPPAN URBANIZATION

VISHNU-MITTRE

1. The Harappan Civilization and the Need for a New Approach

INTRODUCTION

KNOWLEDGE of the Harappan Civilization has advanced considerably since Charles Masson first reported the vast mounds of Harappa in 1826. A valuable mass of information relating to town planning and architecture, arts and crafts and the way of life of the Harappans emerged between 1924 and 1929 (Marshall 1931) from the description of artifacts and from inferences drawn therefrom. The subsequent excavators followed almost the same trends in thought concerning inferential aspects of the artifacts (Vats 1940; Mackay 1943). A school of thought had been founded, and it greatly influenced later excavators. Overwhelmed with the similarities throughout the Harappan area, this school of thought always placed more emphasis upon features of uniformity than upon the contrasting ones. This civilization was believed to be exotic and strictly urban. The vast expansion, material advancement and economic prosperity of the Harappans was attributed to a wet climate, the drying up of which was believed to have caused its decline.

These thoughts have reigned supreme in the minds of many archaeologists in spite of excavations at several more sites which have demonstrated meaningful variability within the culture. The discovery of non-urban sites, the recognition of indigenous features in this civilization (Sankalia 1974) and the strong disputation of the earlier concept of a wet climate (Raikes 1964), etc., gave birth to a new school of thought. These two schools have grown and become rigid in the course of time.

New disciplines such as Palynology, Paleobotany and ^{14}C dating were harnessed to throw fresh light on the origin, spread and decline of the Harappans, the climatic background of the civilization, the food habits of the people, chronology, art and architecture. But lamentably, in spite of providing a decisively fresh perspective, the trend has been to follow the beaten track opened by either of the two schools of thought. The gulf between these two schools has widened even though frequent seminars exclusively devoted to this culture have been held. The most recent was in 1978 in Karachi.

Divergence of opinion may be a sign of progress, but rigidity is certainly not. Why cannot the specialists and protagonists of these schools sit together and sort out their differences by identifying areas into which intensive research can be directed with a view to bridging the gap? There is now an immense stock of data and it is time for a healthy "taking of stock." This can bring a reorientation of thought and fresh approaches which will solve the problems that have been neglected so far. This small communication by a non-archaeologist is an attempt to draw the attention of experts to certain fresh approaches, which I believe, may answer several of the questions concerning the life and culture of the Harappans.

The Harappan Culture flourished in a vast tract of the land which today ranges from coastal to continental plains and uplands extending into the sub-Himalayan region. Within this area today there are patches of dry deciduous forest, desert communities and salt marsh vegetation. The rainfall pattern is much varied from isohyets of 10 to 60 centimeters.

The isotherms are similar. The region also varies physiographically. Did a similar varying pattern exist during the Harappan times, or was it much different from today? This has been a matter of serious enquiry since the first site was excavated. There is an answer to the question, but it is concealed by a vast and inscrutable body of data. Long strides will be made in the understanding of the Harappans if a systematic approach is taken in this area of research.

LOCAL AND REGIONAL VARIABILITY

The contemporary local and regional variability in the Harappan Culture has been a neglected field. Owing largely to this neglect it has not been possible to reconstruct the rate and direction of the Harappan development and its geographical expanse. As a result, causes for the extinction or diffusion of the Harappan Culture have eluded the experts. Finally, the complexity of the Harappan environment has never been considered since one has been generally concerned only with wet or dry climate.

The uniformity of weights and measures, and the common features in architecture, town planning, art, religion, script and seals, etc., have become such an obsession that archaeologists have lost sight of features which perhaps distinguished local settlements from one another and from those distantly located.

The qualitative and quantitative assessment of material data between the metropolitan towns or cities and the smaller settlements, the life patterns of the inhabitants and the environment and socio-economy are certain to provide valuable information. It is these areas in which new research is needed since only this will solve the profound and tantalizing problems of the way in which this culture developed, how it was maintained and the manner it declined or was "diffused" into subsequent cultures. The role of the large settlement sites vis-a-vis town/city or village places and trading and cultural contacts are other important features on which light can be thrown. Even with "competent dullness" which was "technically the peer of the rest," meaningful local and regional variation must have occurred. The gradual and successive development of the Harappan Culture from the Pre-Harappans, the retention and subsequent modification of Pre-Harappan traits and the ultimate abandonment of the nonadaptable features which led to the emergence of an exclusively Harappan Culture can be revealed through qualitative and quantitative analysis. Some of the Harappan traditions were first established by the Pre-Harappans at certain sites. The presence of great walls around Pre-Harappan settlements as at Kot Diji and Kalibangan and their use of dried bricks of a standard size $(3:2:1)$ are interesting; though some features were modified later by the Harappans (Allchin and Allchin 1968). The extent to which these aspects were restricted to few sites, and if so, what the level of development was, should be a matter of enquiry.

Precise knowledge of the alignment in the layout of the streets at Mohenjodaro is particularly lacking. The layout of the settlement was in some respects different at Lothal. The use of baked and sun-dried bricks varies between Harappa, Mohenjodaro and Kalibangan. At Kalibangan baked bricks were reserved for wells, drains and bathrooms; at Mohenjodaro sun-dried bricks were used for filling and at Harappa they alternated with burnt bricks course by course. Further, the buildings of the citadel mounds, or their vicinity, show considerable variation (Allchin and Allchin 1968).

The plant economy of the Harappans finds considerable geographical differences: wheat and barley at Mohenjodaro, Chanhudaro and Harappa; only barley at Kalibangan; rice and millets at Lothal, Rangpur and Surkotada, and at the latter site particularly, there were enormous quantities of seeds of wild plants, grasses, sedges and other weeds (Vishnu-Mittre and Savithri 1978: 67).

There may be other local and regional variable features, and these could be highly meaningful.

THE RATE AND DIRECTION OF ADVANCEMENT

The Harappan Culture, whether indigenous or not, must have commenced at one center wherefrom its spread was gradual, radiating subsequently in various directions, the Harappans eventually colonized a vast area. In the virgin areas it reached, it met with environmental features different from those in the source area. The colonization in a virgin area was thus conditioned by local environment factors, the adaptability to which must be read in the variability of settlement and variable patterns of life style, art and architecture, food habits and pottery. It is essential to establish this fact so that the directions of advancement of this culture can be mapped. One can no longer get away with the concept that "the Harappan

Culture appeared with a bang."

The rate of advancement can best be reconstructed from radiocarbon dates. There are in all over 70 radiocarbon dates available for the Harappan Culture. Slightly over 17 sites have been dated, some of them copiously. Kalibangan, for instance, has 30 dates and others have one to seven; however most sites have not been copiously dated (Sankalia 1974).

The present ^{14}C dates suggest that the Pre-Harappans lived together with the Harappans for a fairly long time at Kalibangan. At Bara and Mitathal the culture preceding the Harappans also continued after them. Did the Kalibangan Pre-Harappans come from Kot Diji or Bara and Mitathal? Wherever they came from one ought to know the amount of time they took to reach and settle at Kalibangan.

Likewise, the Harappans at Mohenjodaro and Lothal were contemporaries; whereas those at Kalibangan and Damb Sadaat II preceded them by about 200 years. And at Surkotada they were later than Lothal.

The close of the Harappan Phase has been estimated to have been around 1700 B.C. with the exception of Banawali. There it was 1300–1400 B.C. With extrapolation, however, it has been estimated that 2300–2000 B.C. was the span of time in the nuclear regions and 2000 B.C. to 1650 or 1700 B.C. for the peripheral regions. A major question that confronts one here is: Has the last word been said on the span of the Harappans?

Within the picture that has emerged from ^{14}C dates, indications are apparent that the determination of cultural variability, accompanied by a series of radiocarbon dates from freshly dug sites can help measure the rate of development of the Harappan Culture and map the directions of its advancement. The continuation of Pre-Harappans into the Harappan Culture followed by the Post-Harappan at Amri of Chanhudaro and the overlap between the Pre-Harappans and Harappans at certain sites (e.g., Kalibangan) strongly suggest that the Harappan Culture did not appear with a bang. Rather, it evolved gradually from the pre-existing Pre-Harappan Culture. Considerable variability seems to have been involved here. Some sites have only the Pre-Harappan Culture. Other places show it developing into the Harappan Culture. Some sites have Harappan Culture only, and some have the late phases of the Harappans followed by subsequent cultures. The abrupt appearance of Harappans at a particular site may be due to the colonization of that site by a culture at a particular stage of development. Likewise, the disappearance of a cultural complex may involve the movement of its people. An overview of the entire picture suggests that neither the development nor the decline from one phase to another was simultaneous. Local and regional factors determined that the colonization of a site would take place at a certain phase of the Harappan development and its arrest or further development thereafter was similarly determined. It is high time that the dates are reinvestigated with freshly reoriented attitudes. No longer can one be obsessed with the idea of an abrupt end to the Harappan Culture. The data show that at Amri the Mature Harappan is succeeded by the Jhukar and Jhangar Cultures respectively. The picture is the same at Chanhudaro. Likewise there is evidence of the continuation or survival of this culture at Rangpur, where the Post-Harappan Period is marked by new pottery styles. The interval between these phases is marked by floods which perhaps forced the Harappans to abandon their site (Sankalia 1974).

At Somnath, the settlement on a thick flood deposit starts ca. 2000–1800 B.C. The culture has similarities to the Late Harappan and continues with the Prabhas Ware until 1500 B.C., when the pot shapes are copied from the Harappan Ware. The occupation continues until the first century B.C. (Sankalia 1974).

These instances once again show that the Harappan decline was neither a uniform nor a simultaneous event. Further, the culture diffused into succeeding cultures in which should be included the Cemetery H, Ochre Colored Pottery (OCP), the Copper Hoards and Painted Gray Ware (PGW). The diffusion was also partial, as stray Harappan finds have been discovered. The qualitative and quantitative analyses of material will help in determining the directions taken by the Harappan Culture.

THE ENVIRONMENT OF THE HARAPPANS

The rigidity of the two schools of thought referred to earlier has centered around the issue of a purely wet or dry climate during the Harappan times: wet during the Mature Harappan Period and dry during the period of degeneration. The debate over the years has offered strong, though refutable, arguments for and against each position. The hard fact that cannot be denied is that the Harappan stage was in many ways very different, particularly in geographical expansion, art, architecture, etc., from its antecedents and the Post-Harappan Cultures. This would not have been possible without a favorable environment, which according to one school, is believed to have been appreciably wet. The word humidity is also used to express wetness. Estimates for the amount of precipitation are often given but not for humidity. And the relation between the two is not realised at all. For instance, Delhi with 667 millimeters of total precipitation has a 48 mean average humidity, and Shri Ganganagar in West Rajasthan with 218 millimeters of precipitation has a 47 mean average humidity. Bikaner and Jodhpur have the same humidity of 41 whereas rainfall is 291, and 361 millimeters respectively. Dwarka in Gujarat has 73 humidity with 354 millimeters of rainfall. Etawah in Uttar Pradesh has 77 humidity with 758 millimeters of rainfall. But, all these areas are characterized by the Northern Tropical Thorn Forest and are semiarid to arid.

In my opinion enough has been said about climate. A climate of division has been created and the two schools have almost reached a point of no return. Obsessed to the extreme with climate, the search for the environment of the Harappans has been overlooked: climate is indeed a part of environment but it includes many other things as well. It is a complex whole of many interesting factors which influence every organism. All that surrounds and affects an organism is its environment. There are biotic (inter- and intraspecific competition) and abiotic (soil, atmosphere, light, temperature, precipitation, etc.) components of the environment.

As part of the biotic component, especially for man, the psychology, level of tolerance and adjustability play an important role apart from competition.

Man inhabits regions with or without a congenial environment. People living in both hot and cold deserts and arctic alpine regions show the extent of their tolerance and adjustment to a harsh and most inhospitable climate. The Indian desert is not as bad as elsewhere, since in the extreme it still has a rainfall of 10–25 centimeters. Between 17 and four persons per square kilometer inhabit the region and in several cases they have to fetch water for their daily needs from a distance of several kilometers. They have adjusted to nature. In the sandy region of northern Gujarat, the banks of the rivers and streams are complicated by a network of small rivulets and *nallas* which extend with each monsoon. The villages along their banks are constantly forced to move further inland. They do this but still do not permanently abandon the region.

Artemisia plants are known to possess alkaloids which repel sheep and goat and in normal circumstances these plants are left untouched. But in the harsh climate of Ladakh, *Artemisias* are not spared because of the paucity of other edible herbs (Duthie 1893).

The district of Kutch, with widespread saline marshes, the Little and the Great Ranns, where several Harappan settlement sites have been discovered, has a population of over 850,000 with 16 persons per square kilometer. A large part of its area (44,136 square kilometers) is a wasteland even though 5,149,000 hectares are under cultivation in millet, cotton, pulses and groundnut, etc. (Gaussen *et al.* 1968). And there are nearly 50 important towns and quite a large number of villages.

Several more instances of this kind may be cited of biotic and human tolerance and adjustment to the adverse vagaries of environment.

Water is the first essential for any biotic element and that explains human settlements along rivers, streams, or their tributaries. It is this riverine environment to which man owes the progress and decline of his civilizations. However harsh and inhospitable the climate may be, it is compensated for by the presence of water in the riverine environment. Wells may also be dug to further ameliorate the situation. Natural phenomena causing shifts in the river courses or their drying up have been the chief cause for the weathering out of a civilization. No matter how dry the climate may be it does not necessarily cause a river or stream to dry up. Any change in the source can be responsible for this. There is thus a need to study the impact of earth movements which result in changes in river courses or their sources. The lack of a continuous water supply may let loose the degeneration of a flourishing culture and reduce it eventually to nomadism.

Human influence in changing riverine environments to man's detriment may have far-reaching consequences. Hystera village in Chomu Tehsil of Jaipur District, about 45 kilometers northwest of Jaipur on the left bank of River Manda, is a typical example. Records reveal that nearly 300 years ago Hystera was a populous (7000 agricultural families) and prosperous village, famous for calico printing. Now there are only 1800 families. In addition to the written records there are the ruins of a fort, buildings, mosques, and the dry river, all of which speak of the village's former prosperity. This debacle resulted from bad management on the part of the villagers. Their ruthless cutting of vegetation caused soil erosion, resulting in the renewed activity of sand dunes and their encroachment on the productive lands. This turned their prosperous village of 300 years ago into a deserted one (Sankhala 1964).

Another interesting case of human interference can be cited in the territory between Lakhpat, Sahara and Mundan in Kutch, extending to a few miles north of Sindri which is now desert. Prior to A.D. 1800 it was a fertile tract and grew rice which yielded good revenue. Further, the channel from Lakhpat to Alibandar was navigable in A.D. 1808. The channel, called Puran, was once a considerable and perennial river across the western Rann to the sea via Lakhpat and Kori creek. At an earlier date, shortly after 1762, the ruler of Sind constructed a bund or barrage at Mora to divert the river into his territory. This resulted in salinity and the desertification of this territory in Kutch (Raverty 1892–97; Oldham 1926). Rice has not been cultivated there since then.

History is witness to the greater prosperity during the 16th and 17th centuries in Agra, then North India's largest commercial center, Cambay and several towns in the Rajasthan desert and Sind have lost much of their prosperity at the hands of man himself—his neglect and interference. Today, only ruins stand as a testimony supported by historical records to flourishing trade and commerce in these places.

The area of Okhamandel in Jamnagar District was once densely forested and fruits of *Tamarindus indicus* were exported from there. It was destroyed by Mohammad of Gazni in the 11th century A.D. Now tamarind fruits are not even available for domestic use here (Gaussen *et al.* 1968: 29–30).

Indigo and *Lathyrus odoratus,* both legumes, the root nodules of which help in the natural fertilization of soil, were once widely cultivated in the western region of the Subcontinent. Their cultivation was stopped by the British and this adversely affected soil fertility.

The gigantic ruins of Mundore Fort and several others, approximately seven kilometers in circuit, and castles and estates in the heart of the desert in Pokurna, Jodhpur, Jaisalmer and Saurashtra are testimony to flourishing prosperity in recent history (Todd 1829: 559–67).

Are these events due to human interference and the mismanagement of natural resources, or have there been changes in precipitation and temperature in the centuries preceding the present? No records of such changes in climate are available. The situation has been aggravated by the frequency of famines, one almost every seventh year.

These examples emphasize the need to re-examine in a new way the causes of the degeneration of the Harappan Culture. It may have been their overuse and mismanagement of natural resources, interference with natural phenomena accompanied by earth movements, which may have proved detrimental to their flourishing civilization, eventually settling in nomadism during the Late Phase. Thus, at some sites the degeneration appears to continue and develop into different cultures. But they still retain the Harappan imprint. Other groups moved out, radiated into different directions and mingled with other cultures imparting to them some Harappan impact.

The present, indeed, is the key to the past. But, the immediate present has witnessed changes due to factors which were perhaps not operative during the Harappan times. So the comparison is not fair and could be misleading. There has to be a base period for comparison, just as 1950 is the base year for ^{14}C dates. The 15th to 18th centuries can be considered suitable for the purpose.

Whatever be the base year, the fact that should not be overlooked is that there have been climatic and environmental fluctuations during even the last few centuries. Their impact on plant, animal and human communities, as well as their distribution, have not been properly assessed for comparative purposes with times several millennia ago.

Precipitation is very erratic in the arid region of Rajasthan. From 1875–1960 there have been eight years with a precipitation deficit of 50–83 percent of the norm. There were also nearly eight years when rainfall was 50 to 120 percent in excess of the norm (Datta and George 1964). From 1891 to 1960 Bhuj and Jodhpur experienced six to seven shifts to a semiarid climate. At each place there was a change to a dry subhumid climate: in 1917 at Jodhpur and in 1926 at Bhuj (Subramaniam 1964). A general trend to more congenial climate was observed from 1941–50; whereas the decades between 1911 and 1921, 1931 and 1940 were characterized by severe aridity. The year 1899 saw a famine in Rajasthan; 1899-1900 at

Ajmer (Subramaniam 1964).

The recent analysis of trends in climatic change in Rajasthan during 1891–1975 (Krishnan 1977) reveals that:

1) The below-normal rainfall spell from 1962–71 is comparable to a very significant below-normal rainfall spell from 1895–1905. The overall pattern shows a decrease from 1956 to 1969 and an increase thereafter. But at Churu, and to some extent at Jhunjhunu, just the reverse happened: increasing trend during 1957 to 1963 and a decreasing trend thereafter.

2) The period 1970–80 has been one with excessive rainfall (in 1970, 1973, 1975, 1976, etc.). During the surplus rainfall year of 1944 Barmer and Jaisalmer came under the subhumid category; but Bikaner, Phalodi and Ganganagar continued to be in the arid zone. During the high deficit rainfall of 1941, arid zone conditions prevailed in the entire state except in the Banswara and Jhalawar regions.

3) During 1901–70 the aridity index line of 80 shifted to the east in the first and second decades, particularly in Ganganagar, Bikaner, Churu and Jodhpur Districts; but no change was noticed in Barmer and Jalore Districts. Different decades from 1920 to 1970 witnessed minor oscillations comparatively more marked in the north (Churu District) and in the south (Jalore District).

A decreasing trend in summer temperature, and an increasing trend in winter temperature, was observed from 1960–61 in Jodhpur. There was a steep fall in wind speed from 1941–47 and gradual increase thereafter followed by a decline from 1952–1975.

The availability of surplus water in Jodhpur for runoff and the recharge of aquifers was steady during the period 1901–40; maximum during 1941–50; and decreased thereafter. The smallest figure (81 millimeters) was recorded during 1961–70. The pattern is consistent with the pattern of decreasing rainfall during this decade. Decade by decade surplus water for runoff and the recharge of aquifers is shown in Table 1.1.

It would also be of interest to know of instances of seismic activity. The year 1899 had the worst earthquake in Gujarat and Kutch (Oldham 1926). This may have caused river discharge fluctuations, changes in lake levels, changes in rainfall and temperature. Some of these may be local but others are regional in character. Unfortunately data are not available.

Many of these changes last over a decade or so. Some are also believed to be related to sunspot activity (Jagannathan and Raghavendra 1964). Short-term fluctuations have a direct economic significance, particularly in regard to crop yields, which may vary. Long and severe fluctuations may have a substantial influence on the life and distribution of plants and animals. But this can only happen if the duration and degree go beyond the threshold of biota tolerance.

It is reasonable to believe that short-term environmental changes, as observed during the last few hundred years, also occurred in the past, together with man's mismanagement of natural resources. The total, cumulated impact of all these should be considered the chief cause for the rise and fall of civilizations. Other factors such as war, may also be considered. But one does not have sufficient means to reconstruct short-term environmental alterations at archaeological sites. No matter how closely spaced a pollen sample may be it can represent several decades, and the reconstruction of decade to decade environmental changes is not possible with this tool. Can it be done through the study of stratigraphy and nature of sediments exposed in trenches at archaeological sites?

The estimated time span for the Harappans in the nuclear and the peripheral regions is each about 300 years. To believe that the environment remained static during those three centuries would be untenable in the light of present knowledge, as already stated. An individual site, or a group of sites, had its own environmental context, and it is this context that should be reconstructed and compared or contrasted with contexts elsewhere.

The desertion of the gigantic forts and castles in the heart of the Rajasthan desert and the construction of new ones not distant from the ruins, is indeed due to alterations in the environmental contexts rather than a change in climate.

The Harappans living at Lothal and Rangpur were recurrently affected by floods from 2450 B.C. to

Table 1.1

	1901–10	1911–20	1921–30	1931–40	1941–50	1951–60	1961–70
Number of surplus years	2	3	4	3	4	2	3
Total surplus water in millimeters	376	365	341	326	555	143	81

(Krishnan 1977: Table 4).

1600 B.C. but they continued to struggle and reconstruct. At Surkotada, not very far from there, the Harappans never experienced such a calamity and the conflagration between Periods II and III did not result in degeneration but the adoption and enrichment of Harappan traits, the construction of massive ramparts and an increase in copper objects. Nothing of this kind happened at Kalibangan as the environmental contexts were different there. A much different environmental context governed the undisturbed continuation of the cultural complex of the Harappans along the three-hundred-mile strip of the Hakra between the fourth millennium and the first millennium B.C. (Mughal 1980).

The varying environmental contexts in different parts of the Harappan Empire governed cultural processes, some of which led to urbanization, social and economic stratification, intensification of specialized activities as well as the organized exploitation of natural resources. An overview of all the discoveries sees these cultural processes at different stages of development and decline. It is a cultural complex in the real sense of the word. Recognition of it in the Early, Middle and Late Harappan Phases has attained a rigidity of attitudes which have eclipsed the understanding of the real perspectives. With hardened attitudes over the years, as often happens, one has failed to make use of the facts available.

For instance, one has not realized from the *Rigveda* and the later Vedic texts, that the Aryans were the first observers of the Harappan sites: the ruined mounds and cities along the banks of the Sarasvati and Drishadvati Rivers. They even named them: Naitandava, Vyarna, etc. Their ruination was not caused by the Aryans and the statement in *Taittiriya Brahman* (II, 4, 6, 8) is just a casual one that "The people who lived here were expelled by you, Oh Agni, and have migrated to other lands." The Aryans did encounter the dark-skinned, snub-nosed worshippers of Sisna deva who were rich in cattle and lived in Puras. Through battle and fire the Aryans did destroy their cities, Narmini for instance. They saw the local inhabitants flee rather than fight them. What about the chronology of the Aryans and what about the cultural complex they encountered and fought and destroyed? Knowing nothing of that, one makes much out of the slender evidence from the Harappan sites. Is one really justified in stretching the evidence that far?

The origin of lakes in the northern part of the Rajasthan desert about 10,000 years ago is believed to have been due to a prevailing wet climate at that time. The factual support for this belief is derived from meager stratigraphic and palynological evidence (Singh *et al.* 1974). Sambhar Lake, from which the stratigraphic evidence is derived, is in fact, as the geographical survey of the region reveals, an abandoned meandering river channel. This was choked by invading sands, suggesting that the environment then governing the movement of dunes, must have been dry or arid, rather than wet. The subsequent proportional decrease of the meager fresh water pollen suggests the progressive increase in aridity, resulting in a proportional increase in the salinity of the lake. Further, the simultaneous increase in the pollen of herbs, shrubs and trees, and of exotic pollen transported from the Himalayas in the north and Mount Abu in the south, suggests a further increase in aridity, and an environment charged with high speed winds and dust storms during the time period corresponding to that of the Harappan Civilization (Vishnu-Mittre 1978).

The varied environmental contexts helped the evolution, and subsequently the devolution, of the Harappan cultural complex. During devolution, there set in the evolution of new cultural complexes following the alterations in the environmental context. One strong, and common, element of the environmental context was the riverine environment. This was altered with the change in river courses along the banks of which the Harappans had lived (Wilhemy 1969). Readjustments to the alterations in the other elements of the environment kept the wheel of cultural processes moving, sometimes fast, sometimes slow, but to and fro.

During the course of adjustment, old traits were modified or abandoned and new ones evolved. For instance, in the later Harappan tradition most metal tools, mother goddess figurines, standard cubical weights and square steatite seals disappeared and changes were brought about in pottery. The cultural processes continued into PGW times at Bhagwanpura and Dadheri. The discovery, and use of iron, necessitated the abandonment or modification of old traits, pottery and elements of art and architecture, suiting them to the new environmental contexts. A qualitative and quantitative approach to variability of traits is certain to bring forth much new information. Together with a fresh approach one must keep the environmental contexts in view, and abandon rigid and stereotyped attitudes.

CONCLUSION AND SUMMARY

This paper urges the examination of the immense data at hand with a reorientation of thought and a fresh approach. Radiocarbon dates, and the qualitative and quantitative assessment of contemporary local and regional variability against the shared features of the Harappan cultural complex from one site to another should be worked out to determine the rate of local and regional development of the culture and to reconstruct the directions of its geographical expanse. Work along these lines will, it is believed, go a long way in solving many baffling problems that have confronted one for years. These include the interrelationships between the Pre-Harappan and Mature Harappan and the diffusionary processes at work during the later phase of the Harappan Culture. The various excavated sites should be looked at as colonizations by the Harappans at a particular stage in the development of the cultural complex. This was governed by local and regional environmental contexts, which either allowed further development of the complex or arrested it.

It would be advisable to designate the Harappan Civilization a cultural complex rather than dividing it into three phases: Pre-Harappan, Mature Harappan and Late Harappan. The entire complex shows a development of traditions which were either retained and modified, or abandoned because of their non-utility, and replaced by new ones. The trend of development of traditions is progressive or retrogressive depending upon the environmental context and this is apparent in the various levels or stages of development observed at the sites excavated. They should be treated as parts of the entire cultural complex, and in their stages of development should be treated as features with trends towards urbanization in the background of the struggle against environmental contexts and their ultimate adjustment to it.

Viewed in this light it would appear that the various processes of evolution and devolution of the cultural complex can be reconstructed if the sites are not considered isolated, either locally or regionally. Evidence has come forth from the commencement of the Pre-Harappans from a preceding culture; of Pre-Harappans living together with the Harappans; and of Harappans passing through the Late Harappans into the PGW Culture. Conditioned as the evolution or devolution processes were by the environmental contexts, differing locally and regionally, the events of initial development, maturity and decline could not have been simultaneous in the entire Harappan Empire. This aspect can be more clearly brought out by the qualitative and quantitative assessment of the traits.

It is inadequate to use wet or dry climate to explain processes of evolution and devolution. It is more important to reconstruct the entire environmental context of each site, keeping in view the psychology, the level of tolerance and adjustability of man to the vagaries of environment. Man's interference with, his exploitation of natural resources and his mismanagement, are other features which should not be overlooked.

Short-term fluctuations in the environment during the past few centuries are very suggestive that the naive, rigid attitudes about wet and dry climate should be altered. These fluctuations have a duration of a decade or so. Their cumulating impact on contemporary societies must be borne in mind to interpret the data on the Harappan cultural complex. All means should be used to determine short-term fluctuations in the past. Indeed, a new approach is needed here.

BIBLIOGRAPHY

Allchin, B. and F.R. Allchin, 1968
The Birth of Indian Civilization. Harmondsworth: Penguin.

Datta, R.K. and C.J. George, 1964
Some Climatological and Synoptic Features of the Arid Zones of Rajasthan. In *Proceedings of the Symposium on Problems of the Indian Arid Zone, Jodhpur.* Pp. 347-53. Delhi: Government of India.

Duthie, J.F., 1893
Report on a Botanical Tour in Kashmir. *Records of the Botanical Survey of India* 1 (1): 1.

Gaussen, H. *et al.*, 1968
Notice de la Feuille Kathiawar. *Travaux de la Section Scientifique et Technique De L'Institut Francais.* Pondicherry: Institut Francais.

Jagannatham, P. and V.K. Raghavendra, 1964
Wet Spells in Rajasthan. In *Proceedings of the Symposium on Problems of the Indian Arid Zone, Jodhpur.* Pp. 363-67. Delhi: Government of India.

Krishnan, A., 1977
A Climatic Analysis of the Arid Zone of North West India. In *Desertification and its Control.* Pp. 42-57. Delhi: Indian Council for Agricultural Research.

Mackay, E.J.H., 1943
Chanhudaro Excavations, 1935-36. American Oriental Series 20. New Haven: American Oriental Society.

Marshall, Sir John, ed., 1931
Mohenjodaro and the Indus Civilization. 2 vols. London: Arthur Probsthain.

Mughal, M.R., 1980
New Archaeological Evidence from Bahawalpur. *Man and Environment,* Vol. 4: 93-98.

Oldham, R.D., 1926
The Cutch (Kachh) Earthquake of 16th June 1819 with a Revision of the Great Earthquake of 12th June 1897. *Memoirs of the Geological Survey of India* 46 (2): 1-77.

Raikes, R.L., 1964
The End of the Ancient Cities of the Indus. *American Anthropologist* 66: 284-99.

Raverty, H.G., 1892
The Mihran of Sind and its Tributaries: A geographical and historical study. *Journal of the Asiatic Society of Bengal* 61: 155-508.

Sankalia, H.D., 1974
Prehistory and Protohistory of India and Pakistan. 2nd ed. Poona: Deccan College Postgraduate and Research Institute.

Sankhala, K.S., 1964
Sand Dune Formation at Hastura. In *Proceedings of the Symposium on the Problems of the Indian Arid Zones, Jodhpur.* Pp. 197-200. Delhi: Government of India.

Singh, G. *et al.*, 1974
Late Quaternary History of Vegetation and Climate of the Rajasthan Desert, India. *Philosophical Transactions of the Royal Society.* 267. Pp. 467-501. London.

Subramaniam, A.R., 1964
Drought and Aridity Studies of the Indian Arid Zones. In *Proceedings of the Symposium on the Problems of the Indian Arid Zones, Jodhpur.* Pp. 398-401. Delhi: Government of India.

Todd, J., 1829
Annals and Antiquities of Rajasthan. 2 vols. London: Routledge and Kegan Paul.

Vats, M.S., 1940
Excavations at Harappa. 2 vols. Delhi: Government of India.

Vishnu-Mittre, 1978
Palaeoecology of the Rajasthan Desert During the Last 10,000 Years. *Palaeobotanist* 25: 549-58.

Vishnu-Mittre and R. Savithri, 1978
Palaeobotanical and Pollen Analytical Investigations. *Indian Archaeology: A review, 1972-73.* Pp. 67-68. Delhi: Archaeological Survey of India.

Wilhemy, H., 1969
Urstromtal am Ostrand der Indusebene und der 'Sarasvati-Problem.' *Zeitschrift fur Geomorphologie,* Supplementband 8: 76-93.

JIM G. SHAFFER

2. Harappan Culture: A Reconsideration

INTRODUCTION

FIFTY years ago, the discovery of ancient cultural remains at Harappa and Mohenjodaro thrust the Harappan Culture upon the archaeological world. Although scholars were aware of the antiquity of cultural development in the South Asian Subcontinent, few were adequately prepared to cope with the nature and scope of cultural phenomena revealed by these and subsequent excavations in the Indus Valley. At the time of the discovery of the Harappan Culture, many scholars felt that technological and social innovations which resulted in urban literate cultures occurred initially in Mesopotamia and then diffused to other areas of the Old World where indigenous populations adapted them to local conditions. Besides diffusion of technological and social innovations, the other explanation most used by archaeologists of an earlier period to account for culture change was a more abstract theory about universal, or unilineal, evolution, exemplified by the various writings of V. Gordon Childe. However, when dealing with the explanation of particular cultural sequences, most archaeologists used what has been called cyclic models of cultural development. This model is based on an analogy of the life cycle of living organisms (see Nisbet 1969 for discussion); that is, every culture undergoes a developmental sequence of origin (birth), fluorescence (maturity) and decline (death). All cultures were subject to this cycle of stages. Any similar traits exhibited by different cultures were taken to mean that similar cultural processes were responsible for them or that diffusion had taken place. Since Mesopotamia was viewed as exemplifying the innovations which result in the development of early urban civilization, the social record retrieved there through archaeology could be applied to any area which had urban centers—especially an area as geographically close as the Indus Valley. Metallurgy, urban centers and literacy were associated with extensive external trade, centralization of political and economic organization, and the development of hereditary elites in the Mesopotamia area, and archaeologists, until recently, have never questioned that the same traits are exemplified by the Harappan data.

The high level of technological sophistication, the well-organized appearance of the architectural units, and the striking similarity in objects of material culture between widely separated sites recorded for the Harappan Culture were traits which could be compared to the final phases of early urbanization and state development in Mesopotamia. It was noted, however, that these traits were much more pronounced in the Indus Valley than in Mesopotamia. In particular, the traits of stylistic similarity and well organized architectural layout of settlements in a culture which encompassed such a vast geographical distribution (far larger than anything in Mesopotamia) suggested to early investigators that here was an example of an early urban literate culture and one also demonstrating the presence of a rigidly stratified, centralized and authoritarian government. Early interpretations about an Harappan Empire, with twin city capitals and a uniform and conservative culture were first comprehensively discussed in Piggott's (1950) general synthesis on the archaeology of South Asia. In one form or another, these same interpretations about the nature of the Harappan Culture have been repeated in nearly every synthesis on the culture to date. The uncritical acceptance of these *interpreta-*

tions by South Asian archaeologists has resulted in preconceived notions about the nature of the archaeological data, which in turn has been used to substantiate the original interpretations. This unquestioning transference of interpretation to studies of Harappan Culture hampers attempts to let the Harappan data "speak" for itself. The purpose of this paper is to examine some of these preconceived notions about Harappan Culture in light of recent data and analysis.

THE CURRENT STATE OF INTERPRETATION

A review of protohistoric archaeological research in northern South Asia shows that the major point of interpretation of any site or cultural complex is how it relates to the Mature Harappan. The usual, and often the only, question asked of the data is whether it constitutes an example of Early, Mature or Late Harappan cultural development. Usually this question is addressed through trait analysis of material artifacts which are compared for similarities and differences to those recorded for the Mature Harappan. Once this relationship with the Mature Harappan is established, cultural data is analyzed either within the context of western diffusionary social influences or as the life cycle inherent in any given culture group—the group is born, lives and dies at some point in time. This approach has limited the interpretation of Harappan Culture and affected the perspective of what constitutes cultural development in the general South Asian context. Two schools of thought have developed: those which see the Mature Harappan as an intrusive cultural development versus those proposing an indigenous cultural development. Related to this issue is how to evaluate the three known cultural complexes which are stratigraphically and chronologically earlier than the Mature Harappan. Debate about the developmental role played by Amri, Kot Diji and Sothi cultural complexes in the formation of the Mature Harappan has pre-occupied South Asian archaeology for the last twenty years. Many (e.g., Wheeler 1968) deny that any genetic cultural linkage exists between these cultures and what has been called the Mature Harappan. Others (e.g., Mughal 1970) maintain that while singly none of these complexes is a direct ancestor to the Mature Harappan, if all three are combined into a single, albeit diverse, cultural complex, they do share enough characteristics with the Mature Harappan to be considered an early phase of the Harappan Culture. This debate is currently unresolved. The point being made is that an overriding concern of how these cultures fit into a cyclic model of development of the Mature Harappan restricts the types of data collected, limits analysis and curtails the focus of research.

Research related to these three cultural complexes has been stratigraphical, chronological and typological in nature. Stratigraphic and chronological data have been utilized to demonstrate the greater antiquity of Amri, Kot Diji and Sothi complexes with respect to the Mature Harappan. Developmental relationships between these complexes and the Mature Harappan have usually been based on typological studies of material culture. Such studies emphasize the similarities and differences which can be defined between the material culture of the Mature Harappan and the artifacts associated with Amri, Kot Diji and Sothi complexes. As a result, one has an idea of the relative and absolute chronology for these complexes, and an extensive knowledge of material culture similarities and differences which exist between them as a group and the Mature Harappan. However, one knows very little about the Amri, Kot Diji or Sothi economics, settlement patterns, or about the political, social or religious organizations. In other words, more is known about the similarities and differences between the Mature Harappan and these groups than is known about the total cultural configuration of any particular social unit or group as a whole. The present data base is so limited that even if a definite cultural-social link could be established between one, or all of these complexes, and the Mature Harappan, it would still not be possible to explain how the link is defined through time, i.e., what changes occurred to create the Mature Harappan Culture.

The focus on the link between the Amri, Kot Diji and Sothi culture complexes and the Mature Harappan has been at the expense of addressing critical issues of the early protohistoric period in South Asia. First, how can the presence of these cultures in the Indus Valley be accounted for? What is the nature of the social, political, religious and economic organization of these complexes? Do Amri, Kot Diji and Sothi represent distinct cultural entities or are they regional variants of a basic cultural pattern? Since these complexes maintained some degree of interaction among themselves (evidenced by intrusive/trade items as well as similarities among some objects of material culture), what was the nature of these interaction networks, and how were they maintained through time? The questions of regional diversity and maintenance of interaction networks are important to understand not only the nature of these cultural complexes, but also that of the Mature Harappan. One of the major characteristics of the Mature Harappan is the presumed establishment of homogenous cultural traits throughout the Indus Valley. Although the homogeneity of Mature Harappan material culture has been overstated, its continuity in material culture style and types contrasts to the more obvious regional diversity of the Amri, Kot Diji and Sothi complexes. It is possible that the homogeneity of Mature Harappan material culture reflects, or was a capitalization of, the interaction networks established by the Amri, Kot Diji and Sothi complexes.

Using cyclic models of development for interpreting Harappan Culture has resulted in the uncritical application of theories and concepts concerned with the development of urban literate civilizations in Mesopotamia (and other areas) to the South Asian context. As a result data on Harappan Culture has been forced into a framework supporting preconceived theories about early urban civilizations. The highly subjective interpretations of Piggott's (1950) general synthesis of the Harappan Culture are perpetuated to the extent that no other interpretation is considered possible, let alone valid. The central issue here is whether Mature Harappan traits such as the homogenous material culture, developed craft specialities (metallurgy, lapidary work, pottery, etc.), specialized public architecture (defensive walls, granaries, great bath, etc.), literacy, extensive external trade, and a grid-patterned urban center reflect a highly stratified society with centralized authority. In Mesopotamia similar culture traits are associated with the development of social-political elites, centralization of authority (sacred and/or secular), and the rise of early states which individually underwent cyclic patterns of development. A similar situation has been assumed for the Indus Valley. Recent excavations and reinterpretations of existing data on the Mature Harappan clearly indicate that the Mesopotamian models, even when adjusted for local factors, are not applicable to the South Asian context. The application of such models rests on a conceptualization of the nature of the Mature Harappan Culture unsupported by the data. I now want to consider the nature of Harappan Culture as indicated by the available data.

Data are limited in the sense that most interpretations are based on the excavations at Mohenjodaro and Harappa. Subsequent comparable excavations have been attempted at Lothal and Kalibangan, but definitive reports on these sites are not yet published. Perhaps no other "early civilization" has been so *thoroughly* reconstructed on the basis of two site reports as the Mature Harappan. With the known number of Mature Harappan sites approaching 200, the weakness of relying mainly on data from Mohenjodaro and Harappa becomes more apparent. Also, interpretation of the Mature Harappan has been significantly biased by the nearly exclusive attention given by excavators to the large, presumable urban, sites of this culture. As Fairservis (1975: 241-42) has noted, knowledge about Mature Harappan urban centers has been collected at the expense of knowledge about the equally important rural aspects of this culture. Another important factor overlooked in most evaluations of the Mature Harappan is that the site of Mohenjodaro, because of its large size (almost five times larger than Harappa) and several unique features (i.e., the great bath, granary style, etc.), may not even be representative of Mature Harappan urban sites. Failure to recognize these biases in the data results in uncritical distortions and interpretations about Mature Harappan Culture.

Some material artifacts of the Harappan Culture can be considered. Architecture, although technically an aspect of material culture, will be discussed separately. The main analytical framework for Mature Harappan material culture was established by Piggott (1950: 135-42), who chose to emphasize the uniformity in style and technology definable among such objects as ceramics, metal tools, seals and weights. According to Piggott such uniformity correlates with a "... a monotonous regularity of a highly-organized community under some strong system of centralized government, controlling production and distribution and no doubt levying a system of tolls and customs throughout the territory under its rule" (1950: 136). Piggott felt that this uniformity reflected a basically conservative attitude toward culture change, one reflected in the Mature Harappan Culture to such a degree that he felt it had entered a stage of cultural stagnation. This interpretation of Mature Harappan material culture is somewhat reflected in all subsequent summaries on the culture. Of course, there exists a definite Harappan style and regularity in the types of objects associated with Mature Harappan settlements. However, it is possible that the uniformity of such objects has been overemphasized, and similarities which exist do not necessarily reflect a conservative cultural framework nor are they necessarily indicative of centralized types of political organization. Explorations and excavations in the eastern Mature Harappan sites have demonstrated that among the ceramics, some degree of regional variation does exist. At Surkotada (Joshi 1972) for example, Mature Harappan decorated pottery was found in association with a distinct regional style of ceramics. It is possible that the traditional emphasis upon the very distinctive Harappan black-on-red pottery has prevented the definition of regional ceramic variations which manifest themselves among the non-decorative or non-black-on-red ceramics. At the Mature Harappan site of Allahdino (a small site near Karachi) the distinctive Harappan black-on-red ceramic type was restricted to specific vessel shapes and sizes, and quantitatively constituted less than one percent of the pottery found. It is possible that the cultural rules governing the manufacture and distribution of the distinctive black-on-red decorated pottery were significantly different, and varied independently, from those which governed other types of pottery.

The current evidence indicates that regional variations can be defined among Mature Harappan ceramics. However, a similar situation does not seem to apply to other material culture objects such as metal tools, lithics, figurines, seals, weights and beads. Whenever these objects are found in a Mature Harappan context, they do reflect a pronounced degree of homogeneity in style and technique of manufacture. In assessing the importance of this homogeneity, the recent reanalysis of material from Mohenjodaro and Harappa by Fentress (1976) is worth noting. Fentress (1976: 205-63) was able to determine differences between sites based upon the proportional ratios of some artifact types when compared to an expected ratio based on the volume of excavated earth, 2 : 1 (Mohenjodaro : Harappa). Among the intaglio stamp seals, a between-site comparative ratio of 3 : 1 exists while the seal impressions had a reverse ratio of 1 : 3. In addition, a wider range of variation in seal type and symbols exist for Harappa when compared with Mohenjodaro. Anthropomorphic ceramic figurines were found to correspond closely to the expected between-site ratio of 2 : 1 but zoomorphic figurines were present in a ratio of almost 1 : 1. Male figurines had a higher frequency at Harappa than Mohenjodaro. In general Fentress maintains that figurines found at Mohenjodaro were also more elaborate than those at Harappa. Only stone weights were found to occur in the expected between-site ratio of 2 : 1. However, of the five metal categories examined (jewelry, tools, figurines, tablets, and vessels) none conforms to the expected between-site ratio. Ratios for these metal categories ranged from 4 : 1 to 33 : 1 with Harappa having proportionately less metal. Fentress also indicates that "Within the sites the DK Area of Mohenjodaro showed a high concentration of metal, while the high mound at Mohenjodaro showed very little compared to the high mound at Harappa" (1976: 260). There were certain tool and metal types that were mutually exclusive between the two sites. Finally, metal vessels were numerous, but vessel forms were distinct between the sites. Although Fentress' study has methodological limitations, it demonstrates that the importance attached to stylistic and technological similarities of the Mature Harappan hinders recognition of the frequency differences of various artifacts which exist at the two sites and hinders recognition of frequency differences which may exist between Mohenjodaro, Harappa and other Harappan sites. Such artifact frequency differences may reflect regional variations in man-to-land relationships, or functional differences among sites. It is increasingly apparent that characterizing Mature Harappan material culture as "monotonously uniform" is misleading and an oversimplification of the archaeological record.

Although regional variation exists for some artifact categories, a pronounced stylistic and technological similarity is definable in other material culture categories. Assessing the similarity is complicated by the fact that the geographical distribution of the Mature Harappan encompasses an area larger than any comparable or contemporary early civilization in the Old World. Such widespread cultural similarity has been attributed to the existence of a strong centralized government enforcing rules governing production, and to the innate conservate perspective of the culture (i.e., Piggott 1950). The absence of corroborating archaeological data indicates that alternative explanations may be possible. Specifically, it is suggested here that this similarity in style and manufacture among objects of Mature Harappan material culture reflects the existence of an extensive and intensive *internal* distribution and communication system (Shaffer in press). The quantity and variety of objects involved encompassing such a vast geographic area clearly suggests that regular avenues of communication and interaction were maintained among settlements of Mature Harappan affiliation. The fact that objects manufactured from materials with limited sources of origin (semiprecious stones, metals, etc.) were involved with this interaction system suggests that the broad-based Harappan Culture may have rested on an *internal* trading network. The extent of such an internal network is indicated by the variety and quantity of similar objects found throughout the vast geographical region occupied by the Mature Harappan settlements. The intensity or importance of such a system is only beginning to be appreciated. While it is expected that such large urban centers as Mohenjodaro, Harappa and Kalibangan would be involved in such an internal network, the excavation at Allahdino demonstrated that even the very small, presumably rural, types of settlements were equally integrated in such a network. Excavations at Allahdino demonstrated the presence of almost every major artifact category of the Mature Harappan Culture, including quantities of metal objects (including silver and gold) and semi-precious stones. At the same time, despite extensive excavations at the site, there is no evidence to indicate that any of these objects, including ceramics, were manufactured at the site. The present evidence suggests that almost all major categories of material culture objects at Allahdino were manufactured elsewhere, and came to the site via its residents who were participants in an internal Harappan trading network(s). The fact that the system involved the distribution of objects commonly used in daily activities, such as pottery, as well as objects of more limited function (jewelry), indicates that this internal distribution system was crucial to every phase of Harappan adaptation, whether urban or rural. The existence of such an internal artifact distribution network would account for the similarity found in Mature Harappan material culture and explain the development of the regional diversity noted above.

A similar problem exists when interpreting data dealing with Harappan architectural features. For example, the idea that only centralized social authority permits organizing personnel and material to build those kinds of structures is reflected in a recent summary of the Harappa Culture:

The archaeological evidence does support a view of an authoritarian, hierarchical, social and political system: the extraordinary cultural unity maintained over that vast geographical expanse could not have been possible without a high degree of centralized authority. The large granaries, efficient drainage system, and planned settlements required central control (Lamberg-Karlovsky and Sabloff 1979: 203).

To be precise, the data indicates that "granaries" have actually only been identified at Mohenjodaro and Harappa (at Lothal this issue was avoided by designating one structure as a "warehouse"). Other than interpreting them as granaries, the two structures have little in common (Fentress 1976: 133-83 for extensive discussion of various traits). Architecturally there is no similarity between the two buildings so designated. At Mohenjodaro the granary is a rectangular series of mud-brick platforms separated by narrow corridors, while the Harappa structure is two long blocks of subdivided rectangular units separated by a central aisle. If uniformity in material culture was an important Mature Harappan trait then it certainly is not reflected in the construction of what are presumably two important public architectural units! The artifacts associated with these units "...indicate no particular special function either in the form of grains, storage jars or otherwise" (Fentress 1976: 179). Structures associated with the so-called "granaries" at these sites are completely different in nature. At Mohenjodaro the granary is found on the high mound in the context of other public units, while at Harappa the granary is found on the low mound surrounded by ordinary domestic structures. The Mohenjodaro unit would have needed an elaborate wooden superstructure for which there is currently no archaeological evidence. The so-called "loading dock" at the Mohenjodaro structure faces a narrow congested street, making it very unlikely that it could have so functioned as a grain transfer or distribution area (see also Jansen 1979 for discussion on this point). In summary there is nothing in the existing archaeological record to indicate that either structure definitely functioned as a granary, nor that of themselves they reflect a strongly centralized government or a redistributive economy. Yet there is no doubt that these are important architectural units and understanding what they represent is crucial to one's perspective on the nature of the Mature Harappan Culture.

In other architectural features, the Mature Harappan "gridiron layout" (Wheeler 1966: 23) of urban centers is said to reflect the existence of centralized authority and a highly developed sense of town-planning. Jansen's (1979) restudy of the Mohenjodaro excavations demonstrates that the gridiron layout existed more in Wheeler's mind than in Mohenjodaro's actual design.

> One recognizes that there is no actual proof for the famous 'grid pattern'. Only the north-south axis of First Street is evident. The second axis to the east is not proved. All other streets turn corners and do not fit into a 'gridiron lay-out'. But the general orientation of all structures, except that in trench 'M', is according to the cardinal directions. The same system of 'turning corners' may be recognised on entering the houses. In general there are no straight axes to enter (1979: 414).

Indeed, a review of published excavation plans reveals that the vast majority of the gridiron layout at Harappan sites is represented by dotted lines through unexcavated areas rather than the solid lines of actually excavated streets. One cannot help questioning to what extent the presumed existence of a gridiron street plan has influenced the placing of these "dotted line" streets through unexcavated areas. The existence of a cultural norm prescribing the orientation of all buildings according to the cardinal directions would of itself produce a superficial "gridiron pattern," without the existence of centralized authority or a developed sense of town planning. As with the so-called granaries, the current assumptions about Harappan town planning are not clearly warranted by existing archaeological data. If the more usual interpretations of Mature Harappan Culture are insufficient, it is best to re-examine the available data to see if alternative explanations may be proposed.

ALTERNATIVE EXPLANATIONS

One of the more striking aspects of Mature Harappan material culture is the quantity of metal objects. Excavations produced almost 2000 metal artifacts at Mohenjodaro over 1000 at Harappa. No doubt if more detailed excavation techniques had been used, and all the more fragmentary metal examples recorded, the count of metal artifacts would have been even larger. Even the small Harappan site of Allahdino has a tremendous number of metal artifacts. Types of metal smelted by the Mature Harappans included copper-bronze, gold, silver, lead and more rarely electrum. The ratio of functional to non-functional (jewelry) items is difficult to determine since a single necklace or belt can contain hundreds of metal beads. However, if one discounts beads, there appears to be a very high incidence of functional metal tool types (i.e. points, knives, chisels, etc.). It is difficult, of course, to definitely ascribe a utilitarian status to these objects, however, two associated aspects of these artifacts suggest their utilitarian nature. Agrawal's (1971: 168) study of metal artifacts indicates that the process of alloying was understood, although the bronze objects demonstrated a wide variation in the percentages of metals added to copper to make bronze. He found that tin-bronze was mainly confined to knives, axes and chisels, with other objects having a lower percentage of metal additives. He feels that this reflects an inability by the Harappans to control the correct metal proportions which, indeed, may have been the case. At the same time, this differential ratio of copper to other alloying metals may reflect functional variations. In other words, tool types whose utilitarian function would have benefited from hardness would have the higher amounts of metal additives needed to produce that hardness. Tool types whose utilitarian function was not so dependent upon hardness had smaller amounts of metal additives. A combination of tin-bronze confined to tools such as chisels and axes reflects a cultural decision in the same way that tools whose utilitarian function was not dependent upon hardness but on sharpness (i.e., points, razors, fishhooks, etc.) would have had fewer metal additives. Given the rarity of tin in the environment, metalsmiths may have been forced to make the most economical use possible of this rare metal. Varying ratios of copper to other metals in the manufacture of bronze objects may not reflect technological limitations, but rather a detailed knowledge of how to produce a functional utilitarian object with the greatest economy of materials.

Two recent studies (Hoffman and Cleland 1977; and Cleland 1977) of the lithic artifacts from Harappan and related sites (Amri, Kot Diji, Sarai Khola, Gumla, etc.) also support the hypothesis that manufacture of metal objects in a Mature Harappan context was directed toward the production of functionally utilitarian items. Cleland came to the following conclusion after an extensive analysis of the lithic artifacts from Early and Mature Harappan sites:

> Lithic technology during this period declined quantitatively and in terms of functional variabi-

lity. Although still important in production, the number of tasks in which chipped stone tools were used declined. Contemporaneously utilitarian copper-bronze tools became widely distributed. It has been suggested herein that these two trends were causally linked, i.e. that metal tools were replacing stone (1977: 175).

In their analysis of the Allahdino lithics, Hoffman and Cleland came to a similar conclusion:

> Not only in the general paucity and simplicity of its lithic industry, but in specific morphological categories, such as point tools and heavy-duty cutting tools, Allahdino presents a striking contrast to other Chalcolithic and Bronze Age sites to the west. We strongly suspect that this general poverty, far from belittling the general level of Harappan industry, hints at the greater importance of copper/bronze tools in the Harappan world at a time when they were apparently the plaything of the elite classes farther to the west. Perhaps this difference is merely an artifact of differing techniques of recovery, but, at this point in time, there is good reason to suspect that copper and bronze tools were not only relatively more abundant in Harappan society, but were manufactured and redistributed according to a basically different set of social and economic rules (1977: 60).

It is very likely that Harappan metal tools were manufactured and distributed so that they could be utilized in daily utilitarian activities. Metal tools were thus a part of the utilitarian activities performed in both the large urban centers such as Mohenjodaro and the much smaller, seemingly more rural, settlements such as Allahdino.

The utilitarian nature and the broad-based distribution of these metal objects within the social group is indicated by the context in which they are found distributed within a site. As noted above, Fentress states that the highest frequency of metal objects was in the habitation area at Mohenjodaro—not in the high mound with all of its public or monumental architectural units. Similarly, at Harappa, Fentress states that metal artifacts are relatively evenly distributed throughout the site, rather than being concentrated in any particular area. At Allahdino, as at Harappa, metal artifacts were found distributed throughout the site in a variety of contexts: inside structures and outside structures (in streets, drains, and trash deposits). Even a gold, silver and carnelian beaded belt crammed into a small, plain red jar was located on the floor of a structure. At present there appears to be no definite association of metal artifacts with any particular area of a Harappan site or type of architecture within a particular site. Although the sample is limited, another striking characteristic of Harappan metal artifacts is their rare occurrence in graves. Other than a few beads or blades, metal objects are seldom found associated with burials. Precious and semiprecious stone objects are also rare in Harappan cemeteries. These stone artifacts seem to have similar characteristics of distribution and context in Harappan sites as the metal artifacts, i.e., in all places. To sum up, it appears that except for obvious items of jewelry, metal artifacts were manufactured for use in daily activities and were available to a broad segment of Harappan society, urban or rural. A similar distribution and access to items manufactured from semiprecious stones may also be postulated.

Other data shedding light on the Mature Harappan Culture are emerging from the Allahdino excavations. All major categories of Harappan material culture, except anthropomorphic figurines, have been located in quantity at this small site. This includes semiprecious stones and precious metals. Structures at Allahdino are oriented to the cardinal directions, separated by streets, and are functionally distinct (although at present one is unable to make specific functional designations). Numerous hydraulic features, including drains, wells and bathrooms, are found. One large structure with a mud-brick platform at one end and a deep well at the other may represent some type of public architectural unit. Absence of any indication of local manufacture for most objects of material culture found at the site indicates that the inhabitants of Allahdino had access to, and participated in, the extensive Harappan internal trading noted earlier (see Shaffer in press). Yet another significant aspect of Allahdino was the location of several seals, one sealing, and several examples of Harappan script incised and painted on potsherds. These examples of Harappan script located at Allahdino suggest that literacy was present in a small site context and may have played an important part in daily activities there. The point to note is that qualitatively there is little difference between Allahdino and the large urban centers of the Mature Harappan Culture such as Mohenjodaro. All the essential characteristics of the urban center are duplicated at this smaller site, including literacy. It would appear from the available data (albeit it is limited) that there was no sharp cultural dichotomy separating the large urban centers and smaller, presumably rural, settlements (see Fairservis 1975: 299-300).

From this brief discussion, a very different picture of the nature of the Mature Harappan Culture is beginning to emerge. Traditionally early urban literate cultures are associated with the development of pronounced social stratification and concentration of wealth and power in the hands of few social, presumably hereditary, elites. Archaeologically, this type of social pattern is symbolized in the appearance of "palaces," "temples," and "royal tombs" with associated wealth objects (metals, semi- and precious stones, works of art, etc.). Metal objects in the Mesopotamian context are usually interpreted as representing status symbols, and as a means of concentrating wealth in a limited number of relatively portable objects. The function of metal artifacts in early Mesopotamian cultures is viewed as being mainly symbolic rather than utilitarian. This is a distinct contrast to the Mature Harappan Culture where the primary function for a vast number of metal artifacts appears to have been utilitarian rather than symbolic. Such a contrasting difference in functional roles for metal artifacts is in part due to the fact that the distribution zone for the Mature Harappan Culture incorporates areas which contained natural deposits of these metals. Therefore, metal artifacts were more readily available to Mature Harappans than they were to Mesopotamian groups, which had to obtain metals from geographically and socially foreign areas. Indeed, all of the commodities associated with wealth and status in Mesopotamia can be found within the distribution zone of the Mature Harappan save two: lapis lazuli and tin. It is clear that the emphasis for the Mature Harappan Culture was upon internal exchange and distribution rather than external exchange. Mention must be made here of the recently discovered Mature Harappan site of Shortugai on the Oxus River in Afghanistan. This site has been quickly interpreted by some to demonstrate the importance and existence of external trade for the Harappan Culture (Kohl 1978). However, as argued elsewhere (Shaffer in press), this site could equally represent an attempt by the Harappans to incorporate more effectively a commodity not found (lapis lazuli and perhaps tin) within the geographical boundaries of the existing internal exchange network. If external trade, or interaction with foreign cultural groups, was a primary purpose for the settlement of Shortugai, then the relative paucity of Harappan type objects in the contemporary sites of Turkmenistan is puzzling. Even more puzzling in this respect is the absence of any Harappan type artifacts at Shahr-i Sokhta, Mundigak, Said Qala Tepe, and Deh Morasi Ghaundai which are geographically closer to the Indus Valley. I do not deny, however, that some form of direct, or more likely indirect, contact took place between the Mature Harappan and cultural groups located to the west. Such contact is documented by the few Harappan artifacts found in Mesopotamia, and more recently, at Tepe Yahya (see Chakrabarti in press for discussion). What I do maintain is that external exchange networks did not have the same socioeconomic significance in the Mature Harappan context that they did in Mesopotamia or the Iranian Plateau, and that for the Mature Harappan Culture, the development and maintenance of internal networks is a critical issue for understanding the cultural processes at work in the greater Indus Valley.

The production of objects of personal adornment (jewelry) from metals and semiprecious stones indicates, however, that such commodities were not entirely without symbolic meaning for the Mature Harappan Culture. Beads, mirrors and pins would have little utilitarian value in the harvesting of grains or the building of a house. Yet, the frequency and distribution context of these objects also indicate a significant cultural contrast with Mesopotamia and other groups to the west. Since such objects have little utilitarian value but, at the same time do represent a considerable technological effort in manufacture, their acquisition very likely bestowed some social distinction on the social unit (individual or group) able to procure them. That such objects, and metal tools also, could be accumulated is indicated by finding occasional clusters of these items within a site (or "hordes" as they are commonly called). Unlike cultures to the west, such items in the Mature Harappan context are not found in association with any particular type of architecture, area of the site or burials. The absence of such objects in most burials, and their statistical insignificance when found in burials, is important to note. Although such items may fall within the cultural category of "wealth objects," the distribution of these objects within the social group was quite different between the Harappan and western cultures. The failure to define specific contextual associations for these items indicates that a relatively broad segment of Harappan society had access to and the ability to procure such objects, unlike in Mesopotamia where the distribution of such items was increasingly restricted to a limited range of social units. Absence of such objects in Harappan burials may indicate that: (1) such wealth objects were not hereditary; (2) they were not considered particularly important indicators of social status; (3) the objects were redistributed at the time of death; (4) There was an absence of well-defined social stratification; or (5) some other cultural rule at present unknown was at work designating their presence or absence in burials. If wealth was not hereditary, or if wealth and power were constantly fluctuating between units of any social group, this might also account for the inability to identify "palaces," "temples" or "royal tombs" in the Harappan context. At present, however, the data are too limited to form a more comprehensive picture of the nature of the Mature Harappan social organization. The data do indicate that if pronounced social stratification was present in Mature Harappan Culture, it is reflected in a different, as yet undetected, set of archaeological traits than is the case in Mesopotamia. And, it is quite possible that the "road" to an urban literate culture in the Indus Valley represents a unique achievement in urbanization. It could be that in the Indus Valley, a technologically advanced, urban, literate culture was achieved without the usually associated social organization based on hereditary elites, centralized political government (states, empires) and warfare.

No overview of the Harappan Culture is possible without some reference to its final phase—the Late Harappan. This is the most poorly understood period of Harappan cultural development. It is often referred to as a period of "decline" or "degeneration" which witnessed the end of urban centers in this geographical area. Such an interpretation reflects the dominant influence of the cyclic model of cultural development: what is born must eventually die. Moreover, the archaeological sequence of events in the Sind (especially those recorded at Mohenjodaro) have to a great extent governed interpretations for this phase. Yet, Late Harappan sites have a very broad distribution within the geographical area recorded for Harappan Culture. The data on the Late Harappan is so limited that only the barest essentials of chronological boundaries and material culture traits are known. Certainly, such subjective evaluations as "decline" and "degenerate" are unwarranted until a fuller archaeological record is available for examination. Cultural changes distinguish the Late from the Mature Harappan Phase, but the exact nature of these changes and the processes responsible for them are at present unknown. Even the often stated disappearance of urban centers noted for the Late Harappan is an assumption. While urban centers may have ceased to exist in the Sind, it is impossible to assert that this was the situation for the entire area covered by the Harappan Culture during this phase. Certainly, until some of the large Medieval and Early Historic sites which also have associated Late Harappan ceramics are excavated, and the extent of the Late Harappan settlement determined, it is inappropriate to conclude that urban centers were absent during the Late Harappan Culture. A systematic research program involving large-scale, horizontal excavations at Late Harappan sites is one of the most critical needs in South Asian archaeology today.

CONCLUSION

This discussion has attempted to demonstrate that the uncritical application of cyclic models of culture change in general, and those developed for Mesopotamia in particular, to Harappan Culture has resulted in significant distortions about the nature of the Harappan Culture. Early interpretations of the Mature Harappan Culture have been uncritically accepted and propagated to the extent that preconceived notions about the nature of Mature Harappan Culture have significantly influenced interpretations of archaeological data, both new and old. Together, these factors have resulted, I believe, in an overall theoretical stagnation concerning analysis of the data available on Mature Harappan Culture. For too long, one has let preconceived notions about the nature of Harappan Culture dictate what the archaeological data will reveal. It is time to view the archaeological data for what it is, and not what one thinks it is. Recent studies are just beginning to indicate the real importance of Harappan studies, showing that in South Asia, a unique experiment in the development of urban, literate culture, was underway. Such a culture was highly attuned to local conditions and not a mirror image of Mesopotamia's urban experiment or, for that matter, of any other region which witnessed the development of comparable cultural achievements.

BIBLIOGRAPHY

Agrawal, D.P., 1971
The Copper Bronze Age in India. Delhi: Munshiram Manoharlal.

Chakrabarti, Dilip, in press
External Trade During the Harappan Period: Evidence and hypothesis. In *Indus Civilization: Problems and Issues.* B.B. Lal and S.C. Malik, eds. Simla: Indian Institute of Advanced Study.

Cleland, J., 1977
Chalcolithic and Bronze Age Chipped Stone Industries of the Indus Region: An analysis of variability and change. Ph.D. dissertation, Department of Anthropology, University of Virginia.

Fairservis, W.A., 1975
The Roots of Ancient India. 2d. ed. Chicago: University of Chicago Press.

Fentress, Marcia, 1976
Resource Access, Exchange Systems, and Regional Interaction in the Indus Valley: An investigation of archaeological variability at Harappa and Mohenjodaro. Ph.D. dissertation, Department of Oriental Studies, University of Pennsylvania.

Hoffman, M. and J. Cleland, 1977
Excavations at Allahdino II, The Lithic Industry. New York: Walter A. Fairservis, American Museum of Natural History.

Jansen, Michael, 1979
Architectural Problems of the Harappan Culture. In *South Asian Archaeology: 1977.* Maurizio Taddei, ed. Pp. 405-31. Instituto Universitario Orientale. Seminario di Studi Asiatici, Series Minor VI: Naples.

Joshi, J.P., 1972
Excavations at Sur Kotada and New Light on the Harappan Migration. *Journal of the Oriental Institute, University of Baroda* 22: 98-144.

Kohl, P., 1978
The Balance of Trade in Southwestern Asia in the Mid-third Millennium B.C. *Current Anthropology* 19: 463-92.

Lamberg-Karlovsky, C.C. and J. Sabloff, 1979
Ancient Civilizations: The Near East and Mesoamerica. Menlo Park: Benjamin Cummings.

Mughal, M.R., 1970
The Early Harappan Period in the Greater Indus Valley and Northern Baluchistan (c. 3000-2400 B.C.). Ph.D. dissertation, Anthropology Department, University of Pennsylvania.

Nisbet, Robert A., 1969
Social Change and History. New York: Oxford.

Piggott, S., 1950
Prehistoric India. Baltimore: Penguin Books.

Shaffer, J., in press
Harappan External Trade: A critical assessment. In *Indus Civilization: Problems and issues.* B.B. Lal and S.C. Malik, eds. Simla: Indian Institute of Advanced Study.

Wheeler, Sir Mortimer, 1966
Civilizations of the Indus Valley and Beyond. New York: McGraw-Hill.

Wheeler, Sir Mortimer, 1968
The Indus Civilization. 3rd ed. Supplementary volume to the Cambridge History of India. Cambridge: The University Press.

S.P. GUPTA

3. The Late Harappan: A Study in Cultural Dynamics

PART I

What happens when the urban fabric of a culture disintegrates? People, by and large, leave the urban settlements and migrate elsewhere. Similarly, material culture becomes poor. But what items of culture are still prone to persist? Is there any pattern in this process? Two case studies are being undertaken to answer these questions. One from India and the other from Soviet Central Asia: the Harappan Culture Cycle and the Altin Culture (Namazga V Bronze Age) Cycle. These examples, it is hoped, will explain, at least partly, the dynamics of the Late Harappan Culture complexes. In this context one more question is touched upon in light of the fact that, broadly speaking, both Soviet Central Asia and India passed through two cycles of urbanization; the first belonging to the third millennium and the second belonging largely to the late second and early first millennium. Are any proccesual parallels observed between the two otherwise independent cycles? One may go even a step further and ask if at some point in time they converged. After all, these two dynamic areas are geographically not far removed. In fact, there are a few definite pieces of evidence to show that the cultures in these regions interacted closely.

To begin with, during the Late Bronze Age there was a marked decrease in human occupation in the traditional strongholds in these two culture areas. This followed a period of fluorescence. In Turkmenia, Altin Depe was reduced from 114 to three acres and Namazga Depe dropped from 170 acres to 3.5 acres (Gupta 1979 II: 175ff.). In eastern Iran at Shahr-i Sokhta the occupied area shrank from 80 hectares to five hectares (Biscioni, Salvatori and Tosi 1977). In the Indian Subcontinent, Mohenjodaro was reduced from 85 hectares to approximately three hectares, and Lothal was reduced from 4.75 hectares to approximately two hectares. Thus, broadly speaking, during the Late Harappan period of the second millennium the population decreased considerably on most urban settlements. While some people may have perished, others seemed to have migrated to different places. It is equally possible that some sites were only temporarily deserted and some people may have vainly gone back to the old towns, while others may have been attracted to other villages existing in the neighborhood. Some may have even broken ground and founded new settlements. In fact, the number of people who did the latter appears to be the largest. Those who struggled hard to remain in the towns sometimes occupied areas nearby or only a portion of the old settlement because of limited population and economic resources. Examples of all these patterns are available in archaeological record.

At Mohenjodaro there are several cases of violent death (Marshall 1931) and uncared-for dead bodies (Dales 1964). A number of Pre- (or Early) Harappan sites in Haryana and Bahawalpur are found to have been occupied by the Late Harappans, some of whom may have been those who had deserted sites like Harappa and Kalibangan; although this is not always easy to prove archaeologically. Sites like Chanhudaro and Harappa were, however, occupied by two different kinds of "Late Harappans," the Jhukar and the Cemetery H People, respectively; after, of course, a definite break in occupation. At places like Mitathal in Haryana, the Late Harappans occupied the Siswal (a Sothi or Kalibangan I complex) village (Bisht 1976a: 21). In recent years Suraj Bhan and Shaffer (1978) have located 59 Late Harappan sites (single culture sites, showing in unmistakable terms the occupation of new lands) in a comparatively small area of Haryana between the towns of Narwana, Yamuna Nagar, Jind and Panipat. In Haryana, as a whole, up to 1977, Suraj Bhan (in press) counted 133 Late Harappan (Mitathal II B) sites: 43 in the Sarasvati Valley, 51 in the Drishadvati Valley, seven in the Sabi Valley and 32 in the Yamuna Valley. It is significant to note that in the same region there are only 36 Mature Harappan sites (Late Siswal): three in the Sarasvati Valley, 22 in the Drishadvati Valley, three in the Sabi Valley and eight in the Yamuna Valley. At Banawali the Late Harappans (sometimes called Post-Harappan) occupied areas partly used by the Harappan settlers and partly beyond those fortifications (Bisht 1978: 87). At Shahr-i Sokhta (Biscioni, Salvatori and Tosi 1977) the post-firing period (IV: 2000-1800 B.C.) witnessed the occupation of only pockets of the town, that is, the southeast and northwest edges of the central plateau. In Period III the occupation shifted from the eastern residential areas to one in the west.

From these examples the next notable fact that emerges is that the regions which had once been "centers of attraction" became, during the Late Harappan times, "areas of isolation." The lower Indus and the Ghaggar-Hakra basins which were thickly inhabited during the Mature Harappan times, were now thinly populated.

Now, when does an "area of attraction" become "an area of isolation"? Scholars usually take it to be an ecological phenomenon because a shift of this kind is usually seen in the perspective of geographical model (Subbarao 1956). But, the process of disintegration of the Harappan Culture discussed here is primarily a cultural phenomenon. Environmental causes were secondary. If environmental factors had been decisive in the downfall of civilizations, Mesopotamia would have been deserted long ago, since hydrological changes were quite pronounced there. The geological record indicates that only parts of Rajasthan (Sambhar Lake) and Sind (i.e., the arid and semiarid areas) experienced a short dry period from 1800 B.C. to 1500 B.C. (G. Singh 1971: 188-89). There is absolutely no evidence of any major climatic change affecting the Punjab, Haryana or Gujarat. This, of course, does not negate the pressure of local hydrological changes, such as the one that the Ghaggar-Hakra system experienced (Raikes 1964; Wilhelmy 1969). Therefore, it is only when the social fabric of a culture begins to disintegrate that urbanism cannot be held fast and areas of attraction are reduced to areas of isolation. Natural causes are contributory, not decisive in this process. The Late Harappan, at least in areas beyond the extreme arid and semiarid belts, is, therefore, to be viewed primarily within a process of "cultural disintegration" and "cultural transformation" or "cultural readjustment," and not as a product of catastrophic climatic change coupled with the mythical invasion of the Aryans or even the migration of barbaric nomadic hordes from Iran. It may, however, be reiterated that local hydrological changes may have adversely affected the prospects of a few local towns such as Kalibangan where such changes hastened the people to leave their traditional metropolises (Lal 1979: 95). This inference is fully supported by the fact that the areas which are supposed to have experienced the greatest hardship due not to aridity, but to floods (Raikes 1964), for example the towns below the Sukkur barrage (Mohenjodaro, Chanhudaro, etc.) have yielded evidence of Late Harappan occupation. Other regions, such as the Punjab and Rajasthan, where Harappa and Kalibangan are located, have not yielded evidence of Late Harappan occupation. The settlements were deserted once and for all during the Mature Phase of the Harappan Civilization. Even if the desertion of Kalibangan is assigned to a shift in the Ghaggar River (Lal 1979) no such argument can be valid for Harappa on the Ravi. The desertion of Harappa shall remain enigmatic to hydrologists since it can be explained only on socioeconomic grounds. These are, of course, not as convincingly verifiable as the hydrological postulates; but such inferences are quite obvious to archaeologists.

Now, if the cultural decline of a people is accompanied by sociopsychological aversion to the land on which they lived earlier; or, if during the period of decline the people were pressed because of a marked fall in the productivity of the land due to human factors, such as overgrazing, etc., the diffusion of a population follows. In Soviet Central Asia, the Altin people moved into the Murgab Valley and colonized it during the Late Altin or Namazga VI (Gupta 1979 II: 180) times. In Rajasthan the Ghaggar basin was,

The Late Harappan: A Study in Cultural Dynamics

by and large, deserted, and the Harappans moved toward Haryana in the east. In Gujarat a slightly different kind of situation is met with, probably because it is devoid of large rivers like the Indus and Ghaggar. Here, there was a sudden spurt of new settlements during the Late Harappan. For example, there were only about 13 sites of the Mature Harappan Period in the entire state. But Rajkot District alone has 20 Late Harappan settlements (Chitalwala 1979: 115). The same is true of other areas as well (Possehl 1974) and there are now over 200 Late Harappan sites in Gujarat. Obviously, the limited number of Mature Harappan sites could not disintegrate into so many settlements, even conceding the possibility of a higher population growth rate for this period, because the Gujarat Harappan sites were very small as compared to the Sind and Punjab sites (Chakrabarti 1979). Lothal may not have accommodated more than 2,000 to 3,000 people during its peak period. Mohenjodaro, on the other hand, may have had a population of 40,000 to 50,000 people during the same period (Fairservis 1967: 33; Chakrabarti 1979). The larger number of Late Harappan sites is, therefore, to be seen as resulting from a process of social disintegration followed by geo-cultural readjustment by a people in the same area which had once witnessed a few urban centers.

A somewhat similar phenomenon is observable in eastern Haryana (U.V. Singh in press; Suraj Bhan 1973, 1976, in press; Suraj Bhan and Shaffer 1978) and western Uttar Pradesh (Dikshit in press; 1979a, 1979b). There are only two or three Mature Harappan sites in these regions while the number of Late Harappan sites is about 60. If the so-called OCP sites are included (e.g., Ambakhedi and Bahadarabad) the number increases to more than 75. It should be noted that for our purposes OCP is, in fact, a Late Harappan variant.

The upper plains of the Ganga-Yamuna *Doab* held 50 sites as of 1972 (Deshpande in press) none of the status of even a small town. It is, however, extremely significant to note that most of the sites found in Saharanpur District are located at a distance of eight to 12 kilometers from one another and their occupational deposits are not more than 0.75 to 1.50 meters. The Late Harappan sites in the adjoining District of Muzaffarnagar are equally small and located in small river valleys after every eight kilometers or so.

In the wake of the movement of people and the occupation of new lands pockets of new settlements can develop, particularly in areas once deserted. In the submontane region of Soviet Central Asia a few sites were redeveloped (Gupta 1979 II: 180 ff.). Similarly, in India the Bahawalpur region on the Ghaggar was reoccupied during the Late Harappan, Cemetery H times. A pocket of more than 72 sites developed in a small area of Cholistan, with the greatest concentration in the vicinity of Derawar. Significantly enough, the same area produced a number of Mature Harappan sites but only a few Early Harappan settlements (Mughal 1978, 1980). A small pocket of Jhukar settlements also developed in Sind at places like Jhukar, Amri, Mohenjodaro and Chanhudaro (Fairservis 1971: Appendix F).

Why do settlement pockets develop and how do they differ from newly founded sites resulting from diffusion, sometimes called "colonization"? Archaeological evidence appears to favor the theory of "past association." That is, an emotional attachment to the region in which a group of people had once lived may once again bring them to the area; of course, only if environmental conditions favor it. In other words, this precludes serious environmental constraints. In such examples a love for traditional items is inherent, i.e., things of the past reappear, though not always in identical terms. Thus, such sites are prone to show a continuation of old traditions much more effectively than newly poineered sites do. This appears to be the reason that Cemetery H and Jhukar sites have more Harappan affinity (Mughal 1980) than those of the Late Harappan in Gujarat, Haryana and Uttar Pradesh (Dikshit 1979a, 1979b). This also probably explains the adoption of Harappan painted designs by the Rang Mahal people, some 2000 years later (Rydh 1959), in the early centuries A.D.

This phenomenon has, of course, also been explained by the dictum "the farther something is from the center, the more dilute its character will become." For example, the Late Harappan sites of eastern Haryana and western Uttar Pradesh are distantly removed from Harappa, and, therefore, they do not show a very close Harappan affinity. But this is too simple an explanation. First, there is not as much difference between the settlement patterns of Haryana and the Indus as is sometimes asserted. Second, the settlement of Rakhigarhi was in no way smaller than Harappa. Banawali and Balu were also sizable (Suraj Bhan in press; Bisht 1976b; Suraj Bhan and Shaffer 1978). Finally, it was the process of deurbanization, coupled with diffusion in time and space, which inherently caused the loss of more and more Mature Harappan features.

The Late Harappan problem in the Punjab, particularly in the Sutlej basin, at sites like Ropar, Bara, Sanghol, Katpalon, Nagar, Dadheri and Chandigarh, is extremely complex. Bisht (1976a) sees Cemetery H pottery in Sanghol IB. Joshi (in press) says that Nagar and Dadheri have a typical Late Harappan complex. Dikshit (1979a, 1979b) finds OCP plus Late Harappan at Katpalon. Y.D. Sharma (1976) is not favorably inclined to these observations; instead, he takes all of them to the Pre-Harappan Bara traditions. However, he (Sharma in press) agrees with Suraj Bhan that at places like Mitathal (II B) in Haryana, the Pre-Harappan Bara pottery belongs to the Late Harappan times. As indicated elsewhere (Gupta 1975-76) the Pre-Harappan complex in the Punjab (Sutlej basin) came, in all probability, from Rajasthan (Kalibangan) and it is possible that even the Harappan and Late Harappan were later than the Ghaggar basin facies.

There are also Harappan sites on the western borderlands of the Indus Valley, in the hilly tracts of Baluchistan and Afghanistan. With only a few exceptions, however, the borderland sites were "secondary" in the sense that they were established as posts for commercial purposes (e.g., Shortugai), or they were small stray settlements such as Pandi Wahi. Other settlements in this area were like Mundigak. These were basically local culture sites with some Harappan elements. Their ability to survive was determined by the existence of sizable Mature Harappan sites in the foothills and the Indus basin. Places like Dabar Kot, Gumla and Rahman Dheri, sustained them economically and, possibly even socially. Obviously, with the decline of large Mature Harappan settlements the other borderland sites could hardly sustain themselves. Thus, the Late Harappan, as understood from more central areas, simply did not exist in the Baluchistan-Afghanistan hilly tracts.

The picture that emerges from this discussion is that when a civilization of the Harappan type declines due to forces other than political (i.e., invasion, etc.) a definite culture process (diffusion, etc.) sets in. This leads to new settlement patterns, such as the clustering of villages in newly occupied areas, which are clearly identifiable in the archaeological record. The emergence of the Late Harappan was thus not a haphazard process. There were conscious efforts on the part of the people to readjust their life to the new hydrological and socioeconomic conditions which the second millennium brought to the Indian Subcontinent.

PART II

The second question posed at the outset was: What items of material culture are prone to *persist* when urban cultures decline? But before this is answered let a counter question be entertained as well: What items of material culture are lost easily and quickly, or even gradually and what conditions promote this? The following is suggested as an answer to these questions.

Public structures, large domestic buildings, objects of fine art, trade items from distant lands (both raw materials and finished goods), drainage systems and other civic amenities, and, of course, writing, seals and other items of authority are lost earlier than other items. There is a reason for this. Urbanism is a product of material prosperity regulated by political authority through its control of economic channels and organs of corporate life, such as guilds of professionals, and municipalities. The Late Harappan levels of Mohenjodaro clearly demonstrate the breakdown of the machinery that controlled trade and civil government. That is, squatters houses were built over the granary as well as over the citadel without any regard to municipal regulations (Marshall 1931). After some time even these houses were deserted.

Does this mean that when the urban fabric of a culture disintegrates nothing worthwhile in it is prone to *persist*? Unless violently suppressed over several generations, this does not appear to be the case. It is more so when the decay is gradual. What actually happens is that people try to preserve, and they most consciously put all their efforts to preserve their oral traditions, such as mythology and folk songs. This is an area where political efforts are not needed at all. But this is not easy to prove archaeologically, unless some kind of written record or objects of plastic art are preserved, and this is seemingly not the case with the Harappans. In the Late Harappan, both are by and large absent except, of course, for a few terracotta figurines. There are too few of these for any generalization. In addition to oral traditions, some crafts may also persist, but on a reduced scale. The small amounts of metal and faience from places like

The Late Harappan: A Study in Cultural Dynamics

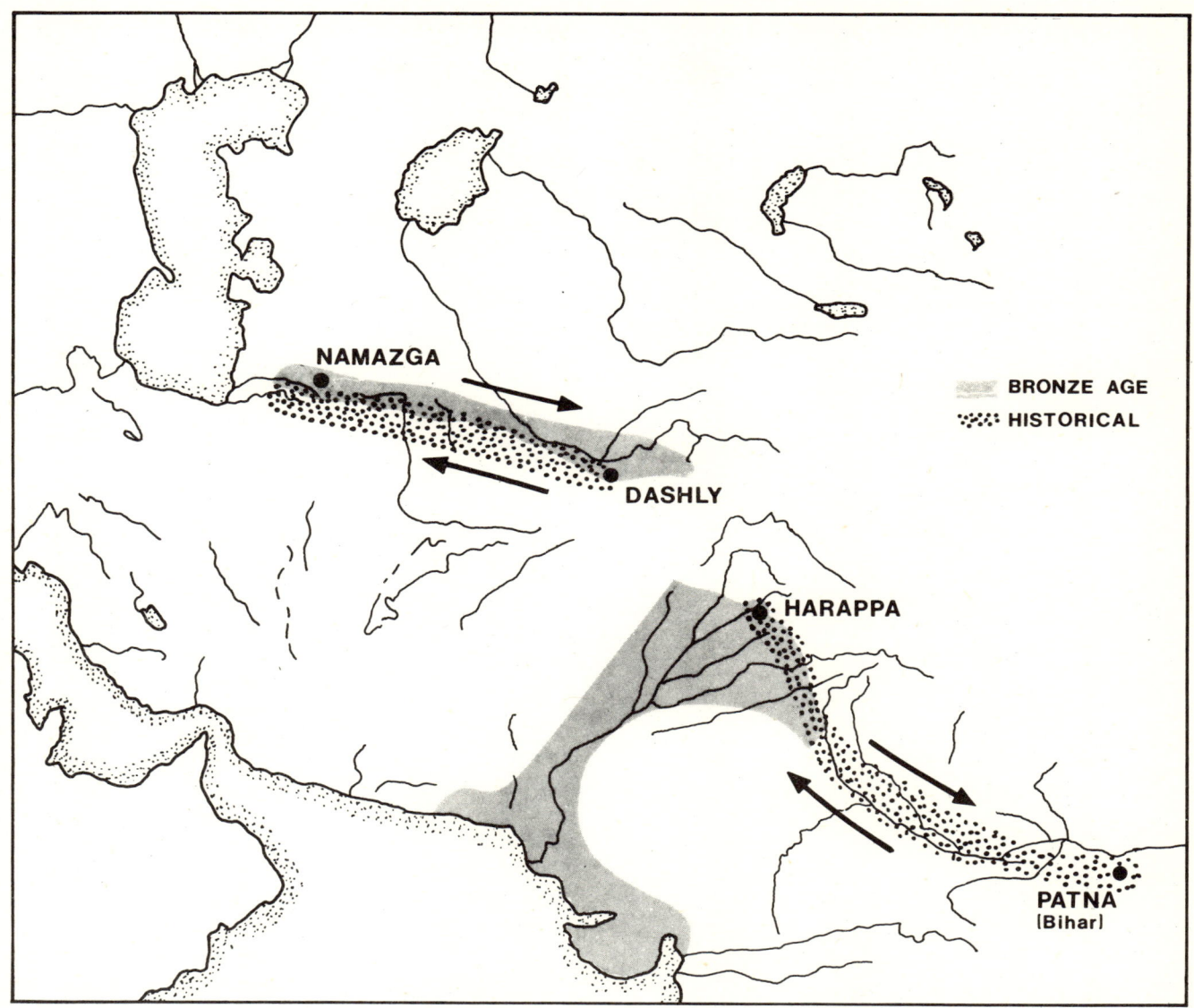

Fig. 3.1. Bronze Age and historical patterns in Central Asia and India.

Rangpur IIB-C, Lothal B, Dadheri, and Bhagwanpura indicate this. There also are uninscribed seals from Jhukar, another Late Harappan complex. Agriculture and animal husbandry, basic to the subsistence economy, is also generally preserved, albeit sometimes a little altered. Techniques for making huts, mud and mud-brick houses of one or two units are also preserved. Thus, phenomena like the Late Harappan represent village cultures which have inherited certain crafts and techniques as well as a large corpus of oral traditions from the preceding urban stage. One of the real strengths of such cultures is their wealth of traditional history and lore which can also be augmented with fresh formulations. Whether the Vedic traditions belong to the Late Harappan Phase or not, traditions of this general kind did belong to such cultural forms. Pundit Madho Swarup Vats, the excavator of Harappa, tried to see Vedic concepts and rituals dealing with life after death in the painted panels on burial jars from Late Harappan Cemetery H (Vats 1940). The same concepts can be traced to the Avestan traditions when considering

Namazga VI (Masson and Sarianidi 1972: 162). In fact, the roots of various iconographic forms emerging in the plastic art of later traditions (e.g., Brahmanic icons of Siva and non-Brahmanic icons of Vrishabha [bull], Naga [serpent] and Yaksha) may be traced back to oral traditions. These were, of course, codified, but at a very late date, in the two great epics, the *Ramayana* and the *Mahabharata* as well as in the *Puranas* and the *Jatakas*. Marshall had a point when he traced the origin of water, tree and animal worship in the Hinduism of historical times to the Harappan complex (Marshall 1931). While making this suggestion he was well aware of the archaeological gap between the two urban cycles; but he bridged this by drawing attention to the continuance of oral traditions.

The picture that emerges from this discussion is simple: *When an urban culture declines without external political interference, as was the case with the Harappans, the cultural items which are prone to persist include basic crafts relating to stone, bone and clay as well as the knowledge of agriculture and animal husbandry. It may also include, in some areas at least, crafts like metallurgy and glazing (faience). But the most important item which we may not always be in a position to prove archaeologically, save indirectly, is the preservation of oral traditions.*

Thus, when an urban culture like that of the Harappans or Altins declines, in terms of material items, it often gains in terms of moral culture. The Late Harappan and Late Altin (Namazga VI) cultural dynamics are very good case studies in this respect. Similarly, when an urban culture declines the people tend to return to Neolithic-Chalcolithic patterns and readjust themselves within either the region of their urban phase, often in pockets, or in new areas where they migrate but where they may or may not succeed. There are examples of both. For example, in the Rajkot District of Gujarat the new settlements remained small and apparently lacked substance (Chitalwala 1979). In Haryana some of the settlements did very well (Joshi in press; Suraj Bhan in press; Suraj Bhan and Shaffer 1978), sometimes surviving through the Early Iron Phase. At other times they wore out under their own weight. Sometimes they came into contact with new cultural styles and gave forth new dimensions in the process of acculturation. This can be clearly observed at Bhagwanpura in Haryana where the Late Harappan came into contact with the Painted Gray Ware complex or a Bahadarabad and Ambakhedi (Dikshit 1979b) where they met the OCP Complex. The cultural dynamics of the Late Harappan has yet one more dimension. It was not just a static unified stage of devolution from the Harappan format. Within its total range one has a tremendous amount of variety, particularly in Gujarat where a mosaic of painted and plain wares has been found. These include the Prabhas and Lustrous Red Wares (Rao 1961, 1973). Obviously, innovative tendencies do not die when the urban fabric of a culture declines. But, possibly, such a culture has to wait for proper stimulus from the outside to effectively cross-fertilize. The second cycle of urbanism in India had, therefore, to wait for nearly a millennium, if not more.

PART III

The third question: How does the second urbanization of India compare with the second urbanization of Soviet Central Asia? In India the second urbanization may be taken to begin with the firm establishment of the 16 *Mahajanapadas,* the large, generally fortified, townships of the seventh-sixth century B.C. with large estates attached to them. In Central Asia it may be taken to begin with the establishment of fortified settlements in the middle of the late second millennium B.C. (Namazga VI, Sappali-Dashly sites of Bactria). There is, therefore, a gap of 1,000 to 700 years between the second urbanization of India and the second urbanization of Central Asia. To that extent, our case is thus one of parallelism and not congruence. There are five observations that pertain to this case of parallelism.

1) Both of them start from the same place: full-fledged Bronze Age cities developed in their respective western regions. That is, the Punjab in India and South Turkmenia in Central Asia. But, the second cycle of the Late Bronze Age-Early Iron Age cities developed in the eastern region: Uttar Pradesh and Bihar in India and Bactria in Central Asia and Afghanistan.

2) The cities of the first urbanization in this part of the world developed in *both* large river valleys (the Indus) and in the smaller submontane river basins (Kopet Dagh rivers). During the second urbanization only large rivers and their tributaries fostered the growth of cities—the Ganga system in India and the Oxus system in Central Asia and Afghanistan.

3) While the diffusionary direction of the first

urbanization was from the west to the east (from the Punjab to Uttar Pradesh in India, and from Turkmenia to Tadjikistan in Central Asia) the diffusionary direction of the second urbanization was from the east to the west (from Madhyadesh, that is, Uttar Pradesh/Bihar to the Punjab in India, and from Bactria to South Turkmenia in Central Asia).

4) While it cannot definitely be said that the king was the pivot of the first urbanization, for the second urbanization this can definitely be asserted; the emperor was the pivot, at least to begin with. In India (Majumdar 1951: 1-35) the directional change in polity ran from 16 *Mahajanapadas* (Kasi, Kosal, Vrijji, etc.) to four kingdoms (Kosala, Avanti, Vatsa and Magadha) and subsequently, from four kingdoms to one empire (Magadha in Bihar). In Central Asia (Gupta 1979 II: 194-219) the many Bactrian towns of the Sappali-Dashly complex of the second millennium B.C. led to the four ancient kingdoms of Bactria, Margiana, Parthia, and Hyrcania. These emerged during the early part of the first millennium B.C. The unified empire of the Persians of the sixth-fifth century B.C. emerged, in turn, from these four kingdoms. *The directional changes were, therefore, more or less the same.*

5) Although one is dealing with a case of the parallel development of two cultural complexes (Indian and Central Asian), these areas do not appear to have developed in complete mutual isolation. There was some contact, some filtering of cultural traits, some mutual awareness during the Late Harappan Period of the second half of the second millennium B.C. This is borne out from the following few points (Gupta 1979 II: chapter 3):

At Mehrgarh, on the Bolan River in the Kachi area of Baluchistan, there is a cemetery with typical Namazga VI or Sappali-Dashly (same as Bactrian) pottery, including bowls-on-stand and pedestaled bowls. At Ghaligai, and several other sites of the Gandhara Grave Culture, there are a few comparable Bactrian bowl shapes in Stratum V of 1400-800 B.C. Although at our present stage of knowledge none of these shapes appear to have come to northern India, the east of the Indus, two things may be noted for future guidance. The first is the occurrence of pedestaled bowls at Post-Harappan Chalcolithic sites of the second millennium B.C. such as Navadatoli in Central India (Sankalia 1974: 434 ff.). The second is the occurrence of Saka-Parthian red ware and bronze, open-mouthed pedestaled cups at Taxila (Marshall 1951) during the first century B.C./A.D. These examples are apparently meaningless because of the marked space gap in the former case and great chronological divergencies in the latter example; but, as noted at the outset, these are noted here only for future reference. The reason is that in the Indian context, as Prof. Sankalia has repeatedly stressed, these materials are by and large enigmatic in the entire gamut of Indian ceramics. Some explanation has, therefore, to be found for them and it is at this point that the position taken here has real significance. After all, similar cultural processes in two neighboring areas admit, at least theoretically, a situation, irrespective of the time factor, of echo.

The problem has also been looked at from another point of view. Some have thought of the movement of people and ideas from Central Asia into India during the second millennium B.C. in the light of literary evidence in the *Avesta* and *Rigveda* (Gupta 1979 II: 230). This is admittedly a moot point. The original home of the Vedic Aryans is often located outside India, along the northeastern side of the Caspian (e.g., R. Ghirshman). But this is completely rejected by many Russian and Italian authors (e.g., Y.Y. Kuzmina, K.F. Smirov, and M. Tosi; Gupta 1979 II: Appendices). Still the discovery (Jarrige, personal communication) of early second millennium B.C. Bactrian pottery (Dashly-Sappali or Namazga VI) in the graveyards of Mehrgarh goes a long way to prove that the ancient Bactrians did move far and wide, from northernmost to southernmost Afghanistan, and beyond to Baluchistan. The Quetta/Kachi region on the Bolan has the greatest potential for the cultural interaction of many peoples, and sites like Mehrgarh have begun to throw significant light on this problem.

CONCLUSION

The Late Harappan and Early Iron Age of India thus present a very interesting case study when compared to the Late Bronze Age/Early Iron Age of Soviet Central Asia and the Afghan-Iranian borderlands. A cultural process conforming to a definite pattern (eastward diffusion and the creation of pockets of settlements) developed between the prehistoric and historical cycles of urbanization in these regions. A clearer understanding of this pattern, and of its significance, would be most rewarding. At the moment the belief is that the Late Harappan is not at all a new culture complex. It is the result of the breakdown of the urban fabric of the Harappa Culture and, therefore, it represents a stage of readjustment by an urban system to the rural setting without losing its basic ethos which was preserved in oral tradition. The innovations probably lie in some of the Vedic texts and the overall Vedic Culture Complex. In the present paper the attempt has been only to evaluate a mass of disjoined data to arrive at a sense for the broad directional changes which marked the cultural dynamics of the Late Harappan; to be exact, of the second millennium.

BIBLIOGRAPHY

Biscioni, R., S. Salvatori and M. Tosi, 1977
Shahr-i Sokhta: The prehistoric settlement and the chronological sequence. In *La Citta' Brusiata del Deserto Salato*. P. Basaglia *et al.* Pp. 103-12. Venezia: Erizzo.

Bisht, R.S., 1976a
Transformation of Harappa Culture in the Punjab with Special Reference to the Excavations at Sanghol and Chandigarh. In *Archaeological Congress and Seminar, 1972*. U.V. Singh, ed. Pp. 16-22. Kurukshetra: Kurukshetra University.

Bisht, R.S., 1976b
Banawali. Chandigarh: Public Relations Department, Government of Haryana.

Bisht, R.S., 1978
Banawali: A New Harappan Site in Haryana. *Man and Environment* 2: 86-88.

Bisht, R.S. and S. Asthana, 1979
Banawali and Some Other Recently Excavated Harappan Sites in India. In *South Asian Archaeology, 1977*. Maurizio Taddei, ed. Pp. 223-40. Instituto Universitario Orientale, Seminario di Studi Asiatici, Series Minor VI: Naples.

Chakrabarti, Dilip K., 1979
Size of Harappan Settlements. In *Essays in Indian Protohistory*. D.P. Agrawal and D.K. Chakrabarti, eds. Pp. 205-15. Delhi: B.R. Publishing Corp.

Chitalwala, Y.M., 1979
Harappan and Post-Harappan Settlement Patterns in the Rajkot District of Saurashtra. In *Essays in Indian Protohistory*. D.P. Agrawal and D.K. Chakrabarti, eds. Pp. 113-21. Delhi: B.R. Publishing Corp.

Dales, G.F., 1964
The Mythical Massacre at Mohenjodaro. *Expedition* 16 (3): 36-43.

Deshpande, M.N., in press
The Harappan Culture in Ganga-Yamuna Doab. In *Indus Civilization: Problems and issues*. B.B. Lal and S.C. Malik, eds. Simla: Indian Institute of Advanced Study.

Dikshit, K.N., 1979a
The Ochre Colored Ware Settlement in the Ganga-Yamuna Doab. In *Essays in Indian Protohistory*. D.P. Agrawal and D.K. Chakrabarti, eds. Pp. 285-99. Delhi: B.R. Publishing Corp.

Dikshit, K.N., 1979b
The Late Harappan Culture in India. In *Essays in Indian Protohistory*. D.P. Agrawal and D.K. Chakrabarti, eds. Pp. 23-133. Delhi: B.R. Publishing Corp.

Dikshit, K.N., in press
The Chronological Problem of the Late Harappans with Special Reference to Western Uttar Pradesh. In *Indus Civilization: Problems and issues*. B.B. Lal and S.C. Malik, eds. Simla: Indian Institute of Advanced Study.

Fairservis, W.A., 1967
The Origin, Character and Decline of an Early Civilization. *Novitates* 2302. New York: American Museum of Natural History.

Fairservis, W.A., 1971
The Roots of Ancient India. New York: Macmillan.

Gupta, S.P., 1975-76
"Origin of the Form of Harappa Culture: A New Proposition". *Puratattva* 8: 141–46.

Gupta, S.P., 1979
The Archaeology of Soviet Central Asia and the Indo-Iranian Borderlands. Vol. II (Protohistory). Delhi: B.R. Publishing Corp.

Joshi, J.P., in press
Overlap of Late Harappan Culture and Painted Grey Ware Culture in Light of Recent Excavations in Haryana, Punjab and Jammu. In *Indus Civilization: Problems and issues*. B.B. Lal and S.C. Malik, eds. Simla: Indian Institute of Advanced Study.

Lal, B.B., 1979
  Kalibangan and the Indus Civilization. In *Essays in Indian Protohistory*. D.P. Agrawal and D.K. Chakrabarti, eds. Pp. 65-97. Delhi: B.R. Publishing Corp.

Mackay, E.J.H., 1937
  Further Excavations at Mohenjodaro. 2 vols. Delhi: Government of India.

Majumdar, R.C., ed., 1951
  The Age of Imperial Unity. Bombay: Bhartiya Vidya Bhavan.

Marshall, Sir John, ed., 1931
  Mohenjodaro and the Indus Civilization. 3 vols. Arthur Probsthain.

Marshall, Sir John, 1951
  Taxila. 3 vols. Cambridge: Cambridge University Press.

Masson, V.M. and I. Sarianidi, 1972
  Central Asia: South Turkmenia before the Achaemenids. London: Thames and Hudson.

Mughal, M.R., 1978
  Four Years of Archaeological Discoveries in Cholistan. Unpublished lecture given at the Lahore Museum, February 21. Cyclostyled copy.

Mughal, M.R., 1980
  New Archaeological Evidence from Bahawalpur. *Man and Environment*, 4: 93-98.

Possehl, G.L., 1974
  Variation and Change in the Indus Civilization. Ph.D. dissertation, Department of Anthropology, University of Chicago.

Raikes, R., 1964
  The End of the Ancient Cities of the Indus. *American Anthropologist* 66 (2): 284-99.

Rao, S.R., 1961
  Ceramics of the Indus Valley in Gujarat. *Marg* 14(3): 18-27.

Rao, S.R., 1963
  Excavations at Rangpur and other Explorations in Gujarat. *Ancient India* 18-19: 5-207.

Rao, S.R., 1973
  Lothal and the Indus Civilization. Bombay: Asia Publishing.

Rydh, Hana, 1959
  Rang Mahal. Lund: CWK Gleerup Publishers.

Sankalia, H.D., 1974
  Prehistory and Protohistory of India and Pakistan. Poona: Deccan College.

Sharma, Y.D., 1976
  Transformation of the Harappa Culture in the Punjab. In *Archaeological Congress and Seminar, 1972*. U.V. Singh, ed. Pp. 5-15. Kurukshetra: Kurukshetra University.

Sharma, Y.D., in press
  Bara and the So-called Late Harappa Cultures of the Punjab. In *Indus Civilization: Problems and issues*. B.B. Lal and S.C. Malik, eds. Simla: Indian Institute of Advanced Study.

Singh, G., 1971
  The Indus Valley Culture. *Archaeology and Physical Anthropology in Oceania* 6 (2): 177-89.

Singh, U.V., in press
  Late Harappan Culture as Revealed by the Excavations at Mirzapur and Daulatpur, District Kurukshetra. In *Indus Civilization: Problems and issues*. B.B. Lal and S.C. Malik, eds. Simla: Indian Institute of Advanced Study.

Subbarao, B. 1956
  The Personality of India. Baroda: M.S. University of Baroda.

Suraj Bhan, 1973
  The Sequence and Spread of Prehistoric Cultures in the Upper Sarasvati Basin. In *Radiocarbon and Indian Archaeology*. D.P. Agrawal and A. Ghosh, eds. Pp. 252-63. Bombay: Tata Institute of Fundamental Research.

Suraj Bhan, 1976
  Transformation of the Harappa Culture in Haryana. In *Archaeological Congress and Seminar Papers, 1972*. U.V. Singh, ed. Pp. 23-30. Kurukshetra: Kurukshetra University.

Suraj Bhan, in press
  The Protohistoric Settlement Pattern in Haryana. In *Indus Civilization: Problems and issues*. B.B. Lal and S.C. Malik, eds. Simla: Indian Institute of Advanced Study.

Suraj Bhan and J. Shaffer, 1978
  New Discoveries in Northern Haryana. *Man and Environment* 2: 59-68.

Tosi, M., 1969
  Preliminary Report on the Second Campaign at Shahr-i Sokhta. *East and West* 19 (3-4): 283-86.

Vats, M.S., 1940
  Excavations at Harappa. 2 vols. Delhi: Government of India.

Wilhelmy, H., 1969
  Urstromtal am Ostrand der Indusebene und der Sarasvati-Problem. *Zeitschrift fur Geomorphologie*, Supplementband 8: 76-91.

C.C. LAMBERG-KARLOVSKY

4. Sumer, Elam and the Indus: Three Urban Processes Equal One Structure?

IN THIS paper I shall attempt to point out the similarities and dissimilarities in the structural processes that characterized the urban development of the Harappan Civilization, Central Asia, southern Iran (Elam), and Mesopotamia (Sumer).[1] All of these areas are perceived by archaeologists as distinctive centers of indigenous urban and state development which were, at different times, either directly or indirectly in contact with each other (Gupta 1979; Lamberg-Karlovsky and Tosi 1973). Within the last decade it has become evident that developments in one of the above regions affected the cultural systems of neighboring and even distant areas.

The analysis will focus upon the period of early urban formation in an attempt to isolate similar structural processes which characterized each region. Such an attempt moves away from earlier efforts which searched for isolated similarities in ceramics, seals, metals, etc., in order to build a comparative stratigraphy of time-space systematics involved in questions of diffusion versus independent invention. It is the search for structural similarities which characterized each region that leads to the isolation of a general uniform process. If a structural similarity can be found which characterized each area, it is probable that a general explanation is applicable to its understanding.

In order to establish a structural equivalence between the culture areas already noted, I shall contrast within the three distinctive regions, the processes of: (a) primary urbanization, (b) primary incorporation, and (c) secondary involvement. By "primary urbanization" I mean the descriptive process which leads to urbanization within the area under review. "Primary incorporation" refers to the process which brings neighboring communities (at times the colonization of distant communities within distinctive culture areas) under the direct political and/or economic influence of the primary urban center(s). Lastly, by "secondary involvement" I mean archaeological sites which merely indicate an archaeological contact situation, one based on a repertoire of *very* limited typological similarities to distinctively different primary urban centers. Such an approach is necessarily abstract and takes for granted that sites such as Uruk, Susa, Altin Depe, and Harappa were primary urban centers of the Sumerian, proto-Elamite, Turanian, and Indus regions respectively. It is not my purpose to review the process of urbanization in each area, either theoretically or substantively, but rather to review the structure which each process took and compare it with that of other distinctive areas. Such an attempt, preliminary and premature as it might be, focuses upon the structural similarities and differences which characterized each area.

It is fundamentally important to recognize that the development of the proto-Elamite cities of southwestern Iran, though still very little understood, is inextricably interwoven with contemporary developments in neighboring Sumer. This fact is of fundamental significance and sets the first structural difference between the Elamite/Sumerian urban process and that of the Turanian and Harappan. Neither of the latter two culture areas were situated geographically adjacent to, nor chronologically contemporary with, a distinctive, though interacting, urban process of the type that characterized early Sumer and Elam. Sites of southern Mesopotamia (Sumer), such as Uruk, appear to maintain a slight chronological priority over those (i.e., Susa) of Khuzistan (Elam), in the development of writing, defensive structures, and regional hierarchies of settlement. Nevertheless, within two or three centuries the proto-Elamites, as evidenced at Susa, appear to have developed their own distinctive form of writing, settlement hierarchies, and material culture which can readily be distinguished from that of Sumer. Pierre Amiet (1979) has recently offered an interesting proposition for isolating ethnic boundaries separating not only Sumer from Elam but attempting to distinguish such boundary conditions within Elam itself. Amiet writes of Elam:

> Cultural and occasionally political integration into Mesopotamia lasted during virtually the latter part of the third millennium, with the exception of the brief break of Puzur-Inshushinak's reign, when a new script adapted to the national language [Elamite] was adopted and used concurrently with the Akkadian writing and language. This fact is significant in the linguistic and ethnic duality of Susiana.... In addition, during the periods of integration into Mesopotamia a related phenomenon occurred, namely the appearance of national dynasties [Elamite], outside Susa, first in Awan then in Simashki. Finally, exactly as Puzur-Inshushinak, who was to become the last king of Awan, conquered Susa when the dynasty of Agade declined, the kings of Simashki united the Elamite country after the downfall of the dynasty of Ur (1979: 197).

Any consideration which entails a discussion of the urban process in Sumer and Elam *must* take into account the stimulus-response nature of Sumerian-Elamite relations. The ethnic and linguistic diversity which characterized these neighboring communities may have in fact played an important role in setting conditions for conflict, integration, and political centralization within and between Sumer and Elam.

Following the nearly contemporaneous state formations in Elam (Khuzistan) (Wright and Johnson 1975) and Sumer (Adams and Nissen 1972) an identical phenomenon can be observed occurring in each: the incorporation of distinctive cultures into their sphere of influence by *direct* colonization. Thus, by 3200 B.C. the Sumerian fortified colony at Habuba Kabira is established within a distinctive cultural region of northern Syria (Strommenger 1976). Similarly, by 3000 B.C. the proto-Elamites established a colony in the equally distinctive cultural area around Tepe Yahya in southeastern Iran (Lamberg-Karlovsky 1978). These are not the only sites evidencing such colonization by the Sumerians and Elamites. The process is, in fact, a widely recognized one which has been recently discussed by Weiss and Young (1975), Amiet (1979), Strommenger (1976), Lamberg-Karlovsky (1976) and years ago by Ghirshman for the Elamite colonization of Sialk (1954: 45-50).

Structurally one can review the situation this way: Following the *interrelated* processes of primary urbanization and state formation, Sumer and Elam became independently involved with colonizing "foreign" communities. From Elam sites such as Tal-i Malyan, Tepe Yahya, Tepe Sialk, and Tal-i Ghazir, each with an earlier *distinctive* material culture and widely dispersed on the Iranian Plateau, have imposed on them a proto-Elamite colony. From Sumer the sites of Habuba Kabira (Strommenger 1976) and Godin Tepe (Weiss and Young 1975: 1-18) are directly colonized by Sumerians. Both Sumer and Elam, following primary urbanization, undertake an attempt at expansive colonization. The factors that led to the colonization are still poorly understood but an attempt at political expansion to control the resources and populations of foreign areas are typically advanced as the reasons inspiring such colonization.

The attempt at colonization (following primary urbanization and state development) led to the "primary incorporation" of the indigenous culture into the political and economic sphere of the colonizing culture. Thus, there can be no doubt that the site of Habuba Kabira, with its Sumerian material inventory (including tablets), or Tepe Yahya with its proto-Elamite material inventory (with tablets as well) represent a primary incorporation of these previously distinctive culture areas into the respective political and economic spheres of Sumer and Elam. There can also be little doubt that the presence of these colonies within distinctive culture areas led to an acculturative process between the culture of the indigenous populations and the colonizing culture. The effects of this acculturative process, which is referred to as "secondary involvement," may be seen in the isolated presence of a few rare artifacts characteristic of the colonizing culture but found in archaeological sites of the indigenous culture. Examples of this include the

Sumer, Elam and the Indus

single proto-Elamite tablet and limited sealings found at Shahr-i Sokhta or the single tablet from Hissar. Unlike Yahya, neither of these sites was colonized directly. Neither has the full complement of ceramics, seals, sealings, and tablets been found which allows for an identity between Susa and Yahya. Rather, the materials at places like Hissar or Sokhta appear as *rare* instances within an indigenous tradition of material culture. The presence of these rare items on scattered sites around the colony, however, point to a process of acculturation and "secondary involvement" of the nearby region with the colonizing culture. One may now ask whether this structural similarity between Sumer and Elam bears any relationship to the aspects of primary urbanization in the Turanian and Harappan Civilizations.

The important and distinctive nature of the primary urban development which characterized Soviet Central Asia has become a recent recognition, resulting from the research of Soviet colleagues over the past three decades (Masson and Sarianidi 1972; Tosi 1974; Lamberg-Karlovsky 1978).

The Late Chalcolithic Cultures of South Turkmenia, that is the Namazga III and Geoksyurian Culture complexes, suggest an aspect of primary urbanization dated to 3200-2700 B.C. This would be approximately contemporary with or perhaps a century or so later than, the period of primary urbanization and colonization which characterized Sumer and Elam.

Soviet archaeologists have repeatedly attempted to derive the increasing cultural complexity which characterized this South Turkmenian Late Chalcolithic as resulting from a series of tribal migrations from Iran, which were themselves the results of cultural developments in Mesopotamia. The indirect outcome of these tribal migrations emanating from Iran, it is held, resulted in improved irrigation systems, enlargement of house units, and a remodeling of village plans (Masson and Sarianidi 1972). This view, which derives the increasing cultural complexity of Central Asia from Iranian tribal migrations has been aptly criticized by Gupta (1979), Tosi (1974), and Lamberg-Karlovsky (1973). In fact, today most archaeologists follow the views of Khlopin (1974) who was the first Soviet archaeologist to interpret this Late Chalcolithic Central Asian cultural complexity as representing an indigenous urban process with only the most distant, if any, parallels and influences from such sites as Susa, Sialk, Hissar, etc., on the Iranian Plateau.

The primary urbanization which characterizes the Namazga III period is derived from the excavations of Geoksyur I, Chong Depe, and Kahpuz Depe in the Tedzen Delta and from a line of settlements at the northern foothills of the Kopet Dagh mountains: Kara Depe, Gara Depe, Namazga Depe, Ulug Depe, Altin Depe and Serahs.

The increasing number of sites in the Tedzen Delta from Namazga I to III times, the hierarchy of settlements with Geoksyur I being the largest (the Soviets characterize it as a "capital" town in Namazga III times), the increase in metal objects and increasing efficiency of irrigation systems (Lisitsina 1965), all attest to a transformation of increasing cultural complexity characteristic of an indigenous primary urbanization. In addition, Soviet archaeologists excavating Kara Depe point out important qualitative changes characteristic of the Namazga III period. Houses become multichambered units, each with a distinctive courtyard; a characteristic difference from the earlier typical one-room house. The excavators see in this an important social shift from the nuclear family to accommodations of extended family groups united by kinship and economic ties within a more integrated and centralized community. By the late third millennium (Namazga V) southern Turkmenia achieves a fully urban status as evidenced by the excavations at Altin Depe, with its large "ziggurat" and other structures necessitating corporate labor and indicative of administrative functions (Masson 1967, 1968).

One may now ask if following the initial phases of primary urbanization in South Turkmenia there was an attempt at expansive colonization and the acculturation of distant cultures, as characterized by early Sumer and Elam. Was there, in other words, a structural similarity in the process of urbanization in this area? I turn to two sites to suggest a qualified "yes." Excavations at Mundigak and Shahr-i Sokhta both suggest a primary incorporation by the Namazga III-IV cultural complex. Tosi (Lamberg-Karlovsky and Tosi 1973) has argued that in the initial settlement of Shahr-i Sokhta, 40 percent of the total material, including painted pottery, was derived from the South Turkmenian sites. In fact, he argues for a direct colonization of Seistan and the delta of the Helmand from South Turkmenia bringing about the initial settlement of Shahr-i Sokhta. Similarly, in Mundigak III and IV there are substantial parallels in material culture which tie the site closely to those of South

Turkmenia. The archaeological evidence strongly suggests a primary incorporation by direct colonization from South Turkmenia to Shahr-i Sokhta. The presence of identical ceramic types and metal compartmented seals at such sites as Damb Sadaat II-III (Namazga III-IV), Said Qala Tepe, and Gumla II on the Indus Plain, are suggestive of a secondary involvement in the acculturative process in these areas of indigenous culture with those of the primary urban centers of southern Turkmenia.

The reasons for this expansive colonization to Shahr-i Sokhta and the increasing interaction with the indigenous cultures of the Indo-Iranian borderlands is as imperfectly understood as that which brought about the same process in Sumer and Elam. One explanation, which is an imperfect one for the understanding of its entirety within the Indo-Iranian borderlands, rests upon the total abandonment of the settlements of the Tedzen Delta during the last phases of Namazga III and their suggested southern migration to Seistan and Shahr-i Sokhta. The causes for the abandonment of these settlements has been argued as resulting from the changing of the courses of the hydrological system of the Tedzen Delta caused by the silting up of the channels and neotectonic phenomena. It is hard to accept, however, that such a localized phenomenon within South Turkmenia would have accounted for the primary incorporation and secondary involvement of so many sites in the Indo-Iranian borderlands.

The evidence for direct colonization of, for example Habuba Kabira by the Sumerians or Tepe Yahya by the proto-Elamites, remains far more convincing than that of Shahr-i Sokhta by the Namazga III/Geoksyurian cultural complex (Turanian). Nevertheless, the evidence suggests that the initial process of urbanization in each area was followed by an expansive interaction and/or colonization of "foreign" indigenous cultures. One may fairly ask, prior to investigating the Indus area, whether one can observe a structural similarity in what happened on the different sites following colonization? The answer would appear to be an unequivocal "yes." The sites "colonized" (Yahya, Sialk, Shahr-i Sokhta, Habuba Kabira, *et al.*) in *all* regions were without exception abandoned by the colonists with the communities reverting to their indigenous culture. It would appear that after a century or two at the most, colonization ceased to be carried out and the areas colonized were abandoned. The cause of the withdrawal from the colonies remains elusive though it has been suggested for at least one instance that "the administrative costs, and expenditure incurred, assuring safe transport of goods and personnel, were higher than the economic return gained from the 'colonies' " (Lamberg-Karlovsky 1978: 119).

I might add that this bureaucratic collapse in maintaining the colonies might be "turned on its head" to provide an explanation for the initial colonizing. Explanations have favored the establishment of colonies to control local resources. As an alternative I suggest that the developing state experienced an expansive growth of a bureaucracy. That is, the growth of a managerial class which can readily expand and/or be adopted beyond the limits of its own territorial development. It is not impossible that in these cases a bureaucratic structure, as a self-contained entity, expanded beyond its own territorial limits and was imposed and/or adopted in "foreign" areas. The explosive growth of this managerial bureaucracy had within it the seeds of its own destruction. Its rapid development, within a century or two, ultimately led to its collapse, for it had overextended its own ability to maintain the costs of its existence beyond the frontiers of its creations.

To what extent are the structural similarities of processes involving primary urbanization, primary incorporation, and secondary involvement noted for Sumer, Elam and Turan similar and/or dissimilar to the situation of the Indus Civilization?

Our first important consideration deals with comparative chronology. In the cases of Sumer and Elam the processes contrasted above deal with the time from Late Uruk to Early Dynastic I, that is approximately 3200-2900 B.C. The Namazga III-Geoksyurian complex (Turanian) refers to a period at about 3000-2700 B.C.; thus overlapping only the later part of the Sumerian-Elamite process. For aspects of primary urbanization within the area of the Indus the dates are again slightly later: 2800-2500 B.C. Thus, as a general observation, it appears that as one moves from west to east the process of urbanization occurs at a *slightly later* date. This phenomenon has in the past been interpreted as resulting from the diffusion of urban traits from the west to the east. Such a process is explicitly stated in Sir Mortimer Wheeler's famous phrase in considering the rise of the Indus Civilization (Wheeler 1968: 135).

But it can at least be averred that, however translated, the *idea* of civilization came to the Indus from the Euphrates and Tigris, and gave the Harappans their initial direction, or at least informed their purpose.

The west to east sloping chronology remains today the strongest, and perhaps only, logic for maintaining this diffusionary conception. Most archaeologists would argue for an essentially independent process of primary urbanization in the Indus area, while not denying that external contact took place (for a recent review, see Gupta 1979).

Recently Dr. Rafique Mughal (1973: 15) has suggested:

> Thus, before the rise of large cities of the Indus Civilization, a wide-spread cultural phenomenon had already set a permanent and uniform pattern of essential elements.

This "uniform pattern of essential elements" Mughal (1970) termed the "Early Harappan" and incorporated sites such as Harappa, Kot Diji, Gumla, Kalibangan, Amri, Sarai Khola, Jalilpur, etc. This Early Harappan remains chronologically poorly defined, being dated by only a few ^{14}C dates, all of which would confirm an early third millennium date for its inception. Such a date suggests that the process of primary urbanization in this area was roughly contemporaneous with the Namazga III/Geoksyurian Complex and only a few centuries later than that of Sumer and Elam.

To what extent following primary urbanization can one document, as in Sumer, Elam, and Central Asia, the replicating process of "primary incorporation by colonization" and sites of "secondary involvement?" In both cases one can answer in the affirmative. The recent discovery of Indus sites in the vicinity of Shortugai near the Oxus River represents not only the furthest northern expansion of the Mature Indus Civilization but a clear colonization of that indigenous area (Francfort and Pottier 1978). The excavators of the sites have suggested that the colonization of these northern settlements was brought about by the desire of the Indus Civilization to exploit resources (copper) and control the trade of lapis lazuli. Additionally it can be pointed out that several of the Early Harappan sites were reoccupied (colonized?) by the Mature Indus Civilization. Thus, the direct stratigraphic superposition of Mature Indus occupations over the local indigenous cultures at Kalibangan, Kot Diji, Amri, Bala Kot, etc., indicate that following primary urbanization (the Early Harappan) these sites were directly incorporated into the cultural system of the Indus Civilization.

Evidence for "secondary involvement" with the Indus Civilization can be documented through the presence of undoubted Indus material remains in areas beyond its direct geographical expanse. Thus, the discovery of Indus seals, one with an inscription, at Altin Depe in Central Asia (Masson 1977) or the presence of an Indus inscription impressed on a sherd from Tepe Yahya (Lamberg-Karlovsky 1978) are rare, even unique finds, but indicate a distant communication with these areas. There is little evidence, however, to suggest that these isolated finds, helpful only in establishing a time-space framework, indicate important social, political or economic communication with these areas.

The question of Mesopotamian-Indus relations has long been a topic of concern. The total absence of clear Mesopotamian materials in the Indus is in ready contrast to the presence of numerous Indus seals on many sites in Mesopotamia. Should the equation of the place name Meluhha, mentioned in Mesopotamian texts, be the Indus Civilization then the recent argument for the acculturation of Harappan peoples in Mesopotamia obtains firmer ground (Parpola, Parpola and Brunswig 1977: 129–65). Adequate methods, from strictly archaeological material remains, for deriving the extent and nature of acculturation still remain to be worked out. One may suggest, however, one instance in which archaeological evidence may be suggestive of acculturation. Seals in the Indus are almost exclusively square while those of Mesopotamia are cylindrical. Their distinctive form and style have long been recognized and allow for easy identification. Two "Indus" seals from Mesopotamia suggest an acculturation of form and style with Mesopotamian products. A glazed steatite *cylinder* seal from Tell Asmar depicting an elephant, rhinoceros, and crocodile (*gharial*) is well known for its Indus style (Frankfort 1939: 50, Fig. 32). Only three cylinder seals are reported by Mackay (1935: 192, Pl. M: 10, 11) as being recovered from Mohenjodaro, compared to the over 300 square seals. The cylindrical form of the Tell Asmar seal with the classical Indus motif is, with one from Ur, unique. Additionally, one can point out that the convention by which the elephants feet are rendered and the network of lines extending over the body, head and trunk (normally restricted on Indus seals to the ears) is without parallel on Indus seals. I would suggest this: the Mesopotamian seal *form* (cylindrical), with aberrant Indus *style*, is not an imported Indus object (as suggested by Frankfort 1939: 305) but a product made in Mesopotamia by a local craftsman under instructions from a Harappan. The end product was a cylinder seal incorporating the basics of Indus style but neither the artisan (Mesopotamian) nor client (Harappan) got the seal quite right—the compromise of acculturation. The only other example, the cylindrical seal from Ur, shows a Brahmi bull at its manger, a second unidentifiable creature, a tree motif, and a scorpion. Scorpions never appear on Indus seals; but they are most definitely a very common motif on those from Mesopotamia. Again, I would suggest this to be a product of direct acculturation— much as one might argue in an another direction for the bearded bull depicted on a fragmentary silver vessel from the Fullol Hoard, in Afghanistan, being a distinctive Mesopotamian motif adopted on the silver vessels from Fullol (Tosi and Wardak 1972). Such evidence of iconographic adaptation of foreign symbolism suggests a more direct communication of ideas than the isolated finds of objects of Indus manufacture at Altin Depe or Tepe Yahya.

CONCLUSIONS

This paper is necessarily an abstract, a preliminary study, encompassing a large geographical area within one of the most complex archaeological regions of the Old World. I have attempted to point out, without full documentation, that there were important structural similarities in the urban processes which characterized Sumer, Elam, Turan, and the Indus. Most important among these are:

1) Areas of primary urbanization were characterized by considerable ethnic diversity. The archaeological evidence supports clear cultural distinctions between North and South Mesopotamia, Sumer and Elam, North Baluchistan and the Indus, Turan and the Hilmand Civilization, etc. Each of these regions of primary urbanization, far from indicating a cultural homogeneity, are characterized by inter- and intraregional differences, highly suggestive of ethnic diversity (clearly indicated for Sumer where texts are available).

2) Within each of the areas of primary urbanization, and perhaps resultant from the ethnic diversity which characterized them, there is substantial evidence for conflict and warfare. Clearest evidence for this comes from Egypt (ca. 3000 B.C.) and Sumer-Elam (ca. 2800 B.C.) where texts indicate the enmity and warfare which characterized the period of primary urbanization and political centralization in these areas. The first fortification systems constructed around such Early Harappan sites as Kalibangan, Kot Diji, Rahman Dheri, etc., further indicate conflict conditions at this time within this area.

3) Following the period of primary urbanization, distantly inhabited regions were colonized. This represents the primary incorporation of these regions into the urban economic and political spheres of influence. Typically, the establishment of these colonies, and the increasing interregional interaction, has been understood in terms of a desire for resource control; the need to control particular resources, particularly of an elite nature, to validate the status distinctions within the emerging urban centers. Without taking exception to this view, I can point out that the increasing tendency toward political centralization and conflict resolution led to the growth of managerial bureaucracy. The formal structuring of this bureaucracy may also have facilitated methods of conflict resolution. The increasing formalization of a bureaucratic structure at a time of increasing levels of decision making, may have in its own right been exported and adopted in distant areas as a valued good. This suggests that institutional structures, within any social order, can be exported and adopted as a commodity.

4) Without exception the "colonies" indicative of primary incorporation and the intensification of interregional contacts that they represent, "collapse." That is to say, after 100-200 years they abandon the region. The understanding of this phenomenon is elusive. Perhaps the managerial bureaucracy which made it initially possible had overextended itself and the "costs" of their maintenance exceeded "profits." Perhaps internal tensions within the region of each primary urban center regained stronger internal integration after a period of rapid growth requiring abandonment of their "colonies." Perhaps, the "foreign" areas, for different reasons, expelled the colony in favor of earlier managerial systems. What is evident, however, is that during the period of colonization the indigenous culture became secondarily involved with the colony. This secondary involvement can be seen in the single finds of "foreign" materials in distant places, i.e., Indus stamp seals at Altin Depe, following colonization at Shortugai.

5) The common process following urbanization

in Mesopotamia, Elam, the Indus, and perhaps Turan involved the establishment of colonies in distant regions with an increase in regional interaction. There was then an abandonment of the colonies and a collapse of the interregional integration. Thus, structural similarities are evident and they suggest a common process. The explanation for that process is now a fundamental problem to be resolved.

6) Much of this paper concerns center-periphery relations and the observation that within the centers of Sumer, Elam, Turan, and the Indus there was an expansion to the indigenous peripheral cultures. This expansion was characterized by direct colonization of the peripheral cultures by populations from the centers of more advanced civilization. It can be hypothesized that the impingement of the centers on the periphery results from multiple and interacting factors: (1) the desire of the center for the control of the flow of resources; (2) rulers of the centers attempting to prevent the tendencies of the periphery to coalesce into broader centralized political frameworks; (3) expansive tendencies among the elite of centers to structure hierarchies in the periphery; (4) the arrangement of status sets (the development of symbols of common political and cultural entity) to expand the essentially political aspects over the periphery in maintaining the centers normative definition of the political, economic, and social institutions; and (5) to allow for the custodianship of principle kin groups from the centers of expansion of their "cosmic" order—the moral and social order.

The results of such colonization, the permeation of the peripheries by centers results in an acculturative process involving: (1) forms of administration by laws derived from the centers; (2) regulatory aspects in maintaining peace; (3) exaction of taxes; and (4) maintenance of cultural and/or religious links, effected by increasing kinship ties.

NOTE

[1] These processes have been discussed by a number of authors such as Oats and Oats (1976), Oats (1978), Postgate (1977), Adams (1966), Redman (1979), Wright and Johnson (1975) and Lamberg-Karlovsky (1978).

BIBLIOGRAPHY

Adams, Robert McC., 1966
   The Evolution of Urban Society. Chicago: Aldine.
Adams, Robert McC. and Hans J. Nissen, 1972
   The Uruk Countryside. Chicago: University of Chicago Press.
Amiet, P., 1979
   Archaeological Discontinuity and Ethnic Duality in Elam. *Antiquity* 53: 195–204.
Frankfort, H., 1939
   Cylinder Seals. London: Macmillan and Co.
Francfort, H.P. and M.H. Pottier, 1978
   Sondage Preliminarie sur l'Establissement Protohistorique Harappan et Post-Harappan du Shortugai (Afghanistan du N.E.). *Arts Asiatiques* 34: 29-86.
Ghirshman, R., 1954
   Iran. Baltimore: Pelican Books.
Gupta, S.P., 1979
   Archaeology of Soviet Central Asia and the Indian Borderlands. 2 vols. Delhi: B.R. Publishing Corp.
Khlopin, I.N., 1974
   Ancient Farmers in the Tedzen Delta. *East and West* 24 (1-2): 51-87.
Lamberg-Karlovsky, C.C., 1972
   Tepe Yahya 1971: Mesopotamia and the Indo-Iranian borderlands. *Iran* 10: 42-48.
Lamberg-Karlovsky, C.C., 1973
   Prehistoric Central Asia: A review. *Antiquity* 47 (185): 42-48.
Lamberg-Karlovsky, C.C., 1976
   Foreign Relations in the Third Millennium at Tepe Yahya. In *Le Plateau Iranien et L'Asie Centrale des Origines a la Conquete Islamique*. J. Deshayes, ed. Pp. 33-43. Paris: CNRS.

Lamberg-Karlovsky, C.C., 1978
 The Proto-Elamites on the Iranian Plateau. *Antiquity* 52 (205): 114-20.

Lamberg-Karlovsky, C.C. and M. Tosi, 1973
 Shahr-i Sokhta and Tepe Yahya: Tracks on the earliest history of the Iranian plateau. *East and West* 23 (1-2): 21-57.

Lisitsina, G.N., 1965
 Orosayemove Zemledeliy Epokhi Eneloithia na Yuge Turkmenii (Irrigation Agriculture in the Neolithic of South Turkmenia). Moscow.

Mackay, E.J.H., 1935
 Early Indus Civilization. London: Lovat, Dickson and Thompson.

Masson, V.M., 1967
 Proto-Urban Culture of Central Asia: Altin Tepe along with analogies with Indus, Afghan, and Mesopotamia. *Sovietskaja Arkeologia* 3.

Masson, V.M., 1968
 The Urban Revolution in Southern Turkmenia. *Antiquity* 42: 178-87.

Masson, V.M., 1977
 Proto-Indian Seal from Altin Tepe. *Vestnik Drevnii Istorii* 31: 147-55.

Masson, V.M. and V. Sarianidi, 1972
 Central Asia Before the Achaemenids. London: Thames and Hudson.

Mughal, M.R., 1970
 The Early Harappan Period in the Greater Indus Valley and Northern Baluchistan (3000-2400 B.C.). Ph.D. dissertation, Anthropology Department, University of Pennsylvania.

Mughal, M.R., 1973
 The Present State of Research on the Indus Valley Civilization. *Proceedings of the International Symposium on Mohenjodaro*. Pp. 1-28. Karachi: National Book Trust.

Oats, D. and J. Oats, 1976
 The Rise of Civilization. Oxford: Elsevier Phaidon.

Oats, J., 1978
 Mesopotamian Social Organization: Archaeological and philological evidence. In *The Evolution of Social Systems*, J. Friedman and M.J. Rowlands, eds. Pp. 457-86. Pittsburgh: University of Pittsburgh Press.

Parpola, S., A. Parpola and R. Brunswig, 1977
 The Meluhha Village. *Journal of the Economic and Social History of the Orient* 20 (2): 129-65.

Postgate, N., 1977
 The First Empires. Oxford: Elsevier Phaidon.

Redman, C., 1979
 The Rise of Civilization. San Francisco: W.H. Freeman and Co.

Strommenger, E., 1976
 Funfter Vorlaufiger Bericht uber di von der Deutsche Orient-Gesellschaft mit Mitteln der Stiftung Volkswagenwerke in Habuba Kabira unternommenen Archaeologischen Untersuchungen (Kampagnen 1973, 1974, 1975). *Mitteilungen Deutsche Orient Gesellschaft* 108: 5-22.

Tosi, M., 1974
 The Northeastern Frontier of the Ancient Near East. *Mesopotamia* 8-9: 21-76.

Tosi, M. and R. Wardak, 1972
 The Fullol Hoard: A find from Bronze Age Afghanistan. *East and West* 22 (1-2): 9-17.

Weiss, H. and T.C. Young, 1975
 The Merchants of Susa: Godin V and plateau-lowlands relations in the late fourth millennium B.C. *Iran* 13: 1-19.

Wheeler, Sir Mortimer, 1968
 The Indus Civilization. 3rd ed. Supplementary volume to the Cambridge History of India. Cambridge: The University Press.

Wright, H. and G. Johnson, 1975
 Population, Exchange and Early State Formation in Southwestern Iran. *American Anthropologist* 77: 266-89.

K.V. SOUNDARA RAJAN

5. Motivations for Early Indian Urbanization: An Examination

It is common knowledge that the establishment of urban settlements in India, as elsewhere, followed a riparian pattern wherein major river valleys were colonized first. The Indo-Gangetic Plain has been occupied by several cultures of which the Indus Civilization poses to be the oldest and parent model for urban life and material prosperity. Urbanization, it is needless to add, was not a preconceived or universalized scheme, but an exclusive, original process, decided as much by antecedent conditions as by ecological compulsions. At the time of the rise of the Harappan Civilization, in the Indus Valley, a large part of the rest of India was passing through discrete stages of a pastoral neolithism, often coeval with one or the other facets of the Indus Culture. Urbanization did not reach the Ganges system, however, much prior to the end of the second millennium B.C.

The oldest literary heritage of our land gives the pride of place to the authors of the Vedic hymns who had established themselves in parts of the Punjab and Haryana. When the process of their expansion, acculturation and gradual urbanization had run its course from their *quondam* pastoral life, one finds the residents of the northern plains in the *entire* Ganges Valley were heirs to a rich heritage of a Vedic-Brahmanical, epic-historic, religio-cultural synthesis. Between *Brahmavarta* and *Aryavarta*, thus, was witnessed a spatial, sociocultural shift and metamorphosis.

In this context, trade, religion and art became the main preoccupations of the people, given a fairly stable and efficient polity which, though, was carrying the germs of a truly monarchical system. The earlier systems of society had no such polity but were a coordination of vocational skills in the civic centers; however the primarily agricultural pattern in the villages was uncoordinated in comparison. Leadership of the civic or rural communities was not crystallized into a particular coterie or tribe. In fact, even the republican states *(Mahajanapadas),* which became increasingly important during the period of the first colonization of the Ganges Valley, do not seem to have had: (a) hereditary claim to social office, (b) socially fixed, rigid status, (c) firmly defined territorial jurisdiction[1]—the first among the several traits of a monarchical system. There was neither a conscious trend toward "expansionism" nor any superior socio-economic viability characterizing their spread. It might even be appropriate to concede that a hereditary monarchical system was a sequel to the consolidation of the Vedic culture. This was a "nationalization," at the hands of the Vedic sages and schools, of the prevalent planned, temporal programs of the urban centers, into whose mold was squeezed a new flow of organized spiritualism which the former lacked. This may explain why the Chalcolithic Cultures of the post-Indus Valley period were disparate in character, being the mutations of the indigenous, chthonic groups in which neither *culture* nor *cult* played any special part which could impart a self-generative momentum to the society. On the other hand, the early Iron Age urban cultures of the Ganges Valley were able to form an integration of religious, economic and political institutions. Unlike the Indus Civilization or the Chalcolithic settlements, the early Iron Age habitations had a *polity,* expressed in terms of geographical jurisdiction, internal cohesion, defensive and offensive works and a systematized religious orientation (by either the king or an elite) of which the last (namely, religion) was *different* from the diversified nature of the cults of the people.

Thus, one may be tempted to state that the urban trends evinced by the Harappan Civilization were a face lift, a window dressing and a draconian insistence on a regimented pattern. It seemingly did not have its firm roots in an urban matrix, nor did it seem to have any clear liaison between the ruling elite and the rural folk, between the civic overlords and the peasant proprietors of the villages. It was something like a stringent, centralized oligarchy, which had invented a disciplined civic model, with a consumer policy for drawing the agricultural surplus of the villages. Thus, the so-called standardization of the structures, pottery and antiquities of the Harappan Culture may be essentially an index of the *vogues* created by the craft guilds of the city-states.

Taking a parallel analog in the early historic trade modes in Southern India, it can be seen that the southern guilds dealt with virtually every commodity produced in the countryside, pooled them, vended them within and even outside India. The surplus of this trade-built capital they used as munificent religious donations for Jainism, Buddhism and other religions. They even advertised their philanthropy through inscribed records. Similarly, even the Harappan villages were the deliberate products of a consumer-oriented regulation. Their cultural trappings were a mere urban veneer. That which went by the appellation of "Pre-Harappan," whether at Kot Diji, Kalibangan or Amri, was a similar series, though more discrete and less systematized than the Harappan, of craft production, including pottery for daily life. Thus these antecendent Harappan stages were "Pre-Harappan" in a strictly cultural sense, in addition to the temporal sense. Trade and civic organizations were what was missing in them. Since the bulk of the trade transactions of the Harappans went toward catering to, and underwriting the coeval village economy and nexus, when the trade balance eventually broke down, everything broke down. Economic disintegration thus, was one of the vital reasons for the disappearance of what could be termed as the "high life style" of the Harappan Culture seen in its period of primacy between 2600 B.C. and 1900 B.C.

The existence of people contemporary with the Indus Civilization in its mature stages in Gujarat, Central India and the Deccan has become increasingly clear with recent archaeological research. The continuance of the Late Stone Age microlithic or stone-using cultures well into the Chalcolithic and later even into the tribal stages (despite the advent of urbanization) represents a clear process of *recession*. Cultural expansion, after the rootless *melange* of Post-Harappan Cultures, into consistent urbanization and growth, is seen most diffused only from the secondary stage (of Iron Age) in the Ganges Valley. The sites reflecting the Post-Harappan *milieu* are the largest in this region, smaller in the Punjab and smaller yet in the Deccan. Rajasthan, Gujarat and Central India did have the development of iron technology but these regions did not seem to have reached an urban balance, socioculturally speaking. Based on the above, the problems are: (1) Did the Chalcolithic stage of the protohistoric cultures in India vitally contribute to the advancement of the society as a whole, toward eventual urbanization (in the stage antecedent to their Chalcolithic acculturation)? (2) Did the Indus Culture bequeath its seemingly systematized urban traits to the Chalcolithic and the Iron Age urbanization? (3) Which were the epicenters of the ecological and social motivations which distinguished indigenous developments and intrusive patterns during the third and second millennia B.C. in northern as well as southern India?

It has been variously held that urban growth in India was a product or concomittant of: (1) the consolidation of political power, (2) economic or money power, or (3) that no truly urban cities existed, the vast population was rural and only drifts toward town life occurred. The first view seemingly ignores the fact that there could be cities without regular urbanization. The second point ignores the fact that trade does not spend or invest its surplus *only* in cities, but everywhere. The city was not absolutely necessary for the prosperity of trade either. As regards the last point, it may be stated that cities have existed at all times, on a sociocultural basis, where consumer goods were in demand and where "white collar" jobs, to take a modern term, alone existed. But it should indeed be asked if a city is essentially a political center? A pilgrim city of today, like Kasi, is an exception to this idea. Is it an economic center, for trade alone? There are several conventional market cities or towns which are exceptions to this. Is the city an artificial place where some floating, drift population gathers and diversifies its wants? The answer seems to be that the base of a city is:

1) its topographical advantage;
2) high consumer potential;
3) unquestioned cultural, religious or spiritual sanctity; and
4) where civic control is, even otherwise, well established; which is self-governing and therefore not directly linked with a ruler or a political power center.

The cumulative results of the above could make a city mainly a trade center, with (a) civic, (b) exchange, (c) consumer, and (d) cultural functions. It is likely that after each city was formed, political power shifted into the one most strategically placed. In early historic context, around the sixth century B.C and after, the city was first a secular and temporal civic center. It is fortified only in the subsequent stage, thus becoming a political and military center. As a sequel to this development, unregimented civic amenities and free life are lost in such centers. But they do shift to towns and villages, where greater freedom exists due to the absence of metropolitan compulsions. Fortified cities can be identified with power centers, but secular and temporal graces can be witnessed only in towns and villages. In a subsequent stage, the fortified city itself is superseded by, and modified into, larger metropolitan and suburban complexes which draw from the villages and thereby seek to revitalize trade. Considered in this light, urbanization is the capacity for the widest habitational spectrum, with cultural differentiation. It is the capacity to promote thought, art and leisure activities and artisans like musicians, painters, perfumers, entertainers, sportsmen and caterers. None of these is politically motivated and they can exist only under the shadow of economic affluence, created either from the surplus of agricultural produce from rural areas or by trade surplus from inter-city or other exchange processes. Mere political or military power centers have never become cities with urban flowering. They develop into cantonments.

In the Harappan context, the city was concomittantly the center of politico-religious power. The Pre-Harappan stage was devoid of this dichotomy of political cum civic center between the city consumer and the suburban retailer.

The implications of a fortification in a town, especially in the earliest Harappan context, are seemingly different from those of the second (Iron Age) urbanization. It is to be noted that the twin mounds of the Harappan sites, with separate fortified enclosures, and the later Iron Age fort-cities, should be basically different. The close liaison implied in the latter, with the citadel located *within* the city-fort, is not seen in the Harappan case. Hence, there is a likelihood that there was an absence of regular civic or community administration of the people—only their management and control for the benefit of the "citadel" people.

Hence, to recapitulate, Pre-Harappan Culture was not urban. The Harappan Culture was an urban dichotomy with political control and civic consumer potential as its highlights. The Post-Harappan lapsed into a degenerate consumer situation, with village-type community status and was otherwise much like the Pre-Harappan. The clock had come a full circle.

In the second stage of urbanization, the city outside the citadel was painstakingly built by tradesmen as a civic center, with cultural amenities, topographical advantages and spiritual sidelights. In fact, *srenis* might have been directly in charge of these civic centers. Then, with increasing political might, they were taken over by political overlords.

Trade was not under the capricious leadership of the state—autonomy was clearly accepted. It is this that gave rise to the well-known series of autonomous trade guilds. These served as a bridge between the chieftain and the people and helped in the decentralization of the fiscal and revenue programs of the state. It is not yet clear if the role of the trader in the Harappan Civilization was comparable. The overwhelming importance of trade, however, is fairly obvious and there might have been a very close relationship between the chief of the city-state and the trading agency. One is not yet in a position to partition from material finds the secular, mercantile and religious segments of the Harappan civic organism. As and when one finds the means of achieving this, one will be nearer an understanding of the actual urban "model" it represents. It has recently been argued, mainly it would seem to avoid placing Harappan town planning into a rigid mold, that the Indus town pattern was not identical everywhere, as at Mohenjodaro, Harappa, Lothal, Surkotada, etc. This view may be laudable enough as a desire to investigate the background of how and why the Harappan civic plan developed. But it is obvious that the Harappan city pattern was, as already shown, different from both the early historic town planning, and the proto- or Pre-Harappan pattern (e.g., Kot

Diji or Kalibangan or elsewhere). There is no need either to consider all the cities as representing one pattern. There were undoubted metropolises like Mohenjodaro, Harappa and Kalibangan, port towns like Lothal and Rangpur, and trade outposts along coasts. Other settlements were in comparatively less inhabited areas, as at Desalpur, Surkotada and Sutkagendor. This is why the pattern differs. Similarity was in the "trade objective" that united them. It has recently been argued that models for these cities can be found in the upper Sarasvati Basin (present Bahawalpur region) in Pre-Harappan times. But there is no evidence available for trade or economic viability of these places during the Pre-Harappan. It would perhaps be fair, to a limited degree, to postulate that, in the final analysis, the origins of Harappan cities should be explored in the immediate region in which the cities themselves developed. But the full explanation of the city organization and layout will come from an understanding of the cumulative impact of several factors, economic, political, cultural, etc.; and West Asia need not in entirety be a region out of bounds for influencing such a phenomenon.

Here again, it is worthwhile examining another analog: the earliest "megalithic" tomb type(s) of India, which are mainly, to be seen in the lower Deccan. The inspiration for these doubtless came to India from the West Asian and Mediterranean regions, through obvious agencies of trade. But, the first megalith type is not known in India since there is a minimum chronological gap of at least half a millennium between the later series of megaliths of the West and the earliest in India. The latter can be placed toward the end of the first quarter of the first millennium B.C., or a little earlier. Nor were the models for Indian megaliths just imitations of a *single* western archetype. The reason for this is that there must be an equation between the model and the contemporary sociocultural base of the adopting region. This equation varies across time and space. Returning to Harappan urbanization, the Indus model was intended to be a trade-oriented urban standardization. This did not exist in the antecedent (Pre-Harappan) stage but developed in the Harappan age due to several visible and invisible factors, as clearly held by Wheeler. In trade-supported city centers (like, for example, Singapore or Hongkong, on a modern analogy), there is always an elite way of life in the upper strata of the community. A rural, or less-consumer based, sector of people will also exist in a substandard urban condition, but these people will always be controlled by the elites. There is no class or caste difference here, there is no religious superiority, there is no antecedent base for it. It is consumerism that separates the upper class from the lower, bestowing the leadership for organization, in the hands of the higher rank, and making it also tend thereby to control the masses. Religious groups may have been trying to strengthen the hand of the elites, by their own exclusive character, but they have no pervasive influence—on either the controlling elite or on the masses. The folk cults of the masses, on the other hand, continue to reign, more as a concession from the upper (technocratic) stratum to the lower (agricultural) groups. In due course, they get into one or more firm religious preferences, on the basis of the transformation or absorption of folk cults by the elite groups, grafting them into their own religion's beliefs and creating a "vogue" for them. There was no institutionalized or well-organized religion, as such, in the Harappan cities of India. The terracottas, etc., do show the germ of a cult but these belong to the folk order. To that extent the Harappan city-state was indeed secular. The religious trend, it would seem, reached these cities, in a significant way, at about the beginning of the second millennium B.C., and, growing in momentum, upset the Harappan secular, urban, consumer-oriented agriculture-exploiting economy by the middle of that millennium. This led to its decay and the rise of new masters in the form of a new religious and an intellectual elite. One is not able to see and touch them yet by using archaeological tools; although their presence is felt in the Ganges Valley during the succeeding centuries in specific institutions and the compartmentalization of social participation witnessed in no uncertain terms, and inspired in this regard, by a firmly and categorically postulated ethicomoral manual—the *Smriti* code—as its cohorts. The socialization process of urbanization was consummated here; whatever be its own repercussions on society in the subsequent stage—that is, the age of the protestant creeds of Mahavira and Gautama.

Please see the Appendix attached to this paper for a summary of the issues discussed here.

SUMMARY

Harappan Urbanization

This was probably a conditioned, secular, consumer-oriented, agricultural-exchange economy—a stringently disciplined oligarchy of political, trade and technocrat coterie. Its Pre-Harappan stages themselves did not have the germs of this conditioned urbanization system. Its motivations, thus, though perhaps caused by special leadership traits, may have been inspired though not fashioned on contemporary external centers of civilization.

On the other hand, the Iron Age urbanization had its motivations caused by certain non-Harappan trends and forces which had prevailed in India in the second-first millennium B.C. which stimulated both the head and the heart, and had a universalized social purpose. They thus promoted a polity, art, thought and national or sovereignty concepts, for the first time, on a pan-Indian basis, with the State liaising with trade groups as well as citizens.

APPENDIX

Comparative aetiology of Harappan and Iron Age urbanization differentiae

Harappan urbanization	Iron Age urbanization	
	Early	Late
1	2	3
Citadel and city separately walled	Citadel and city unified	Improved unification
Trade independent of civic leadership (?)—largely maritime and external	Trade independent of political control and both inland and maritime	State trade and tax for revenue
Civic leadership combining spiritual role also	Republican/monarchical leadership hardening into dynastic rule with religious aura	Dynastic king—God rule
Civic standardization of structures—brick size systematized—sanitation	Fort palace—civic center concept—brick sizes vary—no centralized sanitation	Extreme variation in construction—minimal civic sanitation
Uniform pottery types by centralized technical control of vogue and production	Marked variation and proliferation of pottery forms and types—*deluxe* wares registering economic disparities with localized private kiln production	Varied qualities and mass production of local wares imported techniques and local imitation
Organized religion only marginally apparent	Evolving and vibrant religion assimilated by society—institutionalized by law codes (?)	State preoccupied with religion and a social obsession with cults
Craft resources pooled and crafts processed by the city-state into standard patterns	Craft resources and process a private enterprise but under caste groups concerned	Craft resources state-owned or controlled but workmanship in caste groups
No standing army or war machinery or defense works in city layout	Defense part of social structure under king and his army, wars a regular phenomenon	Defense-like kingship on regional basis and advanced defense tactics and machinery available

(*Contd.*)

1	2	3
Writing limited, exclusive non-alphabetical and not a social tool	Literacy on oral tradition but germs of regular writing noticeable	Extensive alphabetical public and private written records
Weights and probably measures of a graded range occur but no coinage, as barter system alone prevailed in the agricultural exchange economy that prevailed. No stable self-sustaining monetary system existed. Gold used only for ornaments	Weights and measures as well as coinage prevailed in gold and silver standard in some form. This further reflects a regular buyer and seller economy based on a monetary system which could, by its state control produce rich and poor classes	A more stable but a more centrifugal and fluctuating economy, divided into several autonomous regional systems each under a powerful political leader or king
Religious statuary in stone almost non-existent but effigies in terracotta in limited quantities occur, was it folk- (?) or fetish-based (?) and not reflecting communal religion though produced for some spiritual trends. Metal statuary, minimal and probably secular	Profuse stone, metal and terracotta figurines suggesting religious groups in society of un-unified character. Mostly folk but with unseen influences from sacerdotal religions	Religious art well consolidated mostly under state patronage of temples side by side with eschatelogical and secular trends
No private property seemingly existed except perhaps in villages, of land use but open to demand of produce and animals for exchange—trade by city-states	Private property implied and inferred by socio-religious codes, of both movable and immovable categories. Transport system expanded and regulated for military and civil needs	Highly competitive social class and caste disparities with professional occupation on caste basis decentralized to village levels but under monolithic state control

NOTE

[1] The *Ayudhajivis* mentioned in the *vartika* of *Ashtadhyayi* of Panini (and applicable later to the *Malava* and the *Yaudhaya ganas*) involved groups not claiming any administrative apparatus but mainly of peripatetic mercenary status.

BIBLIOGRAPHY

Formal citations have been omitted from this paper. The sources listed below are all fundamental in a documentation of the position outlined here. In addition, however, the yearly reports in *Indian Archaeology: A review* should be consulted, especially between 1961 and 1968. Numbers five through eight of the journal *Puratattva* are important as well.

Allchin B. and F.R. Allchin, 1968
    The Birth of Indian Civilization. Harmondsworth: Penguin.

Ghosh, A., 1973
    City in Early Historical India. Simla: Indian Institute of Advanced Study.

Gupta, S.P. and K.S. Ramachandran, eds., 1976
    Mahabharata: Myth and Reality. Delhi: B.R. Publishing Corp.

Mughal, M.R., 1978
    Four Years of Archaeological Discoveries in Cholistan. Lecture presented at the Lahore Museum, 21 February 1978. Cyclostyled copy.

Wheeler, Sir Mortimer, 1968
    The Indus Civilization. 3rd ed. Supplementary volume to the Cambridge History of India. Cambridge: The University Press.

PART II

RESULTS OF RECENT FIELDWORK

JEAN-FRANÇOIS JARRIGE

6. Excavations at Mehrgarh: Their Significance for Understanding the Background of the Harappan Civilization

UNTIL very recently archaeological research in Baluchistan was very fragmentary. Despite the pioneering work of W. A. Fairservis and B. de Cardi, the absence of large-scale excavation left a rather distorted image of cultural developments on the western fringes of the Indus Valley in the millennia before the Harappan Civilization. Sir Mortimer Wheeler, in reference to the genesis of Harappan Civilization, said: "In the present context the ill-sorted industries and cultures of the hills are of no immediate concern save as a back-curtain to the main scene" (Wheeler 1968: 9). And C. A. Reed could declare: "On the basis of present knowledge no evidence exists for the presence of agriculture in India before 5000 B. P." (1977: 917).

Prior to the work at Mehrgarh one had to admit that while several parts of Baluchistan are well suited to primitive agriculture, the deserts, mountains and distance from more "central" regions had obstructed the introduction of farming for several millennia. Apparently Baluchistan, and the other parts of the northwestern Subcontinent were devoid of early Neolithic occupation, if one were to put aside the scanty evidence from Kili Ghul Mohammad. A farming economy reached these areas only after 4000 B.C. Western India and Pakistan were thus considered marginal areas affected by cultural innovations from Western and Central Asia only via diffusion. There was apparently a fundamental contrast between the two main civilizations of Ancient Asia. On the one side, urban growth in Mesopotamia and Susiana was thought to be the result of deep cultural processes originating in the Neolithic. On the other side, though it was possible to emphasize some genetic links between the Indus Civilization and the Pre-Harappan Cultures, the change from village to city was thought to suggest that an external factor played a fundamental part in the process. Sir Mortimer Wheeler suggested that direct influences from Mesopotamia could be discarded. But he accepted a notion that civilization reached the Indus from Mesopotamia as a stimulating factor initiating a deep transformation.

In 1974 a decision was made to excavate Mehrgarh in Kachi District, Baluchistan. The plan was to undertake a large, horizontal excavation at a site occupying a very important geographical position which could bring together sufficient elements to build a reliable model for understanding the cultural background of the Harappan Civilization. Mehrgarh is an important site at the foot of the Bolan Pass in the Kachi Plain, which though belonging to the Baluchistan Province, is still very much a part of the Indus system (Fig. 6.1). The site covers an area of about 500 acres with only Pre-Harappan remains (Fig. 6.2). It had obviously been occupied for a very long time. Thus, by excavating a sufficient sample of this huge site we were confident that we would be able to build a solid chronological framework with deep significance for understanding the socioeconomic background of the Harappan Civilization.

After five excavation campaigns at Mehrgarh we

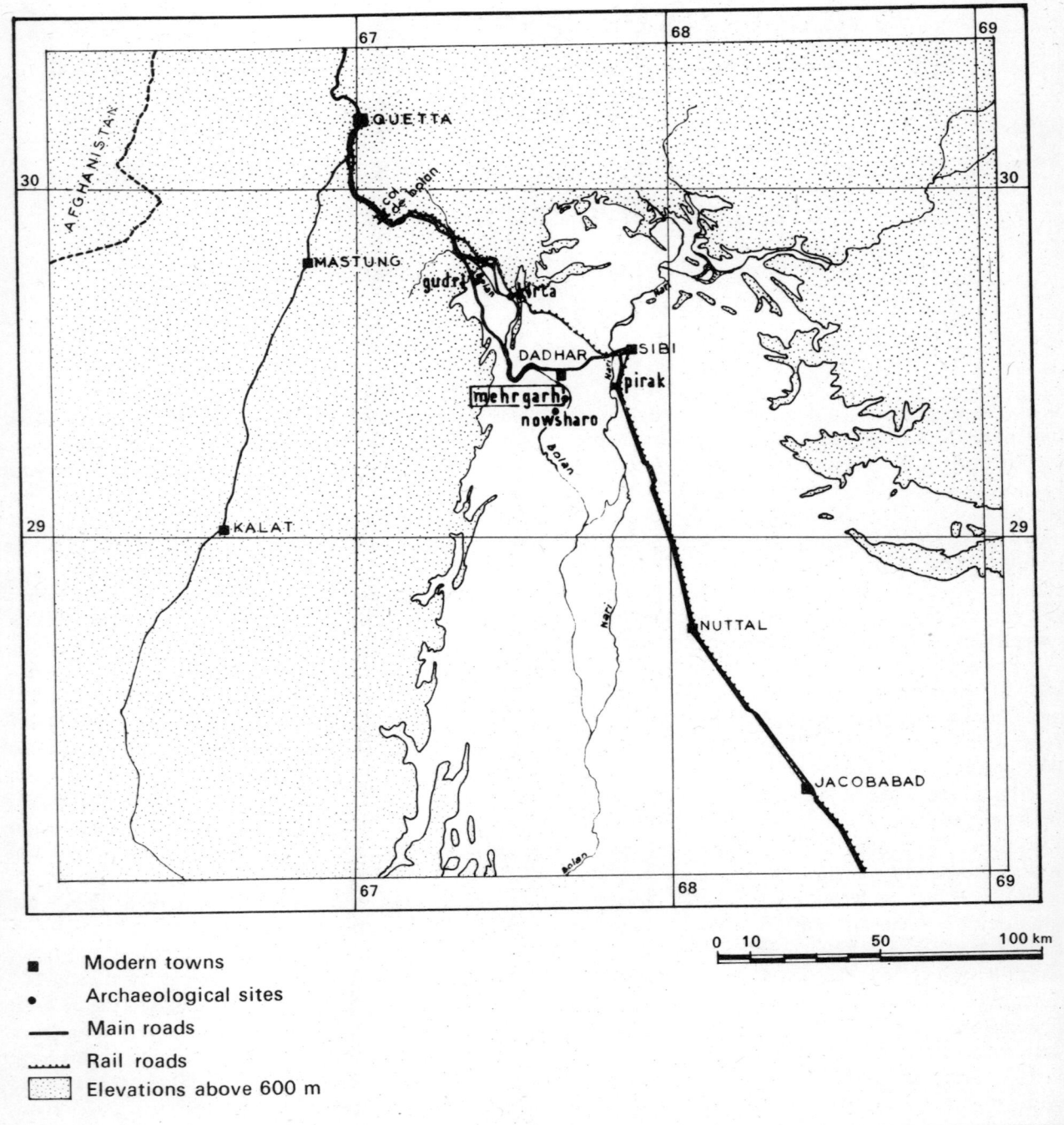

Fig. 6.1. Map of the Kachi Plain.

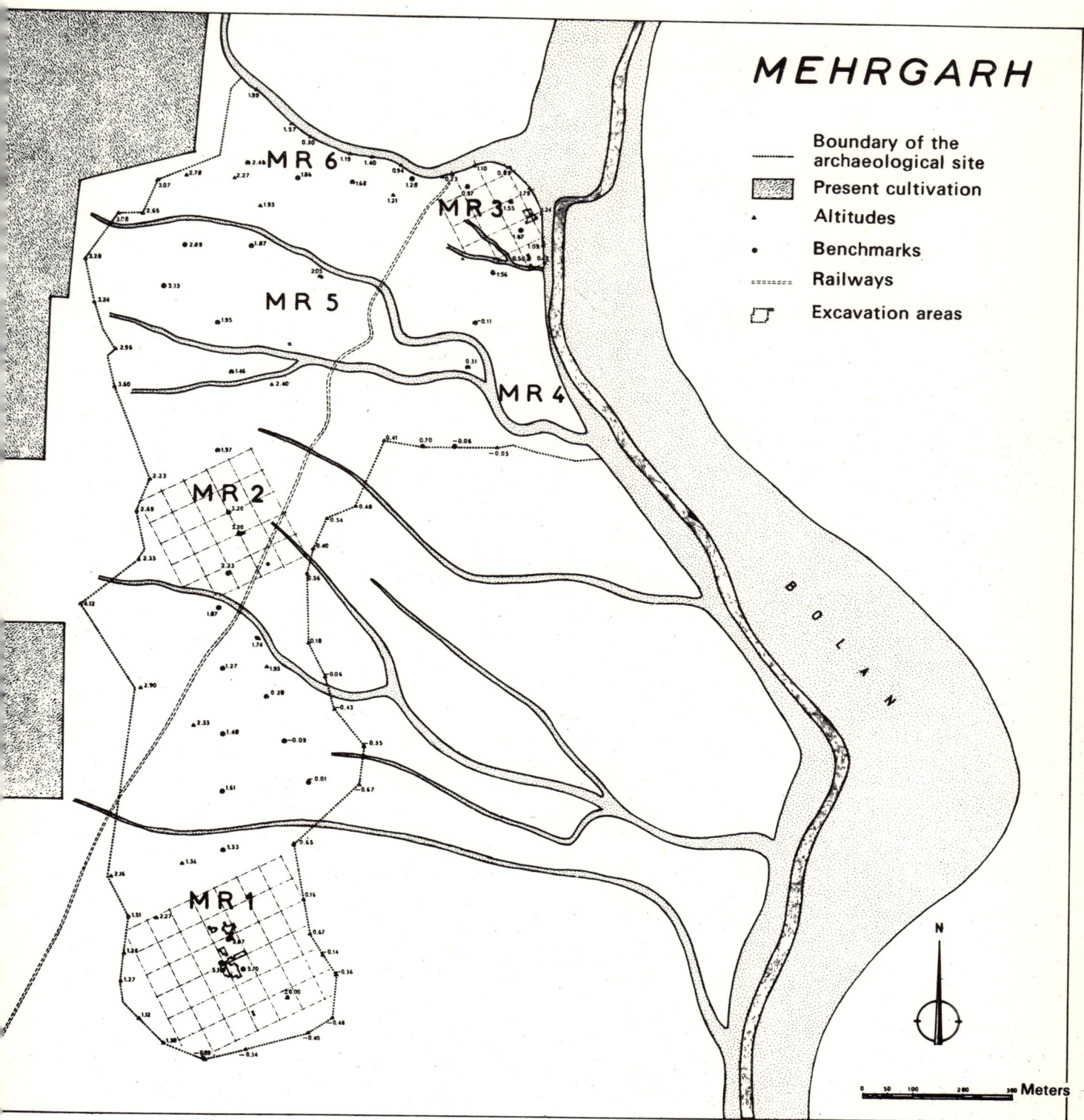

Fig. 6.2. Map of the site of Mehrgarh.

now have evidence of continuous occupation for more than three millennia prior to the Harappan Civilization. The sequence demonstrates that the Kachi Plain is an area with a long cultural tradition and its own regional characteristics.

At the 1977 meeting of South Asian Archaeologists in Naples we announced the discovery of an aceramic Neolithic site at Mehrgarh (Jarrige and Lechevallier 1979). This has been designated Mehrgarh Mound Three (Fig. 6.2). A section cut by the Bolan River revealed 10 meters of Neolithic deposit. The top levels of this settlement dated to ca. 5000 B.C. (radiocarbon determination with MASCA calibration factors added). We still have no date for the lower layers but we assume that the beginning of the settlement is as early as the seventh millennium. For the time being only the upper layers have been extensively excavated, but in a large sounding undertaken during the 1978-79 season, five meters of Neolithic deposits were excavated. It is hoped that virgin soil was reached in this area during the 1979-80 season. The 1978-79 sounding confirmed the fact that the deposits are aceramic. Several layers of mud-brick architecture have been exposed here showing the sedentary character of the settlement. Sickle elements and grinding stones were recovered from the upper levels along with cereal impressions in lumps of clay (Pl. 6.1) which have been studied by L. Costantini. Impressions of two-row hulled barley (*Hordeum distichum*), six-row barley (*H. vulgare* and *H. vulgare* var. *nudum*), eincorn wheat (*Triticum monococcum*), emmer wheat (*T. dicoccum*) and bread wheat (*T. durum/aestivum*) suggest that agriculture in Baluchistan was diversified and well developed by the end of the sixth millennium.

The faunal remains from the upper two meters of the Neolithic deposit have been studied by Richard Meadow. He finds a marked shift over time from an assemblage dominated by bones of hunted animals [e.g., gazelle (*Gazella dorcas*, Pl. 6.2), wild sheep (*Ovis orientalis*), swamp deer (*Cervus duvauceli*) and cattle (*Bos namadicus?*)] to one characterized almost exclusively by domesticated species [e.g., sheep (*Ovis ares*), goats and most importantly, cattle (Pl. 6.3)]. The identification of two bones from the water buffalo (*Bos bubalis*) from these same levels makes it the earliest evidence for this animal in South Asia.

Flint artifacts are the most numerous find in this period, with approximately 15,000 pieces. These belong to an industry dominated by blades and bladelets, geometric microliths, lunates, or a characteristic trapeze with a curved back. The microlithic types represent about four percent of the collection. This lithic industry shares many common features with epipalaeolithic sites in the Near East.

Nearly 700 square meters of the upper levels of the aceramic community have been exposed. These produced large rectangular buildings symmetrically divided into a number of rooms. Some of the buildings have small square compartments without doors that must have been storehouses (Pl. 6.4). Interspaced among these buildings are large cemeteries (Pl. 6.5). Some of the burials contain baskets coated with bitumen (Pl. 6.6). They also have ornaments of local stone, shell and bone (Pl. 6.7). Beads of imported semiprecious stone, such as turquoise, (Pl. 6.8) and lapis lazuli, are also present. Another of the interments is associated with a copper bead giving interesting evidence for the use of metal in an aceramic context. Red ochre is commonly associated with the burials and in one case the traces of a red ochre-colored textile were visible on the bones. Cakes of red ochre were also found as grave goods along with polished stone axes, stone vessels, flint cores, blades and microliths.

On the southern edge of the Neolithic settlement a sloping deposit contained about twelve potsherds in a very coarse chaff-tempered ware. This is so far the first evidence of pottery in this part of Mehrgarh and it seems to come slightly later than the top level of the Mehrgarh Mound Three Neolithic settlement.

South of the Neolithic settlement are the remains of a fifth millennium occupation. A large rectangular building has been exposed with the same type of long plano-convex bricks used during the earlier Neolithic phase (Pl. 6.9). It is divided into 10 narrow compartments, symmetrically disposed on each side of a narrow corridor. This building, which is preserved in some places to a height of one meter, has no door and seems to have been used as a storeroom, just as were the buildings mentioned in the Neolithic settlement. Its use as a granary would explain the large number of barley and wheat imprints noticed in the compartments. Two very well preserved sickles with three bladelets hafted slantwise in bitumen have also been found in one of the compartments. Outside this building, along the western wall, a large fireplace was found to contain several hundred charred grains. These are presently being studied by L. Constantini who has already identified several kinds of wheat

Excavations at Mehrgarh

including *Triticum aestivum-compactum* and barley. Some of the seeds have been identified as cotton (cf. *Gossypium* sp.). But these seeds are very carbonized, often broken and are in such a bad state of preservation that it is difficult to know if they belong to the wild or cultivated species. But their occurrence among the other seeds of cultivated cereals, in a fireplace apparently associated with a "granary," would suggest that their presence is not accidental. It therefore cannot be denied that cotton was cultivated in the fifth millennium for either its oil or fibrous properties. But, a certain amount of caution is called for in this matter and further information on the cotton from Mehrgarh is awaited.

Along the southern wall of the "granary" are the remains of a steatite cutter's workshop. This has various stone tools, including a few drills. On the eastern side of the same building, heaps of bones were mixed with ashes. About one hundred bone awls were collected here (Pl. 6.10). It seems that a bone industry was associated with the garbage resulting from intense butchering activity. Thus, the awls may have been used for working animal skins on this very spot.

A limited number of sherds in a fine burnished red ware have also been found in and outside the building. Most of the vessels are pear-shaped jars. It is interesting to note that these pots were shaped on a rotating device, probably a wheel, and extended with dabber. Two human figurines in clay were also found. They are very stylized; one is in a seated position, the other, which is truncated, is decorated with small discs pasted around its base (Pl. 6.11). Another terracotta figurine is of a stylized four-legged animal, and it comes from the same area within the site. These figurines, to which one must add a lower part of a seated example from the Neolithic levels of Mehrgarh Mound Three, demonstrate that representations of humans and animals are to be found in the earliest cultural assemblages known in Baluchistan. By the very end of this period (Period II in the general sequence at Mehrgarh), comes the first occurrence of painted pottery. This is definitely wheel-thrown, with very simple geometric patterns in the Kili Ghul Mohammad II style. It is associated with a large number of handmade sherds, some of them with basket marks.

The discoveries made at Mehrgarh in the deposits of the fifth and sixth millennia have a deep significance. They reveal the great antiquity of a farming economy, of craft specialization and of long distance contacts (turquoise, lapis lazuli and sea shells) in Baluchistan. Further excavations in the deepest Neolithic deposits, so far unexplored, will throw new light on the part played by the northwestern regions of the Indo-Pakistan Subcontinent in the cultural processes which led to the development of the earliest farming communities. The cultural traditions of the third and fourth millennia in Baluchistan and the Indus Valley are deeply rooted in local traditions beginning with a very early Neolithic.

At the beginning of the fourth millennium B.C. Mehrgarh (Period III) becomes a mass production center for wheel-turned pottery. The vessels, often of a fine fabric, are decorated with geometric motifs of the Kili Ghul Mohammad III style, or with caprid and bird representations of the Togau style (Pl. 6.12). Workshops where lapis lazuli, turquoise, carnelian and sea shell were worked are also associated with this period which marks an important stage in the development of craft activities. The presence of several microdrills in green stone (phtanite) found in association with stone beads is worthy of note (Pl. 6.13). This is so far the earliest evidence for these tools of remarkable workmanship. Their ends are slightly hollow and highly polished, suggesting the use of a bow drill. Tools like these are found in later contexts at Shahr-i Sokhta, Shahdad as well as Indus sites such as Chanhudaro (Mackay 1937).

This period can be considered a phase of technological innovation, and one within which there was a diversification of agriculture. It witnesses the earliest appearance of oats (*Avena* sp.) and the addition of *Triticum sphaerococcum* to the group of wheats already present in earlier times.

At about 3500 B.C. the main period of occupation (IV) at Mehrgarh begins. This phase is known in Baluchistan through the pioneering work of W. A. Fairservis who designated it "Damb Sadaat I." Domestic buildings with small, low doors and open spaces where household activities were carried on, have been exposed (Pl. 6.14). The floors of these open spaces, where many fragments of large storage jars were found, are full of barley imprints. In this period there are beautiful examples of polychrome pottery with geometric decorations in red, white and black. Large, semiconical vessels on small pedestals, decorated with intricate geometrical patterns in bright colors are masterpieces (Pl. 6.15). Some of the painted pottery is decorated with the geometric motifs of the Togau B and D styles. But the painted wares, which represented almost 30 percent of the sherds in Period III, now account for less than 15 percent. At the same time there is a remarkable development in the range of shapes in plain ware. This includes "eggshell" goblets and sturdy storage jars. The first stamp seals of terracotta and bone occur in Period IV. The female figurines, which still resemble the early Chalcolithic prototypes, now have pendulous breasts.

By about 3200 B.C. a phase is reached which is well known in the Indo-Iranian borderlands. This period marks the beginning of Shahr-i Sokhta in Eastern Iran, of Period III at Mundigak and of Damb Sadaat II in the Quetta Valley. This period, which extends from 3200 to 2500 B.C. has already been dealt with, in previous papers on Mehrgarh VI and VII (Jarrige 1979: 85–87; Jarrige and Lechevallier 1979: 501–34). During this time Mehrgarh is a part of a large interaction zone extending over most of the Indo-Iranian borderlands. The mass production of pottery and terracotta figurines is one of the main activities of the site. Some of the finest specimens of the Faiz Mohammad style Black on Gray Ware have been found close to kiln areas. The human figurines, with diversity in hairdressing, a variety of ornaments and painted in yellow, reflect the existence of a rather sophisticated society. The remains of a huge brick platform faced with a plastered wall is probably connected to a monumental complex. During this period there are some indications of urbanization similar to those noted at Rahman Dheri by the team from the University of Peshawar.

The upper levels of Mehrgarh, with a cultural assemblage corresponding to Damb Sadaat III in the Quetta Valley, have an increase in the percentage of micaceous pottery in the Kot Dijian fabric. Triangular terracotta cakes, long parallel-sided blades (reaching a length of 18 centimeters) and several other elements which will be found in the Mature Harappan cultural assemblage, begin here.

Mehrgarh has produced a long history of man's adaptation to the Indus Valley. This begins with the earliest settling by farming peoples, and goes through the middle of the third millennium. Just prior to 2500 B.C. the site is integrated into the Early Harappan as defined by Dr. M.R. Mughal (1970). Mehrgarh is then abandoned. But, eight kilometers to the south, at Nowsharo, there is a Mature Harappan site which indicates that the Kachi Plain was definitely a part of the Harappan territory.

BIBLIOGRAPHY

Jarrige, J.F., 1979
   Excavations at Mehrgarh, Pakistan. In *South Asian Archaeology, 1975*. J.E. van Lohuizen-de Leeuw, ed. Pp. 76–87. Leiden: E.J. Brill.

Jarrige, J.F. and M. Lechevallier, 1979
   Excavations at Mehrgarh, Baluchistan: Their significance in the prehistoric context of the Indo-Pakistani borderlands. In *South Asian Archaeology, 1977*. Maurizio Taddei, ed. Pp. 463–536. Instituto Universitario Orientale, Seminario di Studi Asiatici, Series Minor IV, Naples.

Mackay, E.J.H., 1937
   Bead Making in Ancient Sind. *Journal of the American Oriental Society* 57: 1–15.

Mughal, M.R., 1970
   The Early Harappan Period in the Greater Indus Valley and Northern Baluchistan (3000–2400 B.C.). Ph.D. dissertation, Anthropology Department, University of Pennsylvania.

Reed, C.A., 1977
   Origin of Agriculture. The Hague: Mouton.

Wheeler, Sir Mortimer, 1968
   The Indus Civilization. 3rd ed. Supplementary Volume to the Cambridge History of India. Cambridge: The University Press.

M. RAFIQUE MUGHAL

7. Recent Archaeological Research in the Cholistan Desert

INTRODUCTION

In 1974, the Department of Archaeology and Museums, Pakistan launched a major program of field research in the Cholistan Desert of former Bahawalpur State in the East-Central Indus Valley. The purpose of this preliminary survey was to locate and identify the full range of archaeological remains in this little-known region. The Cholistan Desert, an area of extreme aridity, was originally watered on its western fringes by a river now called the Hakra in Pakistan and the Ghaggar in India. Of particular interest was the now dry bed of this river.

A part of this region was first explored by Sir Aurel Stein in 1941 (Stein 1942). In 1955 Henry Field (1959) re-examined a part of Stein's track. On the Indian side, the dry bed of the Ghaggar River was surveyed by A. Ghosh (1952) and later by B.B. Lal and B.K. Thapar, who extensively excavated the Harappan site of Kalibangan. A zone along the Sutlej River was explored by K.N. Dikshit and the area near Anupgarh and Nohar on the Ghaggar river reviewed by Katy F. Dalal (1980). The major work in Haryana and the Punjab (east) was carried out by Suraj Bhan (1973 and 1975) which he continued in 1977 with Jim G. Shaffer (Suraj Bhan and Shaffer 1978).

RECENT SURVEYS

Our surveys were concentrated along 300 miles of the dry bed of the Hakra River, within an approximately 10 to 15-mile-wide strip (Mughal 1980a. b). The project was directed by the author for four seasons between 1974 and 1977. Beginning at the Indian border near Fort Abbas, we covered 110 miles, to Fort Derawar, during the first season. The settlement pattern that emerged from the first season's work was most encouraging in terms of understanding the character, distribution and location of various sites of the Harappan Civilization. The highest concentration of sites was found around Fort Derawar and to its southwest (Figs. 7.1 and 7.2), an area which had not been previously explored. As the work progressed, the pivotal importance of this region began to emerge. It is now clear that this is a key region for understanding the developmental stages of the Harappan (or Indus) Civilization.

THE SITES

A total of 414 sites have been mapped along 300 miles of the Hakra River bed (Mughal in press). They range in time from at least the fourth millennium B.C. to the Medieval Period. The protohistoric sites fall into the various periods of development (Table 7.1).

The sites cover the long, continuous sequence of development and change of the Indus Civilization, encompassing the period from the fourth to the beginning of the first millennium B.C. The protohistoric settlement pattern in Cholistan has largely remained undisturbed to the present time and it is an important laboratory for the study of prehistory. The main features of each cultural phase are briefly reviewed in the following pages.

Fig. 7.2. Ancient sites in the Central Hakra region.

Table 7.1

Approximate time range	Cultural association	Number of sites
Fourth millennium B.C.	Hakra Wares (Jalilpur I related)	99
Early third millennium B.C.	Early Harappan (Kot Diji related)	40
Mid and late third millennium B.C.	Mature Harappan (Mohenjodaro and Harappan related)	174
Early second millennium B.C. and later	Late Harappan (Cemetery H related)	50
End second and early first millennium B.C.	Post or non-Harappan (Painted Gray and Black-and-Red Wares related)	14

Note: Some sites have more than one cultural phase.

KEY TO THE MAPS OF SITES

Site No.	Name of site	Site No.	Name of site	Site No.	Name of site
1.	Raowali	27.	Gamanwala	54.	Wariyal–F
2.	Chak 258 HL	28.	Ladulai	55.	Wariyal–H
3.	Chak 265 HR	29.	Gujranwala	56.	Wariyal–G
4.	Ahmadwala Toba	30.	Chak 337 HR	57.	Hanaswala
5.	Channanwala Ther	31.	Kandianwali	58.	Guddal–B
6.	Theriwala	32.	Chapliwala (West)	59.	Guddal Ther
6A.	Bahadrianwala	33.	Chapliwala (East)	60.	Guddal–A
7.	Phulra Fort	34.	Chapuwala	61.	Wakkarwala
8.	Chak 270 HR	35.	Chak 341	62.	Bokhariyanwala
9.	Chak 271 HR	36.	Jathewali	63.	Bokhariyanwala–A
10.	R.D. 66	37.	Chak 353 (West)	64.	Bazariwala
11.	Rajuwala	38.	Mansura	65.	Jatoiwala–A
12.	Sandhanawala	39.	Chak 323 HR	66.	Jatoiwala–B
13.	Satkui (East)	40.	Satwali	67.	Kuchanwala
14.	Satkui (West)	41.	Gharanwali	68.	Ahmadwala Ther
15.	Chak 280 HR	42.	Jalwali	69.	Lal Patel
16.	Chak 281 HR	43.	Trillar	70.	Tarsoolwala
17.	Quraish Ther	44.	Akhera	71.	Jatoiwala Ther
18.	Chak 285 HR	45.	Malhalewala Ther	72.	Hakim Ali Ther
19.	Chak 298 HR	46.	Bokharaiwala	73.	Chak 88
20.	Mirgarh Fort	47.	Mojgarh Fort	74.	Chak 88A (West)
21.	Jamgarh Fort	48.	Mojgarh Ther	75.	Chak 69
22.	Chak 308 HR	49.	Chipwala	76.	Kudwala
23.	Chak 314 HR	50.	Kalepar (Bhoot)	77.	Wariyal–A
24.	Kirarwali	51.	Khewtal	78.	Wariyal–B
25.	Chak 315 HR	52.	Wariyal Ther	79.	Wariyal–D
26.	Marot Fort	53.	Wariyal–E	80.	Wariyal–C

Site No.	Name of site	Site No.	Name of site	Site No.	Name of site
81.	Gharaiyanwala	127.	Bagrauwala Ther	174.	Hotewala–II
82.	Ali Mohd Wala Ther	128.	Bara Fort	175.	Hotewala Ther–A
83.	Chak 45	129.	Bara Ther	176.	Hotewala Ther–B
84.	Maujhalwala	130.	Dingarh Fort	177.	Garakwala
85.	Chak 45B (North)	131.	Dabli (West)	178.	Jamuwali–A
86.	Chak 45A (South)	132.	Dabli (East)	179.	Jamuwali–B
87.	Chak 44	133.	Sullewala	180.	Mubarakwala Ther
88.	Boharwala Ther	134.	Cheelanwali	181.	Butewala
89.	Chak 51	135.	Cheelanwala–B	182.	Lunida–II
90.	Kaliyar	136.	Killianwali–D	183.	Lunida–I
91.	Rohatwala	137.	Jiwaiwali	184.	Sanukewala–II
92.	Chak 103	138.	Waddanwala	185.	Sanukewala
93.	Chak 107	139.	Bahilawala–C	186.	Sanukewala–III
94.	Chak 61 (East)	140.	Bahilawala–B	187.	Kalharwala
95.	Chak 61 (West)	141.	Bahilawala Ther	188.	Drigwala
96.	Lurewala	142.	Nahranwala	189.	Kalharwala–B
97.	Ratta Ther	143.	Turawewali–C	190.	Kaiyanwala–II
98.	Dunkkian	144.	Turawewali Theri	190A.	Trekoe
99.	Turanwala	145.	Turawewali–B	191.	Kaiyanwala–I
100.	Phukhi Ther	146.	Khingarwali	192.	Dilwashwala
101.	Kuruwala	146A.	Naharwali–B	193.	Payunewali Bhit–II
102.	Shahiwala	147.	Khan Kandewala–A	194.	Payunewali Bhit–III
103.	Sui Vihar	148.	Khan Kandewala–E	195.	Payuna Bhit
103A.	Zahir Pir Tibba	149.	Akkanwali Theri	195A.	Mehruband Ther
104.	Kotla Musa Khan	150.	Khan Kandewala–B	196.	Qadir Bux Theri
105.	Uchh Sharif	151.	Khan Kandewala–D	197.	Shikarwala Ther
106.	Mehmudabad	152.	Achharwala	198.	Litanwala
107.	Sukkarwala	153.	Wavriwala	199.	Goongal Mar
108.	Chak 75	154.	Waddanwali	200.	Magrejewali
109.	Chak 76	155.	Killianwali–C	201.	Bazariwali–C
110.	Dundkianwali	156.	Killianwali–B	202.	Bazariwali–B
111.	Shaikhanwala Ther	157.	Killanwali	203.	Bazariwali–A
112.	Dabli Theri	158.	Bandwali	204.	Singharwali
113.	Chak 97	159.	Lundwali–III	205.	Gadiwali
114.	Siddhuwali–E (or Lumrywala)	160.	Dhedaniwala Ther	206.	Mahiwali
115.	Siddhuwali–F	161.	Lundewali–IV	207.	Thoom Thali
116.	Bulbaliwala	162.	Lundewali–II	208.	Derawar Fort
117.	Khohi Siddhuwali	163.	Lundewala Ther	209.	Derawar Ther
118.	Siddhuwala Ther	164.	Jalwali–A	210.	Chaudhryanwala
119.	Siddhuwali–B	165.	Khan Kandewala–C	211.	Jhumtiwala
120.	Siddhuwali–C	166.	Jalwali–B	212.	Charhoyanwala
121.	Siddhuwali–D	167.	Changalawala–C	213.	Ghumharianwala
122.	Khatranwali–II	168.	Changalawala Ther	214.	Marechiwala
123.	Khatranwali–I	169.	Naharwali	215.	Merechi Kanda
124.	Chak 131	170.	Oinwala Ther	216.	Merechi Kanda–II
125.	Mirana	171.	Changalawala–B	216A.	Garewala
126.	Rawewala	172.	Daiwala	217.	Merechi Kanda–III
		173.	Gopawala	218.	Luppewala–III

Site No.	Name of site	Site No.	Name of site	Site No.	Name of site
219.	Lathwala	267.	Musafarwali	311.	Khiplewali–II
220.	Lathwala–II	268.	Gamuwala Ther	312.	Khiplewali
221.	Luppewala	269.	Gamuwala Dahar	313.	Khiplewala
222.	Luppewala–II	270.	Gamuwali	313A.	Khiplewala
223.	Chiheywali	271.	Mehrianwala Ther	314.	Jhandewala–II
224.	Baggewali	272.	Mehrianwali–II	315.	Jhandewala Ther
225.	Gajjuwala–II	273.	Adhi–III	316.	Burhanewala Ther
226.	Gajjuwala Ther	274.	Adhi–II	317.	Mashinewala
227.	Sadwala Kanda	275.	Adhi–I	318.	Develiwala–II
228.	Hasilwala Ther	276.	Bhootanwala–C	319.	Develiwala Ther
229.	Niwaniwala Ther (West)	277.	Bhootanwala–A & B	320.	Mehwali
230.	Niwaniwala Ther (East)	277A.	Bhootanwali–II	321.	Mehwali–II
231.	Niwaniwala–II	278.	Bhootanwali	322.	Mahawala Ther
232.	Niwaniwala–III	279.	Noor Shah Ther	323.	Barula–II
233.	Azimwala–II	280.	Ambrawala Ther	324.	Barula–I
234.	Azimwali	281.	Ambrawali	325.	Ganweriwala
235.	Azimwali–A	282.	Ghaziwala Ther	326.	Bilewali
236.	Azimwali–B	283.	Laluwala Ther	327.	Thoriwala
237.	Azimwali–C	284.	Baghwala Ther	327A.	Tharwala
238.	Shidiwala–A	284A.	Sanghewala	328.	Safuwala–III
239.	Batoorwala	285.	Sohniwali	329.	Safuwala–IV
240.	Khanpuri–II	286.	Sohniwali–II	330.	Safuwala Ther
241.	Sauransanda	287.	Khiplewala–II	331.	Safuwala–II
242.	Khanpuri	288.	Jawaiwala–II	332.	Valwala–II
243.	Kikriwala Ther	289.	Jawaiwala Ther	333.	Valwali
244.	Abduwali	290.	Kuppianwala	334.	Thakowala
245.	Kikri	291.	Chorewala	335.	Dhuhinwala Ther
246.	Kikri–II	292.	Lakhman	336.	Dhuni
247.	Bhagriwala	293.	Jhalar	337.	Duhienwala Qila
248.	Qasaiwala	294.	Jafawala–III	338.	Dhuni (South)
249.	Tharulawala Ther	295.	Chandnewala–III	339.	Moniwala
250.	Janiwali	295A.	Jafewali Theri	340.	Gaddawala Ther
251.	Dadwala–II	296.	Jafawala	341.	Jejalam
252.	Dadwala Ther	297.	Jafawala–II	342.	Rajbai
253.	Runwali	298.	Rahmanwali	343.	Shadiwala Ther
254.	Darkhanwala Ther	299.	Barriwala Ther	344.	Sheikhwali
255.	Darkhanwala–II	300.	Rappwala Ther	345.	Karowala
256.	Sheruwala–II	300A.	Chakwali	346.	Sanasiwala
257.	Sheruwala Ther	301.	Badalwala–II	347.	Khairgarh Fort
258.	Chandnewala Ther	302.	Badalwala	348.	Khairgarh Ther
259.	Chandnewala–II	303.	Jangipar	349.	Malluwali–I
260.	Sheruwala–III	304.	Badalwala–III	350.	Malluwali–II
261.	Chikrala	305.	Badalwala–IV	351.	Onchi Ther
262.	Parhara	306.	Badalwala–V	351A.	Kot Ghunia
263.	Parharewala–A	307.	Mehrindawala Ther	352.	Shah Garh Ther
264.	Chore	308.	Sheikhri–II	353.	Ratta–I
265.	Wasuwala Ther	309.	Bootewali	353A.	Chak 124
266.	Musafarwali–II	310.	Khiplewali–III	354.	Ratta–III

Site No.	Name of site	Site No.	Name of site	Site No.	Name of site
354A.	Chak 121	360.	Ghatoro	366.	Chak 143 P
355.	Ratta–II	361.	Pattan Minara	367.	Kot Murid
356.	Baggapura Ther	362.	Bhagla Fort	368.	Nawan Kot
357.	Baggapura–II	363.	Jummewala Tibba	369.	Khangarh Fort
358.	Chak 112 P	364.	Chak 139 P	370.	Rukanpur
359.	Machki Fort	365.	Falji Fort		

Note: Among 414 sites listed, the map shows 385 sites. In the map, an area about thirty miles long on southwest and entire desert on south containing sites of the Medieval Period are omitted. The sites not shown on the map are: Medieval/Early Historical = 14, Hakra = 5, Mature Harappan = 8, and Late Harappan = 2. The final report on Bahawalpur Survey (in press), however, contains details of all the listed sites.

THE HAKRA WARES PERIOD

The oldest known cultural assemblage in Cholistan is represented by 99 sites of varying dimensions. These settlements are generally low mounds in lesser Cholistan (Bahawalnagar and Bahawalpur Districts) and are located close to, or in, the *dahars* (mud flats). In greater Cholistan (Rahimyar Khan District), they also occur on sand dunes. This assemblage has been called "Hakra" because of the initial area of discovery and the great concentration of sites along the Hakra flood plain.

Hakra ceramics are very distinctive. They are both wheelmade and handmade red wares with a variety of surface treatments. The most frequent and conspicuous pottery types include: (a) those treated on the external surface with a secondary coating of mud mixed with bits of pottery called "mud applique" (Pl. 7.1); and (b) pottery with a series of incised lines on the external surface called Hakra Incised (Pl. 7.2). Most of the Hakra Mud Applique Ware consists of handmade, thick-bodied vessels tempered with clay. There are also some wheelmade, thin-bodied pots with a fine fabric. The thin-bodied pottery has an everted rim and is painted in black on a deep red or chocolate slip which is confined to the shoulder just below the rim. The resemblance of the Hakra Mud Applique Ware in vessel form and surface treatment to some of the handmade pottery from the earliest levels of Amri IA (Casal 1964: Fig. 45) is most striking. At Amri, this pottery occurs in levels which would certainly date to earlier than 3500 B.C. by radiocarbon. Also included in the Hakra Wares is red pottery with a black slip all over the body. The black slip on many specimens appears to be burnished to a glossy finish. A Hakra Wares site called RD 89, located just few kilometers east of Pakistan's border in Anupgarh Tehsil in Indian territory, has yielded precisely identical black-slipped or burnished pottery along with Hakra Mud Applique and Incised Pottery (Dalal 1980: Figs. 8 and 9). Material comparable to this Hakra black-slipped or burnished pottery is not yet known in the Greater Indus Valley at fourth millennium B.C. sites. However, the exposed levels at Periano Ghundai in the Zhob Valley of northern Baluchistan (west of the Gomal Pass) that have been grouped under the term "Periano A" (Mughal 1972a: 140) yielded black burnished/slipped pottery in association with a handmade basket-marked ware.

The Hakra Wares assemblage also includes a small percentage of distinctive buff wares. These were wheelmade and painted black in a style that recalls the fourth millennium B.C. ceramic tradition of the Pakistan-Iranian borderlands.

It is too early to say whether or not the combined form and decorative styles of the Hakra Wares indicate the beginnings of the diagnostic Kot Dijian ceramic assemblage. It is known, however, that such pottery forms overlap the Kot Dijian Wares at Jalilpur (Mughal 1972b and 1974).

Other finds of the period include: animal figurines with short, joined legs including those of bulls and cows; shell and terracotta bangles with triangular and rectangular sections; fragments of grinding stones; bits of copper and a great number of other implements. The lithic industry has parallel-sided blades, most of which have reworked edges; microblades, borers, leaf-shaped arrowheads, scrapers and cores (Pl. 7.3). Typologically it appears to compare well with the lithic materials from Jalilpur I and II, the Neolithic Period I of Sarai Khola (Halim 1972), Gumla I (Dani 1971) and even Rahman Dheri (Khan 1979).

The Hakra Wares sites are heavily concentrated

around Derawar Fort and to the southwest with a few sites to the east of Derawar. Most of the sites are single period settlements with only Hakra Wares; but two (Nos. 67 and 142 on Fig. 7.1) were occupied in the succeeding Early Harappan Period and four sites (Nos. 184, 233, 327 and 336) have Mature Harappan remains. None of the Hakra Period sites was occupied during the Late Harappan Period. Among 99 sites, 52.5 percent were camp sites; 45.4 percent were settlements; while 2 percent contain kilns within the settlement areas.

THE EARLY HARAPPAN PERIOD

The cultural phase that follows the Hakra Wares Period in Cholistan is represented by characteristic Kot Dijian ceramics and associated materials. These are already well known from other sites in the Greater Indus Valley and can be assigned by radiocarbon dating to the early third millennium B.C. Within the Greater Indus Valley there is a basic similarity of material culture at this time, despite the presence of some regional variation. Equally to the point, however, is the apparent continuity of development in the material culture between this Early Harappan and the succeeding Mature Period. Thus, Kot Diji and Kot Diji-related sites in Pakistan and parts of India together constitute the full Early Harappan Period, or the early urban, formative stage of the Harappan Civilization. It was during the Early Harappan Period that cultural processes leading to full urbanization began (Mughal 1980b).

In terms of material culture, continuity of several ceramic forms in the Early Harappan and Mature Harappan levels of Kot Diji is fully documented. A very recent reanalysis of small finds from the type site (Kot Diji) also clearly demonstrates this continuity throughout the lower (Early Harappan) and upper (Mature Harappan) levels. There are, however, certain exceptions (Mughal 1980a: 95 and 1980b).

Forty sites of the Early Harappan Period have been located in Cholistan. Most of these have a single occupation with ceramics related to the Kot Dijian, Kalibangan I, Siswal A (Suraj Bhan 1972) and Binjor 1 and 3 (Dalal 1980) (Pls. 7.4 and 7.5). They are also comparable in form and surface treatment to pottery from Jalilpur II, Sarai Khola II, Gumla II-IV, Rahman Dheri and other contemporary sites in Bannu Basin and Taxila Valley (Mughal in press). Only three sites (Nos. 12, 109 and 270) were re-occupied during the Mature Harappan Period in Cholistan. This is a pattern found elsewhere in the Greater Indus Valley and Baluchistan.

The Early Harappan Period is marked by an increase in the size and number of functionally articulated sites, at least as compared to the preceding Hakra Wares Period. There is a very sharp decline in the number of camp sites: 7.5 percent of the total during the Early Harappan Period against 52.5 percent during the Hakra Period. There is a slight increase (57.5 percent) in the frequency of purely settlement sites. But, the interesting change is an increase to 35 percent in multifunctional settlements, that is, those combining residential functions with specialized/industrial activities. In the Hakra Wares Period only two percent of the sites were of this type. This shift seems to be significant in terms of socio-cultural changes that occurred by the beginning of the Early Harappan Period in Cholistan.

About 60 percent of the Early Harappan sites here are smaller than five hectares in overall size. Twenty-five percent are between five and ten hectares. One site, Gamanwala (No. 27 on Fig. 7.1) spreads over an area of 27.3 hectares, while another Early Harappan site, Jalwali (No. 42) is 22.5 hectares in size. Gamanwala is so far the largest known settlement of the Early Harappan Period. It is larger than Rahman Dheri (21.7 hectares), and also Kalibangan, where the total area occupied during the Early (KLB-I) and Mature (KLB-II) Harappan Period measures 22 hectares, excluding the cemetery area. Gamanwala is close to half the size of Harappa (which is 65 hectares or 160.6 acres without cemeteries) and was certainly not a small town. It is thus evident that during the Early Harappan Period, large settlements—towns, if not large cities—emerged amidst a cluster of smaller settlements. This is a distinctive feature of Harappan settlement patterns, especially in Cholistan, where original cultural patterns have remained largely intact.

During the Early Harappan Period the main focus of occupation appears to have been between Yazman and Fort Abbas, where there are few settlements of the Hakra Wares Period. This pattern seems to extend across the border in India past Kalibangan, to Banawali near Fatehbad, and even beyond, along the ancient course of the Chautang River in Hissar and Rohtak districts. The succeeding Mature, or fully urbanized stage of the Harappan Civilization, is marked by a major shift in the settlement pattern along the Hakra as regards area of settlement concentration.

THE MATURE HARAPPAN PERIOD

This phase of cultural development is best represented at the cities of the Indus Civilization and at 174 sites in Cholistan (Pls. 7.6, 7.7 and 7.8). The most striking aspects of the Mature Harappan Period in Cholistan are: (1) a general shift of sites from the northeast to the southwest, around and beyond Derawar Fort, (2) an increase in the number (47.7 percent of the total), size and height of settlement sites, among which at least one (No. 325), Ganweriwala at 81.5 hectares in size, is essentially the same size as Mohenjodaro, and (3) a profusion of industrial sites (45.4 percent) and their clear separation from habitation areas. However, sites combining both residential and industrial functions (19 percent out of 47.7 percent total settlements) also occur. In the preceding Early Harappan Period industrial areas were located close to, but outside the residential area at fourteen sites or 35 percent of the total number in that period. Although this feature persists in the Mature Harappan Period, some industrial areas at this time were demarcated exclusively for craft activities such as the firing of pottery, bricks, small terracotta objects, the glazing of faience objects and the melting, if not smelting, of copper. Cholistan, it may be pointed out, is located close to the copper sources of Rajasthan.* The Khetri-Singhana source in Jhunjhunu District was reportedly worked during Mauryan and Mughal times; although it is not certain that these sources were also worked in the protohistoric times. It may, however, be added that Sir Aurel Stein found a copper ingot at the (Late) Harappan site of Siddhuwala Ther (No. 118 on Fig. 7.1), located near Derawar. This site also contains numerous kilns.

The emergence of separate Mature Harappan industrial sites, or production centers, and the increased number of kilns during the Mature Harappan Period are indicative of: (1) marked social stratification, (2) the intensification of specialized activities responsible for making standardized products on a large scale, and (3) the existence of intersettlement trade or exchange.

The maximum expansion of the Harappan Civilization outside the primary Indus River Valley occurred in Mature times. After reaching a fully urbanized stage at its core, which may have been the central part of the Indus Valley, it spread towards the Baluch Hills, and along the Arabian Sea Coast. This corresponds in time to intense Harappan long distance sea trade or exchange.

THE LATE HARAPPAN PERIOD

By about the middle of the second millennium B.C. there are changes in Harappan material culture. These resulted from readjustments or changes in the socioeconomic and political organization of Harappan society. These may have been caused by: (1) the gradual depletion of economic resources resulting from the overutilization of land, (2) changes in the hydrographic pattern of the Indus Valley, (3) increased population pressures, (4) insecurity created by invading or intruding groups of people, or (5) a combination of various causes. But, whatever the reasons, it is certain that the pan-Indus integration of the Greater Indus Valley, which climaxed during the Mature Harappan Period, was weakened but not destroyed by the mid-second millennium.

The population regrouped and adjusted to the changed situation in the three principal regions. It thus managed to survive in a recognizable form for a considerable period of time, but some changes are reflected in the material culture found in each region of Harappan concentration: the Cemetery H Culture in the Punjab; the Jhukar Culture in Sind; and the Degenerate, Post or Late Harappan Culture in Gujarat. Regional differentiations, still within the Harappan ceramic tradition, can be seen in the pottery of each group. However, the characteristic square steatite seals with script, standard cubical weights, "mother-goddess" figurines and most metal tools disappeared.

In the upper Indus Valley, a distinctive body of ceramics was recovered from the surface of Harappa, as well as from a cemetery designated "H" at the same site. Similar material has been reported from two sites found by Stein in Bahawalpur. Indian archaeologists have also located and probed several sites with the Cemetery H Ware. These are generally located in the Punjab (east), even to the east of the Yamuna River, suggesting a spread of the Harappan

---

*Editor's note: See R.C. Agrawala's paper in this volume for a discussion of these sources.

tradition during the second millennium B.C. Until this research in Bahawalpur, the Late Harappan Phase was virtually unknown in Pakistan.

The recent survey of Bahawalpur has brought to light 50 sites with Cemetery H-related materials. Cemetery H material is essentially confined to the upper Indus Valley, just as the Jhukar-related materials of the Late Harappan Period generally occur in the lower Indus region.

In Cholistan the sites of the Late Harappan Period (Cemetery H-related) are large, high settlement mounds near the Hakra bed. There are also small sites concentrated around Derawar where the Hakra River once formed an inner delta as with the Helmand River in Seistan. There is an apparent constriction of site concentration in Cholistan during the Late Harappan occupation, as compared to that of the Mature Harappan (see Fig. 7.1). But it should be emphasized that Late Harappan sites are concentrated in the very same area where Mature Harappan sites are located, but where there are few Early Harappan settlements.

Exclusively industrial sites account for only 18 percent of total of Late Harappan sites. Settlement sites, and settlements with kilns or specialized activities areas, represent 28 percent of the total. Camp sites which decreased to only 5.7 percent in the Mature Harappan Period, increase markedly to 26 percent in the Late Harappan times.

Some sites with classic Cemetery H materials are high mounds. For example, the highest parts of Lurewala (No. 96), Shahiwala (No. 102) and Kudwala (No. 76) are respectively 41, 42, 46 feet above plain level. Without excavation, it has not been possible to determine how much of the occupation on these high mounds belongs to the Late Harappan Phase. Some sites, however, are quite extensive, spreading over 20, even 38 hectares.

The beautiful red pottery (Pls. 7.9 and 7.10) is often treated with a thick glossy slip and painted with black designs. Many vessel forms and other materials from the Late Harappan settlements in Cholistan compare well with what is known from contemporary sites in Pakistan and India. New wares of the Late Harappan Period include one with raised knob-like, elongated decorations. These form regular patterns on the external surface which appear to have been made on a thick secondary layer of clay. This type of ware has been christened "Harappan Wet." Its parallels in the Greater Indus Valley come only from Harappa where a complete vessel with similar surface treatment was found in association with burial pots of Stratum I (Vats 1940; Pl. LIX, 10).

THE POST OR NON-HARAPPAN PERIOD

Settlements of this period are concentrated in northeastern Cholistan where 14 sites with the well-known Painted Gray Ware (PGW) have been identified. This is the first time that PGW has been found in Pakistan. It is reported from 320 sites in India. These are located in northern Rajasthan, Haryana, the Punjab and western Uttar Pradesh (Tripathi 1975). The date of PGW and its cultural association have provoked a great deal of controversy that has led to considerable field research in India. It is generally assigned to the end of the second and the beginning of the first millennium B.C. (Lal 1977-78; 1978). although differing opinions still exist. Early excavations revealed a hiatus between the Late Harappan and the PGW assemblages, but recent work at Bhagwanpura, Dadheri and a few other sites has led to the claim of continuity between the Harappan tradition and the PGW Period (Joshi 1978). Connected to this is the question of the Black and Red Wares as regards their association with PGW in western Uttar Pradesh and eastern Rajasthan and their significance in the context of contemporary assemblages of East Punjab.

PGW sites in Cholistan are generally located in the middle of the former Hakra River bed. With the exception of one site (Satwali, No. 40), which covers 13.7 hectares, all the settlements are less than four hectares in size.

The classic PGW ceramic (Pl. 7.11) never constitutes more than five percent of the total surface collections from any site. The remaining pottery consists of red wares, often with stamped and relief designs on the external surface (Pl. 7.12), few black and red potsherds and dishes in red ware resembling the PGW form.

CONCLUSION

This survey of Cholistan has yielded a wealth of information on the cultural sequence in the central Indus Valley. It has given a new perspective and orientation for planning future research on the Indus Civilization. Sites of various periods, and their concentration or distribution, provides a reliable basis for reconstructing various changes in the course of the Hakra River, often identified with the Sarasvati of the Vedic period. The hydrographic history of the Sutlej-Yamuna Divide has often been discussed during the last one hundred years. This is summarized by Lambrick (1964) and Wilhelmy (1969). However, the most recent reconstruction of the changing courses of the Sarasvati, as proposed by Bimal Ghose and his colleagues (1979 and 1980), will require confirmation by archaeological or other dateable evidence.

On the Pakistan side, archaeological evidence now available overwhelmingly affirms that the Hakra was a perennial river through all its course in Bahawalpur during the fourth millennium B.C. (Hakra Period) and the early third millennium B.C. (Early Harappan Period). About the middle of the third millennium B.C., the water supply in the northeastern portion of the Hakra, roughly between Fort Abbas and Yazman (near Kudwala) was considerably diminished or cut-off. But, abundant water in the lower (southwestern) part of this stream was still available, apparently through a channel from the Sutlej; this is attested by the heavy clustering of sites in that area during the late third and early second millennium B.C. (Mature and Late Harappan Periods respectively). About the end of the second, or not later than the beginning of the first millennium B.C., the entire course of the Hakra seems to have dried up and a physical environment similar to that of present day in Cholistan set in. This forced the people to abandon most of the Hakra flood plain. A few Painted Gray Ware settlements, most of them smaller than four hectares in size, are located along the upper part of the Hakra River. These were sustained by a meager water supply reaching there with seasonal regularity from the Ghaggar.

Though the physical environment of Cholistan has changed since protohistoric times, the original mosaic of the settlement pattern is well preserved. The recent field research reported here has revealed functionally differentiated sites within chronologically defined cultural horizons. This will enable one to recognize and reconstruct changes in this region that have not yet been recognized elsewhere in South Asia. Furthermore, archaeological evidence is a reliable guide for the history of dune formation in Bahawalpur. For example, the presence of Hakra Ware sites on top of old, reddish-brown sand, as observed on the south and southwest of Derawar, would seem to indicate that the Cholistan part of the Thar Desert had already advanced close to Derawar prior to the fourth millennium B.C.

NOTE

Dr. Mughal was not a participant in the Srinagar conference. His work in Cholistan is so important, however, that this paper was solicited.

BIBLIOGRAPHY

Casal, J.M., 1964
Fouilles d'Amri. 2 vols. Paris: Commission des Fouilles Archeologiques.

Dalal, Katy Feroze, 1980
A Short History of Archaeological Explorations in Bikaner and Bahawalpur Along the 'Lost' Sarasvati River. *Indica* 17(1): 1–40.

Dani, Ahmad Hasan, 1971
Excavations in the Gomal Valley. *Ancient Pakistan* 5: 1–177.

Field, Henry, 1959
An Anthropological Reconnaissance in West Pakistan. Papers of the Peabody Museum, 52. Cambridge Mass.: Harvard University.

Ghose, B., A. Kar and Zahid Hussein, 1979
The Lost Course of the Sarasvati River in the Great Indian Desert: New evidence from Landsat imagery. *The Geographical Journal* 145 (3): 446–51.

Ghose, B., A. Kar and Zahid Hussein, 1980
Comparative Role of the Aravalli and the Himalayan River Systems in the Fluvial Sedimentation of the Rajasthan Desert. *Man and Environment* 4: 8–12.

Ghosh, A., 1952
The Rajputana Desert: Its archaeological aspect. *Bulletin of the National Institute of Sciences of India* 1: 37–42.

Halim, Muhammad Abdul, 1972
Excavations at Sarai Khola (Part 2). *Pakistan Archaeology* 8: 1–112.

Joshi, J.P., 1978
Interlocking of Late Harappa Culture and Painted Grey Ware Culture in Light of Recent Excavations. *Man and Environment* 2: 98–101.

Khan, Farid, 1979
A Preliminary Report on the Microlithic Blade Industry from Rahman Dheri. In *South Asian Archaeology* 1977, M. Taddei, ed. 1:375–403. Instituto Universitario Orientale, Seminario di Studi Asiatici, Series Minor VI, Naples.

Lal, B.B., 1978
The Indo-Aryan Hypothesis vis-a-vis Indian Archaeology. *Journal of Central Asia* 1: 21–41.

Lal, B.B., 1977-78
Did the Painted Grey Ware Continue up to the Mauryan Times? Puratattva 9: 64-80.

Lambrick, H.T., 1964
Sind: A General Introduction. Vol. 1. Hyderabad, Pakistan, Sindhi Adabi Board.

Mughal, M.R., 1972a
Explorations in Northern Baluchistan. *Pakistan Archaeology* 8: 137–51.

Mughal, M.R., 1972b
Excavations at Jalilpur. *Pakistan Archaeology* 8: 117–24.

Mughal, M.R., 1974
New Evidence of the Early Harappan Culture From Jalilpur. *Pakistan Archaeology* 27 (2): 106–13.

Mughal, M.R., 1980a
New Archaeological Evidence From Bahawalpur. *Man and Environment* 4: 93–98.

Mughal, M.R., 1980b
The Origins of the Indus Civilization. *Sindhological Studies,* Summer: 1–10.

Mughal, M.R., in press
Archaeological Surveys in Bahawalpur. *Pakistan Archaeology.*

Stein, Sir Mark Aurel, 1942
A survey of ancient sites along the "lost" Sarasvati River. *The Geographical Journal* 99: 173–82.

Suraj Bhan, 1972
Siswal: A Pre-Harappan site in Drishadvati Valley. *Puratattva* 5: 44–46.

Suraj Bhan, 1973
The Sequence and Spread of Prehistoric Cultures in the Upper Sarasvati Basin. In *Radiocarbon and Indian Archaeology.* D.P. Agrawal and A. Ghosh, eds. Pp. 252–63. Bombay: Tata Institute of Fundamental Research.

Suraj Bhan, 1975
Excavations at Mitathal (1968) and Other Explorations in the Sutlej-Yamuna Divide. Kurukshetra: Kurukshetra University.

Suraj Bhan and Jim Shaffer, 1978
New Discoveries in Northern Haryana. *Man and Environment* 2: 59–68.

Tripathi, Vibha, 1975
The Painted Grey Ware: An Iron Age culture of northern India. Delhi: Concept Publishers.

Vats, M.S., 1940
Excavations at Harappa. 2 vols. Delhi: Government of India.

Wilhelmy, H., 1969
Urstromtal am Ostrand der Indusebene und der Sarasvati-Problem. *Zeitschrift fur Geomorphologie,* Supplementband 8: 76-93.

GEORGE F. DALES

8. Mohenjodaro Miscellany: Some Unpublished, Forgotten, or Misinterpreted Features

NO SITE of the ancient Indus Civilization has received more archaeological and scholarly attention than Mohenjodaro. Most widely known are the large-scale excavations directed from 1922 to 1927 by Sir John Marshall (1931) and from 1927 to 1931 by Ernest Mackay (1938), the publications of which provide the basic archaeological data for the study of the site. Also, well known are the excavations conducted in 1950 on the so-called Citadel Mound by Sir Mortimer Wheeler (1950, 1968). And finally in 1964-65 the University of Pennsylvania Museum sponsored excavations along the western edge of the old HR Area (Dales 1965a, 1965b, 1966). These latter excavations were conducted just prior to the imposition of a total moratorium on new work at the site by the Government of Pakistan, a restriction that will probably continue indefinitely.[1]

Less well known, in fact, virtually unknown, are extensive excavations conducted from 1932 to 1934 by Mr. Q.M. Moneer, Custodian of the Mohenjodaro Museum and Mr. K.N. Puri, Custodian of the site. The only published reference to their excavations is a brief notice in the 1930-34 Annual Report of the Archaeological Survey of India (Government of India 1930-34: 51). In addition to continuing work in the immediate vicinity of Mackay's excavations in the DK Area, Mr. Moneer opened an extensive new plot directly east of the VS Area (Fig. 8.1). The brief notice states that "As, unfortunately there is no photographer and no draftsman attached to the site anymore, no illustrations can be given to these latter diggings" (Government of India 1930-34: 51). Largely forgotten, these excavations are known today in the records of the Department of Archaeology as the DK-B, or Moneer Site.

If all the results of these years of digging were published one would undoubtedly know considerably more about the city. It is probably not too inaccurate to estimate that between one-third and one-half of the excavated data has not been published or at least not in detail. As an offender myself, I can speak without malice on this topic.

As impressive as is the original three-volume report edited by Sir John Marshall, it is not a complete report on the 1922 to 1927 excavations. Reports from some of his field supervisors were never completed or for various reasons were not included in these volumes. The most serious losses are the reports on the work of Mr. Vats in the VS Area in 1922-23 and the reports of Mr. Banerji on his work in the Stupa Area in 1922-23 and at Sites Two and Three.

Mackay's two-volume report is admirably more detailed than Marshall's, nonetheless, subsequent studies of the collections in museums and in the Archaeological Survey of India storerooms have identified considerable numbers of unpublished artifacts from his excavations.

Most lamentable is the absence of a detailed report on the 1950 excavations of Sir Mortimer Wheeler. The implications of his purported discovery of a "State Granary" and of "Citadel Fortifications" are crucial for any interpretation of the nature and function of Mohenjodaro as a city. There is no end to the speculation these claims have aroused but it is impossible to reach objective conclusions with the published details. Some of this data has recently been

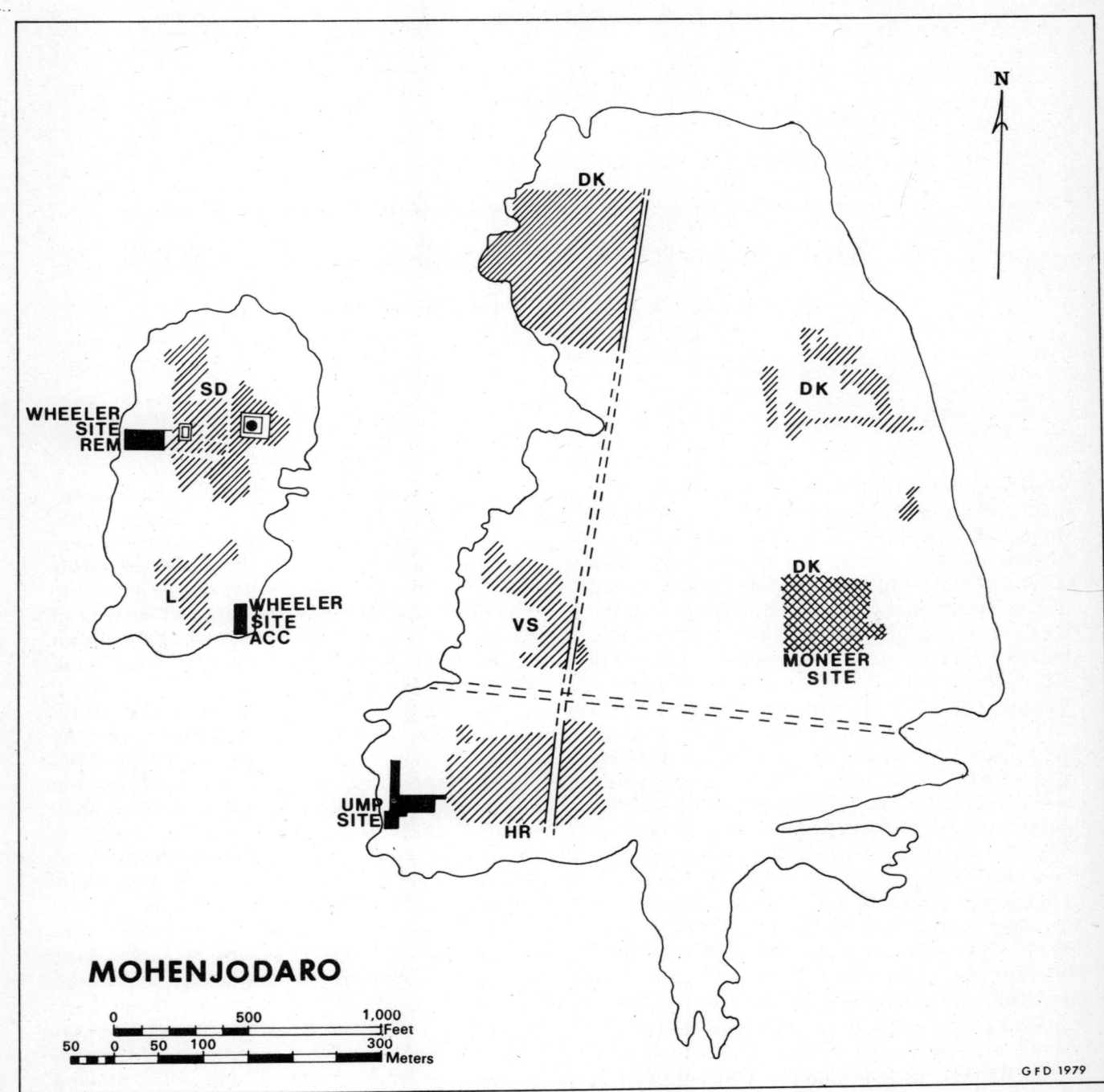

Fig. 8.1. Site plan of Mohenjodaro.

rediscovered as I will describe later in this paper.

The lack of any records or reports on the excavations of Moneer and Puri comprises serious loss of potentially valuable data. The Moneer Site is extensive—almost half the area of the HR excavations. It is noteworthy that it is not indicated on any of the published plans of the site or mentioned in any descriptions of the city. Recently, its very existence was rediscovered independently by A. Parpola and I. Mahadevan during their studies of seals and inscribed artifacts in collections in Pakistan and India. Parpola (1972: 13) studied over 400 unpublished seals, "a special group being the seals from the DK-B and DK-I Areas of Mohenjodaro." Mahadevan (1977: 4) mentions finding photographs of unpublished seals from Mohenjodaro in the Photo Library of the Archaeological Survey in New Delhi. He informs me (personal communication) that excavation was also done sometime between 1935 and 1940. He found no mention of the excavator's name but he thinks the work area was designated DK-B. Seals and other antiquities were found by Mahadevan in New Delhi. Photographs of these objects as well as a part of the excavations were found in the Photo Album, Sind, Vol. XXVI (1935-40). There is thus some confusion as to exactly where the excavations designated DI-1, DI-i, or DK-B or Moneer Site were conducted. I was told directly by the Director of Archaeology in Karachi that the area so designated on Figure 8.1 is the DK-B/Moneer Site.

Both Parpola's and Mahadevan's interests were only in the inscribed artifacts and it was not until the winter of 1978-79 that the Moneer Site itself attracted serious attention. Dr. Michael Jansen, the archaeological architect directing a detailed study of the Mohenjodaro architecture, came upon a detailed plan of the site prepared by a Dutch engineering firm in 1968 as part of the preliminary work for developing a conservation program for the site (UNESCO 1968). The plan, drawn from aerial photographs of the site, clearly shows the Moneer Site with an approximation of the architectural plan. The plan is important also because it is the only one that has detailed contours in metric measurements and shows the locations of all the borings and test drillings used in formulating a master plan for preserving the site (UNESCO and Government of Pakistan 1968).[2] A former superintendent at Mohenjodaro, Mohammad Siddique, has informed me that some of the pottery and objects from the Moneer excavations are in the Mohenjodaro Museum storeroom and that he has personally done the best he could to arrange and catalog the collection. Unfortunately, there are no records giving specific proveniences for any of it. Mr. Mahadevan informs me that what is probably the balance of the excavated artifacts is in Delhi with the Archaeological Survey of India.

Dr. Jansen and I visited the Moneer Site in February 1979 and were astounded at what we saw. The size of this neglected excavation is impressive enough in itself but the general appearance of the architecture gave a very different feeling than those experienced from other parts of the city. The structures seem smaller, with thinner walls in general, and though neatly oriented and arranged along straight streets and lanes, they seem to be more crowded. This is an impressionistic view only and must be checked by actual measurements.

A most peculiar feature of the structures is what appear to be triangular shaped corbelled holes through most of the walls just above the floor level. Dr. Jansen has informed me that some of these are modern creations intended by the conservators of the site to promote drainage. But some of them must be ancient. I have found two published references to similar apertures at Mohenjodaro and none at other Harappan sites. The first example is in Room 78 of House XIII in VS Area (Marshall 1931: 20-21, 219, Pl. VI and LV, b) where it looks like a crawl-hole about a meter high and just wide enough for a man to pass through. It is completely blocked with brickwork and Marshall suggests that it belonged to an earlier building level.[3] The second example is seen in House V, Block 2 of HR Area, Section B, between Rooms 49 and 54 (Marshall 1931: 190, Pl. LIV, b). It appears to have been a corbelled doorway, eight feet four inches high and two feet five inches wide, but it also is completely blocked with brick-work.[4] It is curious that this presumed doorway is almost identical in construction and dimensions with the famous corbelled drain associated with the Great Bath (Marshall 1931: 134, Pl. XXII-XXIV).[5] Whether this is a mere coincidence, related somehow to the Harappan's limited knowledge of constructing arches or whether there is something fundamental about the functions of these two passageways which is not clearly understood, requires further investigation.

Another peculiar architectural feature at the Moneer Site is an apparent modification of the well known, ubiquitous bathing (or ablution) floors with their finely constructed brick floor and drains. These are common at most other parts of Mohenjodaro but at the Moneer Site they have an interesting added feature. Outside one wall of these washrooms there is usually a small flight of brick steps. They are so arranged that they could provide an easy means for a servant, or member of the family, to pour water on the bather, thus making these more like shower rooms rather than ordinary washrooms. A perusal of Marshall's and Mackay's Mohenjodaro reports, and those of other Indus Civilization sites, turned up very few similar arrangements and for none of them have the excavators suggested whether the steps were used for any purpose other than gaining access to a presumed second story. At Harappa, for example, only a few bath floors are reported (Vats 1940: 21, Pl. III) and they are located, oddly enough, in the central aisle bisecting the granary. The plan shows clearly that one of these bathing floors has a small set of steps constructed directly next to it.

The Mohenjodaro publications indicate only six locations where wash floors and steps are associated. Three of these are in the Lower Town and three are in the SD Area on the Stupa Mound. The clearest examples of wash floor with steps combinations are seen in the remarkable series of eight chambers in Area SD, Block 6, north of the Great Bath (Mackay 1938: 18-20, Pl. III, b and d). These are unique in having the flights of steps constructed inside one corner of the washroom itself. Mackay interprets the room as ablution chambers above which the priests lived. The steps were used merely for getting to the second story. Without any direct knowledge of the ancient religious beliefs and practices of the Harappans it is meaningless to attempt to refute this, or any other interpretation, but the evidence from similar structures at other parts of Mohenjodaro suggests to me a purpose for the steps more directly related to the function of the bathing floors themselves.

In Block 2 of the SD Area, south of the stupa, another exceptionally well-built bathroom is described (Marshall 1931: 147, Pl. XXVII, XXVIII, b). The excavator notes that "this bath, which is situated a little below the level of the surrounding rooms, was entered from above by a short stairway in its southeastern corner...." Given the incredible complexity of the architectural remains at Mohenjodaro, it is just as reasonable to suggest that this bathroom with its steps belongs to the floor level of an earlier structure. The third bathroom is seen in Room 5, Block 5 of the SD Area south of the stupa (Marshall 1931: 149, Pl. XXVII). Nothing is mentioned in Marshall's text but the plan of the area shows clearly a set of steps at the northwest corner of the wash floor.

In the Lower Town, DK Area, G Section (northern portion), Block 23, House III, Room 15 (Mackay 1939: 155-56, Pl. XIII, XXII, 1) a flight of steps, with four remaining treads, is seen at the east side of a paved wash floor. Mackay describes the room as a "privy" and suggests that the steps "probably led up to a privy of the next phase." Marshall describes a similar situation in House VIII, HR Area, Section A (Marshall 1931: 18-19, Pl. IV, V, a) where a bath floor has a set of steps leading up directly from it. He explains the steps as leading up to a later building level and sees no direct connection between them and the wash floor. In House LIII, Block 7, B Section of the HR Area, Marshall describes another possibly related bathing complex where in the portico of the house there is a staircase "the tiny chamber under which may have done duty as a privy" (Marshall 1931: 209, Pl. XXXIX).

It is possible that a careful examination of the numerous examples of wash floor-steps combinations in the Moneer Site may help elucidate this aspect of daily life at Mohenjodaro.

Thus, it seems, the Moneer Site may provide significant new insights into the living arrangements and practices of the Mohenjodaroans. The apparent differences in architectural detail with the other excavated parts of the city may be temporal, or more important if true, they may reflect some degree of socioeconomic stratification in the population not noticed in the other excavated parts of the city.

Dr. Jansen will make a detailed survey of the Moneer Site which will be an especially important aspect of his long-range project to document fully the architectural remains of Mohenjodaro. With the present moratorium on new excavations at the site and the ceaseless battle between the forces of natural deterioration and the efforts to preserve and reconstruct the remains, Jansen's documentation project takes on special importance. It is, under the present circumstances, the only way to learn significant new information that was overlooked, unrecorded or unpublished in the earlier excavations.

Adjunct to Dr. Jansen's project is the research of Dr. Anna Sarcina of Torino, Italy, who has completed an important study of the domestic architecture of Mohenjodaro (Sarcina 1979). Her analysis of different house types will be published in the journal *Mesopotamia*. It is hoped that her theoretical scheme can be tested in the field as part of Jansen's architectural project.

As for other new information and re-evaluations of old data, I wish to mention a few of the points concerning us now as we are preparing the final reports on the University Museum (Philadelphia) excavations along the western edge of HR Area.[6]

The first volume under preparation is devoted to the pottery. The ceramics are being classified and described according to the system developed during our recent four-year project at Balakot, Pakistan (Dales, 1974, 1979). The approach differs from other classifications and descriptions of Indus ceramics in that we are treating the material holistically as an integrated industry—a major industry at Mohenjodaro involving complex technological skills and aesthetic preferences not treated in detail in earlier reports. A number of distinctive manufacturing techniques, not recognized in earlier studies, set off the Harappan industry as something quite different from contemporaneous industries in neighboring regions. The more complete and detailed publication of the full range of vessel forms and surface decorations will help abrogate statements about the "unimaginative and unadventurous" character of Indus ceramics. There is no question as to the high degree of standardization and the mass production aspect of the industry, but a closer look at it gives a better appreciation of its sophistication and variability.

One of the problems that has led to the impression of monotony and dull uniformity in the Mohenjodaro ceramic industry is that few of the earlier studies could treat the material with much temporal perspective. As Sir Mortimer Wheeler put it, the so-called uniformity of the pottery, and of the civilization as a whole, is due as much to "archaic methods of research as to any inherent conservatism in the ancient craftsmen" (Wheeler 1968: 94). This problem will be dealt with specifically in our Mohenjodaro reports, thanks partly to the fortuitous discovery of some of the long-forgotten records of Wheeler's 1950 excavations on the Citadel Mound.

I was fortunate in 1976, during a sabbatical leave in England, to learn of the location of some of these important unpublished records. The British Academy and Professor Raymond Allchin put me on to Professor Leslie Alcock at the University of Glasgow who had been Wheeler's principal assistant during the 1950 excavations. He had in his possession the drawings and descriptions of the pottery from the excavations at the so-called Granary and Fortifications. After Sir Mortimer's personal involvement in Mohenjodaro had waned, the excavation records were stored and virtually forgotten. Some of them at least, are now being rediscovered and the sad occasion of Sir Mortimer's death has rekindled interest in his important work at Mohenjodaro. Professor Alcock has generously agreed to collaborate on a joint volume including the pottery from both the University of Pennsylvania and Wheeler's excavations. The 25-year-old drawings had to be completely redone[7] and Professor Alcock has updated and partially revised the catalog and text. This provides an excellent opportunity to study fairly long sequences of ceramic development from functionally different parts of the site. The Wheeler pottery will be presented in four groupings with the earliest coming from his deep sounding just to the west of the "Granary" (his Site REM) and the latest coming from the "Fortifications" (his Site ACC) at the southeastern corner of the Citadel Mound. The volume will provide a small but hopefully significant tribute to Wheeler's own work at Mohenjodaro and to the enthusiasm and support he so persuasively offered others to continue research on the Indus Civilization.

One interesting result of our study of the ceramics from the University Museum excavations is the identifying of apparently non-Harappan pottery in the upper Harappan levels. Especially significant is the presence of Jhukar-style pottery similar to that described from the earlier excavations at Jhukar (Majumdar 1934: 5-11), Chanhudaro (Mackay 1943), and Amri (Casal 1964). We have at least a dozen examples of stylistically non-Harappan painted pottery from well-stratified Harappan contexts, several of which are identical to published examples of the Jhukar-style pottery.[8]

There is corroborative evidence from other sites in Pakistan that the usually assumed Post-Harappan position of Jhukar is questionable. To be sure, at Chanhudaro, the excavator states that the Jhukar occupation was separated from the latest Harappan by several centuries, but elsewhere he mentions that the Jhukar people sometimes reoccupied Harappan dwellings. Mackay appears to have been puzzled by the Jhukar presence. On the one hand he stresses the radical difference between the Jhukar painted pottery and that of the Harappans (Mackay 1943: 25) but on the other hand he emphasizes the continuity between the two cultures.

> If we were not so well acquainted with the craftsmanship of the peoples of the Harappa culture as it is exemplified at Mohenjodaro and Harappa, we might have found it difficult to distinguish between the products of the Jhukar people and those of the Harappan people in the Chanhudaro mound (Mackay 1943: ix).

At Amri, Casal postulated a Period III-D Jhukar, but states that no actual archaeological strata of this phase have been found in the excavations. He sees Jhukar as a late manifestation of Harappan rather than as a new cultural successor.

At Jhukar itself, new excavations by the Pakistan Department of Archaeology from 1972 through 1974[9] discount the interpretation of Jhukar being temporarily and culturally distinct from Harappan. The results of the excavations have not been published but they were discussed in detail at the International Symposium on the Indus Civilization held in Karachi in January 1979. There Dr. Mughal firmly stated his impression that Jhukar is nothing more than a pottery style that occurs archaeologically with Mature and Late Harappan and not after it and that it has much in common with the Harappan ceramics. This may be overstated but even so it is based on direct observation of the excavations at Jhukar and first-hand study of all the ceramics. At the very least, these new excavations corroborate the evidence from Mohenjodaro that there is no significant temporal separation between Jhukar and Harappan.

Part of the dilemma over Jhukar results from the selective manner in which the evidence has been published with the emphasis on the spectacular and the unique, especially with the painted decorations. The recent excavations at Jhukar provide the opportunity for the study of the complete ceramic industry including the more numerous examples of unpainted types. Provisionally it seems clear that Jhukar pottery has some typological and stylistic connections with the Harappan but that it definitely was manufactured separately, and has its own distinctive repertory of basic forms (implying a degree of functional differentiation from Harappan ceramics), and its own level of technological competency.

A recent study of the Chanhudaro pottery in the Boston Museum of Fine Arts by Berkeley graduate student Jonathan Mark Kenoyer makes it clear that the Jhukar pottery is readily identifiable because of its distinctive vegetable-tempered paste, its thin red matte slips, its painted decorations in purplish-brown to black, and its generally crude craftsmanship. And, with the exception of the dish-on-stand form, the Chanhudaro Jhukar pottery is quite different from the Harappan forms.

The implication is that what one usually calls Jhukar is not Post-Harappan and may instead be a manifestation of interaction between the Urban Harappans and a closely allied, but culturally differentiated, group of peoples living locally in northern and central Sind. An analogy might be suggested with the Kulli-Harappan symbiosis wherein one sees a geographically peripheral population interacting peacefully with the Harappans, perhaps imitating certain Harappan forms and styles and, at Balakot, Nindowari and other sites having a physical presence in the Harappan settlements, all the while retaining its basic cultural identity. A scenario such as this seems reasonable, else one is forced to postulate a Harappanization of the entire Indus Valley and much of Baluchistan—an unlikely possibility, as unrealistic as talking about the total Indianization of South and Southeast Asia.

Just how closely, if at all, related the Jhukar phenomenon is to the decline and devolution of the Mature Harappan is unknown in cultural and historical terms. But temporarily, to judge from the archaeological evidence, Jhukar is not the Post-Harappan development it was once thought to represent.

Walter Fairservis in his earlier study (1975: 353) agrees with this general assessment of the chronological, historical and cultural position of Jhukar. The Allchins, on the other hand (1968: 145-47), see Jhukar as a Post-Harappan continuation of local traditions, carried on by the local survivors of the barbarian invasions (Aryan) that overwhelmed the Harappans. Now in the face of collective evidence from the various sites where Jhukar material is found, this must be regarded as a minority opinion. Any final verdict depends first of all on the full publication of the recently excavated material from Jhukar itself.

The major, and controlling, factor in the University Museum excavations is the stratigraphic and chronological sequence of the architecture and depositional remains. Any architectural and stratigraphic discussion of Mohenjodaro is difficult, even under the best of circumstances. The 1964-65 excavations were not conducted under the best of circumstances and the post-excavation work was saddened and curtailed by the untimely death of our architect Aubrey Trik. The preliminary reports described how the excavations were conducted along the western edge of the HR Area (Fig. 8.1). One curtailed season of excavation was completed before the government moratorium on new work was imposed. While many significant new discoveries were made (Fig. 8.2) it has been difficult to assess them as fully as would be desirable. Especially serious is that some crucial details of relative stratigraphy were not worked out during that single season. It was not until the winter of 1978-79 that the opportunity was afforded to return to the site with experienced architects to complete the recording of the excavations. Dr. Michael Jansen and Mr. Jurgen Philips of Aachen, West Germany,[10] worked with me to retrieve as many of the surviving unrecorded architectural and stratigraphic details as possible. The final plans, elevations, and sections are now being prepared.

Fig. 8.2. Remains of wooden door jambs and reconstruction of doorway. University of Pennsylvania excavations, 1964-65.

The opportunity to work again with these long-neglected records allowed for considerable reassessment of the nature and significance of the architectural features uncovered. Jansen and Philips have provided essential insights into some of the main interpretative problems. One of the principal advances in one's understanding concerns the massive fired brick wall uncovered at the base of the mound at present ground level. In the heat of discovery, I—to paraphrase Sir Mortimer—"lightheartedly suggested" that the City Wall of the Lower Town had been discovered. This solid brick wall, some two meters thick and more than ten meters high, is actually but a segment of other massive and complex architectural features delineating the eastern side of a wide street. This street, which can be traced for a couple hundred meters, is almost identical in dimensions and orientation to the famous First Street that runs north-south through the DK, VS and HR Areas. Fragmentary remains of fired brick structures, directly at or just below present plain level, form the western side of this street. This provides further substantiation that at least the main traffic arteries of the city were intentionally planned and laid out in a systematic manner.

The presence of this major street along the present base of the Lower Town does not obviate another suggestion made in our preliminary reports that a canal or branch of the river bisected the city plan. One of the deep borings made in 1965 in the low empty area between the Lower Town and the Citadel Mound revealed the presence of only water-laid deposits from the surface down some 40 feet to virgin soil. This suggestion of a canal having run through the city goes back to the earliest excavators. Mackay (1938: 4) mentioned the excavations of R.D. Banerji (never published) at Site Three to the northeast of the Stupa Mound which appeared to be constructed as a small fort or a landing-loading platform for small boats. Further work at Site Three and along the edges of the mounds bordering this assumed canal should have high priority if excavations are ever permitted to resume.

To return to the architectural discoveries made in 1964-65: descriptions have been provided in the preliminary reports of the gigantic mud-brick platform that dominates that section of the western edge of the Lower Town. This, and the large fired brick wall that provides a facing for the platform, substantiate the abundant evidence from other parts of Mohenjodaro that it was necessary for the inhabitants to raise the occupation level constantly as defense against floods. As for the existence of a formal city wall it is best to stick with the interpretation offered by Sir Mortimer that "For the present it would be premature to conjecture that the Lower City was fortified in a military sense, though it is increasingly clear that massive flood-defences were undertaken" (Wheeler 1968: 47).

Certainly the currently most debated—but not debatable—phenomenon concerning the life and destiny of Mohenjodaro is that of the nature and extent of flooding. Contrary to some prevailing opinions, the Mohenjodaro floods were not invented by Mr. Robert L. Raikes and myself in 1964. Not a single excavator or serious student of Mohenjodaro has denied the presence of massive disruptive floods throughout the history of the city. There is, however, disagreement over the cause and nature of these floods. This is the problem that Mr. Raikes originally focused on and on which we collaborated during the University Museum excavations (Raikes 1964, 1965; Raikes and Dales 1977; Dales and Raikes 1968).

Despite some serious, and often well-reasoned objections to the Raikes hypothesis (Possehl 1967; Lambrick 1967; and others) it is still, given the admittedly small amount of scientifically-collected evidence, the only hypothesis that accounts for the complex multifarious anomalies involved. The most recent statement on the issues and problems involved has been published by Raikes and myself (1977) in the *Journal of the Palaeontological Society of India*. Mr. Raikes and I would appreciate constructive criticism, comments, and suggestions. Hopefully an opportunity will come in the not too distant future to continue and expand the scientific field investigations this crucial problem deserves.

This paper has focused on a few of the numerous aspects of Mohenjodaro which are receiving fresh study. It is hoped that wholesome discussions and criticisms of the newly published data and interpretations will ensue and that the furtherance of research on the Indus Civilization will be encouraged.

NOTES

[1] This has been imposed by the Government of Pakistan to allow all of the limited resources to be directed toward the staggering job of conservation and preservation of the already excavated remains.

[2] It is unfortunate that this detailed plan was not the one published in the *Master Plan for the Preservation of Mohenjodaro* or in other official publications of the project. All these publications have used the incomplete plan published by Mackay in 1938. The aerial photographs were taken sometime between February 1965 and the publishing of the UNESCO map in 1968 because they show the 1964-65 excavations of the University Museum.

[3] The reconstruction drawing of Hall 76 of this same building (Marshall 1931: Pl. LXIII) shows four corbelled niches in the north wall. Actually the corbelling was only conjectured by Marshall. Indeed Mackay thought these were vertical chutes extending up to the roof to provide fresh air circulation. At any rate, the niches do not pierce the wall and apparently are unrelated to the enigmatic corbelled apertures under discussion.

[4] Little evidence survives at Mohenjodaro for the construction of doorways. We were fortunate in our 1964-65 excavations to have uncovered the charred remains of the jambs of a doorway associated with a room at the crest of the HR Mound (Fig. 8.2). They were cut with L-shaped section from logs having a diameter of at least 30 centimeters. Although preserved to a maximum height of only about 30 centimeters, it is logical to assume that the top of the doorway had a wooden lintel rather than a corbelled arch.

[5] It measures approximately seven feet six inches high by two feet six inches wide according to the drawing. Oddly, this unique architectural feature is only summarily mentioned in the text.

[6] To be terminologically consistent with the earlier excavation reports, this should be called the DL or DS Area but I prefer to call it the UMP Area.

[7] I wish here to acknowledge the weeks of work volunteered to this task by my wife, Barbara.

[8] I thank Dr. M. Rafique Mughal for helping with these identifications.

[9] Directed by Gulzar Mohammed, 1972-73 and by M. Rafique Mughal and Gulzar Mohammed in 1973-74.

[10] Jansen is with the Department of History of

Architecture and Architectural Preservation, and Philips is with the Geodatisches Institut, both at the Rheinisch-Westfalische Technische Hochschule, Aachen, West Germany. The field study at Mohenjodaro was supported by a grant from the Smithsonian Foreign Currency Program.

BIBLIOGRAPHY

Allchin, B. and F.R. Allchin, 1968
  The Birth of Indian Civilization. Baltimore: Penguin Books.
Casal, J.M., 1964
  Fouilles d'Amri. 2 vols. Paris: Librairie C. Klincksieck.
Dales, G.F., 1965a
  Re-opening Mohenjo-daro Excavations. *Illustrated London News* May 29: 25-27.
Dales, G.F., 1965b
  New Investigations at Mohenjo-daro. *Archaeology* 18(2): 145-50.
Dales, G.F., 1966
  The Decline of the Harappans. *Scientific American* 214(5): 92-100.
Dales, G.F., 1974
  Excavations at Balakot, Pakistan 1973. *Journal of Field Archaeology* 1(1-2): 3-22.
Dales, G.F., 1979
  The Balakot Project: Summary of four years of excavation in Pakistan. *Man and Environment* 3: 45-53.
Dales, G.F. and R.L. Raikes, 1968
  The Mohenjo-daro Floods: A Rejoinder. *American Anthropologist* 70(5): 957-61.
Fairservis, W.A. Jr., 1975
  The Roots of Ancient India. 2nd ed. Chicago: University of Chicago Press.
Government of India, 1930-34
  Annual Report of the Archaeological Survey of India, 1930-34. New Delhi.
Lambrick, H.T., 1967
  The Indus Flood-Plain and the 'Indus' Civilization. *Geographical Journal* 133: 483-94.
Mackay, E.J.H., 1938
  Further Excavations at Mohenjodaro. 2 vols. Delhi: Government of India.
Mackay, E.J.H., 1943
  Chanhudaro Excavations 1935-36. American Oriental Series 20. New Haven: American Oriental Society.
Mahadevan, I., 1977
  The Indus Script: Texts, Concordance and Tables. Memoirs of the Archaeological Survey of India, 77. New Delhi.
Majumdar, N.G., 1934
  Explorations in Sind. Memoirs of the Archaeological Survey of India, 48. New Delhi.
Marshall, Sir John, ed., 1931
  Mohenjodaro and the Indus Civilization. 3 vols. London: Arthur Probsthain.
Parpola, A., 1972
  In: *Newsletter 5.* The Scandinavian Institute of Asian Studies, Copenhagen.
Possehl, G., 1967
  The Mohenjo-daro Floods: A Reply. *American Anthropologist* 69(1): 32-40.
Raikes, R.L., 1964
  The End of the Ancient Cities of the Indus. *American Anthropologist* 66(2): 284-99.
Raikes, R.L., 1965
  The Mohenjo-daro Floods. *Antiquity* 38 (155): 196-203.
Raikes, R.L. and G.F. Dales, 1977
  The Mohenjo-daro Floods Reconsidered. *Journal of the Palaeontological Society of India* 20: 251-60.
Sarcina, A., 1979
  The Private House at Mohenjodaro. In *South Asian Archaeology, 1977.* Maurizio Taddei, ed. Pp. 433-64. Instituto Universitario Orientale, Seminario di Studi Asiatici, Series Minor VI, Naples.
UNESCO, 1968
  Mohenjo Daro—Pakistan. Site plan, scale 1:2000, dated 26-8-1968, prepared by Engineering Consultant Dwars Heederik & Verhey, Ltd. Amersfoort, The Netherlands (Sheet No. 3.27.07.04).
UNESCO and Government of Pakistan, 1968
  Master Plan for the Preservation of Mohenjodaro. Paris: Karachi.
Vats, M.S., 1940
  Excavations at Harappa. 2 vols. Delhi: Government of India.
Wheeler, Sir Mortimer, 1950
  Preliminary reports in *Illustrated London News.*

May 20: 782-83; May 27: 813-16; June 3: 854-55.

Wheeler, Sir Mortimer, 1968
The Indus Civilization, 3rd ed. Supplementary Volume to the Cambridge History of India. Cambridge: The University Press.

WALTER A. FAIRSERVIS, JR.

9. Allahdino: An Excavation of a Small Harappan Site

SITES IN THE KARACHI AREA

The Harappan site of Allahdino is one of five now known in the former Federal District of Karachi (Fig. 9.1). Two of these are found on the east bank of the perennial Hab River which marks the boundary between Karachi and the District of Las Bela. Pir Shah Jurio is a small site located on the western tip of a crescent-shaped ridge standing some 15 meters above the Hab River approximately five kilometers from the Arabian Sea. Hab Chauki, about 23 kilometers north of Pir Shah Jurio, is situated on a spur of the Lyari border range overlooking the Hab. It is a low-lying small mound surrounded by alluvial soils. The remaining three sites are found to the east of Karachi some 35 kilometers away and are situated in the basin of the semiperennial Malir River. This river system drains an area in the Kohistan of considerable magnitude and in consequence the catch basin is responsible for an extraordinary quantity of underground water. So great is this amount that up to Partition the Malir system was able to provide Karachi with almost two-thirds of its water supply. Pumping of this water provides irrigation water for the Damlotti and Malir agricultural developments—the most prosperous ones locally. The water table is found in the Malir area at about 15 meters, rising in wells to about six meters below the surface in a good year. The Malir River in flood season is a formidable stream and capable of regularly filling local reservoirs.

The site of Amiliano was discovered by Majumdar in 1934. It is located in a pocket of soil found in the broken country which lies along the western borders of the main Malir drainage. Considerably higher than that drainage it receives water naturally only during a rainfall period. It is a flat-lying pebbled site suggesting a short, single occupation. No structures, except a small pile of sandstone slabs, are indicated for this site.

Hasan Wali is about 15 kilometers to the southwest of Amiliano just south of the old Thano Bulla Khan Road. It is located on a sandstone outcrop overlooking a narrow belt of alluvial soil which widens as it trends toward the west. This terminates at the eastern bank of the Bazaar Nadi, a small usually dry tributary of the Malir. Near the site, and lying across the alluvium, are a series of superimposed stone and mud dams, the earlier of which are of considerable antiquity. Associated with the earlier dam (gabarbund?) are the clay bicones familiar at Harappan sites, evidencing the possibility that the earlier dam might very well be Harappan, as indeed the position of this site also suggests. Hasan Wali is a moderately large settlement which fans out from a high point with a central stone structure that immediately overlooks the alluvium. Stone walls run in a number of directions showing that buildings with stone foundations were characteristic of the site. Considerable deflation has taken place owing to the site's exposed position; but all the evidence suggests that ancient occupation was short and for one period only. Plans have been drawn of the exposed structures and will be included in the overall Allahdino report.

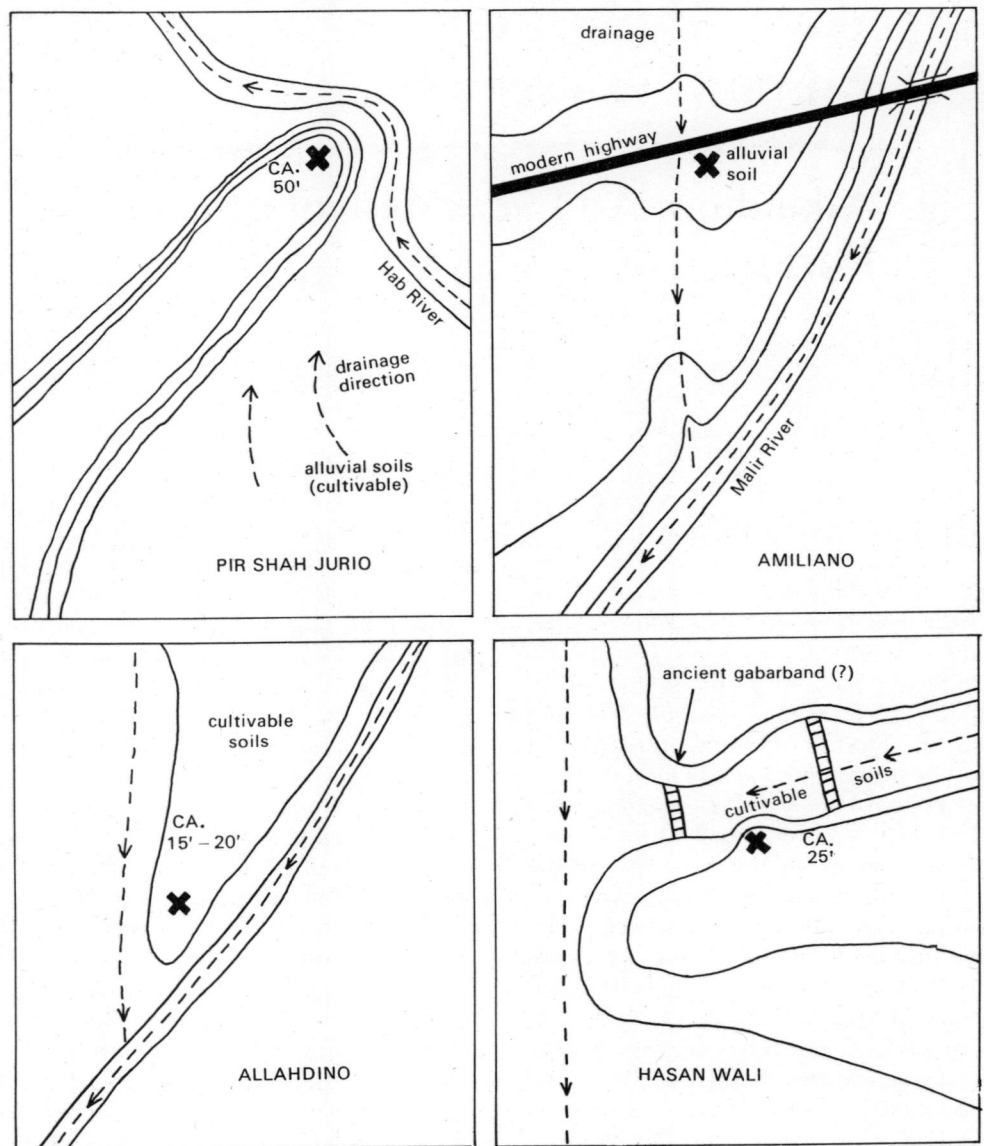

Fig. 9.1. Sites and drainage patterns in the Karachi region.

ALLAHDINO

Allahdino is a low silt mound rising about two meters above the modern alluvium. The site extends no more than 100 meters in any direction. Its position is in the midst of modern cultivation, three to five meters above the present flood plain of the Malir River and that of its tributary the Bazaar Nadi. Allahdino is close to the junction of the present beds of these streams and is about 15 kilometers south of Amiliano. Of the five Harappan sites of the Karachi region, Allahdino offers the most promise of excavation return. It is in a relatively protected situation and its size promotes the possibility that a reasonable sample can be taken. It is also important in that its position within the modern alluvium is in striking contrast to the

Allahdino: An Excavation of a Small Harappan Site

other sites. Pir Shah Jurio and Hasan Wali are above and outside the cultivable alluvium. Hab Chauki and Amiliano are in the midst of very small pockets of cultivable alluvium but are to a degree isolated from the more important tracts of cultivable land in the region. Only Allahdino's location indicates the man/land relationship emphasized at Mohenjodaro, Harappa, and other riverine-oriented sites.

The study of these Karachi District sites is important for several reasons. First, it will reveal much about the Harappan Civilization's internal character. Also, the sites stand at an intermediate position between Baluchistan and Sind and are close to the traditional sea and overland trade routes which converge on the Karachi area. It is hardly likely that if extensive commerce moved along these routes in the Harappan times that the sites of the Karachi region would not reflect its influence in some way or another.

The excavation strategy at Allahdino was to clear one level as completely as possible. It is known of course that non-Harappan, or Early Harappan, sites of Amrian type occur in the region (Orangi, Hasan Wali II, and sites along the Hab River for example) and it would not be unexpected given the situation elsewhere to find Amrian material in the lower levels at Allahdino. Though in actual fact one did not, this possibility seemed far less important than an effort to reveal the character of Harappan occupation at one level; something surely needed in the study of the Indus Civilization. Allahdino's size also makes possible the excavation of the entire site, thus ensuring the recovery of a "complete" sample. It has been growing clearer and clearer that excavations on parts of sites of a given period do not, as a rule, produce sufficient evidence by which to truly assess cultural character. However statistically valid a random sampling might be, it is suspect when one has to deal with most human activities as the history of sociology evidences. In order to handle this problem a quantitative method was adopted which required that all excavated earth be screened and that a rigorous control over fragmentary material be exercised. Even thumbnail-size copper stains *in situ* were recorded as if they were actual objects. After three-and-a-half seasons of work the amount of recovered material is impressive: more than 300,000 potsherds, 24,000 bicones, 2,600 terracotta triangles, 1,500 bangles, 196 pieces of copper or bronze, etc. The same technique was of course maintained for faunal material, slag, exotic unused stone and the like. Flotation and soil analysis were carried out as well. All material was recorded in the same way, *in situ* or in fill. This helps create a distributional picture where, for example, the density of artifact or non-artifactual material may serve as an indicator of specific functional locations. It also gives an opportunity to test the validity of random sampling in the archaeology of the borderlands, wherever it occurs. At least one more full season at Allahdino is planned, however, before this can be done.

ARCHITECTURE

At the central, highest part of the site, an open court measuring approximately 20 meters by eight meters was uncovered. The most distinctive feature of this court is a stone-built well (Well A) in the middle of the southern wall. The well has a small opening (ca. 60 by 90 centimeters) and a Harappan intersecting circle "bath tub" was attached to its southern side. This well stood at least 1.25 meters higher than a surrounding pavement which at one phase of the site's existence probably covered the entire court. The well, however, appears to have been a part of rectangular Building IV. South of Building IV is a complex of small rooms which is temporarily called Building VII. This is apparently joined to Building IV by another and similar well (Well B). Building VII has a broad brick platform with two square pits and a third rectangular in plan. There are also stone walls and rooms along its southern margin. In one of these rooms a small pot was found *in situ* which contained a jewelry cache of five necklaces and eleven copper finger rings of coiled wire. The necklaces had silver beads (both barrelform and disc) as well as carnelian, agate, jasper and copper beads and spacers. A tiny gold earring was also found in this cache.

Access to the central court was made possible through open passageways left between the surrounding buildings. Of these, Buildings I and II are the most impressive. Building I, the largest on the site, is still not completely excavated and in its latest phase may have been modified from an earlier, still poorly defined building. It appears to have been characterized by two east-west running wings joined by a platform and drain complex on the east and by a stone wall complex on the west. The latter is only partially excavated. The whole centered around an inner court in which there may have been some subsidiary (or earlier) structures. The northern wing was made up of compartments, the western half of which contained storage vessels, including a fine classic Harappan black on red vessel similar to the one shown in the famous frontispiece of Mackey's publication on Chanhudaro. There is some suggestion that access to these compartments was via some stone steps.

Building II contained a stone-lined bathroom complete with covered drains, and outlets to the north. Between Buildings I and II there are remnants of a paving which is presumed to have been joined to the paving of the central court at a late phase of the site's existence. Most striking is the presence of a drain system represented by two stone-lined channels which join to the south at the head of the alley between Buildings I and II. A large stone slab, still in place, was apparently used to direct water from one channel to the other.

Building III, at the western end of the central court, appears to have been used for the manufacture of clay bicones and other baked clay objects. It contained clear evidence for ovens in compartments in both its northwestern and southeastern sections. Building V appears to have been used as a "warehouse" of some kind since large storage vessels were found there. But, it also contained considerable habitation debris. Building VI is still unexcavated but a line of stone wells suggests a separate structure.

Certain features of this complex of buildings at Allahdino can be noted.

1) All the buildings have some portion of their structure in stone.

2) There appears to be no regular pattern of brick laying: header-header, stretcher-stretcher, and header-stretcher bonding all occur, even in the same building.

3) There are functional differences among the structures.

4) There is a formality of plan which integrates the structures. There is a general absence of haphazardness both in the way the buildings were constructed and the way they relate one to another.

5) The thickness of walls in Buildings I, II and probably III, as well as the smallness of many of the "rooms" in these structures, argues for a second story in at least some of these buildings.

6) There was no perimeter, or enclosing wall around the site.

IRRIGATION

One of the most intriguing problems which Allahdino raises, and perhaps solves, is the question of the smallness of the openings in the two wells. Well A was traced to a depth of about 4.3 meters or some 1.25 meters into the virgin soil before the stone construction stopped. Clearly the well builders had a special purpose for this kind of construction. What was this?

As outlined earlier, the immense catch basin of the Malir system produces a large underground reservoir. The modern open pump wells, some of which are 30 meters or more across, fluctuate seasonally according to the amount of water in the reservoir. However, as is well known, water in wells rises higher than the surrounding water table because of hydrostatic pressure. The smaller the well diameter the higher the water will rise. Modern wells in the Damlotti area fluctuate in water height as much as 10 meters or more. Even in the larger wells the water surface may reach to within six meters of the modern land surface.

It is suggested then that the Harappan wells were deliberately kept small in diameter so that the water level would not only rise higher but would indeed *overflow* in artesian fashion. The well openings are certainly too small to conveniently lower containers through them. But there is another important factor. The central well is located at the highest part of the site. Any runoff from that well could be channeled wherever one wished because of the slope of the surrounding site. In the case of the divided drain to the north, a regular flow of well water could be moved with precision through the stone channels into the surrounding fields via earth-cut ditches; again *because of the slope of the site itself.* In the modern situation well water is pumped out onto a platform above the surrounding fields and guided into those fields by a channel which slopes down from the platform. The neatness of this idea in the Allahdino case is that it accounts for the narrowness of the well, the strategic location of the well at the top of the site, and the bifurcation of the drains with their movable sluice block. It also makes site location understandable. Since Allahdino is five or more meters above the Malir River, water for the cultivation of the surrounding alluvium must be brought to the fields in some regular fashion. Alternatives to meet this need are not attractive. One could hypothesize an irrigation canal which takes off from a contour above Allahdino; but this would mean a canal at least 20 to 25 kilometers long. One could argue for greater rainfall, which may be valid; but for which the evidence at

Allahdino: An Excavation of a Small Harappan Site

Allahdino is at least still uncertain. One could postulate the regular use of some water-raising devices, like the *shaduf* or the Persian Wheel; but there is no evidence for these. On the face of it I believe that the argument as outlined above for well-water irrigation is plausible. An additional observation might be added that immediately north of Allahdino the slope of the land is from east to west, or across the greatest extent of cultivable land.

OTHER CONSIDERATIONS

The stratigraphy of the site leans heavily upon the work of Jim Shaffer who cut a sondage in quadrant J-6. It appears that there was an early phase when Harappan cattle pastoralists settled the site. This was followed by a major construction period during which Buildings I, II, III and probably IV, were created. These were embellished somewhat later by the addition of the more flimsy structures on the south. None of the buildings, however, remained static during its life as all of them have indications of rebuilding and wall modification as one might expect in the life of any structure. The site was abandoned suddenly as the jewelry cache and the basically intact walls of the various buildings suggest. Apparently the collapse of the superstructure did much to preserve the foundations and the contents of many of the rooms. Later visitors to the place left little evidence for their passing except some burned spots which marked their fires and an occasional line of postholes, such as in plan of Building II, quadrant G-5, and Building I, quadrant F-4. The conformity and continuity of artifacts and structures evidences a short time span for Harappan occupation which I suspect was no more than a hundred years at the most.

The scale of the site is modest and the fact that several of the structures are specifically functional rather than generally habitational, as well as the possibility of an irrigational premise as outlined above, gives the impression that the population living on the site was no more than eighty or so. One suspects numerous scattered households were satellite to sites like Allahdino and Hasan Wali. In turn these sites served the extended community by providing collective labor for functions such as milling, irrigation, religious services, administration, storage, etc.

ARTIFACTS

An ongoing study of the interior diameter of fragments of clay bangles has indicated so far that the hand breadth of the bangle wearers was about five centimeters. This evidence suggests that the women who are presumed to have worn them were very slender and perhaps under five feet four inches in height.

There is evidence for cattle, goats and sheep, the water buffalo, possibly the donkey, and for grain-eating rodents. There were also gallinaceous fowl, as well as fish and possibly the monitor lizard. Flotation results have not been truly satisfactory. Wheat, and perhaps barley, is attested and a legume of some unidentifiable kind was found; but nothing else has been isolated. One hopes to improve on this by utilizing newer flotation methods in a subsequent season.

The seals and graffiti attest to the fact that not only was the Harappan script well known to the inhabitants of Allahdino, but that the social organization for which the seals are representative was in vogue there. There are "unicorn" bull seals, and both the elephant and the rhinoceros. If, as I have discussed in the first preliminary report for Allahdino (Fairservis 1976), these larger motifs in the seals generally represent sodalities in the society, it is clear that the Allahdino settlement was highly organized under a leadership familiar on a larger scale at Mohenjodaro and elsewhere. In the same context, the repetition of the -capped knot sign 𐀀 on sealing 73-156, and on three unicorn bullseals 73-105, 73-32, and 74-177, which I would read as settlement chief (*urtal*), is not at variance with the sense that the polity of the Harappans revolved around shared and specialized authority as is not uncommon in later manifestations of village India.

TRADE

If one draws a series of concentric circles representing 10 kilometer units with Allahdino at their center it can be said that 95 percent of all materials found on the site could have been obtained within 50 kilometers. Flint deposits have been located within seven kilometers of Allahdino. Shell and fish are obtainable both in the Malir Basin and the coast of the Arabian Sea. Copper, agate, jasper and carnelian are found in the Lyari Hills, the Porali Basin, the Kohistan, and the Hab River Valley. On estimate, about 10 kilograms of copper artifacts were found at Allahdino. Only the gold and silver are not locally obtainable among all the materials that have been identified.

However, until qualitative analysis of these materials is completed one cannot exclude the possibility that at least some of the manufactured articles are the consequence of trade. While copper slag is attested at Allahdino it is scattered and sparse and no furnace has yet been found there. However, it is doubtful on the face of the overall evidence that trade was significant either in the location of the site or deeply involved in its functions.

SUMMARY

Allahdino, and by allusion the other Malir sites, was a settlement created to serve a community whose population was resident in households scattered over the landscape and presumed to be largely engaged in agriculture and cattle pastoralism. Ancient Allahdino provided various functions including local administration, the manufacture of clay artifacts and irrigation water. The households were probably no more than three kilometers from the central site and a constant interplay between Allahdino and the household was maintained. Local natural resources were sufficient for most material needs and specialists living at Allahdino both obtained and converted these materials. Interaction among the Malir, and with other Harappan sites of the region, moved objects and services through a network which is characteristic of Harappan settlement almost everywhere. Ultimately, regional networks connect with one another reinforcing both the conformity of Harappan Culture and its continuity even far from the Indus River Valley itself. This is a model which hopefully one can continue to test as work is finalized at Allahdino.

BIBLIOGRAPHY

Fairservis, W.A., 1976
Excavations at Allahdino I: Seals and inscribed material. New York: Walter A. Fairservis, American Museum of Natural History.

R.S. BISHT

10. Excavations at Banawali: 1974-77

INTRODUCTION

The excavations at Banawali (lat. 29°37'5" north; long. 75°23'6" east) in Hissar District, Haryana, during the four seasons 1974-77, have revealed a threefold cultural sequence; Pre-Indus, Indus and Post-Indus. This material is important in assessing the role played by the Pre-Indus Culture during the Mature Indus times and thereafter. It also places more light on the tangled mass of Chalcolithic materials gathered in Haryana and the Punjab, besides adding a new Pre-Indus settlement and another Indus fort-town in the eastern part of the valley of the "lost" Sarasvati. Over the last six decades the consistent efforts of a number of field workers have led to the gathering of a good deal of archaeological data bearing on the protohistory of the Subcontinent and the neighboring countries of Iran, Afghanistan, the U.S.S.R. and in the Persian Gulf. Needless to say, the most spectacular discovery so far relates to the phenomenal emergence and spread of the Indus Culture which as yet stands in majestic isolation, evading precise clues as to its ancestry and progeny. But, like all preceding and succeeding cultures, it still remains nameless, despite the claims of India and Iran to a long and most ancient literary tradition. No archaeological materials have so far been conclusively associated with the Vedic, Avestan, or, for that matter, with the Epic Age. Nor can any of the Pre-Indus, Post-Indus, or Early Iron Age cultures be convincingly identified with any age or phase known in literature. Therefore, conclusions on the history of Pre-Buddhist times are exceedingly difficult to arrive at and are often debatable.

Before turning to Banawali, it is appropriate to say something about Haryana and its special role in this story. Geographically, Haryana forms a part of the Indo-Gangetic Divide and partakes of river systems of both the Indus and the Ganges. Furthermore, it is the natural and most convenient corridor between these two valleys, both of which are circumscribed by strong geographical barriers. The Indus Valley forms a great triangle. The rugged and inhospitable mountain ranges of the Kirthar and Sulaiman, which have always allowed successive groups of peoples through their narrow passes, stretch as the baseline along the west. The formidable Himalayas lie as the northeastern arm. On the south the Arabian Sea bounds the valley. The marshes of the Rann of Kutch in the southeast and the sandy wastes of the Thar Desert extending northward and northeastward, interspersed with the outcrops and the hilly terrain of the Aravallis, make up the southeastern border. It is here that the Himalayas and the Aravallis come sharply closer forming a nearly 200 kilometer-wide gateway connecting the two most fertile and eventful valleys of India. The Ganges Valley too, in its turn, is bounded by the Himalayas in the north, by the Vindhyas in the south, and, anciently, by densely wooded marshes of the east. The Bay of Bengal lies to its south and a north-south oriented chain of the steep mountains is further east. This exceedingly strategic location made Haryana a very lively transit zone, an area of compulsive and strong interactions, with a constant flow of two-way traffic in men, materials and ideas since the unknown past. It is all the more important in the context of the Indus Valley which has had a very special relevance in regard to the development of early human cultures in the Subcontinent. Geographically speaking, Haryana is an eastern extension of the Indus Plains, forming in fact the apex of the region.

The natural barriers of the Indus Valley channeled the movement of people of developing cultures as well as the advance of marching hordes, toward the rich plains of Haryana before entering the Ganges Valley or the highlands of Central India. The route running along the Himalayas instantly brought them here from the northwest or from the hills beyond, as did the route running north along the River Sarasvati. The latter route was useful for those moving from the Arabian Sea coast, Sind, the centrally located Sind-Sagar *doab,* or from the connected passes of the Baluchi hills. Thus the "lost" Sarasvati traversed the Indus Plains diagonally and connected the southern sea with the Siwalik foothills on the Yamuna.

Materially, Haryana and its adjoining regions abound in natural wealth. The Aravallis are rich in copper, iron, minerals and other raw materials. The copper (Agrawal 1970; 1971: 145; Agrawal, Magabandhu and Shekhar 1976; Agrawala 1978; Hegde 1968) and other minerals are said to have been commercially exploited during protohistoric times. That apart, these hills together with the Himalayas and the intervening riverine plains must have offered a variegated wealth of flora and fauna most of which have since vanished due to prolonged human interference and overexploitation. The riparian plain is rich in fertile land and water. It is presently blessed with two perennial rivers—the Yamuna and Ghaggar—in addition to a few shorter hill streams and seasonal torrents. But, in antiquity there should have been other perennial rivers such as the Sarasvati, and its two tributaries, the Drishadvati and the Apaya, all of Rigvedic fame. Their now dry beds are still traceable in Haryana and northern Rajasthan (Bhargava 1964: 52-101). The Sarasvati in particular has received the most intimate affection, reverence and imagery from the Rigvedic seers and the later poets. The *Rigveda* explicitly refers to its flowing from the hills to the sea (*Rigveda* VII. 95.2) and having a string of settlements on its banks (*Rigveda* VII. 96.2). During the later Vedic period, it had started drying up as recorded in the *Mahabharata* (Vana Parvan LXXXII: CXXX, and Salys XXXV), *Panchavimsa Brahmana* (XXV. 101), *Latyayana Srauta Sutra* (X. 15.1), *Baudhayana Dharma Sutra* (I. 2.9), and *Manava Dharma Sastra* (II. 21). Topographical studies as well as archaeological investigations of late have since amply borne out this fact. In the course of his extensive exploration in North and Central Haryana, and in some parts of the northeast Punjab (India), the present author has observed that the Sarasvati and its tributaries had probably been extensively harnessed. Protohistoric man apparently dug canals for irrigating fields and storing water in large ponds. The existence of a network of abandoned canals and river beds, dotted with numerous Chalcolithic and Early Iron Age sites, in the Sarasvati Valley in Haryana bears testimony to this. It also indicates large-scale deforestation, claiming land for agricultural purposes. In addition, the *Mahabharata* bears evidence that when the center of political activity shifted to the Ganges Valley, the Kurus maintained cattle land in this area.

Such large-scale exploitation of natural resources must have seriously disturbed the prevalent ecobalance and set most of those streams that were not fed by the snow on the path of gradual desiccation. However, the upper course of the Sarasvati, right from Adi Badri in the Siwaliks, traditionally held as its sources, to Bahar, running past Kapalmochan, Bhagwanpura, Thanesar-Kurukshetra and Pehoa (ancient Prithudaka), is still seasonally alive. At Bahar it has lately been taken by the Ghaggar. Its old course, which now runs parallel to that of the Ghaggar, is still traceable and forms the Sottar Valley now famous for yielding bumper crops and potable subsoil water. This valley, which is two to four kilometers wide, and even more at places, runs through the districts of Jind, Hissar and Sirsa in Haryana until it meets the modern Ghaggar near the Rajasthan border. Before protective bunds and the present network of roads were built along with irrigation and stormwater canals along the entire length and breadth of the Sottar Valley, it used to occasionally carry a volume of water during the rainy season. It is still publicly known variously as the Rangoi, Nai, Nadi, or Hakra Ban. A series of mounds runs along both its banks. The mound of Banawali is one of those on the northern flank.

THE SITE

Banawali is located on the time-honored "Northern Highway." This connected the Ganges Valley, the Himalayan regions and Central India with the passes of the northwestern hills and the Arabian Sea located across the Indus Plains. It lost some of its importance in the recent past when Sher Shah Sur (1539-45) developed a more northerly route because of increased desertic conditions in this region, in addition to other factors.

Excavations at Banawali: 1974-77

The approximate straight line distances (in kilometers) and directions from Banawali to well-known Harappan towns are: Kalibangan, 120 west by south; Mohenjodaro, 740 west southwest; Harappa, 260 west northwest; Roopnagar (formerly Rupar), 180 northeast; Mitathal, 110 southeast; and Rakhigarhi (a very extensive and prospective site in district Jind, Haryana), 80 east northeast. The mound at Banawali stands about half a kilometer south southwest of the village of the same name. It spreads over an area of about 400 by 400 meters and rises to a height of 10 meters from the surrounding area. In its present form it is a single mound. The marginally truncated southern side and the extensively leveled western and northern flanks have now been appropriated for agriculture. The twin mounds, as observed by Suraj Bhan (1975: 95, fn. 2), are not vouched for by the local folk who saw it prior to the recent despoliation. The south-central part of the mound is conspicuously higher than other parts. The sides on the east, west and south are very steep. So are both the corner margins along the northern face, the central portion of which, however, descends gradually into a shallow depression only to rise again for a short length and then stretch out for about 100 meters. More or less similarly, the eastern and western slopes too, after the sharp descent, fan out over nearly 150 meters on either side. On the south the side drops down sharply to terminate on the level plain. The excavations reveal that the higher segment generally conceals the Indus citadel built over the rubble of the Pre-Indus settlement. In the southern half of the western flank the Indus remains have been almost completely removed and the underlying Pre-Indus remains stand exposed on the surface, whereas the northern half contains only Harappan relics. The Post-Indus habitation spreads out over the eastern flank beyond the ankle of the mound.

The cultural assemblage (Bisht in press: 1 ff; 1978: 86-88; 1976b; 1977) gathered during four field seasons at Banawali has been divided into three periods:

Period I : Pre-Indus or Kalibangan Culture
Period II : Indus Culture
Period III : Post-Indus or Banawali-Bara Culture

PERIOD I: PRE-INDUS/KALIBANGAN CULTURE

The Pre-Indus levels were sounded on the truncated western flank. These are three meters thick, although they might be deeper toward the center of the mound. The excavated material bears an overall likeness to that from Kalibangan I, the type-site, as described by Lal and Thapar (1967: 78-88; Lal 1969: 15-16; Thapar 1965: 135-38; 1969; 1975).

The settlement was founded on alluvium. Although the area under operation was too small to provide much information on town planning, some system seems to have been followed since the structures are oriented to cardinal directions. The house walls, in most cases, were built of single bricks. Thus the houses should have been single-storied, quite low and squat, probably with light thatched roofs, lacking mud terracing. The bricks, both fired (Pl. 10.1) and sun-dried (Pl. 10.2), were meticulously standardized, conforming to the ratio 1:2:3. This ratio was observed earlier at Kalibangan. But, the dimensions at Banawali are 12 by 24 by 36 centimeters and 13 by 26 by 39 centimeters as compared to 10 by 20 by 30 centimeters at Kalibangan. In addition, there is one aberrant size: 24 by 24 centimeters, the thickness remaining still indeterminate. However, the succession of structural phases remains as yet to be built up. The most interesting structure so far exposed is a two-meter wide brick-on-edge pathway which, curiously enough, runs along the inner side of the defensive wall of the Indus citadel (Pl. 10.3) and, on the present showing, it limits the Pre-Indus settlement on the north. It should therefore not be surprising if the Indus wall is found to conceal within it the enclosure wall of the antecedent period, as is the case in places at Kalibangan. Another noteworthy structure is a partially uncovered house complex with several hearths, ovens and fire pits in the room (Pl. 10.4). Excessive fire activity in this area has reddened house floors there. Surely, it should be a workshop, plausibly that of a metalsmith. One more interesting feature is the presence of precisely circular pits, both large and small, neatly cut deep into the house floors. In one case, a pit rim was lined with mud bricks and its walls were thickly plastered. Most of these pits yield fine bluish ash, occasionally mixed with charred grains; although the pits themselves show no sign of firing. These might be the storage silos or bins. The paucity, or near absence, of large storage jars lends further credence to this surmise.

The ceramic inventory records all six Kalibangan fabrics, including the methods of surface dressing, shapes and many of the decorative motifs (Pl. 10.5). Additionally, there are pottery lugs and loop-handles. Certain ceramic vessels have an incised decoration of shallow multiple wavy or vertical lines, deep-cut sigmas or casually done criss-cross patterns executed on the exterior. Fabric "D" Incised Ware is also found (Pl. 10.6).

Copper is scarce. Points and awls of bone are numerous. The lithic industry is represented by a solitary microblade of chalcedony. Characteristic clay bangles with triangular, as well as square cross-sections, blackish gray color, are duly found in addition to round examples, red in color. Among other important antiquities are beads of gold, semiprecious stones, steatite (including disc beads), faience, shell, bone and clay; bangles of shell, faience and copper; animal figurines of terracotta; clay balls; stone pebbles and other miscellaneous objects. However, the most significant find is a sherd depicting a canopied cart with spoked wheels (Pl. 10.7). Many sherds are found with engraved or fingernail marks on the base and occasionally on the exterior. Similar marks have already been observed on other pottery, chronologically and genetically ascribable to Pre-Indus times, from Baluchistan and South Afghanistan. These are illustrated and briefly discussed by Fairservis (1971: 142, 144 Fig. 35) who tends to take them as either potter's marks or trade marks. Lal (1969) also notes them. Such marks are also prevalent on the Pre-Harappan ceramics of the Indus Valley. Some of them are quite complex and can be derived from naturistic or stylized animal forms. They are likely to have been auspicious signs. Banawali I has also yielded a stone weight, perhaps the first of its kind. Its weight is 87.855 grams. Although it does not fit the binary system of Indus weights, it closely approximates a sum a hundred times the supposed Indus unit weight of 0.857 grams (Marshall 1931: 590-91; Mackay 1943: 602, 606, Table III).

Preliminary studies made in small segments of two quadrants may point to the transformation of the Pre-Indus ceramics and the marginal appearance of Indus pottery. If this is the case, it should denote that a phase of vigorous cultural interaction was taking place during the transition. This phenomenon is represented by a thin deposit of only about 50 centimeters. The buff and light red fabrics of the Pre-Indus ceramics tend to be more matted and pinkish red or buff in color and heavier and thicker in texture in these areas. Predilection for painting as well as the use of white pigment seems to decline. Luxuriant motifs give way to simpler designs and there is generally a restraint in decoration. In addition, mundanely utilitarian Indus shapes make their appearance, although the Classic Harappan forms and decoration are not present. In one quadrant, bricks of both Pre-Indus and Indus sizes are found to have been used side by side in construction.

However, only further work at the site will help to properly evaluate the real import of this seemingly transitional phase that has been observed at Banawali. The presence of such a transitional phase has already been established at Amri (Casal 1964) and Kot Diji (Khan 1965). It was also pointed out at Mitathal (Suraj Bhan 1975: 15, 18, 81) and Siswal (Suraj Bhan 1975: 103), where Harappan pottery makes its "intrusive" or "limited" appearance in the existing local cultures of Pre-Indus genre. This phenomenon is altogether absent at Kalibangan, despite the fact that the Pre-Indus ceramic tradition continued into the middle levels of the succeeding Indus Culture. For the present, it is probably best for this phase to remain a shadowy entity at Banawali, pending further confirmation through excavations.

PERIOD II: MATURE INDUS CULTURE

With proverbial dramatic precocity the full-bloomed Indus Culture makes its appearance at Banawali. This includes its essential cultural appurtenances: town-planning and architecture, ceramics, seals, script, weights, clay figurines, terracotta "cakes," items of ornament and miscellaneous knick-knacks and tools. The older ceramic tradition continues throughout Period II as a culture-companion but in reduced frequency. New pottery elements, indicating other sources, also enter the pottery corpus.

Excavations have indicated that the entire Indus town at Banawali was securely enclosed by massive defenses, the eastern arm of which has already been determined for a length of nearly one hundred meters along the base of the mound. Dimensions of this town have been ascertained through excavations. It extends over not less than 275 and 130 meters respectively along the north-south and east-west axes, while its extent towards the north and west may continue ever farther. Within the walled town there is a fortified acropolis, a regular road system and well-defined residential sectors. The acropolis stands out pre-eminently on higher ground built up by the accumulation of Pre-Indus debris. It overlooks "down town" stretching beyond the fortifications toward the north, east and to the riverside on the south. Surface contours suggest that the acropolis may share a common wall with the town along the riverside. However, one is not certain whether there is a similar arrangement on the west where the original contours of the mound have lately been substantially eroded. On present showing, the citadel appears to occupy the southwestern quarter (or the south-central segment), of the town and thus simulates the general layout of the Indus town of Lothal; albeit with the difference that the Lothal acropolis appropriates the southeastern quarter of the town. Only the high podium upon which it was built segregates it from the "lower town." Whereas at Banawali, the eastern and northern arms together with northeastern turn of the defenses of the citadel (Pls. 10.8 and 10.9) have been extensively laid bare. Their width ranges from 5.4 to seven meters. The two squarish bastions that were unearthed along the east wall project towards the "down town." By the side of the bastion at the northeastern corner, a 1.5 meter wide opening with a built-in *pucca* drain pierces the defensive wall. It is not unlikely that it served as both the postern entrance and as a stormwater drain. As to the entrance it may be mentioned that it has links to the two major roads, both 5.4 meters wide and running north-south on either side of the defense wall. In addition a 1.5 meter wide alley, coming from the residential blocks of the "upper town," passes through this opening by cutting across both the major roads at right angles. It runs further eastwards between the house blocks of the "lower town." Another entry point is found across the northern arm in the form of a 1.5 meter *pucca* ramp leading one up from the "down town" onto the citadel (Pl. 10.10).

The "lower town," which has been subjected to more soundings than the acropolis, indicates that roads played a significant role in the civic planning. Major roads run not only on both sides of the citadel wall, but also along the inner side of the town wall to the east. Even the roads distantly removed run parallel to the general plan. They scrupulously follow the orientation of the citadel defenses even though they have to negotiate awkward turns in order to maintain conformity. The flanking residential sectors also follow suit at the cost of convenience and simplified planning. This is manifest in the plan of the part of the lower town that is located in the tortuous northwestern corner of the wall of the acropolis. Normally, two longitudinal roads bound a row of single house blocks which, at least on one side, are separated by narrow latitudinal alleys. It may be mentioned that the "lower town," which is narrowest—70 meters in breadth—in the southeastern quarter, has as many as three major roads, each as wide as 5.5 meters, whereas there are only two rows of house blocks in between. The total area covered by roads is thus as much as one-fourth of the whole. Such planning would have imparted to the township an air of pleasant lightness.

Houses are normally large and spacious, containing several rooms meant variously for sleeping, sitting, storage, kitchen, toilet and worship. There is usually a courtyard, and at times a corridor, in a house. In at least one case, a sitting room was paved with mud bricks. It is this room which yielded the famous inscribed seal depicting the horned tiger. The toilet of this house was provided with a wash basin placed on a high place in a corner near the drain which carried off waste water into a sullage jar placed outside on the street. This was normal practice at Banawali. Surely, this house (Pls. 10.11 a and b) belonged to a rich merchant as it has yielded more than one seal, a few weights and a large number of jars half embedded in the house floors. Another large house (Pl. 10.12) may have belonged to a jewelry dealer as it produced numerous beads including etched carnelian examples, those of gold and lapis lazuli as well as their imitations. There were also many small weights. A house was generally provided with a room containing a square fireplace, with or without brick lining, but with a longish cone of clay placed in the center. This was also noticed at Kalibangan. Another noteworthy feature is the presence of small cubicles in the massive walls. These generally measure one by one meter and sometimes two by one meters, and no doors. These were most plausibly blind vaults or bins meant for valuables, or foodgrains. If this is so, there should have been one or two openings. One of these was probably at some distance below the ceiling. This was used to feed in material. The other was just above the floor level and was used to gain access to the food grains. Only this postulate explains the probable use of such small cubicles which are otherwise too small to be regular storerooms. One of the rooms had a platform constructed against a wall. It also had a curious fireplace with thin, vertical mud walls.

In most cases, the house walls near ground level were strenghtened with a lining of bricks placed vertically, or a footwork of rammed earth. This protected them against underscoring caused by natural agencies or vandalism of small animals or playful children. On the road side there were sometimes platforms or brick-lined fodder tubs. All structures, as a rule, were neatly plastered with mud, usually mixed with ash, straw or cow dung.

So far, Banawali II has five, or probably six, successive building phases (Pl. 10.13). As found elsewhere in the Indus context, the original layout of the town was maintained most zealously throughout the lifetime of the culture. However, a public drainage system is conspicuously absent at Banawali and individuals must have been called on to maintain a high standard of hygiene. They did this by depositing household refuse at fixed points and by draining sullage into soakage jars placed on the street. From there the garbage might have been removed by municipal scavengers. The composition of road materials indicates that there is very little household refuse there. Occasional undulations in the roads seem to have been filled in with earth laden with heavier matter such as **potsherds** and waste terracotta nodules, etc. Fallen debris from a collapsed house were probably promptly thrown out of the town. Nothing was obtained about door sills or leafs, nor about the roofing method. Some of the houses had walls as thick as one meter. These might have been double storied as such examples are not wanting in the rural Punjab even today.

Bricks, both baked and sun-dried, were carefully molded into various sizes which, except the wedge-shaped examples, form two broad groups and always give the ratio of 1:2:4 as regards thickness, width and length. The smaller bricks, which variously measure 6 by 12 by 24 centimeters; 6.5 by 13 by 26; 7 by 14 by 28; 7.5 by 15 by 30 or 8 by 16 by 32, were used in constructing residential houses. The larger ones, 10 by 20 by 40 centimeters; 11 by 22 by 44; 12 by 24 by 48 and 12.5 by 25 by 50, were used in massive structures such as defenses. Fired bricks are normally used in drains, wells and bathing platforms; places with a constant use of water.

Classic Indus ceramics come in all their manifestations (Pls. 10.14 and 10.15). Three other distinct wares of separate origins flourished alongside these. The most distinguished of these is the group of Kalibangan Wares which continue into the Harappan Period. In this process, Kalibangan Fabrics C and D gradually merge with Indus Wares to which they bear a remarkable resemblance in technological finesse and general appearance. On the other hand, Fabrics A, B and E influence each other and undergo a marked devolution already underway during the supposed Intermediate Phase which will be briefly discussed later. On the whole these ceramics survive throughout Period II. They retain much of their pristine characteristics including forms and surface decoration. However, these wares are not dominant in either number or types. Basically, they were used to make unassuming and commonplace forms such as vases, cooking vessels, small jars, basins and bowls in particular. During this period, as noted earlier, the ceramics tend to be more of a dull matt red, or pinkish red in color and are usually treated with either a dilute wash or no wash at all. The use of white paint seems to have been discarded early in Period II. This ceramic corpus compares well with that of Mitathal I and II A (Suraj Bhan 1975: 18-23, and 27-31) and Siswal "B" (Suraj Bhan 1975: 108), which Suraj Bhan calls "Late Siswal Ware."

A second non-classic Harappan pottery group is represented by a sprinkling of Red Ware sherds. These are distinct because of their unusually thick and heavy fabric and a subdued oily surface which was occasionally burnished. Technically, its family-likeness lies in the controversial Bara Ware which is consistently a principal associate of the Indus Culture in the upper regions of the Punjab and Haryana as is evident at Roopnagar (Ropar) I, Sanghol IA, Chandigarh and Mirzapur near Kurukshetra (Singh in press: 3). As circumstances indicate, Bara Ware might be a derivative of a separate Pre-Indus culture group. During Post-Indus times it attained phenomenal perfection in technique and variegation in painting. During this time it enjoyed a wide distribution in the Indo-Gangetic Divide and further eastwards.

The third ceramic class is an uninspiring dull red ware with a poor matt surface, thin walls and a coarse texture. The usual forms are vessels and cooking *handis* which often have an incised decoration or applique bands with cut-marks or pinchings on the shoulder. Sometimes these occur together and sometimes independently. When these occur together the bands enclose, underline, or overline the incised zone which usually contains deeply incised parallel horizontal lines subsequently cut through by vertical or oblique strokes, or wavy incisions. These patterns are later found to have been simulated by the Harappan potters on their own Indus Red Wares. However, the patterns which occur first on a duller ware seem to be comparable to those from Ahar (Sankalia, Deo and Ansari 1969). Decoration by way of incisions also occurs in Pre-Indus contexts, but that is not comparable to the case under discussion. This technique of embellishment later becomes the hallmark of the

Bara Ware of Post-Indus times.

Certain antiquities of Period II deserve special mention. Banawali has yielded about ten steatite seals and one terracotta sealing (Pl. 10.16). Exquisite examples of great artistic achievement, and a high degree of literacy, these seals are a definitive pointer to the commercial importance of Banawali. They also throw welcome light on their probable owners since they have only come from the lower town, not the citadel. To be more precise, these seals were generally recovered from houses which on the basis of their contents (noted elsewhere in the paper) have been tentatively attributed to a trader or a jeweler. It is also important to note that the site is very rich in lapis lazuli and gold. Gold plated terracotta beads were also found. Surprisingly, a vast number of lapis lazuli beads, and their imitations in paste, indicate that the trade in lapis was possibly both lucrative and brisk, contrary to the general belief that it was dwindling during Harappan times (Chakrabarti 1978: 54, 56). Etched carnelian beads are also plentiful. Of course, there are numerous examples of beads, inlays and studs in semiprecious stones, shall, bone, faience, steatite and clay. The enormity and variety of steatite beads is impressive. Faience was generally used to make bangles, *pipal* leaf-shaped earrings or small beads. Clay was also used to make bangles, anklets and an assortment of ornaments. Some of the terracotta human figurines from Banawali throw light on the style of personal decoration; but no new information is added in this regard (Pl. 10.17).

Equally revealing is the impressive range of small weights which broadly form four groups: (1) cubes and square prisms usually made of stone (Pl. 10.18); (2) gamesman-types of stone and bone (or ivory or antler) (Pl. 10.19); (3) clay pyramids; and (4) spheroid pebbles with plane bases and tops. Barring the last-mentioned examples, the other types come in a baffling range of size in the lower denominations. Of course, most of them fall within the known Indus weight system. Two specimens are of special interest. One is a perfect cube of stone that weighs 0.216 grams. This approximates one-fourth of Hemmy's Indus weight unit of 0.857 grams (Mackay 1943: 602, 606, Table III). It is exactly six times the weight of a rice grain at 0.036 grams (Marshall 1931: 596). The second specimen is a slightly chipped micro-gamesman type of green stone that weighs 0.68 grams. When intact, it should have weighed 0.072 grams, or twice a rice grain, which supports Hemmy's proposition that the Indus weight system was based on the rice grain (Marshall 1931: 596).

Banawali has also produced a unique tool made out of the coil of the spine of an animal. In addition to the natural central hole, it has two slit-holes, carefully cut through the bone along the diameter. These run into each other crosswise. With the aid of this survey instrument one can draw not only straight lines, but also certain angles. The author has seen a similar device in the Chalcolithic assemblage from Chirand (Saran, Bihar).

Terracotta figurines and other miscellaneous objects from Banawali II are, as a rule, all known Indus types. There are typical Indus figurines of Mother Goddesses represented by one complete specimen, one headless body, two ornate heads and certain pot-bellied specimens (Pl. 10.20). In addition, human figurines include carelessly made and highly stylized forms in a seated posture. Amongst the animals (Pls. 10.21 and 10.22) are terracotta of the bull, buffalo, ram, deer, rhinoceros, dog, tiger and birds. The bull figurines clearly outnumber all others. These are generally quite stylized and simplified forms; although a few are modeled quite realistically and sensitively. Certain bull figurines have slender and elongated bodies, muzzle mouths and conjoined long legs. These recall the painted figure of a deer executed on a pottery piece from the Pre-Indus levels of Kalibangan. M.R. Mughal has found animal figurines with conjoined legs in the assemblage anterior to the Kot Dijian, or his Early Harappan Culture (Mughal 1980). Such figurines are surely of Pre-Indus inspiration. Of course, some of these specimens are modeled realistically and artistically. Next in number are the bird forms. These come as bird whistles and pedestaled eagles or falcons with outstretched wings and tails. A few animal figurines were fitted with wheels (Pl. 10.23). Toy cart frames, including a few solid clay platforms, are abundant (Pl. 10.24). A few clay "cakes," nodules and sherds have engraved forms and symbols as well. One sherd has a beautifully engraved figure of a bull. In one case a human form is delineated in simplistic folk tradition. The body is shown as two opposed triangles, and hands and legs as lines.

Among the tools, there are objects of copper: arrowheads, spearheads, a fragmentary sickle blade, the typical razor, chisels, rings, double spiraled and simple pins, ear/nose rings and fish hooks (Pls. 10.25 and 10.26). There are points, a knife and scrapers of bone. Chert blades and fluted cores and flakes are also present. Other objects include clay net-sinkers, balls, pallets, sling balls, longish cones and solid wheels made of clay, besides numerous other household implements.

It should be restated that this period has five or six successive structural phases in a deposit of 4.5 meters. Three charcoal samples from one quadrant have given the following dates based on the 5730 year half-life. The reference year is 1950.

Laboratory Number	Locus	Date
1. PRL-204	(10) 1.13-1.28 MBS	1400 B.C. ±130 years[1]
2. PRL-205	(12) 1.3 to 1.6 MBS	1960 B.C. ±160 years
3. PRL-205	(14) 1.7 MBS	1980 B.C. ±190 years[2]

These dates cover the penultimate phase of the citadel wall, and are comparable to the third building phase of the residential area. The first sample was collected just below the previous year's last excavated stratum. This was left exposed during the rainy season, hence there is strong chance of contamination. However, the following two dates are absolutely consistent and are ascribable to the upper middle levels of the Indus deposit. If one assigns the date of ca. 1800/1750 B.C. to the final phase, the beginning might be dated to about 2300 B.C. or so. As far as the other two dates [1240 B.C. + 110 (PRL ^{14}C Date List I/1976, 2) (Cyclostyled) and 1400 B.C. + 130 (PRL ^{14}C Date List III/1975, 2)] are concerned, the former comes from a disturbed trench and the latter subsequently turned out to belong to a pottery kiln of the following period.

It is not out of place to mention here that Kalibangan has nine successive Mature Harappan construction phases. Thus, the duration of the Indus Culture at Kalibangan should surely be longer than that at Banawali. But one has no data to find out which of the building phases of these two places should be coeval, nor does one know whether or not the beginning or the end of the settlements of these sites was simultaneous. It is also not known whether the town at Banawali started later and ended earlier. It is not unlikely, in the face of the facts, that the Pre-Indus deposit at Banawali is twice as thick as that at Kalibangan. At Banawali the Indus Culture is followed by a Post-Indus Culture, the authors of which may have overcome the Indus inhabitants, but this is not yet substantiated. Nor have the lower levels of Period III been adequately probed. Hence the precise relationship between the two cultures will remain unresolved until further work has been done.

It is certain however that Banawali was an important administrative headquarters or provincial capital and a prosperous trading center along the Sarasvati during the Indus times. Materially, the area must have been producing surplus food and the town is nicely located for trade in raw materials from the Aravallis as well as the Himalayas. The copper fields of North Rajasthan are also close at hand.

PERIOD III: POST-INDUS BANAWALI-BARA CULTURE

Period III is stratigraphically posterior to the Indus Culture. Post-Indus material is found in pits and kilns dug into Indus cultural debris on the top of the mound. There is also a settlement of Period III against the eastern wall of the Indus town. So much so that toward the end of this period the accumulation attained the extant height of the defensive wall. Then, regular structures are found raised and refuse pits and hearths dug into the defense wall itself (Pl. 10.27). Moreover, this period is explicitly devoid of all urban attributes and the classic, diagnostic objects which characterize the preceding period. Hence, one prefers to call it "Post-Indus," although it has widely been designated "Late Harappan" by a majority of authors. One would have liked to call it "Bara" alone, had that not been overshadowed by the controversy with regard to its chronological position and cultural status. The Banawali material of the Period III, in its present showing, is undoubtedly closely akin to that of the Bara Culture which Y.D. Sharma has made familiar to the archaeological world through his various illustrations and notes (Sharma 1955-56: 121-29; 1964: 7-10, 21-25, 71-72; 1973: 222-30; 1976: 10-12; also, Indian Archaeology: A review 1953-54: 6-7; 1954-55: 9-11). Tentatively, therefore, it is christened as the "Banawali-Bara Culture," of course, Post-Indus in time scale.

Bricks were not used as building material in Period III, and structures were made of packed earth; however they roughly follow the cardinal directions as noticed in Sanghol IB. The Pre-Indus tradition of digging large underground silos and small pits meticulously cut and perfectly circular with vertical, straight sides is again a common practice. In addition, corn bins made of clay as well as lime, and *tandoors* and ovens are normally found in every house (Bisht 1976a: 17; in press: 3, 4, 7, 8; Indian Archaeology: A review 1968-69: 25; 1969-70: 9; 1970-71: 30; Suraj Bhan 1975: 8-13, 17, 33-58, 111-15).

Interestingly, houses are usually found to have been kept so neat and tidy that no layers of ash or waste materials are generally met with through the successive floor levels. Another diagnostic, yet curious artifact, is a clay object that gradually tapers upwards from the square base and ultimately turns towards a side terminating into two short, horn-like prongs. It is usually found placed in the center of a hearth. This object has been found widely distributed at cognate sites. At times, the lower body of a vessel or a roughly straight-sided pottery stand is found to have been placed in a fire pit.

The ceramics are the most distinctly identifiable item of the cultural equipment of Period III (Pl. 10.28). In fact, as noted earlier, the assemblage occurs sporadically during the preceding period. The personality of these ceramics is markedly punctuated by an astounding resurgence of most of the painted motifs and pottery forms of the Pre-Indus tradition. There is an exuberance of painting and the gainful employment of the advanced Harappan technology. Unusually, rather unnecessarily, there is a thick, heavy, and yet very attractive ware that is oily to the touch and glossy in appearance. The classic Indus types and designs summarily disappear, and only utilitarian pots having roots in Pre-Indus times survive. The surface is generally dressed with a slip which ranges in color from subdued plum-red to purple, or from glowing buff to bright orange. Further, all forms undergo a phenomenal evolution. As a rule, the rim tends to be markedly thick, so as to become collared, beaded, squared, or ellipsoid. At times, it tends to be outturned, horizontally splayed-out, or to develop a molded profile. It occasionally has a deep undercut. Certain dishes-on-stand develop a drooping rim with an outward curve. Among other characteristics are the wide use of incised patterns and the roughening of the lower body in certain pots (Bisht 1976a: 17, 21; in press: 7–8). In addition, Cemetery H pottery, or its inspired forms, designs or features have also been noted at Banawali and elsewhere (Bisht 1976a: 21; Deshpande 1965: 10, 11, 128–77; Suraj Bhan 1973: 259–62; 1975: 33). There is also a burnished gray ware with a somewhat coarse texture generally used for the dish-on-stand. This vessel usually has a cylindrical stem, either hollow or solid. There is also gray or blackish, as well as a red ware of crude texture, tempered with sand or chaff or both.

Thus, multiple traditions went into the making of the Banawali-Bara Ware. But its parentage probably lies in a distinct ware which is a necessary appendage to the Indus assemblage at Roopnagar and the principal ceramics of the Indus-associated Sanghol IA (Bisht 1976a: 17–21) and Alamgirpur I. It is plausibly a local version or variety of the as yet little known Pre-Indus pottery, perhaps a near cognate of the Pre-Defense Harappa Ware which shares many traits with the various contemporary Chalcolithic Cultures.

Of the antiquities, the qualitative and quantitative profusion of faience ornaments is most impressive: bangles, anklets, rings, beads and *pipal*-leaf-shaped earrings. These and beads of semiprecious stones are fine examples of skillful artistry. The faience usually has a shiny silvery coat. One wonders whether or not the production centers which might have been manufacturing for foreign markets during the Indus times diverted their goods to the home markets following the collapse of the Indus economy. The Indus script, seals, clay bangles, steatite disc beads, chert weights, and for that matter, stone blades or any other aspect of an allied lithic industry are conspicuous by their absence. Copper is not plentiful, even rare. The classic triangular "cakes" disappear, but biconvex *idlis,* longish nodules and balls of clay are plentiful.

A sound sense of the inner chronology of the Banawali-Bara Culture at Banawali and its precise relationship with the antecedent period require further fieldwork. This was left incomplete during the last excavation since its identification was only made toward the close of the campaign there. However, it is certain that in the upper levels the pottery has perceptible signs of deterioration. It loses the natural verve and warmth of surface treatment and decoration. Most of the pottery tends to be dull or clumsily purplish or blackish red in color. The fabric is heavier and thick and in many cases it is soft-fired and tends to be ochreous in look and feel. In addition there is a handmade red ware which is thick, coarse, ill-fired and tempered with sand and chaff. This is generally employed in making large basins and jars. A gritty grayish ware is also occasionally encountered.

Period III at Banawali is also identifiable with

Sanghol I B Mitathal II B and partly with Daulatpur I (Singh in press: 6–7) Bhagwanpura IA (Joshi in press: 4–6, 23; 1978: 98, 101) and Dadheri IA (Joshi in press: 12–13, 23; 1978: 99–101). The two last mentioned phases probably represent the later life of the culture when degeneration had already set in. However, the Bara Culture with which it has a strong generic relationship, has been purposefully included with Banawali III. One wants to avoid confusion, resulting from the controversy that happens of late to surround the individuality of the Bara Culture. One feels, however, that the upper half of the deposit at Bara should belong to the period presently under discussion. More or less similarly, Chandigarh which has yielded classic Indus pottery and script, as well as other traits, also contains the Banawali-Bara Ware; but its stratigraphic status is indeterminate as the deposit is reportedly a disturbed one. However, the ceramics of Period III bear strong affinity with Cemetery H pottery. Likewise, the total equippage has much to share with that of Ambkheri in the Ganges Valley in the east, the Jhukar Culture in Sind (Mackay 1943: 103–31) and Lothal B, Rangpur II C and III (Rao 1963: 22–25, 59–61, 86–120; 1973: 181–82) in Gujarat. Significantly, some of the illustrated sherds from Mohenjodaro, a few of which are certainly from the upper levels, also belong to this phase. This leaves little doubt there was a settlement there, possibly not large, which somehow escaped the notice of the excavators. Much of it may have been washed away due to the erosion over the centuries.

In conclusion, the pottery is the most diagnostic and assertive antiquity of this period. The most noticeable features of Period III are the shapes and the painted motifs which are totally different from the classic Indus ceramics. They are, curiously enough, close to Pre-Indus pots. In addition, the tendentious thickening of the ware and the rims, as well as the basal rims in preference to this, and the featureless or gently out-curved or hooked ones of the antecedent period. Broadly speaking, these characteristics, in addition to many ceramic types and painted motifs and the more or less similar socioeconomic stage of development are also generally observed in contemporary cultures widely distributed in the upper and central Ganges Valley, Central India, parts of Rajasthan, Gujarat, Saurashtra and the Deccan. Sometimes, influences trickling into the remote areas in the south and the east have also been pointed out by various scholars in different contexts. Generally, the Chalcolithic, or cognate and allied cultures, which were flourishing in the areas mentioned above are believed or have been shown to fall in the broad chronological framework of Post-Indus times.

No radiocarbon dates are available for Period III. Stratigraphically, it is Post-Indus, as indicated earlier by the findings at Sanghol (Bisht 1976a: 20, 21; in press: 7, 8) and Mitathal (Suraj Bhan 1969: 7; 1975: 17), and subsequently confirmed at Banawali. The upper limit of the period has been finally detected with its dovetailing with PGW at Bhagwanpura and Dadheri (Joshi in press: 12-13; 1978: 101). Taking into account that the total thickness of cultural debris at Banawali is two to 2.5 meters it should be well within justifiable limits to assign it a tentative time-bracket of ca. 1700-1400 B.C.

On the whole, this period witnesses an overall disintegration of cities and towns and the emergence of smaller, more nebulous settlements concentrated in fertile areas. So far neither fortified sites nor towns worth the name have come to light. The glamour of social life and flourishing trade were life ways of the past. There appears to have been a phenomenal lack of standards and a rarity of art forms and materials. It was only toward the later half of the period that it developed a new style and in plastic art as seen at Bhagwanpura. Thus, it betrays a bias in favor of a rural economy in which there is little room for large-scale and diversified industrial production. This registered a sudden fall. Further, it amply demonstrates that there should be some serious inherent weakness in the socioeconomic mechanism of the preceding period. That is why, when it broke down, the whole structure crumbled under its sheer weight and society once again relapsed in its pastoral and agricultural lifestyle.

NOTES

[1] Published in PRL ^{14}C Date List III/1975, 2 (cyclostyled).

[2] Published in PRL ^{14}C Date List I/1976, 2 (cyclostyled).

BIBLIOGRAPHY

Agrawal, D.P., 1970
Metal Technology of the Harappa Culture and its Socioeconomic Implications. *Indian Journal of the History of Science* 5 (2): 238-52.

Agrawal, D.P., 1971
The Copper Bronze Age in India. Delhi: Munshiram Manoharlal.

Agrawal, D.P., C. Margabandhu and N.C. Shekhar, 1976
Ancient Copper Working: Some new C^{14} dates. *Indian Journal of the History of Science* 11 (2): 7-8.

Agrawala, R.C., 1978
Copper Celts and an Indus Arrow-head from Kulhade-Ka-Johad. *Man and Environment* 2: 123.

Bhargava, M.L., 1964
The Geography of Rigvedic India. Lucknow: Upper India Publishing House.

Bisht, R.S., 1976a
Transformation of the Harappan Culture in Punjab with Special Reference to the Excavations at Sanghol and Chandigarh. In *Archaeological Congress and Seminar: 1972*. U.V. Singh, ed. Pp. 16-22. Kurukshetra: Kurukshetra University.

Bisht, R.S., 1976b
Banawali. Chandigarh: Public Relations Department, Government of Haryana.

Bisht, R.S., 1977
Banawali: A look back into the Pre-Indus and Indus Civilizations. Chandigarh: Special Board of Archaeology, Government of Haryana.

Bisht, R.S., 1978
Banawali: A new Harappan site in Haryana. *Man and Environment* 2: 86-88.

Bisht, R.S., in press
Harappa Culture in Punjab: A study in perspective. In *Indus Civilization: Problems and issues*. B.B. Lal and S.C. Malik, eds. Simla: Indian Institute of Advanced Study.

Casal, Jean-Marie, 1964
Fouilles d'Amri. 2 vols. Paris: Librairie C. Klincksieck.

Chakrabarti, D.K., 1978
Lapis Lazuli in Early India. *Man and Environment* 2: 51-58.

Deshpande, M.N., 1965
Comments on: The Indus Civilization: Its origins, authors, extent and chronology. In *Indian Prehistory: 1964*. V.N. Misra and M.S. Mate, eds. P. 128. Poona: Deccan College.

Deshpande, M.N., in press
The Harappan Settlements in Ganga-Yamuna Doab. In *Indus Civilization: Problems and issues*. B.B. Lal and S.C. Malik, eds. Simla: Indian Institute of Advanced Study.

Fairservis, Walter A., 1971
The Roots of Ancient India. New York: Macmillan and Co.

Hegde, K.T.M., 1969
Technical Studies in Copper Artifacts from Ahar. In *Excavations at Ahar*. H.D. Sankalia, S.B. Deo, Z.D. Ansari. Pp. 238-52. Poona: Deccan College.

Indian Archaeology: A review (IAR), 1953-54
Rupar, District Ambala. Pp. 6-7. Delhi: Archaeological Survey of India.

Indian Archaeology: A review (IAR), 1954-55
Bara and Salura, District Ambala. Pp. 9-11. Delhi Archaeological Survey of India.

Indian Archaeology: A review (IAR), 1968-69
Excavation at Sanghol, District Ludhiana. P. 25. Delhi: Archaeological Survey of India.

Indian Archaeology: A review (IAR), 1969-70
Excavation at Sanghol, District Ludhiana. Pp. 31-32. Delhi: Archaeological Survey of India.

Indian Archaeology: A review (IAR), 1970-71
Excavation at Sanghol, District Ludhiana. Pp. 30-31. Delhi: Archaeological Survey of India.

Joshi, J.P., 1978
Interlocking of Late Harappa Culture and Painted Grey Ware Culture in Light of Recent Excavations. *Man and Environment* 2: 96-101.

Joshi, J.P., in press
Overlap of Late Harappa Culture and Painted Grey Culture in Light of Recent Excavations in Haryana, Punjab and Jammu. In *Indus Civilization: Problems and issues*. B.B. Lal and S.C. Malik, eds. Simla: Indian Institute of Advanced Study.

Khan, F.A., 1965
Excavations at Kot Diji. *Pakistan Archaeology* 2: 13-85.

Lal, B.B., 1969
Fresh Light on the Indus Civilization. *Science and Culture* 35: 15-16.

Lal, B.B. and B.K. Thapar, 1967
Excavation at Kalibangan: New light on the Indus Civilization. *Cultural Forum* 9 (4): 78-88.

Mackay, E.J.H., 1943
  Chanhudaro Excavations, 1935-36. American Oriental Series 20. New Haven: American Oriental Society.
Marshall, Sir John, editor, 1931
  Mohenjodaro and the Indus Civilization. 3 vols. London: Arthur Probsthain.
Mughal, M.R., 1980
  New Archaeological Evidence from Bahawalpur. *Man and Environment* 4: 93-98.
Rao, S.R., 1963
  Excavations at Rangpur and other Explorations in Gujarat. *Ancient India* 18-19: 5-207.
Rao, S.R., 1973
  Lothal and the Indus Civilization. Bombay: Asia Publishing.
Sankalia, H.D., S.B. Deo and Z.D. Ansari, 1969
  Excavations at Ahar. Poona: Deccan College.
Sharma, Y.D., 1955-56
  Past Patterns of Living as Unfolded by Excavations at Rupar. *Lalit Kala* 1-2: 121-29.
Sharma, Y.D., 1964
  Protohistoric Remains. *Archaeological Remains, Monuments and Museums* Pp. 7-10. Delhi: Archaeological Survey of India.
Sharma, Y.D., 1971
  Comments in the Seminar on OCP and NBP. *Puratattva* 5: 21-24.
Sharma, Y.D., 1973
  The Value of Common Painted Ceramic Designs from Different Sites as a Guide to Chronology with Special Reference to the Pottery from Bara (Punjab). In *Radiocarbon and Indian Archaeology.* D.P. Agrawal and A. Ghosh, eds. Pp. 222-30. Bombay: Tata Institute of Fundamental Research.
Sharma, Y.D., 1976
  Transformation of the Harappan Culture in Punjab. In *Archaeological Congress and Seminar: 1972.* U.V. Singh, ed. Pp. 10-12. Kurukshetra: Kurukshetra University.
Singh, U.V., in press
  Late Harappan Culture as Revealed by the Excavations at Mirzapur and Daulatpur, District Kurukshetra (Haryana). In *Indus Civilization: Problems and issues.* B.B. Lal and S.C. Malik, eds. Simla: Indian Institute of Advanced Study.
Suraj Bhan, 1967
  New Light on the Ochre Colored Ware Culture. *Research Bulletin (Arts) Punjab University* 57 (3): 1-9.
Suraj Bhan, 1969
  Excavations at Mitathal (Hissar) 1968. *Journal of Haryana Studies* 1 (1): 1-15.
Suraj Bhan, 1973
  The Sequence and Spread of Prehistoric Cultures in the Upper Sarasvati Basin. In *Radiocarbon and Indian Archaeology.* D.P. Agrawal and A. Ghosh, eds. Pp. 252-63. Bombay: Tata Institute of Fundamental Research.
Suraj Bhan, 1975
  Excavations at Mitathal (1968) and Other Explorations in the Sutlej-Yamuna Divide. Kurukshetra: Kurukshetra University.
Thapar, B.K., 1965
  Comments on: The Indus Civilization: Its origins, authors, and extent and chronology. In *Indian Prehistory: 1964.* V.N. Misra and M.S. Mate, eds. Pp. 135-38. Poona: Deccan College.
Thapar, B.K., 1969
  The Pre-Harappan Pottery of Kalibangan: An appraisal of its interrelationship. In *Potteries in Ancient India.* B.P. Sinha, ed. Pp. 251-56. Patna: Patna University.
Thapar, B.K., 1975
  Kalibangan: A Harappan metropolis beyond the Indus Valley. *Expedition* 17 (2): 19-32.

R.C. AGRAWALA and VIJAY KUMAR

11. Ganeshwar-Jodhpura Culture: New Traits in Indian Archaeology

In 1972-73 the authors conducted archaeological excavations at Jodhpura (lat. 27°31′ north; long. 76°5′ east) in Tehsil Kotputli, District Jaipur, Rajasthan (IAR 1972-73, 1973-74; Kumar 1977; Agrawala and Kumar 1976). The site is located 98 kilometers from Jaipur town. Jodhpura mound is situated on the right bank of the Sabi River. The operations confirmed the stratigraphic position of unpainted Black and Red Ware which precedes Painted Gray Ware (PGW). This is also the case at Noh (District Bharatpur, Rajasthan) and Atranjikhera (District Etah, U.P.). The Jodhpura excavations produced a thick deposit of OCP. This is a painted red slipped ware with profuse incised designs on the exterior. It is stratigraphically prior to the Black and Red Ware, thus fixing the former in a well-defined horizon. Carbon samples run by the Physical Research Laboratory at Ahmedabad produced a date between 2500 and 2200 B.C. for the upper OCP levels at Jodhpura and Dr. D.P. Agrawal (Agrawal *et al.*, 1978; Agrawal and Kusumgar 1979) rightly christened it the *Jodhpura Culture* of the Pre-Harappan Period. The beginning of the OCP at Jodhpura may therefore be pushed back to about 2700-2800 B.C. It is worth noting that Jodhpura is situated barely 15 kilometers from Bairat (District Jaipur)—the old capital of Matsya Desa.

On 30 November 1977 a team of state archaeologists led by Shri R.C. Agrawala (Director, Archaeology and Museums, Jaipur, Rajasthan) examined copper material in the Sub-Treasury at Neem-ka-Thana in Sikar District of Rajasthan. The Treasury contained 60 flat copper celts from a "hoard" in the region. They measured 20 to 25 centimeters in length and can be associated with the Indus Valley complex. This was an outstanding discovery, the first of its kind not only in Rajasthan but in all of India. On further enquiries the authors and others rushed to the site near Ganeshwar (about 15 kilometers from Neem-ka-Thana) where these copper axes had been made more than four thousand years ago. OCP sherds littered the small mounds outside Ganeshwar village (lat. 37°40′ north; long. 75°51.30′ east). The site is about 250 kilometers from the Indus Valley site of Kalibangan and 160 kilometers from Bhadra, both in Ganganagar District of Rajasthan (Fig. 11.1). The distance between Jaipur and Ganeshwar is hardly 150 kilometers.

Further exploration in the vicinity of Ganeshwar required excavation of the mounds to the north of the Sanskrit School outside the village. By the beginning of 1979 these explorations and excavations became very rewarding because by then about 1000 copper objects in association with OCP had been found. These included copper arrow heads, rings, bangles, spear heads, chisels, balls, celts and the like. They are all made of copper derived from local mines. This is the first time in the history of Indian archaeology that such a rich find of prehistoric copper objects has been found at a single small site. But equally to the point is that the site is near the mines and in association with OCP from beginning to end. The thin blades, arrow heads and fish hooks are also characteristic of Indus sites and have not been found in the copper hoard sites of western Uttar Pradesh. The presence of a round terracotta cake at Ganeshwar is also important in this regard. The principal varieties of Ganeshwar

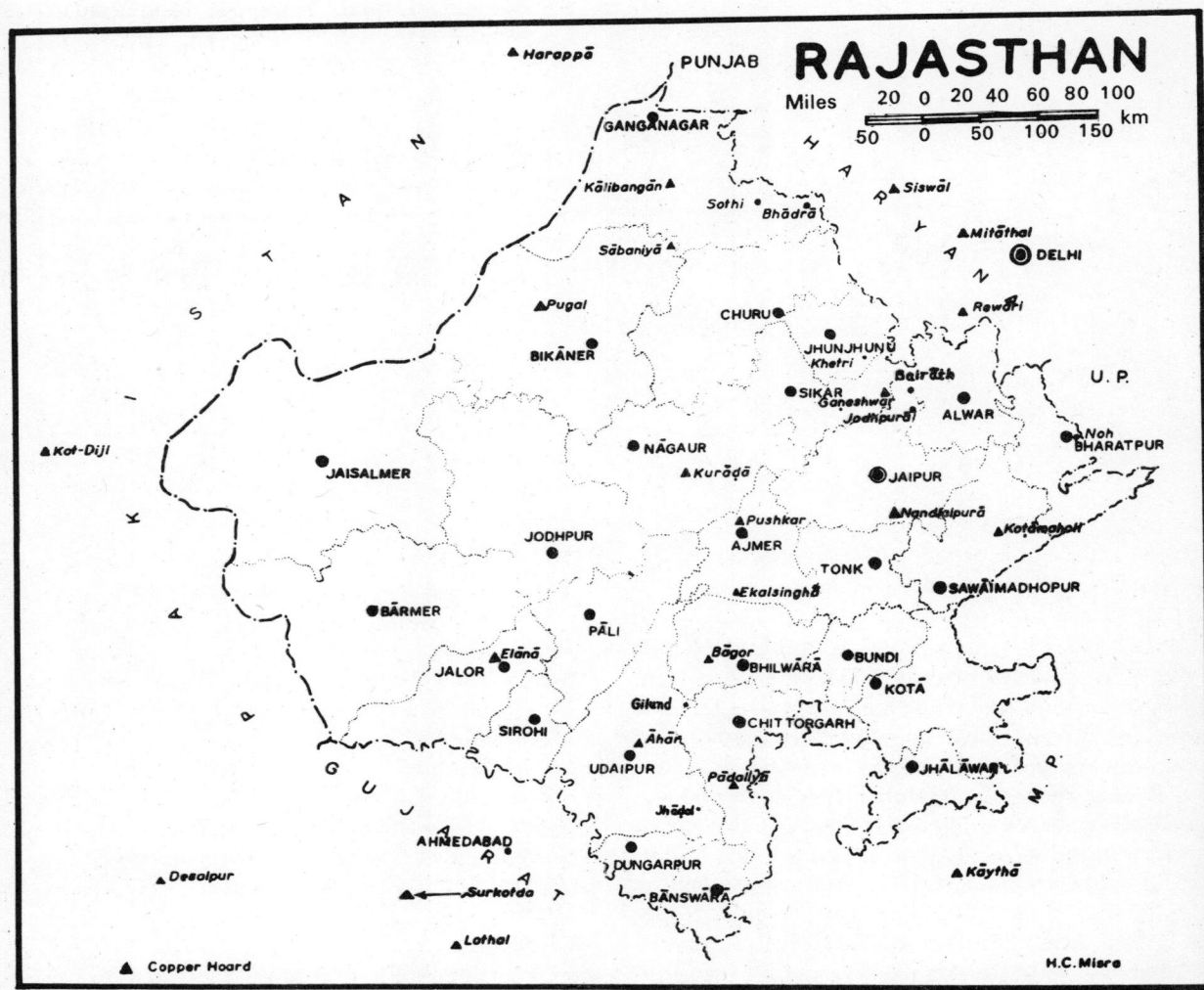

Fig. 11.1. Protohistoric copper sites in Rajasthan. Second and third millennia B.C.

copper objects are described as follows:

Arrow Heads (Pls. 11.1 and 11.2). Cut from thin copper sheets, like those of Indus sites, the Ganeshwar arrow heads are rich and varied in size and shape. Most of them are of the barbed variety. A solitary exception is a tanged specimen from the surface. These arrow heads were fixed to a wooden shaft and secured with a whitish adhesive. This can still be seen on both the sides of arrow heads along with prominent wood impressions. Arrow heads like these have been collected from distant mounds, proving that they were actually once used for hunting purposes. Most of the examples have sharp points so that they could kill birds with a single stroke. But, quite a number have a curved tip which is very unusual. They were probably meant for hunting a flock of birds. One copper arrow head of this kind was excavated from Harappan levels at Banawali,[1] Haryana (Fig. 11.2). None of the copper arrow heads from Ganeshwar has a perforation for hafting. But contemporary arrow heads from Bagor (Fig. 11.3) (District Bhilwara, Rajasthan) were provided with two holes each (Misra 1970). This allowed them to be fixed to the wooden shaft with the help of a thin wire. The Ganeshwar variety of copper arrow head (without holes) was found in negligible numbers at

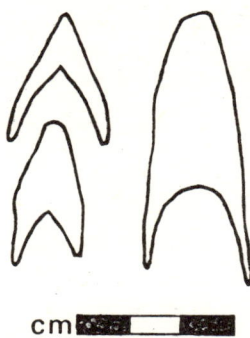

Fig. 11.2. Arrow heads from Banawali (Rajasthan). The larger example resembles those from Ganeshwar.

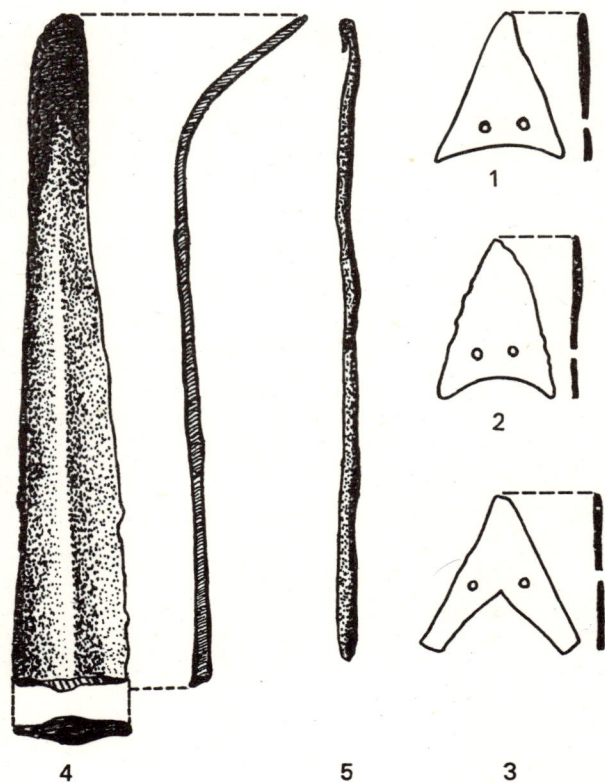

Fig. 11.3. Copper objects from Bagor (Rajasthan). Period II (2800–2000 B.C.).

Kalibangan, Lothal, Harappa, Mohenjodaro and Chanhudaro (Marshall 1931: Pl. CXLII, no. 13; Mackay 1938: Pls. CXXI, CXXVII, CXXXIII; Vats 1940: 383-84, Pl. CXXV, nos. 13-14). There are approximately 400 arrow heads of this style from Ganeshwar alone. This suggests that it was a local product and not one inspired by examples from the west. In fact, major sites like Mohenjodaro and Harappa have produced not more than twenty arrow heads each. But then, hunting may not have been an important activity in these urban settings—a fact which highlights the importance of the Ganeshwar finds.

The discovery of microliths with copper arrow heads at Ganeshwar suggests that the people of Ganeshwar, though they had developed a metallurgical technology, were still in a hunting stage. With rich copper mines nearby, they were able to exploit and successfully work this local resource as early as the third millennium B.C. But, even with this technology the OCP-using people at Ganeshwar were still hunting with the help of their many varieties of arrow heads (Pls. 11.1 and 11.2). The shapes of Indus arrow heads bear a close affinity to those from Ganeshwar. Artistically, some of the shapes of Ganeshwar arrow heads are unique (Pl. 11.2). They range in size from five to 6.5 centimeters in length. Comparable types have yet to be reported from areas west of the Indus Valley.

Copper arrow heads from Ganeshwar were analyzed by Dr. K.K. Tripathi of the Geological Survey of India, Jaipur. His results are as follows: copper 96.5 percent, silver 0.3 percent, arsenic 1 percent, lead 0.03 percent, tin 0.2 percent, nickel 0.04 percent, zinc 0.25 percent, iron 0.2 percent.

Spear Heads (Pl. 11.3). The Ganeshwar copper spear heads are generally very thin. There are, however, a few thick examples. Comparable objects were also found at Harappa and Mohenjodaro. They were attached to wooden shafts before actual use.

Fish Hooks (Pl. 11.4). The Ganeshwar copper fish hooks, numbering about 50, are usually not provided with a tang. A few years ago one example of a similar fish hook was recovered from the microlithic site Budha Pushkar in Ajmer District of Rajasthan by Mrs. Bridget Allchin (Allchin, Goudie and Hegde 1978: 143, Fig. 10.2). These fish hooks were also found at Harappa and Mohenjodaro in the early levels (Mackay 1938: Pls. CXXXII, no. 21 and CXXIV, no. 29; Vats 1940: CXXV, no. 28). Similar fish hooks were recovered from Banawali as well.

Shri J.P. Joshi, Director of Explorations and Excavations, Archaeological Survey of India in New Delhi has very kindly informed us of the discovery of copper arrow heads in the Pre-Harappan levels, and fish hooks in the Harappan levels, at Kalibangan. As noted, this site is about 250 kilometers from Ganeshwar (Fig. 11.1) and linked to it via the Kantali River which has its source near Ganeshwar. This river once joined the Drishadvati somewhere near Nohar-Sothi-Bhadra in Ganganagar District of Rajasthan. Thus, the copper objects from Kalibangan, 1200 in number, seem to have been manufactured and supplied by the people of the Ganeshwar-Khetri region. The Khetri copper mines are hardly 60 kilometers from Ganeshwar.

This proves beyond doubt that copper technology was well developed during the Pre-Harappan Period in the Ganeshwar-Khetri area as early as 2700 B.C. This is a date not far removed in time from Bagor (2800-2000 B.C.), a site that has yielded several copper objects, including the three arrow heads noted above. Viewed in this light, it is clear that the OCP-using people at Ganeshwar had evolved a full fledged copper technology by the third millennium B.C.

The copper objects from Ganeshwar were neither the products of Harappan refugees nor those of wandering itinerants. Exploitation of the nearby copper mines (smelting, casting, etc.) could not have been done by outsiders. It was the arduous job of those who lived in the region to explore the local mines. They also perfected their copper technology. The Indus people undoubtedly received copper and finished objects from the Ganeshwar region. Copper ingots were also sent to be made use of according to daily needs and requirements. Thus, most of the copper and copper artifacts for neighboring places in Pakistan, Punjab and Haryana was supplied from the Sikar-Jhunjhunu Districts of Rajasthan. Other sources of Harappan copper in the west cannot, of course, be denied.

Spiral-headed Pins. Ganeshwar also yielded a few fragmentary pins which were characteristic of Harappan Culture.

Celts (Pls. 11.5 and 11.6). The copper celts from Ganeshwar contain only a nominal quantity of tin as shown by the following details furnished by the Chemical Laboratory of the Geological Survey of India at Jaipur:

1) Copper	97%
2) Silver	0.2%
3) Arsenic	0.3%
4) Lead	1%
5) Tin	0.1%
6) Nickel	0.6%
7) Zinc	0.1%

The average weight of a Ganeshwar celt is approximately one to 1.5 kilograms. All these flat celts were prepared from molds by the *cireperdu* technique. The butt portion of the celts have round indentations in groups of four, five, six, eight, nine, 12 and as many as 15 in different combinations of one, two, three, four and six dots (Pls. 11.5 and 11.6). The varied permutations and combinations of dots recall somewhat similar marks on the Chalcolithic celts from Navdatoli (Wheeler 1959: Pl. 25) and Kayatha (Ansari and Dhavalikar 1975: 150). At Kayatha these celts were assigned a date of 2000–1800 B.C. by ^{14}C determinations. There was also incised pottery from these levels—a point of some significance which will be noted later. Copper celts with circular impressions also come from copper hoard sites in western Uttar Pradesh (Thaplyal and Shukla 1976). But there is no doubt that the Ganeshwar celts are the most numerous of this kind, suggesting that the parallel types at other sites were supplied from this part of Rajasthan. The name of a small village Kulhade-ka-Johad (Pond of Axes) near Ganeshwar bears testimony to the survival of a tradition of axe (*kulhada*) manufacture in this region. The indentations on these objects were made with pointed copper drills which have been found at Ganeshwar (Pl. 11.7).

ROUTES OF COMMUNICATION

There are rich copper mines at Dariba, Ahirwala, Baleshwar, Chiplata, Behar, Mothooka; all of which are in the vicinity of Ganeshwar. It will be recalled that the Kantali River has its source in this same area and that it once seems to have joined the ancient Drishadvati River near Nohar-Bhadra in the north. The Dohan River originated to the north of the Baleshwar copper mines in Neem-ka-Thana Tehsil, and Dr. Suraj Bhan (1972, 1973, 1975) discovered a number of protohistoric sites on this river in Haryana. There is a third river, the Kasaunti, (Krishnavati) also originating from the nearby Baleshwar-Dariba copper hills. Besides this, the Sota River, a tributary of the Sabi, takes its origin southeast of the Ahirwala-Dariba copper mines. It was via these rivers and streams that the ancient copper tools prepared in the Sikar region of Rajasthan seem to have been taken to different places in Haryana, Punjab and Uttar Pradesh. There is also a land route from Ganeshwar to Sothi-Bhadra (Fig. 11.1) via Neem-ka-Thana, Khetri, Chirawa and Rajgarh. Similarly, both Hissar and Bhiwani were connected with Rajgarh by road. Travel to these places in days gone by could be via both the land-river routes cited above. The site of Mitathal (near Bhiwani, Haryana) is not very far from Ganeshwar and has already yielded interesting copper objects. These include a celt, a chopper type *parasu*, rings, even a harpoon. Two long, heavy copper bar-celts, reported by Rewari and preserved in the Gurukul Museum at Jhajjar, bear close resemblance in size and shape, to the six specimens acquired in 1973 from Nandlalpura (near Chaksu, Jaipur District) by the Rajasthan State Department of Archaeology and Museums, Jaipur.

The availability of copper in the Sikar-Jhunjhunu area was responsible for the presence of ancient sites. These are very near the copper sources. We should not suggest that crude copper ores were carried to far off places. The discovery of a rich hoard of 60 copper celts (50 acquired by the State Department of Archaeology and Museums and two by the Geological Survey of India, Jaipur) at Ganeshwar proves beyond doubt that finished goods were prepared near Ganeshwar, wherefrom they were supplied to different places. The existence of a number of hot and cold water springs, around the Ganeshwar, Dariba, Baleshwar, Ahirwala, Chiplata copper mines, all the more suggests the suitability of the area for both habitation and operational purposes, including the extraction of copper ores, smelting and metal casting.

Ganeshwar falls on the most direct, shortest route connecting Delhi-Indraprastha with the Pre-Harappan site of Kot Diji. This route goes via Rewari, Narnaul, Neem-ka-Thana, Parbatsar-Kurada (incorrectly called Khurdi), Nagaur, Phalodi, Pokaran, Jaisalmer, Ghotaru, Mithrau, Sangrar, Alor, Sukhar Rohri, Khairpur and then Kot Diji. The road distance between Jaisalmer and Kot Diji is about 300 kilometers; the latter is, of course, not far from Mohenjodaro. Jaisalmer is well connected with Hyderabad (Sind), via Mirpur Khas as late as the British Period. Harappa is similarly easy to reach from Kalibangan through the Ghaggar (Hakra) and Sutlej Valleys. Kalibangan is approximately 250 kilometers from Ganeshwar. The Sikar-Jhunjhunu copper deposits of the Khetri belt were thus in easy reach for the Indus population, from both Harappa and Mohenjodaro. Sir John Marshall has rightly stated that: "Other stones in use both at Mohenjodaro and Harappa were the fine grained yellow Jaisalmer stone, all three of them almost certainly came from Rajputana" (Marshall 1931: 31). That was possible only through trade. Impurity patterns in the Khetri copper ores when compared to those of Harappan copper-bronze artifacts, have led scholars like M.S. Vats and D.P. Agrawal (1971: 175) to the conclusion that "the Khetri-Rajputana mines are not only nearest of all to Harappa and Mohenjodaro, but also fulfill the test for key elements: i.e. nickle and arsenic" (Vats 1940: 379).[2] It is very likely, therefore, that these mines supplied the bulk of the metal, and even copper objects, to the Indus Valley sites.

The Ganeshwar copper finds (Agrawala 1978a, 1978b, 1979a, 1979b) also help in the proper assessment of so-called Khurdi hoard from Nagaur District of Rajasthan. The correct name for the find spot of 103 copper objects is "Kurada," which is located not very far from the Budha Pushkar site referred to above. This unique copper hoard from Rajasthan was originally made up of seven flat celts, 11 chisels, 21 curved blades of Ahar-Mitathal type, 55 rings, four plain copper bowls and five channel-spouted bowls. Of these only one celt, one chisel, one plain bowl, one channel-spouted bowl and two rings (10 objects in all) are preserved in the Government Museum at Jodhpur (Rajasthan). The curved blades, cut from thin copper sheets, were used as delicate choppers, similar to those excavated by R.C. Agrawala at Ahar (District Udaipur, Rajasthan) and by Suraj Bhan at Mitathal (District Bhiwani, Haryana). They can be dated to the second millennium B.C. What the Kalibangan excavators have described as an indeterminate curved blade, from the Pre-Harappan levels (Thapar 1975) seems to have originally been a copper chopper.[3] A close examination of the Kurada celt has brought to light the existence of four indentations, three in a single line and one below. This recalls Ganeshwar celts. The channel-spouted bowls from Kurada, prepared from thin copper sheets, recall a vessel in metal from Iran (Mughal 1972: 143, fn. 37; Hakemi 1972). This may suggest that these vessels were made for western demand.

OCP

The OCP (Pls. 11.8 through 11.11) from Ganeshwar and Jodhpura is identical in shapes and designs. The term OCP is now a misnomer; it is in fact red slipped painted pottery with profuse linear designs, executed with the help of a sharp, short, comb-like instrument. This was used to make horizontal oblique grooves, latticed designs and the like, on the exterior of vessels. This can also be seen on some of the Pre-Harappan fabrics at Kalibangan I, Sothi, Siswal, Bara and several sites in the Punjab, Haryana and western Uttar Pradesh. As many as eight thermoluminescence dates ranging between 2650 B.C. and 1180 B.C. (three prior to 2000 B.C., three between 2000-1500 B.C. and 1500 B.C. and two between 1500 B.C. and 1180 B.C.) are available for this ceramic. Thus, the copper hoards of Uttar Pradesh have a central date of 2000-1500 B.C. as rightly suggested by Thapar (1973), Gaur (1971-72, 1973) and others.[4]

It appears that this particular pottery had its origin in the Sikar-Jaipur regions of Rajasthan where two carbon dates for the upper OCP levels assign it to a period as early as 2500-2200 B.C., as already noted above. OCP traits moved from this part of Rajasthan to western Uttar Pradesh through the River Sabi, its tributaries, which were well connected with the Yamuna in days gone by. The incised and painted pottery in this part of Rajasthan, being early in date, is closely associated with Pre-Harappan and Harappan type copper objects. The typical copper harpoon, anthropomorphic figure and copper sword, so characteristic of the Copper Hoard Culture of western Uttar Pradesh, was a later development, consequent to the movement of the OCP people to the northeast from the Jodhpura-Ganeshwar region. It is therefore hardly possible to agree with the scholars who suggest that OCP is an extension of the central *Doab* complex through Sota and Sabi, the tributaries of Yamuna (Dikshit 1979). The crucial site of Ganeshwar, so abundant in OCP and copper artifacts, is situated just at the source of the Kantali River. It is thus absolutely wrong to think that OCP is absent in the Kantali Valley.

Our explorations in 1979 along this river even brought to light a Painted Gray Ware and Black and Red Ware site. This is on the right bank of Kantali itself, at Sonari-Jodhpur (District Jhunjhunu), about 25 kilometers from Ganeshwar. Further explorations are likely to throw more light on the problem. It appears that Painted Gray Ware penetrated as far as Sonari-Jodhpur through the upward course of the Dohan River, the source of which is not very far from the newly discovered site of Sonari-Jodhpur. The River Dohan itself is a part of the Sabi, Sota and Kasanti complex. The Dohan was joined by the Nai River from the north and one branch of the Drishadvati from the south. All these eventually fell into the Najafgarh Lake, which some scholars are tempted to identify with the Arvavat Sea of Vedic literature or the Dvaitavana Lake of the *Satapatha Brahmana* (Bhargava 1964: 13-14, 26-27, 47-51). These rivers played a great role in the diffusion and transformation of protohistoric cultures in Rajasthan, Haryana and western Uttar Pradesh, during the second and third millennia B.C.

It is also clear from the above that the authors of OCP did not belong to the same stock as the Pre-Harappan or Harappan people in the Indus Valley. Rather, they seem to have been a people indigenous to the Ganeshwar-Khetri region of Rajasthan. They were essentially experts in copper technology and supplied surplus copper objects to the east and west. This took place at a stage when there was substantial water in the Rivers Sabi, Sota, Kasaunti, Dohan and Kantali, all originating from the Sikar-Jhunjhunu Districts of Rajasthan.

Viewed in this light, the excavations and explorations at Ganeshwar have added a new horizon to Pre-Harappan copper technology. This can be dated to the period 2800-2000 B.C. There should now be no hesitation in calling it the "Ganeshwar-Jodhpura Culture." It is absolutely wrong to suggest that the Pre-Harappan Cultures were poor in metals. The richness of copper objects, both from Kalibangan and Ganeshwar, is quite evident. And, Ganeshwar was not likely to have been the only copper site of its type in the Khetri belt. There might have been many more such centers specializing in the manufacture of copper tools, pots and pans during the Pre-Harappan, Harappan and subsequent periods.

In addition to the unique copper-producing center of Ganeshwar there are many more protohistoric sites in Rajasthan. The state is thus a part of the Copper Map (Lal 1951: 21) of India (Fig. 11.1).

1) Pind Padliya, District Chittor

Six copper celts of Ganeshwar type were discovered in 1978 and acquired for the State Directorate of Archaeology and Museums, Jaipur. This Ahar Culture site is situated not far from the copper deposits of Bhinder and Bhadesara (Agrawala 1979a). Long celts of this kind are unusual in the Ahar complex.

2) Ahar, District Udaipur

The copper objects include flat celts of the short,

very light variety as discussed by H.D. Sankalia, S.B. Deo, and Z.D. Ansari (1969: 199-203). Earlier excavations by R.C. Agrawala at the site brought to light a thin knife blade in the lowest levels, dated to about 2100 B.C. There were also two copper choppers of the Mitathal type. The copper mines of Matoon and Umara, hardly 12 kilometers from the site, might have been tapped by the Aharians.

3) Bagor, District Bhilwara

Period II (2800-2000 B.C.) produced three barbed copper arrow heads with holes, a spear, an awl, etc., from a grave. The famous Pur-Dariba copper mines are at a stone's throw from Bagor.

4) Jhadol, District Udaipur (near Jai Samand Lake)

Vestiges of copper, in association with Ahar pottery, were discovered here with the assistance of Sri R.K. Biswas, G.S.I., Jaipur. The State Department of Archaeology further discovered contemporary sites at Bespura and Utpuria on the bank of a rivulet named the Tidi. This is a tributary of the River Gomti which falls into the River Som on the border of Dungarpur District in southern Rajasthan. There are two Ahar sites here (Karelia and Aspura) which were discovered by the Custodian, Ahar Museum in November 1979. This proves that the Ahar Culture had an extension to the Gomti and Soma belts to the south of Udaipur. This widens the horizon of Ahar Culture for the first time.

5) Kurada, District Nagaur

Incorrectly spelled "Kurdi" this unique copper hoard originally consisting of 103 objects enumerated above. Channel-spouted copper bowls from this place are quite unique in the realm of Indian archaeology.

6) Kalibangan, District Ganganagar

The Archaeological Survey of India recovered about 50 copper objects from the Pre-Harappan levels. More than 1200 copper specimens came from the Mature Harappan levels. This was kindly communicated by Sri J.P. Joshi on behalf of the Director General of Archaeological Survey of India. This also bears testimony to a flourishing copper industry in Rajasthan during the third millennium B.C. (see Pl. 11.12).

7) Sabania, District Bikaner

Two long copper celts from this site, with Indus script, are now preserved in the Gurukul Museum at Jhajjar (Haryana). Sabania is not very far from Kalibangan.

8) Pugal, District Bikaner

In 1979 Dr. Das Sharma of G.S.I. Jaipur discovered microliths and some fragments of copper arrow heads at Pugal. This was on the trade route to Bahawalpur (Pakistan) during historic times.

9) Nandlalpura, near Chaksu, District Jaipur

Six heavy bar celts, about 28 centimeters long, unlike those from the copper hoard of the Ganga-Yamuna *Doab,* were acquired at Nandlalpura in 1973. Two of the specimens from the Rewari-Narnaul area (on the border of Ganeshwar) are preserved in the Gurukul Museum at Jhajjar (Agrawala 1979a). These heavy bar celts, with both ends sharpened, seem to have been prepared for extracting ores, though no such tools have been discovered at Ganeshwar so far.

10) Elana, District Jalore

One copper flat celt was discovered in 1978 in a field outside the village of Elana (Agrawala 1979a), which is situated on the bank of the Jawai River. This is a tributary of River Luni, which, originating from the Pushkar-Ajmer area, falls into the Rann of Kutch. There are a number of Indus sites in Kutch.

11) Budha Pushkar, District Ajmer

An Indus type fish hook without a tang, and bearing a close resemblance to the Ganeshwar specimens was reported here by Mrs. Allchin a few years back.

12) Ekalasimgha, District Ajmer

In January 1979, a heavy bar celt was found in a field and acquired for the Directorate of Archaeology and Museums, Rajasthan, Jaipur. The site is only a few miles away from Barli River and the Khari (a tributary to the Banas) on the border of Bhilwara District. The unusual, heavy bar celt may belong to the Ahar complex.

13) Kota-Maholi, District Sawai Madhopur

The State Department of Archaeology and Museums recently acquired (September 1979) eight copper celts reported to be from Kota-Maholi Village, about 16 kilometers from Karauli town. They are a light variety and appear to have been used as agricultural implements like the modern *khurpis.* The site, when examined by the authors, yielded microliths as well. Kota-Maholi is not far from the Chambal River.

DISCUSSION

No copper harpoons, anthropomorphic figures or swords typical of the Copper Hoard Culture of the Ganga-Yamuna *Doab* have been reported from any part of Rajasthan. But the major copper deposits in the Ganeshwar-Khetri area suggest that even these second millennium objects may have been made in Rajasthan. The Aharians of course exploited the local ores of Udaipur-Bhilwara Districts, where a number of copper mines have been located. These are near Ahar Culture sites. It is, therefore, not plausible to suggest that Khetri copper ores were used to make Ahar artifacts. As late as 1951 Rajasthan was considered to be a blank with respect to protohistoric copper artifacts. But today we know that it played a great role in copper technology during the second and third millennia B.C.

ACKNOWLEDGMENTS

The authors are extremely thankful to Messrs. Harish Chandra Misra, Vijaya Kumar and M.S. Khangrot for assistance in the field, drawings and photography. The photographs have been kindly supplied by the Director, Archaeology and Museums, Rajasthan, Jaipur and are copyright of the Department. Grateful thanks are also due to Sri J.P. Joshi, Director, Archaeological Survey of India, New Delhi for furnishing the very important and valuable data on the copper objects from Kalibangan, Rajasthan. The Geological Survey of India Laboratory at Jaipur and P.R.L. Ahmedabad very kindly analyzed the Ganeshwar copper celt and Jodhpura charcoal for ^{14}C data respectively.

NOTES

Mr. R.C. Agrawala and Mr. Vijay Kumar were not participants in the Srinagar Conference. Their work on Ganeshwar-Jodhpura Culture is so important however, that this paper was solicited.

[1]The Banawali arrow heads from Harappan levels were examined by R.C. Agrawala in the office of the Director of Archaeology and Museums, Haryana, Chandigarh with the kind courtesy of the Director, Shri O.P. Bharadwaj, I.A.S., and Shri Saran, Deputy Director. The specimen with a curved top has not yet been published. Ganeshwar has, of course, yielded several copper arrow heads of this variety, suggesting links with the Indus complex.

[2]Dr. Agrawal has recently traced arsenic alloying in the copper hoards from Uttar Pradesh as well (Agrawal 1974).

[3]The important comparison between the Kalibangan chopper with the Khurdi (?), Mitathal, and Ahar specimens was first made by the senior author in his 1977 paper presented at the symposium titled "Indus Civilization: Problems and Issues" held in Simla at the Indian Institute of Advanced Study. The Khurdi example is illustrated in Ghosh (1961: 12, Pl. IIIB). Sankalia (1962: 82, Fig. 10) illustrates the channel-spouted copper bowl which is conspicuous by its absence from other Indian sites.

[4]For incised pottery at Sothi, Bara and other sites see Ghosh (1965). Y.D. Sharma covers the Bara Wares (1976). Editor's note: see also Y.D. Sharma's paper in this volume for illustrations of the wares in question.

BIBLIOGRAPHY

Agrawal, D.P., 1971
The Copper Bronze Age in India. Delhi: Munshiram Manoharlal.

Agrawal, D.P., 1974
Alloying in the Copper Hoards. *Bulletin of Museums and Archaeology in Uttar Pradesh* 14: 13-18.

Agrawal, D.P. and S. Kusumgar, 1979
Radiocarbon Chronology of Indian Proto-historic Cultures. In *Essays in Indian Protohistory*, D.P. Agrawal and D.K. Chakrabarti, eds. Pp. 371-86. Delhi: B.R. Publishing Corp.

Agrawal, D.P. et al., 1978
Chronology of Indian Prehistory from the Mesolithic to the Iron Age. *Journal of Human Evolution* 7: 37-44.

Agrawala, R.C., 1978a
Archaeological Discoveries at Ganeshwar, Rajasthan. *Archaeological Studies* 3: 72-75.

Agrawala, R.C., 1978b
Copper Celts and an Indus Arrow Head from Kulhade-Ka-Johad, District Sikar, Rajasthan. *Man and Environment* 2: 123-24.

Agrawala, R.C., 1979a
More Copper Finds from Rajasthan. *Man and Environment* 3: 91-92.

Agrawala, R.C., 1979b
Three Copper Objects From Ganeshwar, Rajasthan. *Journal of the Oriental Institute, University of Baroda* 28 (3-4): 159-60.

Agrawala, R.C. and V. Kumar, 1976
The Problem of PGW and Iron in Northeastern Rajasthan. In *Mahabharata: Myth and reality*. S.P. Gupta and K.S. Ramachandran, eds. Pp. 241-44. Delhi: B.R. Publishing Corp.

Allchin, B., A. Goudie and K.T.M. Hegde, 1978
The Prehistory and Palaeography of the Great Indian Desert. New York: Academic Press.

Ansari, Z.D. and M.K. Dhavalikar, 1975
Excavations at Kayatha. Poona: Deccan College.

Bhargava, Manohar Lal, 1964
The Geography of Rigvedic India. Lucknow: Upper India Publishing House.

Dikshit, K.N., 1979
Late Harappan Cultures in India. In *Essays in Indian Protohistory*. D.P. Agrawal and D.K. Chakrabarti, eds. Pp. 123-33. Delhi: B.R. Publishing Corp.

Gaur, R.C., 1971-72
Comments on the Symposium on OCP and NBP. *Puratattva* 5: 10-12.

Gaur, R.C., 1973
Lal Qila Excavations and the OCP Problem. In *Radiocarbon and Indian Archaeology*. D.P. Agrawal and A. Ghosh, eds. Pp. 154-62. Bombay: Tata Institute of Fundamental Research.

Gaur, R.C., 1974
The Ochre Colored Pottery: An assessment of the evidence. In *South Asian Archaeology, 1973*. J.E. van Lohuizen-de Leeuw and J.J.M. Ubaghs, eds. Pp. 53-62. Leiden: E.J. Brill.

Ghosh, A., 1961
Handbook to the Centenary: Exhibition of the Archaeological Survey of India. Delhi: Archaeological Survey of India.

Ghosh, A., 1965
The Indus Civilization: Its origins, authors, extent and chronology. In *Indian Prehistory: 1964*. V.N. Misra and M.S. Mate, eds. Pp. 113-24. Poona: Deccan College.

Hakemi, A., 1972
Catalogue de L'Exposition: Lut, xabis (Shahdad). *Premier Symposium Annuel de la Recherche Archaeologique en Iran*. Tehran: Department of Archaeology.

Indian Archaeology: A review (IAR), 1972-73
Excavation at Jodhpura, District Jaipur. Pp. 29-30. Delhi: Archaeological Survey of India.

Indian Archaeology: A review (IAR), 1973-74
Exploration in Districts Jaipur and Sikar. Pp. 23-24. Delhi: Archaeological Survey of India.

Kumar, V., 1977
Excavations at Jodhpura. *Journal of the Rajasthan Institute of Historical Research* 15 (1): 28-33.

Lal, B.B., 1951
Further Copper Hoards from the Gangetic Basin and a Review of the Problem. *Ancient India* 7: 20-39.

Mackay, E.J.H., 1938
Further Excavations at Mohenjodaro. 2 vols. Delhi: Government of India.

Marshall, Sir John, editor, 1931
Mohenjodaro and the Indus Civilization. 3 vols. London: Arthur Probsthain.

Misra, V.N., 1970
> Cultural Significance of Three Copper Arrow Heads from Rajasthan. *Journal of Near Eastern Studies* 29 (4): 221-32.

Misra, V.N., 1973
> A New Prehistoric Ceramic from Rajasthan. *East and West* 23 (3-4): 295-305.

Mughal, M.R., 1972
> Explorations in Northern Baluchistan. *Pakistan Archaeology* 8: 137-58.

Sankalia, H.D., 1962
> *Indian Archaeology Today*. Bombay: Asia Publishing.

Sankalia, H.D., S.B. Deo and Z.D. Ansari, 1969
> *Excavations at Ahar*. Poona: Deccan College.

Sharma, Y.D., 1976
> Transformation of Harappan Culture in Punjab. In *Archaeological Congress and Seminar Papers, 1972*. U.V. Singh, ed. Pp. 5-15. Kurukshetra: Kurukshetra University.

Suraj Bhan, 1972
> Changes in the Course of the Yamuna and Their Bearing on the Protohistoric Cultures of Haryana. In *Archaeological Congress and Seminar Papers*. S.B. Deo, ed. Pp. 125-28. Nagpur: Nagpur University.

Suraj Bhan, 1973
> The Sequence and Spread of Prehistoric Cultures in the Upper Sarasvati Basin. In *Radiocarbon and Indian Archaeology*. D.P. Agrawal and A. Ghosh, eds. Pp. 252-63. Bombay: Tata Institute of Fundamental Research.

Suraj Bhan, 1975
> *Excavations at Mitathal*. Kurukshetra: Kurukshetra University.

Thapar, B.K., 1973
> Recent Excavations in India. In *Indologen-Tagung, 1971*. H. Hartel and V. Moellor, eds. Pp. 23-46. Weisbaden: Franz Steiner Verlag GBMH.

Thapar, B.K., 1975
> Kalibangan: An Harappan metropolis beyond the Indus Valley. *Expedition* 17(2): 19-32.

Thaplyal, K.K. and S.P. Shukla, 1976
> Copper Celts with Circular Depressions: Some observations. In *Archaeological Congress and Seminar Papers, 1972*. U.V. Singh, ed. Pp. 98-100. Kurukshetra: Kurukshetra University.

Vats, M.S., 1940
> *Excavations at Harappa*. 2 vols. Delhi: Government of India.

Wheeler, Sir Mortimer, 1959
> *Early India and Pakistan to Ashoka*. London: Thames and Hudson.

B.P. SINHA

12. Harappan Fallout (?) in the Mid-Gangetic Valley

ALAMGIRPUR, Bara, Hulas, Ambkheri and the like are, as far as one knows, the easternmost extension of the Harappan Culture. G.R. Sharma's (1960) claim that the earliest level of Kausambi has rudiments of Harappan burnt brick fortification revements and other elements of architecture, has been strongly controverted, most convincingly by Ghosh (1973) and Lal (in this volume). But even Lal concedes that after the fall of the Harappan urban civilization, the communities dispersed in different directions and some of the common non-urban traits appear to have infiltrated into, and mixed with, the cultural traditions of various communities. Post-Harappan Cultures even in the Punjab, Haryana and western Uttar Pradesh, lack characteristic Harappan features like towns with elaborate planning, drainage and road systems, writing, varied designs in black on red pottery, burnt brick structures, bronze vessels and terracotta cakes.

It would be strange if the entire Harappan gamut, after blazing a luminous tail, completely disappeared as a meteor, leaving no trace behind. For example, it has been observed that many Harappan religious traits, though apparently not found in early Vedic traditions, can in many ways be seen as precursors of later Hinduism. While sophisticated, specialized urban features could not be adopted or adapted by succeeding village communities with lesser skills and poorer resources, some ceramic types and other features not distinctly urban could percolate into regions even far removed from distant Harappan settlements. This may have been via roaming potters selling their wares, and incidentally their ideas. This may be seen in later Chalcolithic Cultures at places like Rangpur, Navadatoli, Jorwe, Siswal and Mitathal with some close, and some distant, affinities with the Harappan ceramic tradition. This is evidenced most clearly in pottery forms and the technique of painting in black on red.

The central and eastern Gangetic Valley has so far been treated as free of even indirect Late Harappan influence or affinity (Dikshit 1979). In this short paper I want to draw the attention of scholars to the possibility of Harappan fallouts in the Mid-Gangetic Valley. Chirand, situated on the northern bank of the Ganges in Saran District of North Bihar, has yielded remains of a Neolithic Culture, provisionally dated to 2500-1500 B.C. (Sankalia 1974: 304). Following the Neolithic without a break is a rich Chalcolithic Culture with the characteristic Black and Red Ware and pottery painted white in the Ahar tradition. Copper is associated with these levels. Iron appears in a later phase of the culture; but NBP Ware is absent. Chalcolithic Chirand has a rich ceramic assemblage in which the dish-on-stand is a prominent type. The exact purpose of this form is not clear; although some have taken it to have been a fruit stand. One cannot be certain of any connection with religion or ritual. However, the Harappan perforated dish, not found at Chirand, could have had a ritual association, and the term "offering stand" may be a reasonable one. The bowl-on-stand or dish-on-stand may have been a table ware, or a drawingroom ware for more well-to-do people.

The dish-on-stand is a characteristic, if not diagnostic, Harappan form. As S. Piggott has observed:

"The presence of sherds of this type of vessel on a site marks the presence of the Harappan Civilization *as surely* as 'Samian' pottery betokens Roman occupation in Europe" (1950: 193; my emphasis). It is true that the dish-on-stand has been found in Pre- (or Early) Harappan Kalibangan I and in the same contexts at Amri and Kot Diji. But, it has also come from the deepest, earliest trenches at Mohenjodaro which could be earlier than Kalibangan I. After all, it has been suggested that the Harappans spread north and south from Mohenjodaro in Sind while in search of cultivable flood plain. They may even have gone to Harappa, Kalibangan and Lothal. Anyway, the fact that many Kalibangan I features are similar to those of the Mature Harappan leaves open the possibility of contact between Mohenjodaro and this settlement. The earliest ^{14}C date for Kalibangan I is TF-155, 2370±120 B.C. (Agrawal and Kusumgar 1974: 88) which is clearly later than the lowest levels of Mohenjodaro; even though there are not yet radiocarbon determinations available from these strata. The point to be made is that none of this controverts the view that this form is a distinctive type of Harappan pottery (Manchanda 1972: 6). The dish-on-stand has been found in Fabric C of Kalibangan I. This ware is thought to be close to the Mature Harappan fabric (Lal 1979: 72 and 73 Fig. 3, nos. 4-5) and so is late in Kalibangan I. This point is not even weakened by the presence of the dish-on-stand at Amri or Kot Diji. It is significant that it has not come from either Amri IA, the lower levels of Kot Diji, or Predefense Harappa for that matter. Its presence in Amri IB and later, Pre-Harappan Kot Diji may only mean that there was, once again, contact between these sites and Mohenjodaro which eventually overwhelmed them with the full impact of the Harappan Culture.

The occurrence of the dish-on-stand in the Post-Harappan Chalcolithic Culture of Rangpur, Ahar and Navadatoli does not conflict with the characterization of the type as Harappan. All these sites are very late in date and it could be that these vessels result from direct contact with the displaced, roving Harappan potters. Or they may be due to stimulus diffusion or culture contact.

The dish- and/or bowl-on-stand has been reported from Bara, Ambkheri, Hulas, and Baragaon in Saharanpur District and from Alamgirpur in Meerut District. Fragments of stands with broad bases have also been found at the OCP sites of Atranjikhera and Bahadarabad. R.C. Gaur (1969a: 97) reporting on the OCP complex at Atranjikhera says: "Although no complete dish on stand has been found the sherds do indicate their existence." No dish-on-stand has been reported from the Black and Red Ware complex at Atranjikhera (Gaur 1969b: 112). Some apparent dish-on-stand sherds have been reported from Kausambi IA (Misra 1969: 204).

Further east, at Chirand in the Mid-Ganges Valley, numerous examples of both the dish- and the bowl-on-stand have been found. These occur in the earliest Chalcolithic levels in three fabrics: (1) Black Ware (Fig. 12.1), (2) Black and Red Ware, and (3) Red Ware. The ^{14}C dates for Chalcolithic Period II at Chirand range between 1650±100 and 715±105 (Agrawal and Kusumgar 1974: 114). There are both the squat and the long-stemmed dish-on-stand. The presence of the squat dish-on-stand in Post-Harappan Chalcolithic Chirand tends to refute the view that the complete absence of the squat type in Kalibangan makes that site later than other Pre-Harappan sites (Manchanda 1972: 192). Many of the stems have corrugation-like moldings round their upper parts. But the most distinctive feature is cream-painted dots on the flaring base in some cases. On one of many variants of the Harappan dish-on-stand there are broad bands of red painted on the stem and other surfaces. This painting may be over a red or cream slip or directly on a plain surface. This feature is found only in Mohenjodaro, and appears to have gone out of use by the time the type infiltrated to other Harappan sites. In many cases horizontal bands or slanting lines to the right and left set between horizontal lines are painted in black on the stem. In one Chanhudaro example one finds set within the bracket of black bands a series of loops, ladders or leaf designs painted in black on the flaring base. At Alamgirpur there is a near parallel to a Chirand example with the dish painted with horizontal bands and dots in black. A similarly painted dish has been reported from Ambkheri. In the Chirand examples the dots are yellowish cream not black. This is the individuality of the Chirand type.

While there are several dishes-on-stand, there are only a few examples of the bowl-on-stand at Chirand. This form is frequently found at Harappa, Lothal A and Mohenjodaro. Krishna Deva (1969: 110) may not be far from right in holding that the Chirand dish-on-stand is a derivative type from the Mature Harappan Culture. The dish-on-stand has been found in graves at Mohenjodaro, Harappa, Lothal, Kalibangan and

Harappan Fallout (?) in the Mid-Gangetic Valley

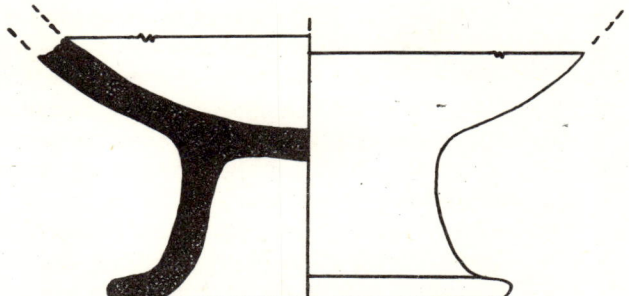

Fig. 12.1. Chirand Chalcolithic. Black Ware bowl-on-stand.

Amri. Similar examples are known from Cemetery A at Kish. But in Chirand there is no association of this vessel type with a burial, and it was probably a purely secular ware here. There is no evidence of soot on the inner surface of the dish. Thus it cannot be taken to have served as an offering firestand in any ritualistic way. Even in the Harappan context the tall-stemmed dish-on-stand is found in several examples in the homes of the well-to-do people of the cities. In Chirand the tall-stemmed type also predominates. It appears that this example was popular with the Chalcolithic village folk as a ware of distinction. Only horizontal excavations on a large scale will reveal settlement patterns and the existence of socio-economic strata pinpointing the greater popularity of this type with the better placed sections of the populations.

It may be noted that the dish-on-stand has been found in the course of explorations at Manjhi, west of Chirand, but in the same district. It has also been noticed in explorations at Maner, almost opposite Chirand on the southern bank of the Ganges, about 30 kilometers west of Patna. It is also present at Champa on the Ganges in Bhagalpur District of South Bihar. But it is significant to observe that in course of excavations further south at Sonepur in Gaya District no dish-on-stand was found though a very rich Chalcolithic Culture with Black on Red Ware as the predominant ceramic was excavated. However the remains of this vessel have been reported from Pandu Rajar Dhibi in West Bengal. The route of its spread appears to have been along the Ganges.

Another find from the Chirand Chalcolithic which is reminiscent of a Harappan prototype is the button-based goblet (Fig. 12.2, no. 14). This example is a Black Slipped Ware. It is very narrow with a slightly bulging belly, constricted at the top with narrow mouth. Exact parallels to this may be found at Mohenjodaro, Chanhudaro and Harappa where they have been called tall vases (although none of them is more than three inches high!). These concave/convex vessels have a beaded base. Manchanda (1972: 117, Figs. 270, 272) illustrates Mature Harappan examples which recall those from Chirand.

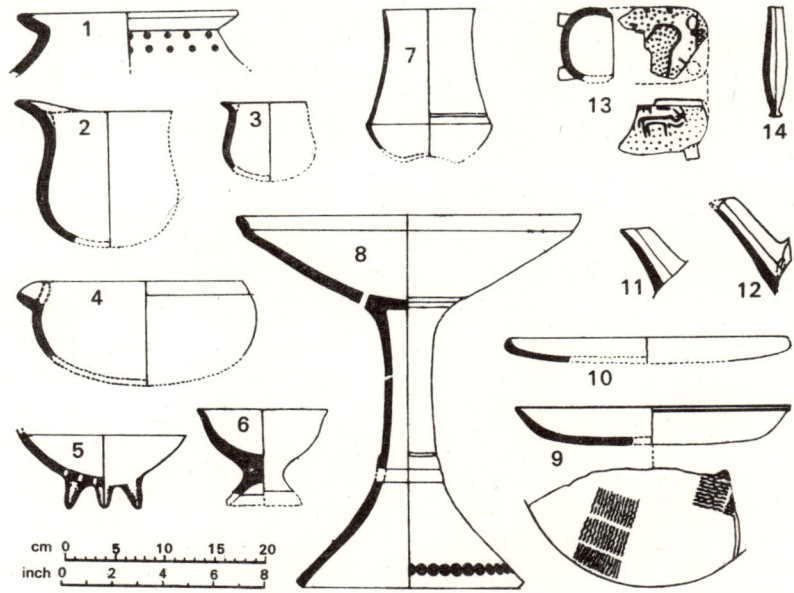

Fig. 12.2. Chirand Chalcolithic. No. 6 is a painted dish-on-stand. No. 14 is a button-based goblet (tall vase?).

Knobbed ware is another Harappan ceramic of which there are numerous examples from Chirand (Fig. 12.3). Here it occurs in a red and a black ware; however both fabrics are confined to the Neolithic levels of the site. This can be taken to indicate that the Neolithic of Chirand was contemporaneous with the Harappan. Unpainted Red Ware jar covers, or lids, with knobs which are once again reminiscent of Harappan types have also been found. The lids from the site are, however, not the dish type with the knob in the center.

There is an exceptionally rich and exquisitely manufactured bead assemblage from Neolithic Chirand. Beads made of steatite, agate, chalcedony, banded agate and jasper come in numerous shapes: barrel, cylindrical, spherical; some with minute holes. This assemblage is indicative of a high proficiency in bead manufacture not met with in other Neolithic sites in India. In fact it recalls the excellence of Harappan craftsmanship. But, whether or not the art of bead manufacture in Neolithic Chirand had direct, or even indirect, inspiration from the Harappan tradition is too complex an issue on which to even speculate at this time. Just the distribution of finds over an immense area raises more questions than it answers.

In conclusion it may be observed that there are some ceramic types and traditions associated with Early (Pre-) and Mature Harappans which are present in Chalcolithic Chirand, particularly dish-on-stand. This vessel form is spread from Alamgirpur to Chirand and is dotted along the Ganges-Yamuna Valley at Saharanpur, Atranjikhera and Kausambi. Chirand specimens are, however, numerous, better preserved and have more varieties than the other Post-Harappan sites in the Ganges. It must also be noted that the Chirand potters added their own individuality by painting in cream and selecting designs like a succession of solid large dots not met with anywhere else. It is obvious that while the design and the painting concept were taken from the Harappan tradition, new features were also introduced disproving a slavish imitation of a nonindigenous tradition.

Harappan urban civilization disappeared toward the middle of the 17th century B.C. There is, however, no doubt that many of the Harappan traditions not related to architecture and sophisticated urbanism infiltrated into regions beyond their geographical

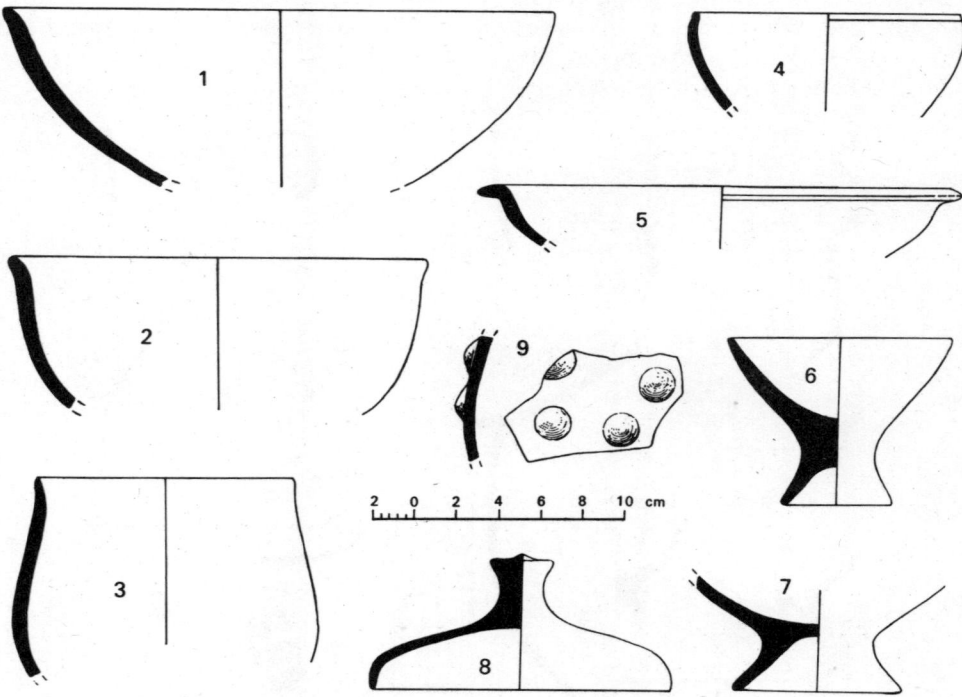

Fig. 12.3. Chirand Neolithic. No. 9 is knobbed ware.

limits. Here they were continuously adapted to by later rural Chalcolithic communities in the Mid-Gangetic Valley, for example. The dynamics of this mechanism are not clearly known; but the fact of its presence cannot be overlooked.

BIBLIOGRAPHY

Agrawal, D.P. and Sheila Kusumgar, 1974
Prehistoric Chronology and Radiocarbon Dating in India. Delhi: Munshiram Manoharlal.

Dikshit, K.N., 1979
Late Harappan Cultures in India. In *Essays in Indian Protohistory.* D.P. Agrawal and D.K. Chakrabarti. eds. Pp. 123-33. Delhi: B.R. Publishing Corp.

Gaur, R.C., 1969a
The Ochre Colored Pottery from Atranjikhera and its Significance. In *Potteries in Ancient India.* B.P. Sinha, ed. Pp. 95-111. Patna: Department of Ancient Indian History and Archaeology, Patna University.

Gaur, R.C., 1969b
Nature of the Pottery Complex of Black and Red Ware Phase at Atranjikhera. In *Potteries of Ancient India.* B.P. Sinha, ed. Pp. 112-17. Patna: Department of Ancient Indian History and Archaeology, Patna University.

Ghosh, A., 1973
The City in Early Historical India. Simla: Indian Institute of Advanced Study.

Krishna-Deva, 1969
Discussion of B.S. Verma's paper titled Black and Red Ware in Bihar. In *Potteries in Ancient India.* B.P. Sinha, ed. P. 110. Patna: Department of Ancient Indian History and Archaeology, Patna University.

Lal, B.B., 1979
Kalibangan and the Indus Civilization. In *Essays in Indian Protohistory.* D.P. Agrawal and D.K. Chakrabarti, eds. Pp. 65-97. Delhi: B.R. Publishing Corp.

Manchanda, Omi, 1972
A Study of the Harappan Pottery. Delhi: Oriental Publishers.

Misra, V.D., 1969
Pottery of Kausambi. In *Potteries in Ancient India.* B.P. Sinha, ed. Pp. 203-23. Patna: Department of Ancient Indian History and Archaeology, Patna University.

Piggott, S., 1950
Prehistoric India. Baltimore: Penguin Books.

Sankalia, H.D., 1974
The Prehistory and Protohistory of India and Pakistan. 2nd ed. Poona: Deccan College Postgraduate and Research Institute.

Sharma, G.R., 1960
The Excavations at Kausambi (1957-59). Allahabad: Allahabad University.

Sinha, B.P., ed., 1969
Potteries in Ancient India. Patna: Department of Ancient Indian History and Archaeology, Patna University.

Y.D. SHARMA

13. Harappan Complex on the Sutlej (India)

DATA FROM FIELDWORK

With the excavation of Harappa and Mohenjodaro, and the discovery of other related sites on the Indus and Ravi in the twenties of the current century, it was expected that the Harappan Civilization also spread along the other rivers of the Indus system. Manda on the right bank of the Chenab was discovered only recently (Joshi 1978, in press; Joshi and Madhu Bala, in this volume). Practically no Harappan or related site is known on the Beas proper, but several sites lie in a row along the Ravi-Beas *doab,* and along the East Bein which joins the Beas. The Sutlej-Ghaggar *doab* is replete with such sites, the more important of which are briefly described on the following pages (Fig. 13.1).

KOTLA NIHANG (lat. 30°57' north; long. 76°32' east)

The first archaeologist to report the discovery of a Harappan site on the Sutlej was M.S. Vats (1929–30, 1940), the original excavator of Harappa. In 1929 he put in a few trenches at Kotla Nihang Khan, two kilometers southeast of the district town of Ropar (earlier spelt Rupar). He concluded that the new discovery extended the zone of the Harappan Civilization to the *doab* between the Sutlej and the Yamuna.

The site was partially excavated again in 1955 by the present writer (Sharma 1971, 1976). Measuring approximately 260 meters east-west and 100 meters north-south, the site may be divided into two contiguous sectors: the western covered by the present village, and the eastern outside it (Fig. 13.2). The latter with one meter of deposit, abounds in typical Mature Harappan pottery: e.g., dish-on-stand with "drum"-shaped stem, scored Indus goblet with pointed base, elliptical footed goblet, shallow flat dish (*thali*) with flaring sides, wide-mouthed large storage jar with concave profile above the base and a cup with a perforated handle (Figs. 13.3 and 13.4). Bara Ware is present here in small amounts in the upper layers and on the surface. In the two-meter thick western sector Mature Harappan pottery is associated with Bara Ware from the bottom to top. The two sectors could not be linked by a connecting trench. It seems, however, that initially, in Phase I, the Harappans occupied the eastern area, but with the advent of the Barans, in Phase II, a large settlement grew in the western area.

Fragmentary walls of standard-sized kiln-burnt bricks occur all over the site. In one trench in the western sector they were assigned to four structural phases. In the eastern sector there were four small oval kilns or furnaces in a row (Pl. 13.1). Small objects were perhaps baked here; although only fragmentary terracotta bangles were picked up from them. The small objects of common use include bangles of terracotta, faience, steatite paste and bone; beads of faience, paste, shell and semiprecious stones, including carnelian; blades and a weight of chert; triangular terracotta cakes, animal figurines, cart frames and wheels, antimony rods; and a ring, and pins of copper.

DHER MAJRA (lat. 29°55' north; long. 70°50' east)

Dher Majra, known as Bikkun in the earlier records

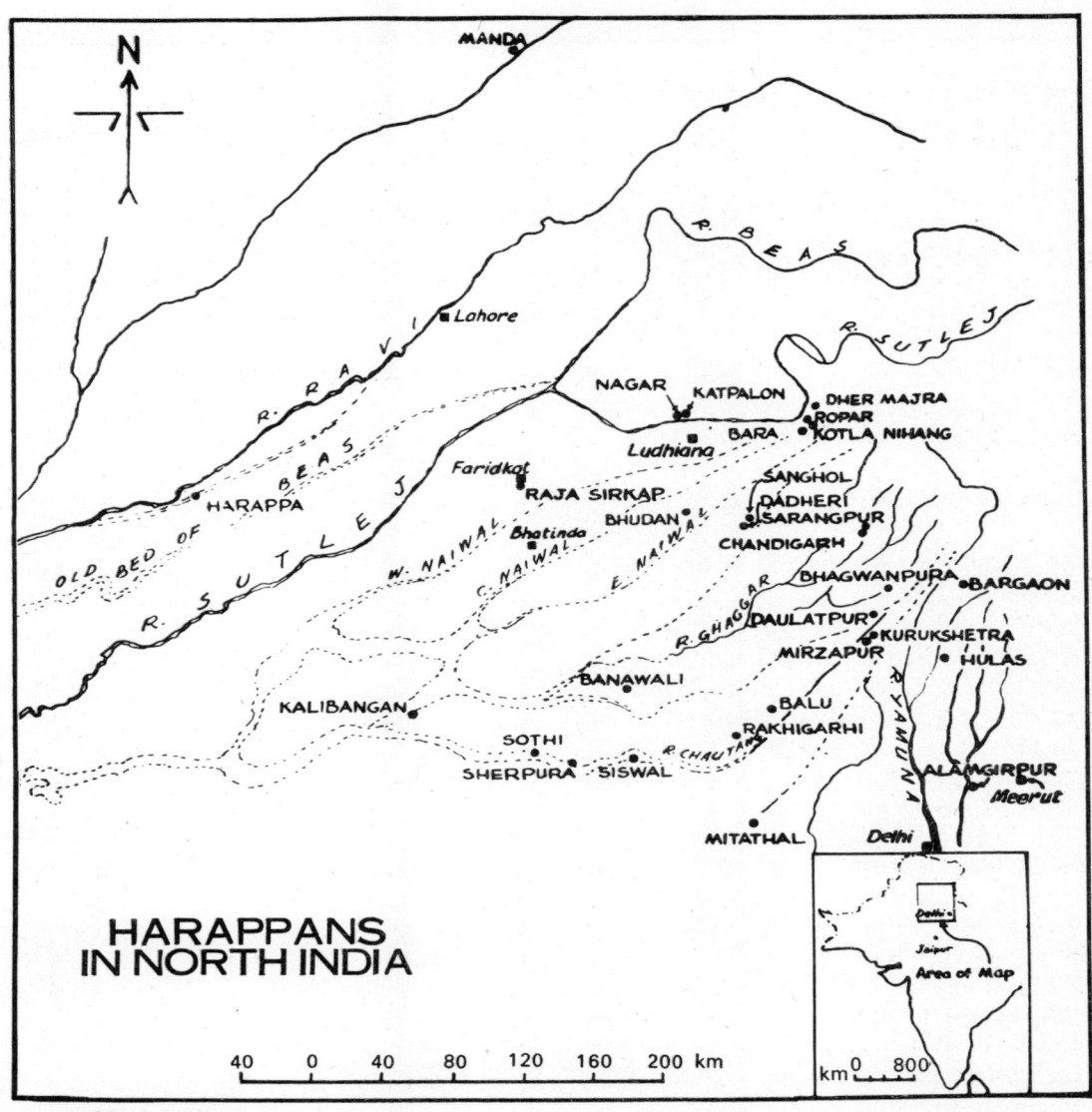

Fig. 13.1. Map of Harappans in North India.

of the Archaeological Survey of India, is on an arm of a monsoon rivulet known as the Kanahan Nadi, which together with the Sirsa, joins the Sutlej five kilometers northeast of Ropar. The site was discovered by Munshi Sadar Din, perhaps in the thirties. It measures 105 meters by 90 meters. Soundings were made there by Olaf Prufer in 1951. He felt that the settlement had not only the remains of the Harappan Culture, but also a number of Post-Harappan Phases, among which he included the Cemetery H Culture.

On reassessment, Prufer's material from Dher Majra is mainly from the Bara Culture, with some new types of the same category, as one finds at any excavated site. There is neither Cemetery H pottery, nor any Mature Harappan pottery or other objects. Out of the 1200 beads found at Dher Majra, agate accounts for the largest number, although carnelian, emerald, crystal, lapis lazuli, steatite and faience are also present. Faience bangles occur in large numbers, as at Bara. Toy cart wheels, some with raised hub, mar-

Harappan Complex on the Sutlej (India)

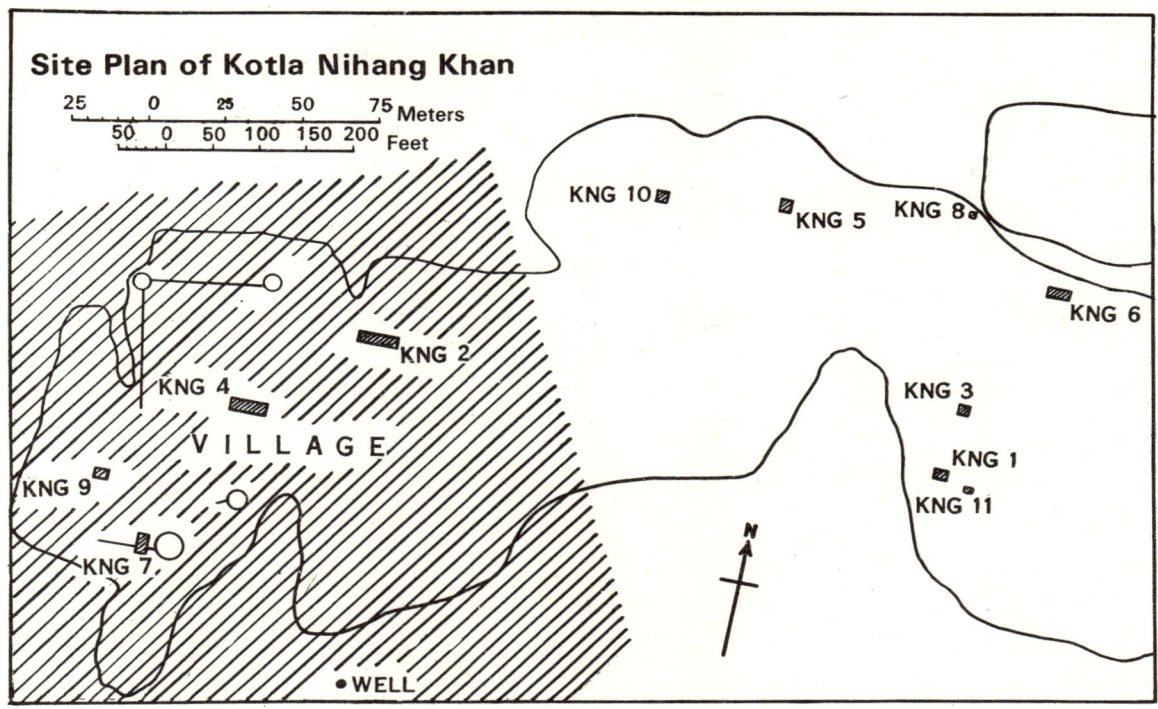

Fig. 13.2. Kotla Nihang: Site plan.

bles, gamesmen, a human figurine and a fragmentary animal figurine are among the terracotta objects. No terracotta cakes were found by the excavator; although the present writer picked up some pieces from eroded sections of the site. Two brick sizes were recorded: 30.5 by 19 by 5 centimeters and 28 by 14 by 6.5 centimeters, the latter conforming to the standard Harappan size. Bronze or copper objects included rods, a fragmentary bangle and a toothpick with a hole. A bracelet with an incised design reported by the excavator from the top layer, may not belong to the original deposits.

BARA (lat. 30°17′ north; long. 76°47′ east)

Six kilometers southwest of Ropar, the mound at Bara lies on the left bank of a monsoon rivulet known as Budki Nadi. The ancient mound presently measures 550 meters north-south and 300 meters east-west. The present writer excavated some trenches here in 1955 and again in 1971 (IAR 1954–55a: 9–11; Sharma 1971, 1973, 1976, in press a). The four meters of deposit belong to one very distinct culture, although they may well be divided into lower, middle and upper levels.

It is the pottery of Bara that is most distinctive (Figs. 13.5 through 13.8). Made of well levigated, fine- to medium-grained clay, it is all wheel turned, with a self-slip or an applied slip, a dull brown in color. Designs are painted in dull chocolate or black, and are incised with wooden points or brushes (Fig. 13.6, nos. 30–40). Paring is present (Fig. 13.5, no. 17) but more characteristic is a technique of drawing designs with a blunt point on a smooth surface. These designs acquire a sheen or burnished appearance when fired (Fig. 13.8, nos. 60, 61, 63, 65, 69). Even the Harappans adopted this technique; although it does not appear to be in evidence in the Indus Valley proper. Cooking utensils or water jars are incised on the shoulder and rusticated at the base in a wet ware technique with honey-combed ridges, brushed spirals or finger patchwork (Fig. 13.6, nos. 30, 35, 37, 40).

Bara pottery has parallels with Harappan ceramics in thick wares, such as the dish-on-stand, basin or large bowl with flaring sides and a variety of rims including the undercut types, and large storage jars with bulging or bluntly carinated profiles. Thin sectioned pots like the oval or round vases with a disc base have a general resemblance to Harappan examples. While the majority of Harappan pottery is plain,

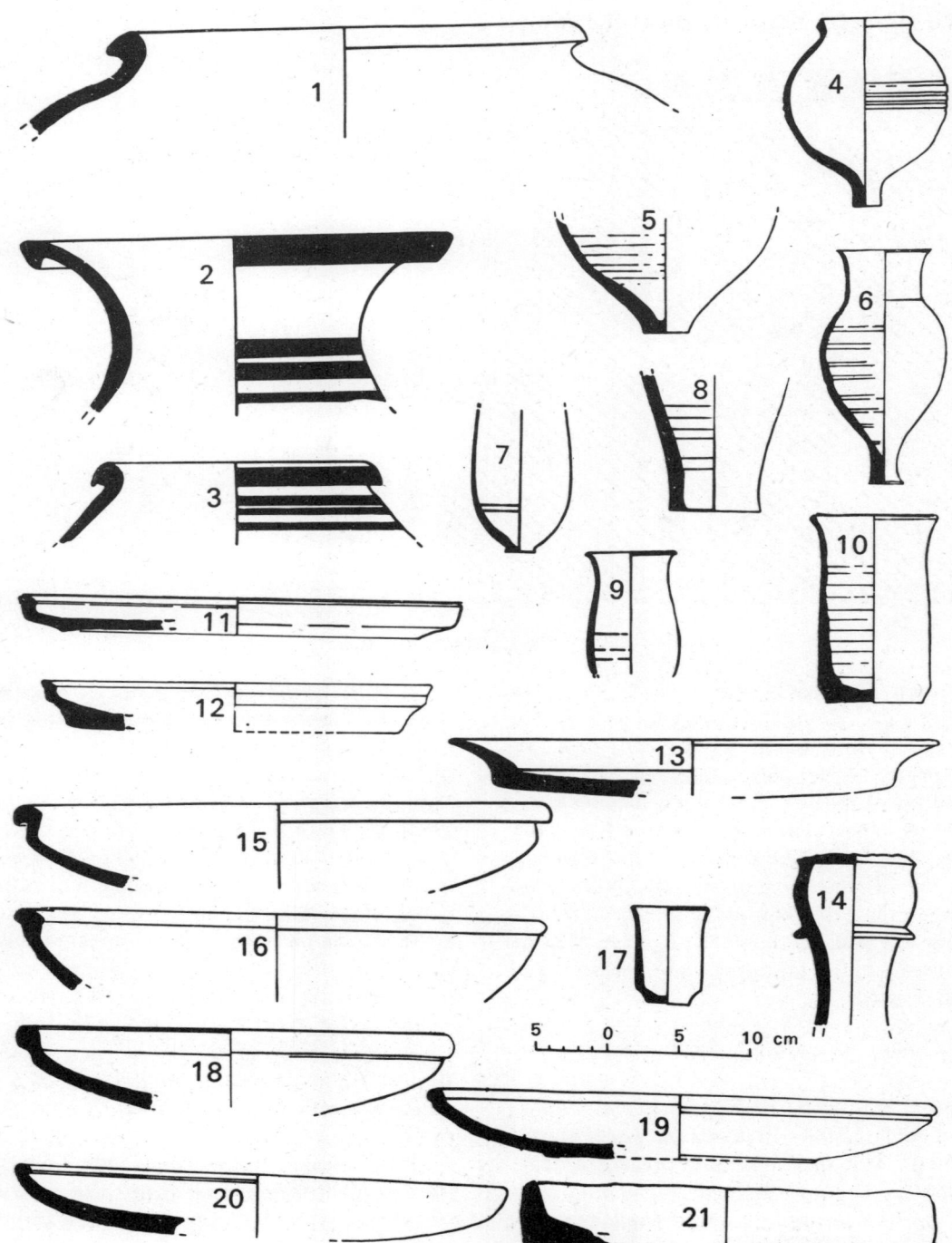

Fig. 13.3. Kotla Nihang: Harappan pottery. Scale 1:4

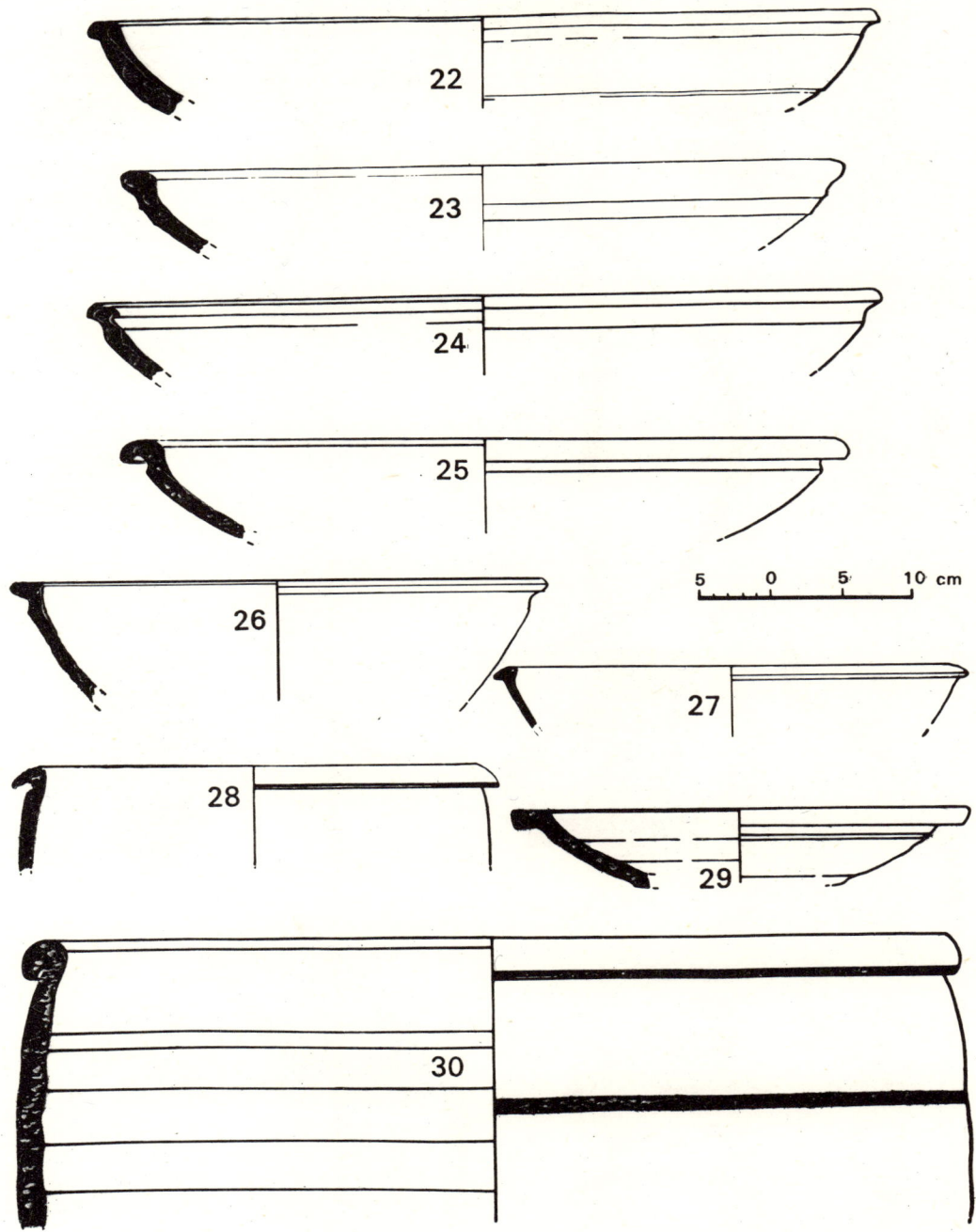

Fig. 13.4. Kotla Nihang: Harappan pottery. Scale 1:4.

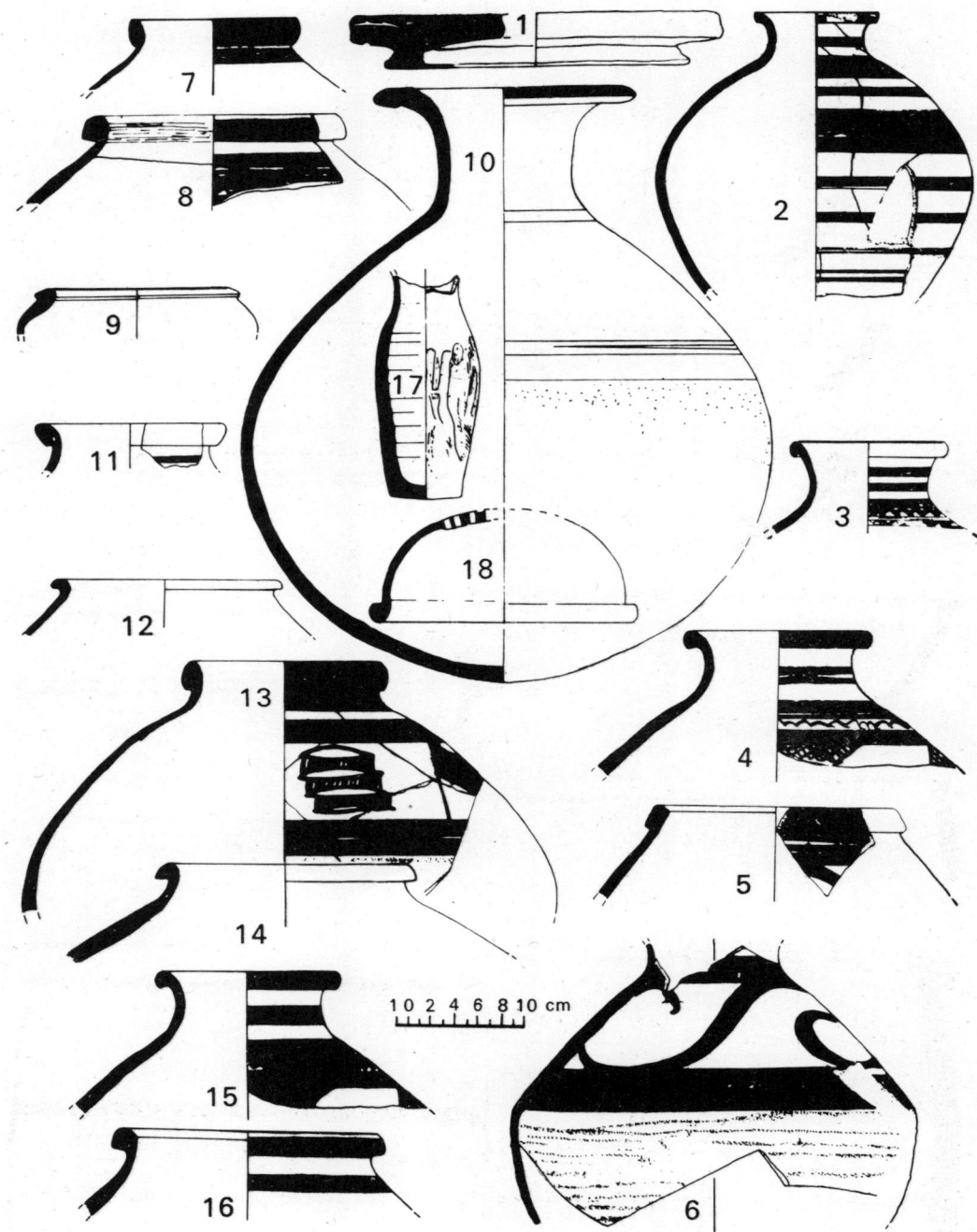

Fig. 13.5. Bara: Pottery. Scale 1:5.

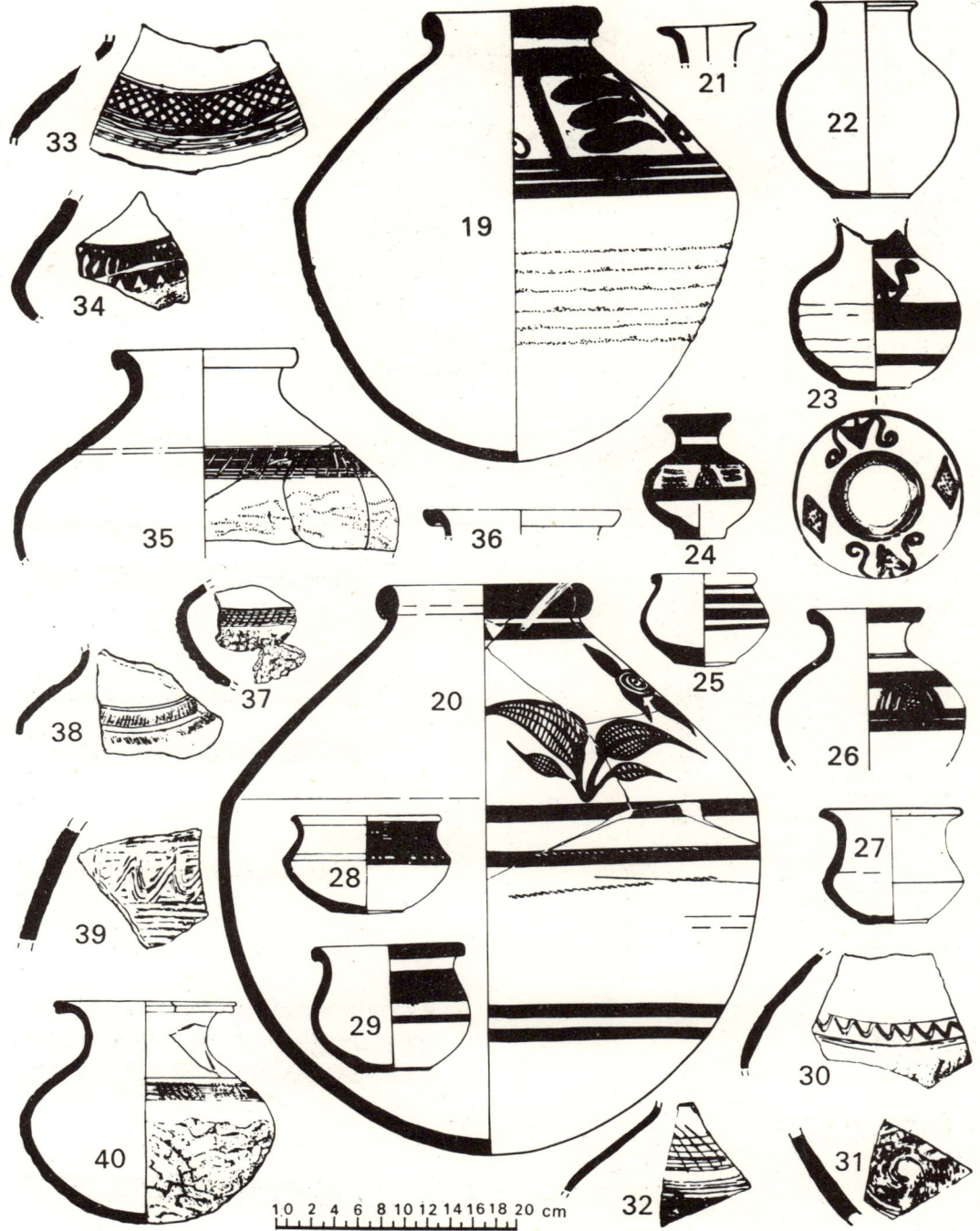

Fig. 13.6. Bara: Pottery. Scale 1:5.

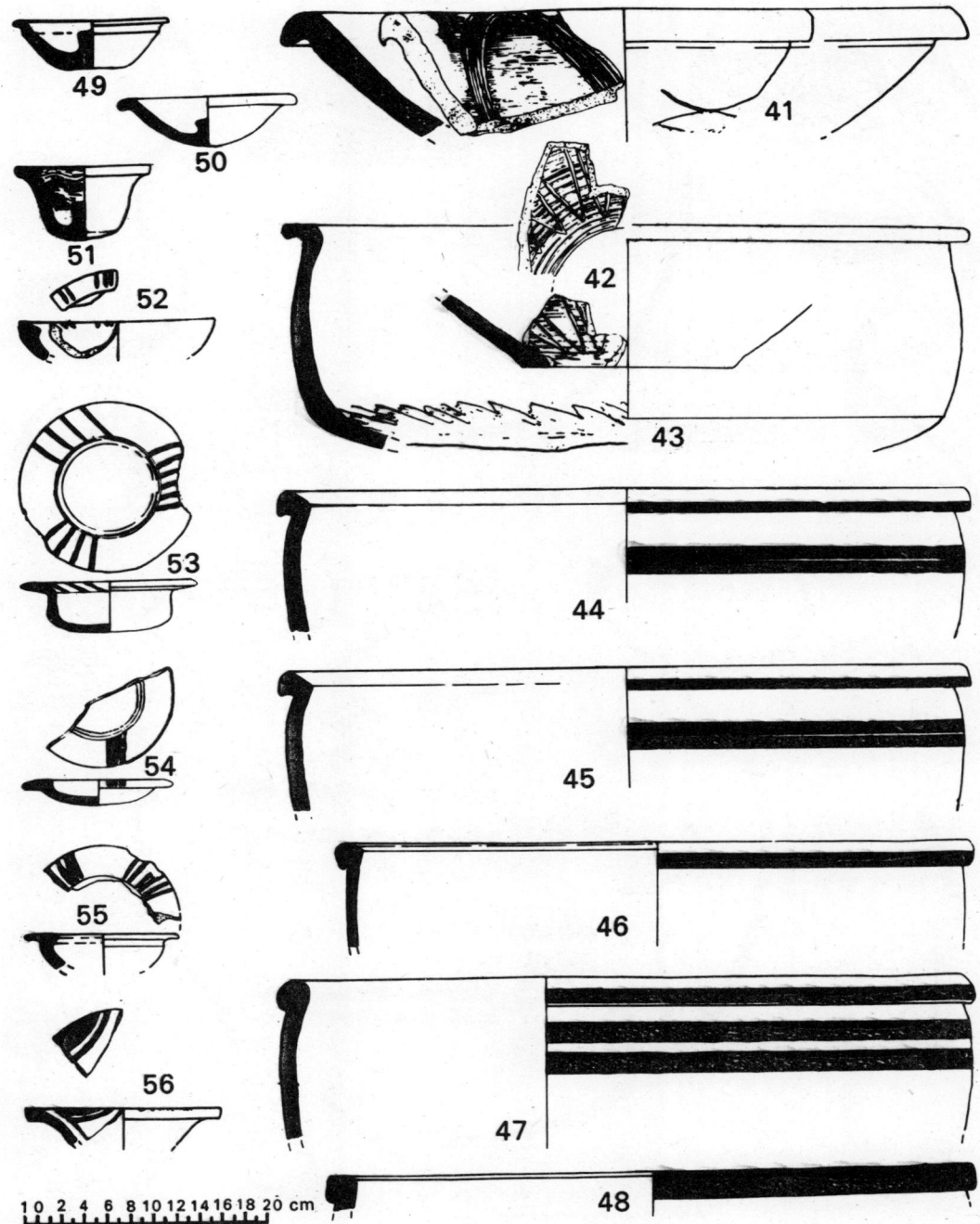

Fig. 13.7. Bara: Pottery. Scale 1:5.

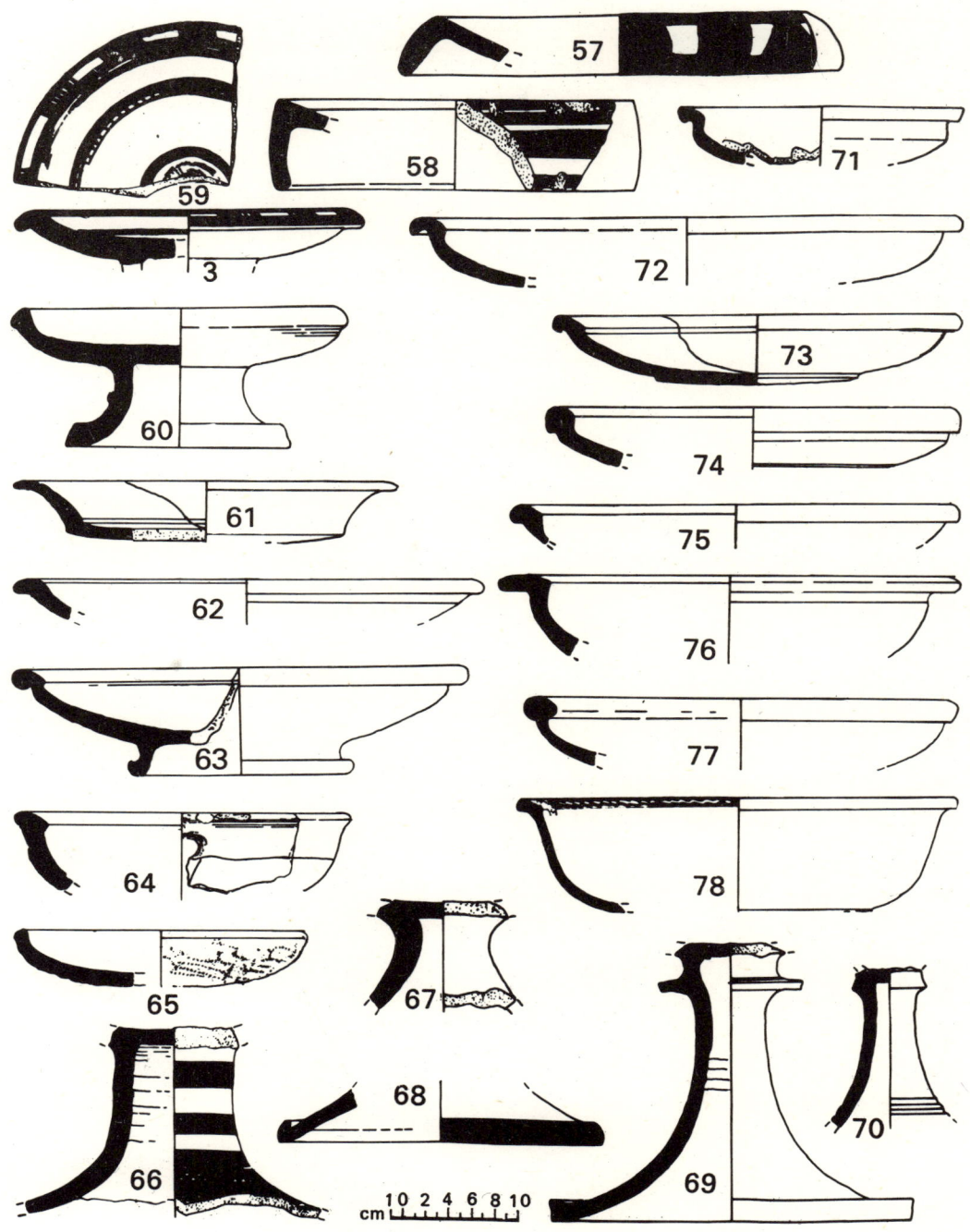

Fig. 13.8. Bara: Pottery. Scale 1:5.

undecorated pots are rare in the Bara assemblage. Even the parallel shapes have certain features which distinguish them from Harappan counterparts. For instance, the stem of the Bara dish-on-stand is short and wide (Fig. 13.8, nos. 60, 67), and even if long it has a projecting ledge in place of a plain or drum-shaped stem (Fig. 13.8, no. 69). The sloping or drooping rim of the dish or basin and the internal incised designs of the basin, and pedestaled base of bowl and dish are also distinguishing peculiarities of the Bara Ware (Fig. 13.7, nos. 41–49; Fig. 13.8, nos. 57, 58, 63). Among the Mature Harappan shapes that are absent in the Bara Culture (not the site of Bara) are the Indus goblet with pointed base, shallow flat dish with flaring sides (*thali*), wide-mouthed large storage jar with concave profile above the base, perforated jar, "S"-profiled jar and the cup with a perforated handle. Bara Ware also includes some shapes that are common in Pre-Harappan and Harappan pottery, such as the carinated dish with flaring and externally concave sides, a small cylindrical beaker with concave sides, the knobbed lid and a lid with an out-turned rim, often painted with a single or double arc, or a series of strokes (Fig. 13.7, nos. 49–51, 53–56; Fig. 13.8, no. 61).

The Bara painted motifs include the "horn" or "bowl"-like curve crowned by an arrowhead or other motif (comparable with Mundigak IV, 3; Casal, 1961: Fig. 102, no. 485), opposed triangles or semicircles, "willow" leaves in vertical or horizontal series, wavy lines enclosing "eyes" or lozenges, cross-hatched "nets," loops with humps surmounted by lines, grouped triangles, squares or rectangles with alternate hatching in different directions, solid dots enclosed by horizontal bands, "eyes" fringed by vertical lines, "wings" surmounted by lines, the square with "bastions" or scrolls at corners, chain and plain wide band at the neck. The petaled rosette, a twig with needle leaves, the frond, an unidentified oval leaf with a long, pointed tip (Fig. 13.6, no. 20) and a plantain-like tree provide floral motifs. Fish are common; birds and animals are rare. Most of the painted designs are absent in the Harappan repertoire, but occur on Pre-Harappan pottery (Sharma 1973). Also absent are typical painted Harappan designs like intersecting circles, opposed loops enclosing a "cross"-shaped motif, *pipal* leaf, peacock and fish scale.

The characteristic ware described above is present at Bara from bottom to top, but in the middle levels Harappan contact is clear. There are some distinct Mature Harappan forms: the scored Indus goblet, the elliptical goblet with footed base, the vase with a button base, the beaker, perforated jar and a sieve with an animal-headed handle (Fig. 13.9). In the upper levels the repertoire of painted designs is poor and the incisions are shallow.

Houses are made of *kankar* stone and mud bricks (44 by 22 by 11 centimeters). Burnt clay lumps with reed impressions are evidence for wattle and daub huts.

Triangular cakes, bull figurines, bangles and beads are among objects of terracotta. Agate and carnelian are additionally used for beads. Faience, however, is by far the most popular material for bangles, bracelets and certain other knick-knacks. Bronze was evidently in short supply, since only a fragmentary bangle, a fish hook and pieces of wire were recovered.

The most puzzling artifact is an unidentified terracotta object, 10 centimeters square at base and 17.5 centimeters high. It has a tapering outline with two bifurcated curved terminals at the top and three

Fig. 13.9. Bara: Harappan pottery.

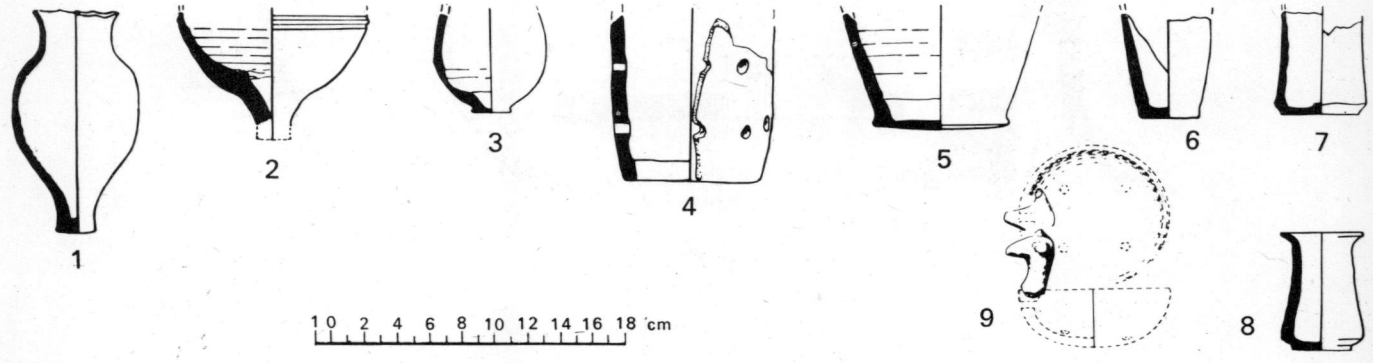

Harappan Complex on the Sutlej (India)

finger depressions on the front and back (Fig. 13.10). The object is also reported from Sanghol and Chandigarh.

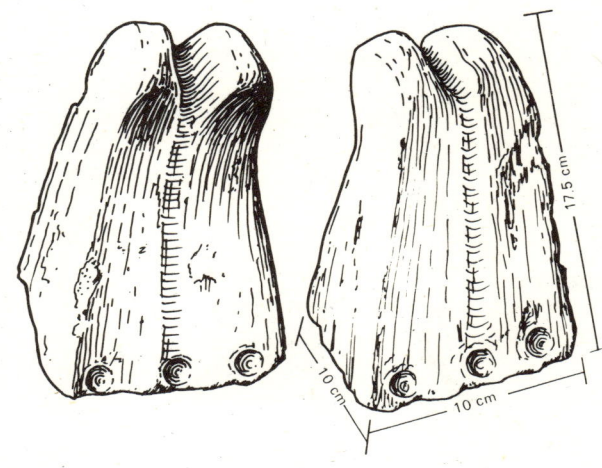

Fig. 13.10. Bara: Unidentified terracotta object.

ROPAR (lat. 30°58′ north; long. 76°32′ east)

The site of Ropar has three mounds: the northern, southern, and western (Fig. 13.11). The present writer excavated the site from 1953 to 1955 (IAR 1953-54: 6–7; 1954–55b: 9; Sharma 1955–56, 1976). Over the southern mound rises the present town, and it could be tapped only marginally. The small western mound conceals the Harappan cemetery, largely disturbed by later occupants. It is the northern mound, 21 meters high, that was excavated at several points. The operations yielded a sequence of six periods; of which, one is concerned with the lowest one here.

Ropar I is described as Harappan, but the variation of contents and/or emphasis in its different levels suggests that its deposits be divided into two phases, IA and IB. In an earlier paper I suggested three phases (Sharma 1976), but one of these is a sectoral variation and it is better not to give it a separate designation. Trench RPR-1, and its lateral extensions on the northern fringes of the mound, produced the lowest two layers, (numbered 35B and 35A) in a representative section. These strata yielded Pre-Harappan pottery, particularly examples of Fabrics A, B and D of Kalibangan I (Figs. 13.12 and 13.13). These levels are designated IA. A medium-sized vase of matt red ware, with a wide black band painted at its concave neck is the hallmark of these levels (Fig. 13.12, no. 17). A jar with a grooved middle profile (Fig. 13.12, nos. 9, 12, 19) is infrequent, but has to be taken note of because of its Pre-Harappan affiliation. Vases with a wide black band at the neck are characteristic of Predefense Harappa, Amri, Kot Diji I, Sarai Khola

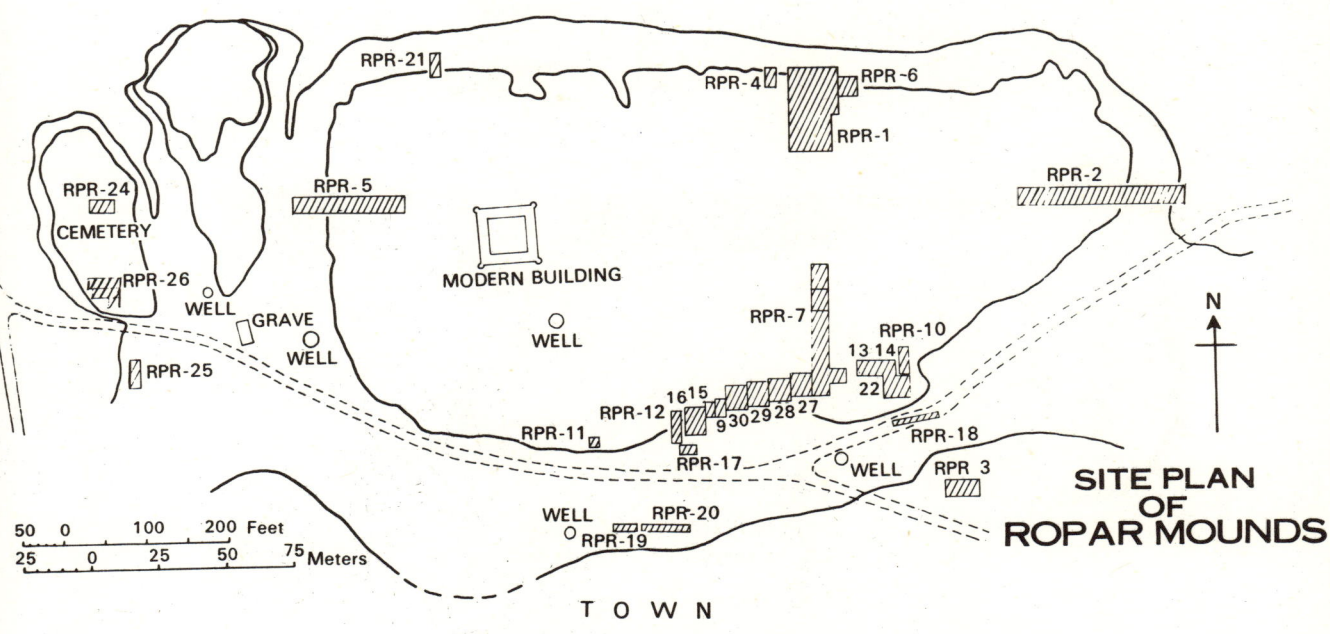

Fig. 13.11. Ropar: Plan of mounds.

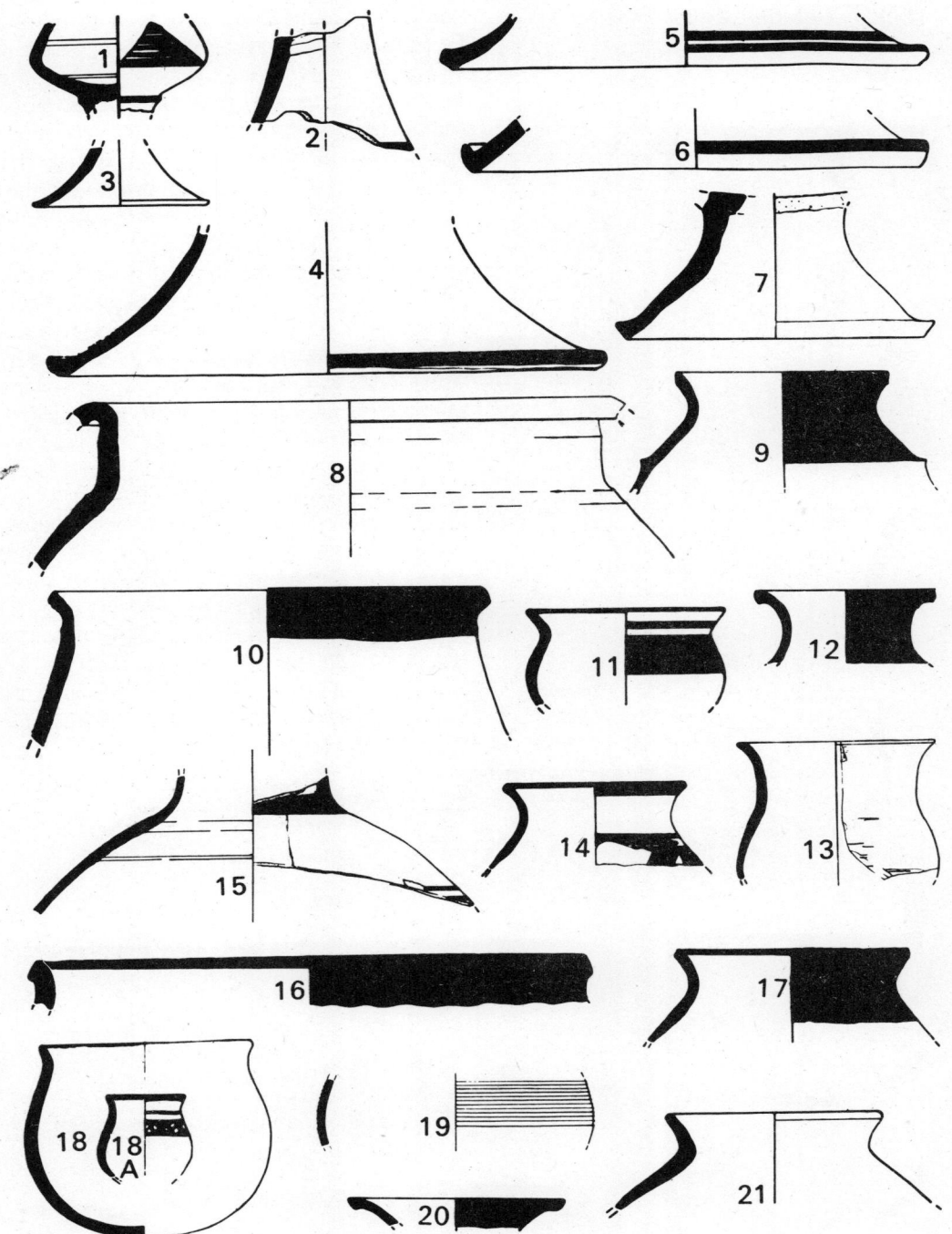

Fig. 13.12. Ropar: Pottery from IA levels. Scale 1:4.

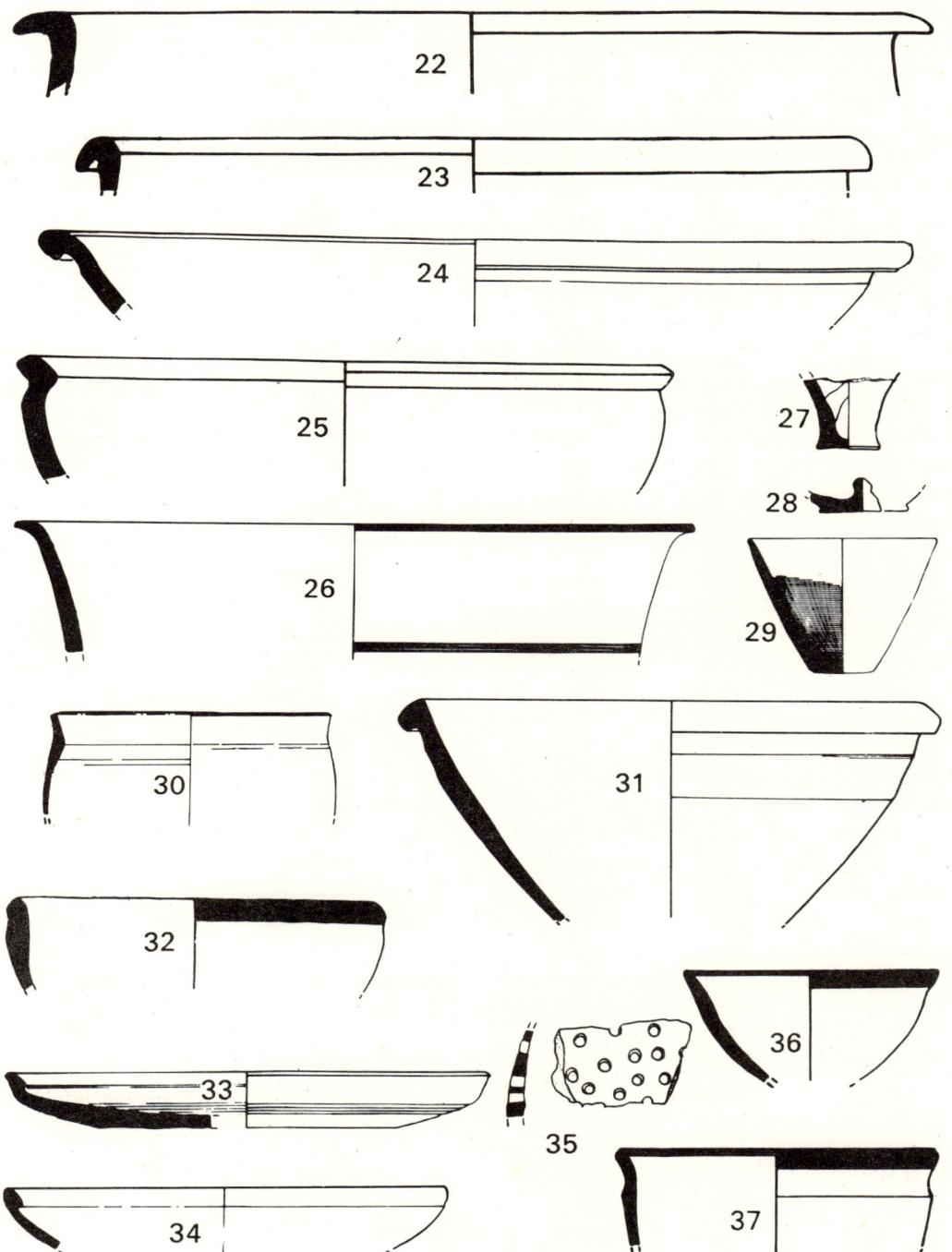

Fig. 13.13. Ropar: Pottery from IA levels. Scale 1:4.

II, Kalibangan I and Siswal. They are also reported from Mohenjodaro. Jars with grooved bodies or shoulders are reported from Predefense Harappa, Sarai Khola II and Jalipur (Mughal 1973: Fig. 3, Pls. IV and V). But with these Pre-Harappan wares are also associated some Mature Harappan pottery forms, a jar (Pl. 13.2) and a heavy broken celt of bronze (Pl. 13.3), terracotta bangles and beads of steatite paste and carnelian, which shows that IA is a phase in which the Pre-Harappans held on to their pottery, but they had borrowed other articles of everyday use from the Mature Harappans. The result of the contact between the poorly equipped Pre-Harappans and the fully urbanized Harappans was that the former gradually lost their identity. The Harappans had probably already come into contact with the Barans, whose presence may be traced in the pottery ensemble of IA. An intrusive element can be detected in flaring-sided bowls of Black and Red Ware, one of which also has burnished lines on the interior (Fig. 13.13, no. 29).

Above the IA levels in RPR-1 the pottery assemblage is a mixed one with both Mature Harappan and Bara Wares. Two bronze celts and a small spear head (Pl. 13.3), chert weights and a tiny inscribed steatite seal (Pl. 13.4) are other important finds. This mixed stratum has been designated IB.

Phases IA/IB were also found stratified on the eastern slope of the mound in RPR-2. But in this location there were only traces of IA. The IB level had, again, a mixed Harappan-Baran ceramic assemblage; but the Bara pottery is predominant. Some idea of this predominance can be gained from an examination of the painted designs from the two trenches (Fig. 13.14). RPR-2 was particularly rich in bronze and chert. A spear head, arrow head (Pl. 13.3), bangle, ring, razor blades (Pl. 13.5) and chert weights and cores were recovered.

The small steatite seal with script symbols has already been mentioned. A sealing with the impressions of three different Mature Harappan seals carrying the bull and legend (Pl. 13.6), were also found. Indus script graffiti on pottery (Pl. 13.7), beads and bangles of faience, triangular terracotta cakes, wheels and cart frames are other characteristic Mature Harappan objects.

In IA levels of RPR-1 only one mud brick wall of three courses was noticed. The bricks were irregular in size, but had a uniform thickness of 10 centimeters. In RPR-2 a pebble wall was the only structural remain in the excavated area. But seven structures assignable to five phases were recorded in IB levels in RPR-1 and its extension. They were differently built of mud brick, kiln-burnt brick and *kankar* stone. One of the well-built rooms from the lower levels had a plinth base of *kankar* stones and pebbles and a superstructure of mud bricks (Pl. 13.8).

The cemetery of the Harappans was a smaller version of Cemetery R-37 at Harappa. Most of the burials, with the head usually to the north-west, contained typical vessels (Figs. 13.15 and 13.16). Some of the skeletons had personal ornaments. A faience bangle was intact on the left wrist of one of the interred, and there was a copper ring on the middle finger of the right hand of another. One grave pit contained the skeleton of a dog below that of a human being, possibly its master. Bara pottery, occurring promiscuously in the graves, is limited and it is uncertain if one and the same cemetery was used both by the Harappans and the Barans.

SANGHOL (lat. 30°45′ north; long. 76°20′ east)

Sanghol in Ludhiana District lies close to a now dry water course, possibly an ancient bed of the Sutlej or one of its defunct tributaries. It was excavated from 1969 to 1973 by R.S. Bisht (IAR 1968–69: 25–26; 1969–70: 31–32; 1970–71a: 30–31; 1971–72: 39–40; 1972–73: 28; Bisht 1976, in press). The site yielded a sequence of six periods, of which the lowest is relevant here. According to the revised estimate of the excavator, Period I is to be divided into Subperiods IA and IB. Subperiod IA has evidence for limited contact with the Harappans in the form of a chert weight and a few Harappan sherds. The assemblage is otherwise non-Harappan. Subperiod IB has a considerable amount of Bara Ware, but there is also Cemetery H Ware. Houses were made of packed clay, but sun-dried bricks of 55 by 35 by 10 centimeters size were in isolated evidence. Mud floors, hearths and circular pits for storage and dumping, of Subperiod IA were sited right on natural soil. In Subperiod IB houses were built afresh on the old plans. There was no change in building material. Copper chisels, bone needles, round and triangular terracotta cakes, faience bangles, beads of faience, steatite and agate and earrings of faience were other articles found.

Excavations were resumed here in 1978 by G.B. Sharma, who confirmed Bisht's period sequence, but divided Period I into three Subperiods IA, IB and IC

Fig. 13.14. Ropar: Painted designs from IB levels. Scale 1:4. A. from RPR-2; B. from RPR-1.

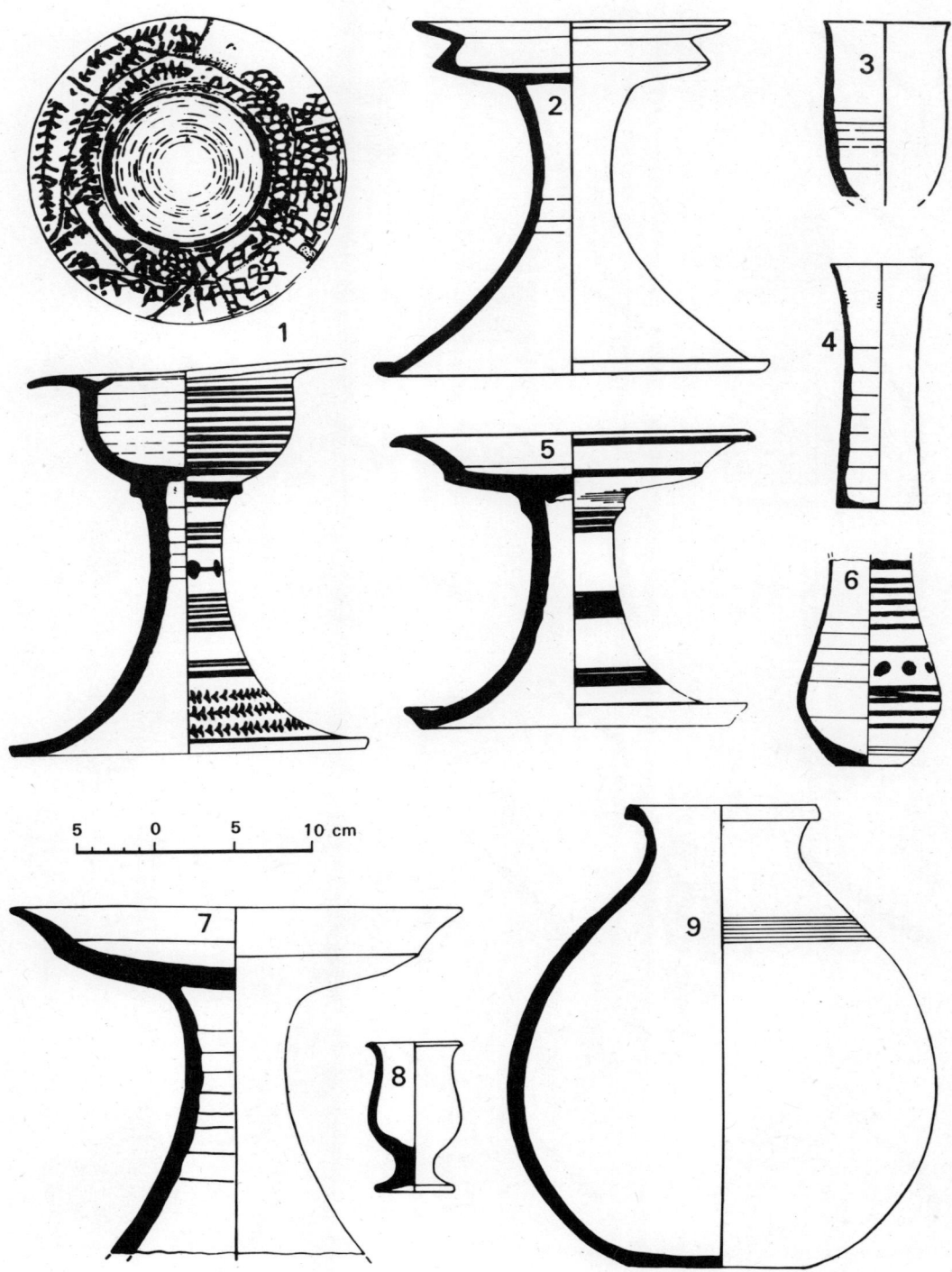

Fig. 13.15. Ropar: Pottery from cemetery. Scale 1:4.

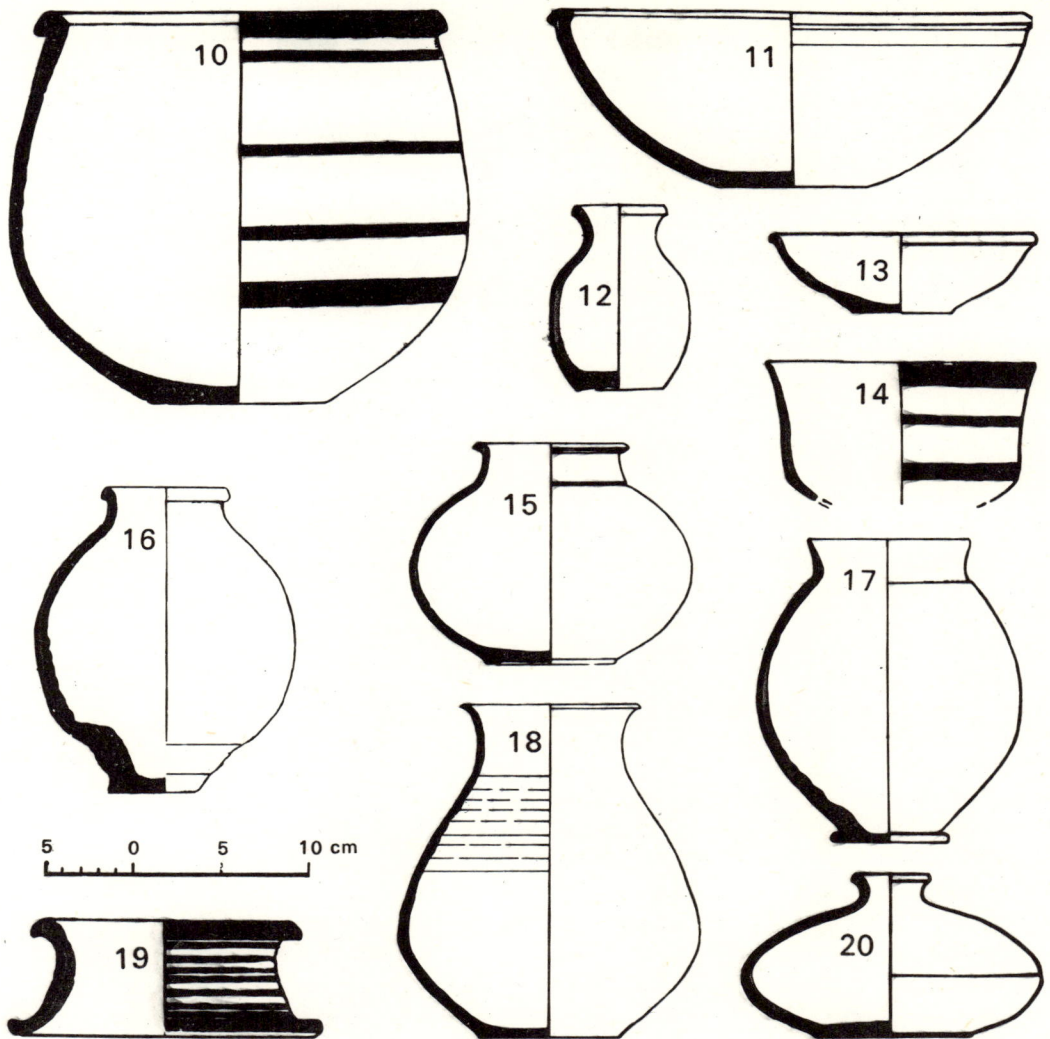

Fig. 13.16. Ropar: Pottery from cemetery. Scale 1:4.

(personal communication). His IA yielded Bara Ware without structures; IB has Bara Ware with structures; and IC has evidence for an overlap of the Bara and Painted Gray Ware Cultures. Particularly interesting in the resumed excavation was a potter's establishment with a kiln and a circular storage pit lined with mud bricks. There was also a furnace or fireplace, which was used again and again while debris continued to pile up around it over a long period (Pl. 13.9). The kiln contained some unbaked pottery and terracotta cakes. Three phases of sun-dried brick walls are also reported from the site. The bricks are 40 by 20 by 10 centimeters.

CHANDIGARH (lat. 30°40′ north; long. 76°50′ east)

In sector 17-C of Chandigarh a Harappan cemetery was discovered while the foundations of a building were being excavated in 1969 (Lalman, 1971). The burials were on the same model as those at Ropar; but the bodies were oriented north-south, with the head to the north. Subsequently, while digging the foundations for a parking place, the remains of a settlement came to notice at an adjacent site. Salvage operations were carried out here by the Archaeological Survey of India in collaboration with the Department of

Archaeology and Museums of the Government of Punjab (IAR 1970–71b: 7–8; Ghosh 1971; Pande 1972–73). No clearcut stratification was observed, but underlying a thick deposit of clean silt, 1.5 meters thick, was another 1.5 meters of cultural debris, with predominantly Bara Wares. Although there were vessel forms, four inscribed sherds were found. Two of these had full inscriptions, and the other two had a single graffito each. All were written in Harappan script. Among other objects that were found are terracotta toy cart frames, wheels, bull figurines, beads and bangles, bangles of copper and faience and beads of paste and agate.

OTHER EXCAVATED SITES

Sarangpur was superficially excavated by Suraj Bhan (1967) who has stated it to be a Siswal B site. He also excavated Bhudan near Maler Kotla (Bhan and Shaffer 1978). According to him "Bhudan I is divisible into three phases: IA, IB and IC. Phases IA and IB are represented by Early and Late Siswal complexes respectively. Bhudan IC is marked by the intrusion of a Late Harappan occupation within an otherwise continuous Siswal tradition." (Suraj Bhan and Shaffer 1978: 67).

An overlap of the Bara and Painted Gray Ware Cultures was first laid bare by J.P. Joshi at Bhagwanpura on the right bank of the Sarasvati in Kurukshetra District of Haryana. He reported the same sequence at Dadheri in Ludhiana District. At Nagar and Katpalon in Jullundur District the overlap phase began with the original occupation of the site (Joshi 1978, in press).

At present a total of 73 sites with Pre-Harappan, Harappan and/or Baran affinities are recorded in the Punjab (Madhu Bala 1978). Eleven of these lie south of the Ravi in the Amritsar and Gurdaspur Districts, perhaps along an older bed of the Ravi. Eight are along the East Bein, a tributary of the Sutlej. Thirty more are along the Sutlej and 34 along the Ghaggar. Some of the sites that are known are not on the list referred to above. Exploration is still in progress, and new sites still come on to the record from time to time.

Pre-Harappan pottery has been reported from Ropar, Sarangpur, Bhudan and Raja Sirkap. Raja Sirkap was first noticed in 1958–59 (IAR 1958–59: 73). The surface collection made from the site by G.B. Sharma has been examined by the writer through the courtesy of the collector (Figs. 13.17 and 13.18). It suggests that the character of settlement here may be different from that of Kalibangan I. Pots of Kalibangan Fabrics A and B are rare. Fabric D, with large, thick jars and basins with spaced grooving or other incised designs on the interior, is the most common. In fact, the thick sectioned forms in Red and Gray Wares are the most noticeable. A match of the bowl with a flanged rim (Fig. 13.17, no. 8) is reported from Sharpura by K.N. Dikshit (1980). It is comparable to one from Kot Diji (Khan 1965: Fig. 24, no. 10). The paucity of thin pottery at Raja Sirkap is striking. The site is, however, rich in bowl forms particularly those with a hollow below the rim (Fig. 13.17, nos. 11–17). There is a large number of thick pale red or dusty red sherds painted with leafy or floral motifs, which are outlined in black and filled in with white. White also occurs between black bands (Fig. 13.18, nos. 40–42).

Varieties of terracotta cakes or flinging missiles (Pl. 13.10) resemble those at Kalibangan. These are: round cakes with a depressed center and lenticular section (not illustrated), triangles, small ovals with single or double finger depressions forming a grip on both surfaces, similar but larger types, and large ovals with straightened sides and depressions for a grip.

BASIC ELEMENTS OF THE SUTLEJ HARAPPAN COMPLEX

The Bara Culture overlaps the Mature Harappan on the one end and PGW on the other. It accordingly has two distinct phases: Early and Late. The excavated and explored material from the Sutlej breaks up into four basic elements: Pre-Harappan, Harappan, Early Baran and Late Baran. The Late Baran is succeeded by the Painted Gray Ware Culture. Each of these elements exists either singly, or in combination with one of the remaining elements, with the result that a variety of cultural complexions are produced. These are broadly:

1) Pre-Harappan
2) Pre-Harappan plus Harappan
3) Early Baran
4) Harappan plus Early Baran
5) Late Baran
6) Late Baran plus Painted Gray Ware

PRE-HARAPPAN

Two facets are present in the Pre-Harappan: genuinely Pre-Harappan, and a mere survival in later times.

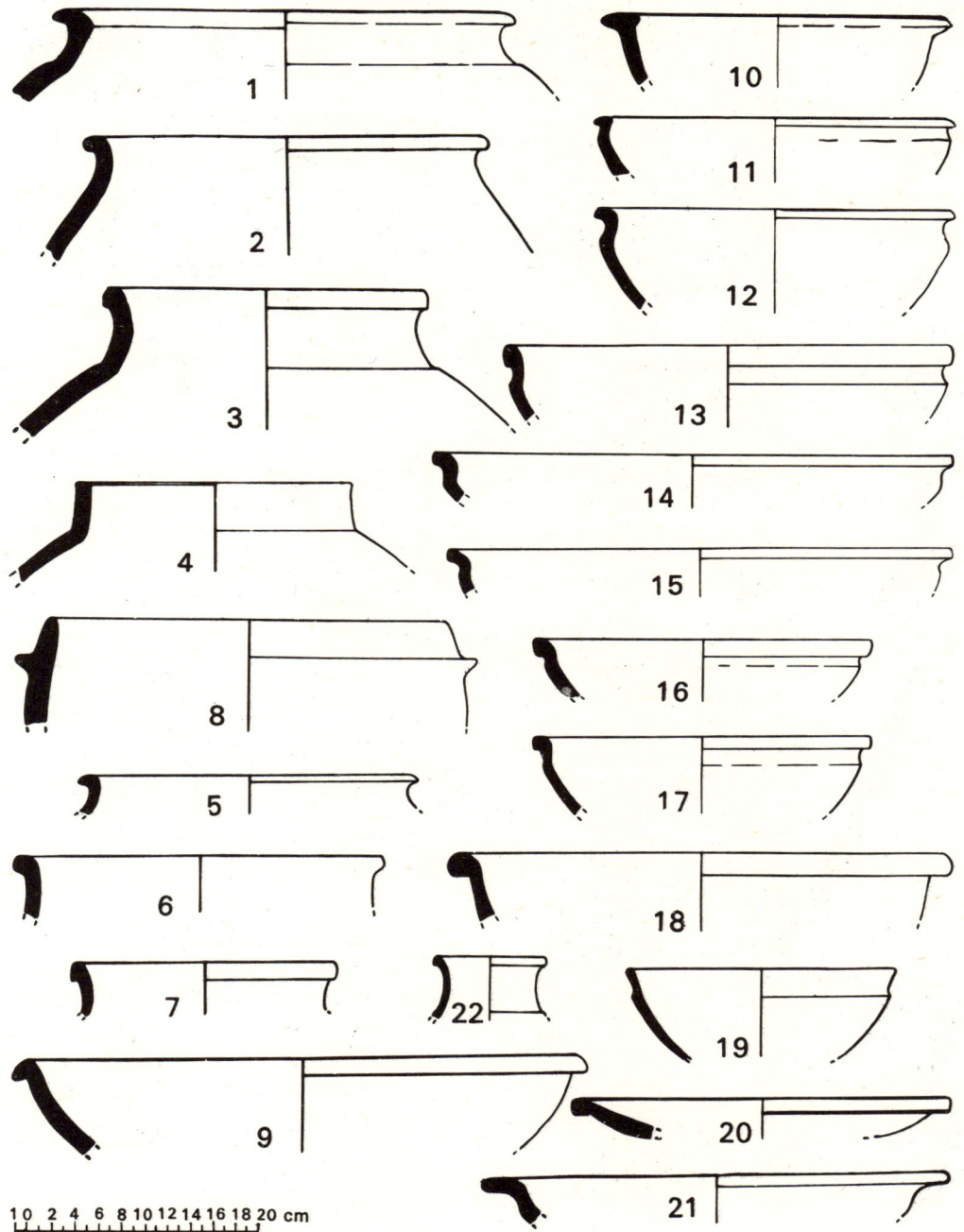

Fig. 13.17. Raja Sirkap: Pottery from surface exploration. Scale 1:5.

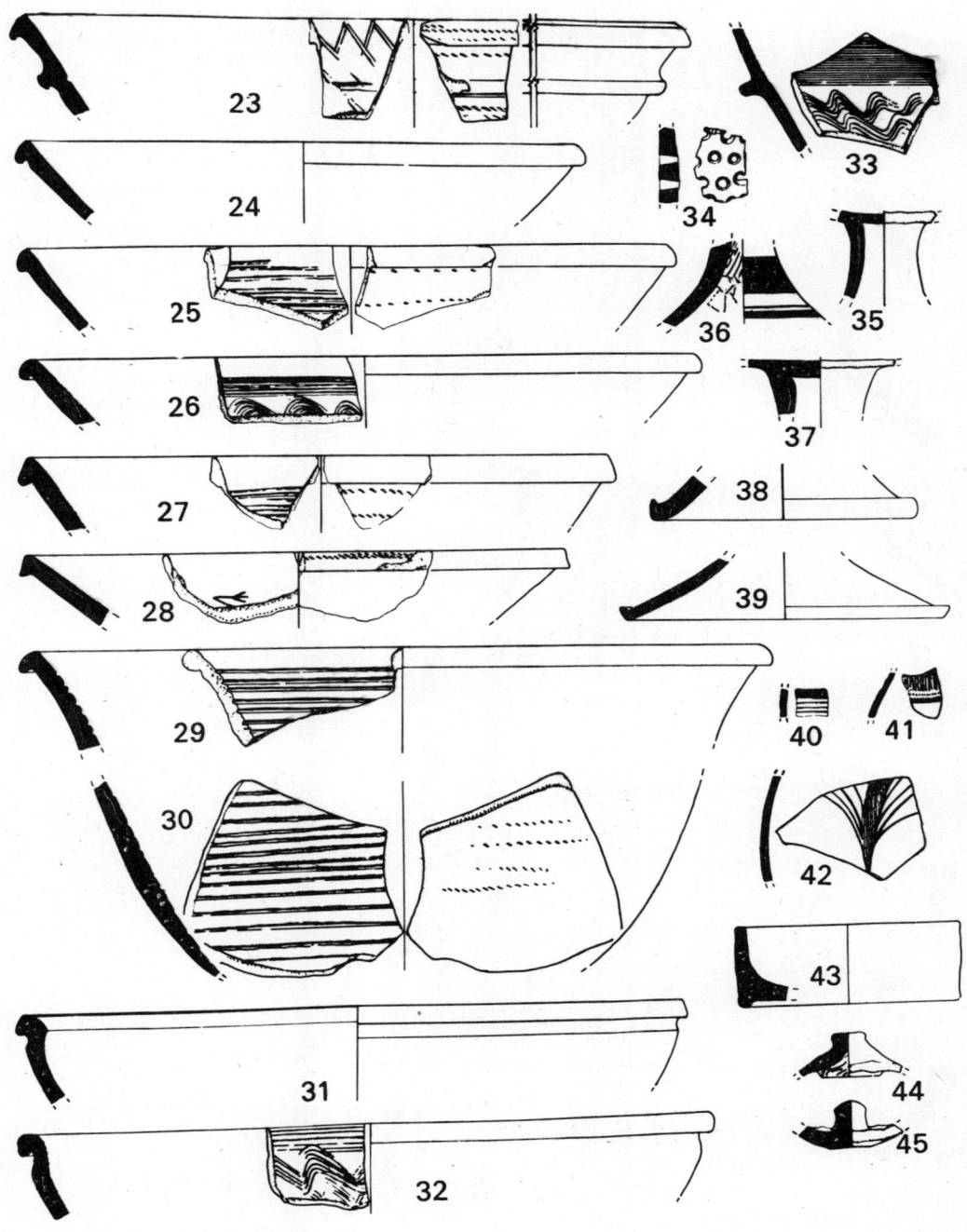

Fig. 13.18. Raja Sirkap: Pottery from surface exploration. Scale 1:5.

Among the sites so far excavated, Suraj Bhan reports the occurrence of Early and Late Siswal from Budhan (Suraj Bhan and Shaffer 1978: 67 n.) and from Sarangpur (Suraj Bhan 1967). Suraj Bhan and Shaffer (1978: 62) have also reported the discovery of Balu in District Jind, Haryana. This site is currently being excavated by a team from Kurukshetra University. They have found a continuous Pre-Harappan deposit from bottom to top, with some contact with the Mature Harappan in the middle levels and with the Baran in the upper levels (personal discussion and examination of material with U.V. Singh and his colleagues). It would appear, therefore, that the Pre-Harappan tradition exemplified by the Sothi or Kalibangan I Culture survived to late times, perhaps in isolated places. Sarangpur may also represent such a survival. As for Bhudan IB, Bhan and Shaffer themselves suggest concomitance of the Siswal and Mature Harappan occupations. If that be so, neither Sarangpur nor Bhudan IB can be genuinely Pre-Harappan.

As already stated, the writer had an opportunity to examine the surface collection from Raja Sirkap in the custody of G.B. Sharma of the Punjab State Archaeology Department. This is apparently a proper Pre-Harappan site; but of a genre different from Sothi of Kalibangan I. While Kalibangan I may be typical of the Sarasvati-Drishadvati region, Raja Sirkap may represent a different movement of the Pre-Harappans.

PRE-HARAPPAN PLUS HARAPPAN

This phase has so far been identified only at Ropar level IA. The indications are that it is the Pre-Harappan habitation on the northern periphery of the site, which has been largely cut away and leveled. The pottery has a close resemblance to that of Kalibangan I, but also includes new forms. Thick sherds with black painted leaf or flower designs filled with white appear to be more popular at Raja Sirkap than at Kalibangan. The Mature Harappan element in Ropar IA is provided by pottery, a bronze jar and celt, steatite, carnelian and agate beads, terracotta cakes, bangles and toy cart frames and wheels. As mentioned earlier, the Pre-Harappans at Ropar were probably a rural group, whose need for sophisticated goods was met by urbanized Harappans.

So far, there is no evidence for a defense work at Ropar. But, with the southern mound still uninvestigated, one does not know if it conceals a twin settlement, as at Kalibangan, Banawali and Rakhigarhi, with or without a defense wall.

A house wall of mud bricks of irregular size, but the uniform thickness of 10 centimeters, conforming to the thickness of Harappan bricks, lends support to the dual character of the first culture at Ropar.

EARLY BARAN

In theory, one would expect that there should exist sites with pure Mature Harappan content in the Sutlej region; however, no site of this type has yet been found. Presently the Early Baran, in more or less unmixed form, is known at Bara and Sanghol, where only limited contact with the Mature Harappan has been identified. The painted motifs on the Bara Ware have exceptional closeness with those on pottery from northern Baluchistan and with certain other Pre-Harappan sites. The middle levels of Bara are ^{14}C dated to 1890 ± 95 B.C. (TF–1205) and the upper levels to 1645 ± 90 B.C. (TF–1207). Another middle level date reads 1845 ± 155 B.C. (TF–1204). Adding another century to the middle level date, so as to arrive at a date for the beginning of the occupation, even a conservative span for Bara site would be 2000–1600 B.C. There is a not unreasonable likelihood that the beginnings may be even another century earlier. These dates also receive confirmation from the fact that typical Mature Harappan shapes occur at Bara as an intrusive element only from the middle levels upward.

The recently announced ^{14}C dates for Sanghol (communication from D.P. Agrawal) range between 1900 ± 160 B.C. (PRL–511) and 1700 ± 150 B.C. (PRL–510) in one trench, and between 1730 ± 160 B.C. (PRL–509) and 1690 ± 160 B.C. (PRL–513) in another. These lend support to the suggested Bara chronology. The excavator informs the writer that the date of 1690 ± 160 B.C. comes from a sample from the middle levels of Period I, while the date of 1900 ± 160 B.C. is from the lowest level. The reasonable span for the Bara Culture at Sanghol would accordingly be 1900–1500 B.C. On the whole this means that compared with the site of Bara, Sanghol might have had a slightly later start and a later finish.

The origins of Bara Culture are by no means clear at present. Separate ceramic traits (potting technique and decoration) can be traced to Quetta, the Zhob Valley (particularly Periano Ghundai), Kot Diji, Pre-defense Harappa and certain other Pre-Harappan sites. This suggests that there is a substantial substratum of the Pre-Harappan tradition in its makeup

(Sharma 1973, 1976: 11). Some Baran pottery shapes have Mature Harappan analogs. The culture is absent on the lower Ghaggar, in the Ganganagar area, and is apparently characteristic of the Sutlej. On the present evidence wherever the Mature Harappan is found on the Sutlej, Bara pottery is found with it in a large or small percentage. This suggests that the Bara Culture runs parallel to the Mature Harappan; at least in the Punjab. At the same time let it be admitted that nowhere has it been found so far underlying the Harappan Culture.

It appears to be a rural phenomenon, which is complementary to the Mature Harappan. This is more than confirmed when considering the 73 sites in the Punjab noted above. If one omits the three with only Pre-Harappan affiliation, and another three where Mature Harappan dominates, 67 sites are left which have possible Bara ranking. One may assume that half of these were Early Baran, and the other half were Late Baran. This would suggest that against two or three towns, there existed more than 33 villages, which contributed to the economy of the former. The find at Ropar of a full-fledged sealing with impressions of three different seals suggests that Ropar was certainly a trading center of some importance. Its situation suggests that it may have received semi-precious stones and other minerals from the hills and may have participated in trade over a wider area.

One would be in a position to define the beginnings of the Bara Culture more accurately if one knew what position Bara holds on the Pakistan side of the border. It is possible that when the cognate Baluchi village cultures descended into the Indus plains, some produced the Urban Harappan society, and others developed into a complementary rural community. The latter may have lacked the luxuries of urban life, but were otherwise a strong element, particularly as producers of agricultural commodities. Continuing down the Indus, this community perhaps turned east along the Sutlej from the junction of the Indus and the Sutlej. Once it had established itself on the Sutlej, it extended south to the upper Sarasvati-Drishadvati area, where it intruded into the Pre-Harappan and Mature Harappan complex, as at Mitathal in IIB levels.

HARAPPAN PLUS EARLY BARAN

It was natural that the Harappans and Early Barans should occasionally converge. The two could live together, particularly because the latter were the agricultural producers, if not also suppliers of certain industrial goods (Sharma 1976: 12, in press b). The result was a pattern that is exemplified at Kotla Nihang, Ropar IB and Chandigarh. At Kotla Nihang, although in the eastern sector Bara Ware has not been noticed in the lower levels, it may be that it has eluded the excavator on account of limited operations. In the western sector, it occurs from the bottom to the top, alongside the Harappan. As shown at Ropar, where the Harappans and Barans lived together, each occupied a different sector of the settlement.

Even the Mature Harappan manifestation on the Sutlej apparently has two forms: one exemplified by Kotla Nihang and the other by Ropar. The difference is not merely one of large and small settlements, or of village and town aspects, or again, of one being earlier than the other; although these factors also count. The difference is in form. To illustrate, Kotla Nihang has a profusion of scored Indus goblets with a pointed base and the shallow dish (Fig. 13.3, nos. 4–5, 11–12). These have a parallel to the type proportions of pottery in the Indus cities. At Ropar the Indus goblet is not present at all, and the shallow dish has a different form, apart from its negligible percentage. The Ropar dish is shallower, with sides that tend to be vertical instead of flaring. The two sites lie within two kilometers of each other. Thus, the difference may be due to two movements of people being involved. Kotla Nihang may represent an earlier movement, perhaps along the Sutlej from its junction with the Indus, while Ropar may have been inhabited by another folk wave from the lower Ghaggar region, possibly at a slightly later date.

Ropar IB has, however, almost all the objects with which one is familiar at Harappa and Mohenjo-daro. If terracotta figurines, including the Mother Goddess are absent at Ropar, this is also true in some measure of other peripheral settlements. Evidence for the layout could not be obtained because of a very restricted area being available for excavation in the lowest levels of a 21-meter high multiperiod site.

Chandigarh was not excavated methodically, the work there being in the nature of salvage operations. But with a cemetery of the Harappan R-37 type, and a mixed repertoire of Harappan and Bara pottery, it apparently represents the Ropar IB phase.

LATE BARANS

No site containing only the Late Bara Culture has

been excavated so far in the Sutlej area. But some idea of its form may be obtained from Bhagwanpura, Dadheri, Nagar and Katpalon, where it overlaps with the Painted Gray Ware. In fact at Bhagwanpura and Dadheri, a preceding phase contains only Late Bara Ware without the association of the Painted Gray Ware. Daulatpur and Mirzapur in the Kurukshetra region may also represent a Late Baran phase (Singh 1977).

LATE BARAN PLUS PAINTED GRAY WARE

At Bhagwanpura on the Sarasvati, a devolved Bara Ware occurs in Subperiod IA. Mature Harappan pottery types are totally absent, nor are there any other objects of that category. Terracotta figurines, including a humped bull, beads of faience and semiprecious stones, bangles of terracotta and faience, and a few pieces of copper are present. Structural activity is evidenced only by platforms erected as protection against floods (Joshi 1978, in press).

There is smooth transition to Subperiod IB in which both the Barans and the Painted Gray Ware people seem to have lived together. The houses of this Subperiod can be placed in three phases: round or semicircular huts followed by mud-walled houses, and finally houses built of kiln-burnt bricks of five different sizes. None of the bricks conform to the Harappan size. Like pottery, articles of everyday use belong to both the cultures.

The excavator reports oval structures of burnt earth, not only from Bhagwanpura, but also from Dadheri, Nagar and Katpalon. To the present writer's mind, these are nothing but small kilns or furnaces like those at Kotla Nihang, Bara and Tarkhanwala Dera in District Ganganagar, although the kiln is made of mud bricks at the latter site.

G.B. Sharma reports an overlap of Bara and Painted Gray Wares from Sanghol. But the Bara Culture here evidences some contact with the Mature Harappans and ^{14}C determinations are fairly early. It is therefore reasonable to surmise that the people here were Early Barans. If so, it is difficult to imagine their overlap with the Painted Gray Ware people.

The devolution of the Bara Ware at Bhagwanpura is apparent from things such as the absence of certain typical early Bara painted motifs, the larger percentage of plain pottery and the introduction of new shapes such as small bowls or solid pedestaled cups with a concavity in base. These cups are absent at Bara proper, but do occur at Alamgirpur, Hulas and Bargaon in Uttar Pradesh.

THE TERM LATE HARAPPAN

"Late Harappan" is a much misused term today, since it has been indiscriminately applied to several pottery traditions in the Indo-Pakistan Subcontinent (Thapar 1975–76). The Bara Culture, without respect to its uncertain genetic relationship, and of the fact that it overlaps both the Mature Harappan and the Painted Gray Ware Cultures, is often labeled "Late Harappan." Such a loose application of the term, without a clearcut definition, creates much confusion. Early Bara, which overlaps the Mature Harappan, can in no way be Late Harappan. It has accordingly been suggested (Sharma in press a) that Late Bara be described as Late Harappan, but the Culture itself be known as Bara. This will ensure that definite assemblage of cultural elements is signified.

CHRONOLOGY

The beginning of Kalibangan I was ca. 2300 B.C. on the basis of ^{14}C determinations. It is reasonable to assume that the Pre-Harappans could have reached the Sutlej region by about 2200 B.C. At the other end, the latest Baran phase, which may be related to the Harappan Culture, albeit indirectly, overlaps Painted Gray Ware. Thus it cannot be much later than 1100 B.C. All the other phases of the Harappan complex on the Sutlej must have flourished within the time bracket 2200–1100 B.C. It is clear that the Early Barans and the Harappans in the Sutlej region were contemporary. At some sites, particularly in rural areas, the Barans lived alone. At other sites, notably the towns, the Barans and Harappans lived together. The following dates are tentatively suggested for the different phases of Harappan-related cultures on the Sutlej:

1) Pre-Harappan: 2200–2100 B.C.
2) Pre-Harappan plus Harappan: 2100–2000 B.C.
3) Early Baran: 2000–1400 B.C.
4) Harappan plus Early Baran: 2000–1400 B.C.
5) Late Baran: 1400–1200 B.C.
6) Late Baran plus Painted Gray Ware: 1200–1100 B.C.

ACKNOWLEDGMENTS

Several of my friends in the Archaeological Survey of India have helped me prepare the illustrations for this paper. My grateful thanks to all of them, particularly to Mr. Sadhu Singh Saar, Mr. Lakshmi Dutt, Mr. L.K. Jain, Mr. S.K. Sharma and Mr. Baljit Lambda.

Except Plates 13.9 and 13.10, which are reproduced here through the courtesy of the Punjab State Archaeology Department, the copyright of other photographs is that of the Archaeological Survey of India.

BIBLIOGRAPHY

Bisht, R.S., 1976
 Transformation of the Harappan Culture in the Punjab with Special Reference to the Excavations at Sanghol and Chandigarh. In *Archaeological Congress and Seminar Papers: 1972*. U.V. Singh, ed. Pp. 16-22. Kurukshetra: Kurukshetra University Press.

Bisht, R.S., in press
 Harappan Culture in Punjab: A study in perspective. In *Indus Civilization: Problems and issues*. B.B. Lal and S.C. Malik, eds. Simla: Indian Institute of Advanced Study.

Casal, Jean-Marie, 1961
 Fouilles de Mundigak. 2 vols. Paris: Librarie C. Klincksieck.

Dikshit, K.N., 1980
 A Critical Review of Pre-Harappan Cultures in the Indo-Pakistan Subcontinent. *Man and Environment* 4: 32–43.

Ghosh, N.C., 1971
 Protohistoric Punjab: More evidence and new theories. *Conflux* 3: 19-20.

Indian Archaeology: A review (IAR), 1953-54
 Rupar, District Ambala. Pp.6-7, Delhi: Archaeological Survey of India.

Indian Archaeology: A review (IAR), 1954-55a
 Bara and Salaura, District Ambala. Pp. 9-11. Delhi: Archaeological Survey of India.

Indian Archaeology: A review (IAR), 1954-55b
 Rupar, district Ambala. P. 9. Delhi: Archaeological Survey of India.

Indian Archaeology: A review (IAR), 1958-59
 Harappan Objects in District Bhatinda. P. 73. Delhi: Archaeological Survey of India.

Indian Archaeology: A review (IAR), 1968-69
 Excavation at Sanghol, District Ludhiana. Pp. 25-26. Delhi: Archaeological Survey of India.

Indian Archaeology: A review (IAR), 1969-70
 Excavation at Sanghol, District Ludhiana. Pp. 31-32. Delhi: Archaeological Survey of India.

Indian Archaeology: A review (IAR), 1970-71a
 Excavation at Sanghol, District Ludhiana. Pp. 30-31. Delhi: Archaeological Survey of India.

Indian Archaeology: A review (IAR), 1970-71b
 Excavation at Chandigarh. Pp. 7-8. Delhi: Archaeological Survey of India.

Indian Archaeology: A review (IAR), 1971-72
 Excavation at Sanghol, District Ludhiana. Pp. 39-40. Delhi: Archaeological Survey of India.

Indian Archaeology: A review (IAR), 1972-73
 Excavation at Sanghol, District Ludhiana. P. 28. Delhi: Archaeological Survey of India.

Joshi, J.P., 1978
 Interlocking of Late Harappan and Painted Grey Ware Culture in the Light of Recent Excavations. *Man and Environment* 2: 98-101.

Joshi, J.P., in press
 Overlap of Late Harappan Culture and Painted Grey Ware Culture in the Light of Recent Excavations in Haryana, Punjab and Jammu. In *Indus Civilization: Problems and issues*. B.B. Lal and S.C. Malik, eds. Simla: Indian Institute of Advanced Study.

Khan, F.A., 1965
 Excavations at Kot Diji. *Pakistan Archaeology* 2: 13-85.

Lalman, 1971
 Discovery of Ancient Chandigarh. *Vishveshvaranand Indological Journal* 9 (2): 368-73.

Madhu Bala, 1978
 A Survey of the Protohistoric Investigation in Punjab and the Emergent Picture. *Indian Anthropologist* 8 (2): 1-30.

Mughal, M.R., 1973
 The Present State of Research on the Indus Valley Civilization. Proceedings of the International

Symposium on Moenjodaro. Pp. 1–28. Karachi: National Book Trust.

Pande, B.M., 1972-73
Inscribed Harappan Pot Sherds from Chandigarh. *Puratattva* 6: 52-55.

Prufer, Olaf, 1952
Nalagarh 1951: Interim report on the excavations carried out at Dher Majra. Calcutta: Jamia Millia Islamia Historical Research Foundation.

Sharma, Y.D., 1955-56
Past Patterns of Living as Unfolded by Excavations at Rupar. *Lalit Kala* 1-2: 121-29.

Sharma. Y.D., 1971
Comments in the Seminar on OCP and NBP. *Puratattva* 5: 21-24.

Sharma. Y.D., 1973
Value of Common Ceramic Designs from Different Sites as a Guide to Chronology with Special Reference to Pottery from Bara (Punjab). In *Radiocarbon and Indian Archaeology.* D.P. Agrawal and A. Ghosh, eds. Pp. 222-30 Bombay: Tata Institute of Fundamental Research.

Sharma. Y.D., 1976
Transformation of the Harappan Culture in the Punjab. In *Archaeological Congress and Seminar Papers: 1972.* U.V. Singh, ed. Pp. 5-15. Kurukshetra: Kurukshetra University.

Sharma, Y.D., in press a
Bara and the So-called Late Harappan Cultures of the Punjab and Haryana. In *Indus Civilization: Problems and Issues.* B.B. Lal and S.C. Malik, eds. Simla: Indian Institute of Advanced Study.

Sharma, Y.D., in press b
The Harappans and the Painted Grey Ware People in the Punjab. Paper read at the XIII Annual Session of the Punjab History Conference.

Singh, U.V., in press
Late Harappan Culture as Revealed by Excavations at Mirzapur and Daulatpur, District Kurukshetra. In *Indus Civilization: Problems and issues.* B.B. Lal and S.C. Malik, eds. Simla: Indian Institute of Advanced Study.

Suraj Bhan, 1967
New Light on the Ochre Colored Ware Culture. *Research Bulletin (Arts) Punjab University* 57 (3): 1-9.

Suraj Bhan and J. Shafer, 1978
New Discoveries in Northern Haryana. *Man and Environment* 2: 59-68.

Thapar, B.K., 1975-76
Editorial. *Puratattva* 8:2.

Vats, M.S., 1929-30
Kotla Nihang. *Annual Report of the Archaeological Survey of India 1929-30.* Pp. 131-32. Delhi: Government of India.

Vats, M.S., 1940
Excavations at Harappa. 2 vols. Delhi: Government of India.

R.N. MEHTA

14. Some Rural Harappan Settlements in Gujarat

INDIAN tradition has evidence for a theory and practice of settlement patterns or organization. A perusal of Kautilya's *Arthashastra* is highly instructive in this matter. The author of this work has instructions for the construction of a royal residence at *Nisanta Pranadhih* in *Vinayadhikarana*. He discusses populating the country, the creation of commercial centers in the *janapadanivesa*, uses of uncultivable land, and the building of forts for protection. There is mention of populating these forts and towns in *janapadanivesa* and *durganivesa*. Military operations and camps, that is the *skandhavaras*, are considered in *sangramikam*. While discussing settlements in *janapadanivesa* he specifies that these villages should be established at a distance of a *krosa* or two so that they can afford mutual protection. These agricultural settlements should also have a population between 100 and 500 families.

Besides these largely agricultural settlements he notes the nonagricultural units appropriate to a territory. These units are tabulated as follows:

Villages	Nonagricultural establishments
800	80 *Sangrahanis*
	4 *Karvatika*
	2 *Dronamukhas*
	1 *Sthaniya*
800	87

In addition to these regulated villages, Kautilya notes outposts and forts, as well as habitats in the forest, isolated habitations on bad land, etc. There are also the nonagricultural habitations of students, teachers, soldiers, miners, traders and the like. As their number is not specified in the *Arthashastra* it can be assumed that they were created according to need. This would lead to more urban settlements.

The picture generated from the study of Kautilya's *Arthashastra* reveals some aspects of a rural urban dichotomy. This dichotomy was further imposed on Indian thinking by following a European model of towns in modern times. An interesting comparison is possible if one takes into consideration the separate existence of *Sangrahani, Karvatika, Dronamukha* and *Sthaniya*. The Indian experience is that these were not purely urban. This view is supported by Kautilya, who notes the presence of agriculturists near the *Durga* and other "urban" settlements. These references indicate the mixed nature of these settlements.

Taking these facts into consideration, the urban proportion of the Mauryan Empire would work out to have been about 10 per cent. This percentage might be made more accurate. It has already been noted that there were other human habitats with urban functions. Assigning some percentage for the settlements of teachers, soldiers, miners, etc., is essential. If one sets this at about five per cent one may not be far wrong, since these functions were carried out by only a small fraction of the population. It has been observed that some villages had one or two trading families, and the same may have been the case with other families of specialists. The other point is that they were not found in all villages. In sum, these features suggest that about five percent additional urban population is called for. These figures indicate that the urban population of the Mauryan Period was about 15 percent of the total. They depended on the remaining 85 percent for their necessities. This 85 percent of the population can be identified as those who dwelled in villages, forests, etc.

This view of settlements within an empire of the

Iron Age seems to be instructive on the situation in the Chalcolithic times. This period, with its copper technology, was a bit weak in food production, as heavy iron implements were not available. They made use of river banks and light soils for agriculture which supplemented the natural food supply. Urbanization existed in these cultures, but its percentage need not be higher than that of the Iron Age Cultures. This technological period is classified as Pre-Harappan, Harappan and Post-Harappan. It can be pointed out here that a site might appear to be Chalcolithic on the basis of limited excavations. But there is a possibility of the coexistence of earlier cultures with later cultures, either in parts of the same settlement or on different settlements in a given region. This requires careful consideration.

Large Chalcolithic settlements are few in number as compared to smaller settlements. But the bigger settlements are usually those that are studied and the smaller settlements are usually neglected. The reasons for this lie both in the sociocultural ethos of the workers, as well as in the basic availability of undisturbed sites. The former lays down the fashions and areas for research. As sociocultural conditions change, the old data are reworked, new data are collected and new viewpoints are introduced. Often this change is considered a new parameter in research. Due to the ethos of today more emphasis is given to urban studies and the analysis of smaller settlements is not undertaken on a sufficient scale to permit a glimpse of the ways of life in these places. However, some research undertaken by the Department of Archaeology, M.S. University of Baroda, in Gujarat, throws some light on it. The discovery of Harappan settlements in this state can be traced to the work of M.S. Vats, who in 1927 identified Harappan elements at the site of Rangpur in Limbdi Taluka. After this initial work, Father Heras noted the site of Somnath; however following this there was a lull in the field for about two decades.

Independence gave an impetus to discovering sites of Indus Culture in India and after 1947 many of their settlements were discovered in places such as Jammu, Kashmir, Punjab, Rajasthan, Gujarat, Madhya Pradesh, Maharashtra, and Uttar Pradesh. The excavations at a few sites have enriched our knowledge of the chronology, foreign relations, and the cultural aspects of the urban life of the Indus Culture.

It is a well-known fact that urban life cannot exist without a strong rural base. The study of this base has received much attention. This lacuna is now slowly being filled through the excavations at rural settlements in different parts of Gujarat. These sites were found in exploration by the staff and students of the Department of Archaeology and Ancient History, M.S. University of Baroda as well as the Archaeological Survey of India and the Department of Archaeology, Gujarat State (Fig 14.1).

Rural settlements are usually comparatively small with a modest thickness of deposit. For example the site of Dhatva in South Gujarat has a radius of about 150 meters and Jokha, a nearby site, is not much larger. Sites like Telod and Mehgam are also small. In Central Gujarat, the site of Nar is of modest size, as are the sites of Jafarabad, Vadgam, etc., in the Bhalbaru area. None of them is more than about 100 meters square. The picture from Kutch is identical to that from other parts of Gujarat.

Sites around Lothal and those in Jamnagar District or central Saurashtra also fall in the same class. In North Gujarat, however, the site of Zekda (Pl. 14.1) was spread over an area measuring about 700 by 200 meters. Large parts of the area were, however bereft of any measurable archaeological deposit. These features pointed out that the habitation was scattered.

A perusal of the thickness of the deposits indicates that some of the sites are a mere scatter of material exposed by the farmer's plough. Such areas often have distinct patches of antiquities. These patches are marked by an ashy color and a scatter of ceramics. They suggest the existence of small huts; this based on an analogy of remains from the recent past. The thickness of deposit at these sites ranges between 50 and 150 centimeters.

These sites have two distinctive features: (1) they are really small settlements, and (2) they probably did not survive for a very long period; at least not long enough to permit a large accumulation of archaeological debris. Both these characteristics rule out the possibility of their being urban centers, which are characterized by good planning, a road system, fortifications, brick buildings on raised platforms, systematic drainage, etc. Minor antiquities like seals and amulets are also indicative of urban functions. In the absence of this material content and the presence of ceramics, graffiti, triangular cakes, terracotta *mushtis,* balls, microbeads, and copper objects typical of the Harappan Culture they have been classified

Some Rural Harappan Settlements in Gujarat

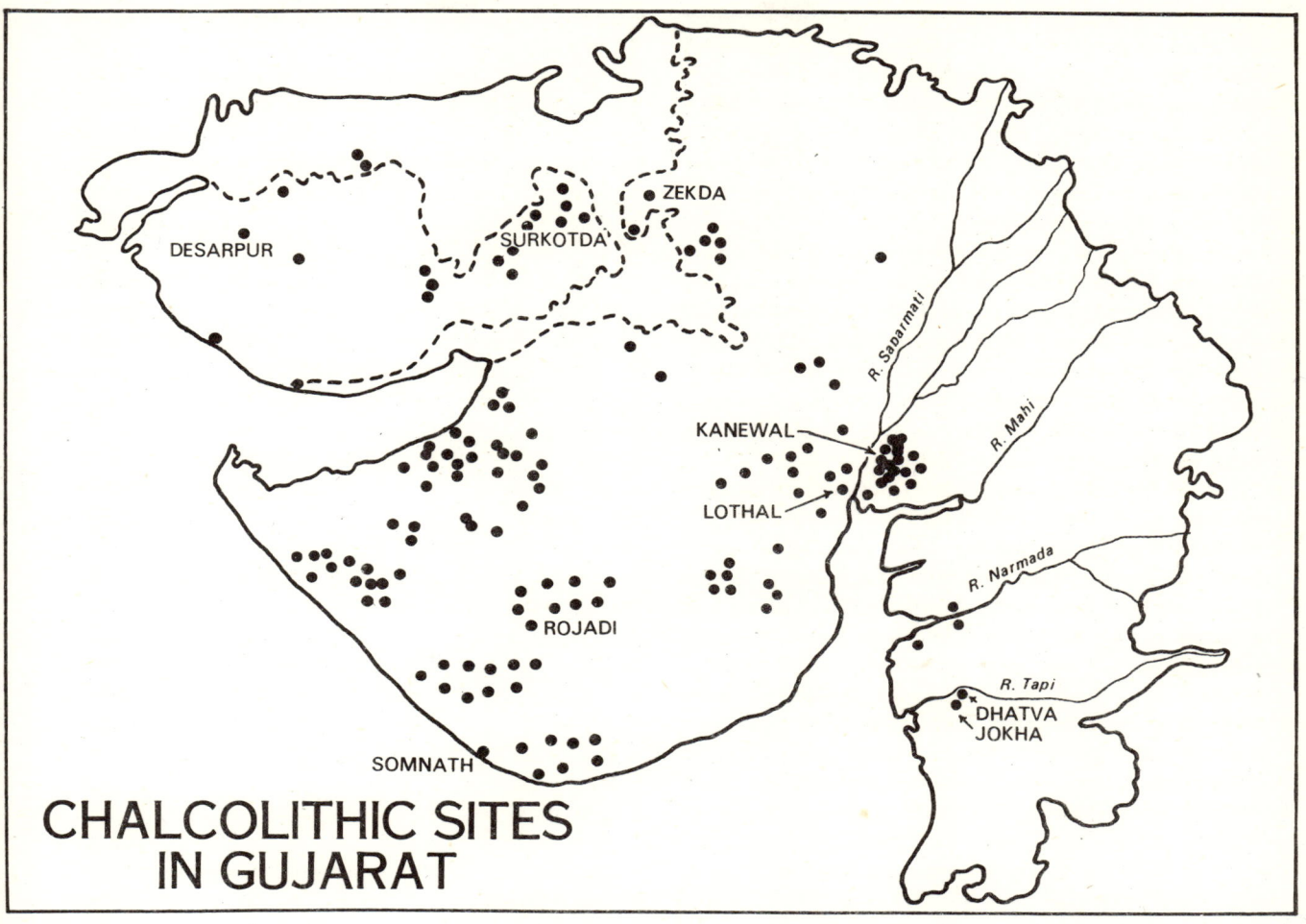

Fig. 14. 1. Chalcolithic sites in Gujarat.

as rural. They also outnumbered the so-called urban centers, and formed the base for their existence. According to the root meaning of "urban" these were "fortified habitations" and by an extension of the notion these places were involved in activities like administration, education, industrial production, trade, and commerce. The small settlements would have been the "service area" supplying basic necessities such as grain, milk and other farm or dairy products as well as forest goods. These materials could have been supplied by farmers, cattle breeders, fishermen, hunters and collectors of food, minerals, and stones. But where and how did these groups live? The answer to this question can be given theoretically: they were the inhabitants of contemporary villages and lived in forests. However, a proper understanding of the past requires exploration and excavation.

The research done on these sites indicates that particular geographical features are associated with these habitations. These include the availability of potable water, a local eminence for relative immunity from monsoon floods, and a convenient vantage point. These settlements are found on a variety of local soils. In South Gujarat, the site of Malvan is on an infertile tract near the River Tapi. The soil on which the habitation began was *kankari*, locally known as *kankaria vago*. The sites of Jokha and Dhatva, located within 50 kilometers of Malvan, are on black cotton soil. The sites at Daheda and Jafarabad in Khira District are on sand dunes. The site of Kanewal (Pl. 14.2) has structures on the dune as well at its base. Sites in *bhal* are on a flat plain. In North Gujarat, the site of Zekda (Pl. 14.1) is on a small sandstone outcrop. A rocky base is also seen at Amra, Lakhabaval and other sites in Saurashtra. These features indicate that the Harappans, and the people of Chalcolithic Culture, used a variety of local situations; however some eminence was considered useful for these settlements.

It appears that natural streams, or tanks were used for potable water. Jokha and Dhatva may have depended on local tanks. Malvan might have had a similar arrangement as it is in the tidal zone. Alternatively it could have utilized the Tapi. Bharuch depended on the Narmada. Jafarabad, Kanewal used the *boda* tank developed by dunes. Zekda seems to have depended on a local stream.

It is a significant fact, that various areas of Gujarat are prone to flood and famine under present-day climatic conditions. While excavating at different sites of the Chalcolithic Period one found soils that are similar to those formed under natural conditions in present-day jungles, river banks and elsewhere. The black soil even now develops on the exposed strata very rapidly. These indicators suggest that the climatic conditions in Gujarat during the Chalcolithic times were not much different from those that prevail today. Often, sites located in favorable environmental situations seem to have been inhabited for longer periods. But field work indicates that there are some gaps in the total cultural sequence. This may be explained by human and natural reasons.

A famine during the 17th century in Gujarat destroyed a large part of the population. As a result many settlements were completely deserted in South Gujarat. Some of these have been recently reoccupied with more favorable climatic conditions. Similar phenomena could explain both the desertion and reoccupation of the sites as well as migrations. They could also explain the gaps in the cultural sequence at different sites.

Excavations have produced some information on the housing pattern of the rural Chalcolithic folk. At Jokha, evidence for mud flooring was available, but the whole house plan was not there. However at Kanewal circular structures were discovered (Fig. 14.2). The evidence at Kesarising's Khetar mound also indicated that the circular structures existed from the beginning of the settlement until its end. At Sai-no-tekro the circular structures indicated a contemporary situation; but only at a specific point on the

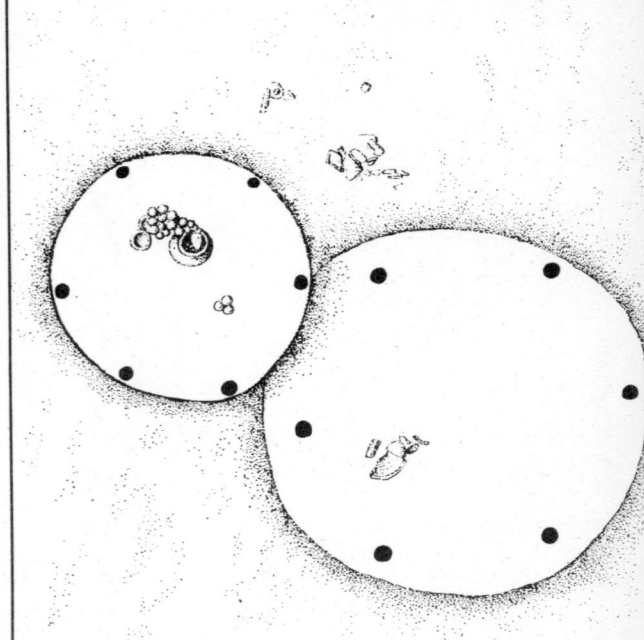

KANEWAL-1977
KESARISING'S KHETAR
TRENCH V · PLAN OF ROUND HUTS

Fig. 14.2. Kanewal, 1977. Kesarising's Khetar trench V. Plan of round huts.

mound. At Zekda evidence for circular structures was also found (Fig. 14.3). They were traced from the beginning to the end of the habitation. These circular structures had two plans. One was an uninterrupted circle. The other was a circle with a rectangular porch attached to it.

These structures had mud walls supported by wooden posts arranged along the circumference of the circle. In at least one case the presence of a central pole was indicated on the plan. At Zekda evidence of a raised water place, called a *paniyara* was available. Evidence for a hearth (*chula*) was also traced. Some burnt wall remnants indicate that they were rather thin and reminiscent of wattle and daub or the type known as *khaparda*, a frame of reeds on which a mud-cowdung mixture is applied.

Three types of structures are usually seen in the country at present. One is the hut (*zupadi parnakuti*) with wattle and daub or *khaparda*. The other is known as a *pidaria* house. It has mud walls. The third house type is of brick which is fairly rare in the rural areas. If

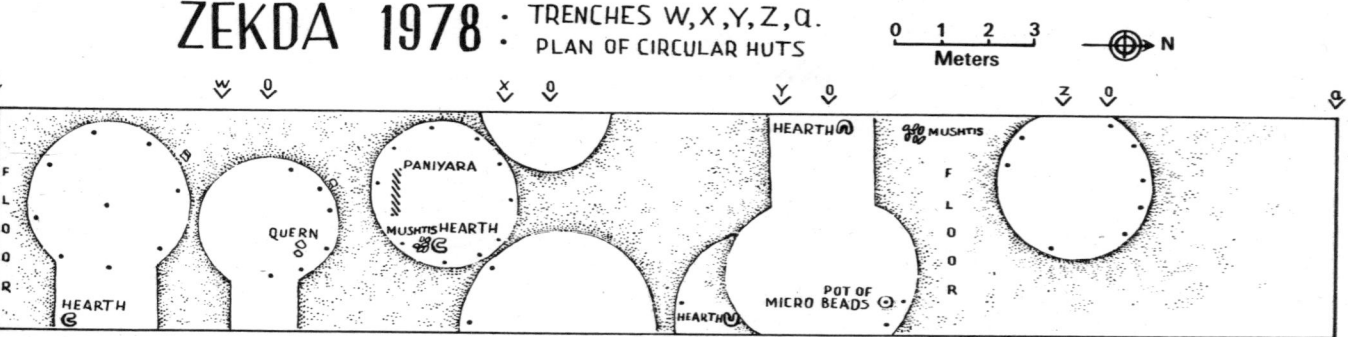

Fig. 14.3. Zekda, 1978. Trenches W, X, Y, Z, A. Plan of circular huts.

this feature of present-day village architecture is considered a phenomenon representing the recent past, it is reasonable to infer that the first two kinds of structures would have been found in the villages of the Chalcolithic Period. This inference is supported by field work.

While excavating, interesting observations were made by local field workers when circular structures were exposed. These circular structures are known as *kuba*. They are seen extensively in the Marwar area of Rajasthan and in Gujarat. They are used by a number of social groups. As some of the workers lived in such houses they helped in the study. Local inquiry indicated that a *kuba* could easily last 50 years, but its floor requires repeated plastering. The thatch roof also requires repairs either every year or every alternate year. As the family expands other *kubas* are constructed in the vicinity. If this tradition of the present-day villages is valid for the past, it could be assumed that a few families occupied different sites in a given area. Villages either grew around these family dwellings, or they were deserted for real or imaginary reasons. This type of movement existed in parts of Gujarat until recently.

The *kuba* is a fire hazard and they are often destroyed by such accidents. Evidence of this was also found at Zekda, Dhatva, Kanewal and other places.

Kubas have a long history so assigning them to a particular chronological horizon has to be done with the minor antiquities found in, or around them. Fortunately at Kanewal and Zekda there were huts with a hearth, typical Harappan ceramics (Figs. 14.4 and 14.5), terracotta balls, dishes-on-stand, microbeads, etc. From the same horizons came triangular cakes, *mushtis*. Harappan pottery includes Red Ware, Buff Ware, as well as ceramics reminiscent of Kot Diji, crude Red Wares, and Incised Wares. Black and Red Wares in crude and refined fabrics were also recovered. Zekda had painted Black and Red Ware, Reserved Slip Ware, etc. Copper, stone beads and stone tools were also discovered. These are all typical Chalcolithic antiquities.

These minor antiquities raise a number of questions of cultural dynamics and affinities. In the Indian situation one has to be a little cautious if one assumes the existence of a cultural group on the basis of a particular type of ceramic industry. The studies of potters, indicate that many of them produce utilitarian wares of several types. Some specialization is noticeable in potters themselves. They also trade their wares. Thus, a variety of ceramics could accumulate on a site. These features seem to point to the fact that several cultural trends, which can be described as old and new, coexisted in these rural settlements.

A reference to the chronological situation over a larger area indicates that at ca. 2000 B.C. Ahar was active, along with Lothal and Mohenjodaro. These sites are all in distinct cultural zones. A question concerning the movement of people therefore becomes relevant. Such movement could bring different cultural groups to a common platform of coexistence. It could cause a recession of one group and the continuation of others in the same area.

Evidence of coexistence is provided by an examination of techniques and materials. The occurrence of a copper knife at the Late Stone Age site of Langhnaj, and the anthropomorphic copper object from Lothal can be cited as evidence for the exchange of materials. The availability of cores with the crested grinding ridge technique from Saurashtra and long fluted cores from Chandaravati can be inter-

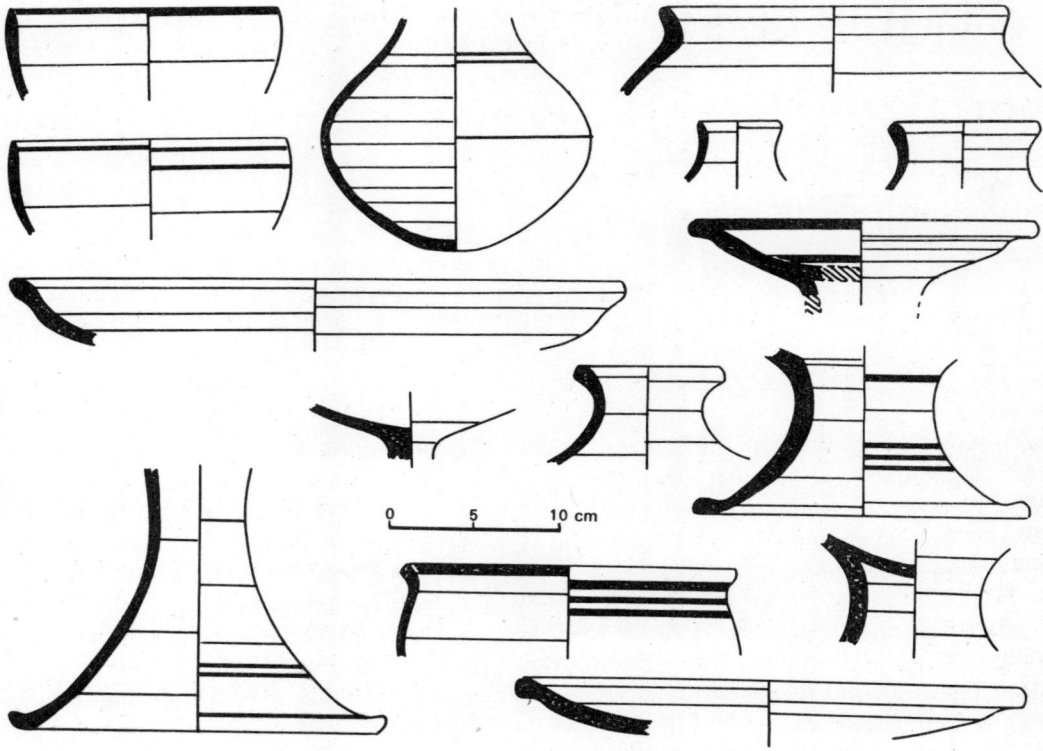

Fig. 14.4. Pottery from Kanewal and Zekda.

preted as evidence for the acceptance of these techniques by the Late Stone Age groups. The production of stone tools, especially short blades and geometric microliths by the villages of Jokha, Dhatva, Kanewal, Zekda, as well as by the urban dwellers at Lothal and Surkotada indicate the acceptance of the Late Stone Age techniques by these Chalcolithic groups. This is partly due to the fact that this technique is suitable for working with the available raw material.

Stratigraphically, there is some interesting evidence for the recession of one group and the continuity of another at Sai-no-tekro at Kanewal. On this sand dune the lower deposit is Late Stone Age material. Two huts of Chalcolithic people were traced over this level. After the destruction of the huts came Late Stone Age tools, cores, flakes, etc. This evidence indicates that after the abandonment of the Chalcolithic villages, the Late Stone Age Cultures continued to exist. The situation reminds one of the historical period.

The historical urban centers like Champaner, Shamlaji, Maheswere, Nagara, Tripuri, and others have clear evidence for the destruction of urban life and the continuation of rural settlement. It is also seen that the cultural groups that received a temporary setback eventually revived their vitality and replaced the later groups. The evacuation of a given area in the time of stress, brought on by either natural or human forces, and its reoccupation is also known. It seems that such a phenomenon is reflected in the evidence from Kanewal.

It would be interesting to analyze the faunal and floral environment of the rural setting. As already discussed, the character of the soils below the Chalcolithic habitations and the present-day earth are similar. The soils developed in forest areas and covering the structures of the 15th-16th centuries are also similar to those that are found below these habitations. If this similarity represents the climatic factors of temperature, humidity, seasonal changes, etc., then it can be concluded that the climate of the Chalcolithic Period was similar to the present. The argument can also be supported by animal remains. These sites have cattle, buffalo, *barasingha, chital,* hog deer, *nilgai,* rhinoceros, pig, dog, varanus, sheep, goat, cheetah and a variety of shells. The

Some Rural Harappan Settlements in Gujarat

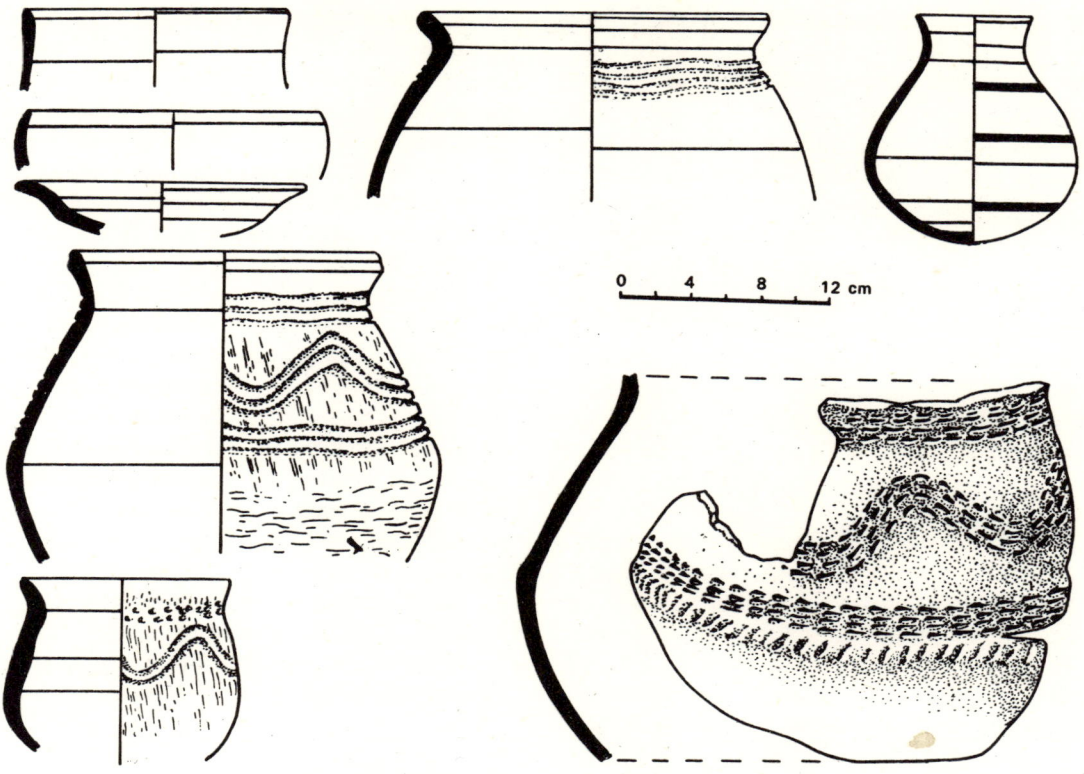

Fig. 14.5. Pottery from Kanewal and Zekda.

presence of all these animals in Gujarat has been established; although some of them are now extinct. But, it is important to note that they were wiped out due to human interference, such as over hunting. They indicate, then, that the environment has been fairly steady for a long period.

The discovery of charred animal bones and those with cut marks give some idea of nonvegetarian eating habits. Domesticated goat, sheep, cattle were eaten as well as deer, *barasingha*, *nilgai*, and pigs. Varanus was also consumed. Even at present, it is considered a delicacy, especially in winter, by some living tribes. The presence of cheetah indicates the existence of wild cats that subsisted on the animals and were in turn the food of man. Today these carnivorous animals are being continuously destroyed by man. The presence of camel and horse is also indicated. So also is the presence of bullocks indicated, being used for transport.

These animal remains also provide interesting environmental data on the basis of their natural habitats and food habits. Hog deer, *chital*, cattle and buffalo, subsist on grass. The goat and *nilgai* require foliage.

The rhinoceros and pigs require marshy areas which develop in natural depressions along streamlets, rivers and between sand dunes. These natural water reservoirs supply drinking water for animals and men, and also produce vegetation like the lecromina croix, as well as wild varieties of edible grains. The lecromina croix was found at Zekda. The presence of rice, wheat and other grains from other sites indicates that along with agriculture, there was the collection of wild grains like *banti sama,* which grow in the areas where lecromina develops.

The environmental picture with foliage, grasslands and marshes is indicative of abundant food resources. Local forests also had an abundant food supply all the year round with fruits, tubers, beans and grains. This broad base of food encouraged the life of *vanprasthas,* who lived in forests, and *unchravritti* of Indian saints. Interestingly, the collection of wild edible seeds can yield a fairly large stock, one which can last for the lean period of the year. Agricultural and cattle breeding activities would further augment this base. The discovery of large storage jars from Kanewal indicate that about 150 kilograms of grain could be stored in each vessel. This storage facility helped the rural population use grains, beans and the like for most of the year.

This collection and storage of food grains at one place is, according to the theory propounded by Bhoja Raja in *Samarangana Sutradhara,* the cause of struggle and the consequent development of *matsyanyaya*. The growth of political power, division of labor, and the development of urban life became necessary to control this *matsyanyaya*.

The presence of lapis lazuli, steatite and such materials that were not locally available would have been brought in by some agency. Copper and stone beads also might have been imported into these settlements. Chank came from the area of Dwarka. The presence of all these materials indicates some system of trade.

Ceramics with graffiti of the Indus script (Pl. 14.3) from these settlements, especially at Kanewal, indicate some form of literacy. These literate village settlers had wide contacts as indicated by the antiquities. These contacts indicate the presence of land routes connecting Gujarat with Sind. This was probably through Thar Parkar and Kutch which were used throughout the historic period. The inland settlements would, of course rule out maritime trade, and emphasize land routes. However, sites like Malvan, or smaller places in Jamnagar do indicate the possibility of maritime movements, especially in eastern Saurashtra and coastal southern Gujarat. The River Tapi might have provided the route to Khandesh. Kutch and Saurashtra might have been similarly connected.

What happened to these groups with the passage of time? This cannot be ascertained by a simple hypothesis. Each site will require its own history. It seems that Jokha was abandoned due to the lack of water. Zekda indicates destruction by fire. Drought and abandonment of some of the sites can also be envisaged. Finding the reasons behind the abandonment of these sites will require careful analysis of the settlement, local topography, climatic and human situation.

Much further work is needed to understand the rural life of the Harappans. Future work on this problem should involve exploration and systematic excavation in different regions of the Indus Culture.

BIBLIOGRAPHY

Agrawala, V.S., 1966
Samarangana Sutradhara of King Bhoja of Dhara. Revised edition of T. Ganpati Sastri, Oriental Series 25.

Joshi, J.P., 1972
Excavations at Sur Kotada and New Light on Harappan Migration. *Journal of the Oriental Institute, University of Baroda* 22: 98-144.

Kangle, R.P., 1969
Kautilya Arthashastra. vol 1. Bombay: University of Bombay.

Mehta, R.N., et al., 1971
Excavations at Jokha. M.S. University of Baroda Archaeology Series 11.

Mehta, R.N., et al., 1975
Excavations at Dhatva. M.S. University of Baroda Archaeology Series 12.

Momin, K.N., 1979
Archaeology of Kheda District. Ph.D. dissertation, Department of Archaeology, M.S. University of Baroda.

Natarajan, D.
Indian Census Through a Hundred Years.

Parikh, R.T., 1978
Archaeology of Banaskantha District (North Gujarat) up to 1500 A.D. Ph.D. dissertation, Department of Archaeology, M.S. University of Baroda.

Rao, S.R., 1973
Lothal and the Indus Civilization. Bombay: Asia Publishing.

Sankalia, H.D., 1973
The Prehistory and Protohistory of India and Pakistan. 2nd ed. Poona: Deccan College Post-Graduate and Research Institute.

Syed, Anis Hashim, 1977
Potters and Ceramic Traditions in the Panchmahals, Baroda and Broach Districts of Gujarat. Ph.D. dissertation, Department of Archaeology, M.S. University of Baroda.

S.A. SALI

15. The Harappans of Daimabad

INTRODUCTION

My discovery of some 50 Late Harappan settlements in the Central Tapti Basin, Dhule District of Maharashtra, proved that the Harappans penetrated the Deccan (Sali 1970, in press). Although the details of the Harappan occupation of the Tapti Valley could not be understood for want of horizontal excavation at a suitable site, the evidence obtained through surface explorations indicated an absence of the urban discipline characteristic of the Mature Harappan. It also suggested that the Harappans who came from Gujarat and settled in this region had lost their prosperity before they reached the northern Deccan. The most important aspect of this discovery, however, was that it made a vast region of the Deccan available for the study of the degenerated phase of the Harappan Culture. It also made it possible to investigate Late Harappan impact on the local, succeeding Chalcolithic Cultures of the region. Research at Daimabad in the upper Godavari Basin has made a beginning toward these ends. This paper will present the evidence for the Late Harappan Phase obtained from the excavation of this site.

THE SITE AND ITS ENVIRONMENT
(Fig. 15.1)

Daimabad (lat. 19°31′ north; long. 74°42′ east) is now located in a deserted village. The modern community was recently amalgamated with the village of Ladgaon in Shrirampur Taluka of Ahmednagar District, Maharashtra. The site is located on the left bank of the Pravara River, a tributary of the Godavari, 18 kilometers southeast of Shrirampur and six kilometers southeast of Padhegaon. Both these settlements are stations on the Daund-Manmad section of the Central Railway. The occupation deposit varies in thickness from place to place. The maximum of five meters of deposit was exposed in Sector I. Occupational material was always found to overlie black cotton soil which developed on the yellow *kankari* silt. This represents the topmost deposit of a 10-meter high alluvial flat developed in a concave loop of the River Pravara during the Late Pleistocene Period. The terrain surrounding the site is a series of Late Pleistocene alluvial flats, one to two kilometers wide, which imperceptibly merge into valley pediments developed on basaltic rocks of Cretaceous-Eocene age. Drainage density is low and most of the local tributaries are monsoon ephimerals. Medium loamy and pedocalic black soils are predominant. The vegetation is the thorny scrub forest characteristic of the semiarid belt.

PREVIOUS WORK

The site was discovered in 1958 by Shri B.P. Bopardikar (IAR 1958–59: 15). Excavation in 1958–59 by Shri M.N. Deshpande revealed evidence for three phases (IAR 1958–59: 15–18). Painted pottery was scarce in Phase I. The main ceramic was a thick coarse Gray Ware, similar to that from Brahmagiri I. Vessel forms included the large globular urn with a flared rim, a basin with a slightly turned-out rim, a spherical bowl and stemmed lid with a pointed or rounded tip. The rim and the tip of the lid was painted with red ochre color. Another associated ware was handmade with incised and applied decorations. A single grave, partly cut by a later pit, but containing

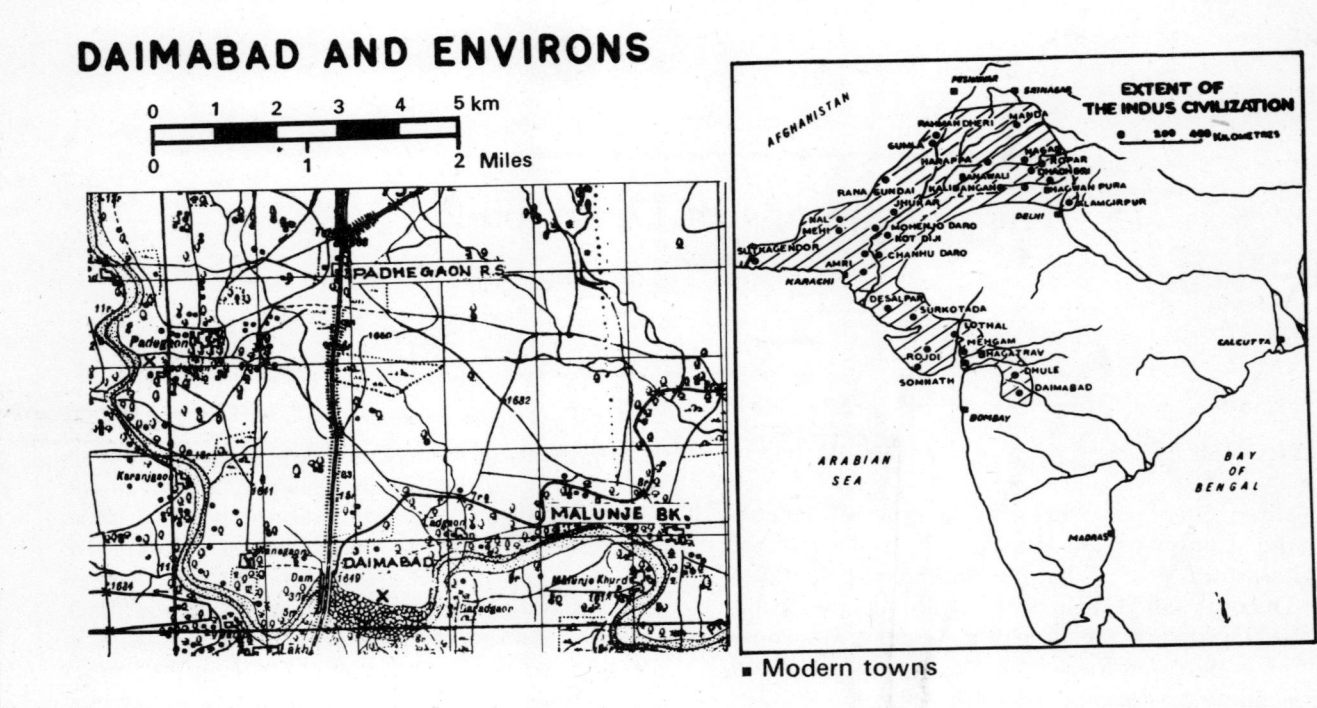

Fig. 15.1. Daimabad and environs.

one skeleton, was found. Chalcedony blades, terracotta beads and semiprecious stones were also found in this, the first occupation.

Phase II was represented by the well-defined Malwa Ware. Of medium fabric, this ceramic was treated with a thin slip which fired brown, deep red, light orange or pink. Vessels were painted in black with geometric designs such as hatched triangles, squares and lozenges, hooks, loops, festoons, etc. The types included in this ware were the subspherical bowl, sometimes with a tubular spout, shallow cup, short-necked *handi*, high-necked jar, and vase with a channel spout. A burial in a specially dug pit with a complete skeleton oriented north-south and without any associated furniture, was found in the levels of this phase. The other finds included a fragmentary celt, a pinhead and a broken knife all of copper, the head of a dog and also a humped bull in terracotta, and beads of semiprecious stone, shell and faience.

Phase III was a Jorwe occupation. Jorwe Ware had a fine fabric, was turned on a fast wheel and was well fired. The main types included the concave-sided carinated bowl, occasionally with a tubular spout, a *handi*-type vase with a flaring mouth and tubular spout, and a vase with a globular body, high neck and beaded rim. The painted designs in black were linear and geometric, although animal motifs were also present. The Burnished Gray Ware and the handmade thick coarse ware of Phase I persisted into this phase. Microlithics, stone maceheads, pottery spindle-whorls, beads of semiprecious stones, a gold coil, two terracotta human figures and a terracotta dog were also found.

Two types of burial practices were in vogue during Phase III: the extended inhumation and the urn burial. One of the two interred skeletons was completely despoiled. The second, oriented north-south, rested on a rammed clay floor in the habitation area. It had no grave goods and it was damaged below the knees. The body had not been placed in a pit; but around it were 14 postholes, suggesting the existence of a canopy over the interment. This is, therefore, probably a case of lying in state prior to burial. In the urn burials the urns are a Burnished Gray Ware with a globular body and flared mouth. These were placed mouth-to-mouth, with a north-south orientation, in a pit just sufficiently large to accommodate them. The skull ribs and lower extremities were placed in the vessel. A single urn burial, with the pot's mouth facing south, was also found. Three urns were placed horizontally for the burial of a mature child. A carinated bowl and a spouted *handi*-type vase were subsidiary vessels.

In 1974 there was the chance discovery of a cache of four solid bronze figures at the site.* This group included a chariot yoked to a pair of bulls driven by a human, an elephant, a rhinoceros and a buffalo. This find necessitated further excavation at the site. In 1974–75, S.R. Rao (1978) renewed the excavation of the site. His main objectives were to reassess the cultural sequence, and determine whether there were cultural contacts with Harappan or Late Harappan settlements. He divided the occupational deposit into three periods, I, II and III.

Period I (1900–1700 B.C.) was divisible into two Subperiods, A and B. Subperiod IA was the first Neolithic settlement and had plain, handmade gray pottery. Subperiod IB was characterized by pottery made on a slow wheel, painted in red on a grayish or red surface. The three main ceramics of Subperiod IB were the Gray Slipped Ware, a dark Gray Burnished Ware and dull Red Ware. A few vessels were turned on a fast wheel. The painted designs included vertical wavy lines drawn in groups, cross-hatched bands and ladders, and an antelope. These designs suggested, according to Rao, contact with the Late Harappans who had by now moved to the Tapti and Godavari Valleys.

Period II (1700–1500 B.C.) was characterized by Malwa Ware and the Cream Slipped Ware. Rao thought that designs such as the hatched diamonds and dancing figures on Malwa Ware were influenced to a large extent by the Late Harappan. During the Period III (1500–1000 B.C.) Malwa Ware decreased and Jorwe Ware increased. The main types Rao found in the Jorwe Ware were stemmed bowls of Rangpur IIC type, concave-convex bowls, spouted vessels and globular jars.

Rao claimed to have identified furnaces used for refining copper. He also thought he had found evidence for the survival of the Indus Script in Periods II and III. The evidence he used for the presence of a simplified script at Daimabad, is the occurrence of Indus symbols on pottery. Most of these signs are identical to the cursive alphabet found during the Late Harappan Phase in Gujarat and the Indus Valley.

EXCAVATIONS AT DAIMABAD
1975–76 to 1978–79

I have excavated at Daimabad for four seasons (1975–76 to 1978–79) and have obtained evidence for a succession of five Chalcolithic Cultures. Each of these is characterized by a distinct class of painted pottery:

Phase I	Savalda Culture
Phase II	Late Harappan Culture
Phase III	Buff and Cream Ware Culture
Phase IV	Malwa Culture
Phase V	Jorwe Culture

People of the Savalda Culture built the first, and smallest, settlement at Daimabad. They occupied a three-hectare strip of black cotton soil near the bank of the Pravara. The largest settlement of 30 hectares was occupied by the last of the Jorwe inhabitants. The other three settlements, including that of the Late Harappans, covered not less than 20 hectares. Ancient Daimabad is thus the largest Chalcolithic site to have been found in Maharashtra. The salient features of each phase are summarized as follows:

Phase I

The Savalda Culture is characterized by Savalda Ware. Of medium to coarse fabric, the ware was made on a slow wheel and has a thick slip with a crackled surface. The color is light brown, chocolate, red and pink. It is chiefly painted in ochre red with occasionally black and white pigments. The designs included arrows, antenae-ended pointed and rounded arrowheads, a harpoon, sword-like designs, plant, deer and fish motifs as well as linear designs such as horizontal bands, radiating lines, groups of short strokes, pointed strokes, wavy lines and oblique strokes. There are very few types: a vase with an out-curved rim and squat globular body, a *handi*-type vase and a vase with a short splayed-out rim. The Burnished Gray Ware, the Black Burnished Corrugated Ware and the handmade Thick Coarse Red Ware with incised and applied decorations are the other ceramics of Phase I.

---

*Editor's note: See M. K. Dhavalikar's paper in this volume for further discussion of this hoard.

The mud-walled Savalda houses were at times rounded on one end. Structures of one, two and three rooms were found. The smallest house, with a single room, measured 3.4 by 1.6 meters. The largest house was seven by five meters. The floors, which were occasionally decorated with fresh water shells, were made of alternating layers of yellow silt and black soil.

Barley was cultivated along with lentil, the common pea, grass pea, black gram, green gram, horse gram and hyacinth bean. They also had copper/bronze rings, beads of carnelian and agate, microliths, tanged bone arrowheads and stone mullers and querns.

Phase II will be described later since it is the main subject matter of this paper.

Phase III

The Buff and Cream Ware which characterized Phase III was generally made on a slow wheel. Only an occasional fast wheel example was met with. Of medium fabric, the clay contained vegetable temper. This was indicated in the core by the presence of air holes. The core also had a band of gray or ivory color suggesting that the ware was underfired. It was treated on the outside with a thin slip which flaked off in places. The painting was generally black with geometric designs such as cross-hatched elongated triangles, diamonds and squares, horizontal bands, groups of wavy lines, comb-like design, circles and animal motifs with stippled bodies.

Fragments of two graduated terracotta rings suggested that the people of this phase had their own measuring system.

They practised symbolic as well as partial burial.

Phase IV

Phase IV was represented by Malwa Ware. Extensive evidence has now come to light at Daimabad to show that the Jorwe Culture was mainly derived from the Malwa. For example, types such as the carinated bowl, the *handi*-type vase with tubular spout, the incurved bowl and the *lota*, which occurred in Malwa Ware, continued to occur in Jorwe Ware. The same is the case with regard to the so-called black painted potter's marks and the graffiti. Similarly, the double-urn burials, so characteristic of the Jorwe Culture of the Upper Godavari Valley, first occurred in the Malwa context. In a double-urn burial of Phase IV one of the Malwa Ware urns was painted with sun, dog and peacock designs. The dog was a favorite animal motif, frequently found on Malwa Ware. One of the examples has a pair of dogs in united position. Another noteworthy scene on one of the potsherds of Malwa Ware is of a man standing in a river with fish and vegetation around him.

Among the structures exposed in the Malwa levels the most interesting is a large mud platform with a channel ending in a soak pit cut into it. This was meant to be used for ablution purposes. There are six types of sacrificial altars including an apsidal, mud-walled structure, called a sacrificial temple. Another altar was made from a series of mud rings. There was also a heart-shaped altar, an oval-shaped altar with a sunken floor, an oval-shaped altar with rounded sides and a rectangular altar. In addition, there were residential rooms closely connected with the religious complex.

The floors of the Malwa houses were decorated with potsherds, by either embedding them on edge or flat. Each house had a low mud step at the entrance, one of which was semicircular, recalling the *chandrashila*.

Phase V

The Jorwe Ware of Phase V at Daimabad comes with all of its characteristic types and painted designs. In addition, there is the Burnished Gray Ware and the handmade thick coarse ware. The Jorwe types from the earliest Phase V levels are deep red in color and have a shiny surface, likened by some to Lustrous Red Ware. But this is the natural outcome of the transition from Malwa to Jorwe. There is neither the true Lustrous Red Ware, nor stemmed bowls of Rangpur IIC type, in this, or any other, phase of Daimabad.

The so-called painted potter's marks on the Jorwe Ware occur only singly here, and many of them are not represented in the list of Indus signs. These marks may have some social or religious significance; but they do not seem to represent a simplified version of the Indus Script.

Structural levels one to five were exposed in this Phase. The houses of structural level four were circular huts with a road and a lane. In the other levels of Phase V they were either rectangular or square. The important features of structural level one included two potter's kilns, one aspsidal sacrificial temple, one crescentic mud structure (perhaps a sacrificial altar), one circular ashpit connected with

The Harappans of Daimabad

rituals relating children, and mud-walled houses. One interesting house exposed in Sector I was seven meters long and 3.5 meters broad. The largest of the houses was found in structural level two (House No. 38). It originally measured nine by five meters, and had five major floor levels. With each successive level the size of the house shrank. One of the fully exposed potter's kilns measured five meters square. It was made up of a platform, an outer mud-wall (1.4 meters high and 50 centimeters broad at the base tapering upward to 15 centimeters), the central ash packing which served as insulation, and the thin inner wall of burnt laminar clay. The kiln was filled with fine gravel used to raise the temperature in the kiln. It had two stoke holes. There were two compartments and on the floor of one were found 15 crushed pots. All save one, which was of handmade ware, were Jorwe Ware. The various painted graffiti on the Jorwe pots from the kiln suggest that they cannot be considered potter's marks, as has been generally held. A huge jar of handmade ware found close to the kiln was profusely decorated in applique with arch designs, human and bull figures as well as reptiles.

Among the important finds from the Jorwe Phase is a unique terracotta covered by a coat of red ochre with the figure of a deified sage and his three consorts united with him. There is also a terracotta cylinder seal with a scene of a procession moving through the jungle. There is a horse drawing a cart, followed by a deer looking majestically to the rear. In front is an animal, perhaps a camel, with a long neck.

CHRONOLOGY

Two lists of Daimabad ^{14}C dates have been received from the Physical Research Laboratory (D.P. Agrawal, personal communication). They are given below as calculated from the 5570 half-life as well as the 5730 value (in parentheses). The dates Before Christ are given as well.

The date of ca. 1400 B.C. for the end of the Malwa and the beginning of the Jorwe (samples PRL 411 and PRL 412) appears to be consistent with the ^{14}C determination of 1400 B.C. obtained from Inamgaon for the beginning of the Jorwe Culture there (Dhavalikar 1977: 46–47).

The sample PRL 420 was collected from a slope. It was buried by a patch of sand and silt deposited in a raingully and so it was suspected to have been contaminated. Hence the date of A.D. 500 is not surprising.

Phase	Sample number	Date
Overlap between Phases IV and V	PRL 411	3230 ± 100 (3320 ± 100) 1370 B.C.
Topmost layer of Phase IV	PRL 412	3250 ± 110 (3340 ± 120) 1390 B.C.
Phase III	PRL 419	2980 ± 110 (3070 ± 110) 1120 B.C.
Phase II	PRL 420	1410 ± 140 (1450 ± 140) 500 A.D.
Phase II	PRL 426	3600 ± 150 (3710 ± 150) 1760 B.C.
Phase III	PRL 428	3400 ± 110 (3500 ± 110) 1550 B.C.
Phase I	PRL 429	3390 ± 150 (3490 ± 160) 1540 B.C.

The date of 1760 B.C. derived from sample PRL 426 is close to what was expected (1800 B.C.) for the upper levels of the Late Harappan Phase at Daimabad. This estimate is based on stratigraphy as well as the date of 1600 B.C. for the beginning of the Malwa Phase in Maharashtra which is based on ^{14}C dates for Inamgaon (Dhavalikar 1977) and the date of 1390 B.C. (or 1400 B.C.) for the topmost layer of the Malwa Phase given by the sample PRL 412 from Daimabad.

The dates from samples PRL 419, PRL 428 and PRL 429 are inconsistent.

PHASE II—THE HARAPPANS OF DAIMABAD

As noted above, Phase II at Daimabad represents a Late Harappan occupation. The deposit of this Phase varies in thickness from a few centimeters at and near the findspot of the bronzes in Sector II to 45 centimeters in Sector IV. In Sector I it was 30 centimeters and in Sector II 20 centimeters. In all sectors the soil color was light brown. Laboratory studies by J.N. Rajaguru (personal communication) show that the Late Harappan occupational deposit at Daimabad underwent weathering, suggesting that the site was unoccupied, although for a short period, after it was deserted by the Harappans and before it was occupied by the people of the Buff and Cream Ware Culture. This occupational deposit was also eroded (Sali in press).

Phase II has the characteristic fine sturdy Late Harappan Red Ware (Pl. 15.1). It is made of fine clay mixed with fine sand and the powder of lime and/or shell was used as a tempering material. The ware was turned on a fast wheel as indicated by the uniformity of the parallel striation marks on the inside. The core of the ware is fairly dense and uniformly light red or brick red in color suggesting that the pottery was baked under controlled, uniform heat under oxidizing conditions. The outside of the ware was treated with a thin slip which is usually red, but occasionally chocolate or light brown, pink and light gray. The black painted designs include horizontal bands on the rim, neck, shoulder and body, crosshatched triangles, groups of vertical wavy and straight lines between horizontal bands, a chain pattern, a buchranian or doublehorn motif, a plant-like motif, interlaced loops painted on the inside of the rim of dish-on-stand, loops, spirals, rows of dots above and below a horizontal band and radiating lines. An interesting design was found on the body of a globular pot lacking only the neck and rim. There were three black bands painted around the body of this vessel. Above the topmost of these bands were two vertical lines painted in black, the upper parts of which had been curved to resemble a snake. Other types (vessel forms) included in this ware are the dish-on-stand, bowl-on-stand, a dish with an internally collared rim, a vase with a beaded rim, a vase with a clubbed rim, a cup or bowl, a vase with a flat base and a vase with a beaked rim.

The associated wares are Ribbed Bichrome, Fine Deep Red, Black and Pale Gray, Burnished Gray Ware and Thick Coarse Ware.

The Ribbed Bichrome Ware (Pl. 15.2) is represented by only a few sherds. It was made from a special paste, very dense in texture and without any tempering material. The core is grayish in color. The slip on one side of the rib was bright chocolate in color, and on the other side it was cream colored. The surface of the latter was painted in black with a loop design. About six sherds were found of the Deep Red Ware (Pl. 15.2). This ware is comparable to that of the Ribbed Bichrome Ware in fabric.

A small number of sherds of the Black and Pale Gray Ware were found. Of fine fabric, the ware is thin and treated internally and externally with a slip which has turned pale gray on the outside and black on the inside. Only one type is represented in this ware: a conical bowl with a carinated neck and featureless rim.

The Burnished Gray Ware is of medium fabric. It was treated with a slip and burnished. The surface colors include gray, ivory, black, pink, brown and their shades. The types met with in this ware are a vase with a flaring rim, a vase with an outcurved rim, a bowl with an almost vertical profile, an incurved bowl, a carinated vase and a dish with a carination below a thin rim. A variety of lids were also found. The rim edge of lids and some of the vases were painted with a horizontal band in red ochre.

The Thick Coarse Ware was handmade with a coarse gritty fabric, pink and light red in color. The ware is decorated on the outside with incised and applied fingertip designs. Those included in this ware are a jar with an outcurved rim, a deep platter or bowl with an almost vertical and thickened rim decorated on the top with fingertip designs and platter with almost vertical sides and a flat rim tip. Embedded in the floor of House Number 17 we found the lower half of a Thick Coarse Ware jar which has a flattish base.

The Late Harappan occupants of Daimabad built both mud-brick and simpler mud-walled structures. Mud bricks were used in two ways: for walls and for a grave. Mud bricks in walls were only attested in fragmentary examples. The size of one of the specimen bricks measured 30 centimeters long by eight centimeters thick. Two other fragmentary bricks were found bonded together with a mortar of black clay. These and other brick fragments were found in a mass which appears to represent the debris from a fallen mud brick wall.

The grave lined with mud brick had an extended human skeleton. This was found in the occupational deposit of Sector I (Pl. 15.3). The ovoid pit bottom of the grave was made in two stages. In the first stage mud brickbats, occasional pebbles and clayey earth were rammed. A layer of clayey earth mixed with fine gravel and burnt clay lumps was spread and rammed over this surface. The floor was then plastered. Full-sized mud bricks and mud brickbats were then placed leaving sufficient space for the corpse to rest on the plastered floor in an extended position. The head is towards the north but tilted to its left. The body was covered with a material like hemp, the fibers of which were found sticking to the skeleton. The grave was then covered with earth mixed with a number of brickbats. This formed tumulus with a stone placed at the point where the head was resting. The sizes of the full mud bricks used in the grave were: (1) 32 cm by 16 cm by 8 cm, and (2) 28 cm by 14 cm by 7 cm. Both sizes have the ratio 1:2:4. Complete mud bricks were found only around the head, since the rest of the grave pit was disturbed by later pits.

The evidence for mud-walled houses in Sector II is fragmentary because most of the walls were disturbed by later occupants. The walls that we found were made of black earth with foundations in the black soil which lay below the light brown occupational deposit of this Phase. The shortest exposed wall measured 45 centimeters long and 43 centimeters broad. The longest wall, lying north-south, was traced to a length of 33 meters, its thickness varying from 30 to 50 centimeters. By using the surviving walls we traced patches of floor in six structures (House Nos. 16 to 21), although the complete plan of a house could not be found. Large patches of finely plastered floors were found in Houses 16, 17, 18 and 20. A circular hearth, 50 centimeters in diameter and 10 centimeters deep, containing ash and charred animal bone fragments was found in House 16. On the floor of this same house was a terracotta button-shaped seal bearing an Indus sign (Pl. 15.4). In adjoining House 17 we found another terracotta button-shaped seal with two Indus signs. The lower half of a vase of Thick Coarse Ware with a flattish base was also found embedded in the floor of this house.

The most important finds which set to rest the Harappan character of Phase II at Daimabad are the two terracotta button-shaped seals and three potsherds, all bearing Indus signs or script. The Indus signs on two of the potsherds were engraved (Pl. 15.5) and on one of the potsherds they were painted in black (Pl. 15.6).

Special mention should also be made of a crescent-shaped Red Ware sherd (Pl. 15.7), which had been ground to its present form. On one side was engraved a scene of a tiger attacking a buffalo from behind. The forceful attack of the tiger and the panic of the buffalo have been excellently depicted. On the other side of this sherd (Pl. 15.7) is a horizontal row of six lozenges with oblique lines inside the upper half of each shape and an open space between the two lower lozenges. The unique engraving on this purposefully-shaped potsherd leads one to surmise that the object represents a cult object. Equally important are the finds of a wornout oval-shaped terracotta cake (Pl. 15.8, no. 7), heart-shaped potsherd (Pl. 15.8, no. 12), the shape being artificial, a "carrot"-type clay cone recovered from House No. 20, a fragmentary terracotta scale with a division of 11 millimeters marked by two incised lines, a circular potsherd with a deeply engraved cross mark on both the sides (Pl. 15.8, no. 10), a fragment of a copper/bronze celt and a bead of gold leaf. We also found pottery objects of indeterminate use, blades of chert and chalcedony, carnelian beads, and others of agate and shell, a shell bangle and a large number of bivalve fresh-water shells.

The author has described (Sali in press) the four bronzes, which on circumstantial and stylistic evidence, can be ascribed to the Late Harappan Phase at Daimabad.

DISCUSSION

The pottery types, the Indus script on terracotta seals and pottery, the mud bricks in the 1:2:4 ratio, the grave pattern, the terracotta cake and the "carrot"-type cone are all undoubtedly Harappan cultural traits. The pottery is an inferior quality if compared to that of the Mature Harappan Phase in Gujarat, Rajasthan and the Indus Valley as well as the Late Harappan pottery in the Tapti Valley. This may be due to the quality of local material. But, the most important aspect of the ceramics is that the Harappan potter produced as fine and sturdy a ware as he could and made traditional Harappan types on the fast wheel to keep up his tradition. He, or she, had not given up the production of Bichrome Ware made from a fine paste. The predominant designs were simple geometric patterns painted in black, as was the practice in the Tapti Valley. There is, however, a single example of the snake pattern as found at Lothal (Rao 1963: Pl. XLVIII, 5). This indicates a continuity of both the ceramic tradition as well as that involving the meaning of particular representations.

The Indus script, on both seals and pottery, has the same form as that which occurs during the Mature Phase elsewhere; although the seal type differs in both material and detail. At Daimabad the seals are of terracotta instead of steatite and the knobs on the back are conical rather than dome-shaped. There is also no hole. The absence of steatite in the region must have been the reason for preparing terracotta seals. The absence of animal representations on these seals is also a noteworthy feature. The idea of preparing seals did, however, survive. It is generally held that the Harappan seals were used for commercial purposes. Trade at Daimabad is, however, very unclear.

As noted above, the mass of mud bricks found by the side of a mud wall in Sector II probably represents fallen debris. Thus the Harappans used mud bricks for construction in the early stage of their arrival at the site. The grave lined in mud brick, with its filling forming a tumulus above surface level, has a parallel at Harappa (Wheeler 1947: 89 and Pl. XXXVII B). A grave lined with mud brick was also found at Lothal (Rao 1973: 147 and Pl. XXXVIII B).

Although a complete plan of a Harappan house has not yet been recovered, the exposed mud walls and their traces, certainly indicate a systematic layout for the community. The Harappans of Daimabad had a system of linear measurements, as attested by the fragment of a terracotta scale. How this fits with other Harappan units of measurement has not yet been studied. The "carrot"-type clay cone recalls other clay cones from Mohenjodaro (Marshall 1931: 475–78, Pl. CXXXIV).

The terracotta cake from Daimabad recalls those from Kalibangan, Lothal and other Harappan sites. Its worn condition need not make it a skin scrubber. Whether the artificially shaped triangular, or heart-shaped, potsherd was meant to be used in place of a triangular terracotta cake is not yet understood; although such a possibility cannot be ruled out.

The deeply engraved plain cross on both the sides of a circular potsherd reminds one of the plain multiple crosses on seals from Mohenjodaro (Marshall 1931: Pl. CXIV, 520 and 528 B).

A majority of the flaked stone blades recovered from Phase II are of chalcedony. There are, however, a few of chert, which is rare in the region. Thus the abundant chalcedony was used in large quantity for producing blades. Yet the occurrence of the small amount of chert is noteworthy since it was the predominant material used for producing blades by the Harappans during the Mature Phase.

The bead of gold leaf, a rare and costly metal, may represent one of the vestiges of their past richness. A piece of slag indicates metal-smelting activities on the site; although no evidence for a copper-smelting furnace has so far been found.

The occurrence of Late Harappan remains in an area measuring about 20 hectares at Daimabad suggests quite a large settlement of "feeble descendants of the Harappans" in the Godavari Basin, several hundred kilometers from the Harappan homeland. This is the largest of Chalcolithic sites known in the Upper Godavari Basin. The possible population of this settlement is an issue which is being studied. If however, the data collected from the surrounding four villages is a guide it may be tentatively presumed that the population of Late Harappan Daimabad was about 7500. So large a settlement should be classed as a small town rather than a village. Daimabad was thus perhaps the only town in the region, the rest of the settlements being villages.

The excavations at Daimabad by the author have yielded unequivocal evidence of the Late Harappan Phase. This discovery has now paved the way for undertaking studies into a set of crucial problems: (1) the end of the Harappans, (2) the allied issue of Harappan contributions to the Chalcolithic Cultures of the Deccan, (3) the distribution of the Harappan settlements on the Deccan and the extent of the southward movement of the Harappan Culture, and (4) the final form of the transformed Harappan Culture in South and Central India as a whole.

There is no evidence at Daimabad which indicates

the transformation of the Late Harappan Culture into a Post-Harappan Culture similar to that at Rangpur in Gujarat. So far the evidence clearly indicates that the Harappans at Daimabad abandoned the site for unknown reasons. Perhaps the desertion was sudden so as not to allow them to carry away the four large bronzes. These were cult objects which they seem to have carried with them from their homeland in the Indus basin as they moved to the Deccan through Gujarat and settled at Daimabad after crossing the Tapti basin. Further movement is clearly implied by this evidence, and coupled with the fact that the Harappans were already in an improverished state when they reached the site we may also surmise that in the course of further movements their cultural equipment was not unlikely to have undergone further change, thus, transforming it into a cultural assemblage quite different from that of the Late Phase with only remote connections to it as a result of changing circumstances and environment.

As the evidence from Daimabad stands there remains much to be studied about the Late Harappans of this place. We need to expose the complete plan of several Harappan houses and better understand the layout of this town. The evidence has shown that the Harappans of Daimabad cultivated wheat, barley, lentils, common peas, and horse gram. But the total picture of the agricultural activities of these people is still very sketchy. The seals with Indus signs have posed a problem concerning the nature of the trade or commerce at Daimabad; that is, if the seals were really meant to be used for commercial purposes. The lump of slag clearly indicates metallurgical activities by the Harappans; but we must know more about these activities in view of the cache of the bronzes mentioned earlier. Although I feel strongly that these bronzes were, as mentioned, brought by the Harappans from their homeland, I also feel it necessary to investigate the possibility that they were manufactured at Daimabad itself. The crescent-shaped potsherd engraved with a scene of a tiger attacking a buffalo, the oval-shaped terracotta cake and the triangular potsherd speak of the religious beliefs of the Harappans of Daimabad, but more evidence in this regard is called for. At Harappa, Kalibangan and Lothal the dead were buried in a cemetery, away from the town. At Daimabad the coffin burial was found inside the settlement. Why, and how, did this change in custom come into being? All these together with other issues will have to be studied in detail.

ACKNOWLEDGMENTS

I am extremely grateful to my *guru* Shri M.N. Deshpande, former Director General, Archaeological Survey of India, for his encouragement, discussion and guidance during the four seasons of excavation at Daimabad. I am also grateful to Shri B.K. Thapar, Director General, Archaeological Survey of India for guidance and discussions on the various aspects of the evidence. Grateful thanks are due to Dr. D.P. Agrawal of the Physical Research Laboratory, Ahmedabad for the ^{14}C dates, to my colleagues Shri M.B.N. Krishna Rao, at present Assistant Superintending Archaeologist, Konarak, and Sarvashri D.R. Patil, D.M. Kulkarni, G.L. Gaikwad, R.S. Trambake and R.D. Ingle, all of the South Western Circle of the Archaeological Survey of India. Thanks are also due to Sarvashri G.K. Mane, G.L. Dharurkar and L.S. Rao who participated in the excavation as trainees, and to Shri G.L. Gaikwad for the photographs.

BIBLIOGRAPHY

Dhavalikar, M.K., 1977
    Inamgaon: The pattern of settlement. *Man and Environment* 1: 46-47.

Indian Archaeology: A review, 1958-59
    Excavation at Daimabad, District Ahmednagar. Pp. 15-18. Delhi: Archaeological Survey of India.

Marshall, Sir John, editor, 1931
    Mohenjodaro and the Indus Civilization. 3 vols. London: Arthur Probsthain.

Rao, S.R., 1962
    Further Excavations at Lothal. *Lalit Kala* 11: 14-30.

Rao, S.R., 1963
    Excavations at Rangpur and other exploration in Gujarat. *Ancient India* 18-19: 5-207.

Rao, S.R., 1973
    Lothal and the Indus Civilization. Bombay: Asia Publishers.

Rao, S.R., 1978
    Late Harappan Daimabad. *Illustrated London News* April: 74-75.

Sali, S.A., 1970
    The Harappa Culture as Revealed Through Surface Exploration in the Central Tapti Basin. *Journal of the Oriental Institute, University of Baroda* 20 (2): 93-101.

Sali, S.A., in press
    The Harappan Contacts in the Deccan. In *Indus Civilization: Problems and issues*. B.B. Lal and S.C. Malik, eds. Simla: Indian Institute of Advanced Study.

Wheeler, Sir Mortimer, 1947
    Harappa 1946: The Defenses and Cemetery R-37. *Ancient India* 3: 59-130.

JAGAT PATI JOSHI and MADHU BALA

16. Manda: A Harappan Site in Jammu and Kashmir

THE SITE AND ITS LOCATION

THE ancient site at Manda, Akhnoor (lat. 36°54′ north; long. 74°48′ east) lies on the right bank of the River Chenab, a tributary of the Indus, on the foothills of Pir Panjal Range. It is about 28 kilometers northwest of Jammu. One has to climb about one kilometer from the local bus stand to reach the site (Fig. 16.1)

ENVIRONMENT

Most of the ancient site is inside the ruined fort of Manda, which was constructed in the 18th century A.D. The area of the fort is about 500 by 500 meters, the northern side of which is occupied by the Tehsildar's office, police station and other government residential quarters. The rest of the area is covered by the remains of the palace, popularly known as Sheesh Mahal. The eastern area is covered by thorny bushes, wild vegetation and *babul* trees. The elevated mound gives a commanding view.

PREVIOUS WORK

In 1973, consequent upon a request made by the military authorities who accidentally found some ancient pottery and coins at Manda Fort, the North Western Circle (then known as the Frontier Circle) of the Archaeological Survey of India put in three trial trenches. These excavations mostly revealed antiquities and remains of the Kushan Period. However, in 1975, the pottery of various levels was again carefully examined and it was found that fragments of perforated jars, goblets and beakers, dish-on-stand in Harappan Red Ware was also found in the collection. Accordingly, in December, 1976 the site was further explored and examined by a team from the Exploration Branch of Archaeological Survey of India led by the senior author. This team had already excavated at Bhagwanpura (District Kurukshetra; Haryana), Dadheri (District Ludhiana), and Katpalon and Nagar (District Jullundur). It had also explored a large region in the Punjab and brought to light the overlap phase of Late Harappan and Painted Gray Ware (Appendix A). Besides re-examining the site at Manda in terms of its Harappan affiliation, the team was also in search of a further possible extension of the Gray Ware, or overlap period in this area. The exploration revealed the existence of Harappan, Late Harappan Red Ware, Gray Ware, and Black Slipped Ware as well as Kushan Wares[1] at Manda.

EXCAVATION

In order to determine the sequence of cultures at Manda, a 20 by six meter trench was laid on 15 April, 1977 at the highest available point in the mound. The trench had a north-south orientation between the overhead water reservoir and Sheesh Mahal. Deep digging was only done in the northern, central and southern sectors of the trench since intervening Kushan structures had to be preserved. The excavations revealed a threefold sequence in a cultural

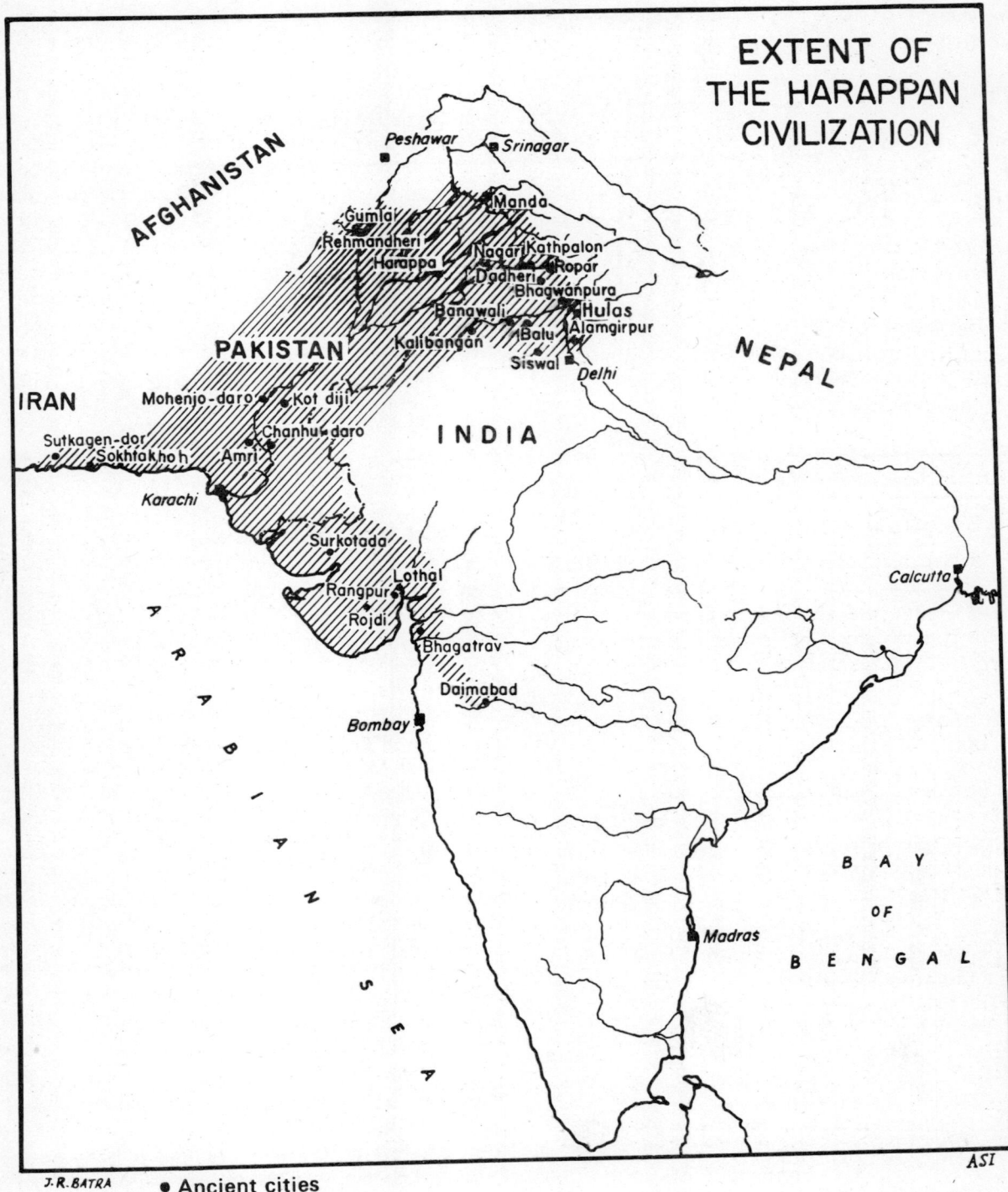

Fig. 16.1. The extent of the Harappan Civilization.

deposit of 9.2 meters (Pl. 16.1). The deep digging, which brought to light the earlier material, was restricted to small areas.

SUBPERIOD IA

This subperiod is marked by the arrival of Harappans represented by a deposit of one to 1.4 meters with eight layers (i.e., 20-27). It is interesting to note that the pottery is generally from two different ceramic traditions: (1) Pre-Harappan Red Ware, and (2) Harappan Red Ware.

1) Pre-Harappan Red Ware

Statistical analysis has revealed that the Pre-Harappan pottery comprises 15 to 25 percent of the total in the earliest levels (Fig. 16.2). It slowly diminishes in the upper levels of this phase.[2] The pottery is Red Ware with coarse, fine and medium fabrics. Some of the sherds are an ochre color and the slip flakes off due to waterlogging. Most of the pottery has a well-oxidized core and was generally treated with an external red slip. Jars with a featureless rim are represented which are medium to miniature in size. Painting is usually on the neck and shoulder in the form of a thick black band; however thin bands are also available. A few sherds show parallel grooves below the painted surface. This pottery is reminiscent of the Predefense (Wheeler 1947: 59-130) phase at Harappa and Kalibangan I (Fabric C). A rusticated ware (mostly jar fragments) is available which is akin to Kalibangan I Fabric B. A ware deeply grooved on the inner surface, possibly in the form of basins or troughs, is comparable to Fabric D of Kalibangan I. The general feel of the pottery brings it nearer to Predefense Harappa. However the presence of Fabric D is interesting (Fig. 16.3; see also IAR 1962-63: 25-28). One sherd of Reserve Slipped Ware (?) was also found.

2) Harappan Red Ware

The bulk of the pottery is Harappan sturdy red ware of medium to fine fabric with painted, unpainted and incised (fine grooves) decoration. The shapes are represented by bowls, dishes-on-stand, cups with footed base, goblets, beakers, basins and jars. No perforated jars were found during the present excavation; however the earlier work did produce them. The design repertoire consists of only horizontal bands in black pigment.

A few sherds of Harappan variety Gray Ware were also found.

The antiquities from Subperiod IA include a copper double spiral-headed pin (Pl. 16.2) 12.8 centimeters in length. This object has West Asian affinities (Piggott 1948). There are also bone arrow heads with a tang, clay bangles, terracotta cakes, potsherds with Harappan graffiti, chert blades, an unfinished seal (three by three centimeters) and a few saddle querns and pestles. Considerable rubble in a horizontal accumulation may suggest a fallen wall in layer number 23 of this period.

SUBPERIOD IB

The next period is designated Subperiod IB. It has a deposit of 1.6 to 1.7 meters consisting of two layers (18 and 19). There are four distinct ceramic traditions in this assemblage: (1) Harappan Red Ware, (2) Gray

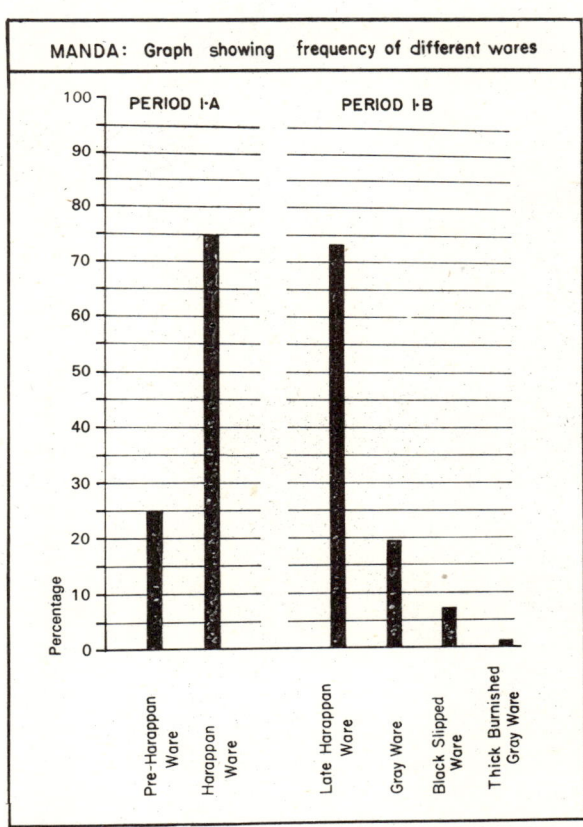

Fig. 16.2. Manda. Graph of ceramic frequencies.

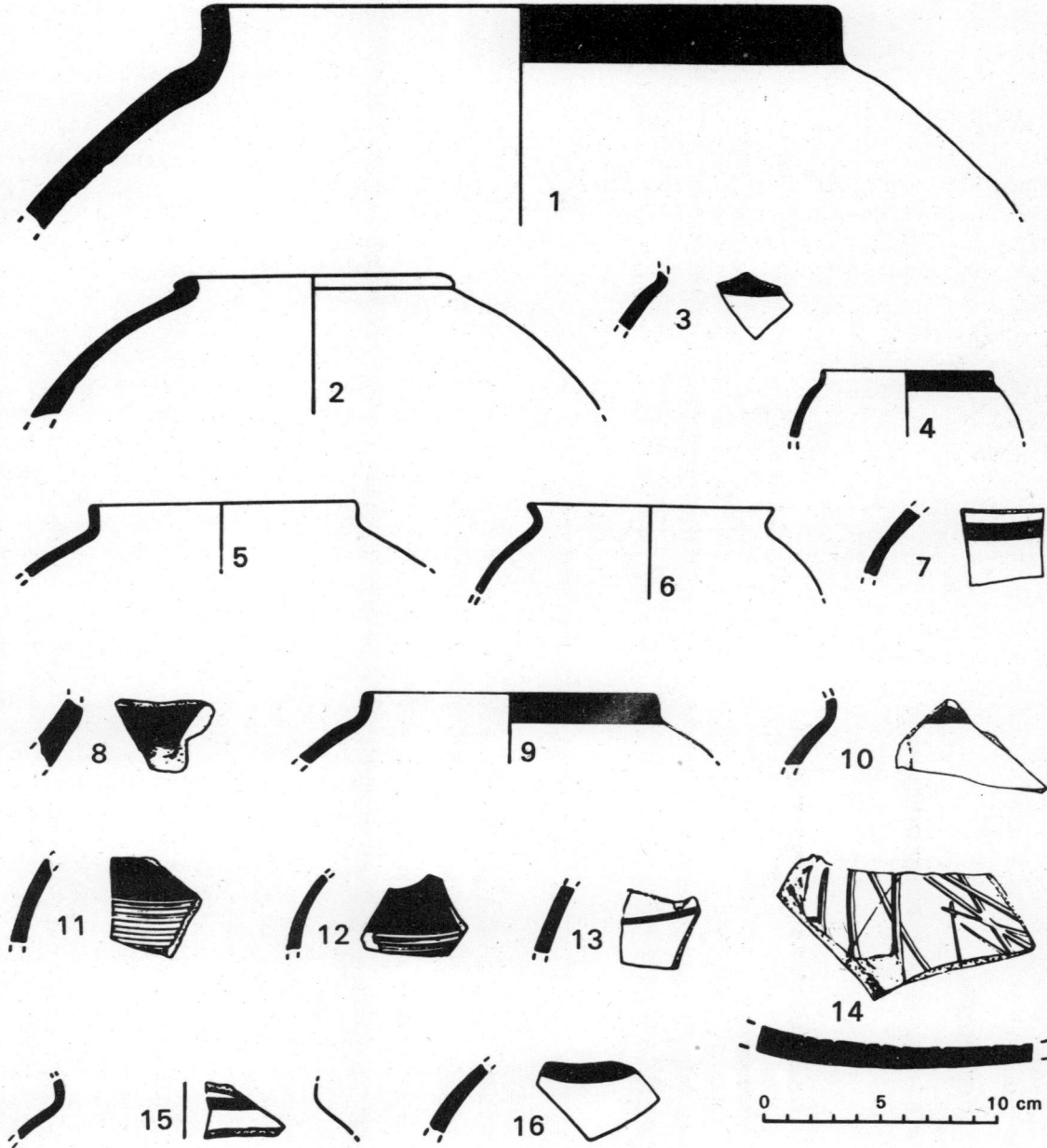

Fig. 16.3. Manda. Pre-Harappan ceramics.

Ware elsewhere generally associated with Painted Gray Ware, (3) a small quantity of Thick Burnished Gray Ware and (4) Black Slipped Ware. No Pre-Harappan Ware is available. Terracotta cakes are also not present. In Harappan Red Ware there are jars, dishes and dishes-on-stand in considerable quantity but beakers and goblets are absent. The Gray Ware is represented by bowls and dishes. Straight-sided bowls also occur in this ware. It may also be mentioned that shapes commonly found in Bara Ware and Cemetery H Ware in varying sites of the Punjab and Haryana were not found in this subperiod during the present excavation. Neither has iron been found in this subperiod. An overall estimation of the ceramics suggests that the Gray Ware generally associated with Painted Gray Ware is seven to 19 percent. Thus there is an interlocking of these two ceramic traditions (Joshi 1978; Madhu Bala 1975) evidently showing the overlap of the two cultures at this site.

PERIOD II

The next period, designated Period II, has a deposit of 1.7 to two meters. There are five layers (13-17) represented by the pottery of the early historical period. This includes dishes, bowls, *handis* with a featureless rim, miniature pots, etc., all in Red Ware. The pottery of this period can be compared with the contemporary types available from many other excavations in northern India.

PERIOD III

Closely following Period II, is Period III with Kushan pottery, both incised and plain. The cultural deposit of 1.7 to 1.9 meters has six layers (7-12). Pottery shapes include jars, dishes, spouted vessels, handled vessels and lids. There is a variety of incised designs in the pottery. A beautiful *swastika* was stamped on one sherd. Vegital and floral motifs are included in the incised and stamped pottery.

The antiquities of Period III include glass bangles, a terracotta figure of a horse with a saddle, votive tanks, beads, stoppers, birds, a lady playing on a small drum (headless and legless), bone arrow heads, stone caskets, iron daggers and arrow heads as well as copper and antimony rods and fragments. A few copper coins and some stone rotary querns are the other interesting finds.

A partially exposed house with walls made of rubble diaper masonry, flanked on both sides of a three-meter wide street, is impressive.

It appears that after the Kushan Period the site remained deserted. The various pits and deposits represented by layers one through six found on the upper levels, represent construction activity of the 18th and 19th century. This is when the fort and the Sheesh Mahal were built by Raja Gulab Singh.

IN SEQUEL

The discovery of the Pre-Harappan pottery with Harappan Ware in Period IA at Manda shows that the Pre-Harappans survived here and coexisted with the Harappans. It is rather significant that this northernmost site of the Harappan Civilization in India has both Pre-Harappan and Harappan remains together in Period IA. To some extent the position is similar to the KLB-2 mound at Kalibangan, where both Pre-Harappan and Harappan remains were found together until the middle levels. Though ^{14}C dates are not available for Period IA the double spiralheaded pin from the middle levels can be dated to ca. 2100 B.C.

There is clear Pre-Harappan evidence in Jammu at Manda. There is also a solitary Red Ware jar with the "horned design" of Pre-Harappan type from Burzhom in the Kashmir Valley. It occurs in a Neolithic context and is a thought-provoking pointer to possible contacts between Neolithic people and the Pre-Harappans. How did this happen? This question needs careful study in future discoveries and analysis. However, it must be borne in mind that chronologically the Pre-Harappans and Harappans are not far removed from the Neolithic time bracket in Kashmir.

At Bhagwanpura and Dadheri the Late Harappan Subperiod is immediately followed by an overlap subperiod (Joshi in press) with Late Harappan Red Ware, Gray Ware and the Painted Gray Ware. But in Subperiod IB at Manda the Mature Harappan Period is immediately followed by the overlap of Late Harappan Ware and Gray Ware. By way of correlation, it appears that the earlier two layers of Subperiod IB of Bhagwanpura are equivalent to Subperiod IB at Manda. At both the places Black Slipped Ware is also available.

The Bara and Cemetery H elements which are available at Bhagwanpura and Dadheri are absent at Manda in Subperiod IB. This may indicate that the intermingling of these elements, or survivals, with the Late Harappans took place only in the Punjab and Haryana and not in the Jammu area. If this is true it is a significant fact since it shows that Manda was beyond the influence of the Barans as such.

Another interesting feature which has come to light in Period IB Manda is the presence of two traditions of Gray Ware: (1) Gray Ware, generally associated with Painted Gray Ware in the Punjab and Haryana, and (2) Burnished Thick Gray Ware. These wares are associated with Late Harappan pottery but without goblets, beakers and terracotta cakes. At this point the evidence from Bhagwanpura IB is significant. Here a Plain Gray Ware precedes by two layers the Painted Grey Ware which is then associated with Late Harappan Ware. At Bhagwanpura the Burnished Thick Gray Ware is not present.

Thus, it appears that the Late Harappans came into contact with a Gray Ware-using people in the first instance and then with Painted Gray Ware people. The time lag is not much but it is meaningful.

A survey of the explored sites in the Punjab, a region which is close to Jammu, suggests that there are a number of Late Harappan sites in addition to those known at Ropar, Kotla Nihang Khan and Charr-Marr-da-Theh. The distribution of these purely Late Harappan sites is: one in Amritsar, three in Jullundur, five in Ludhiana, five in Ropar and six in Patiala. Late Harappan pottery is found along with Painted Gray Ware and Gray Ware at one site in Amritsar, two in Jullundur, six in Ludhiana, twelve in Patiala, one in Ropar and two in Sangrur. Late Harappan pottery with Gray Ware is available at eight sites in Gurdaspur, four sites in Jullundur, five sites in Ludhiana, five sites in Patiala, two sites in Ropar and two sites in Sangrur. Sites with only Gray Ware number eight in Amritsar, ten in Gurdaspur, one in Hoshiarpur, four in Jullundur, two in Ludhiana and two in Patiala. Pure Painted Gray Ware sites are three in Amritsar, six in Jullundur, four in Patiala, fourteen in Ropar and two in Sangrur. Painted Gray Ware with Gray Ware sites number two in Amritsar, one in Hoshiarpur, two in Jullundur, ten in Patiala and one in Sangrur.

The exploration suggests that there are separate sites with the Gray Ware which is generally associated with PGW. These are in District Gurdaspur, where Painted Gray Ware as such is not available. There are presently ten mounds in Gurdaspur with this Gray Ware; however, it is known that as one moves towards the east in the districts of Amritsar, there are eight mounds yielding Gray Ware, four in Jullundur, one in Hoshiarpur, two in Ludhiana and two in Patiala. Thus, the survey shows that separate mounds of Gray Ware become fewer and fewer as one moves from west to east. It has also been observed that at present Painted Gray Ware with Gray Ware and associated Red Ware occurs from Amritsar towards the east. It has been noticed that there is a concentration of Painted Gray Ware sites in District Ropar with four in Patiala, six in Jullundur, two in Sangrur, and three in Amritsar (none in Ludhiana). Patiala District has the largest number of sites—with both Late Harappan and Painted Gray Ware (Madhu Bala 1978).

CHRONOLOGY

No material for absolute dating is available at Manda; however, on the basis of Pre-Harappan Wares the beginning of Subperiod IA can be dated to slightly earlier than about 2350 B.C. and the end of ca. 1750 B.C. The spiral-headed pin suggests a date of ca. 2100 B.C. for the middle levels of Subperiod IA. The beginning of Subperiod IB is then a little earlier than the middle of the second millennium B.C. Manda Subperiod IB anticipates an overlap of Gray Ware with Late Harappan Wares. This compares well with Bhagwanpura IB (earlier levels) where only Gray Ware has been found. As seen in Appendix B (Fig. 16.4) TL dates from Bhagwanpura may support the

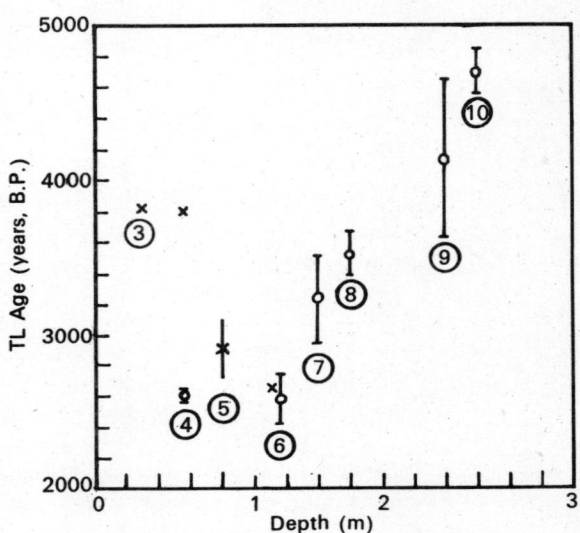

TL dating results for potteries excavated at Bhagwanpura (x-Gray wares, ⊙-Red wares) (The bars indicate the scatter when more than one determination was made; layer numbers are indicated within circles)

Fig. 16.4. Bhagwanpura. TL dates.

view. However, it must be borne in mind that Manda did not have a Bara or Cemetery H element. Whereas it is found with the Gray Ware at Bhagwanpura IB.

On the basis of the finds at Manda Subperiod IB and Bhagwanpura Subperiod IB (earlier levels) it can be concluded that there was a phase of Plain Gray Ware anterior to Painted Gray Ware (Thapar in press). Both these Subperiods have been found to interlock, individually or together, with the Late Harappan in Jammu, Punjab and Haryana. Since this picture is emerging in a region which is geographically well known in the Vedic Period it appears that one may be nearer to an identification of the culture with one of the waves of the Indo-Aryans. This is confirmed by both geography and chronology (i.e., the middle of the second millennium B.C.).

B. B. Lal has dealt in great detail with the problem of the Indo-Aryan movement. One would like to agree with him when he says: "The full picture has yet to emerge but hopefully will emerge" (Lal in press).

APPENDIX A

BHAGWANPURA

The site at Bhagwanpura (lat. 30°04′ north; 76°57′ east) District Kurukshetra, Haryana is situated on the right bank of River Sarasvati. Excavations at this site, in a cultural deposit of 2.7 meters revealed Late Harappan Culture in Subperiod IA. In Subperiod IB the Late Harappan was found interlocked with the Painted Gray Ware Culture (Pl. 16.3).

SUBPERIOD IA

The occupation of Late Harappans in this subperiod was built over raised mud platforms, evidently to protect the habitation from the floods of the Sarasvati. One such mud platform, measuring 4.25 by 10 meters, was exposed in one of the trenches (Pl. 16.4). This platform was provided with a landing step. After an accumulation of 70 to 80 centimeters of deposit the occupation was damaged by a gigantic flood; however the Late Harappans continued to live at the site.

An analysis of pottery from this subperiod indicates that: (1) there is a Red Ware both plain and painted, (2) an Ochre Color Ware is present but comes mostly from the flood effected trenches, (3) there is an Incised Ware with a variety of designs, some of Pre-Harappan lineage, (4) pottery of Bara type is present, (5) Thick Gray Ware, generally associated with Harappan and Late Harappan assemblages is present, and (6) there are some pottery shapes of Cemetery H. The shapes include dish-on-stand, bowls, dishes, jars with everted rims, flanged neck basins, drooping dishes and button-based goblets and cups. Besides the usual geometric and vegetal designs, *pipal* and banana leaves are also painted on pots. The entire pottery corpus appears to be an amalgam of various ceramic traditions. For example, one can compare the shapes with Bara, Bahadarabad, Atranjikhera, Hulas, Siswal IIB, Daulatpur and Raja Karan-ka-Qila.

The antiquities of this subperiod include a terracotta bull with long horns and pinched up hump, a gray to black terracotta consisting of the leg portion of a deity or a human figure, and two more anthropomorphic figurines (Pl. 16.5), wheels with hubs, bangles, copper rods and pins, faience beads and bangles, beads of semiprecious stone and bone pins, etc.

SUBPERIOD IB

Though no stratigraphic break could be discerned, this subperiod is marked by the continued occupation by the Late Harappans and the arrival of Plain Gray Ware using people followed by the Painted Gray Ware using folks. After an accumulation of this overlap culture, some of the habitation was washed away by a flood. This calamity did not prevent both the Late Harappans and the Painted Gray Ware using folks from continuing to live at the site. However, it has been noted that the Late Harappans gradually diminished; but they did not vanish till the end. This may be due to the superiority of the Painted Gray Ware people who slowly entrenched themselves at the site in the late levels of Subperiod IB. During this period of overlap three phases of structural activity could be identified.

At first the people were living in round or semicircular thatched huts (Pl. 16.6). Inside one of the huts we found four saddle querns and different types of pestles on the floor. This may indicate that the house belonged to a corn grinder.

An oval structure of highly burnt earth with a northeast to southwest orientation is also associated with this phase. The structure measures 2.75 by 1.25 meters and has a 10 to 50 centimeter-thick wall and inner depth of 50 centimeters. A large number of pieces of burnt earth, a few potsherds in a sturdy Red Ware and some dome-shaped terracottas, perhaps belonging to the collapsed roof of the structure, were found inside the structure (Pl. 16.7).

In the second structural phase a complete walled house complex with a thick (0.7 to one meter) wall was found (Pl. 16.8). This appears to be a well planned house with 13 rooms. There is a corridor between two sets of rooms and a courtyard on the eastern side. The size of the rooms varies from 1.6 by 1.6 meters to 3.35 by 4.2 meters. Copper objects, faience bangles and beads, terracotta *ghata*-shaped beads, bone styli, terracotta figures, Painted Gray Ware (Pls. 16.9 and 16.10) Plain Gray Ware vessels and Late Harappan pottery were found in this building. A statistical analysis of the pottery revealed that two to five percent of the total corpus was Late Harappan in the rooms of the houses. This shows some social contact between the two groups of people. Two oval shaped structures, size: (1) 1.8 by 0.85 meters, (2) 1.6 by 0.92 meters, are also associated with this phase.

In the third structural phase the houses were built of baked bricks (Pl. 16.11). Vigorous ploughing activity has left no structures but bricks that were found *in situ* are the following dimensions:

1) $1.2 \times 12 \times 18$ cm
2) $12 \times 12 \times 8$ cm
3) $29 \times 22/12 \times 1/2$ cm (wedge shaped)
   $20 \times 20 \times 8$ cm
4) $16 \times 12 \times 4$ cm

Some of the bricks have deep finger marks.

BURIALS

Two skeletons were found in the habitation area of Subperiod IB. Both skeletons had a north-south orientation, with the head to the north, and the face turned to the west. The graves were devoid of any funerary goods. Field study of skeletons made by Shri A. K. Sharma showed that one (Pl. 16.12) of them was an adult of advanced age and the other was a child, of eight to ten years.

Besides the continuance of Late Harappan pottery and antiquities, Subperiod IB yielded Plain Gray Ware in the early levels followed by Painted Gray Ware. PGW is associated with a Red Ware and a limited quantity of a Black Slipped Ware. A Painted Gray Ware with designs in thick lines, is also available from the early and middle levels of the subperiod. The design repertoire is very rich in the Painted Gray Ware (Pl. 16.9) tradition. It includes dots, slashes, horizontal bands, wavy lines, concentric circles, intersecting circles, net designs, honeycomb design, fish scales, lotuses, etc. A unique maltese cross and a set of intersecting circles forming a six- or four-petaled flower have come from Bhagwanpura IB. Gray Ware shapes are: bowls, dishes and straight-sided bowls and basins. It has been noticed for the first time that a few Late Harappan shapes (e.g., bowls, basins, dishes, jars and dish-on-stand) were copied in the Gray Ware.

Other important finds of this subperiod include terracotta anthropomorphic figures with parallels to objects found in the Gandhara Grave Culture I in Pakistan. There is a one-wheeled anthropomorphic figure, wheeled incised terracotta rams (Pls. 16.13, 16.14 and 16.15), birds, dogs, wheels with or without hubs, hopscotches, decorated dishes, ear ornaments, dabbers, violin-shaped Gray Ware mother goddess (Pl. 16.16) used as pendants, bone and ivory needles, pins and styli and one stylus with black pigment on its tip. Some of the bone pins have a very fine polish. Glass bangles in sea blue, white and black are the most impressive finds. Copper bangles, rods, and some indeterminate pieces have also been found. A seal with incised graffiti of Harappan lineage is also available. A large number of terracotta *ghata*-shaped beads, incised biconical beads, decorated faience beads and semiprecious stones deserve special mention. A bull-shaped carnelian pendant, although found on the surface, is most exquisite. Remains of *Equus cabalus* Linn. is another important discovery.

DADHERI

The excavations at Dadheri (lat. 30°40′ north; long. 16°15′ east) District Ludhiana, Punjab have yielded a threefold sequence in a cultural deposit of six meters. In Subperiod IA the Late Harappans built a settlement of huts and mud-walled houses over solid rammed mud platforms. Evidence of a mud wall running east-west in an oblique fashion with a length of 1.7 meters and a width of 0.59 meters has been found. Post holes suggest that people were also living in huts (Pl. 16.17). Evidence of a flood during this period was also recorded. The Late Harappan is represented by a sturdy Red Ware, both painted and plain. The shapes include jars, dishes-on-stand, etc. The design repertoire consists of horizontal bands, crisscross patterns filled in at the arches, hatched lozenges, etc. A large jar with a painted and incised design is one of the most fascinating finds from this level (Pl. 16.18). A considerable amount of incised pottery with a Pre-Harappan lineage has also been found.

Small finds include faience bangles, terracotta wheels, beads, and a painted bull. Copper objects and beads of carnelian and lapis lazuli were also present.

The pottery obtained from Subperiod IB included Painted Gray Ware, Gray Ware, Black Slipped Ware, an associated Red Ware and Late Harappan Ware. The percentage of Black Slipped Ware is much more than that found at Bhagwanpura in a similar context.

The antiquities include faience bangles, beads of semiprecious stone, terracotta wheels and a copper ring. No iron has been found.

In Subperiod IB the excavations have revealed evidence for interesting house types. At first the people were living in semicircular huts as attested by the discovery of post holes. Three oval structures of burnt earth, perhaps of religious character (Pl. 16.19) also came from this phase. These structures probably had a domed roof. In the next stage the houses were built with mud walls. A complete room measuring 1.1 by 2.5 meters from a house-complex has been exposed. The last phase is represented by a wall made of brick bats and brick jelly. Two sizes of bricks with finger impressions have been found. The sizes are: (1) 12 by 12 by seven centimeters, (2) 25 by 20 by five centimeters.

The site was deserted for a long time after Subperiod IB. However, a few sherds of Kushan affinity have been found but no regular habitation as such could be discerned by the present excavation in Period II. The latest Period III represents medieval times.

KATPALON AND NAGAR

Excavations at Katpalon (lat. 31°05′ north; long. 75°52′ east) District Jullundur, Punjab have brought to light a sequence of three cultures in a deposit of six meters. In Period I, Painted Gray Ware has been found interlocked with the Late Harappan Culture. An oval structure in a dilapidated condition was also found in this period. Other finds include copper and antimony rods, terracotta beads and wheels. Late Harappan Ware, Painted Gray Ware and Gray Ware were also there. The succeeding periods, after a break, are Kushan and medieval.

At Nagar (lat. 31°05′ north; long. 75°50′ east) Jullundur District, Punjab has a cultural deposit of five meters. A sequence of three periods has been brought to light. Period I yielded Late Harappan Ware, Painted Gray Ware and Gray Ware. Two oval structures and post holes indicate round and semicircular huts. Other finds include copper objects; bone styli; terracotta animal figurines and ear ornaments in addition to bangles and beads.

Period II is the early historic and Period III belongs to medieval times.

APPENDIX B

TL DATES FROM BHAGWANPURA
(Fig. 16.4)

Dr. K. S. V. Nambi, Dr. R. Sasidharan and Dr. S. D. Soman of the Health Physics Division, Bhaba Atomic Research Center, Bombay, kindly undertook the task of TL dating material from Bhagwanpura (Nambi, Sasidharan and Soman 1979). To aid comparative study and build up hypotheses, extracts from the report are reproduced below. The Red Ware (RW) mentioned in the report is the Late Harappan Red Ware and Gray Ware (GW) also includes Painted Gray Ware.

TL AGES OF BHAGWANPURA POTTERIES

Among the 18 samples excavated, grey wares occur only in the first six layers (up to a depth of about 1.3 m); the red wares are seen less frequently in these layers, but occur exclusively in all layers beyond 1.3 m depth. Fig. 6 shows the TL ages obtained for the grey wares and red wares collected from different layers. A striking difference in the age patterns of the types of wares is quite evident; the GW ages decrease with depth in the region of 0.3 to 1.2 m during which the RW ages remain more or less the same corresponding to the lowest GW age obtained viz., about 2600 years, B.P.: the RW ages on the other hand, increase systematically with depth. (It should be pointed out here that only those RW age results for which more than one estimate could be made have been represented in Fig. 6 [ed. note: Fig. 4 of this report]). Perhaps the red wares belong to the old resident people native to the site and the grey wares to a later settlement, the change-over occurring somewhere between the sixth and seventh layers i.e., between 2600 and 3200 years ago. Bhagwanpura being an ancient site in the domain of the famous Indus Valley civilization, one is reminded of the overlap phase between the late Harappan and Painted Grey Ware cultures that is datable to *circa* 1500 B.C. to 1000 B.C.(ASI, 1978) which is quite close to the TL ages mentioned above.

There remain some six samples (BPR-4, 7, 8, 12, 16 and 18) whose TL ages do not conform to the general trend presented in Fig. 6. It is left to the archaeologists either to reject them totally or partially depending upon individual sample considerations they may have.

TL ages estimated for the Bhagwanpura potteries

Sample code	Depth of find (meters)	TL age year B.P.* (std error, predicted accuracy)
BPR– 1	0.3	3830 (± —, ± 13%)
– 2	0.8	311 (± —, ± 15%)
– 3	0.8	2710 (± —, ± 15%)
– 4	0.55	4038 (± 4%, ± 13%)
– 5	0.55	3814 (± —, ± 14%)
– 6	0.55	2617 (± 1%, ± 16%)
– 7	0.55	1344 (± —, ± 13%)
– 8	0.9	1235 (± —, ± 15%)
– 9	1.1	2649 (± —, ± 15%)
–10	1.15	2742 (± —, ± 16%)
–11	1.18	2434 (± —, ± 17%)
–12	1.3	4868 (± —, ± 12%)
–13	1.4	3241 (± 9%, ± 13%)
–14	1.6	3532 (± 4%, ± 12%)
–15	2.1	4141 (±12%, ± 15%)
–16	2.25	5460 (± —, ± 15%)
–17	2.4	4696 (± 3%, ± 17%)
–18	2.45	3024 (± —, ± 15%)

*Date of measurement: 1978

ACKNOWLEDGMENTS

Grateful thanks are due to all of our colleagues in the Exploration Branch of the Archaeological Survey of India for their kind cooperation and help in the field and headquarters in the preparation of this paper. Finally, the authors express their thanks to Sarvashri J. R. Batra and Vijay Kumar for the drawings and Sarvashri Dhan Pal and H. L. Khatri for neatly typing the paper.

NOTES

[1] With a view to understanding the problem of the relationship of Late Harappan Culture with Painted Gray Ware Culture, excavations at Manda, Bhagwanpura, Dadheri, Katpalon and Nagar and explorations in Jammu and the Punjab were carried out during the field seasons between 1975 and 1977 by a team of the Explorations Branch of the Headquarters Office of the Archaeological Survey of India under J.P. Joshi assisted by Miss Madhu Bala, Sarvashri J.R. Batra, S.N. Jayaswal, G. Laxminaryana, J. Dey, Vijay Kumar and Manohar Lal. Shri A. K. Sharma had exposed and made a field study of human and animal skeletal remains from Bhagwanpura. The material for TL dating from excavations at Bhagwanpura was collected by the present authors and was later analyzed by K. S. V. Nambi, R. Sasidharan and S. D. Soman, Health Physics Division, Bhaba Atomic Research Center, Bombay.

[2] Statistical analysis has been done by Miss Madhu Bala.

BIBLIOGRAPHY

Indian Archaeology: A review (IAR), 1962-63
    Excavations at Kalibangan, District Ganganagar. Pp. 20-31. Delhi: Archaeological Survey of India

Joshi, J.P., 1978
    Interlocking of Late Harappa Culture and Painted Grey Ware Culture in the Light of Recent Excavations. *Man and Environment* 2: 100-103.

Joshi, J.P., in press
    Overlap of Late Harappan Culture and Painted Gray Ware Culture in Light of Recent Excavations in Haryana, Punjab and Jammu. In *Indus Civilization: Problems and issues*. B.B. Lal and S.C. Malik, eds. Simla: Indian Institute of Advanced Study.

Lal, B.B., in press
    The Indo-Aryan Hypothesis Vis-a-Vis Indian Archaeology. Paper read at the seminar on Ethnographic Problems of the Early History of the People of Central Asia and India in the Second Millennium B.C., Dushanbe, U.S.S.R. Cyclostyled copy.

Madhu Bala, 1975
    A Survey of Protohistoric Investigations in Jammu and Kashmir and a Review of the Present Position. *Eastern Anthropologist* 22 (1-2): 13-14.

Madhu Bala, 1978
    A Survey of the Protohistoric Investigation in Punjab and the Emergent Picture. *Indian Anthropologist* 8 (2): 1-30.

Nambi, K.S.V., R. Sasidharan and S.D. Soman, 1979
    Thermoluminescence Dating of Potteries Excavated at Bhagwanpura and Mathura. *Bhaba Atomic Research Center 1013:* Bombay.

Piggott, S., 1948
    Notes on Certain Pins and a Mace Head from Harappa. *Ancient India* 4: 26-40.

Thapar, B.K., in press
    Archaeological Remains of Aryans in Northwestern India. Paper read at the Seminar on Ethnographic Problems of the Early History of the People of Central Asia and India in the Second Millennium B.C. Dushanbe, U.S.S.R. Cyclostyled copy.

Wheeler, Sir Mortimer, 1947
    Harappa 1946: the Defenses and Cemetery R-37. *Ancient India* 3: 58-130.

Y.M. CHITALWALA

17. Harappan Settlements in the Kutch-Saurashtra Region: Patterns of Distribution and Routes of Communication

There is much about the Harappan Civilization which needs to be explained on a scientific basis. But, still one has to be virtually a multiprogrammed computer with data for in-depth studies on such topics as the mechanism of urban growth, geopolitical and sociological explanations for the spread of the Indus people, their settlement and community patterning, economic development and its socioreligious implications. There are many seemingly disparate components of the Harappan Culture that need to be fitted into a logical scheme. One of the important aspects of this culture is the apparent mobility of the Harappans and their proliferation over great distances: from the Afghan/Baluch areas in the north to the borders of Maharashtra in the south. These territories constitute a number of ecozones with different environmental variables and economic incentives which the Harappans had to deal with. It is, therefore, of interest to understand their distribution pattern in the Kutch-Saurashtra region and the mechanisms operative behind this spread.

GEOGRAPHICAL AND ENVIRONMENTAL SETTING

Outside the Indus Valley proper, and territories comprising much of what is Pakistan today, Kutch and Saurashtra have one of the densest concentrations of Harappan settlements anywhere. However, while Kutch and Saurashtra are ecologically speaking, a contiguous unit, geomorphologically and environmentally they stand apart. Kutch forms an intermediate area between Sind and Saurashtra. The Ranns, the great level expanses of salt and sand, separate Kutch from Sind in the north and from Saurashtra in the south. The sea on all sides except in the east, turns Kutch into a kind of closed system. The Ranns are not deserts in the sense the Thar or the Sahara are. They are vast plain-like stretches of sand leveled to an asphalt-like consistency by salty efflorescence and brine. During the monsoons and until the onset of winter, they remain waterlogged and difficult to cross. Another characteristic of the landscape is that Kutch is dotted with low hills. The overall effect of the Ranns, hills, and the sea combined, is one conferring a sense of security.

The most significant rock formation that has direct bearing on the lives of people are sandstones. These are veritable storehouses of underground water. Kutch can survive repeated droughts only because of its reserves of subsoil water. There are no large perennial rivers today; however near the Kori Creek in the northwest, the channel of an effluent of the Indus can be traced up to the Allaha Bund. This was thrown up by an earthquake and cut off the flow of water from the Indus system into Kutch. In the past, the drainage pattern of Kutch, with its overall effect on the configuration of the Ranns, seems to have undergone changes of a rather drastic nature.

As far as Saurashtra is concerned, it shares with Kutch a long coastline with many favorable points for anchorage, but it is not as severely isolated from the rest of India. The preponderant rock formation is basalt, or Deccan Trap, from which the famous black cotton soil is derived and which was possibly one of the more important factors influencing the choice of Harappan site location. The drainage pattern of Saurashtra is radial, with rivers flowing to the sea in all directions from the central hilly region. The larger rivers, like the Bhadar, are perennial and have large tracts of agriculturally rich black soil along their banks. Incidentally, quite a number of large Harappan settlements are located on the banks of the Bhadar.

DISTRIBUTION OF HARAPPAN SETTLEMENTS

The distribution of Harappan settlements in Kutch and Saurashtra differs markedly. Considering that Kutch is only slightly smaller than Saurashtra, the Harappan settlements are few and far between—and most of these are concentrated in eastern Kutch, locally known as Vaged. This is the point nearest to northern Saurashtra. Kotada Dholavira in Khadir and Surkotada appear to be the largest Harappan sites in Kutch, though the former is considerably larger than the latter. Both these sites have evidence for Mature Phase Harappan occupation, as well as the Late Phase. By Mature Phase is meant that the sites did not have any evidence for the general decline in the standard of living from a level comparable to that witnessed at Mohenjodaro or Harappa. There are a few divergences from Harappan norms but these are due to a change of environment and economy. For example Surkotada is not as extensive a city as is Mohenjodaro. In fact it is a small fortified settlement functionally meant to serve as a military outpost (Joshi 1979: 64). As far as Dholavira is concerned, it is located on the margin of the Great Rann of Kutch and therefore, is in the nature of an entrepôt for the Harappans coming from Sind across the Great Rann. Khadir is today an arid land with brackish water in most of its wells. Agriculture is possible only on some patches of ground where sweet water is available. The villages are small and the population seems to be straining the carrying capacity of the environment. The present population of Dholavira, which is near the Kotada mounds, is 750. In view of this fact, it remains to be explained how a large urban settlement, with an area of about two-and-a-half square kilometers, could flourish some 4,500 years ago in such an inhospitable environment.

Pabumath is yet another site located on the margins of the Rann. It is a small Harappan settlement measuring 150 by 150 meters. It is about 20 kilometers from Dholavira as the crow flies. The site has undergone brief excavations and has yielded evidence of four phases of construction. Most of the house foundations are of undressed stone, which remain unchanged from one phase to the next. Before the first phase of construction, the Harappans seem to have cleared the jungle by burning. On top of this burnt layer, they laid the foundations of their first settlement. They came to the site with mature skills for laying house foundations. Since the site is near Dholavira across the Rann, regular communication between the two settlements is likely. The find of a seal with Harappan characters and the "unicorn" motif may add weight to the hypothesis.

As far as the interior part of Kutch is concerned, there is a total of five sites. Desalpar in the northwest is the only excavated site in this group. The site of Khirasara in Nakhatrana Taluka has yielded seals and is a fortified settlement. Then there is the site of Bhedi near the village of Kothara in central Kutch and another near the village of Kakadbhit some 40 kilometers west of Bhuj. Only one coastal site has so far been noted. This is near the village of Navinal near Mundra on the Gulf of Kutch. Of these five sites, Desalpar and Khirasara have yielded evidence for Mature as well as Late Phase occupation. The other three sites were no more than hamlets of the Late Phase of Harappan Culture. The coastal site of Navinal has a deposit only one meter deep. The pottery, including the convex-sided bowl, compares well with the Late Phase of the Saurashtra Harappan. The convex-sided bowl is less frequently found at the Mature Harappan sites in Kutch. Even in Saurashtra this bowl becomes almost a type fossil, with its typically blotchy decoration at Prabhas. This would imply that of all the pottery shapes, the convex-sided bowl became more popular in the later part of the Harappan existence and eventually underwent regional metamorphosis at Prabhas, located on the southern seaboard of Saurashtra.

In Saurashtra the larger excavated sites of the Harappan Culture are those of Lothal, Rangpur and Rojdi. All of these have yielded evidence of Mature as well as Late Phases. Scores of smaller settlements have been found at places like Atkot, Traghda and Hajnali. Excluding Hajnali, most of these small sites belong to the Late Phase. Of 25 sites reported from Kutch, only two or three are exclusively Late Harappan, and none are Post-Harappan, comparable to Rangpur Period II C. The number of sites of Rangpur Period II A (Mature) in Saurashtra increased from 18 to 120 in Period II B-C. This has been attributed in the one place, to an increase in population and secondly, due to a shift in the pattern of land use from *rabi* to *kharif* crops (Possehl 1974: 177-78; Chitalwala 1977: 95). The introduction of *bajra* (*Pennisetum typhoides*) in the Late Harappan Period, corresponded to an increase in population. This added pressure to the environment, led to an intensive system of cropping, and the year round use of land to accrue maximum benefit (Rao 1963: 168-69; Leshnik 1973: 72; Possehl 1974: 153-54; Chitalwala 1977: 96).

It would seem that initially Kutch had all the economic incentives to make the Harappans settle in large urban centers like Kotada Dholavira and strongly garrisoned outposts like Surkotada. Later, however, they found that its economic potential had dwindled and they had to move elsewhere. The paucity of Late Harappan sites points to this fact.

THE PATTERN OF HARAPPAN COMMUNICATIONS

The Harappan Culture has a north-south axis from the hilly Afghan/Baluch areas to the borders of Maharashtra, south of Gujarat. There are four distinct geophysical and ecological zones along this axis. The first two, the Afghan/Baluch areas in the north and the second zone in the Indus Valley and the Makran Coast, form a single land mass. The Ranns together with mainland Kutch make the third zone. To the south lies the final zone, the black soil areas of Saurashtra, mainland Gujarat and Maharashtra with their predominantly basaltic formations. Of these four zones, the second and fourth have environmental variables favoring an agrarian economy. This was the mainstay of Harappan subsistence. Consequently, the Harappan site scatter is densest in these two zones and sparse in the Afghan/Baluch and Kutch zones. In view of this, the nature of the economy at settlements like Dholavira (Khadir) in Kutch must have been based on different incentives than those obtained elsewhere, say in Sind and Saurashtra. The location of Dholavira on the margins of the Rann is quite important in this context. Simple analysis indicates that first, a large urban settlement cannot, by any stretch of imagination, be located next to a hot and howling desert-like environment. Second, Khadir is far too arid to support a large population that is particularly adapted to agricultural pursuits. Third, given the present conditions, the Ranns, which become waterlogged for almost six months in a year, would have made the life of an urban settlement impossible by completely isolating it from the rest of Kutch, and for that matter the rest of India including Sind. The incoming water from the sea during monsoon is too shallow to be negotiable by boat, and too slushy to enable a horse ride. Only camels can trudge along at a snail's pace. These are all geographical and economic disincentives for locating a large township in Khadir. But the fact remains that the edge of the Rann was selected by the Harappans for the location of a major settlement. The relevant question therefore becomes: was the Rann during Harappan times geomorphologically what it is today?

The tradition of the Ranns being an arm of the sea is both persistent and persuasive. Those who live in small villages on the margin of the Ranns speak of ships sailing across their waters bringing goods from distant lands. They nostalgically speak of a rich and benevolent merchant named Jagdusha and his ships with full consignments of gold in their holds, anchoring at many points along the shores of the Ranns. However, no one knows exactly when the Rann was actually a part of the Arabian Sea. Writing in 1907, Robert Siverights refers to Alexander Burnes who learned "That vessels had been known to be wrecked on Pacham and that they came for shelter in heavy weather to the *island* of Khadir" (Siverights 1907: 531). Siverights further says that the Rann was navigable for many hundred years after the Arab conquest. But, by 1361 it is learnt from the historian who accompanied the Sultan Firuz Shah in the year that he led the expedition to Gujarat "the intervening area that was once a marsh was now 'a howling desert'" (Siverights 1907: 531). Siverights, however, does not mention who the historian of Sultan Firuz Shah was, or where he found this reference to Kutch. Mallinath, the great literary critic of the 14th-15th centuries, also mentions Kutch as a marshy region (Gazetteer of India 1971: 1). It is, therefore, clear that in the 14th century the Ranns were what they are at present; although no earlier literary information is available.

Investigations of a purely scientific nature in the spheres of hydrology, archaeology and geology suggest that the Ranns were indeed under a permanent sheet of water at a time when the Harappan Culture was flourishing in Kutch. Based on hydrological studies, S. K. Gupta maintains that "even as late as 2000 years ago Little Rann was about 4 m deep" (Gupta 1977: 205). Geological studies carried out by Roy and Merh bring out the fact that the River Luni, which now flows from Rajasthan and merges into the eastern margins of the Rann of Kutch, once had a greater stream flow (Roy and Merh 1977: 198). Greater flow of fresh water into the Ranns should, in fact, be historically a part of the entire drainage pattern. A greater quantity of fresh water coming into the Ranns would have kept the levels of salinity low and this would mean less salinity of the subsoil water. At present Khadir has reserves of subsoil water, but its high salinity makes it unfit for agriculture or domestic use. If a time is postulated "when the subsoil water was not saline, then a large population can subsist without constraining the carrying capacity of the region" (Chitalwala 1977: 6). Wetter phases of climate during the Harappan Period have been postulated over Rajasthan and western India on the basis of palynological studies carried out by Gurdip Singh (Singh 1971). Withdrawal of this wetter phase over Rajasthan, and possibly Gujarat, must have brought about changes in the ecology, drastically altering the economic infrastructure of the Harappan Civilization in these areas (Chitalwala 1977).

The locational aspect of Dholavira in Khadir has already been discussed. This large Harappan settlement has a twin-mound system of planning. On the mounds one can see ring stones of the type found from Lothal. These were called anchors by Rao (1973). Apart from this, a prosperous industry in making shell objects seems to have been at the site. Numerous pieces of shell bangles, shell discs, ladles and fragments of large marine shells occur on the surface. Today, the nearest seashore to Dholavira would be somewhere near Kandla and Mundra in the south some 100 kilometers away by the shortest route. Since there is no trading post of importance on the southern seaboard of Kutch, a regular trade in seashells cannot be postulated. From excavations at Pabumath, the site nearest Dholavira on the Rann, many objects of shell have been found. Bones belonging to large marine fish (weighing 20 kilograms or more on the basis of vertebrae) have also been found. These facts indicate that the sea was quite near at hand and that exploitation of marine resources was economical.

On the Saurashtra side the small Harappan site of Hajnali is quite interesting. It is located near the junction of the Little Rann, Gulf of Kutch and Saurashtra. At present the site is three kilometers inland from the Gulf. It measures only 60 by 60 meters but has three meters of occupational debris. It does not appear to be a normal habitational mound like a village or a town. From its shape and size it seems to have been made up of a group of large structures; in the manner of a trading post. In fact its location is ideal for discharging such a function. During high tide the waters of the Gulf come close to the site and it seems that in the past it was actually on the Gulf. With the recession of sea level it now stands inland. The name Hajnali is also suggestive in this context. It means "the place of embarkation for pilgrims bound for Haj." Likewise Lothal, with its dockyard and industrial township, is located much inland today, on the southern shore of Saurashtra. The recession of sea level thus had a twofold effect on the Harappan settlements in Kutch and Saurashtra respectively. Settlements like Dholavira and Pabumath, which stood on the seashores during the Harappan times, are now on the margins of the Ranns. Sites like Hajnali and Lothal, also once located on the seacoast, now stand further inland. A study of eustasy suggests there might have been a phase of regression in the level of the sea between 5000 and 3000 B.P. which corresponds with the eclipse of the Mature Phase of the Harappan Civilization (Agrawal and Guzder 1972: 216-22).

Based on the location of Dholavira in Khadir to the north, and Lothal in the south, it can be concluded that these settlements were engaged in sea trade between Sind, Kutch and Saurashtra. Lothal was also trading with the Persian Gulf. It was this interregional and international trade that formed the base of their economy. With the regression of sea level these port cities were left high and dry and their *raison d'etre* (i.e., seabound trade) was lost and their industrial structure destroyed.

This discussion of the Ranns of Kutch and the location of Harappan sites, yields important inferences regarding the routes of Harappan communication between Sind and the Kutch-Saurashtra area. We have examined the evidence that the Ranns were once an extension of the sea. This would make Kutch wholly separate from both Sind and Saurashtra. It would, therefore, appear that all Harappan communications between Sind and Kutch and between Kutch and Saurashtra were essentially seaborne. The port of Dholavira was possibly in trading contact with the Harappan sites like Suktagendor and Sotkakoh on the Makran Coast. Allahdino near Karachi is yet another site which appears to have been a settlement of commercial nature with a "staggering quantity of all artifact categories. Such items as biconical ball, ceramic bangles, toy-cart frames, terracotta triangles and cakes have been found in quantities exceeding 10,000 each" (Shaffer 1979: 25). The number of copper objects found from Allahdino, considering its comparatively small size, also points to the commercial nature of the settlement. It would, therefore, be quite logical to infer that Harappan coastal settlements like Dholavira and Lothal in Kutch and Saurashtra communicated with their counterparts on the Makran Coast. The communication between Dholavira and other Harappan sites, like Pabumath in Kutch, were also carried on across the sea since Khadir was an island. Overland communications were confined to internal contacts between one Harappan settlement and another within Kutch and Saurashtra. One such overland route can be postulated between Pabumath via Lakhapar, Kerasi and Surkotada down to the Little Rann, or the sea as it was during the Harappan times. Another overland route would have started from Desalpar, then moved down to Khirasara and to the south to Navinal on the Gulf of Kutch. The site of Hajnali on the Gulf of Kutch on the Saurashtra side was an entrepôt for cultural and commercial contacts directly from Sind and from across the Gulf. An overland route might have run from Hajnali to Rojdi and along the Bhadar Valley via Atkot to Rangpur and thence to Lothal.

CONCLUSIONS

First and foremost, there is compelling evidence for the Ranns being an area that was under a permanent sheet of water during the time of the Harappans. Only as late as the 14th century it is referred to as being a marshy "howling desert." The combined spectrum of geological, geomorphological and palynological evidence suggests that during the Harappan Period a greater part of western India enjoyed a wetter climatic phase. Riverine stream flow into the Ranns was thus greater than what it is today. Subsequently, with the onset of a dry phase and with the regression of the sea level, the Ranns came into existence and those Harappan settlements which had originally been on the coast found themselves some distance inland. This may be one of the reasons why their economy declined. Second, most of the Mature Harappan settlements in Kutch and Saurashtra were a part of an extensive trading network beginning in Sind. Third, the Harappan settlements in Kutch, like Dholavira and Surkotada, were more dependent on trade and industry than on a purely food-producing economy. Fourth, communication appears to have been on three different lines: (a) overland communication was used between one settlement and another within Kutch and Saurashtra—this communications network was purely regional; (b) contacts between Sind and Kutch, Sind and Saurashtra, and Kutch and Saurashtra were seaborne and essentially interregional; (c) the third type of communication was international, involved with overseas trade between Harappan settlements like Lothal, and the Persian Gulf. Finally, it would be erroneous to assume that when the Harappans arrived in Kutch and Saurashtra they found these areas already populated and by subjugating these populations they founded what is often referred to as the "Harappan Empire." The small number of Harappan sites in Kutch and Saurashtra during the Mature Phase, and their nearness to one or another route of communication, does not indicate any extension of the Harappan state. These areas were either very sparsely populated, if the evidence of Micaceous Red Ware is anything to go by, or they were not populated at all. The Harappans established outposts of civilization in areas which were remote, and free from earlier human habitations. There is no unequivocal evidence to indicate that they lived side by side with local cultures or groups of people who had settled in Kutch or Saurashtra prior to their arrival. In all probability, the political control of the Harappans was limited to their settlements, and the small sustaining areas surrounding them.

BIBLIOGRAPHY

Agrawal, D.P. and S. Guzder, 1972
Quaternary Studies on the Western Coast of India: Preliminary observation. *The Palaeobotanist* 21 (2): 216-22.

Chitalwala, Y.M., 1977
Harappan and Post-Harappan Settlement Patterns. In *Ecology and Archaeology of Western India*. D.P. Agrawal and B.M. Pande, eds. Pp. 93-98. Delhi: Concept Publishing.

Chitalwala, Y.M., in press
Environmental Background of Harappan Culture in Gujarat. *Quaternary Environments with Special Reference to Western India*. Baroda: M.S. University of Baroda.

Gazetteer of India, 1971
Gujarat State, Kutch District. Ahmedabad: Government of Gujarat.

Gupta, S.K., 1977
The Indus Valley Culture as Seen in the Context of Post-Glacial Climate and Ecological Studies in Northwest India. *Archaeology and Physical Anthropology in Oceania* 6.

Joshi, J.P., 1979
The Nature of Settlement of Surkotada. In *Essays in Indian Protohistory*. D.P. Agrawal and D.K. Chakrabarti, eds. Pp. 59-64. Delhi: B.R. Publishing Corp.

Leshnik, L.S., 1973
Land Use and Ecological Factors in Prehistoric Northwest India. In *South Asian Archaeology*. N. Hammond, ed. Pp. 67-84. Park Ridge: Noyes Press.

Possehl, G.L., 1974
Variation and Change in the Indus Civilization: A study of prehistoric Gujarat with special reference to the Post-urban Harappan. Ph.D. dissertation, Anthropology Department, University of Chicago.

Rao, S.R., 1963
Excavations at Rangpur and other Explorations in Gujarat. *Ancient India* 18-19: 5-207.

Rao, S.R., 1973
Lothal and the Indus Civilization. Bombay: Asia Publishing.

Roy, B. and S.S. Merh, 1977
Geomorphology of the Rann of Kutch and Climatic Changes. *Ecology and Archaeology of Western India*. D.P. Agrawal and B.M. Pande, eds. Pp. 195-200. Delhi: Concept Publishing.

Shaffer, Jim G., 1979
The Indus Civilization: New evidence from Pakistan. In *Essays in Indian Protohistory*. D.P. Agrawal and D.K. Chakrabarti, eds. Pp. 17-29. Delhi: B.R. Publishing Corp.

Singh, Gurdip, 1971
The Indus Valley Culture. *Archaeology and Physical Anthropology in Oceania* 6 (2): 177-89.

Siverights, R., 1907
Cutch and the Rann. *Journal of the Royal Geographical Society* 29: 518-39.

PART III

ECOLOGY, TECHNOLOGY AND TRADE

VISHNU-MITTRE and R. SAVITHRI

18. Food Economy of the Harappans

KNOWLEDGE of the Harappan Culture complex has expanded enormously during the last two decades through intensive explorations carried out in the Indian Subcontinent. A fairly large number of new sites has been discovered some of which have widened the geographic expanse of the Harappan Empire far beyond its earlier limits. In spite of this, knowledge of the food economy of this culture complex has not progressed very far. This may be attributed to the lack of carbonized food grains at many of the sites, the rare examination of potsherds and terracotta cakes, the fact that flotation techniques are rarely used, and to the fact that ancient plant remains are frequently not available to archaeobotanists.

There is almost no information on the food economy of the Pre-Harappans (only from Mundigak II, Baluchistan) as compared to that of the Harappans (from Harappa, Mohenjodaro, Chanhudaro, Lothal and Rangpur Period II). In addition there is the recently published information from Kalibangan, Surkotada and Daimabad; however the Banawali food grains remain unexamined. ^{14}C dates for the food grains from Kalibangan and Surkotada would refer them to a Late Harappan Phase.

The presumption that food grains from any level or site of the Harappan Culture suggests the food economy of the entire civilization may well be true; but ought to be supported by evidence. After all, there could have been shifts in the food economy over the course of time at a particular site because of culture contacts or the domestication of wild progenitors. There could also have been different food economies in the various parts of this vast empire, unless it had a uniform climate suited to the cultivation of a particular group of crops. The socio-economic disparities inferred for the Harappans may have, as today, led the elites to exist on superior crops, leaving the poorer classes of the society with inferior foods. There are thus many implications with far reaching significance involved in the study of ancient crops with regard to the life and culture of the Harappans.

Published information on the food economy of the Harappans is available in excavation reports and papers in specialized journals which do not have a wide circulation. In view of the importance of the food economy, and its implications, it is imperative to assemble all the published and unpublished data that is available. An attempt has also been made to procure and re-examine some materials which had been described earlier. This communication is therefore a comprehensive report (within limits of availability of material, of course) on the food economy of the Harappans.

All those colleagues interested in the Harappans are requested to provide, in future, an opportunity for the botanical materials from their sites to be examined. Only this will ensure that a more comprehensive report is prepared. It is unnecessary to ennumerate the advantages that would accrue from such a study, to archaeologists on the one hand, and to agriculturists deeply interested in the history of crops on the other.

This paper is a compilation of the material identified and published earlier by colleagues and by our team. It also includes the results of our reinvestigation of materials from Mohenjodaro and Chanhudaro and a detailed account of the materials from Kalibangan and Surkotada. The Banawali materials examined casually at an exhibition at Purana Qila organized under the auspices of the Archaeological Survey of India are also included. An attempt has been made to arrange the data in chronological order beginning with the Pre-Harappans. The provenance of some of the materials is not given since it could not be obtained.

Usual morphological and statistical methods have been employed in the identification of food remains. Cuticles of plant remains embedded in the terracotta cakes from Kalibangan were extracted and identified by comparison with the cuticular preparations from lemma and palea of modern cereals (Vishnu-Mittre and Savithri 1975). The Kalibangan potsherds with crystals have been found to be devoid of grain or husk impressions, although the crystals have been identified through chemical analysis.

Howsoever inadequate the information is, it still provides a wide-spectrum view of the plant economy of the Harappans which suggests variability in crops grown in various parts of the empire. The analysis of the modern environment, and of the corresponding modern crops, has also yielded very valuable information. In total this information gives us some idea of Harappan cultivation methods, their cropping pattern and the possibility that they used chemicals for the reclamation of the saline/alkaline soils and the like. These topics are discussed in the concluding part of this paper.

THE PRE-HARAPPAN FOOD ECONOMY

Mundigak

Mundigak, Baluchistan

(Casal 1961; Allchin and Allchin 1968; Allchin 1969).

1) Wheat (*Triticum compactum*)
2) Jujube (*Zyzyphus jujuba*)

In the absence of any opportunity to examine these materials and to check the identifications, the following comments have been added which may be of interest.

Modern wheats from cultivated fields in Baluchistan were examined by Howard in 1916. They showed a baffling array of types with a large number of intermediate forms of *T. aestivum*, *T. sphaerococcum*, etc. He further found that the distinction between *T. compactum* (apparently *T. sphaerococcum*) and *T. vulgare*, based upon glume and grain shape, broke down. It is not known if variability was observed in this Pre-Harappan material and whether it could be *T. sphaerococcum*. Both species possess dwarfing genes at the S and C loci which govern their characteristics.

The *Zyzyphus jujuba* Mill occurring in Sind and Baluchistan is believed to be not truly wild. This is not "ber." *Z. mauritiana* Lam (*Z. jujuba* Lam non Mill) is the real "ber" and it is frequently cultivated and self sown. Wild "ber," the fruits of which are eaten, is *Z. nummularia* (Burn f.) Wt and Arn. It is distributed commonly in the hotter parts of Sind, Baluchistan, etc. (Stewart 1972: 469).

THE HARAPPAN FOOD ECONOMY

Harappa

Harappa, District Montgomery, Pakistan

(Vats 1941: 466–67; Allchin 1969; Vishnu-Mittre 1974a)

1) Wheat (*Triticum compactum* and *T. sphaerococcum*)
2) Barley (*Hordeum vulgare* a small-seeded six-rowed variety)
3) Peas (*Pisum arvense* L.)
4) Sesame (*Sesamum indicum*)

Owing to their nonavailability, these materials could not be examined. For diversity of opinion on the botanical identity of Harappa wheat see "Mohenjodaro and Chanhudaro" in this paper.

The identified wheat came from two lumps: (1) No. 5346A, NDF, Great Granary Area in Square I 9/15, depth five feet, in association with Stratum III, (2) No. 12387 V from a trench on southern edge of Mound AB in association with Stratum II. The barley, No. 3429 came from Extension Pits I and II in Mound AB, depth six feet, in association with Stratum III. The peas, No. 8366 came from the hollow of circular Platform P8 in Trench V. Finally a lump of charred sesame, No. 8827, was found in Trench V, Mound F, depth six feet, in association with Stratum III.

Banawali

Banawali, Haryana, India

1) Wheat

The material was seen at an exhibition as stated earlier; but it was not examined.

Lothal

Lothal, Gujarat, India

(Vishnu-Mittre 1961, 1974a; Allchin and Allchin 1968; Allchin 1969).

1) Rice: imprints of husks and spikelets.

Rangpur

Rangpur, Gujarat, India
(Allchin and Allchin 1968; Vishnu-Mittre 1974a)

1) Rice

We have had no opportunity to examine the rice imprints from Lothal and Rangpur to establish whether they belong to a wild or cultivated form. It was earlier noted (Vishnu-Mittre 1961) that they might belong to wild rice, which occurs locally in marshes; however the possibility of rice cultivation cannot be ruled out.

Mohenjodaro and Chanhudaro

Mohenjodaro, Chanhudaro, Sind, Pakistan
The wheat and barley grains from these two sites, not far from each other, are treated together here.

1) Wheat (Pls. 18.1 and 18.2)

The material examined from Mohenjodaro is from a pavement of late date (Marshall 1931) and subsequently dated by radiocarbon to 1650 B.C. (TF-75, 3600±100 years B.P., Agrawal *et al.* 1964). The sample from Chanhudaro is a mixture of two samples, 2345 and 2346. The Mohenjodaro sample consists of 56 entire caryopses of wheat, with several broken fragments, as well as a fragment of a grain of barley. In contrast, the Chanhudaro material consists of an enormous quantity (several hundred) of wheat caryopses, from which 160 caryopses of barley were segregated.

The divergent opinions on the identity of the carbonized wheat grains from these two sites, and from Harappa, necessitated a re-examination of these materials. Stapf (1931) found the Mohenjodaro wheat grains to be variable in size and shape and referred most of them to *Triticum compactum* but the plumpest ones to *T. sphaerococcum*. On the other hand Percival (1921) referred all of them to *T. sphaerococcum* except those from the SD level which he called *T. compactum*. Luthra (1936) referred them to *T. aestivum* subsp. *vulgare*, and *T. aestivum* subsp. *compactum*, and stated that the *T. compactum* of Mohenjodaro was very similar to that from Harappa

(Luthra 1941). Burt (1941) referred the Harappa material to *T. sphaerococcum*. Shaw (1943) examined the Chanhudaro grains that had been preserved in storage bins and referred the rounded and variable grains to *T. sphaerococcum* and the slightly larger ones to the *T. vulgare* type. He also stated that the Harappa and Mohenjodaro wheat grains referred by Luthra to *T. compactum* belonged to *T. sphaerococcum*.

Wheat caryopses of modern *T. sphaerococcum* Perc., *T. compactum* Host and *T. aestivum* L. Syn. *T. vulgare* (Vill.) Host (vide Peterson 1965) were studied by us to prepare a morphostatistical base for the comparative study of the charred grains. The following data are based on 50 or 100 random grains from each species.

Modern Wheat Grains (Table 18.1)

T. compactum Host

The caryopses, about 5–7 by 2–3.5 by 2–3 millimeters have a rounded and broad apex with the base pointed or narrower due to the projection of the embryo. The dorsal surface is flattened and smoothly rounded, and the ventral surface is flat. The ventral furrow running from end to end is deep or superficial.

Table 18.1. Dimensions (in millimeters) of modern wheat grains

No. of grains	Length (L)	Breadth (B)	Thickness (T)
Triticum sphaetococcum			
Humped Grains			
(with constriction)			
50	Average 5.05	2.81	2.81
Humped Grains			
(without constriction)			
50	Average 5.16	2.81	2.71
T. compactum			
50	Average 6.02	2.63	2.38
T. aestivum			
50	Average 6.66	2.92	2.76

L=Length, B=Breadth and T=Thickness in millimeters, in all tables.

T. aestivum L.

The caryopses, about 5.75–7.25 by 2–3.75 by 2–3 millimeters, are slightly narrower toward both ends and slightly broader in the middle. The dorsal surface is smooth and slightly raised. The deep ventral furrow is slightly curved, deeper in the middle and running end to end. The furrow margins, far apart towards the tops, converge at the base. The embryo end is less pointed than in *T. compactum*.

The caryopses of both these species are only slightly different in morphological and size characters. This makes a distinction between them in a dispersed condition, uncertain. A similar conclusion has been reached by Jessen and Helbaek (1944) and Helbaek (1958).

T. sphaerococcum Perc.

The caryopses of shot wheat, about 4–6 by 2–3.5 by 2–3.25 millimeters are short, broad and more or less rounded, with or without a characteristic hump (a raised area on the dorsal surface). The hump is either broadly rounded or vertically raised into a narrow projection. The humped caryopses were found on 97 percent of the sample. Of those, 23 percent had a constricted and 65 percent a nonconstricted hump. Grains without a hump were only three percent of the total.

The distinctive morphological features of the caryopses of *T. sphaerococcum* make them distinguishable from those of the other two species. This is further supported by the various index ratios as given in Table 18.2. For instance L/B, and L/T indices are under two, and B/L index above 0.5, etc., for *T. sphaerococcum* against the indices L/B and L/T above two and the B/L index under 0.45 for the other two species.

Table 18.2. Morphology of the caryopses of modern wheat

No. of grains	Species of *Triticum* examined	L/B	L/T	B/L	B/T	T/L	T/B
50	*T. sphaerococcum* constricted	1.80	1.80	0.56	1.00	0.56	100
50	*T. sphaerococcum* non-constricted	1.84	1.90	0.54	1.00	0.53	96
100	**T. sphaerococcum*	1.76	1.62	0.56	—	0.61	109
100	**T. aestivum*	2.68	3.07	0.37	—	0.32	87
100	**T. compactum*	2.44	3.07	0.40	—	0.32	79
50	*T. compactum*	2.29	2.52	0.44	1.10	0.39	90
50	*T. aestivum*	2.28	2.41	0.44	1.06	0.41	94

*After Vishnu-Mittre 1974.

The dimensions of the Harappan charred wheat grains, together with their identity, are set out in Tables 18.3 and 18.4.

In applying the identification criteria to the carbonized caryopses on Tables 18.3 and 18.4 (56 caryopses from Mohenjodaro and a random 100 caryopses from Chanhudaro) it can be said that:

Twelve grains from Mohenjodaro, and 30 from Chanhudaro were discovered with a dorsal hump (six constricted at Mohenjodaro and 10 at Chanhudaro) with a L/B ratio much under 2 (ranging from 1.5–1.81).

Nearly twelve grains from Mohenjodaro and 17 from Chanhudaro resembled *T. sphaerococcum* in size and shape, were without hump, but had L/B indices under two.

There were six humped grains from Mohenjodaro and two from Chanhudaro that had L/B indices of two or above, like those of *T. compactum* and *T. aestivum*. These can be considered variable forms.

Thirty-two humpless caryopses with L/B indices of two or more came from Mohenjodaro and 54 from Chanhudaro differed in shape and size from *T. sphaerococcum*. These compared well with the *T. aestivum-compactum* group.

Thus, the Harappans at Mohenjodaro and Chanhudaro were growing and consuming grains of both the *T. sphaerococcum* and *T. aestivum/T. compactum* groups.

2) Barley (Pl. 18.3, nos. 1, 3, 4, 7)

For a detailed comparative study of modern barleys and the carbonized specimens see the following section on Kalibangan. Mohenjodaro produced only one broken-hulled grain, whereas from Chanhudaro two hulled (4.3–5 by 2.2 millimeters) and 10 naked (4–5 by 2–3 millimeters) grains of barley were recovered.

3) Rice

There is a report by Andrus and Mohammed (1958) on the occurrence of rice at Harappan sites in Sind and Punjab. We have not been able to trace either the source of this information or the actual specimens.

4) *Pisum arvense*

5) *Brassica juncea*

We did not recover mustard seeds in the material we examined from Chanhudaro.

Kalibangan

Kalibangan, Rajasthan, India

The archaeological provenance of the samples examined is as follows:
Samples
1) KLB-2/XA 17; Locus A17; 8.47×A18, 9.02;

Food Economy of the Harappans

Table 18.3. Dimensions (in millimeters) and index ratios of humped carbonized caryopses with L/B ratios under two
(*T. sphaerococcum*)

No. of grains	Length (L)	Breadth (B)	Thickness (T)	L/B	L/T	B/L	B/T	T/L	T/B
Humped Grains (with constriction)									
Mohenjodaro									
1	4.00	2.25	2.50						
1	4.00	2.50	2.50						
1	4.50	2.50	2.00						
1	4.50	2.50	2.50						
1	4.75	3.00	3.00						
1	5.00	3.00	2.50						
Average	4.46	2.63	2.50	1.70	1.78	0.59	1.05	0.56	0.95
Chanhudaro									
1	4.00	2.75	2.50						
2	4.00	3.00	2.50						
2	4.00	3.00	3.00						
1	4.25	2.50	2.00						
2	4.50	2.75	2.00						
2	5.00	3.00	3.00						
Average	4.32	2.87	2.55	1.50	1.69	0.66	1.12	0.59	0.89
Humped Grains (without constriction)									
Mohenjodaro									
1	4.00	2.50	2.15						
1	4.50	2.50	3.00						
1	5.00	3.00	2.50						
3	5.00	3.00	3.00						
Average	4.75	2.83	2.77	1.68	1.71	0.59	1.02	0.58	0.98
Chanhudaro									
1	4.50	3.00	3.00						
1	5.00	2.75	2.00						
2	5.00	2.75	2.50						
1	5.00	3.00	2.50						
8	5.00	3.00	3.00						
2	5.00	3.50	3.00						
1	5.25	3.00	3.00						
1	5.50	2.75	2.50						
1	5.55	3.00	2.25						
1	5.00	3.00	2.50						
1	5.00	3.00	3.00						
Average	5.04	3.00	2.78	1.65	1.81	0.60	1.08	0.55	0.93
Humpless Grains									
Mohenjodaro									
1	4.00	2.50	2.00						
1	4.50	3.00	2.00						
1	4.50	3.00	3.00						
2	4.75	3.00	2.75						
1	5.00	3.00	2.00						
1	5.00	3.00	2.75						
4	5.00	3.00	2.75						
1	5.15	3.00	2.75						
Average	4.80	2.96	2.58	1.62	1.86	0.62	1.15	0.54	0.87
Chanhudaro									
1	4.50	2.50	2.00						
1	4.75	3.00	2.50						
1	5.00	2.75	2.00						
6	5.00	3.00	2.00						
2	5.00	3.00	3.00						
3	5.00	3.50	2.00						
1	5.00	4.00	3.00						
1	5.50	3.00	3.00						
1	6.00	3.50	3.00						
Average	5.04	3.13	2.32	1.61	2.17	0.62	1.35	0.46	0.74

depth 2.5 meters. Stratum 17 (in three bottles labeled as wheat).

2) KLB-2/XAB; Locus A8, 8.85×A9-5.27, Se. Sector; depth 2.41 meters; Stratum 16 (labeled as gram)

3) KLB-2/XAI; Stratum 25; Depth 4.4 B.B. (brittle charred wood).

4) KLB-1/YAI; Locus YAI; Qdt; I; Depth 1.95 meters, Stratum 3 (labeled as potsherds containing grain and organic material for chemical analysis).

5) KLB-2/Qdr; stratum (terracotta *pai*)

6) KLB-20,566 (terracotta cake).

7) KLB-2/XBI, Stratum 7 (terracotta cake).

The two samples of charred food grains from the early phase of the Harappan Culture dated by radiocarbon to 4040 ± 125 B.P. and 4025 ± 110 B.P. respectively (Agrawal and Kusumgar 1968) were not available for study.

Samples 1, 2, 3, and 5 are from the Harappan Phase whereas sample 4 is from the Pre-Harappan Phase. We are not certain if sample 6 is from the Harappan or the Pre-Harappan occupation. The examination of the two radiocarbon dated samples from the early phase of the Harappan Culture would have thrown light on the food economy of this period, but they were not available for study.

1) Barley (*Hordeum* sp.) (Pl. 18.3, no. 1)

To determine the botanical identity of carbonized

Table 18.4. Dimensions (in millimeters) and index ratios of carbonized caryopses with L/B ratio of two or more
(*T. aestivum, compactum,* etc.)

No. of grains	Length (L)	Breadth (B)	Thickness (T)	L/B	L/T	B/L	B/T	T/L	T/B
Humped Grains (without constriction)									
Mohenjodaro									
2	4.00	2.00	2.00						
1	5.00	2.00	2.00						
1	5.00	2.50	2.50						
1	5.00	2.50	3.00						
1	5.75	2.75	2.75						
Average	4.79	2.29	2.37	2.09	2.02	0.48	0.96	0.49	1.03
Chanhudaro									
1	4.00	2.00	2.00						
1	6.00	3.00	3.00						
Average	5.00	2.50	2.50	2.0	2.0	0.50	1.0	0.50	1.0
Grains without hump but with both ends blunt, furrow straight with parallel margins									
Mohenjodaro									
3	4.00	2.00	2.00						
1	4.00	2.00	2.50						
1	4.50	2.00	2.00						
1	5.00	2.00	2.00						
3	5.00	2.50	2.00						
1	5.50	2.25	2.25						
Average	4.60	2.17	2.07	2.12	2.22	0.47	1.04	0.45	0.95
Chanhudaro									
1	5.00	2.25	2.00						
1	5.00	2.25	3.00						
1	5.00	2.50	2.00						
1	5.50	2.25	2.00						
1	6.00	2.50	2.50						
1	6.00	3.00	2.00						
2	6.00	3.00	3.00						
Average	5.56	2.59	2.43	2.15	2.29	0.46	1.06	0.44	0.94
Grains with both ends tapering, furrow deep, curved, margins wide apart									
Mohenjodaro									
1	4.00	2.00	2.00						
1	4.25	2.00	1.50						
1	4.25	2.00	2.00						
1	4.50	2.00	2.00						
1	4.50	2.25	2.00						
1	4.75	2.00	1.50						
1	5.00	1.75	1.50						
3	5.00	2.00	2.00						
1	5.00	2.50	2.25						
2	5.00	2.50	2.00						
1	5.25	2.50	2.00						
1	6.00	3.00	2.75						
1	6.00	3.00	3.00						
Average	4.90	2.25	2.03	2.18	2.41	0.46	1.11	0.41	0.90
Chanhudaro									
1	4.00	2.00	1.50						
1	5.00	2.00	2.50						
2	5.00	2.50	2.25						
3	5.00	2.50	2.00						
1	5.25	2.25	2.00						
2	5.50	2.25	2.00						
1	5.50	2.50	2.00						
1	5.50	2.75	2.50						
3	5.50	2.50	2.00						
2	5.50	2.00	2.00						
2	5.50	2.25	2.00						
1	5.75	2.50	2.50						
1	5.75	2.75	2.50						
5	6.00	2.50	2.00						
1	5.00	2.50	2.00						
1	6.00	2.75	3.00						
1	6.00	3.00	2.50						
12	6.00	3.00	3.00						
1	6.25	3.00	3.00						
2	6.50	3.00	3.00						
Average	5.67	2.62	2.42	2.16	2.34	0.46	1.08	0.42	0.92

barley, the grains of modern barleys belonging to *Hordeum vulgare* L. and *Hordeum spontaneum* Koch were examined for distinguishing criteria. There are approximately eight species of cultivated barley. These are all grouped under *Hordeum vulgare* considered the cultigen embracing all cultivated types. *H. spontaneum* and *H. agriocrithon* Aberg are wild and believed to be the ancestral forms of cultivated barleys (Anonymous 1959: 118).

The *Hordeum vulgare* complex includes various types of cultivated barley, some with six and some with two rows of fertile spikelets (e.g., *Hordeum vulgare* is a six-rowed barley and *H. distichon* Linn a two-rowed barley. *H. spontaneum* is a two-rowed wild barley, as is *H. agriocrithon,* a six-rowed variety).

In the twenty-four cultivated types of Indian barleys five are two-rowed and 19 are six-rowed. The types are further divided into those with husked (adherence of the lemma to caryopsis) or huskless (that is, "naked") grains. Today the six-rowed husked types are the most widely grown in India. The two-rowed varieties, both husked and huskless, are rarely grown.

Modern Cultivated Barley

Exceptionally small barley grains were recovered from the excavations at Kalibangan. Their seemingly aberrant size and the general problems involved with the accurate identification of ancient food grains, demanded a systematic approach to the proper handling of these remains. Therefore, several samples of modern cultivated barley were obtained from the Indian Agricultural Research Institute for comparative study. The results of this investigation are as follows:

1) Hulled barley

Sample RS-17 from Durgapura, Rajasthan. This sample of six-rowed barley had a majority of grains measuring 10–12 millimeters in length, 3.5–4 millimeters in breadth and 2.5–3 millimeters in thickness. Some of the small grains measured 9–9.5 by 2.5–3.25 by 1.5–2.5 millimeters.

Sample BG-1, Punjab. This sample of six-rowed barley ranged in size as follows: 9–12 by 3–4 by 2–2.25 millimeters.

Sample REB-209, India. Unlike the six-rowed hulled grains in the other samples these samples of barley are slender, thin and flat on the dorsal side. They are angular in cross-section, tapering to a narrow base and less sharply to the blunt apex. Their range in size is: 8–11 by 2–2.75 by 1.5 millimeters.

Sample NP-104, I.A.R.I., New Delhi. This six-rowed barley ranged in size from: 7.5–12 by 3–4 by 1.5–2 millimeters.

Sample DG-2, Delhi. The size range of this six-rowed barley is as follows: 8–13 by 2–3 by 1–3 millimeters.

Naked barley

Sample RS-17, Durgapura, Rajasthan. Grains from a packet of naked barley from the hulled barley noted above are quite diverse in size. Their characteristics are as follows:

Size range: 5–9.5 by 2–4 by 1–4 millimeters.
Small grains: 5–6 by 2–3 by 1–2 millimeters.
Medium grains: 5–7 by 2–3 by 1–2 millimeters.
Large grains: 8–9.5 by 3–4 by 2.5–3.5 millimeters.
Sample C-292, Kanpur. This two-rowed barley was: 5–7 by 2–4 by 1–3 millimeters.

Sample HC-1905, Delhi. A naked barley, this sample ranged in size as follows: 6–9 by 2.5–4 by 1.5–2.5 millimeters.

Sample BHD-45 is a six-rowed barley from Delhi. It measured 6.5–9 by 3–4 by 1.5–2 millimeters.

Sample EB-581, New Delhi is a two-rowed sample with the following dimensions: 5–9 by 3–4.5 by 2–3 millimeters.

Samples from I.A.R.I. Two unnumbered samples from this Institute were examined. They were made up of the polished grains of pearl barley. The grains were rounded. Both ends were round, with the ventral groove superficial and broad. The ventral groove was faint or absent. The embryo and hillum scar had been removed by polishing. They ranged in size from: 4–7 by 3–4 by 2.5 millimeters.

DISCUSSION

The study of these modern varieties of barley has revealed that the small grain size was particularly evident in the sample from Durgapura, Rajasthan (RS-17). It should be noted, however, that the number of small grains is less than the combined sample of medium and large grains from the same locality.

The Kalibangan grains are three to five millimeters smaller than the modern grains of barley. This is in part the result of ancient carbonization. Renfrew (1973) observed that modern grains of naked barley, when carbonized in the laboratory, showed a decrease in length and an increase in breadth. But hulled barley shows a very slight decrease in length since the grain is tightly invested by its lemma. Its breadth remains unchanged. But the European prehistoric carbonized grains of barley are two to three millimeters longer than the modern naked examples and one to two millimeters longer than modern carbonized examples. The Kalibangan carbonized grains are thus much smaller, like the very small grains of the variety grown in Rajasthan.

The hulled grain can be easily separated from the naked grain on a morphological basis. When the palea is lost the surface features of grains with faint longitudinal striping allow them to be distinguished from naked grains, which resemble wheat grains, on the basis of macroscopic transverse rippling on the grain surface. The rippling in hulled grains after the palea has been burnt away is coarse and not transverse.

Carbonized Barley Grains

Carbonized barley kernels comprise the bulk of the plant remains in the Kalibangan sample. They were found in three bottles labeled "wheat." The spike parts and paleae are absent. The grains vary considerably in size. The hulled barley grains outnumber naked forms: for every 100 hulled grains, there are only five naked examples.

Hulled Barley Grains

The hulled forms range in size from 2 by 1 by 1 millimeters to 6 by 4 by 3 millimeters (Table 18.5). But most grains are 4 to 5.75 millimeters in length. Although the palea is lost in most of the specimens due to intense carbonization, their angular cross-section is suggestive of its former presence. The grains are characterized by very faint longitudinal striping or finger print-like impressions most likely resulting from the closely adpressed paleae over the grain surface. Such grains are both twisted and straight. The twisted examples are slightly smaller than those that are straight, suggesting derivation from a six-rowed variety which has twisted lateral grains smaller than the median straight ones. The awns and hoods are absent. The absence of any trace of the palea in several other grains makes it almost impossible to decide if these were straight or twisted.

Table 18.5. Dimensions (in millimeters) of hulled barley grains (*Hordeum* spp.) from Kalibangan

No. of grains	L	B	T	No. of grains	L	B	T
1	2.00	1.00	1.00	1	4.00	4.00	3.00
1	2.75	1.50	1.10	1	4.25	2.50	2.00
1	3.00	2.00	1.50	2	4.25	3.00	2.00
1	3.00	2.00	1.10	1	4.25	3.25	2.00
1	3.25	2.25	2.00	1	4.25	3.50	2.50
1	3.50	1.25	1.00	1	4.50	2.00	1.50
1	3.50	1.75	1.00	1	4.50	3.00	2.00
1	3.50	2.00	1.50	1	4.50	3.50	2.50
1	3.50	2.50	1.75	1	4.75	2.00	1.00
1	3.50	2.75	1.75	2	4.75	4.00	3.00
1	3.50	2.50	2.25	2	5.00	3.00	2.00
1	3.75	1.75	1.50	5	5.00	3.00	2.50
1	3.75	2.00	2.00	2	5.00	3.00	3.00
2	3.75	3.00	2.00	16	5.00	4.00	3.00
1	4.00	1.00	1.00	1	5.00	3.50	2.50
2	4.00	1.10	1.00	1	5.00	3.75	3.00
1	4.00	1.75	1.25	1	5.00	3.00	2.75
1	4.00	1.75	1.50	4	5.00	4.00	2.75
1	4.00	1.50	1.50	1	5.00	3.75	2.75
1	4.00	2.00	1.50	7	5.00	4.00	2.50
1	4.00	2.00	1.00	1	5.00	4.00	2.00
1	4.00	2.50	2.50	1	5.00	4.00	3.50
1	4.00	2.75	2.50	4	6.00	4.00	2.50
2	4.00	3.00	2.00	4	6.00	4.00	3.00
1	4.00	3.00	1.75	1	6.00	3.50	3.00
2	4.00	3.00	2.50	1	6.00	3.00	2.75
1	4.00	2.50	2.50	1	6.00	3.00	2.50
1	4.00	2.75	2.50				
1	4.00	3.25	2.50	100 Average	4.59	3.15	2.32
1	4.00	3.50	1.75				
1	4.00	3.50	2.50				

Naked Barley Grains

The few naked barley grains measure 3 by 2 by 1.5 millimeters to 4.75 by 3 by 2.5 millimeters (Table 18.6). Longitudinal furrows and ridges on the surface of caryopses are absent. They are evenly rounded in cross-section and show certain macroscopic transverse rippling on the grain surface. The transverse rippling usually occurs during the drying of the grain resulting from the contraction of the fruit shell devoid of the paleae. The coarse wrinkling seen in carbonized grains when the palea has been burnt away differs from the transverse rippling in naked grains. The former is caused by the fiber cells of the closely adpressed or fused paleae which might have completely burnt away.

Table 18.6. Dimensions (in millimeters) of naked barley from Kalibangan

No. of grains	L	B	T
1	3.00	2.00	1.50
2	4.00	2.75	2.00
1	4.00	3.00	2.00
1	4.25	3.00	2.50
1	4.75	3.00	2.50
6 Average	4.00	2.75	2.08

The barleys cultivated by the Harappans at Kalibangan were varieties which produced hulled barley grains. The naked barley-producing varieties were less common; they were there as revealed by a few naked barley grains. The presence of twisted hulled grains in them reveals that the hulled barley grains were most probably produced by a six-rowed variety.

2) Wheat (*Triticum* sp.)

Among the barley grains, only five rotund or globose grains with a smooth surface (measuring 4–5.5 by 2.75–3.75 by 2–3 millimeters, Table 18.7) were found to possess a distinct dorsal hump as it occurs in grains of *Triticum sphaerococcum*. Unlike wheat caryopses, the ventral furrow is shallow and does not run from end to end, a characteristic seen in grains of barley only. But unlike barley grains, a thin depression or streak running from the embryo to the apex, seen on the dorsal surface, and the projection of the embryo towards the dorsal end, are not seen in these carbonized grains. These grains possess characteristics intermediate between wheat and barley.

Table 18.7. Dimensions (in millimeters) of carbonized wheat grains from Kalibangan

No. of grains	L	B	T
1	4.00	2.75	2.75
1	4.00	3.00	2.00
1	5.00	2.75	2.75
1	5.00	3.75	2.75
1	5.50	3.00	3.00
5 Average	4.70	3.05	2.65

Their rare occurrence with hundreds of barley grains suggests them to be either aberrant forms or the result of a few wheat plants that may have grown in the barley fields.

Supporting evidence for the occurrence of wheat at Kalibangan has been obtained from the cuticular anatomy of the husk in terracotta cakes and *pai* from this site. The epidermal characters of rice husk are entirely different and husk referrable to that of rice was not found. Sarma's observation that husk in cakes and *paies* belonged to rice could not be established (Sharma 1972; Vishnu-Mittre and Savithri 1975).

3) *Cicer arietinum* (gram) Chickpea (Pl. 18.3, no. 6)

The three carbonized seeds in sample number 2, measuring 5–7 by 5–6 by 4–6 millimeters (Table 18.8) are squat-shaped, angular and pointed at one end. The blunt oblique point formed by the germ (radicle) is well preserved. The hilum is 1.5–2 millimeters long, large, and concave on the flattened side near the pointed end. The seed coat is also well preserved. The seeds are unmistakably those of the chickpea.

Table 18.8. Dimensions (in millimeters) of gram (*Cicer arietinum*) from Kalibangan

No. of seeds	L	B	T
1	5.00	5.00	4.00
1	6.75	6.00	4.75
1	7.00	6.00	6.00

4) *Pisum arvense*. Linn. (Pl. 18.3, no. 5)

The single seed, about 2.5 millimeters in diameter, from sample number 1, is spherical with an ovate hilum, approximately 0.5 millimeters long, flush with the surface of the seed. It resembles that of *Pisum arvense*.

5) Crystals on potsherds (Pl. 18.3, no. 2)

Sticking to the inner surface of the potsherds in sample number 4, otherwise devoid of imprints of any organic matter (husks or spikelets or grains), was found a large number of transparent to dirty clayey crystals. The chemical analysis of these crystals carried out by Shri D.K. Agrawal, Lecturer in the Chemistry Department of Lucknow University has shown them to belong to selenite gypsum in transparent crystalline form.

Surkotada

Surkotada (Period III), near Adesar, Kutch, India (Joshi 1972; Vishnu-Mittre 1974a; Vishnu-Mittre and Savithri 1978).

The charred lumps of carbonized seeds in the earthen pot discovered from Locus XA4 (Qd I, Layer 5, depth 1.6 meters) in Period III are dated to 1660 B.C. (TF-1307; Agrawal 1972; Joshi 1972). Period III ranges in time from 1970 B.C. to 1660 B.C. (TF-1297, TF-1294, TF-1311, TF-1307). The advent of a new culture preceded by a widespread conflagration and characterized by the White Painted Black and Red Ware, resembling that of the Ahar Culture in southeastern Rajasthan, is noticeable during Period III. The residual Harappans at this site appear to have been pushed into the background by the influx of new peoples during this period.

Two of the several charred lumps yielded as many as 574 seeds, an overwhelming majority of which were from wild plants. Only about seven percent were identified as being of cereals.

The wild seeds have only been *tentatively* identified for want of modern comparative materials. Their broad, distinctive morphological features allow some of them to be referred to the following groups of wild plants. Their specific identity, wherever mentioned, is tentative.

1) *Setaria* spp. (Pl. 18.4 nos. 1, 2, 3)

On morphological and comparative grounds derived from a study of 10 modern species of *Setaria*, 40 grains out of 574 have been referred to this genus. It is possible that grains of Italian millet (*S. italica*) the cultivated species and the two wild species, the green millet (*S. viridis* and *S. verticillata*) are included (Vishnu-Mittre and Savithri 1978).

2) *Eleusine coracana* (*ragi*) (Pl. 18.4, no. 4)

A small number of grains compare in all essential characters with those of the finger millet (Savithri and Vishnu-Mittre 1979).

3) *Wild Grasses* (Pl. 18.5, no. 8)

Besides *Setaria* spp., dealt with above, there are as many as 257 obovoid, ovoid, oblong and grooved, 1-2 by 0.5-1 millimeters, seeds of grasses. Fifteen of these, the oblong and terete ones, seem to compare with those of *Phragmites karka*, a reed grass. The remaining seeds may belong to wild grasses like *Andropogon, Brachiaria, Panicum, Echinochola, Eragrostis,* or *Digitaria*. These are species which occur as weeds on disturbed soil in and around cultivated fields and settlement sites, or around sheets of water and moist places.

4) *Sedges* (Pl. 18.5, nos. 2, 4, 5)

Among 47 seeds referred to sedges, two globosely obovoid trigonous and rugose seeds, 1.25 by 1.5 millimeters compare with the seeds of *Scirpus supinus*. Thirteen glumeless nuts, which are biconvex, ovate, shortly beaked, stipitate or trigonous, cylindric, ellipsoid, smooth with narrowed apices compare with those of *Carex* spp. and 38 look like those of *Eriophorum* spp.

5) *Cheno-amaranths*

Among 13 seeds, three circular-lenticular examples with curved embryos compare with those of *Amaranthus* spp. and eight ornamented specimens with those of *Atriplex* spp. probably *griffithii* Moq. var. *stocksii* Boiss, a plant of salt marshes.

6) *Polygonum* spp. (Pl. 18.5, no. 7).

Two hundred and fifteen triangular, ovate, lens-shaped seeds, about 1-1.5 millimeters long seem to belong to this genus on morphological grounds.

7) *Euphorbia* spp. (Pl. 18.5, no. 3)

Twelve obtusely four-angled seeds about one millimeter across compare with those of *Euphorbia pycnostegia* as described by Hooker (1885) in the *Flora of British India*.

THE FOOD ECONOMY OF THE LATE HARAPPANS

Daimabad

Daimabad, District Ahmednagar, Maharashtra (Deshpande 1978)*

---

*Editor's note: See also S.A. Sali's paper in this volume.

The Savalda Culture inhabitants of Daimabad had a food economy consisting of the following plants:
Jowar (*Sorghum* sp.)
Barley (*Hordeum* sp.)
Lentil (*Lens culinaris*)
Period II on the site produced only barley (*Hordeum* sp.).
Period III, following Period II, a barren and weathered deposit ceramically corresponding to Period I at Prakash (ca. 1500 B.C.), had a food economy consisting of:
Barley (*Hordeum* sp.)
Pea (*Pisum* sp.)
Horsegram
Lentil (*Lens culinaris*)
Mung (*Vigna radiatus*)
Indian jujube (*Zyzyphus* sp.)
(Possible latin names are added by us.)

Daulatpur

Daulatpur, District Kurukshetra, Haryana

1) *Vigna mungo* (L.) Hepper (*Phaseolus mungo* L), Urd.

Charred grains from Locus 01, Stratum (5), depth 1.65 meters, referred to Late Harappans, have been identified by us as *Vigna mungo*, Urd.

CONCLUSION

Factual information on the remains of food plants is so scanty and widely scattered that it allows neither the reconstruction of the sequential development of the food economy from the Pre-Harappan to the Late Harappan nor does it provide information on the changing food economy at a particular site through the passage of time and through phases of evolution and devolution of the Harappan Culture.

It has become apparent, howsoever insufficient the evidence is, that in themselves the food grains from Harappan sites could have provided the Harappans with a balanced vegetarian diet: carbohydrates derived from cereals like wheat, barley, millets, etc., proteins from peas, chickpea, *Vigna* and horsegram, and fats from seeds of sesame and mustard. They were also consuming the fruits of jujube. One believes that there were probably other food plants as well, but certain evidence is lacking.

GEOGRAPHICAL VARIABILITY OF CROPS

The presence of wheat at Mundigak, predominantly wheat, with some barley, at Mohenjodaro, Chanhudaro and Harappa, wheat at Banawali, exclusively barley at Kalibangan, the millets *Setaria* and *Eleusine* at Surkotada, and possibly rice at Rangpur and Lothal would suggest that the food economy in the vast Harappan Empire was not a uniform feature; rather, it varied geographically. We cannot overlook, however, the fact that complete information on their food economy still escapes us. But, broadly speaking, the Harappan situation compares well with the modern food economy in western South Asia. This vast region is presently characterized by a variety of climates from arid to subhumid, with gradation both in temperature and precipitation. There is a variety of soils as well. The Harappan crops suggest that a similar situation existed during those times. It is unlikely that the vast region was uniformly wet or dry as is usually believed.

The crops presently cultivated in Baluchistan, Sind and the Punjab (Stewart 1972) are:
Triticum sphaerococcum. Formerly grown in Sind and the Punjab, but now only important in Baluchistan.
Triticum aestivum, *durum* and *trugidum*; *Hordeum distichon*, and *vulgare* are now grown extensively in Sind and the Punjab.
Italian millet (*Setaria italica*) and *bajra* (*Pennisetum typhoides*) are the important millets in parts of Baluchistan.
Paspalum scrobiculatum is important in Sind.
Several varieties of *jowar* (*Sorghum bicolor*) are important in Sind and lower Baluchistan.
Panicum miliaceum (Cheena) and *P. sumatrense* (*miliare* Lamk.) are also found, the latter especially in Sind.
Eleusine coracana is found occasionally on the plains and the lower hills of the Indus delta.
On the Indian side, in the Punjab, Haryana and western Uttar Pradesh, wheat is the predominant crop, grown along with *bajra* and barley. Rice is comparatively unimportant in these regions. *Bajra* is the principal crop in the Rajasthan desert along with *jowar* and barley. Maize, introduced in the historical period is also cultivated. A drawing on a Mohenjodaro potsherd (Marshall 1931 Pl. LXXXVII, photo 5) looks like a *Sorghum* plant and indicates that more crops, particularly millets, may have been grown by the Harappans than we know so far.

ENVIRONMENTAL ANALYSIS OF CROPS

The inferred geographical variability of Harappan crops, if factual, should indicate environmental variability during the Harappan times. The environmental analysis of the comparable modern crops discovered from the Harappan Empire should make this point.

Wheats

Although largely restricted to an area with annual precipitation between 37 and 110 centimeters, a little wheat is grown in regions with less than 22.5 centimeters of rainfall. The rain should be well distributed during the year. Irrigation is essential in desert soils. River alluvium is poor in nitrogen, humus and phosphorus as compared to Indus alluvium which is loamy or sandy loam, alkaline and rich in phosphorus and potash but poor in organic matter and nitrogen. Alluvium yields a good wheat crop, with or without irrigation. Water is a great limiting factor for agriculture in the Rajasthan desert, southern Punjab and Haryana, although the soils are alkaline with high percentage of soluble salts (Anonymous 1976).

According to Rao (1974: 37) many local wheats are tolerant of adverse soil conditions. Also being drought tolerant they are grown in areas of low soil fertility with little precipitation. *Triticum sphaerococcum* particularly, is highly resistant to drought, which explains its former widespread cultivation in northwestern India (Singh 1946). It requires a cool climate at the time of sowing but sufficient warmth devoid of high humidity at the time of grain formation. Desiccating hot winds affect its growth adversely.

Barley

Being both heat and drought resistant, barley is grown in areas too dry or too saline to carry a satisfactory wheat crop. It is the most profitable crop where saline or alkaline conditions prevail (Bakshi and Ranga 1974: 48-49). It requires moderate precipitation and sunny weather. It is tolerant of alkalinity, frost and drought and is less exacting in its nutritive requirements than wheat. It is also grown without manuring. Barley is grown with wheat in the Punjab and Uttar Pradesh as an insurance against weather hazards. It is also grown mixed with gram.

Owing to barley's higher digestibility coefficient, it is regarded as inferior for human consumption. Because of little or no glutin, its flour is mixed with that of wheat to make bread (*chapatties*) (Anonymous 1959).

Sesame

An essential article in Hindu religious ceremonies, this seed requires a warm climate and cannot withstand frost, continued heavy rains or prolonged drought. Waterlogging is highly detrimental to sesame which thrives best on sandy loams like the sandy semidesert soils in Rajasthan, or clayey soils or on black cotton soils of Central India. It is a rotation crop with wheat, gram, cotton, *ragi, jowar,* etc. It is also grown mixed with *bajra, jowar,* cotton, etc., as a measure against total loss. Manuring is done in the mixed cropping pattern (Anonymous 1972).

Setaria italica

This is a crop suited to tracts with low rainfall (50-75 centimeters) which is uncertain both in quantity and distribution. The least touch of frost is fatal to it. Italian millet favors ordinary red loams but also grows on very light ashy soils and black cotton soil. Cultivators grow it alone, or mixed with cotton, *ragi, Dolichos lablab* or in rotation with *Sorghum* and *Pennisetum typhoides*. Manure is seldom applied unless it is under irrigation. But for hoeing or working the crop with a blade harrow no further attention is given. The grain is also used for cage birds. *Setaria glauca* is cultivated on light soils with moderate rainfall without manuring or irrigation (Anonymous 1972).

Eleusine coracana

Much like *Setaria;* but grown in areas with under 625 millimeters of rainfall, irrigation becomes essential. It stands salinity better than any other crop.

Rice

Usually suited to regions where rainfall is adequate it can be grown in tracts with rainfall below 200 millimeters, provided it is compensated with adequate supply of water. Waterlogged conditions are most suitable.

This concise environmental analysis, along with the discussion of crops still grown in Baluchistan, Sind, Punjab, etc., where extremely low rainfall, drought and adverse soil conditions still prevail, makes interesting reading. Water is a great limiting factor in these regions and some sort of irrigation must be practiced. The proximity of river alluvium, if exploited for cultivation, should offset this limiting factor. For the Harappans, exploiting flood plains along the rivers for cultivation water was indeed not a great limiting factor. There is, thus, reason to believe that the precipitation pattern during Harappan times was much like the present, and irrigation, mostly natural, was used along the lines of the present day farming practice in Sind, as described by Lambrick (1967).

The fact that only barley was found at Kalibangan suggests that the environment here was harsher, with saline alkaline soils unsuitable for wheat cultivation. The presence of the most drought-resistant wheat (*Triticum sphaerococcum*) in the rest of the Harappan Empire also suggests the prevalence of drought conditions during Harappan times.

The cultivation of *Setaria* and *Eleusine,* a small fraction of thousands of wild seeds gathered by the Late or Post-Harappans at Surkotada, may be ruled out. These were perhaps cultivated elsewhere in Gujarat, as today.

From the above analysis it appears that environmental variability, much as is seen today, also existed in Harappan times.

STATUS OF RICE IN HARAPPAN FOOD ECONOMY

The Harappans were generally unaware of rice as a crop, except possibly in Gujarat (Lothal and Rangpur) where there is meager evidence for husks in the form of imprints in pottery (wild or cultivated, it is not known). If it was cultivated, the supply of water required for its cultivation may have been derived either from higher rainfall or from rivers and streams in the vicinity. About 150 years ago, under what is essentially the present precipitation pattern, rice, yielding a good revenue, was cultivated in the territory between Lakhpat, Sahera and Mundhan. This was possible because of a sufficient fresh water supply coming through a channel from an affluent of the Indus. Why could not the Harappans at Rangpur and Lothal have done something similar? After all, the territory of Lakhpat is a desert today and no rice has been grown here since 1762 when a bund was constructed at Mora by the ruler of Sind. This diverted the Indus water into his territory (Raverty 1892; Oldham 1926). Considerable quantities of rice were also grown in and near fertile areas of Bikaner (Todd 1832). Thus, if the water requirement is met, rice can be successfully grown, even if precipitation is much lower than required. Still, evidence suggests that the Harappans, over a large part of their empire, were not aware of this crop.

METHODS OF CULTIVATION

There is one example of field preparation through furrowing at Kalibangan (Lal 1971). This does not, however, allow us to generalize that this was a uniform practice over the entire Harappan Empire.

The contemporary observations by Lambrick (1967) that wheat and barley, the principal food grains on the flood plains of the Indus, are cultivated without ploughing, manuring or providing additional water, may be the manner by which the Harappans grew these crops. Fields may also have been surrounded by earth embankments, possibly along the banks of natural flood channels. The natural fertility of the alluvium was exploited together with the annual inundation, just as is done today. This is supported by the absence of tools used for agriculture in the Harappan sites. There is no factual evidence for either a rake or a harrow; although Kosambi believed the latter to have been used (Allchin and Allchin 1968: 260).

In this connection it is interesting to note that eight years of research and experiments at the Punjab Agricultural University, Ludhiana, have recently shown that tilling the land is not essential for the germination and growth of crops like wheat and maize. They have also found that tilling is required only for weed control (*Hindustan Times* May 1, 1979: Union Agricultural Minister Mr. M.S. Barnala's statement in the Lok Sabha, PTI news, April 30, 1979). To achieve this minimum tilling a bullock-drawn till planter has been developed by this university to shear off the soil crust and stubbles, open a furrow, sow the seeds and apply fertilizer in a single run. The bullock cart was known to the Harappans. Perhaps they used it for minimum tilling.

THE USE OF CHEMICAL FERTILIZER

The discovery of gypsum crystals on a potsherd from the Harappan site of Kalibangan is of special interest. The reason that the Kalibangan Harappans gathered gypsum and stored it may be explained through the present day use of this material to reclaim saline lands and render them productive.

Gypsum occurs profusely in the Rajasthan desert. There is also a large number of deposits in Bikaner. Ground gypsum is used in agriculture as a surface plaster for conserving moisture in the soil and for aiding nitrogen absorption from manures. It is also used to reduce the salinity and alkalinity of soils where the sodium ion is replaced by a calcium ion, since gypsum is calcium sulphate ($CaSO_4 2H_2O$). The soils of the Rajasthan desert are usually saline and alkaline. Even the water is saline, with sodium forming 90 percent of the total cations (Raychaudhuri 1964).

In view of this, the possibility that the Harappans in northern Rajasthan used gypsum as a fertilizer becomes all the more plausible.

CROPPING PATTERN

We continue to be unaware of the cropping pattern and the rotation practices of the Harappans. However, the Kalibangan furrowed field suggests mixed cropping. The same may perhaps be suggested by the mixture of wheat and barley, gram and other grains in the samples from Mohenjodaro and Chanhudaro. There is a small proportion of barley in the Mohenjodaro material; but the proportion is about 20 percent in the Chanhudaro sample. The mixed cropping of cereals, like wheat and barley, is practiced even today in the Punjab, Haryana and Uttar Pradesh as an insurance against weather hazards so that if wheat fails to ripen, the hardier barley is sure to yield.

Further, the occurrence of grains of both wheat and barley in the granaries suggests that bread was made from a mixture of both since barley flour alone has little or no glutin and is highly unsuitable for the purpose. Alcoholic drinks may also have been prepared. The dish-on-stand was perhaps used for this purpose.

HARAPPANS: THE FOOD GATHERERS

The new people that arrived at Surkotada when the residual Harappans had been pushed to the background, and the site had been affected by a widespread conflagration, seem to have been food gatherers, as the evidence of thousands of seeds of wild plants would suggest. Characterized by the White Painted Black and Red Ware, these peoples, it is believed, show resemblance with the Ahar Culture (Sankalia 1974). There is, however, scanty evidence of cultigens such as Italian millet and finger millet (*ragi*). The object for collecting such a wide variety of seeds of grasses, sedges, *Polygonum* and other weeds is enigmatic. Were they all used to prepare a gruel, or medicines, or were they gathered to feed cage birds? These questions will remain unanswered until more evidence has been obtained.

IMPACT OF HARAPPAN FOOD ECONOMY ON CONTEMPORARY CULTURES

The Neolithic cultures in Kashmir and Bihar (Chirand dating from 1700 B.C.) and the OCP Ware Culture in western Uttar Pradesh, Punjab, Haryana and northern Rajasthan (Bharatpur) and the Copper Hoard Cultures were all contemporary to and co-existed with the Harappans of north and northwest India. Their chronology is established to either the entire span of the Harappan Civilization, or to the Mid and Late Phases, by ^{14}C and thermoluminiscent dates (Gaur 1973). Recent researches in the Sarasvati and Drishadvati Valleys in Haryana (Suraj Bhan 1973) and Punjab (Deshpande 1978) have brought out the existence of Harappans in the vicinity of the OCP Ware sites. The cultural interrelationship between the two has also been established. This is a region where the annual precipitation ranges from 600 to around 1000 millimeters. The information on the food economy of most of the OCP sites is unknown, except from Atranjikhera (Chaudhury *et al.* 1971) and Bharatpur (materials we examined). A comparable Neolithic food economy is known from Chirand in Bihar (Vishnu-Mittre 1974b), while the Neolithic Burzahomians were food gatherers (Vishnu-Mittre and Savithri in press).

Howsoever insufficient the information on the food economy of the OCP culture is, it included rice, barley and gram at Atranjikhera. Rice, wheat, barley, *Pisum*, etc., are known from the Neolithic food economy at Chirand. Of these wheat, barley, gram and *Pisum* are common to the food economy of the Harappans.

The most ancient records of wheat, barley, gram and *Pisum* are known from western Asia and southern Europe (Greece). Their earliest occurrence in the Indian Subcontinent and Afghanistan predates the OCP Ware Culture. The introduction and spread of these crops beyond the borders of the Harappan Empire should indeed be attributed to the Harappans.

Whether the Harappans acquired these crops from western Asia, or they were domesticated in northwestern India by the cultures preceding the Harappans, is a matter that remains to be settled. The recent archaeobotanical discoveries in Greece have shown that the region for domestication of wheat and barley extended far beyond the Fertile Crescent. It is interesting to note that northwest India is included by cytogeneticists (Darlington and Janaki Ammal 1945) in the vast center in which wheat and barley are believed to have been domesticated. Deeper digging and boring in this region are sure to provide important information in this matter.

Rice is a crop for which the oldest records (both wild and cultivated: Vishnu-Mittre 1978) are now available from the Neolithic of Koldihwa dated by radiocarbon to 7000 years B.P. It was obviously then diffused to the east and west, through North India, and via eastern Rajasthan into Maharashtra and the deep South (Vishnu-Mittre 1978). The Harappans who came in contact with the OCP Ware peoples, or the Neolithic peoples of North India, influenced the latter food economies with wheat and barley, but did not take advantage of rice. The evidence at the present stage suggests that the Harappans did not introduce this crop into their own empire. It can be hoped that the examination of pottery from all the known Harappan sites, and from fresh excavations, will soon throw more light on these observations.

Today, wheat and barley are predominantly cultivated along with *bajra, Sorghum* and gram in the region formerly occupied by the OCP Ware Cultures. Rice is grown comparatively less. A comprehensive examination of pottery and carbonized materials is certain to bring out more information on the Harappan food economy. This information will take us a long way toward a clear understanding of the various aspects of the food economy discussed here.

ACKNOWLEDGMENTS

We are extremely grateful to Professor B.B. Lal, Shri B.K. Thapar, the former and present Directors General of Archaeological Survey of India (A.S.I.), for the materials from Mohenjodaro, Chanhudaro and Kalibangan. Shri J.P. Joshi, presently Director of Explorations, A.S.I., New Delhi, kindly made materials from Surkotada available. We are also extremely grateful to Professor U.V. Singh, Head of the Department of Ancient Indian History, Culture and Archaeology of the University of Kurukshetra for the materials from Daulatpur; to the authorities of the Indian Agricultural Research Institute (I.A.R.I.), New Delhi for the examples of modern crops and to Shri D.K. Agrawal of the Chemistry Department of Lucknow University for the identification of crystals from Kalibangan. It is with pleasure that we record our immense thanks to the officers of A.S.I. and the I.A.R.I., New Delhi for many encouraging and fruitful discussions with them. Our thanks are also due to Miss Chanchala for checking the figures in the tables.

BIBLIOGRAPHY

Agrawal, D.P., 1972
 C-14 Date List: August 1972. Bombay: Tata Institute of Fundamental Research. Mimeographed copy.
Agrawal, D.P. and S. Kusumgar, 1968
 Radiocarbon Dates of Kalibangan Samples. *Current Science* 37 (4): 96-99.
Agrawal, D.P. *et al.,* 1964
 Tata Institute Radiocarbon Date List II. *Radiocarbon* 5 (6): 226-32.
Agrawal, D.P., *et al.,* 1978
 Physical Research Laboratory Radiocarbon Dates: CS-1. *Current Science* 47 (17): 607-10.

Allchin, Bridget and F.R. Allchin, 1968
 The Birth of Indian Civilization. London: Harmondsworth.
Allchin, F.R., 1969
 Early Cultivated Plants in India and Pakistan. In *The Domestication and Exploitation of Plants and Animals.* P. Ucko and G.W. Dimbleby, eds. Pp. 323-29. London: Duckworth.
Andrus, J.R. and A.F. Mohammad, 1958
 The Economy of Pakistan. Oxford: The University Press.
Anonymous, 1959
 The Wealth of India: Raw materials. Vol. V: H-K.

New Delhi: Publications and Information Director, C.S.I.R.

Anonymous, 1972
The Wealth of India: Raw materials. Vol. IX: Ph-So. New Delhi: Publications and Information Director, C.S.I.R.

Anonymous, 1976
The Wealth of India: Raw materials. Vol. X: Sp-W. New Delhi: Publications and Information Director, C.S.I.R.

Bakshi, J.S. and R.S. Ranga, 1974
Barley. In *Evolutionary Studies in World Crops: Diversity and Change in the Indian Subcontinent.* Sir Joseph Hutchinson, ed. Pp. 47-52. Cambridge: Cambridge University Press.

Burt, B.C., 1941
Comment on, Cereals and Fruits. In *Excavations at Harappa.* 2 vols. M.S. Vats. P. 466. Delhi: Government of India.

Casal, Jean-Marie, 1961
Fouilles de Mundigak. 2 vols. Paris: Librarie C. Klincksieck.

Chaudhury, K.A., K.S. Saraswat, S.N. Hasan and R.C. Gaur, 1971
4000-3500 Year Old Barley, Rice and Pulses from Atranjikhera. *Science and Culture* 37: 531.

Darlington, C.D. and E.K. Janaki Ammal, 1945
Chromosome Atlas of Cultivated Plants. London: Allen and Unwin.

Deshpande, M.N., 1978
Report of the Director General for 1974-78. Archaeological Survey of India. Mimeographed copy.

Gaur, R.C., 1973
Lal Qila Excavation and the OCP Problem. In *Radiocarbon and Indian Archaeology.* D.P. Agrawal and A. Ghosh, eds. Pp. 154-62. Bombay: Tata Institute of Fundamental Research.

Helbaek, H., 1958
Plant Economy in Ancient Lachish. In *The Bronze Age Lachish IV.* O. Tufnell *et al.* eds. Pp. 309-17. London: Oxford University Press.

Hooker, J.D., 1885
Flora of British India. Vol. IV. London: L. Reeve and Co.

Howard, G.I.C., 1916
The Wheats of Baluchistan, Khorasan and the Kurram Valley. *Memoirs of the Department of Agriculture in India.* Botanical Series 8: Calcutta.

Jessen, K. and H. Helbaek, 1944
Cereals in Great Britain and Ireland in Prehistoric and Early Historic Times. Kgl. Danm Vidensk. Selsk. Biol. Skrifter, Copenhagen: 1-68.

Joshi, J.P., 1972
Explorations in Kutch and Excavations at Surkotada and New Light on Harappan Migration. *Journal of the Oriental Institute, University of Baroda* 22 (1-2): 98-144.

Lal, B.B., 1971
Perhaps the Earliest Ploughed Field so far Excavated Anywhere in the World. *Puratattva* 4: 1-3.

Lambrick, H.T., 1967
The Indus Flood Plain and the 'Indus' Civilization. *Geographical Journal* 133: 483-94.

Luthra, J.C., 1936
Ancient Wheat and its Variability. *Current Science* 4 (7): 489.

Luthra, J.C., 1941
Comment on, Cereals and Fruits. In *Excavations at Harappa.* 2 Vols. M.S. Vats. P. 467. Delhi: Government of India.

Marshall, John, editor, 1931
Mohenjodaro and the Indus Civilization. 3 Vols. London: Arthur Probsthain.

Percival, J., 1921
The Wheat Plants: A monograph. London: Duckworth.

Peterson, R.F., 1965
Wheat: Botany, cultivation and utilization. New York: Interscience Publishers Inc.

Oldham, R.D., 1926
The Cutch (Kachh) Earthquake of 16th June 1819 with a Revision of the Great Earthquake of 12th June 1897. *Memoirs of the Geological Survey of India* 46 (2): 1-77.

Renfrew, J., 1973
Palaeoethnobotany. London: Methuen.

Rao, M.U., 1974
Wheat. In *Evolutionary Studies and World Crops: Diversity and Change in the Indian Subcontinent.* Sir Joseph Hutchinson, ed. Pp. 33-45. Cambridge: Cambridge University Press.

Raverty, H.G., 1892
The Mihran of Sind and Its Tributaries: A geographical and historical study. *Journal of the Asiatic Society of Bengal* 61: 155-508.

Raychaudhuri, S.P., 1964
Classification and Fertility of Soils of Desert and

Semidesert Regions. In *Proceedings of the Symposium on Problems of the Indian Arid Zone.* Pp. 101-106. New Delhi: Ministry of Education, Government of India.

Sankalia, H.D., 1974
Prehistory and Protohistory of India and Pakistan. 2nd ed. Poona: Deccan College Postgraduate and Research Institute.

Sharma, I.K., 1972
Southeast Asia, India and West Asia: A Study on the beginnings of the food producing stage. In *Archaeological Congress and Seminar Papers.* S.B. Deo, ed. Pp. 95-112. Nagpur: Nagpur University.

Savithri, R., 1976
Studies in Archaeology Together with its Bearing upon Socio-economy and Environment of Indian Protohistoric Cultures. Ph.D. dissertation, Lucknow University.

Savithri, R. and Vishnu-Mittre, 1979
Further Contribution on Protohistoric Ragi (*Eleusine coracana*). *Palaeobotanist* 26 (1).

Shaw, F.J.P., 1943
Vegetable Remains. In *Chanhudaro Excavations, 1935-36.* E.J.H. Mackay. Pp. 250-51. New Haven: American Oriental Series 20.

Singh, R.D. 1946
Triticum sphaerococcum, Perc. (Indian dwarf wheat). *Indian Journal of Genetics & Plant Breeding* 6: 34-47.

Stapf, O. 1931
Comment on, Cereals and Fruits. In *Mohenjodaro and the Indus Civilization.* John Marshall, ed. P. 586. London: Arthur Probsthain.

Stewart, R.R., 1972
An Annotated Catalogue of the Vascular Plants of Pakistan. Karachi: University of Karachi.

Suraj Bhan, 1973
The Sequence and Spread of Prehistoric Cultures on the Upper Sarasvati Basin. In *Radiocarbon and Indian Archaeology.* D.P. Agrawal and A. Ghosh, eds. Pp. 252-63. Bombay: Tata Institute of Fundamental Research.

Todd, James, 1832
Annals and Antiquities of Rajasthan. London: Routledge and Kegan Paul.

Vats, M.S., 1941
Excavations at Harappa. 2 vols. Delhi: Government of India.

Vishnu-Mittre, 1961
Plant Economy in Ancient Maheshwar. *Technical Report on Archaeological Remains, No. 2.* Pp. 13-52. Poona: Deccan College.

Vishnu-Mittre, 1974a
Palaeobotanical Evidence. In *Evolutionary Studies in World Crops: Diversity and change in the Indian Subcontinent.* Sir Joseph Hutchinson, ed. Pp. 3-30. Cambridge: Cambridge University Press.

Vishnu-Mittre, 1974b
Neolithic Plant Economy of Chirand, Bihar. *Palaeobotanist* 22 (1): 18-22.

Vishnu-Mittre, 1978
Origin and History of Agriculture in the Indian Subcontinent. *Journal of Human Evolution* 7: 31-36.

Vishnu-Mittre and R. Savithri, 1975
Supposed Remains of Rice (*Oryza* sp.) in Terracotta Cakes and Pai at Kalibangan, Rajasthan. *Palaeobotanist* 22 (2): 124-26.

Vishnu-Mittre and R. Savithri, 1978
Setaria spp. in the Ancient Plant Economy of India. *Palaeobotanist* 25: 559-62.

Vishnu-Mittre and R. Savithri, in press
Ancient Plant Economy of Burzahom. In *Excavations at Burzahom.* T.N. Khazanchi. New Delhi: Government of India.

D.P. AGRAWAL and R.K. SOOD

19. Ecological Factors and the Harappan Civilization

INTRODUCTION

The Harappan Civilization was spread over a 1.3 million square kilometer area of Pakistan and western India. This area itself has considerable variation in rainfall—from five to sixty centimeters per year—yet, on the whole, the entire area is either arid or semiarid.

There has been considerable debate regarding the degree and extent of climatic change within the zone of the Harappan Civilization. We will briefly review some of the old theories on this matter. Some note will then be taken of the new data on climatic change and paleochannel configurations in Rajasthan and Gujarat. Finally, some direct archaeological implications of the ecological evidence will be considered.

PREVIOUS THEORIES

The older theories of Stein (1937), Marshall (1931), Wheeler (1959) and Piggott (1950) suggested wetter conditions during the Harappan times. These have been critically evaluated elsewhere (Agrawal 1971). On the basis of the extensive remains of *gabarbands* (dams) and human settlements in the Mashkai-Jhalawan area, Stein (1937) inferred more favorable climatic conditions. Piggott also said, "...the inference from the fauna, the wood needed to burn so many million bricks, and the implication of a flourishing agricultural background, all suggest a climate different than today..." (Piggott 1950). Wheeler (1959) emphasized that "broad jungles and intermittent marshes were indeed infested with elephant, tiger, buffalo, rhinoceros and crocodile, familiar to us from their exquisite representations on the Indus seals."

But these arguments did not convince scholars like Fairservis (1967) who pointed out that the three main trees (*Acacia arabica*, *Tamario gallica* and *Prosopis spicigera*) provide an adequate supply of local fuel today and probably did so also during Harappan times. Raikes and Dyson (1961) calculated that only 400 acres of gallery forest would be needed for each rebuilding of Mohenjodaro. Chowdhury and Ghosh (1951) examined the plant remains from Harappa and declared that "these wood remains do not support the theory that a moist tropical forest prevailed in the neighborhood of Harappa." Regarding the faunal evidence, Fairservis (1967) suggested that the Harappan fauna was without exception dependent upon grassland and open forest country. Discussing the *Rhinoceros unicornis* remains from Kalibangan, Banerjee and Chakrabarti (1973) mention the occurrence of the rhino in the Punjab during Mughal times. Recently, Thapar (1977) has cited evidence for the use of unburnt bricks and the occurrence of barley from Kalibangan as proof of a dry climate during the Harappan and Pre-Harappan Periods.

It is obvious from the above that the data which has been available can be used to support both interpretations: for and against climatic change. We will now discuss some evidence on the climatic change which has come to light as well as information on other events leading to drainage changes. Both these points have an ecological significance and have resulted from our recent research.

CLIMATICALLY CONTROLLED ECOLOGICAL FACTORS

Climatic change is a global phenomenon, and due to fears that the entire earth may be entering another Ice Age, many national governments have appointed special commissions to urgently report on the climatic change. Several reports from these scientific committees, appointed by their National Academies, are now available. Those from Australia, Canada and the U.S.A provide especially excellent summaries on this recent paleoclimatic research (Beltzner 1976; National Academy of Science 1975).

Recent research has established beyond any doubt that climate has been continuously changing (Lamb 1977). Even during the last 5000 years significant changes have taken place. For example, there is now clear evidence for glacier expansions between ca. 1000 and ca. 3000 B.C., as well as during the well-known Little Ice Age (Fig. 19.1). Glacier expansions are generally associated with aridity in non-glaciated areas. "The warmest episode in the mid-continent occurred approximately 8000 to 9000 B.P. with evidence of cooling as early as 5500 to 5000 B.P." (Beltzner 1976: 23). Similarly, the report of the National Academy of Sciences of the United States says: "The period from 7000 to 5000 years ago was marked by temperatures warmer than those that prevail today. The last 5000 years is characterized by generally declining temperatures and a trend towards more extensive mountain glaciation (but not ice sheets) in all parts of the world" (National Academy of Science 1975: 132). Similar is the trend of air temperatures at ca. 5500 B.P. as reported by the Australian Academy of Sciences (Australian Academy of Science 1976: 18). Similar climatic data are available for the western and southern hemispheres, but no detailed information is yet available from the tropical areas. It appears though that there is some time lag between the western and eastern hemispheres. The Australian data (Australian Academy of Science 1976) indicate 2000-year cycles of cooling alternating with warm periods (Fig. 19.2) from 6000 B.P. to recent times. The Harappan zone could not have been immune to such global climatic changes and, in fact it was not.

At the moment the best, most substantial paleoclimatic evidence comes from Rajasthan. Singh, working on the sediments of the northern salt lakes of Rajasthan (Lunkaransar, Didwana and Sambar) has shown significant fluctuations in precipitation based on the pollen sequences dated by radiocarbon (Singh et al., 1974). He has indicated that except for the Pre-Holocene aridity, from 10,000 B.P. to about 3500 B.P., Rajasthan was generally wetter than today. Between 5000 and 3500 B.P., a markedly wet period was followed by a severe aridity between 3000 and 2000 B.P. After 2000 B.P., according to Singh, the climate acquired its present character.

Semiarid regions are ideal for observing geomor-

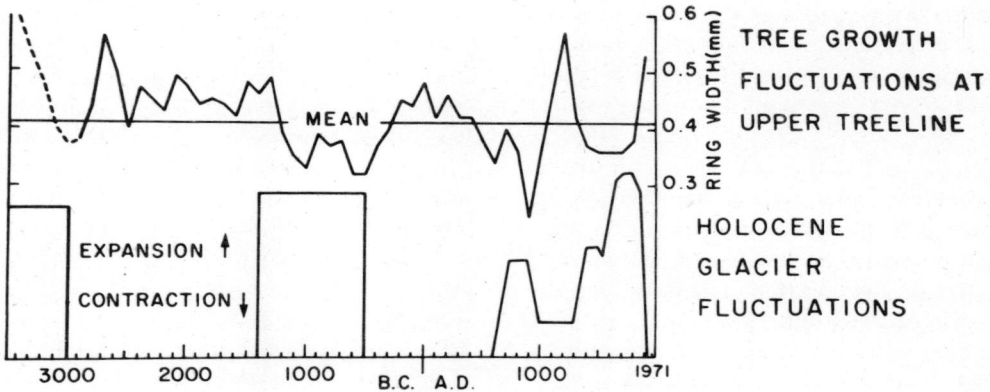

Fig. 19.1. Climatic record of the past 5000 years. The upper curve represents 100-year mean tree ring widths of bristle cone pine at the upper tree line in the White Mountains of California. Positive growth departures indicate warm season temperatures above the long-term mean (after LaMarche). The lower curves represent advance and retreat of Holocene Alaskan Glaciers (National Academy of Science, 1975).

phological manifestations of climatic change. In Rajasthan, an interplay of fluvial and aeolian processes is determined by the precipitation changes. During wetter periods, river and stream channels revived and dunes stabilized. As Verstappan (1970: 104) has pointed out, sand dunes tend to stabilize wherever rainfall exceeds 250 millimeters per year. This postulate was utilized by Allchin, Hegde and Goudie (1972: 451) in their paleogeographic work in the area. They tried to correlate different relict land surfaces with different climatic episodes. They further suggested that microlith-using groups in Rajasthan had inhabited stabilized dunes. Misra has, however, reported microliths in excavated context from the body of dunes (Misra 1977: 31). During the last few years we have carried out an extensive multidisciplinary survey of Rajasthan in collaboration with Poona University and Central Arid Zone Research Institute, Jodhpur. This team has been able to identify various signs of climatic change during the Late Quaternary in Rajasthan. These have been dated by the ^{14}C technique. Calcrete samples from the surfaces of the stabilized dunes near the Pushkar area were collected. These were dated to ca. 5000-6000 B.P., (Agrawal *et al.* in press a, b). The calcrete formation can be taken as the time of dune stabilization, that is a period when more moisture was available. After this phase, there is evidence for fresh dune activity, which, for lack of proper samples, has not been adequately dated. Climatic change is also evidenced from the sedimentation changes in Malhar Rann, as indicated by sedimentological analysis (Agrawal *et al.* in press a, b). Shallow profiles of the aggraded planes have shown almost regular oscillation between sandy silt and *kankarized* sediments. Scanning electron microscopy of quartz grains from these sediments indicates the possibility of aeolian and fluvial conditions alternating with each other (Agrawal *et al.* in press a, b). In Nagar District there are now no perennial rivers; but we have discovered sizable relict river beds which were occupied by Early and Middle Paleolithic man.

In summary, we have been able to work out the broad climatic oscillations in Rajasthan for the Late Quaternary Period. But for the finer oscillations in the Holocene much more data, drawn from multiple sources are being processed, and we hope to give a more definitive picture fairly soon. Even at this early date, however, we have several lines of evidence which indicate that at ca. 5000 B.P., the climate was

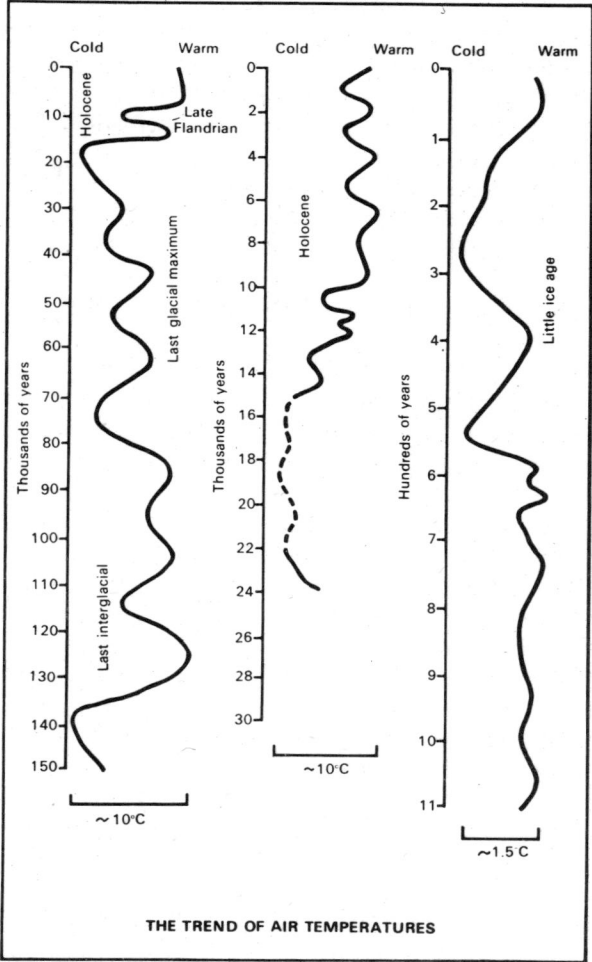

Fig. 19.2. Behavior of air temperature fluctuations during the last 150,000 years. The two right hand curves give detailed fluctuations during the last 30,000 years and 1,100 years respectively (Australian Academy of Science, 1976).

wetter than before in Rajasthan. The onset of aridity can possibly be placed about 3500 B.P.

In semiarid regions where the ecology hangs on a precarious balance, even minor shifts of climate could spell disaster. There is a clear indication of increasing aridity by the middle of the second millennium B.C. which must have put the Harappan Civilization under great stress. In addition to this, there could of course have been other factors: an increase in salinity, a rise of the water table, frequent floods, invasions, etc., especially in the nuclear regions, which may have been responsible for the final collapse of the Harappans.

We feel strongly that paleoclimatic studies such as these should receive attention before building elaborate theories. One should work out the main climatic-cum-environmental changes and then consider theory. Bryson once suggested that climatic change affects vegetation after about 50 years and a botanical change affects culture in another 50 years (Wendland and Bryson 1974). We will have to devote more research to such problems in the future.

TECTONICALLY CONTROLLED CHANGE

When Ghosh (1952) discovered a large number of Chalcolithic settlements on the now dry Ghaggar and Chautang in Rajasthan, it led to speculations about climatic change in the area and the reasons why these rivers dried up. Our recent work has investigated the significance of tectonically caused environmental changes in these areas of Rajasthan (Yashpal, Sood and Agrawal in press). Fluctuations in the paleochannel patterns in this area have been noticed since Oldham's times in the nineteenth century. Dikshit (1977) has chronicled the various hypotheses offered in this matter and several others have discussed the archaeological remains on these now dry rivers (Gupta, Asthana, Amrendranath 1977; Pande 1977). Raikes (1968), without adducing any tangible evidence, even talked of six well-dated diversions of the Yamuna; but the article in which he was to give the technical data to support this contention has not yet appeared. We will not discuss his, or other, theories here but we do want to summarize our new findings, based on Landsat imagery and the field data of other workers. A detailed paper is appearing elsewhere (Yashpal *et al.* in press); we report only our conclusions here.

The Satluj (Sutlej) once flowed into the Ghaggar following a path east of Ropar (Rupar), Sirhing, Patiala and Shatrana (Fig. 19.3). The Ghaggar was a mighty river in the past and had on an average a bed eight kilometers wide. The Satluj, before assuming its present course, was braided into a multitude of channels. This fact is also recorded in the *Mahabharata* in the form of a legend: when Vashishta threw himself into the Satudri (Satluj) it broke into a hundred streams. Since enechelon faults controlled the river course of the Ghaggar, it was prone to drastic changes caused by even minor tectonic movements. The contention that the Satluj once flowed into the Ghaggar is supported by both our work with Landsat imagery and the ground-based field work done by Singh and Ghose (1977).

There was once another major river to the east of the Ghaggar which was frequently changing its course. Three of these courses have been traced, Y1, Y2 and Y3 (Fig. 19.4). The Y1 channel was connected to the Ghaggar. Later it followed the Y2 course merging with the Chautang, which later met the Ghaggar near Suratgarh. The third course (Y3) flowed further east and southeast, finally joining the Ganges, probably through the Chambal. When this Y3 river shifted further east, it left the various lakes in its course which now lie north of Bharatpur (Fig. 19.4). It is probable that it was the Y3 river which eventually took the course of the Yamuna.

These changes in the courses of the various paleochannels are fairly clear, and are supported by published field data. The terminal course of the Ghaggar is, however, far from clear. Near Anupgarh, the ancient Ghaggar bed bifurcates and both the paleochannels come to an abrupt end. The upper one terminates near Marot. The lower one ends as a shallow depression near Beriwala in Pakistan. On the Landsat imagery the lower course looks as if it debouched into the sea, but obviously it was unlikely that the sea was so far inland in Mid-Holocene. It is possible, however, that the chain of tectonic events which diverted the Satluj and the easterly rivers away from the Ghaggar, caused a depression into which the Ghaggar, deprived of its major source of water, died into a lake-like depression.

When the Ghaggar was a perennial river, it is possible that it could have met the eastern Nara and flowed directly into the Rann of Kutch, without meeting the Indus. The paleochannels beyond Marot indicate such a possibility, and it is supported by legend which says that the Sarasvati flowed directly into the sea (Indras 1967).

The presence of archaeological sites in the vicinity of these paleochannels makes it possible to date their active, wet periods. Research by Ghosh (1952), Suraj Bhan (1973), Dikshit (1977: 61), Gupta, Asthana and Amrendranath (1977: 79) and Pande (1977: 55) has already given the outline of this chronology, although much more work needs to be done on this problem. As we understand it now the Ghaggar was alive during the Pre-Harappan and Harappan periods. But, by the Painted Gray Ware (PGW) times it must have been dry, or nearly so, since sites of this period are found within the entrenched river bed. The

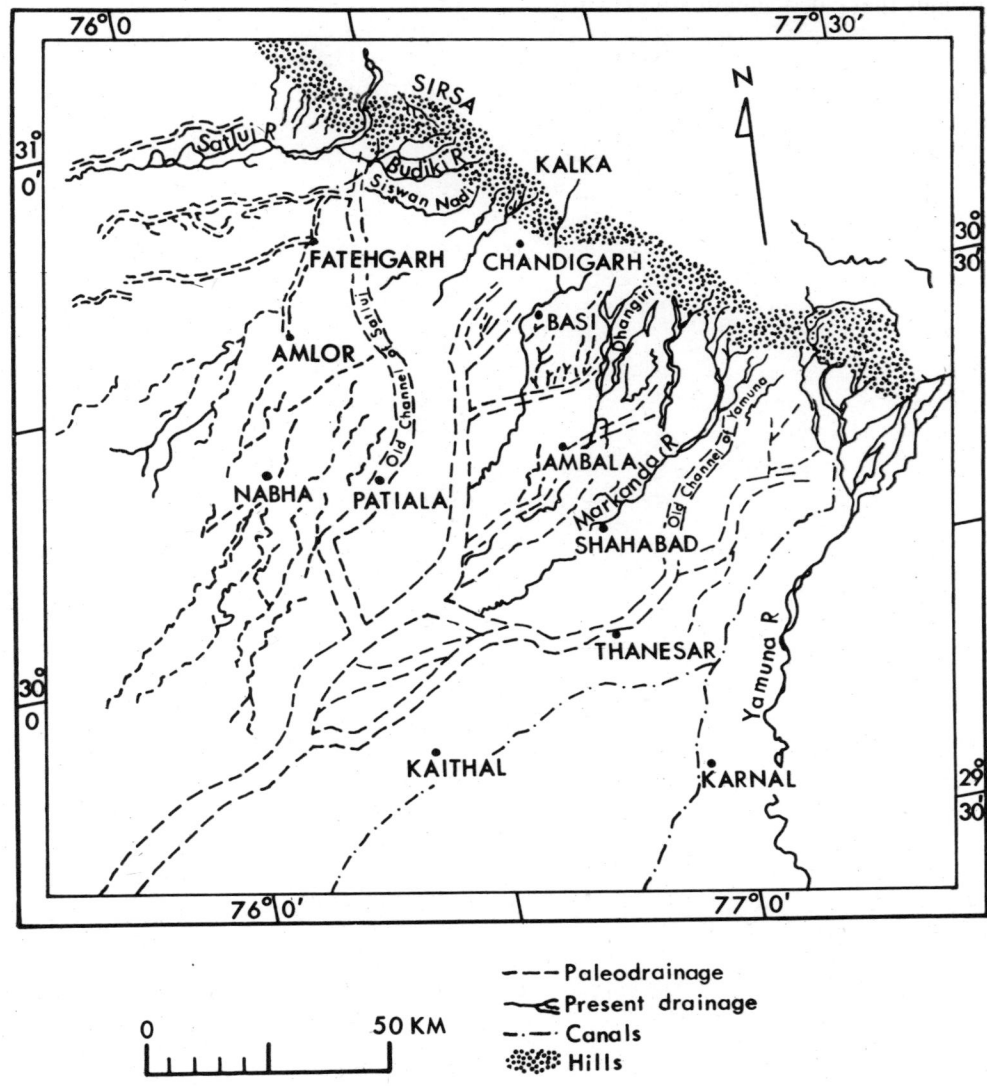

Fig. 19.3. The Indo-Gangetic Divide showing paleo-river channels. Note the old channels of the Satluj.

Chautang has a large number of Late Harappan sites associated with it and the Y3 channel seems to have been a living river during the PGW times. There is not yet sufficient data on the Y1 and Y2 channels for them to be dated.

Considerably more geomorphological and archaeological field work is required to fully document the vagrancy of these rivers. This work should also incorporate chemical/mineralogical analyses of core materials from the beds aimed at detecting the characteristic signatures of the relict rivers. Still it is obvious that in northern and western Rajasthan, tectonically unstable river systems were a major factor confronting human settlements, perhaps from the Pre-Harappan times onwards.

An aerial survey we carried out around Lothal has indicated an annular pattern of drainage which points to tectonic disturbances. We have concluded that either a tectonic uplift, or an eustatic fall, in the sea level was probably responsible for cutting off the Lothal dockyard from its feeder river and eventually from the access to the sea.

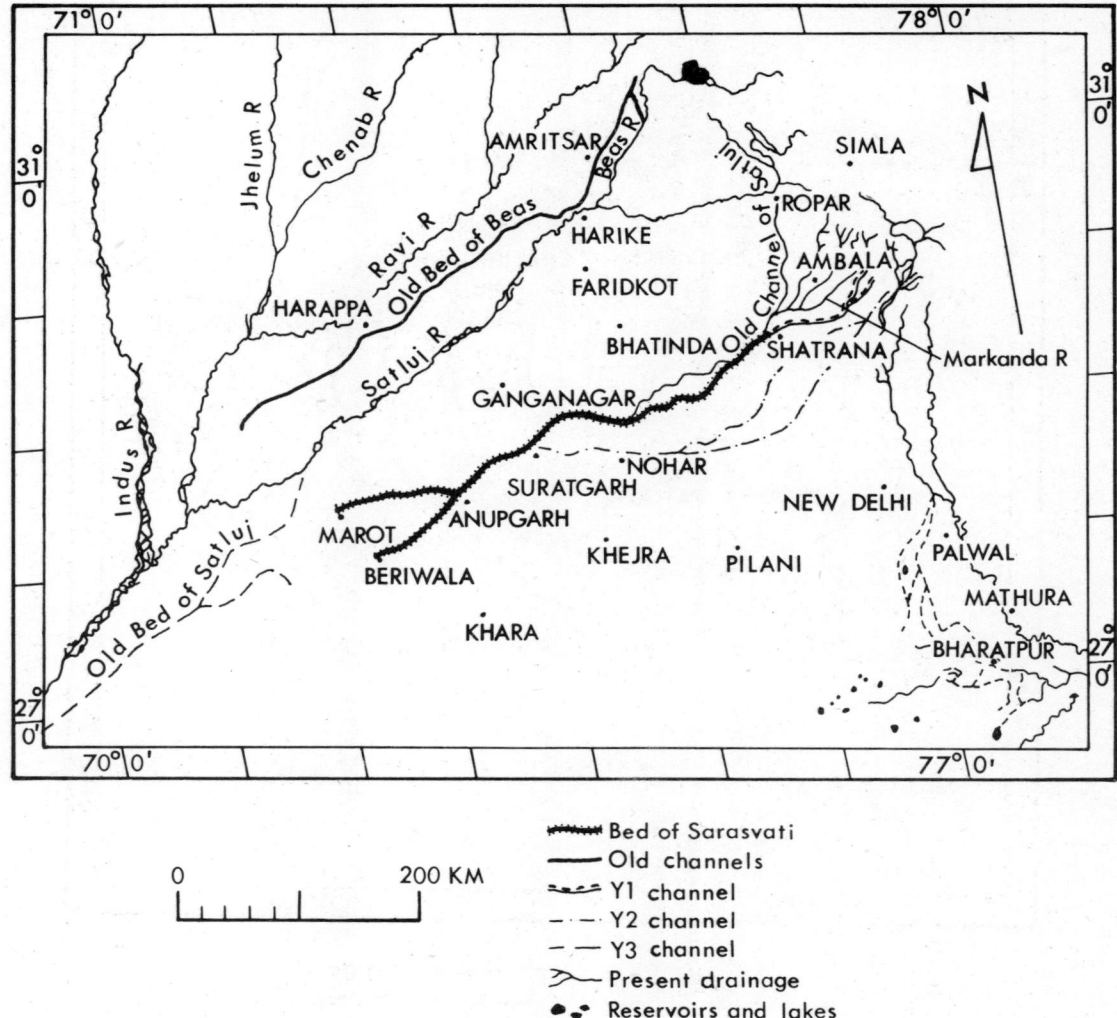

Fig. 19.4. The Indus, the Ghaggar and the Yamuna basins with paleochannels. Note the old courses, Y1, Y2 and Y3 of the paleo-Yamuna.

Another possible disturbance caused by tectonics was the alleged impounding of the Indus and the consequent engulfing of Mohenjodaro under a lake of mud and water (Raikes 1964: 284). Very serious objections have been raised against it by Lambrick (1967), Possehl (1967) and one of the authors (Agrawal 1971). But a lake around Mohenjodaro would have been a calamity since it would have killed the gallery forests, forced animals to migrate, denied any agriculture over a vast area, and made even local travel virtually impossible. It would have also created havoc with sanitation and the disposal of urban refuse (Agrawal 1971). A recent paper of Raikes and Dales (1977: 251) tries to answer some of the criticisms, though not very convincingly.

The formation of a dam like that proposed by Raikes and Dales may be possible and there is a historical case of the Allahbund caused by the 1819 earthquake. But it was breached by the very first flood of the Nara in 1926. How this bund could have lasted for hundreds of years on the Indus is difficult to understand especially with 500,000 cubic feet per second of water pushing at it on a narrow front (Lambrick 1967). Of course, such phenomena are possible in the upper courses of rivers, particularly in the mountainous regions. In fact there are lake remains on the upper reaches of the Indus and the Satluj, some of which have been examined by geologists. These appear to be of Pleistocene date.

SOME ARCHAEOLOGICAL IMPLICATIONS

It is obvious from this discussion that ecological stresses, caused both climatically and tectonically, played an important role in the life and decay of the Harappan Civilization.

Recent studies have tried to build theories using subsistence, population pressure, etc., by assuming that both technology and ecology were constant factors (Flam 1976: 76). Even technological changes need to be better documented (for example, there is evidence of a higher percentage of artifacts made of alloyed copper in the later levels than in the earlier ones), but to categorically declare, "there was no major climatic change in the Indus Valley during the third millennium B.C." (Flam 1976: 81) seems a bit premature. Archaeological theorizing may become easier by keeping several important factors constant, yet one cannot ignore the complexities of the situation. Before building models, one needs to look for, and examine, the paleo-environmental data.

An interesting analysis of the archaeological data has been recently attempted by Chakrabarti. He has calculated and compared the sizes of the various Harappan settlements and finds "a greater concentration of the large sites in the central Indus system, broadly in and around a rough triangle with Mohenjodaro, Harappa and Kalibangan as three points" (Chakrabarti 1979: 207). Between the Satluj and the Yamuna, he finds only smaller settlements. In Gujarat, only Kutch seems to have a concentration of larger sites.

What are the factors responsible for the concentration of larger settlements: agricultural land, raw materials, minerals, or communication/transport facilities? One thing, however, stands out: there is a dearth of village-level settlements, as even the smaller Harappan settlements appear to have an urban character. Towns are known to cater to the industrial and technical requirements, but they do not produce their own food. This is the responsibility of the village. To us it appears that the extreme vagrancy of the rivers in the Indus and the Ghaggar Valleys did not allow traditional villages to grow. Agriculture was probably based on the cover and meander flood plains, which were changing most of the time and therefore required the speed of urban management and resources, like the present day capitalist farming, to cope with the situation.

If Lothal had a dockyard, what determined its location? Was it the timber trade from the hinterland which justified the location of Lothal where it was? Did Lothal become defunct only because of floods, or tectonic uplift, or was it eustatic change that put it out of the reach of the sea?

Through this paper we have tried to focus attention on the ecological studies which should form an integral part of archaeological fieldwork. Only such an approach will allow us a deeper understanding of the Harappan phenomenon.

BIBLIOGRAPHY

Agrawal, D.P., 1971
 The Copper Bronze Age in India. New Delhi: Munshiram Manoharlal.

Agrawal, D.P. et al., in press a
 Quarternary Studies in Rajasthan: Preliminary Results. National Seminar on Quarternary Environment 1977, Baroda.

Agrawal, D.P., et al., in press b
 Multiple Evidence for Climatic Change in Rajasthan. Paper at the International Symposium on Arid Zone Research, 1978, Jodhpur.

Agrawal, D.P. and B.M. Pande, eds., 1977
 Ecology and Archaeology of Western India. Delhi: Concept Publishers.

Allchin, B., K.T.M. Hegde and A. Goudie, 1972
 Prehistory and Environmental Change in Western India. *Man* 7(4): 541-64.

Australian Academy of Science, 1976
 Report of a Climatic Committee. Canberra: Australian Academy of Science.

Banerjee, S. and S. Chakrabarti, 1973
 Remains of the Great One-horned Rhinoceros from Rajasthan. *Science and Culture* 1973: 430.

Beltzner, K., 1976
 Living with Climatic Change. Ottawa: Scientific Council of Canada.

Chakrabarti, D.K., 1979
 Size of the Harappan Settlements. In *Essays in Indian Protohistory*. D.P. Agrawal and D. Chakrabarti, eds. Pp. 205-15. Delhi: B.R. Publishing Corp.

Chowdhury, K.A. and S.S. Ghosh, 1951
 Plant Remains from Harappa. *Ancient India* 7: 3-19.

Dikshit, K.N., 1977
 Distribution and Relationship of Protohistoric Sites Along the Old River Channels of the Ghaggar System. In *Ecology and Archaeology of Western India*. D.P. Agrawal and B.M. Pande, eds. Pp. 61-66. Delhi: Concept Publishers.

Fairservis, W.A., 1967
 The Origin, Character and Decline of an Early Civilization. *Novitates* 2302. New York: American Museum of Natural History.

Flam, L., 1976
 Settlement Subsistence and Population: A dynamic approach to the development of the Indus Valley Civilization. In *Ecological Backgrounds of South Asian Prehistory*. K.A.R. Kennedy and G.L. Possehl, eds. Pp. 76-93. Occasional Papers and Theses of the South Asia Program of Cornell University 4. Ithaca: Cornell University.

Ghosh, A., 1952
 The Rajputana Desert: Its archaeological aspects. *The Bulletin of the National Institute of Science* 1: 37-42.

Gupta, S.P., S. Asthana and Amrendranath, 1977
 PGW Sites in Relation to Old River Beds in Rajasthan. In *Ecology and Archaeology of Western India*. D.P. Agrawal and B.M. Pande, eds. Pp. 79-92. Delhi: Concept Publishers.

Indras, 1967
 Lost Sarasvati. Vallabh Vidyanagar: Sardar Patel University.

Lamb, H.H., 1977
 Climate: Past, Present and Future. London: Methuen.

Lambrick, H.T., 1967
 The Indus Flood Plain and the "Indus" Civilization. *The Geographical Journal* 133 (4): 483.

Marshall, J., editor, 1931
 Mohenjodaro and the Indus Civilization. 3 vols. London: Arthur Probsthain.

Misra, V.N., 1977
 Prehistory and Paleoenvironment of Rajasthan. In *Ecology and Archaeology of Western India*. D.P. Agrawal and B.M. Pande, eds. Pp. 31-34. Delhi: Concept Publishers.

National Academy of Science, 1975
 Understanding Climatic Change. Washington: National Academy of Science.

Oldham, C.F., 1874
 Notes on the Lost River of the Indian Desert. *Calcutta Review* 59: 1-27.

Pande, B.M., 1977
 Archaeological Remains on the Ancient Sarasvati. In *Ecology and Archaeology of Western India*. D.P. Agrawal and B.M. Pande, eds. Pp. 55-60. Delhi: Concept Publishers.

Piggott, S., 1950
 Prehistoric India. Harmondsworth: Penguin.

Possehl, G.L., 1967
 The Mohenjodaro-floods. A reply. *American*

Raikes, R.L., 1964
 The End of the Ancient Cities of the Indus. *American Anthropologist* 66: 284-89.
Raikes, R.L., 1968
 Kalibangan: Death from Natural Causes. *Antiquity* 42 (108): 286-91.
Raikes, R. and G.F. Dales, 1977
 The Mohenjodaro Floods Reconsidered. *Journal of the Palaeontological Society of India* 20: 251-60.
Raikes, R.L. and R.H. Dyson, 1961
 The Prehistoric Climate of Baluchistan and the Indus Valley. *American Anthropologist* 63 (2): 265-81.
Singh, G., R.D. Joshi. S.K. Chopra and A.B. Singh, 1974
 Late Quaternary History of Vegetation and Climate of the Rajasthan Desert. *Philosophical Transactions of the Royal Society* 267(889): 467-501.
Singh, S. and B. Ghose, 1977
 Geomorphology of the Luni Basin and its Palaeoclimatic Inferences. In *Ecology and Archaeology in Western India*. D.P. Agrawal and B.M. Pande, eds. Pp. 135-46. Delhi: Concept Publishers.
Stein, A., 1937
 An Archaeological Reconnaissance in Northwestern India and Southeastern Iran. London: Macmillan.
Suraj Bhan, 1973
 The sequence and spread of prehistoric cultures in the upper Saraswati basin. In *Radiocarbon and Indian Archaeology*. D.P. Agrawal and A. Ghosh, eds. Pp. 252-63. Bombay: Tata Institute of Fundamental Research.
Thapar, B.K., 1977
 Climate During the Period of the Indus Civilization: Evidence from Kalibangan. In *Ecology and Archaeology in Western India*. D.P. Agrawal and B.M. Pande, eds. Pp. 67-74. Delhi: Concept Publishers.
Verstappan, H.T., 1970
 Aeolian Geomorphology of the Thar Desert and Palaeoclimates. *Annals of Geomorphology* 10: 104-20.
Wendland, M.W. and R.A. Bryson, 1974
 Dating climatic episodes of the Holocene. *Quaternary Research* 4: 9-24.
Wheeler, R.E.M., 1959
 Early India and Pakistan. London: Thames and Hudson.
Yashpal, B.S. *et al.*, in press.
 Palaeochannels in North-west India. Paper read at the National Quaternary Seminar, 1979, Baroda.

BRIDGET ALLCHIN

20. Substitute Stones

THERE has always been a strong tendency on the part of archaeologists of South, Central and Western Asia to draw a fairly sharp demarkation line between those who concern themselves primarily with paleolithic studies, and deal with stones, and others who concentrate upon settlements from the Neolithic onwards. These latter scholars devote themselves to the study of pottery, and sometimes also architecture, objects d'art, ancient languages and other more specialized fields. This division is understandable when one recognizes that these two species of archaeology sprang on the one hand from the sciences, via geology and other field sciences, and on the other from the arts, via art history and ancient languages and literature. From quite an early stage the Stone People, or lithophiles, included microlithic industries within their field, and they began to recognize as time went on that these were often associated with Mesolithic Cultures which overlapped, in terms of time, other settled cultures in the world as a whole, or in the region in which they themselves worked. The Pottery People or ceramophiles, steadily worked their way back in time, delving deeper and deeper into the mounds formed by the continuous rebuilding of early towns and cities until they arrived at the preceramic levels. This situation raised, for both parties, a number of problems of terminology, and necessitated some careful thinking, and rethinking, about a variety of questions.

One outcome of the mutual re-evaluation on the part of both species of archaeologists is that some attention is now beginning to be paid to stone artifacts of many kinds that form an important part of all premetal-using cultures. This includes those associated with urban sites and large settlements, and indeed of all cultures prior to the fairly extensive introduction of iron for everyday purposes. Although the basic importance and usefulness of stone artifacts was always accepted, as the terms Neolithic and Chalcolithic clearly show, they once tended to be taken for granted, and were consequently dismissed without detailed consideration. The ceramophiles turned their attention to pottery and other objects of more "cultural significance."

Increasing interest in the beginnings of agriculture, both the domestication of animals and crop raising, and in ecological questions generally, has brought with it the need for a better understanding of the processes involved in the Neolithic transformation. Following from this is a renewed interest in the tools associated with these practices, and the ways in which they differ, if indeed they do differ, from those used by hunter-gatherers. This has lifted the study of stone artifacts onto a new, and somewhat more realistic plain. Instead of studying their shapes and the methods used to make them in a vacuum as old style paleolithic archaeologists or lithophiles were wont to do, it is now easier to see them as important parts of prehistoric man's life. They were tools largely used for making other tools, weapons and objects of wood or bone. They were component parts of composite tools such as arrows, spears, sickles, adzes, hammers, clubs, bolas, digging sticks, querns, mortars, whetstones, and so on. Thus the stone tools begin to come into focus as part of the processes involved in the subsistence and cultural activities of daily life.

In order to further understand the forces that drove some human groups to specialize in new activities, and live in new environments—in the case of the early stages of the Indus Civilization, to live on the strange, flat, unstable and stoneless but highly productive Indus Plain—it is helpful to try to reconstruct the part played by some of these artifacts and analyze the changes in the processes of food production and economic development that they reflect. In doing this it is important to try to project one's mind back to a time and a state of things before the introduction of iron—when mankind as a whole was conditioned to think of stone as serving many of the basic functions of daily life. Today one thinks of iron and steel as serving these functions in the form of knives and other household tools, axes, hammers, spades, and all sorts of carpentering and gardening tools, and so on. The main difference is that by the Harappan Period stone had been in use for tens of thousands of years, man had grown up with it, and he must have been profoundly conditioned to thinking in terms of stone. After all, iron has been in use for only three to four thousand years.

The immediate ancestors of the Harappan Civilization, as one understands the term today, are to be sought in regions around the Indus plains, and especially to the northwest, where stone was, and is, plentiful. They were conditioned to using it for tools and weapons, in a manner inherited from their paleolithic forebears. In many other cases, such as the Kot Dijians, they were also in the habit of employing stone for building house walls and footings, as well as massive town walls. Others used it for building irrigation *bunds* and channels. The inhabitants of the western borderlands today, even in this age of metals, plastic and high technology, continue to use stone for all these purposes, and many more. Boys, too young or too poor to possess fire arms, use stones as ammunition for small catapults, or throw them with great force and accuracy when hunting small birds and animals. They also attach them to a cord, as miniature bolas, to capture alive long-legged cranes and other birds.

Anyone who has taken part in, or read about, the exploration and excavation of early settlements in stonier regions surrounding the Indus plains, whether in the valleys of the northwestern borderlands, the foothills and valleys of the northern Punjab and western Himalayas, the lowlands of Rajasthan, or the hills of western Central India with their numerous caves and rock shelters, will have seen or noted many stone objects among the recorded finds. In some cases these are all that has survived, or at any rate been put on record. In addition to blade- and flake-based stone industries, which show a remarkable uniformity throughout the whole region, there are grinding stones and hammer stones of various types, as well as occasional stone axes, and very often the so-called mace heads or ring stones. Examination of the ring stones shows them all to have been made in a similar manner, that is by choosing a suitable stone and trimming it until it is more or less symmetrical. These are then laboriously pierced by working from each side until the two depressions meet, or almost meet. The surface is further dressed by hammering, and/or grinding and occasionally polishing. Spherical or near spherical stones, evidently worked into shape by a similar process of hammer dressing and grinding are frequently recorded alongside ring stones, and sometimes described as hammer stones. A factory site near Bannu in the N.W.F.P. where both types of stones were produced in considerable numbers during the Kot Dijian times (as well as earlier and probably later) was recently excavated by the Cambridge-Peshawar team as a part of the Bannu Basin Project. The often repeated hypothesis that ring stones were used both as mace heads and weights for digging sticks is supported by rock paintings in parts of India; but there is virtually no other direct evidence within the Subcontinent for either function. In western Asia they occur at sites of various periods and are referred to as mace heads, an identification followed by Marshall with respect to those found at Mohenjodaro and elsewhere, and now widely accepted. In southern Africa they are known to have been made and used as weights for digging sticks, and there is a certain amount of ethnographic evidence from India that points in the same direction; but so far as one knows this has never been fully investigated.

In view of the present day tendency to use selected stones as projectiles, it seems highly probable that ring stones, and spherical stones of various sizes were used in antiquity both as sling missiles and for throwing. Further, many worked stones, including the smaller ring stones may have served as bolas stones. The bolas stone (or stones), being attached to a long cord, is recoverable and therefore can be used again and again. In recent times, in Latin America, it has been recorded that it was held in a small leather bag attached to the end of the cord. This kind of repeated use would explain the very battered state of many spherical, or near spherical stones, found in this type of assemblage. Smaller ring stones, which do not appear to be large enough to serve as mace heads or digging stick weights, could have been attached to a cord and served as light bolas stones for capturing birds, etc., as in the case of the cranes noted above. Spherical and ovoid stones identified as sling pellets, on the basis of western Asiatic parallels, were recorded at Mohenjodaro by Marshall (1931: 35-36), but these appear to be greatly outnumbered by baked clay counterparts which will be discussed now.

It has been suggested that the discovery of copper, or the wider application of its use than hitherto, was one of the causes of the move into the plains, or at least one of the circumstances that made it possible. But how far this was the case, and how far the search for sources of copper may have been the result rather than the cause is questionable, and must remain so until a good deal of more detailed research has been done on the early phases of settlement on the plains and elsewhere.

Copper tools and utensils are a fairly important element in the material equipment of the Mature Indus Culture; but stone continued to be used throughout. Marshall remarked, as have many others following him, that Harappan copper weapons, unlike those of contemporary western Asiatic cultures, were rather ineffective in some respects. He goes on in the same passage to note the absence of arrow heads of stone or bone, "a fact that suggests the bow and arrow could not have been a favorite weapon" (Marshall 1931: 35-36).

In assemblages from urban sites at the beginning of the Mature Phase the range of types of stone artifacts, based upon a flake and blade technology, becomes rather abruptly limited almost exclusively to plain unretouched blades. At contemporary, non-urban sites an extensive range of artifacts went on being made. Throughout the Mature Indus Phase a considerable quantity of very fine stone blades continued to be made and used; although only a very small proportion were trimmed or reworked in any way. There is fairly conclusive evidence at Mohenjodaro, and probably at other sites also, that they, or the cores from which they were struck, were transported to the cities from workshop sites located at the sources of supply many miles distant (Allchin 1976). Thus, there must have been a genuine need for them. Stone objects of many other kinds were also imported. These include utilitarian objects such as querns, bead grinding stones, pallet stones, etc. Other stone objects of artistic and probably religious significance such as *lingas* or rare pieces of sculpture, and stone used for very limited building and constructional purposes (e.g. door sockets, drain covers, and certain other categories) were also imported, but all in strictly limited quantities. The difficulty of obtaining building stones may well have been one of the incentives behind the extensive manufacture and use of baked brick.

Pottery, itself once a substitute for leather and wooden vessels, appears at times to have been used as a substitute for stone. An obvious example of this is to be seen in the grooved pottery which, like Roman mortaria, must have taken the place of stone mortars for certain purposes. As is sometimes the case, the imitation, once developed, seems to have proved more adaptable and more convenient for certain purposes than the original. Other examples of ceramics being used as substitutes for stone can be recognized if one looks at, and thinks about, objects excavated from the major Mature Harappan sites.

There is one particular group of objects that I wish to consider rather more carefully for the purposes of this paper. These are the so-called terracotta sling pellets, terracotta cakes and other related groups of terracotta objects found very widely at Mature Harappan settlements, large and small. They are found rarely, or not at all, at earlier or later sites, nor for that matter in earlier or later levels at the same sites, nor with certain exceptions in contemporary cultures of adjacent regions. The almost universal and particular association of the triangular terracotta cakes with the Mature Harappan Culture has led some scholars, like the late Colonel Gordon and others, to conclude that they had a special significance in connection with ritual bathing or other ablutions (Gordon 1958). While I do not deny this may have been among their uses, I feel that this is altogether too narrow a view of their role especially when considered as part of a whole range of baked clay objects produced in large quantities.

In addition to their association with bathrooms, terracotta cakes are recorded as having been used as infilling, with and without charcoal, beneath brick-paved floors, as hard core for road building (Lal 1979) as well as a whole range of other situations, all of which suggest diversity rather than specialization. Their presence in hearths at Kalibangan (Thapar 1973: 101) may be noted in this connection as having possible religious significance. They also occur in large numbers at Allahdino and in smaller numbers at sites in Gujarat as mentioned in the papers (in this volume) by Professor W. Fairservis and R.N. Mehta respectively. It appears reasonable therefore, to regard them, together with other terracotta nodules produced in fairly large quantities, as substitutes for stone. It is from this basis that certain other, more specific uses of terracotta cakes, pellets, etc., can be considered.

Effective arrow and spear heads of either metal or stone are absent from Mature Harappan sites, but stone sling pellets have been recorded at both Early Indus (or Pre-Harappan) and Mature Indus (or Harappan) sites by Marshall (1931: 173), Mackay (1943 : 168), Wheeler (1968 : 76-77) and others. More recently their presence has been noted at a considerable number of sites of both periods widely distributed in the alluvial plains of the Punjab (personal communication from Dr. Rafique Mughal of the Pakistan Government Department of Archaeology). This suggests that to a certain extent stone for these purposes, or more probably finished stone artifacts, were carried in the course of trade onto the stoneless alluvial plains. Their weight must have made this a laborious and expensive process—much more so than in the case of stone blades which are individually small and light. This in turn suggests that a substitute for stone must have been sought by the plain dwellers. As already pointed out there is no evidence that the substitution was done through the extensive use of spears or arrows of any kind; although it is possible that sharpened hard woods were used for light arrows and spears. Since no wood has been found surviving from Early or Mature Harappan sites, this must remain an open question. But the emphasis upon stones used with catapults, and for throwing, in adjacent regions at the present time strongly suggests that the substitutes came from among the several kinds of terracotta cakes, pellets, etc., that were apparently used by the Harappans for many purposes, and produced in large quantities. Three quite independent observations combine to suggest this hypothesis.

1) There is Marshall's brief, but quite positive discussion of ovoid and spherical terracotta cakes. He identifies these as sling pellets upon the grounds that similar objects are used in contemporary western Asiatic cultures, and the situation in which one concentration of fifty or more was found in a large jar on the citadel at Mohenjodaro:

> Two types of sling-pellets are found at Mohenjodaro: one round and about the size of a marble, the other, which is more rare, ovoid in shape and averaging 2.5 inches long by 1.6 inches in diameter.... This type occurs in all levels. Both types are made by hand with varying degrees of finish. In all cases they were baked. The round pellets may have been propelled by a sling of ordinary type or by means of a bow such as is used in Sind in the present day for killing small birds.... Both ovoid and round sling pellets have been found in early Sumer and Turkestan sites as well as India (Marshall 1931: 466-67).

Marshall's identification of a main group, consisting of two types of terracotta sling pellets, was followed by Mackay and Wheeler. Both of the latter briefly refer to evidence for their use in the defense of cities. Wheeler further mentions finding in 1950 a concentration of 98 pellets at Mohenjodaro at the foot of the citadel mound, in the vicinity of the "great granary" (Wheeler 1968: 76). Another concentration is said to have been found near one of the gateways of Kalibangan (B.K. Thapar, personal communication). None of these excavators, however, considers the further implications of these deductions, nor discusses the questions in much detail. Only Marshall, with his extraordinary gift for seizing upon the significant detail among the mass of material he had to deal with, notes a little further on in the same passage as the one quoted above:

> The sling probably originated in stony country where ammunition would be plentiful. When its use extended to alluvial countries the pellets would naturally have been made of pottery. It is essentially a weapon for open country, and in the hands of a skilled man it is a formidable weapon (Marshall 1931: 467).

More recently the question has been briefly discussed by Sankalia in *New Archaeology: Its scope and application to India*. Here he points to the mention and identification of these objects as sling pellets by Marshall and others. He also sees a need for further research and experimentation as well as consideration of the implications these finds provide regarding Harappan warfare (Sankalia 1977: 68-69).

2) There is also the much more general observation which can be made in the light of all the discoveries made since Marshall's, and even perhaps since Wheeler's time. This is the present day situation which allows one to stand back a little and view the Indus Civilization in a rather wider focus, in relation to its own geographical setting, and to the contemporary cultures to north and northwest. When viewed in this way it is impossible to conceive of the vast area

spanned by sites of the Mature Indus Phase achieving such a level of uniformity of urban culture without some effective political and administrative control of the central region and the military power to maintain it and defend it from incursions from without. The manner in which Mature Indus Culture takes over from earlier cultures at certain peripheral sites, such as Kalibangan and others, tends to support this hypothesis. Therefore it follows that an Harappan army of some size could be raised and armed when necessary. The only armaments that have been found in sufficient numbers to meet the case are sling pellets. Moderate quantities of these are made of stone, and more liberal quantities of hard-baked clay. As Marshall observed, a sling with a supply of stones (or substitute stones) is "a formidable weapon in the hands of skilled man."

Further information supplied by R.N. Mehta and D.K. Chakrabarti supports Marshall's observations on the use of the sling for killing in Sind. Both recalled as young boys having used pellets made of clay, with a double stringed bow for hunting birds: one lived in Gujarat and the other in Bengal. Both say that the pellets were baked in an open fire, not fired in a kiln like pottery or bricks—an observation that might provide an alternative interpretation for those found in hearths at Kalibangan and elsewhere mentioned above. These recollections, and R.N. Mehta's further observation that both stone and baked pellets were used to chase predatory animals such as jackals away from grazing flocks and herds, suggest that they were part of a herdsman's equipment and personal possessions in the Harappan times, as in the less remote past. This in turn provides a possible interpretation of their presence in graves, along with other small objects, that was noted by Gordon (1958: 87).

3) The final observation, which caused me to consider these questions anew, I was able to make in the field thanks to the kindness of Professors F.A. Durrani and Farid Khan of the Department of Archaeology University of Peshawar. In the course of the last two seasons fieldwork they took me, and other members of the British Archaeological Mission, to visit the two sites they excavated near Dera Ismail Khan in the Dera Jat. Although only brief accounts have so far been published, many scholars are familiar, through Professor Durrani's lectures, with the impressive Chalcolithic settlement of Rahman Dheri. This site is laid out on a grid plan, surrounded by a substantial defensive wall, and passed through three phases of unbroken urban occupation which ended somewhat mysteriously around the beginning of the Mature Harappan Phase in the adjacent Indus plains. It may also be recalled that a small site, Hisham Dheri, several hundred meters to the northeast appeared to belong exclusively to the Mature Harappan Period. A small-scale excavation at Hisham Dheri confirmed this, and showed that it was apparently an industrial site, largely given over to the production of triangular terracotta cakes and terracotta sling pellets of the kind identified by Marshall and Wheeler. As the main occupation levels at Rahman Dheri yielded a number of fine stone arrow heads, but few if any terracotta sling pellets or cakes, the relationship of these two sites is highly problematic at first sight. The topmost levels of Rahman Dheri which might have provided further, more precise information have eroded away. But, examined in the light of the earlier observations brought together here, there seems to be one explanation which fits this situation: the town was besieged by an Harappan army and its inhabitants were finally overcome; and that during the seige the Harappan army camped and made its ammunition at Hisham Dheri. This would have been a convenient situation, just out of range of the archers within the city. It is possible that a similar *raison d'etre* may account for isolated Harappan industrial sites elsewhere in Pakistan.

If this hypothesis is accepted, it must lead to a further interesting development of the argument—the Harappans, far from being a nonviolent people, or being without any system of military organization other than that needed to defend their major cities, as has sometimes been suggested, must have had an effective army. How they raised their army is beyond the scope of this paper. It could have come primarily from the population of the cities and surrounding areas of intensive cultivation, or from other communities, such as the seminomadic peoples who must have formed an integral part of the wider Indus Culture, supplying draught animals for cultivation and local transport, and providing the means of long distance transport and trade both inside and outside the confines of the Harappan Empire, as such people did until recently and to some extent still do. But the probability that they had a highly organized, and therefore disciplined, army is inescapable. Indeed, when viewed from without it is in keeping with the character of the Culture as a whole. Further, this hypothesis would agree with the 'expansionist' tendencies in several directions noted by a number of excavators. This is where I shall stop with the suggestion that the concept of substitute stones, and its implications, may have some impact upon the view of the nature and structure of Harappan society.

ACKNOWLEDGMENTS

This paper puts forward observations made over a number of years when visiting Harappan and other early settlements, and traveling in the course of my own research and field work in western India and Pakistan. My gratitude to the Director and officers of the Department of Archaeology, Government of Pakistan for their help and courtesy in making this possible, and in particular for giving me, together with other members of the British Archaeological Mission to Pakistan, the opportunity to visit a number of major Harappan sites in Sind. My thanks to the present Director General of the Archaeological Survey of India, and other officers of the Survey for opportunities I have had over past years to visit Kalibangan and other sites, and to learn about their excavations. Finally, I am grateful to Professors F.A. Durrani and Farid Khan for showing us the sites of Rahman Dheri and Hisham Dheri and allowing us to see the materials in Peshawar.

BIBLIOGRAPHY

Allchin, B., 1976
  Paleolithic Sites in the Plains of Sind and Their Geographical Implications. *The Geographical Journal* 142 (3): 471-89.
Gordon, D.H., 1958
  The Prehistoric Background of Indian Culture. Bombay: Bhulabhai Memorial Institute.
Lal, B.B., 1979
  Kalibangan and the Indus Civilization. In *Essays in Indian Protohistory*. D.P. Agrawal and D.K. Chakrabarti, eds. Pp. 65-97. Delhi: D.K. Publishers.
Mackay, E.J.H., 1943
  Chanhudaro Excavations 1935-36. American Oriental Series 20. New Haven: American Oriental Society.

Marshall, Sir John, editor, 1931
  Mohenjodaro and the Indus Civilization. 3 vols. London: Arthur Probsthain.
Sankalia, H.D., 1977
  New Archaeology: Its scope and application to India. Lucknow: Ethnographic and Folk Culture Society.
Thapar, B.K., 1973
  New Traits of the Indus Civilization at Kalibangan: An appraisal. In *South Asian Archaeology.* Norman Hammond, ed. pp. 85-104. Park Ridge: Noyes Press.
Wheeler, Sir Mortimer, 1968
  The Indus Civilization. 3rd ed. Supplementary volume to the Cambridge History of India. Cambridge: The University Press.

K.T.M. HEGDE, R.V. KARANTH and
S.P. SYCHANTHAVONG

21. On the Composition and Technology of Harappan Microbeads

HARAPPANS loved ornaments. Their stone and terracotta figurines and the human figures carved intaglio on their seals (Marshall 1931: Pl. XXI; Mackay 1938: Pl. LXXV, LXXXVII, XCIV; Rao 1973: Pl. XXXIII) amply demonstrate how much they enjoyed adorning themselves with headbands, earrings, necklaces, bracelets, bangles and waistbands. Apparently, both men and women wore jewelry, an important part of which consisted of beads: a wide variety of beautiful beads. Almost all Harappan sites have yielded large quantities of these trinkets. Indian women who follow *Sanatana Dharma* wear black glass beads as a symbol of *Suasti* in their *Mangalsutra*. Abundance of beads at nearly all Harappan sites makes one wonder if the tradition of wearing beads as a symbol of *Suasti* originated in the Harappan Civilization.

Harappan beads are varied in their shape and material. Some are cylindrical, globular, spheroidal, biconical, segmented or wafer-like. Many a time, they are decorated with trefoil or circular designs. Materials including gold, silver, copper, carnelian, agate, chalcedony, steatite, shell and clay were used. The occurrence of these beads in abundance and in many varieties at nearly all Harappan sites, clearly shows how much they were appreciated. Some of the beads are very elegant and reveal skilled workmanship. They are an index to the sophisticated taste of the Harappans. They also demonstrate deftness, skill, patience and painstaking labor on the part of the craftsmen who made them. Among these fine quality ornaments are Harappan microbeads.

As relics, these tiny beads (Pl. 21.1) are of unique value to students of Harappan technology. They are very small, measuring one to three millimeters in length and one millimeter in external diameter. The diameter of the circular perforation at the center is one-half millimeter. Noting their minute form, Mackay observed (1937: 10) that they indicated craftsmanship of the highest quality, combined with extraordinarily good eyesight. They are hard: six to seven on the Moh Scale. When cleaned in dilute hydrochloric acid they become spotless white, immaculate and beautiful to behold. To the naked eye, they all look alike, uniform and regular in their cylindrical shape. Twisted strands of several strings of these fine beads would undoubtedly make, "à la Ajanta" (Ghosh 1967: Pl. XXII, XXIII, XXIV, XXXI, LXXXI), extremely attractive necklaces, bracelets, bangles or waistbands. No wonder the Harappans prized these beads so highly. The minute form, hardness and attractiveness of the microbeads are a witness to an advanced level of technology that the craftsmen used in their production. However, not much is known of that technology. Therefore carrying out a detailed examination of the beads was considered as a small but essential first step towards understanding that technology.

White microbeads have been recovered in the excavations at Harappa, Chanhudaro, Kalibangan, Lothal, Rojdi and Zekda (Fig. 21.1). However, so far, only the excavator of Chanhudaro has described them in some detail (Mackay 1937: 11, 12). The present study of these beads is based on the examination

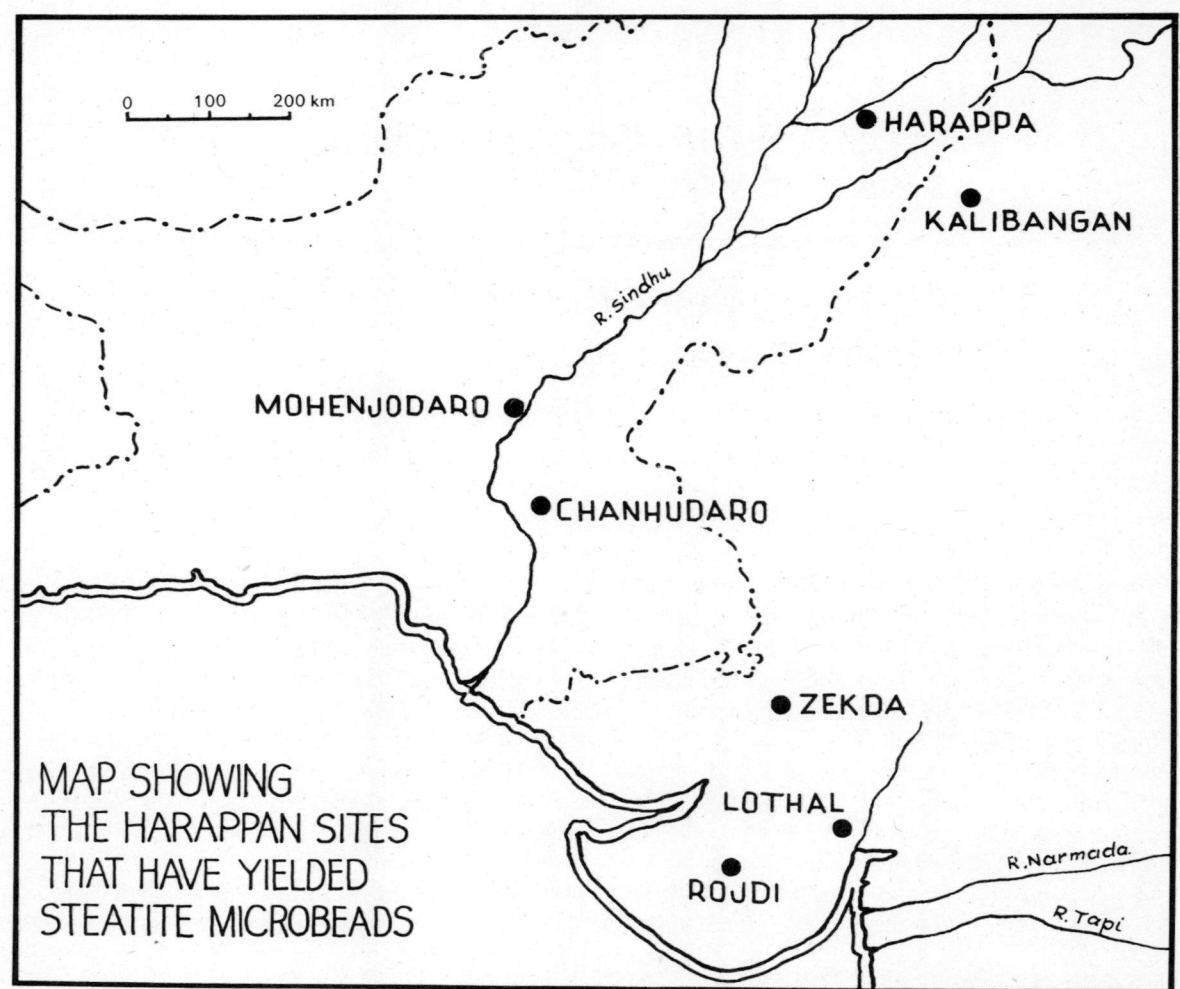

Fig. 21.1. Map showing sites that have yielded steatite microbeads.

of the specimens recovered in the excavation of the Harappan site at Zekda.

Zekda (lat. 23°53′ north; long. 71°26′ east) is an important Harappan site, located in Banaskanta District in the northern part of Gujarat State. Zekda was discovered by Parikh (1978: 188-90) and was excavated by the M.S. University of Baroda, during the field season of 1977-78, under the direction of Professor R.N. Mehta.

The excavation revealed a Harappan habitation of considerable duration. It yielded many characteristic types of Harappan pottery with some of the distinctive decorative motifs, perforated vases, terracotta cakes, chert blades, chert cores with crested ridge flaking, fragments of copper objects, together with the sherds of White Painted Black and Red Ware which is often referred to as "Ahar Ware." This Harappan settlement is, therefore, one of the relatively late Indus settlements, where the material remains of the Harappans merged, without any clear break, into that of the Post-Harappan Cultures. Among other important discoveries made in the excavation of the site are two hoards of microbeads.

The beads were found carefully preserved in two small pots. One of them (Pl. 21.2) was covered with a well-fitting, hollow, cork-like pottery stopper. The other pot (Pl. 21.3) was carefully placed inside another vessel and the outer pot covered with a solid, fitted, baked clay lump. Both the pots were found buried underneath house floors. They were recovered

Pl. 1. Mosaic of Landsat imagery (Punjab, Rajasthan and Haryana).

Pl. 6.1. Imprints of barley on clay from MR. 3 Neolithic. Sixth millennium.

Pl. 6.2. Gazelle bones from MR. 3 Neolithic. Sixth millennium.

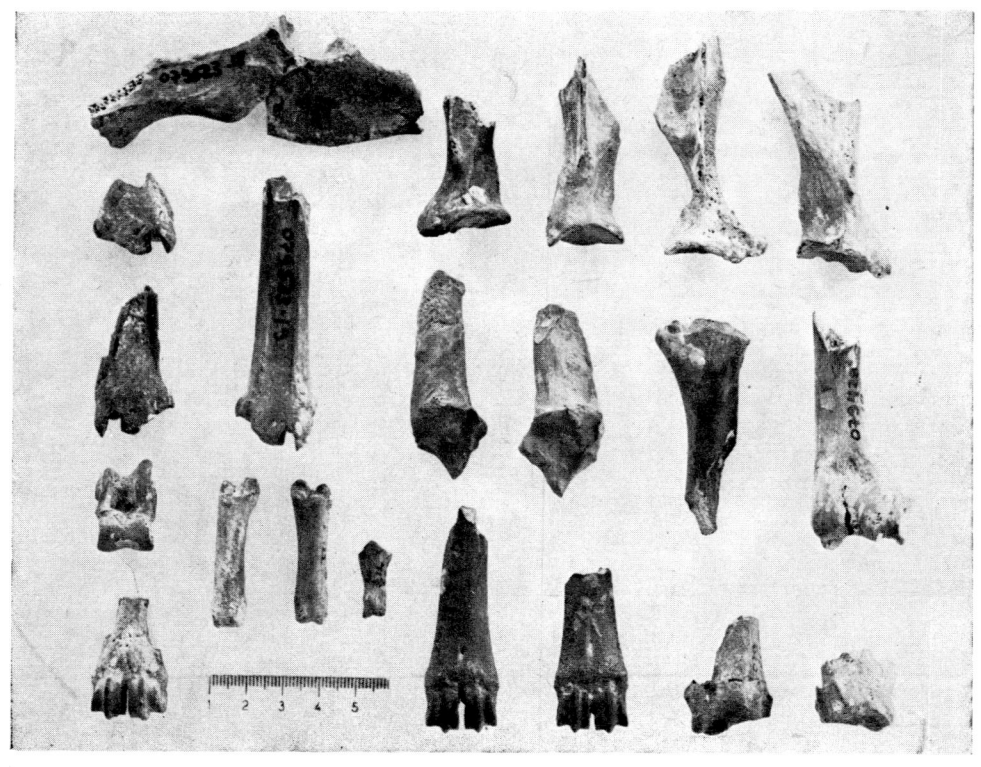

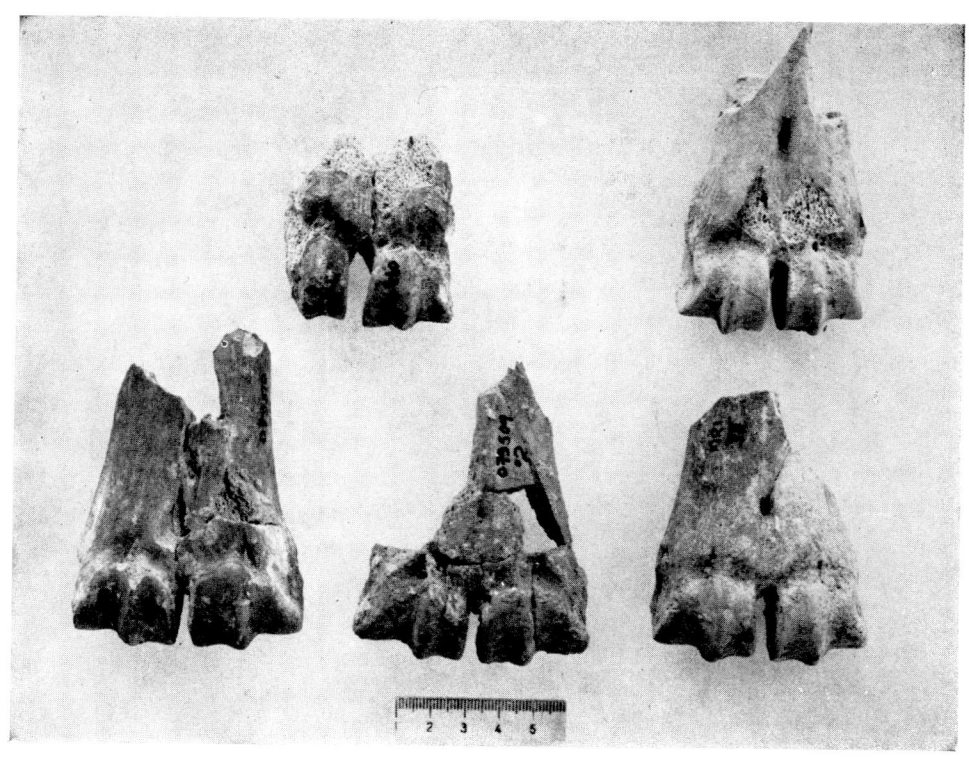

Pl. 6.3. Cattle (Bos) bones from MR. 3 Neolithic. Sixth millennium.

Pl. 6.4. Storeroom from MR. 3 Neolithic. Sixth millennium.

Pl. 6.5. General view of the upper level of MR. 3 with burials on the right side of the foreground. MR. 3 Neolithic. ca. 5000 B.C.

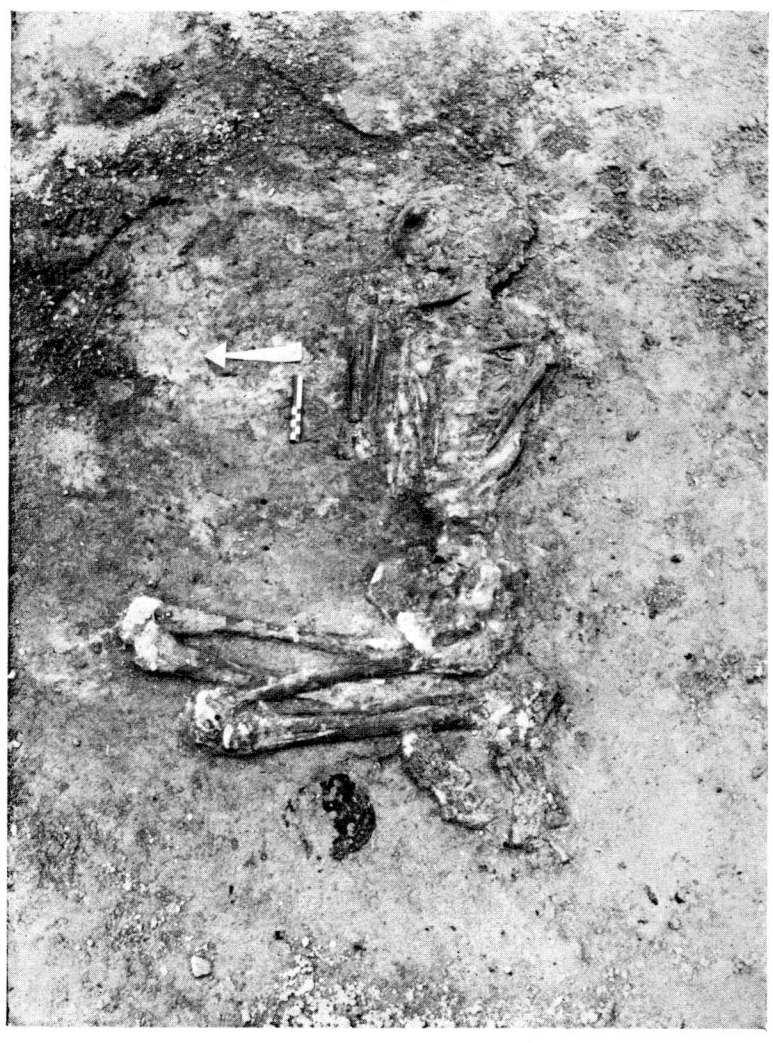

Pl. 6.6. Skeleton from MR. 3 with a basket coated with bitumen. Sixth millennium.

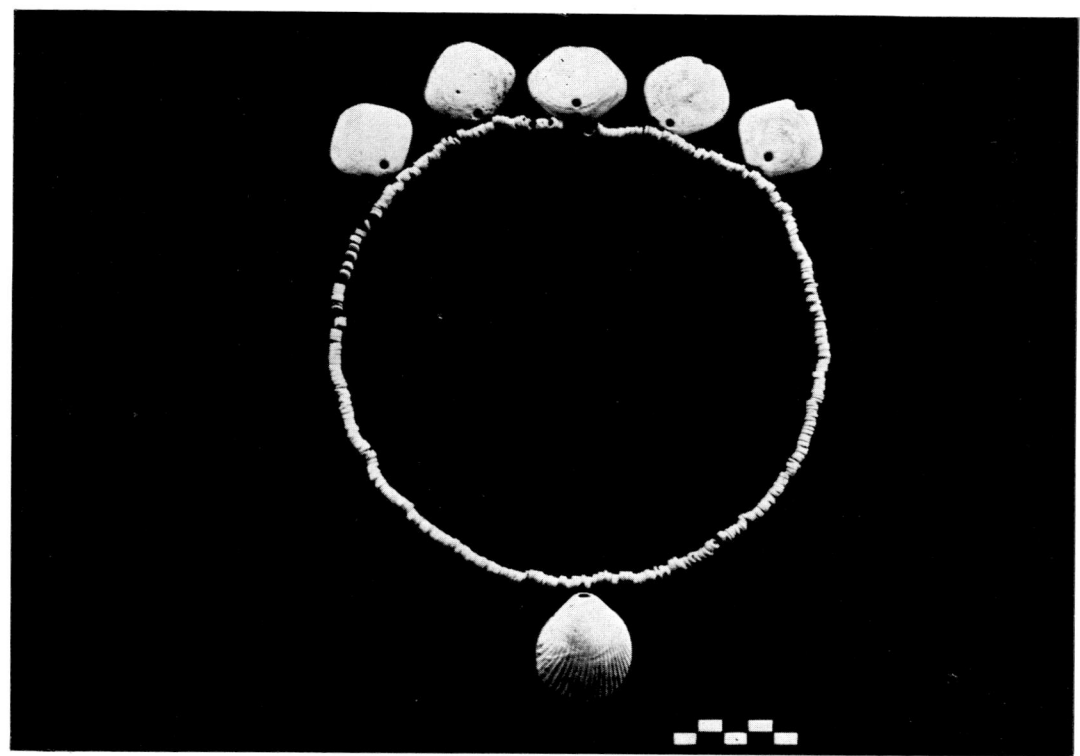

Pl. 6.7. Belt from a grave of **MR. 3** Neolithic. Sixth millennium.

Pl. 6.8. Grave goods from a grave of the upper level of **MR. 3** Neolithic, including a necklace with beads of steatite and turquoise.

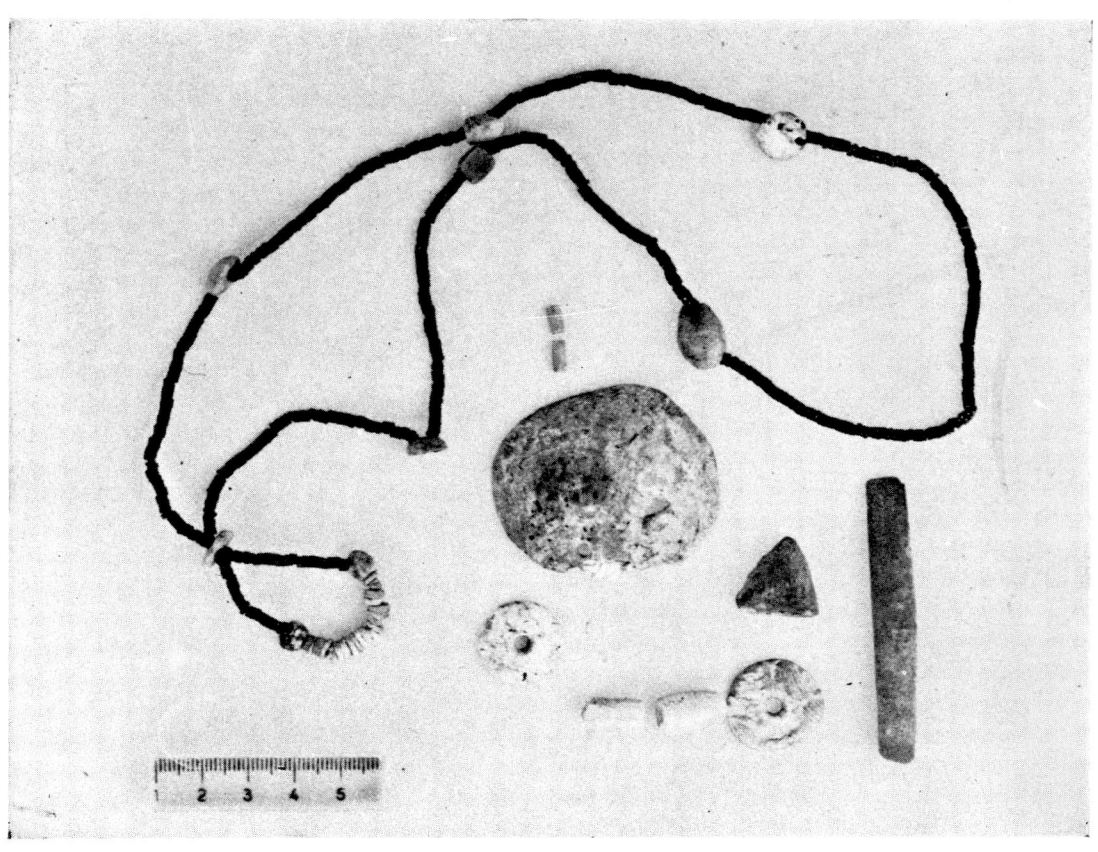

Pl. 6.9. A "granary" in MR. 4. Fifth millennium.

Pl. 6.10. Bone awls from MR. 4. Fifth millennium.

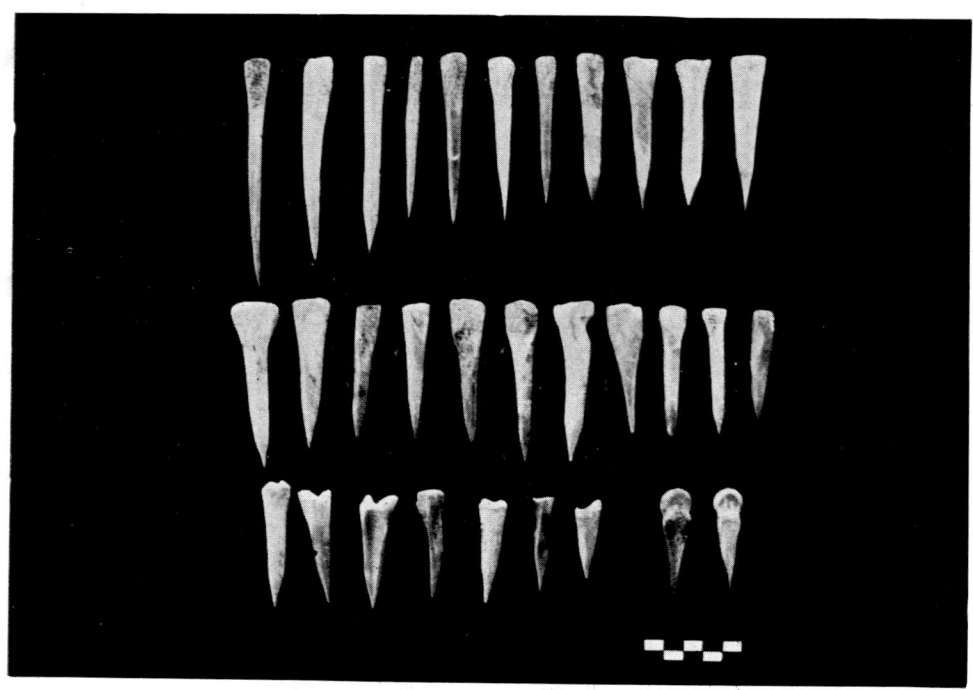

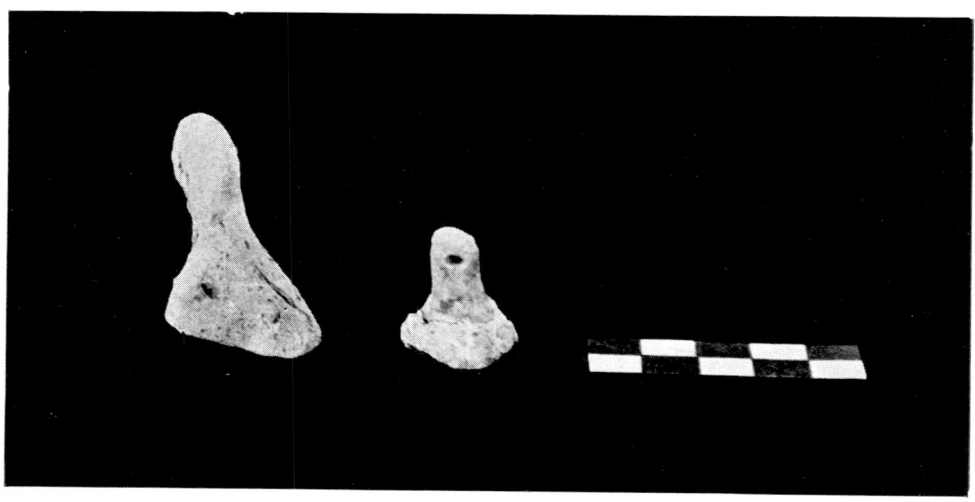

Pl. 6.11. Two human figurines in clay from MR. 4. Fifth millennium.

Pl. 6.12. Painted potsherds from MR. 2. First half of the 4th millennium.

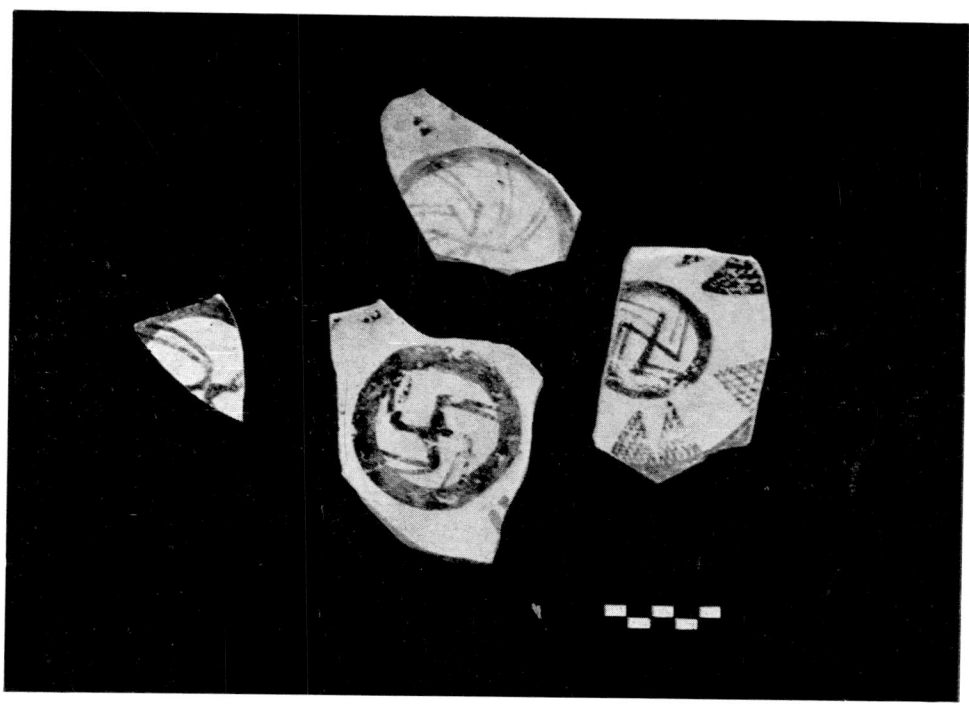

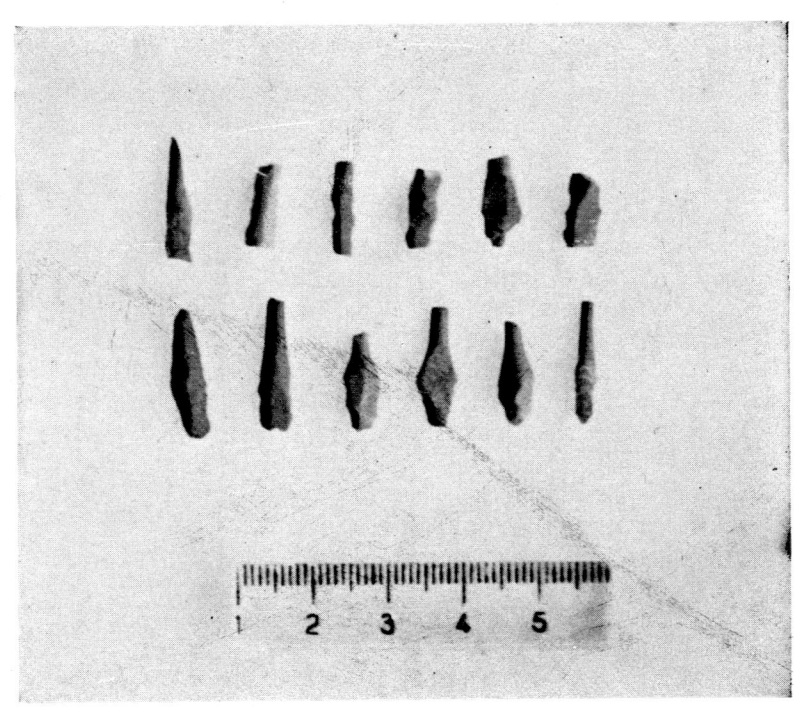

Pl. 6.13. Drills of phtanite. MR. 2. First half of the 4th millennium.

Pl. 6.14. Buildings in MR. 1. Period IV. ca. 3500 B.C.

Pl. 6.15. Polychrome vessel from MR. 1. Period IV. ca. 3500 B.C.

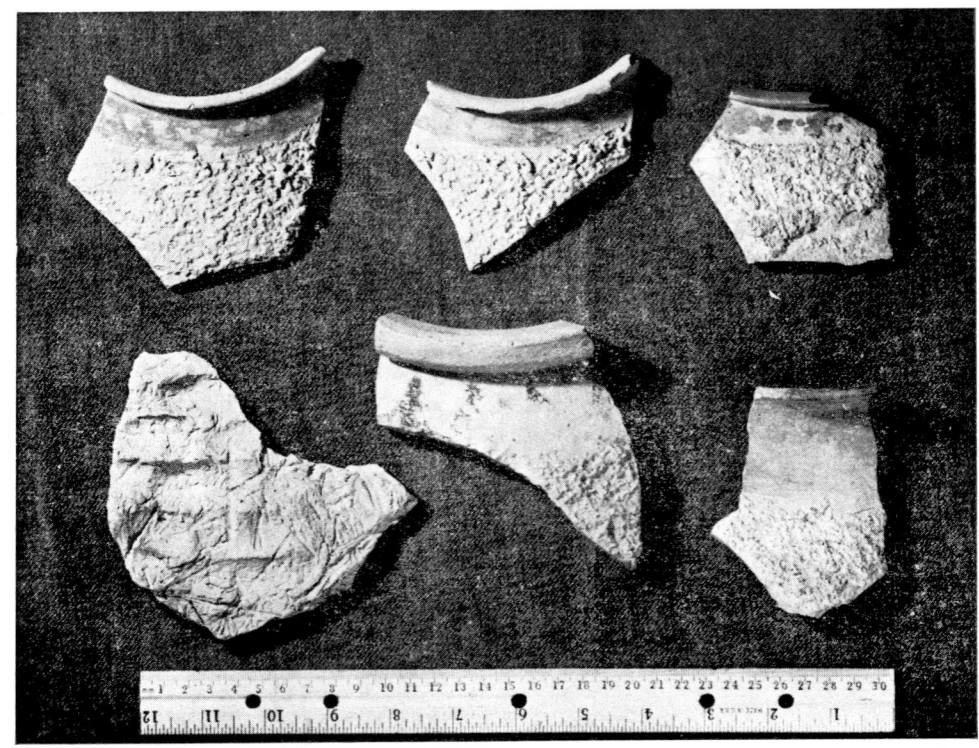

Pl. 7.1. The Hakra Wares. Mud applique pottery with painting in black on red or chocolate slip near the neck. Straw marked disk (extreme lower left) has finger impressions.

Pl. 7.2. The Hakra Wares. Surface treated with multiple incised lines.

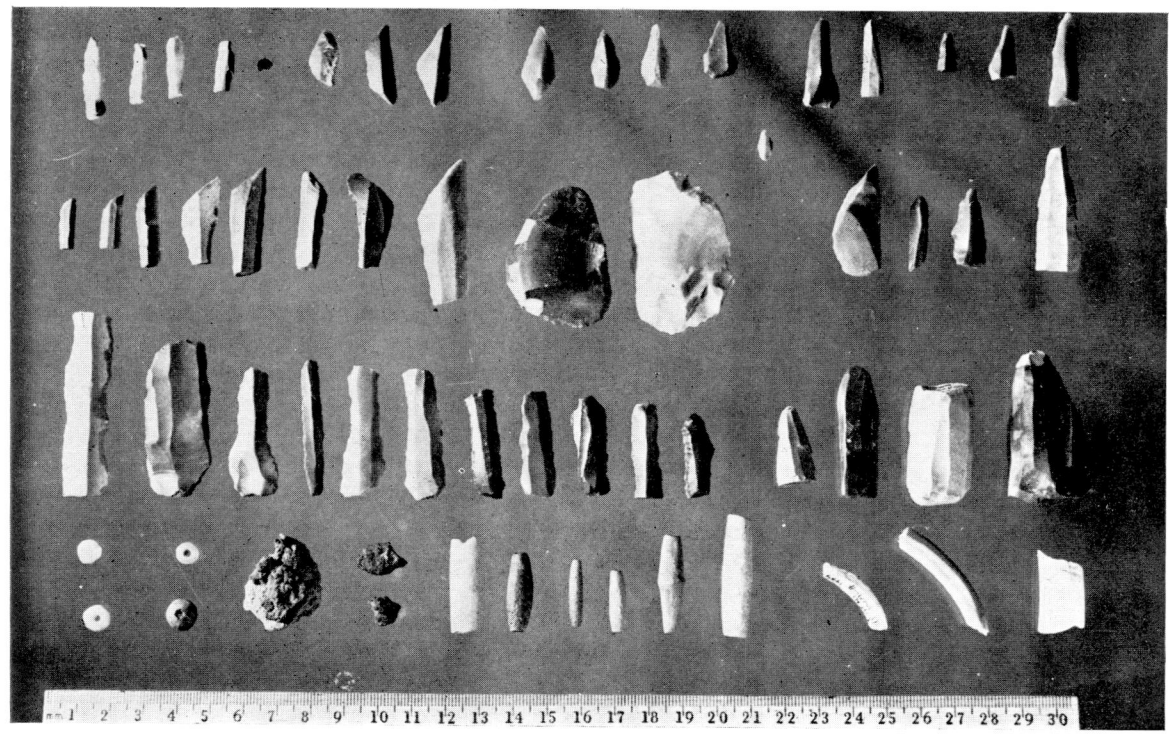

Pl. 7.3. The lithics associated with the Hakra Wares including (from the left in the lowest row) stone beads, copper, cylindrical beads of stone and terracotta and shell bangle pieces.

Pl. 7.4. Pottery of the Early Harappan (Kot Dijian) Period.

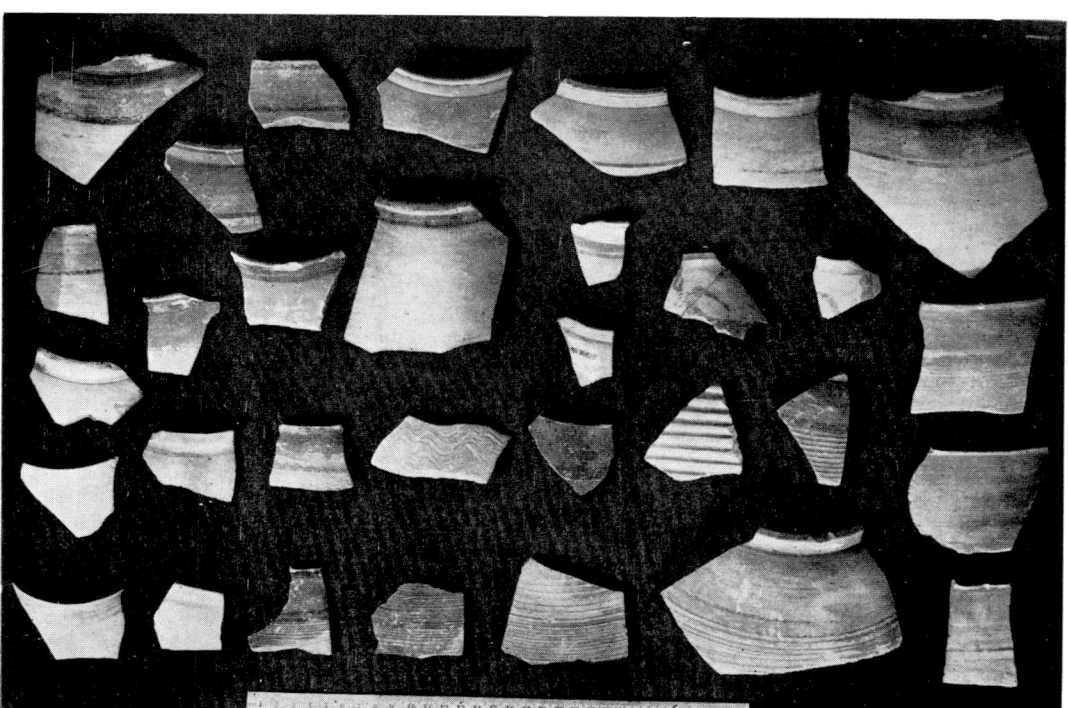

Pl. 7.5. Miscellaneous pottery from Early Harappan sites including mud applique surface treatment in the Hakra Wares style.

Pl. 7.6. Painted pottery from Mature Harappan sites.

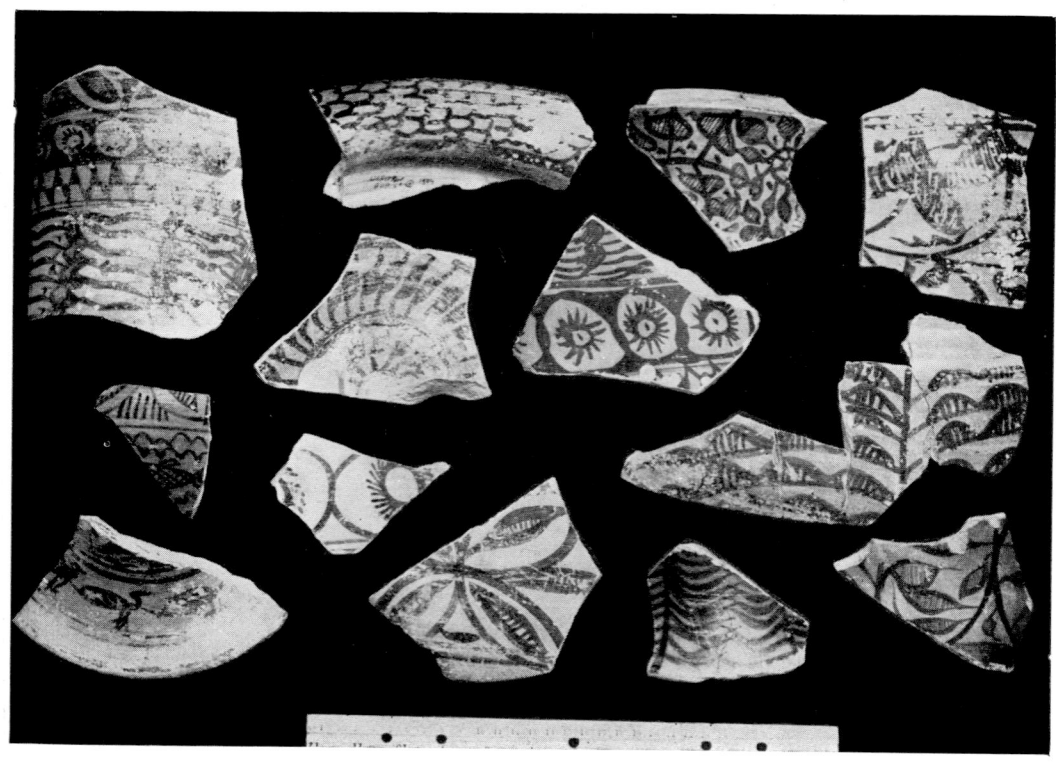

Pl. 7.7. Stone, copper and faience objects from Mature Harappan sites.

Pl. 7.8. Terracotta humped bull figurines and models of the plough—direct evidence for agriculture—from Mature Harappan sites.

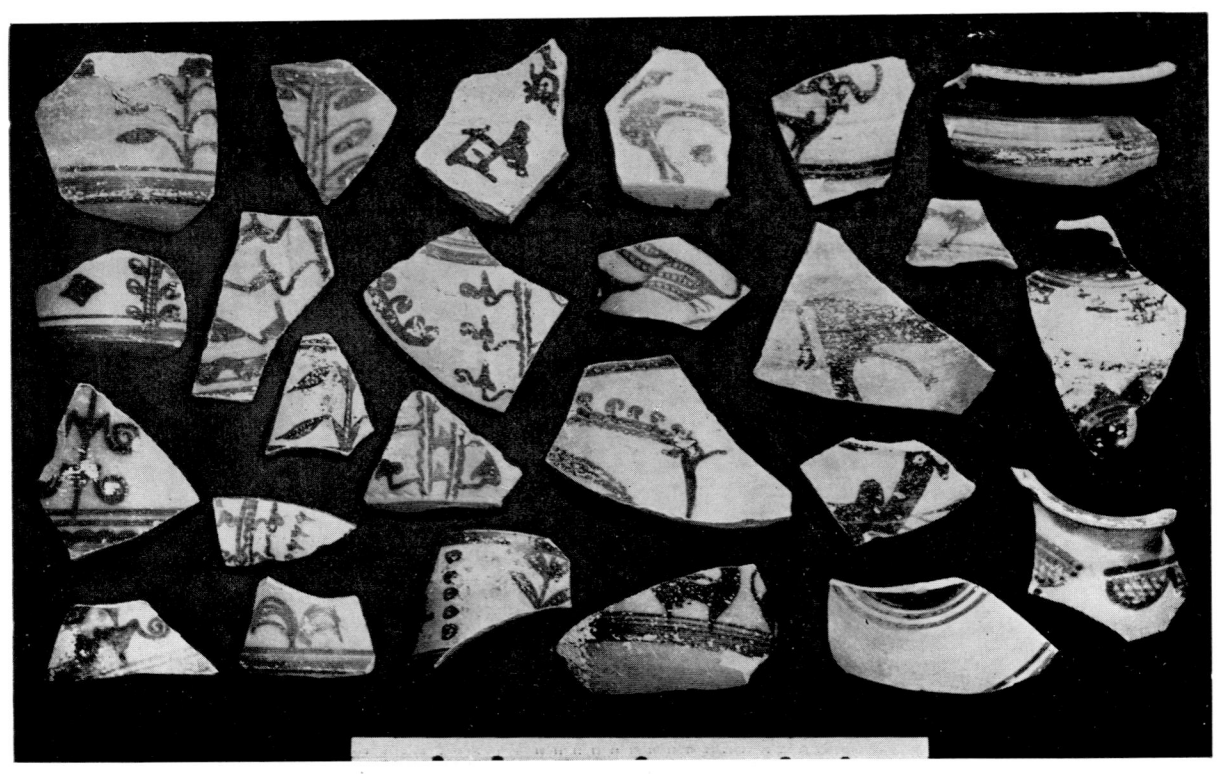

Pl. 7.9. Painted pottery of the Late Harappan Period (Cemetery H related).

Pl. 7.10 Burial pot from Kudwala, a Late Harappan site.

Pl. 7.11. Painted gray and plain gray pottery from PGW sites.

Pl. 7.12. Red pottery with impressed designs from PGW sites.

Pl. 10.1. The baked brick structure of Pre-Indus times may be seen below in excavation. Mud bricks are seen above on the right.

Pl. 10.2. Pre-Indus structures made of bricks of regular size.

Pl. 10.3. Pre-Indus brick-on-edge pathway on the right running along the Indus defensive wall of the citadel, on the left.

Pl. 10.4. A Pre-Indus fireplace lined with mud bricks.

Pl. 10.5. Pre-Indus pottery.

Pl. 10.6. Pre-Indus incised pottery.

Pl. 10.7. Canopied *ratha* painted on a sherd with a Pre-Indus fabric.

Pl. 10.8. The defense wall of the Indus acropolis. The narrow postern entrance, and the bastion projecting toward the "lower town."

Pl. 10.9. The bastion and the narrow passage with a built-in *pucca* drain beside it. The defense wall surrounds the Indus acropolis.

Pl. 10.10. The defense wall separating the acropolis (foreground) from the "down-town" of Indus times. Major roads run along the sides of the wall. A narrow alley is seen in the foreground.

Pl. 10.11a. House of a rich merchant (?).

Pl. 10.11b. Another view of the merchant's (?) house with a paved sitting room and toilet.

Pl. 10.12. Excavated houses in the lower town.

Pl. 10.13. Four successive building phases of a house beside a major road in "the upper town."

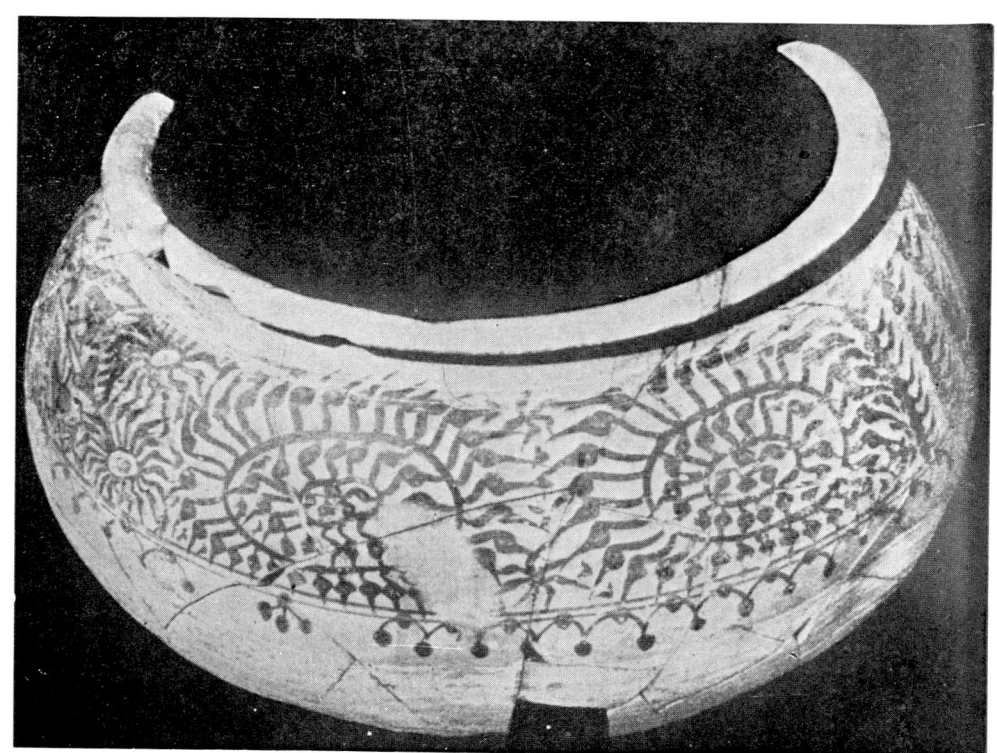

Pl.10.14. Period II pottery.

Pl. 10.15. Indus S-shaped jar.

Pl. 10.16. Indus seal.

Pl. 10.17. Indus antiquities.

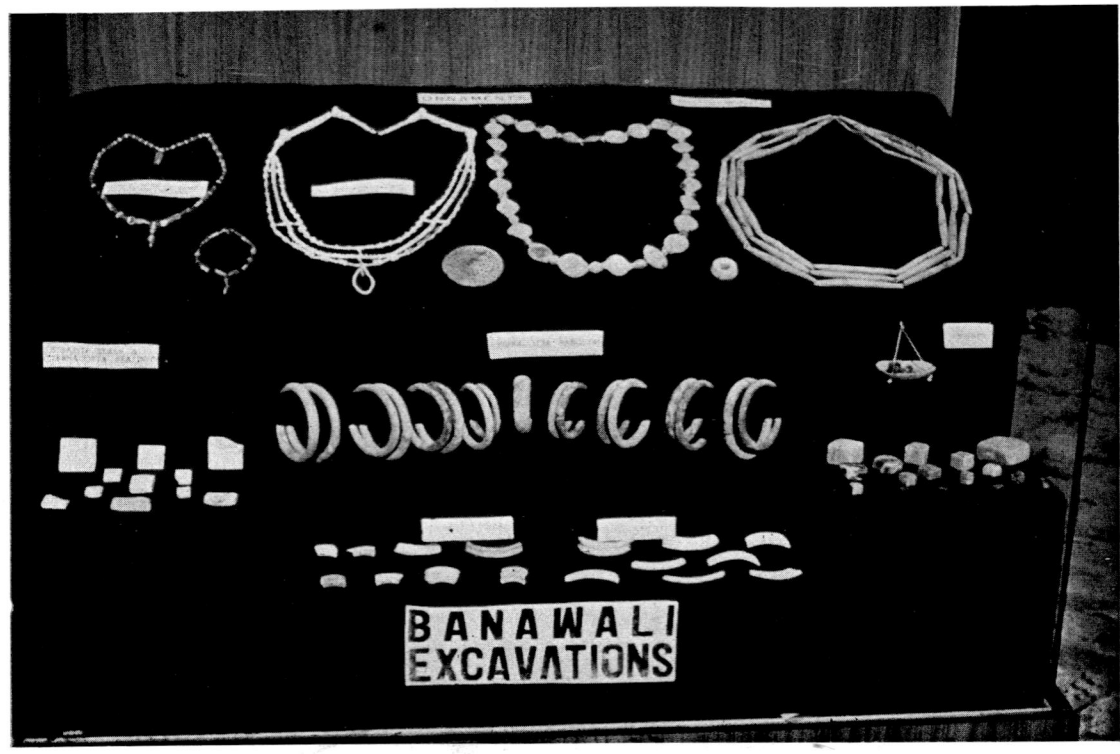

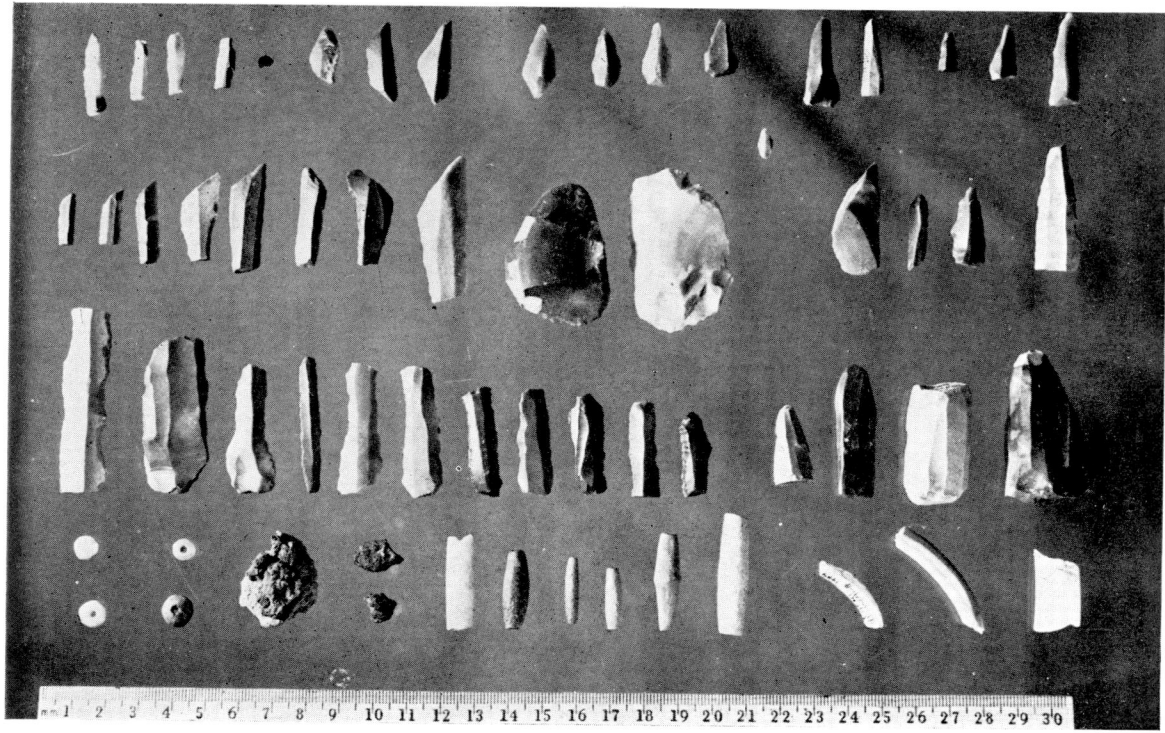

Pl. 7.3. The lithics associated with the Hakra Wares including (from the left in the lowest row) stone beads, copper, cylindrical beads of stone and terracotta and shell bangle pieces.

Pl. 7.4. Pottery of the Early Harappan (Kot Dijian) Period.

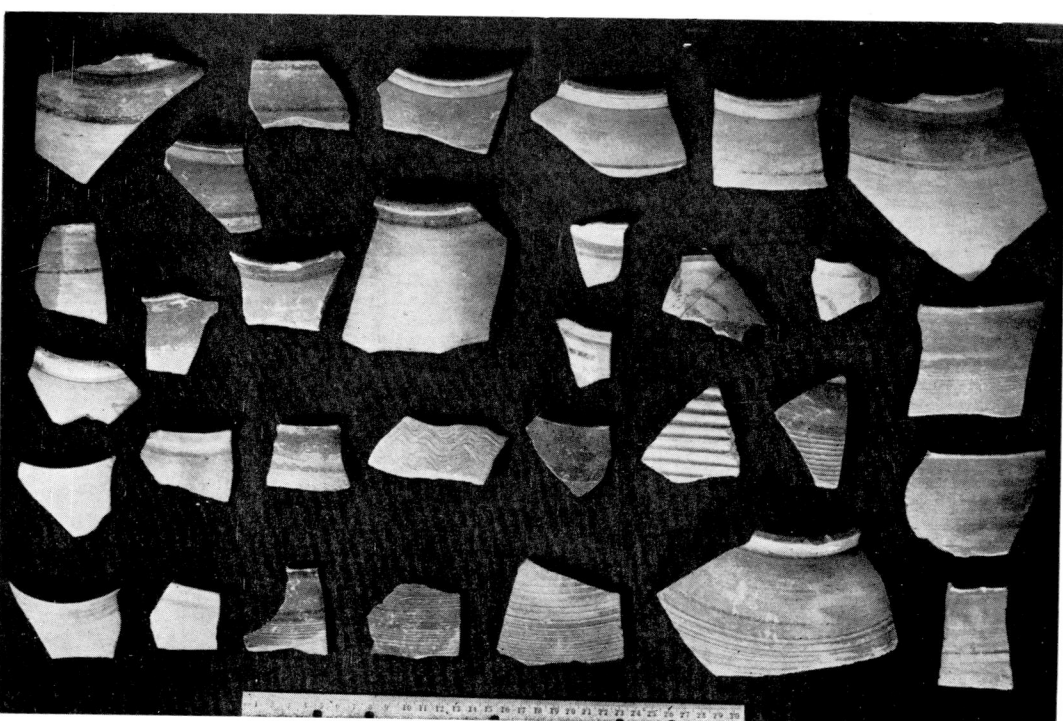

Pl. 7.5. Miscellaneous pottery from Early Harappan sites including mud applique surface treatment in the Hakra Wares style.

Pl. 7.6. Painted pottery from Mature Harappan sites.

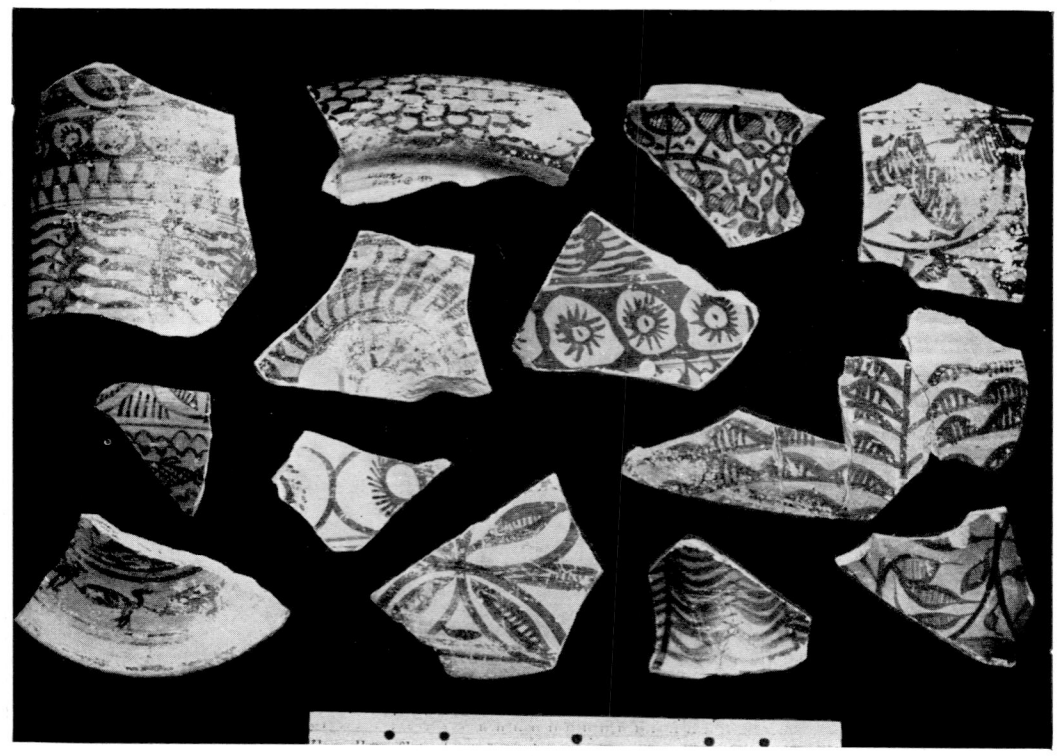

Pl. 7.7. Stone, copper and faience objects from Mature Harappan sites.

Pl. 7.8. Terracotta humped bull figurines and models of the plough—direct evidence for agriculture—from Mature Harappan sites.

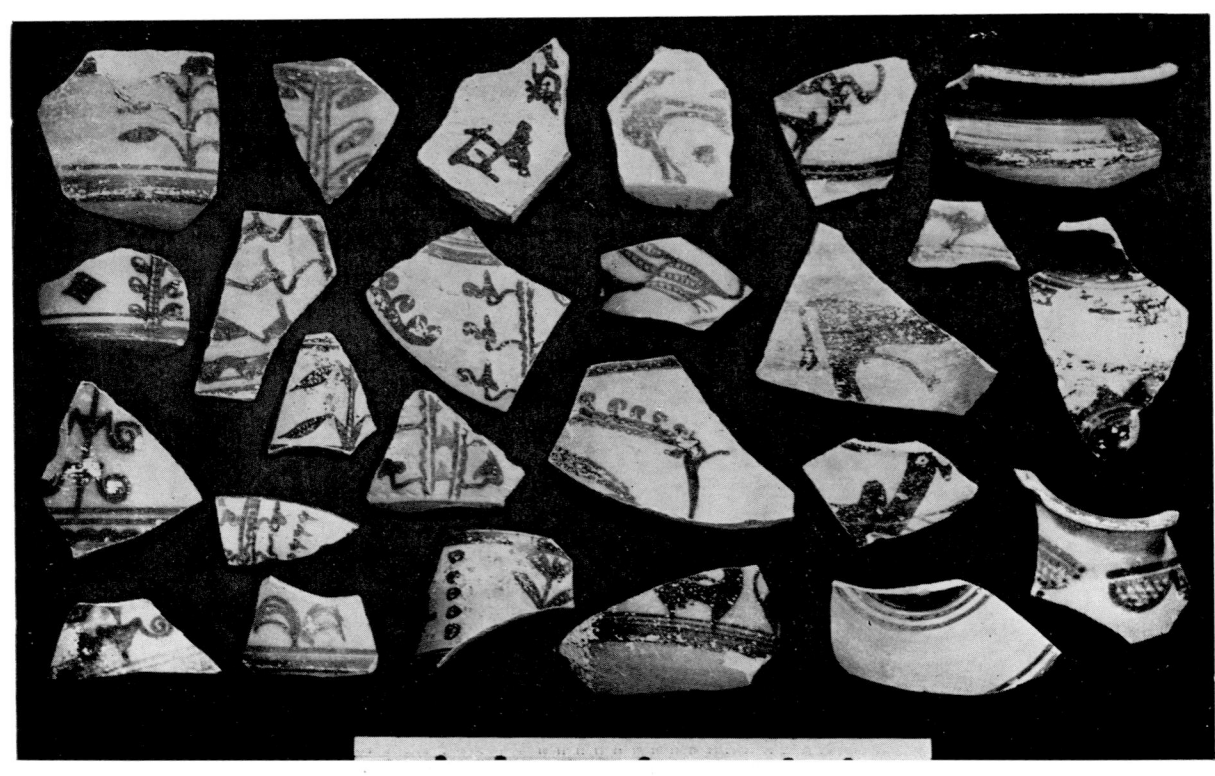

Pl. 7.9. Painted pottery of the Late Harappan Period (Cemetery H related).

Pl. 7.10 Burial pot from Kudwala, a Late Harappan site.

Pl. 7.11. Painted gray and plain gray pottery from PGW sites.

Pl. 7.12. Red pottery with impressed designs from PGW sites.

Pl. 10.1. The baked brick structure of **Pre-Indus** times may be seen below in excavation. Mud bricks are seen above on the right.

Pl. 10.2. Pre-Indus structures made of bricks of regular size.

Pl. 10.3. Pre-Indus brick-on-edge pathway on the right running along the Indus defensive wall of the citadel, on the left.

Pl. 10.4. A Pre-Indus fireplace lined with mud bricks.

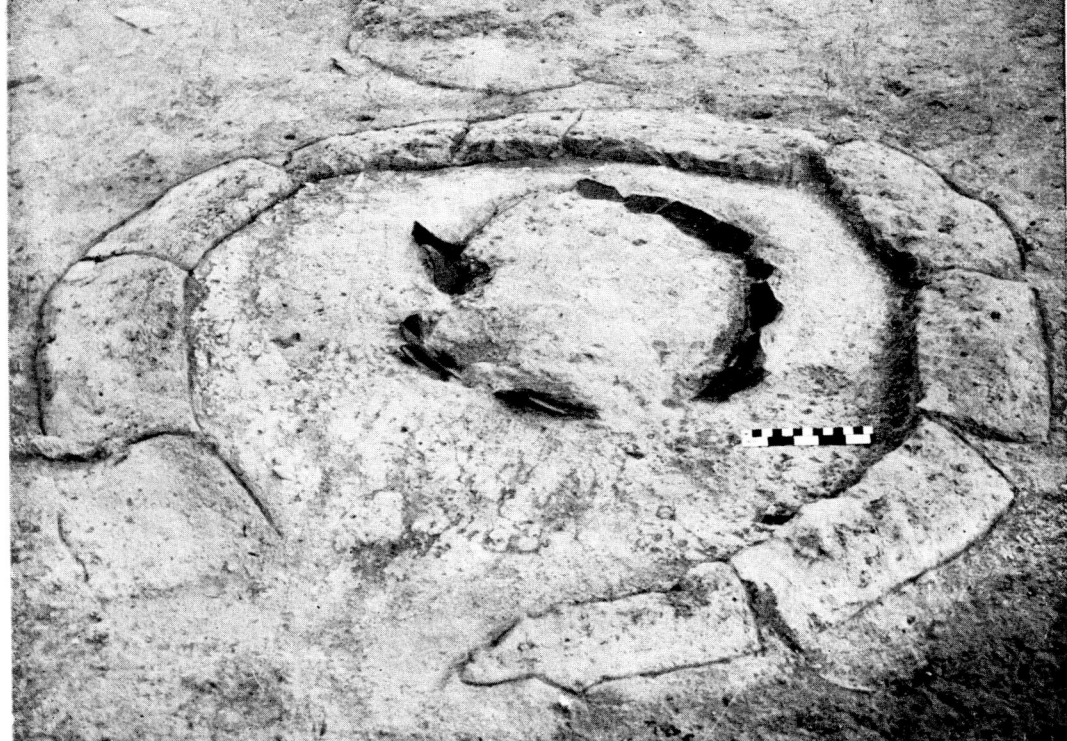

Pl. 10.5. Pre-Indus pottery.

Pl. 10.6. Pre-Indus incised pottery.

Pl. 10.7. Canopied *ratha* painted on a sherd with a Pre-Indus fabric.

Pl. 10.8. The defense wall of the Indus acropolis. The narrow postern entrance, and the bastion projecting toward the "lower town."

Pl. 10.9. The bastion and the narrow passage with a built-in *pucca* drain beside it. The defense wall surrounds the Indus acropolis.

Pl. 10.10. The defense wall separating the acropolis (foreground) from the "down-town" of Indus times. Major roads run along the sides of the wall. A narrow alley is seen in the foreground.

Pl. 10.11a. House of a rich merchant (?).

Pl. 10.11b. Another view of the merchant's (?) house with a paved sitting room and toilet.

Pl. 10.12. Excavated houses in the lower town.

Pl. 10.13. Four successive building phases of a house beside a major road in "the upper town."

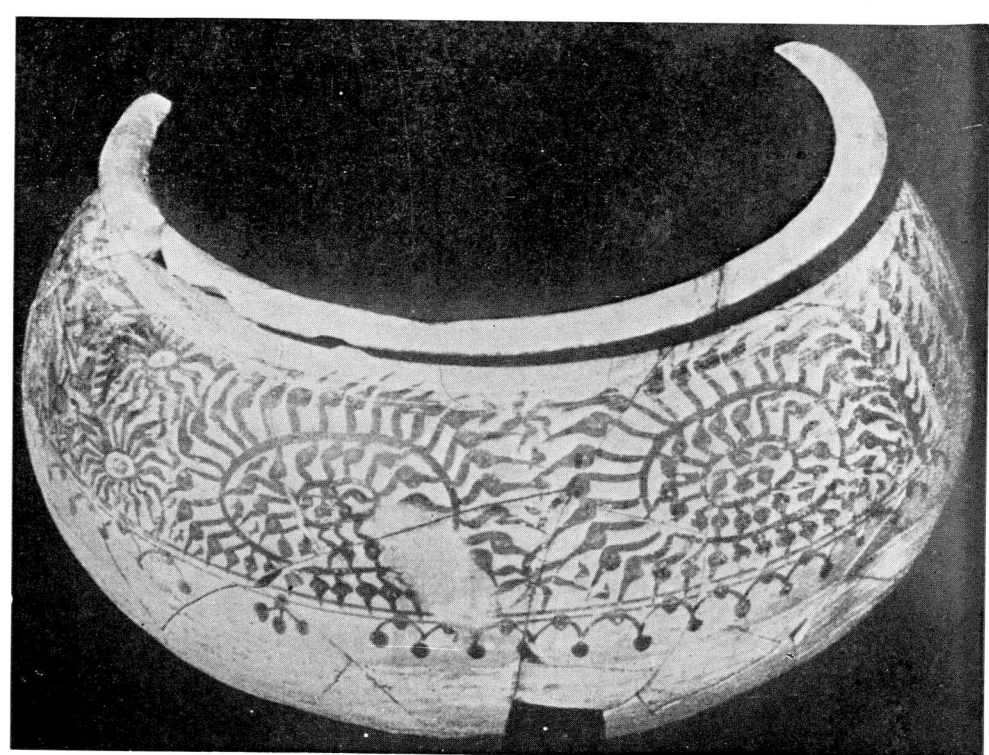

Pl.10.14. Period II pottery.

Pl. 10.15. Indus S-shaped jar.

Pl. 10.16. Indus seal.

Pl. 10.17. Indus antiquities.

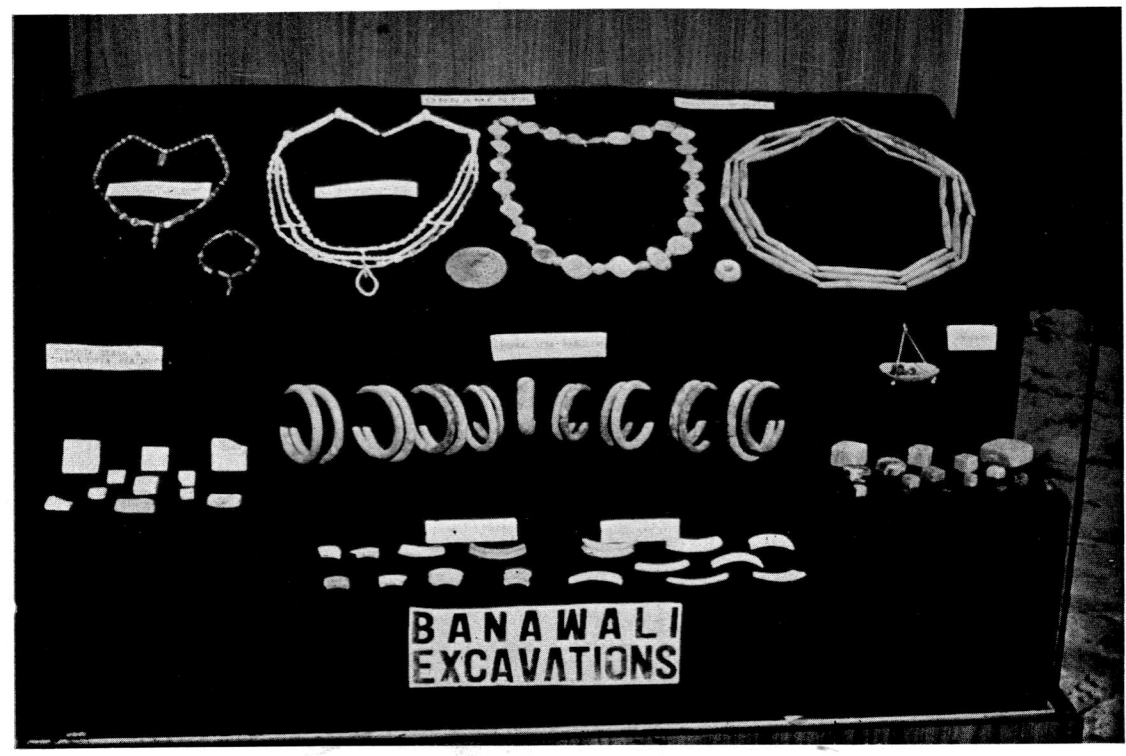

Pl. 10.18. Indus weights.

Pl. 10.19. Indus gamesmen.

Pl. 10.20. Mother goddess.

Pl. 10.21. Bull figurines of the Indus Period.

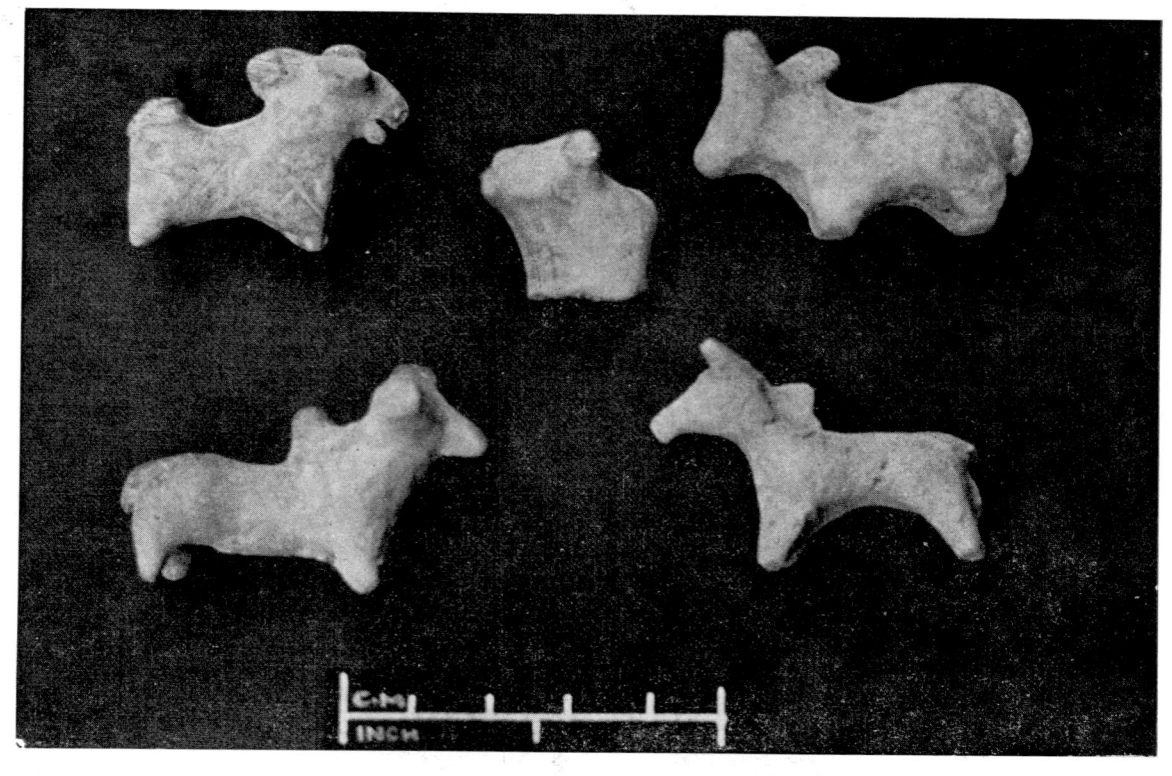

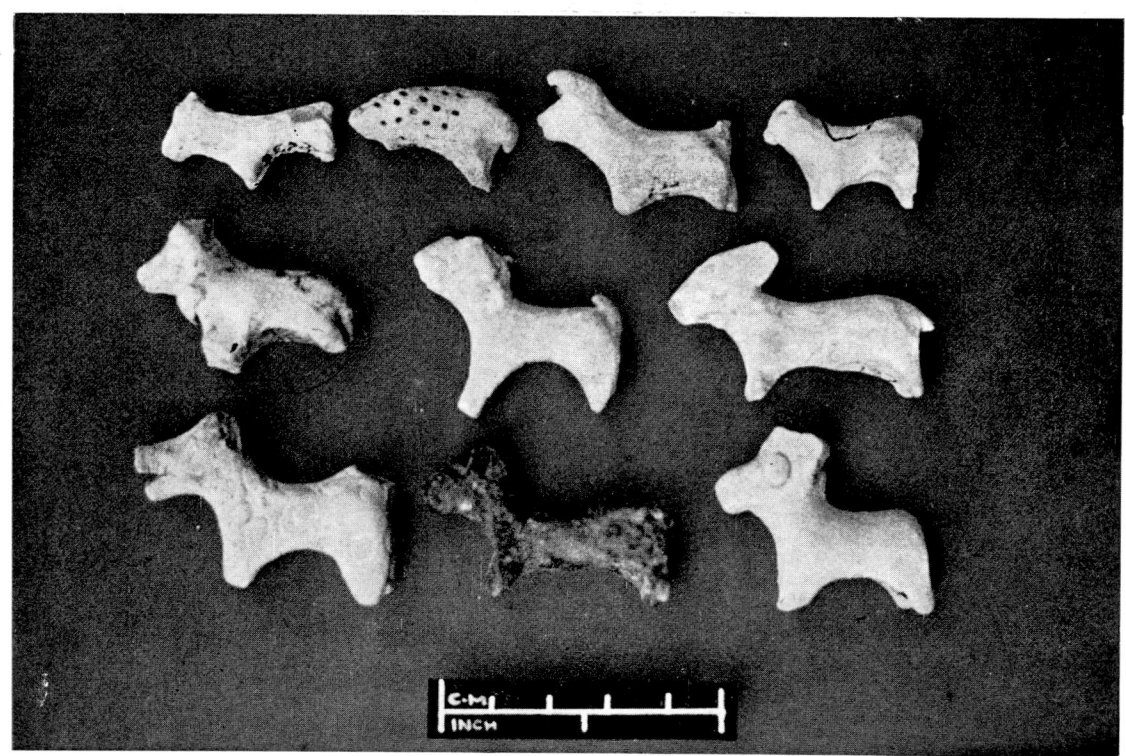

Pl. 10.22. Clay figurines of animals from the Indus levels.

Pl. 10.23. Wheeled terracottas.

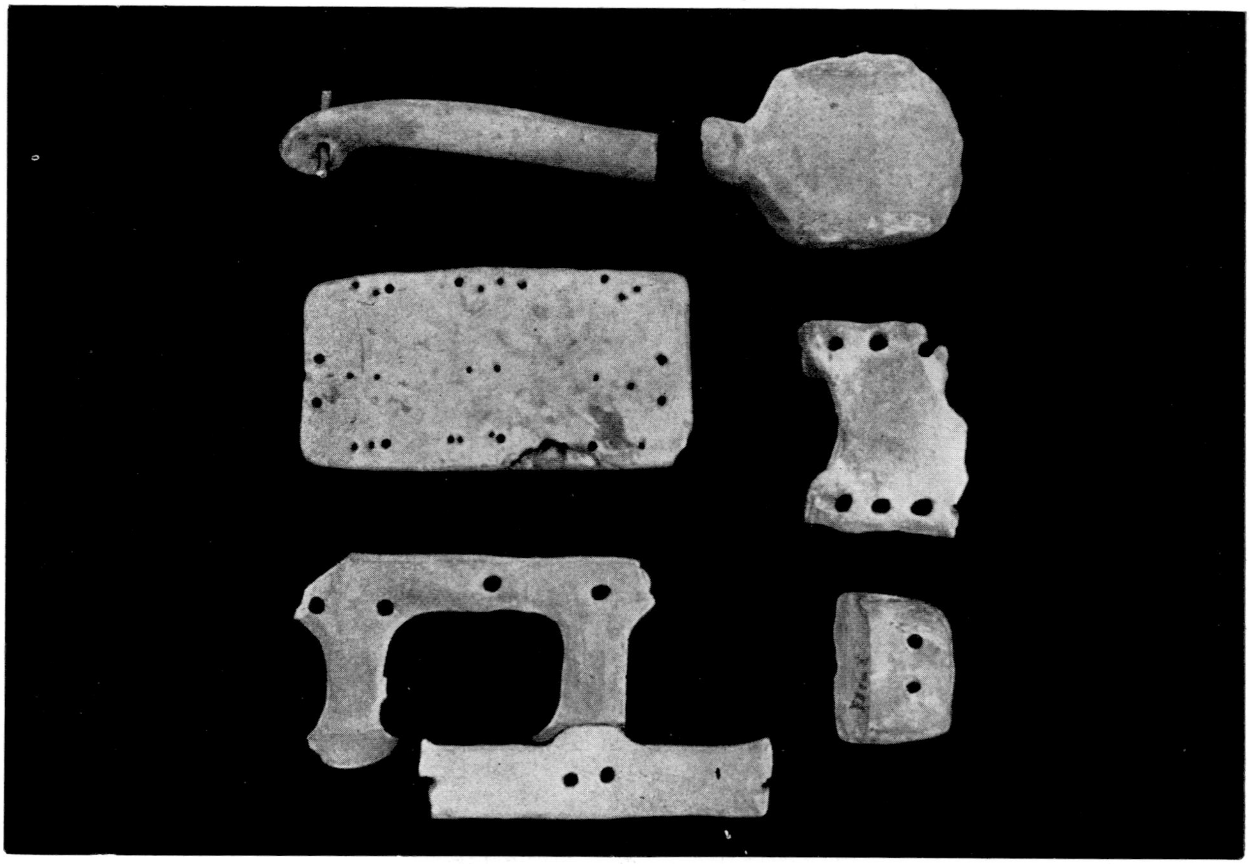

Pl. 10.24. Cart frames and platforms.

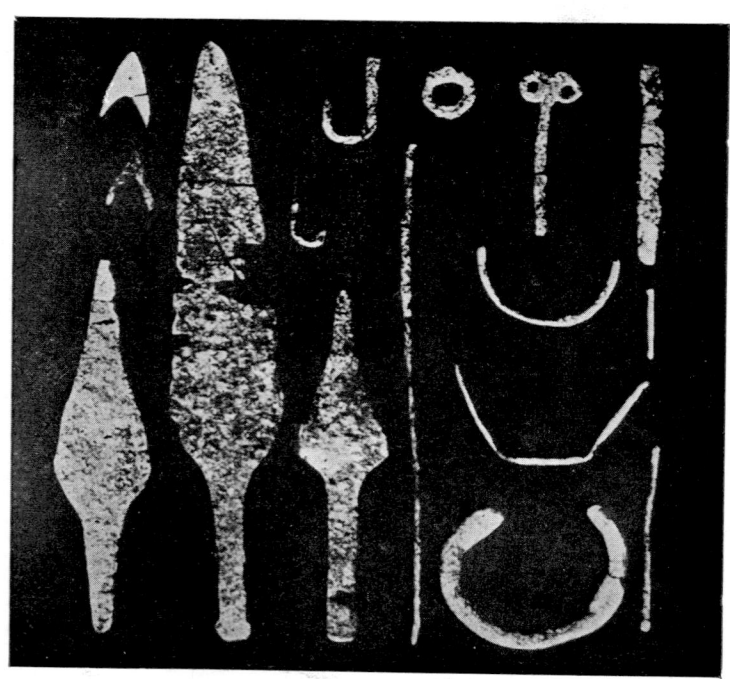

Pl. 10.25. Indus copper implements.

Pl. 10.26. Indus copper implements.

Pl. 10.27. Pits dug into, or near the top of the eastern arm of the town wall of the Indus Period.

Pl. 10.28. Post-Indus Banawali-Bara Ware.

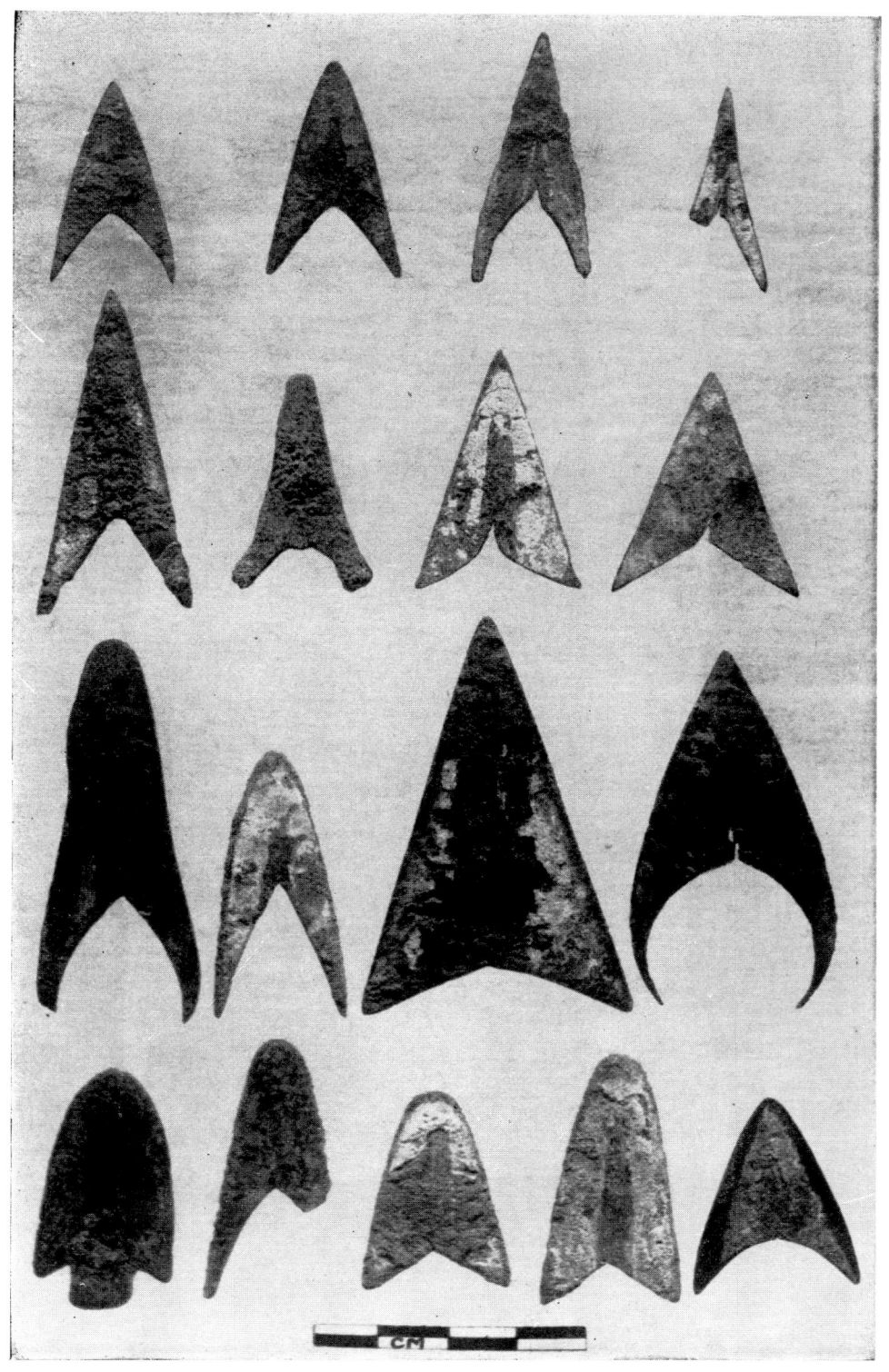

Pl. 11.1. Rich variety of copper arrow heads with wood shaft marks from Ganeshwar (Rajasthan). Third millennium B.C., OCP Complex.

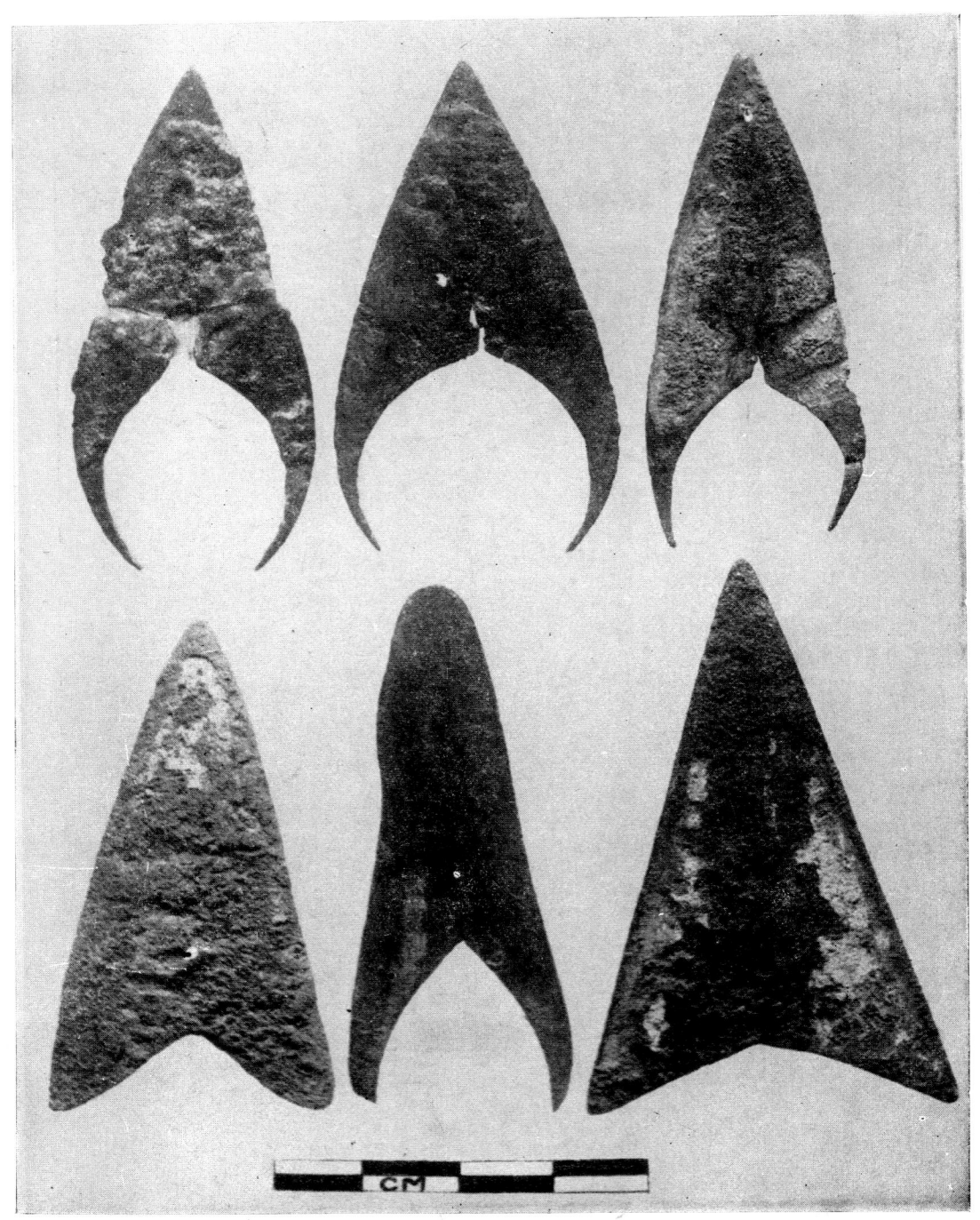

Pl. 11.2. Unique and artistic arrow heads from Ganeshwar. Third millennium B.C., OCP Complex.

Pl. 11.3. Copper blades, knives and spear heads from Ganeshwar (Rajasthan). Third millennium B.C., OCP Complex.

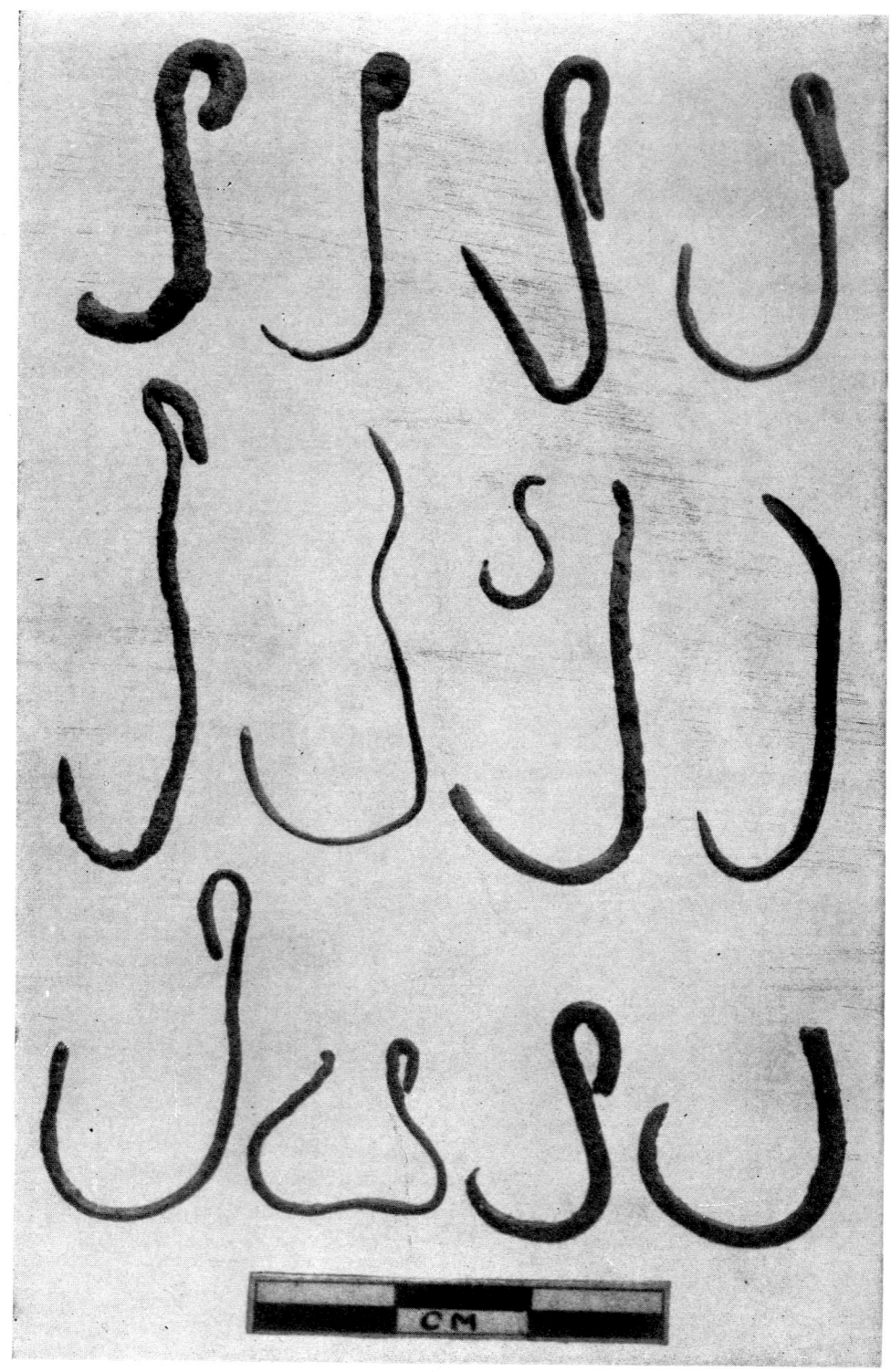

Pl. 11.4. Copper fish hooks from Ganeshwar (Rajasthan). Third millennium B.C., OCP Complex.

Pl. 11.5. Copper celts with various indentations from Ganeshwar (Rajasthan). Third millennium B.C., OCP Complex.

Pl. 11.6. Copper celts with various indentations from **Ganeshwar** (Rajasthan). Third millennium B.C., OCP Complex.

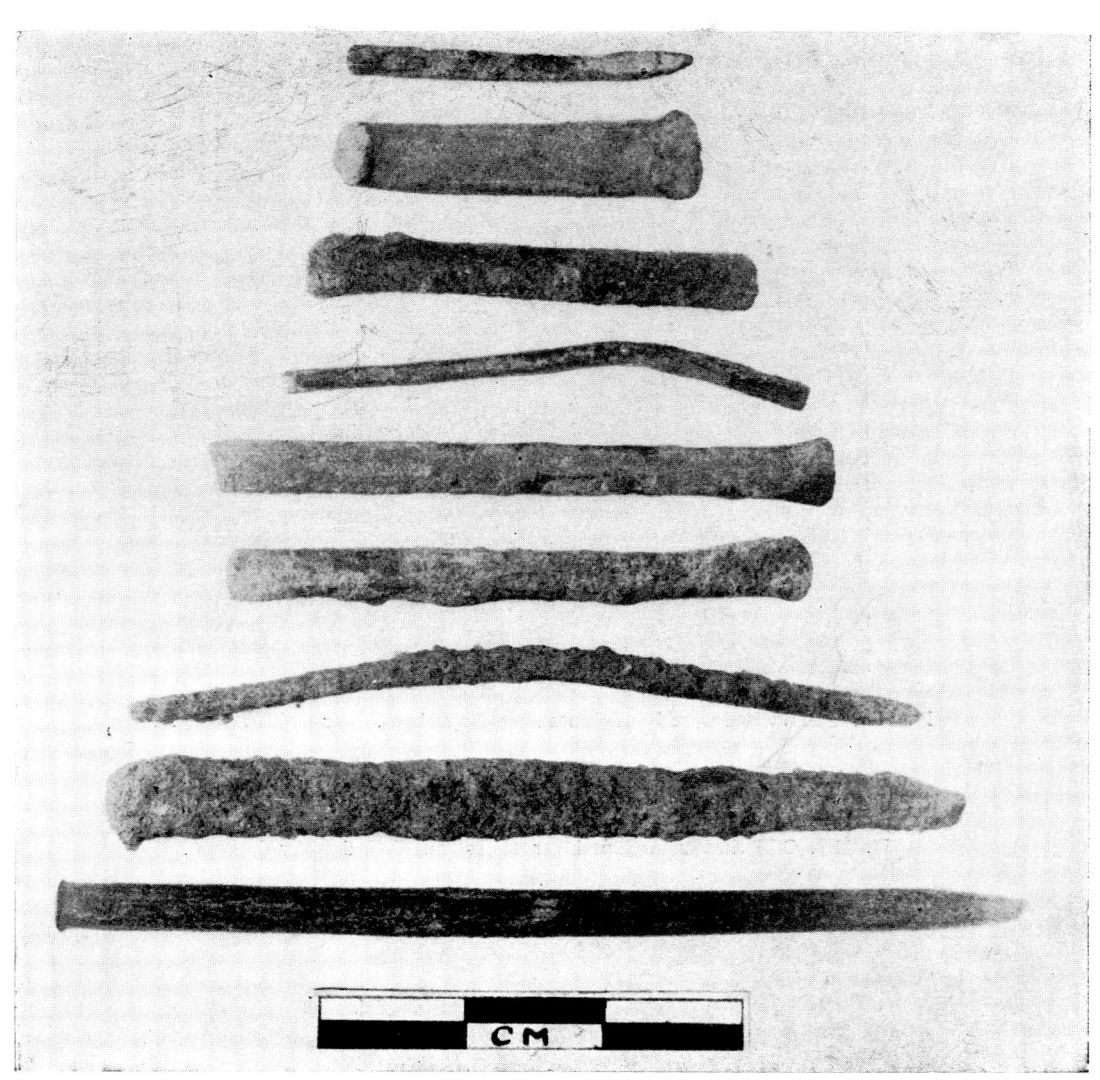

Pl. 11.7. Copper rods, chisels and a drill from Ganeshwar (Rajasthan). Third millennium B.C.

Pl. 11.8. OCP incised ware from Ganeshwar (Rajasthan). Third millennium B.C.

Pl. 11.9. OCP rims from Ganeshwar (Rajasthan). Third millennium B.C.

Pl. 11.10. Painted Red Ware with black designs associated with OCP at Ganeshwar (Rajasthan). Third millennium B.C.

Pl. 11.11. Characteristic graffiti marks incised on the interiors of OCP sherds. Ganeshwar-Jodhpura Culture. From Ganeshwar (Rajasthan). Third millennium B.C.

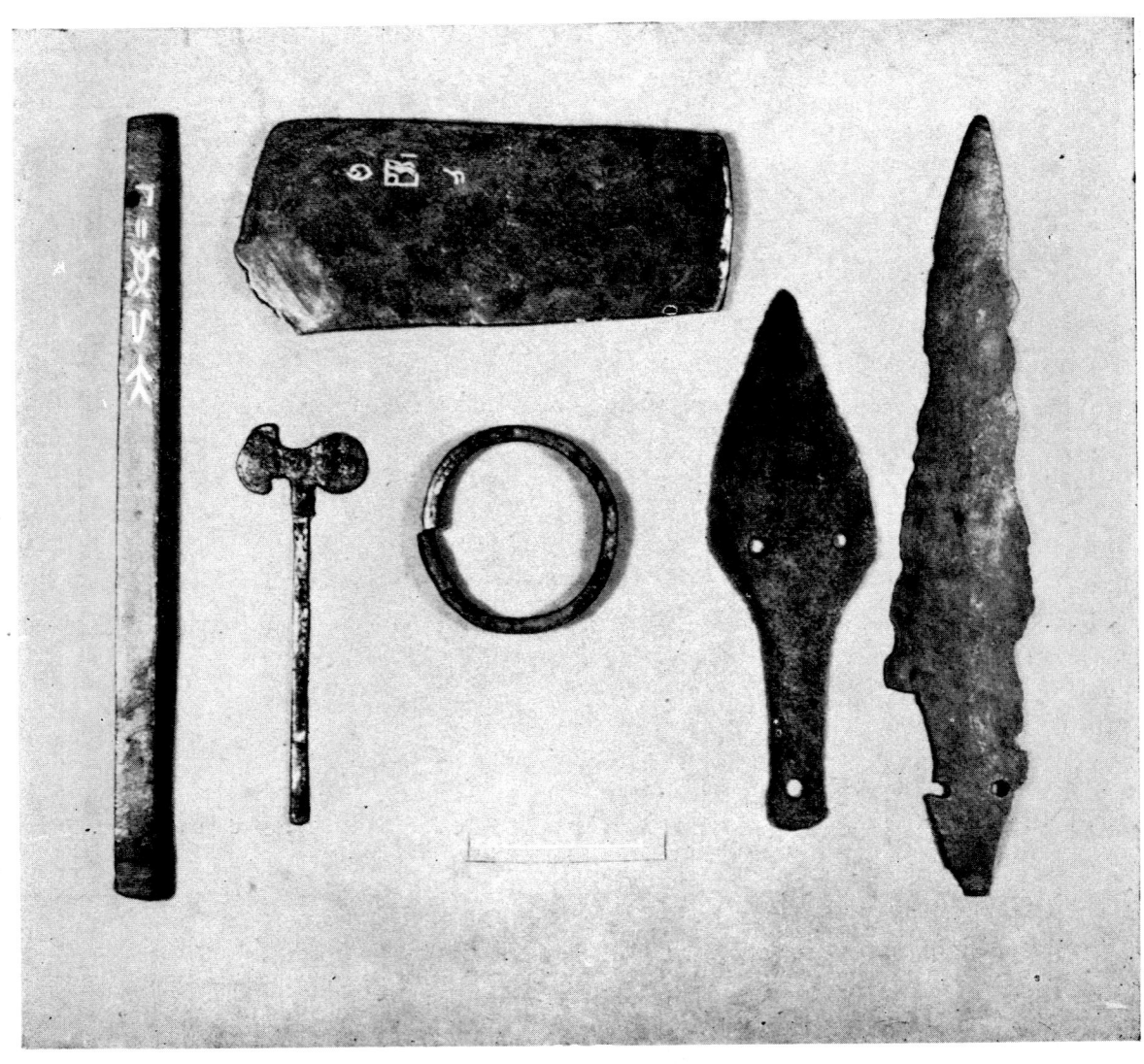

Pl. 11.12. Typical copper objects from the Mature Harappan levels of Kalibangan. Courtesy of B.K. Thapar and the Archaeological Survey of India.

Pl. 13.1. Kotla Nihang: Small kilns in a row.

Pl. 13.2. Ropar: Bronze jar *in situ* in IA level.

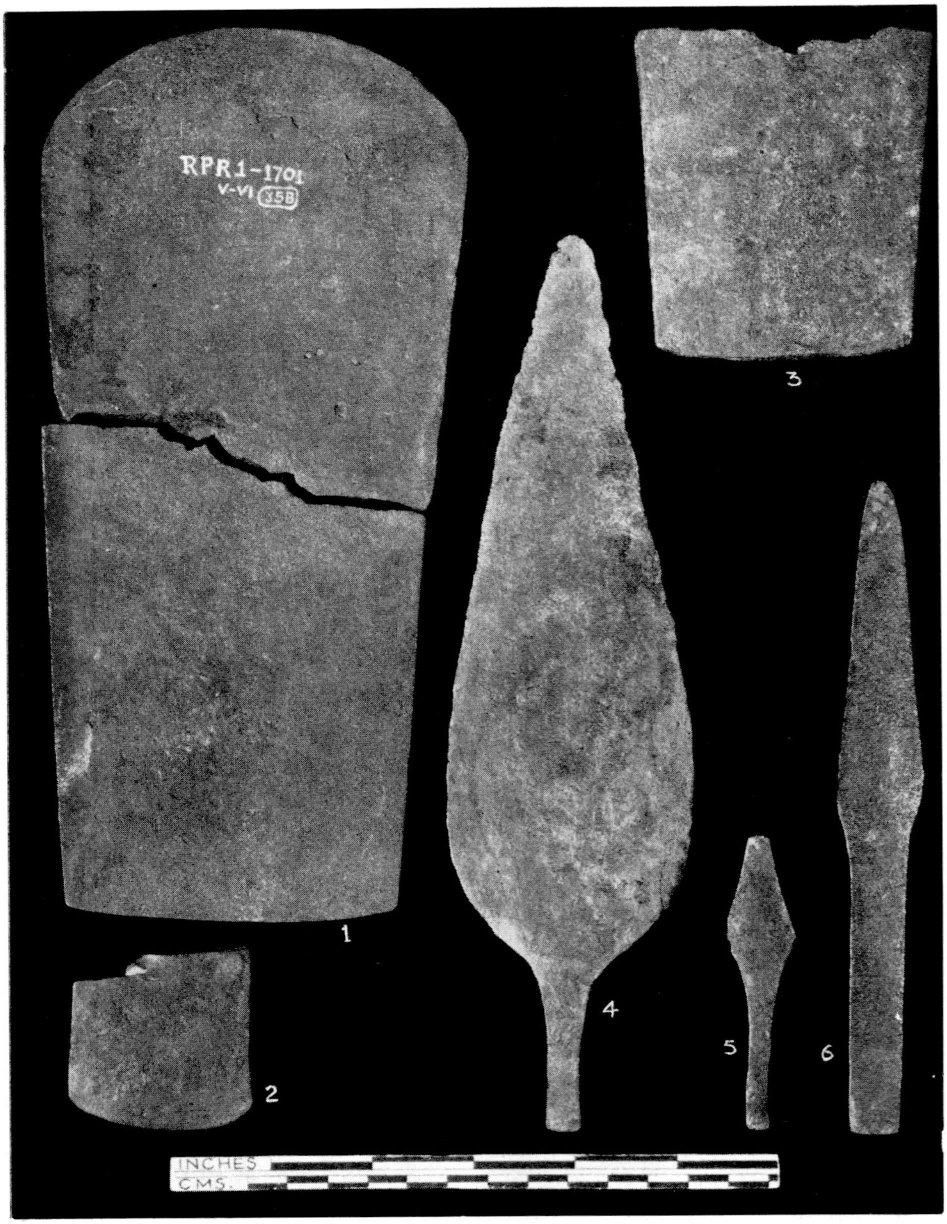

Pl. 13.3. Ropar: Bronze implements from IA and IB levels.

Pl. 13.4. Ropar: Small steatite seals.

Pl. 13.5. Ropar: Bronze razor blades from IB levels.

Pl. 13.6. Ropar: Baked clay sealing with impressions of three seals.

Pl. 13.7. Ropar: Harappan graffiti on sherds.

Pl. 13.8. Ropar: Mud brick walls with stone foundations.

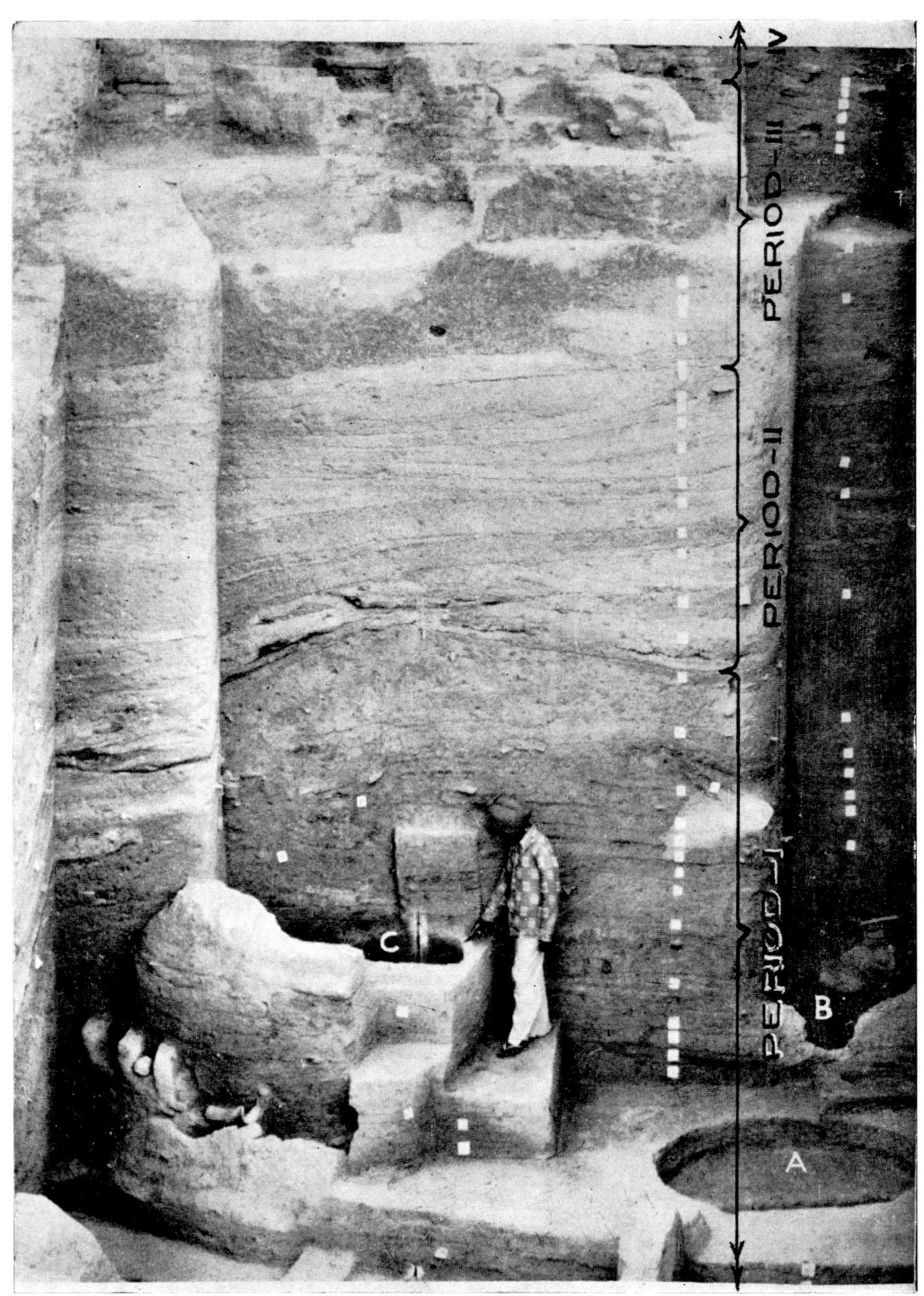

Pl. 13.9. Sanghol: Section cutting with potter's house. A. storage bin; B. kiln; C. fireplace.

Pl. 13.10. Raja Sirkap: Terracotta cakes and missiles.

Pl. 14.1. The site of Zekda.

Pl. 14.2. The site of Kanewal.

Pl. 14.3. Graffiti on pottery from Kanewal.

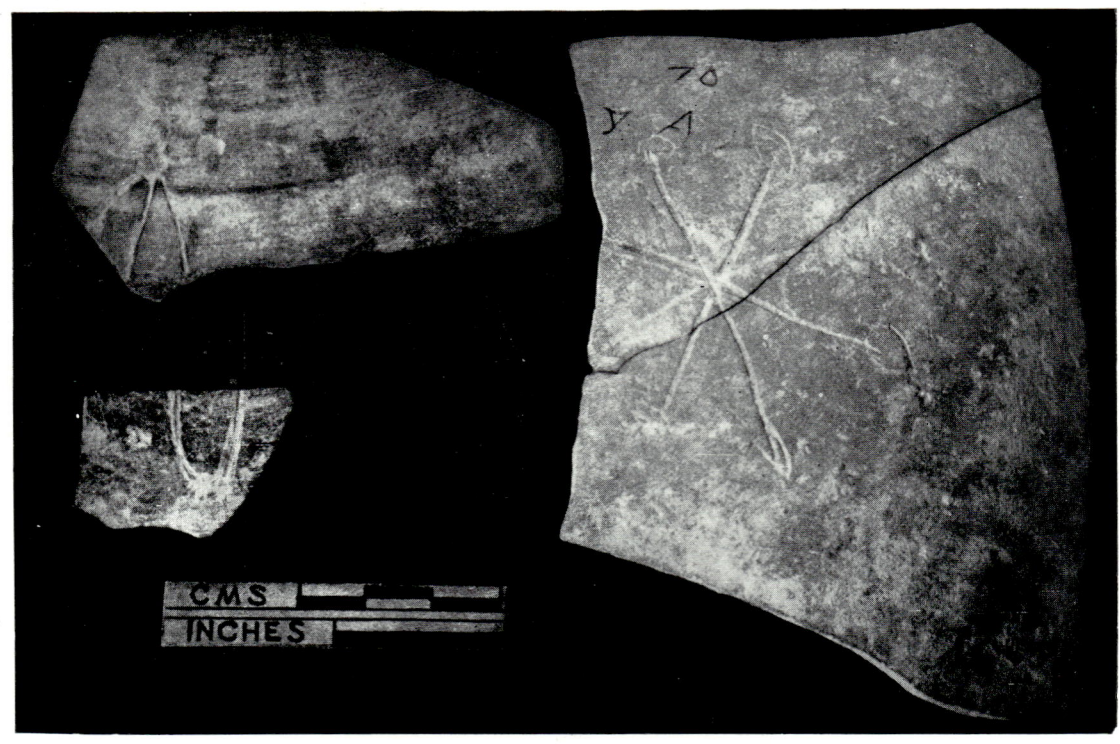

Pl. 15.1. Daimabad Late Harappan Red Ware. Phase II.

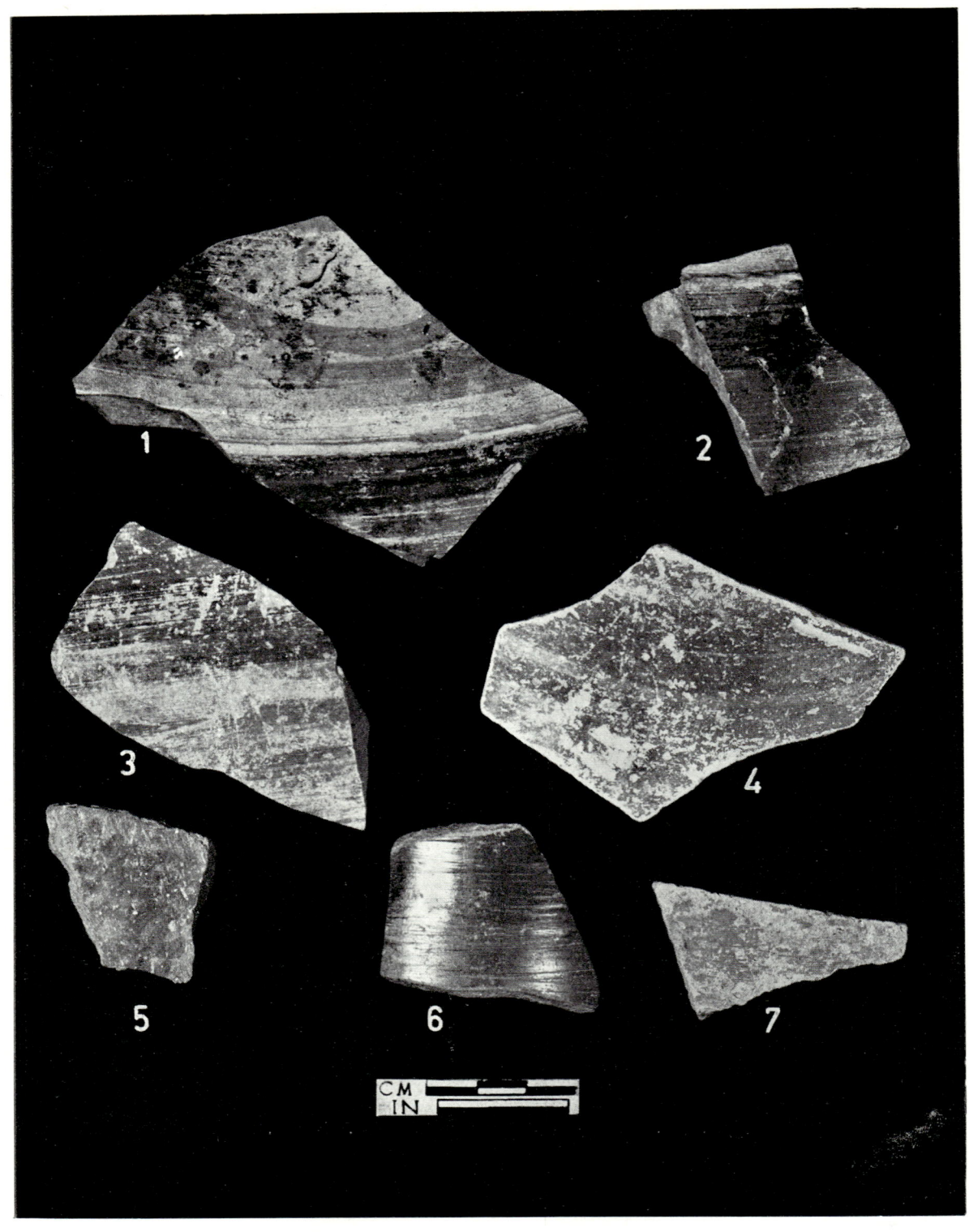

Pl. 15.2. Daimabad Ribbed Bichrome Ware (Nos. 1–3) and Deep Red Ware (Nos. 4–7). Phase II.

Pl. 15.3. Daimabad mud brick lined grave. Phase II.

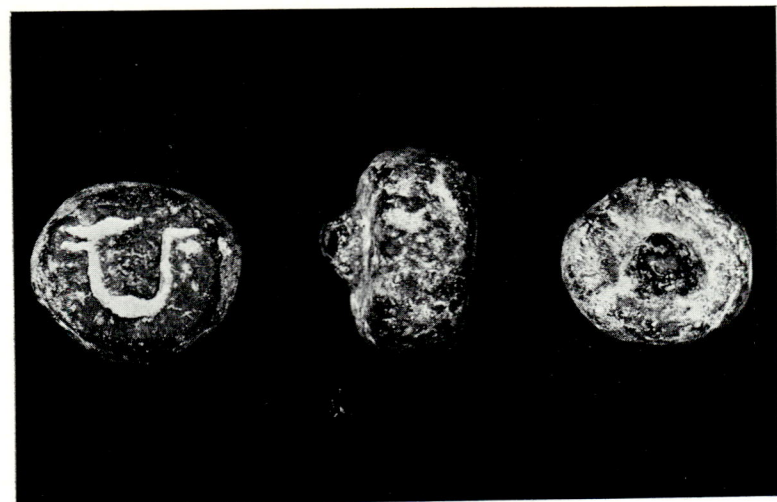

Pl. 15.4. Daimabad button-shaped seal with Indus script. Phase II.

Pl. 15.5. Daimabad potsherd with inscribed Indus script. Phase II.

Pl. 15.6. Daimabad potsherd with painted Indus script. Phase II.

Pl. 15.7. Daimabad. Engraved crescent-shaped potsherd showing obverse and reverse. Phase II

Pl. 15.8. Daimabad. Terracotta cake (No. 7) and other pottery objects. Phase II.

Pl. 16.1. Manda. Stratigraphy.

Pl. 16.2. Manda. Double spiral-headed pin.

Pl. 16.3. Bhagwanpura. Protohistoric plan.

Pl. 16.4. Bhagwanpura. Platform in Subperiod IA.

Pl. 16.5. Bhagwanpura. Figurine.

Pl. 16.6. Bhagwanpura. Circular hut in Subperiod IB.

Pl. 16.7. Bhagwanpura. Structure in Subperiod IB.

Pl. 16.8. Bhagwanpura. Structure in Subperiod IB.

Pl. 16.9. Bhagwanpura. **PGW** in Subperiod IB.

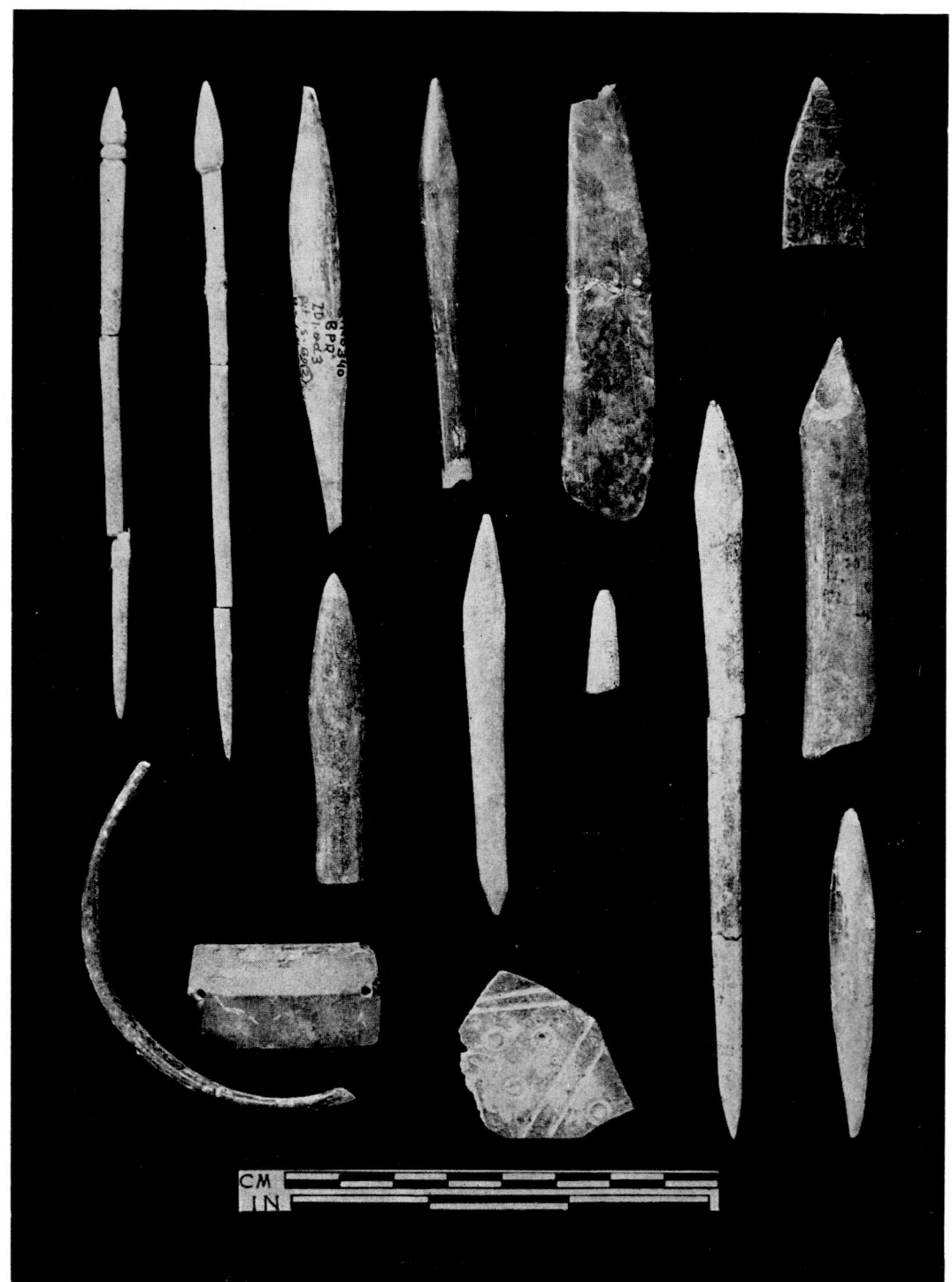

Pl. 16.10. Bhagwanpura. Small finds.

Pl. 16.11. Bhagwanpura. Baked bricks of Subperiod IB.

Pl. 16.12. Bhagwanpura. Burial of an adult.

Pl. 16.13. Bhagwanpura. Incised ram figurines.

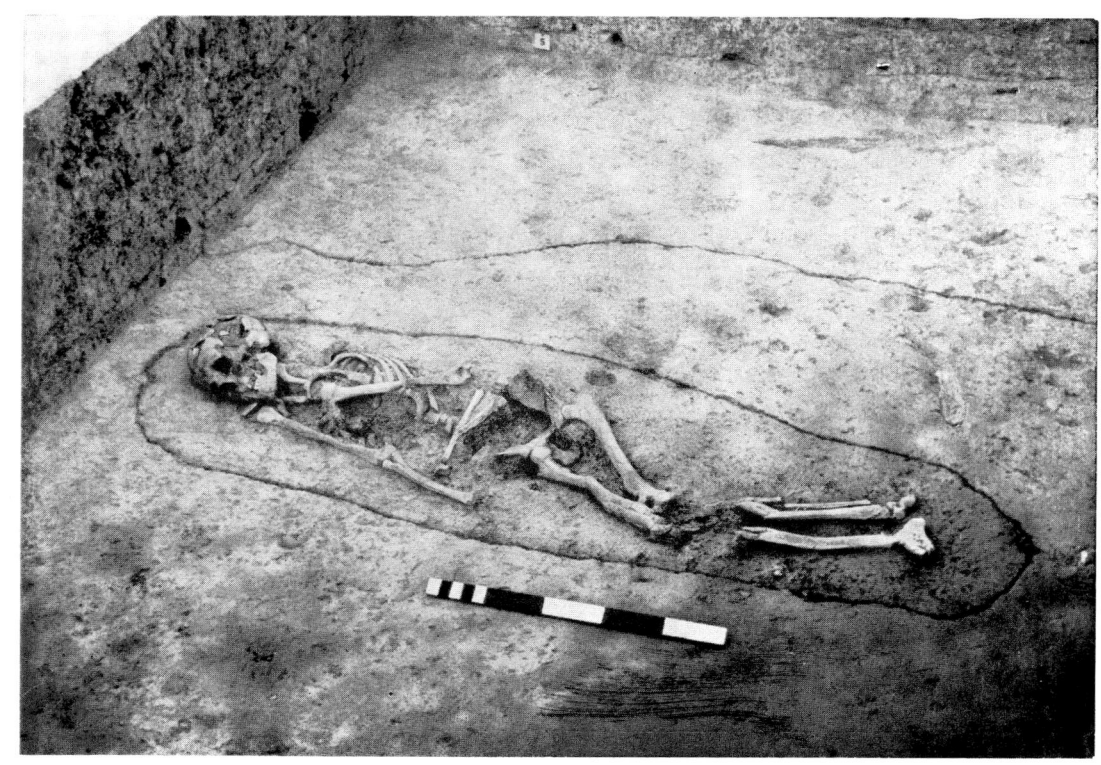

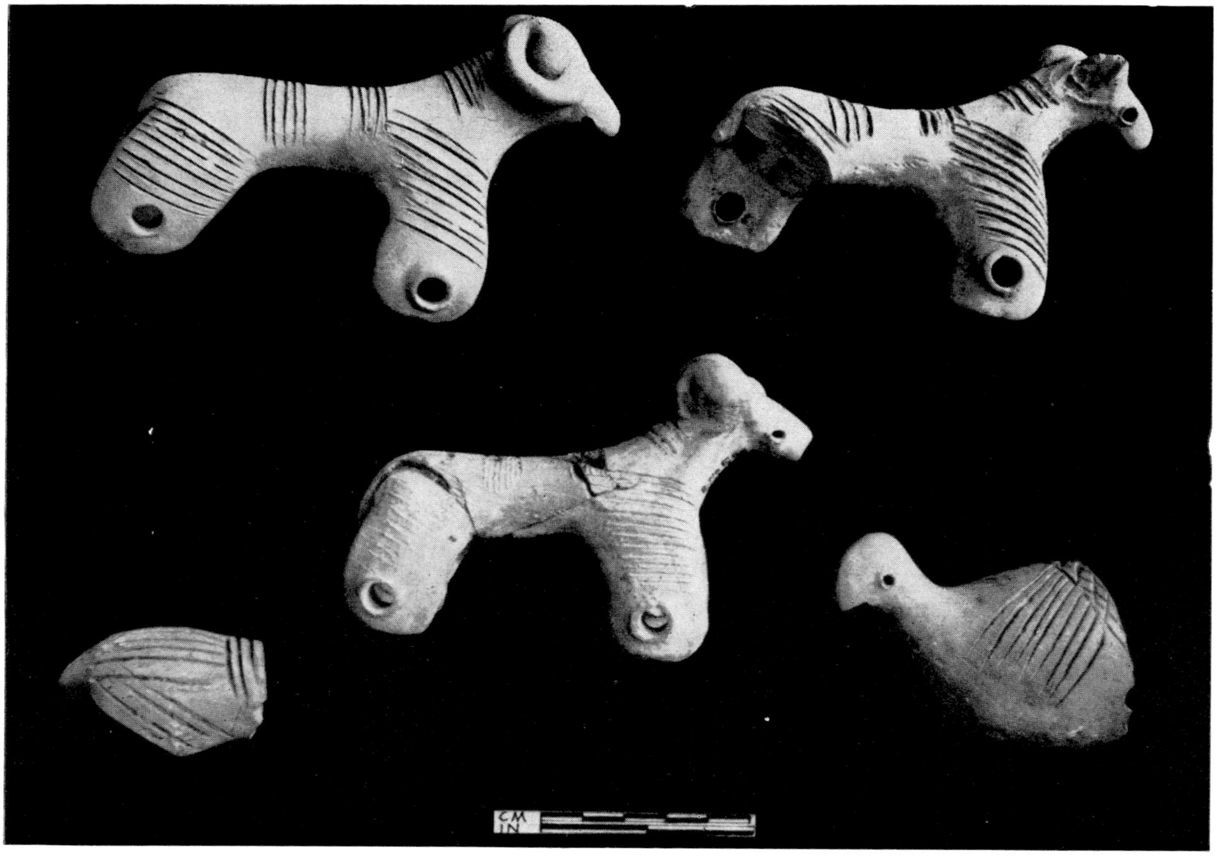

Pl. 16.14. Bhagwanpura. Incised ram figurine on wheels.

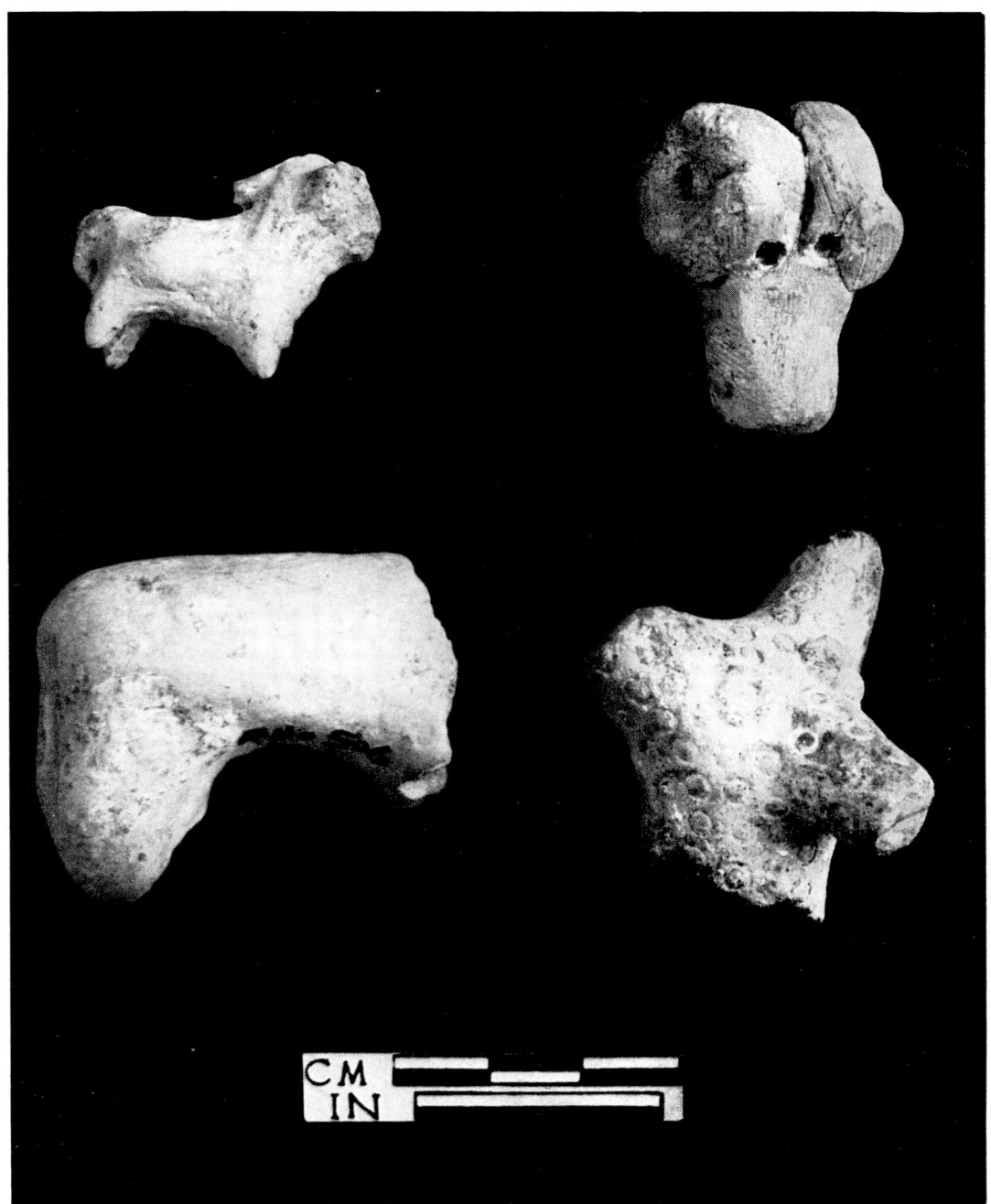

Pl. 16.15. Bhagwanpura. Ram figurines.

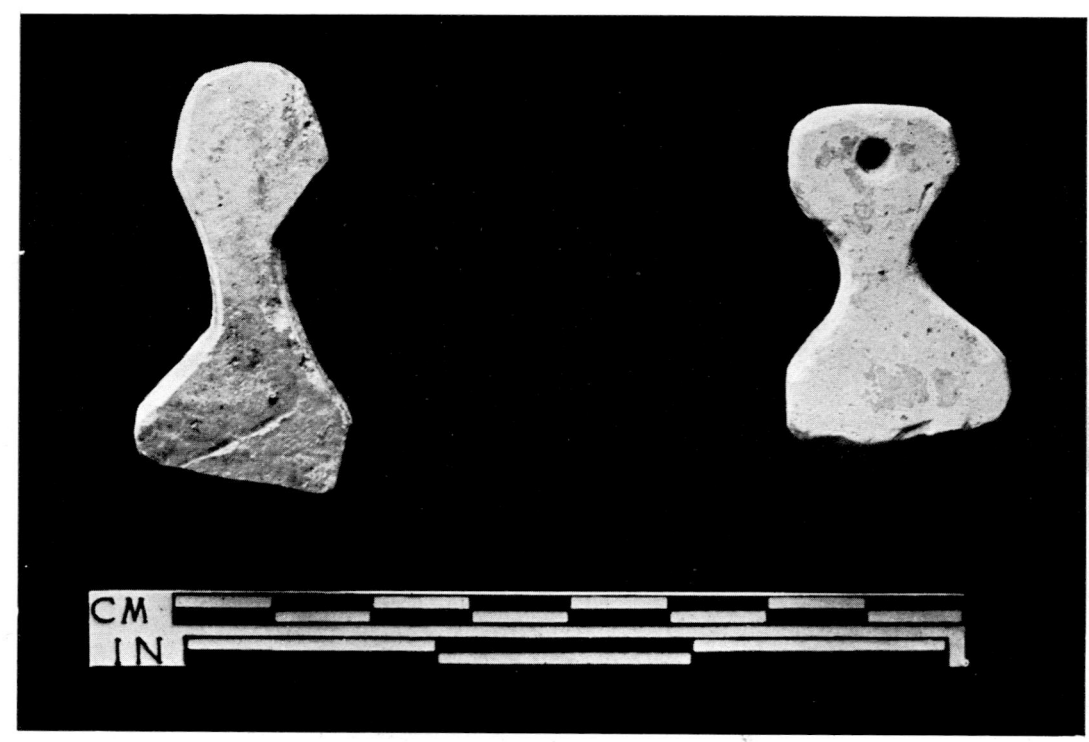

Pl. 16.16. Bhagwanpura. Mother goddess figurines.

Pl. 16.17. Dadheri. Stratigraphy with indications of huts.

Pl. 16.18. Dadheri. Painted and incised pot.

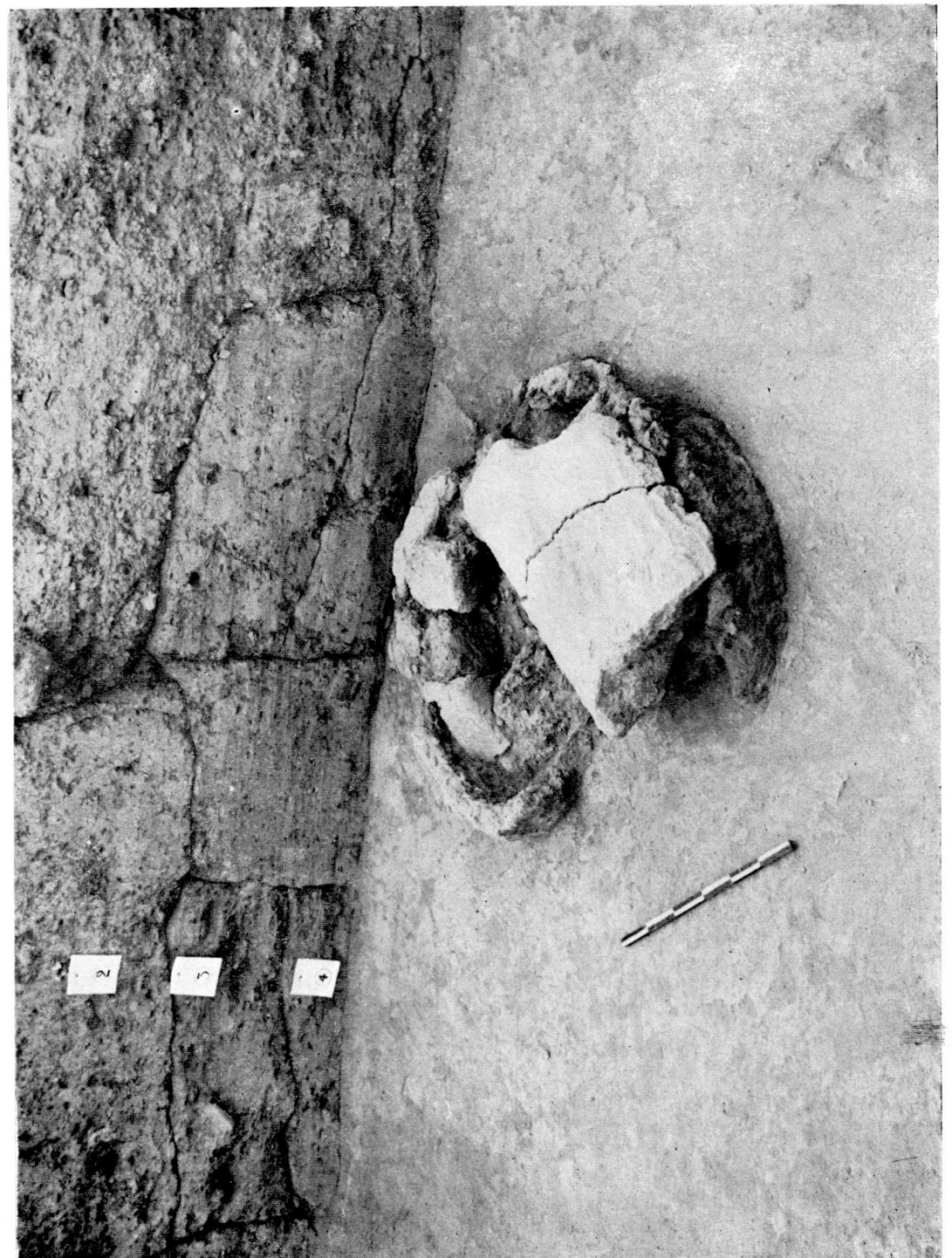

Pl. 16.19. Dadheri. Oval structure of burnt earth.

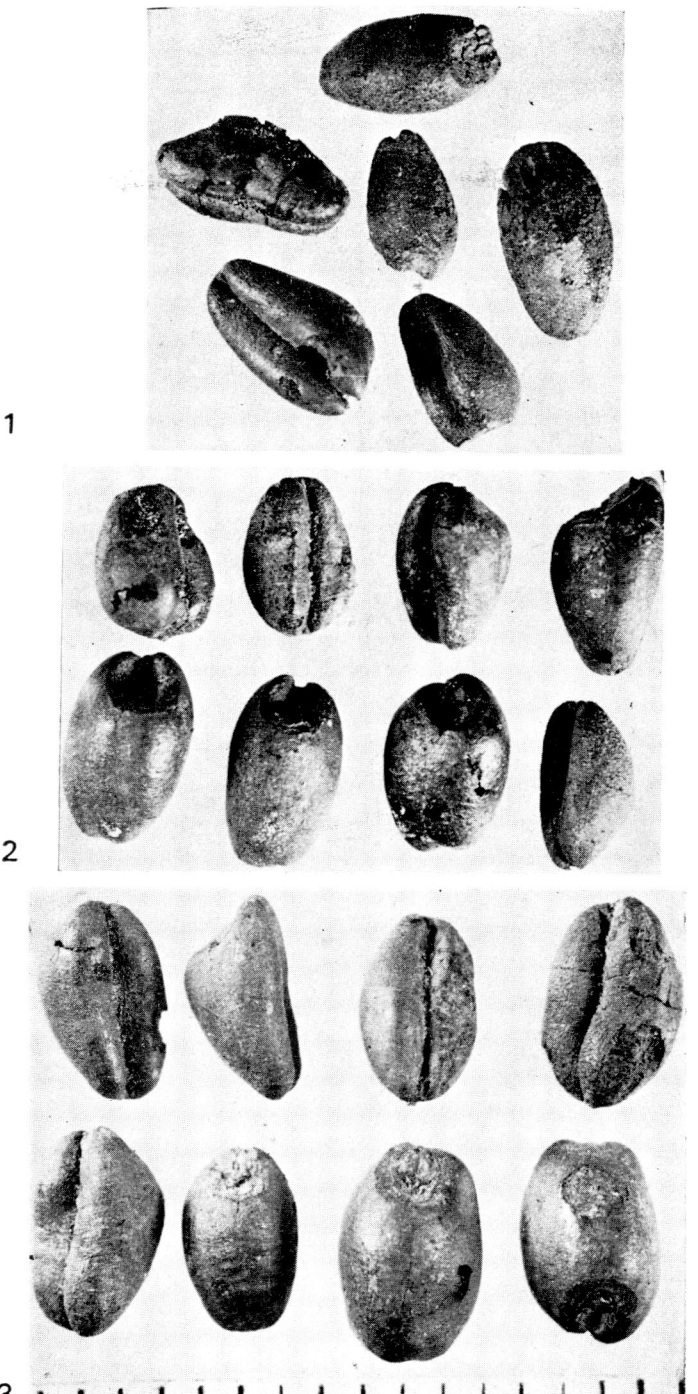

Pl. 18.1. *Trriticum sphaerococcum*, No. 1. From Mohenjodaro. Nos. 2, 3. From Chanhudaro.

Pl. 18.2. *Triticum compactum, vulgare* group. Nos. 1, 2. From Mohenjodaro. No. 3. From Chanhudaro.

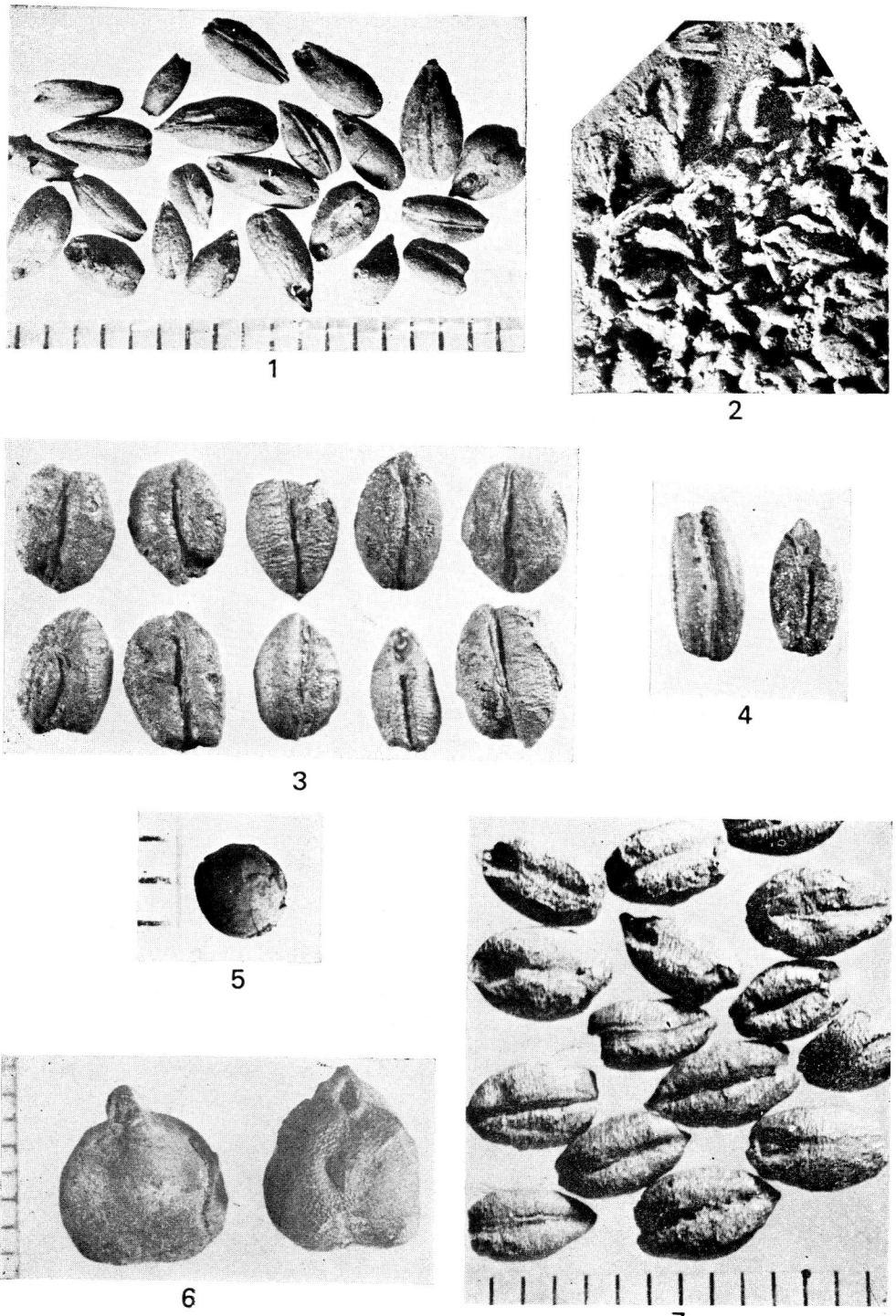

Pl. 18.3. No. 1. Hulled barley from Kalibangan. No. 2. Crystals of gypsum sticking to a potsherd from Kalibangan. Nos. 3, 7. Naked barley from Chanhudaro. No. 4. Hulled barley from Chanhudaro. No. 5. *Fisum arvense* (grass pea) from Kalibangan. No. 6. *Cicer arietinum* (chick pea) from Kalibangan.

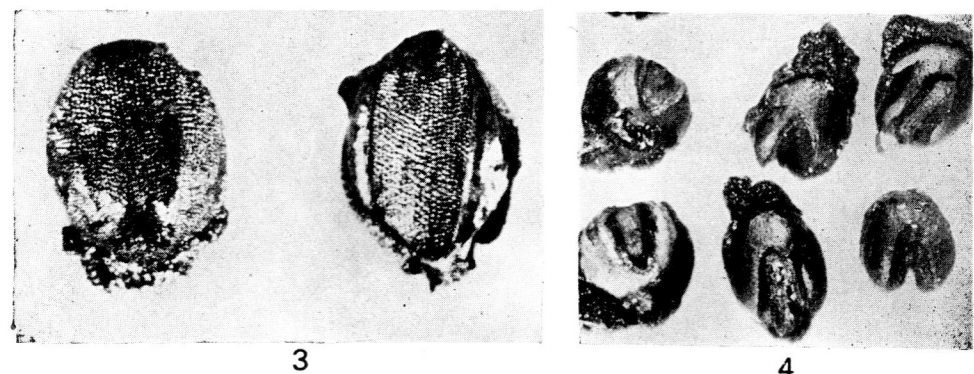

Pl. 18.4. No. 1. Grains of modern *Setaria italica*. No. 2. Spikelets of *Setaria* cf. *italica* from Surkotada. No. 3. Carbonized grains of *Setaria* cf. *italica* from Surkotada. No. 4. Carbonized seeds of *Eleusine* cf. *coracana* (ragi) from Surkotada.

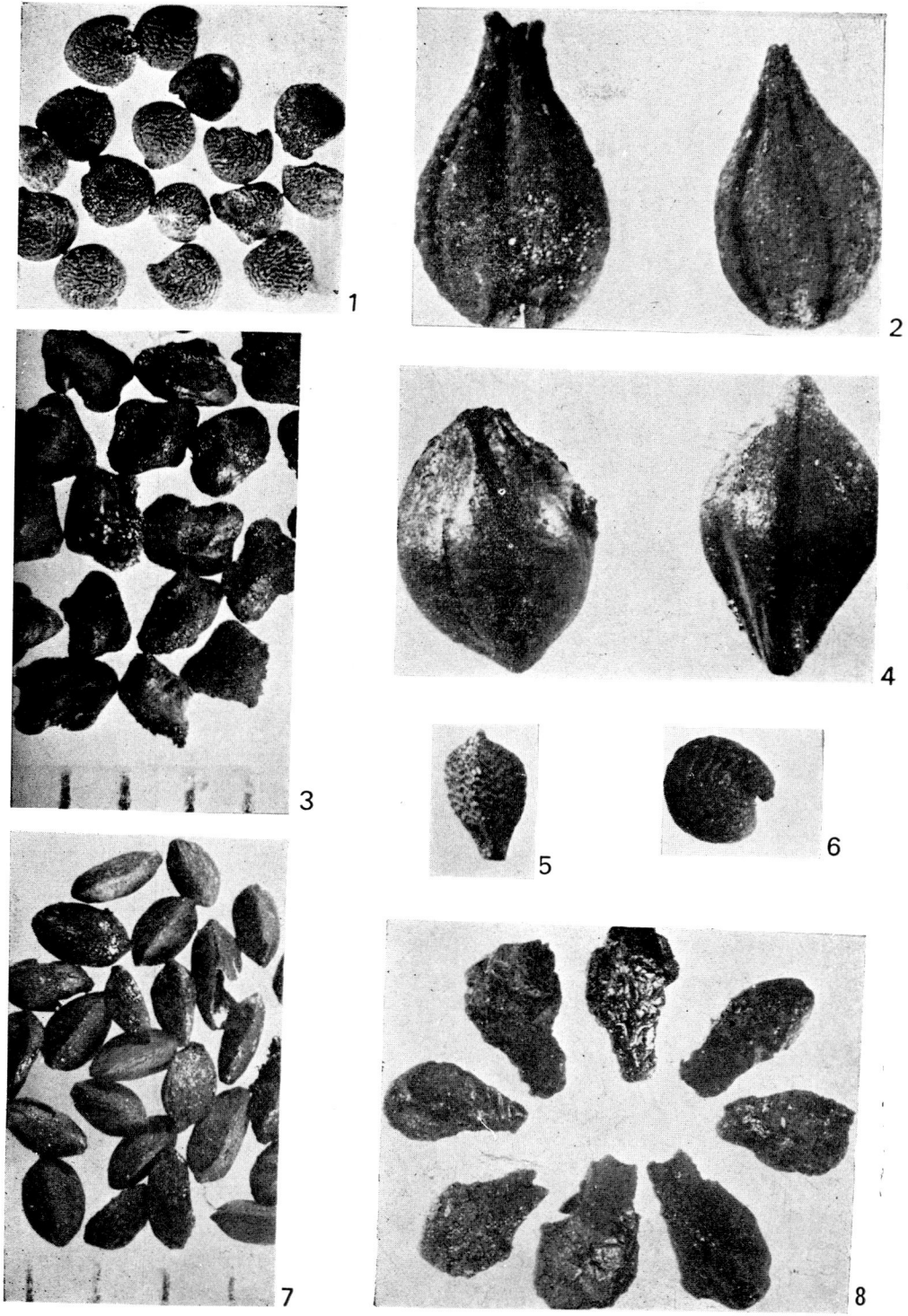

Pl. 18.5. No. 1 *Portulaca* sp. Nos. 2, 4. *Carex* sp. No. 3. *Euphorbia* sp. No. 5. Nuts of *Scirpus supinus*. No. 6. Unidentified. No. 7. *Polygonum* sp. No. 8. Wild grasses.

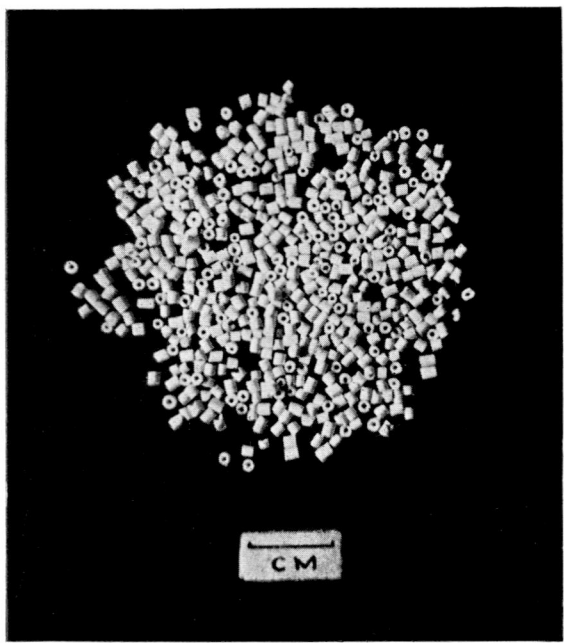

Pl. 21.1. Cleaned microbeads recovered from the Harappan site of Zekda.

Pl. 21.2. Evidence for the careful preservation of microbeads unearthed at Zekda. The beads, mixed with fine ash, were placed inside the miniature jar fitted with a cork-like, hollow, baked clay stopper and buried under a house floor.

Pl. 21.3. Preservation of the microbeads. The miniature pot in the center contained microbeads and ash. It was placed inside the larger pot, whose mouth was covered with a fitted lump of baked clay. The hoard was buried beneath a house floor.

Pl. 21.4. Loosening the stopper on the bead pot: careful dissolution of the lime encrustation.

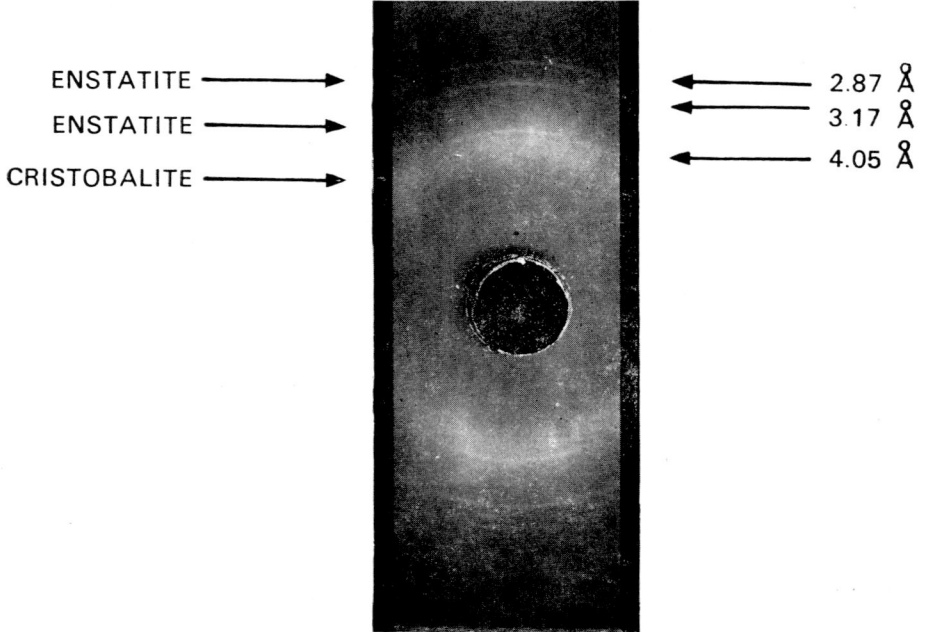

X-ray diffraction patterns obtained on a powdered sample of the beads

Pl. 21.5. X-ray diffraction patterns obtained from a powdered sample of the beads.

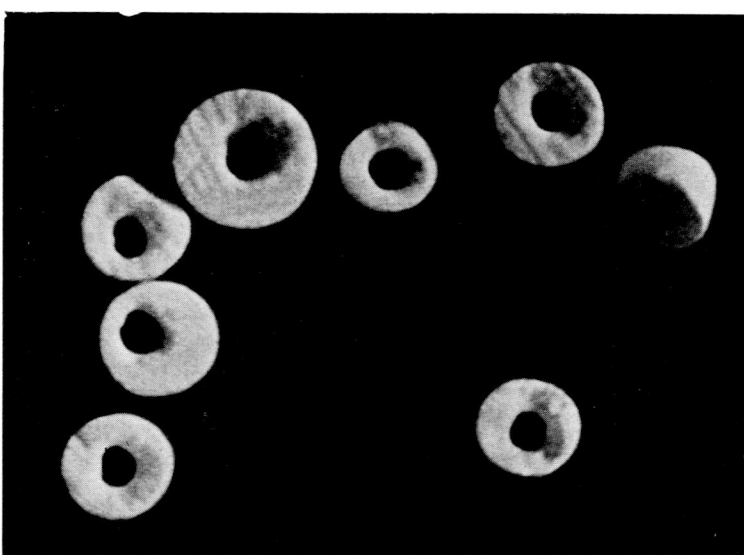

Pl. 21.6. Smooth, straight, even cut edges of the beads (magnified 15 times). This photograph shows that the beads were cut when soft; not after they were hardened and made brittle by baking.

Pl. 21.7. Furrow marks on the length of the beads (magnified 15 times). These striations show that the beads were manufactured by extruding the bead-forming pasty compound through small apertures.

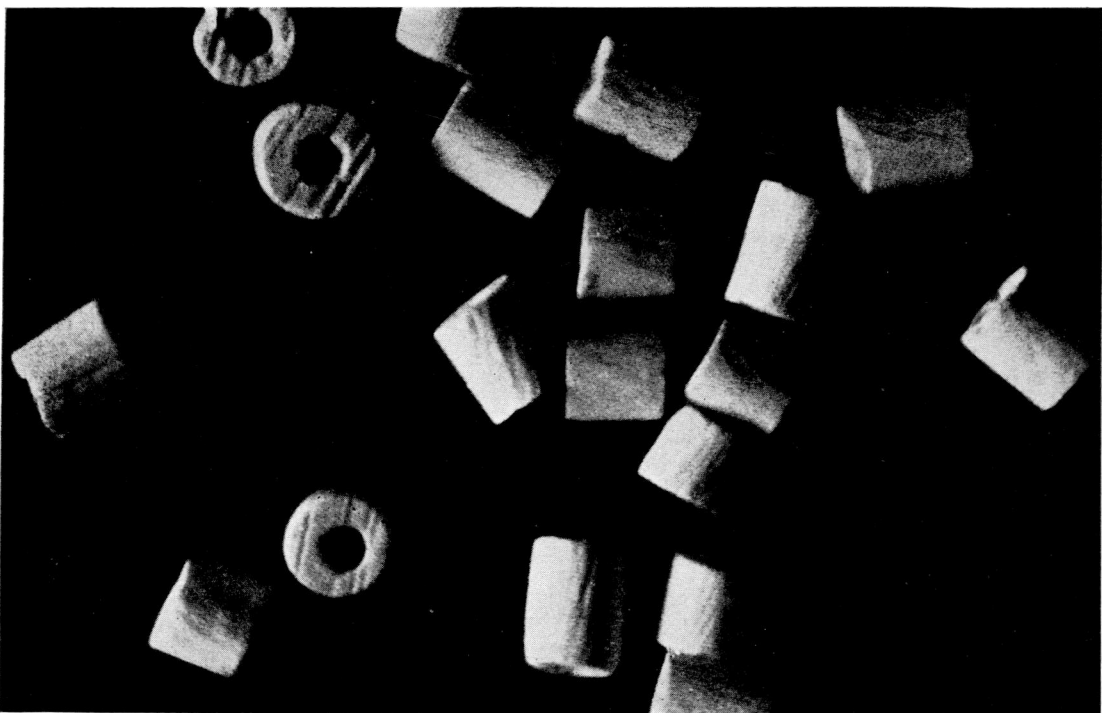

Pl. 24.1. Unfinished long barrel-cylinder beads from Chanhudaro.
Top: 36.1507; Bottom: 36.1564. Boston Museum of Fine Arts.

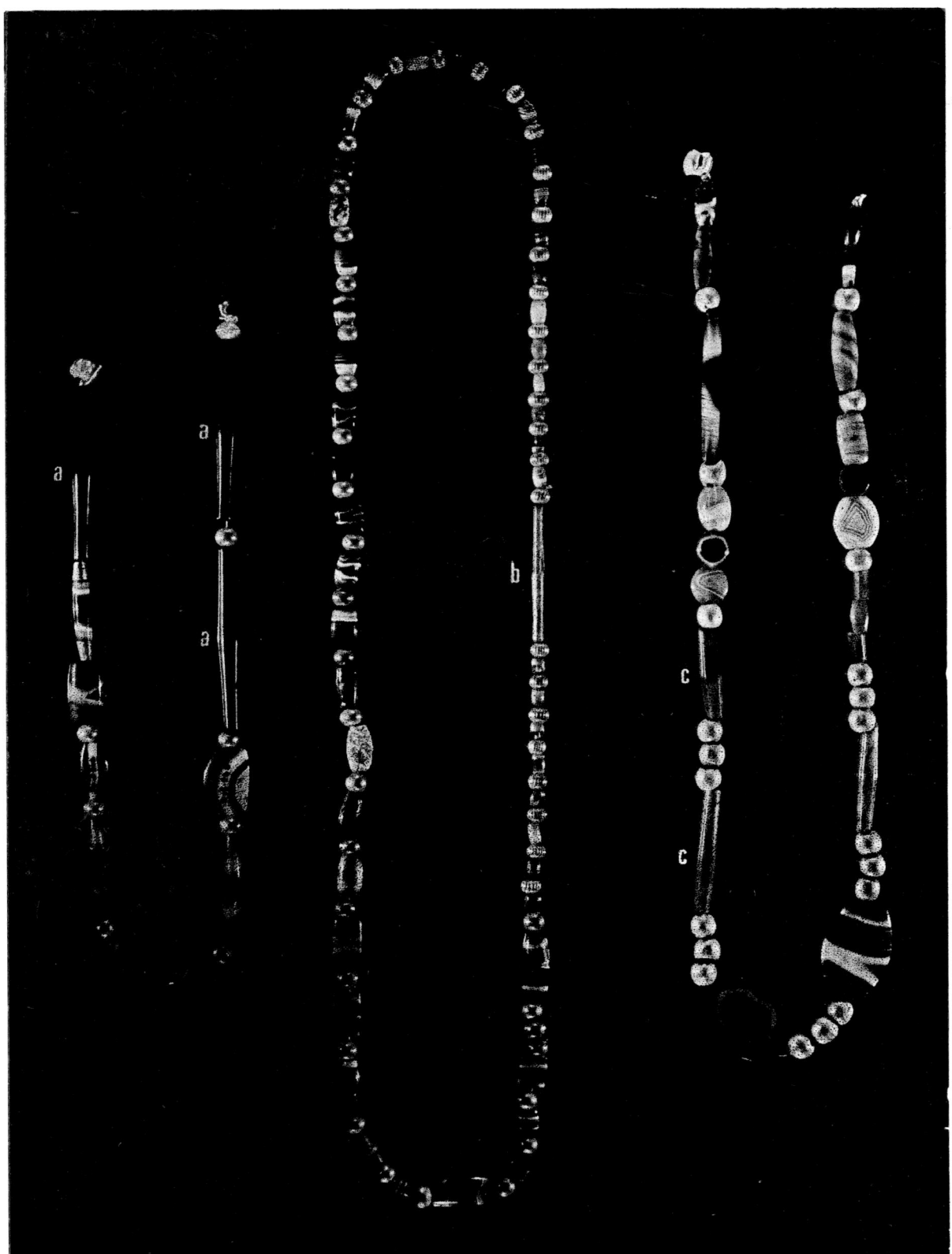

Pl. 24.2. Long barrel-cylinder beads from the Royal Graves of Ur. Akkadian Period. Bead 'b' is 6.4 centimeters in length.

Pl. 27.1. General view of the Kalibangan cemetery with the Citadel Mound in the background. Patches due to salt action indicate the location of graves.

Pl. 27.2. Kalibangan. Extended burial of a child.

Pl. 27.3. Kalibangan. Pot burial in a circular pit.

Pl. 27.4. Kalibangan. Rectangular grave pit containing only pottery.

Pl. 27.5. Kalibangan. A paralytic case.

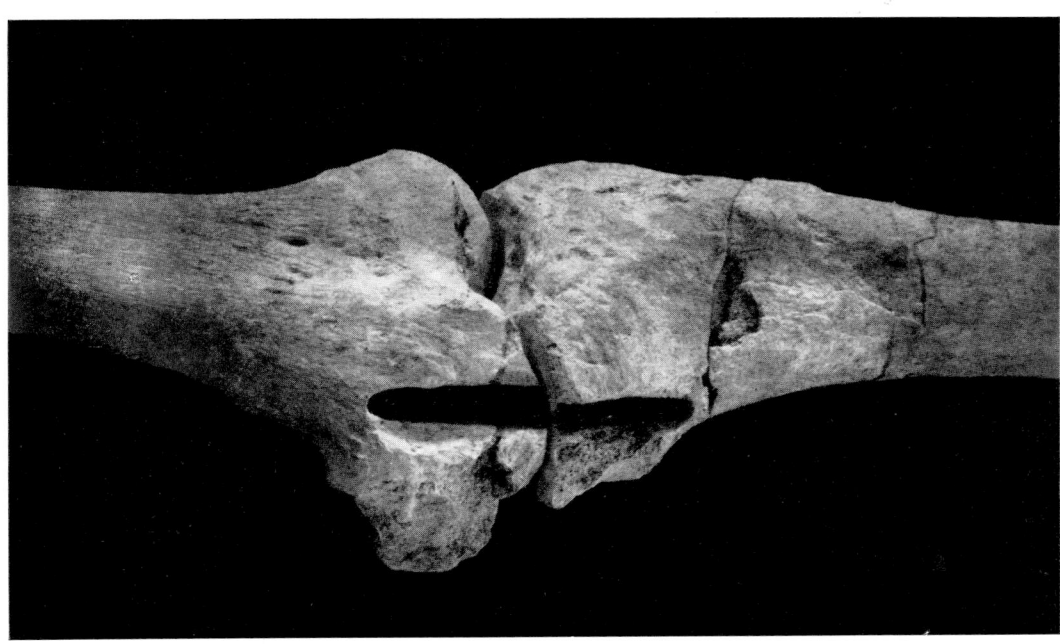

Pl. 27.7. Kalibangan. Deep gash in the knee region of a skeleton.

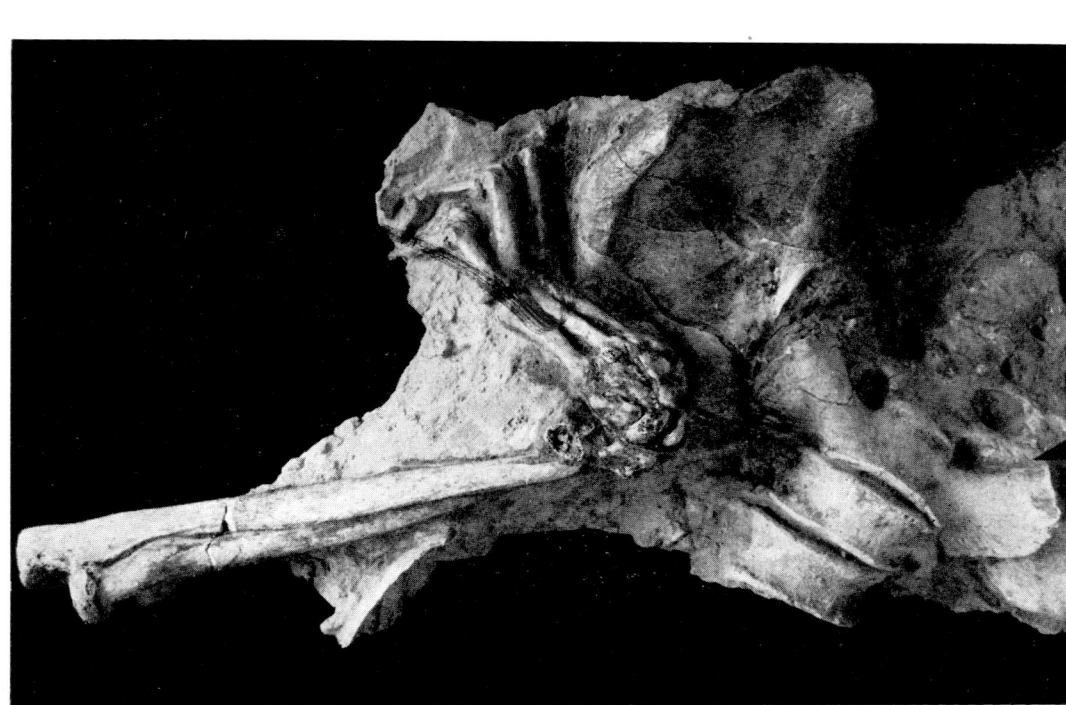

Pl. 27.6. Kalibangan. A crippled hand.

Pl. 35.1. Daimabad chariot and bulls.

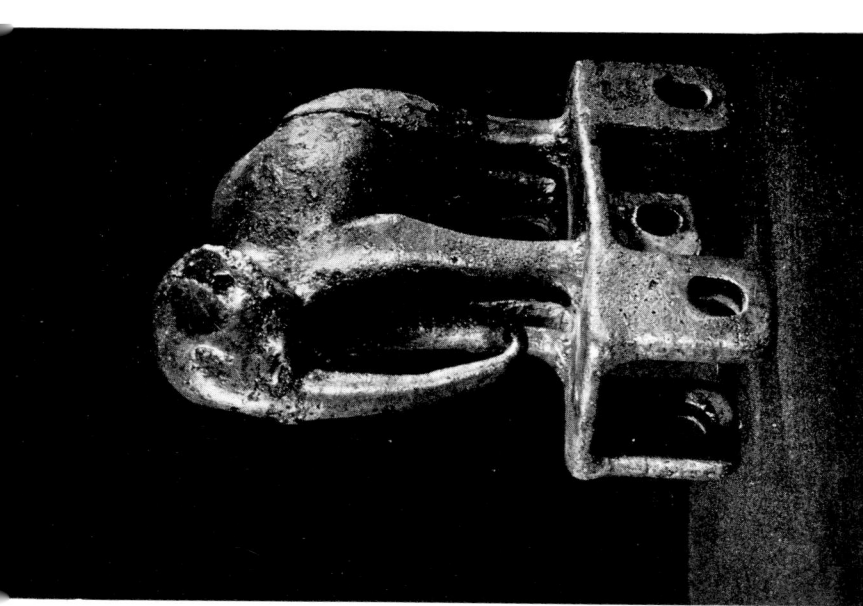

Pl. 35.3. Daimabad elephant.

Pl. 35.2. Daimabad. Detail of the human figure in the chariot.

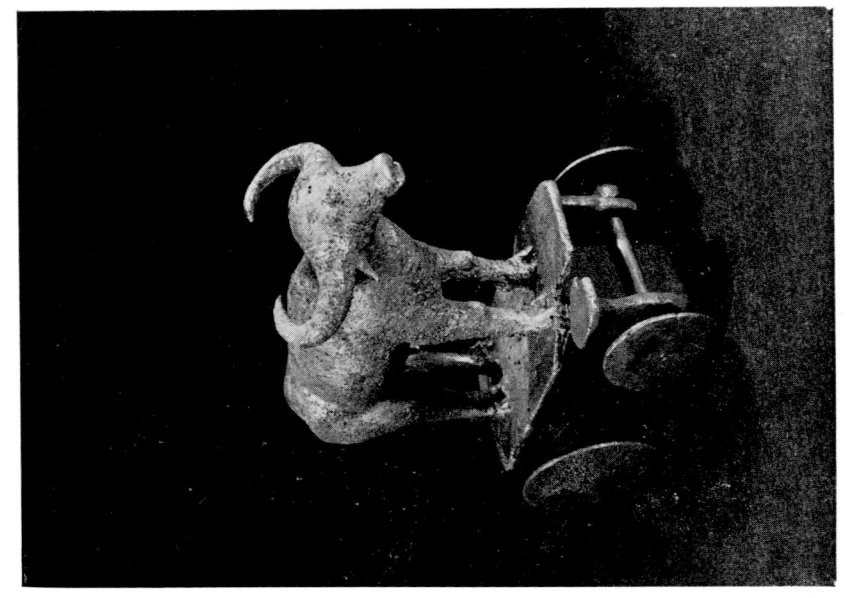

Pl. 35.5. Daimabad water buffalo

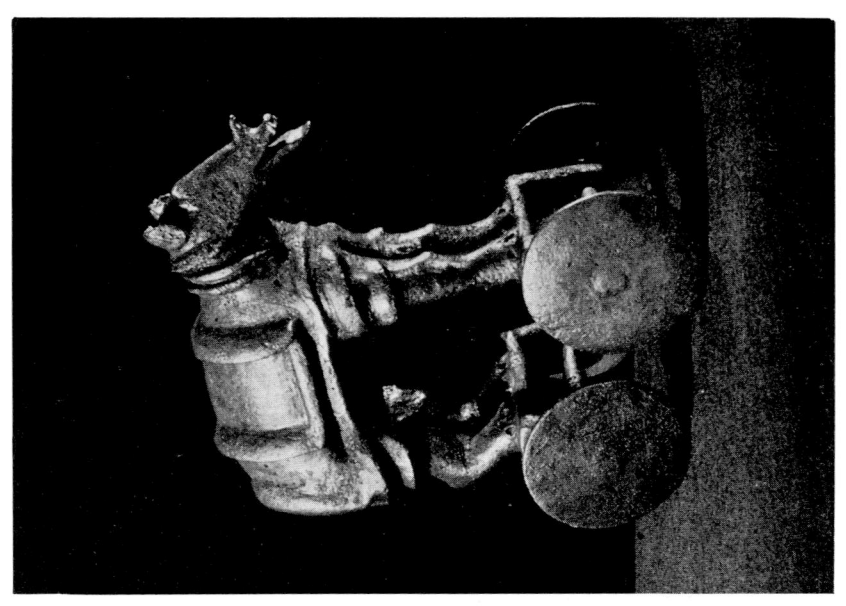

Pl. 35.4. Daimabad rhinoceros.

Pl. 39.1. Charles Masson's signature from Bamiyan.

Seals from Harappa.

C.

A.

B.

Full size.

Pl. 39.2. J.F. Fleet's photograph of seals from Harappa. 'A' is the original Cunningham seal.

Stupa mound, Muhen-jo-daro.

Pl. 39.3. The Stupa Mound at Mohenjodaro as photographed by R.D. Banerji.

Monastery—Muhen-jo-daro

Pl. 39.4. The monastery at Mohenjodaro as photographed by R.D. Banerji.

from layer two of Trench B, cut near the central part of the mound. The great care with which they preserved the beads at Zekda clearly shows how highly the Harappans valued them. At Chanhudaro a hoard of white microbeads was also found in a small pot (Mackay 1937: 12).

The stoppers covering the pots containing the beads recovered in the excavation at Zekda were found to be firmly sealed in the pots because of a superficial accumulation of calcium carbonate. Much care was therefore necessary when loosening the stoppers. In order to ensure that the solvent used to dissolve the carbonate accumulation near the mouth of the pots did not seep into the vessel, whose contents were then not known, the space between the lip and the stopper was covered with a layer of cotton wool. This was kept moist with drops of dilute hydrochloric acid, added at regular intervals (Pl. 21.4). The acid slowly dissolved the carbonate accumulation. When the evolution of carbon dioxide ceased, the used cotton wool was replaced with a fresh layer and the experiment was repeated until the stoppers became loose and could be easily detached.

When the contents of the pots were emptied on plateglass, thousands of microbeads were found carefully embedded in fine ash. There were also two gold beads, probably to be used at the center of the strings. The microbeads were separated from the ash using a set of sieves. The two pots together yielded 109.48 grams of beads and 206.53 grams of ash. Bead-ash ratio was nearly one to two. This was probably deliberate. Ash had apparently been put into the pots along with the beads to ensure that the tiny objects would not be completely scattered if the pots broke. In a one gram sample there were 310 beads. The Zekda pots therefore had approximately 34,000 beads.

EXAMINATION OF THE BEADS

The beads were first washed in dilute hydrochloric acid. Several washings in the acid and distilled water made them clean, even inside the perforation. The clean beads are stark white. They were dried in an oven at 110°C for 24 hours. After drying their hardness was determined. All the heads that were examined ranged between six and seven on the Moh Scale. Their specific gravity could not be determined accurately since it was impossible to drive out all the air bubbles trapped within the perforation when the beads were immersed in water.

A 100 milligram sample of the beads was taken from each of the two pots. These were fused and used for quantitative chemical analysis. The results of the analysis is given in Table 21.1. This shows that the bead material is nearly 60 percent silica, 30 percent magnesia, six percent alumina, less than two percent lime and less than one percent of iron oxide. This composition is interesting.

The chemical test shows that the beads were not made from pure talc (4 MgO 5 SiO_2 H_2O) which is a hydrated silicate of magnesium. If the beads had been made of talc, they would not have contained six percent alumina. The presence of alumina suggests the presence of Kaolinite in the composition of the original material used in the production of the beads. Kaolinite (Al_2O_3 2 SiO_2 2H_2O) is a hydrated silicate of aluminium. It is one of the pure forms of clay. From the percentage composition of the beads, the initial inference was that the Harappan beadmakers deliberately mixed talc and Kaolinite in the ratio of five to one. However, we soon found out that such a material occurred naturally with the metamorphosed ultrabasic rocks. The material is known as talcose steatite. Heron (1953: 371-72, 389) records the occurrence of a long discontinuous schistbelt, rich in various forms of steatite, including talcose steatite, within the Aravalli Hills. This starts from Ambaji in Sabarkanta District, near Zekda, and extends towards the Punjab through Sehore, Ajmer and Jaipur Districts in Rajasthan. We therefore believe that the Harappan beadmakers used the naturally occurring, locally available, talcose steatite as their raw material for producing white microbeads.

To obtain a proof for the above observation, an X-ray diffraction analysis of a powdered sample of the beads was carried out. The X-ray diffraction patterns (Pl. 21.5) revealed the presence of silica in the form of cristobalite and anhydrous magnesium silicate in the form of enstatite. Both were faintly marked on the X-ray plate due to their poor crystallinity. Alumina appeared to be represented by extremely faint lines because of its poor crystallinity coupled with the very small proportion in the sample. Nevertheless, the results are of tremendous value.

When talc is heated below 800°C no appreciable change should be noted by microscopic examination. The first noticeable change occurs in the neighborhood of 850°C, where talc decomposes, giving off its water of crystallization and forms cristobalite and enstatite and becomes hard in the process (Insley and Frechette 1955: 80). We have found that steatite when heated at 900°C for two hours improves its hardness from one to seven on the Moh Scale.

Steatite is a soft stone with a soapy feel. It is therefore known as soapstone. Talc, the chief component mineral of steatite has a hardness of one on the Moh Scale. It can be easily carved. Harappans used it to make many objects which included some of their seals and larger beads. The above analysis shows that they used talcose steatite for making microbeads.

Now the question is: how were these minute beads made? Mackay submitted the white microbeads recovered from Chanhudaro to Beck for their examination in 1936, and commented on the technique of their manufacture: "After carefully examining a modern watchmaker's drill which is capable of drilling holes of 0.01 inch (0.25 millimeters) diameter, it is difficult to believe that either the drill or the bead could have been held by the hand, so I suggest that some form of lathe or jig must have been used" (Mackay 1937: 10). However, it is difficult to visualize the possibility of such fine and precise lathes or jigs within the framework of known Harappan technical infrastructure. The instruments used in the manufacture of the beads necessarily had to be much simpler.

The hardness of the beads (six to seven on the Moh Scale) shows that they were baked at high temperature. The cut edges of the beads on examination at 15 power magnification were found to be even, almost smooth and slightly oblique (Pl. 21.6). If the beads were cut after they were baked, the hard brittle material would have produced rough, uneven, corrugated edges. It therefore appears that the beads were cut before they were hardened by baking.

The sides of the beads when examined under the microscope, were found to be furrowed along their length (Pl. 21.7). These striation marks appear to be slightly twisted. When we examined a few joined beads, that is, two or three beads joined together, cut but not separated, we noticed that the striation marks ran continuously from one bead to the other. Though the beads appeared to the naked eye to be regular in their cylindrical shape, under the microscope they were clearly faceted. Their perforations were also faceted. These observations are most interesting. For, where two beads are found almost joined, with their striation marks coinciding, it appears that they must have followed one another through an aperture. In other words, it appears that the beads were manufactured by extruding the forming material through an aperture(s). The beads are faceted because the nearly circular apertures through which they were extruded were also faceted. They are striated along their length because the apertures were corrugated. The striations have a twist because the composition forming the beads appears to have passed through the aperture under some pressure. F.A. Bannister and G.F. Claringbull, the other two scientists to whom Mackay referred the Chanhudaro beads for their examination in 1936, also considered their manufacture by extrusion. But they did not think it possible because they were not able to visualize how tubes rather than solid rods were produced by such an extrusion process (Mackay 1937: 11).

Table 21.1. Percentage composition of Harappan microbeads recovered from Zekda

Sample No.	SiO_2	MgO	Al_2O_3	CaO	H_2O_3	Total
1	60.80	30.76	5.95	1.58	0.60	99.69
2	59.75	31.42	5.80	1.88	0.77	99.62

CONCLUSION

From the foregoing discussion it has been seen that the beads were made from talcose steatite. They were cut before they were hardened by baking. Their faceted surfaces and the striation marks along their length indicate that they were produced by squeezing a compound under pressure through apertures. This compound appears to have been in a paste form. If it was in a solid form the pressure needed to extrude it through very small openings would have been very high. There is no evidence to believe that the Harappans had the technology necessary to produce such high pressures.

We therefore suggest, keeping in view the known Harappan technological infrastructure, the following simple process as a plausible method for the manufacture of these microbeads. All that is needed is a circular copper or bronze disc with a few one-millimeter diameter perforations near the center. Each perforation must have a copper or bronze wire of 0.5 millimeter diameter with one end soldered or riveted near the perforation and the other end bent and positioned to be at the center of the perforation as shown in figure 21.2. The disc has fine holes at its periphery which allow it to be stitched all around to a

Fig. 21.2. A plausible device that could have been used by the Harappans to manufacture steatite microbeads.

well-knit piece of cloth. If into this device a paste of finely ground talcose steatite is put and the cloth gathered together and squeezed by hand, talcose steatite paste emerges through the perforations as tubes. These soft tubes can be cut as they emerge, at quick intervals, to convert them into microbeads.

Three skillful persons are necessary to do the job: one for squeezing the paste, the second for cutting the soft tubes and the third for collecting the soft microbeads, over a layer of fine ash on a dish, to avoid damaging them. The beads can then be baked at 900 to 1000°C in a kiln to harden them. We have adequate evidence to believe that Harappans had the necessary infrastructure to attempt such a process.

They had copper and bronze discs. There is even evidence of perforated examples (Mackay 1938: Pl. CXXI). They knew both soldering and rivetting. They sometimes soldered the rivet by pouring molten copper or bronze around its base for additional firmness (Marshall 1931: 489). They had cloth (Marshall 1931: 585-86). The soft tubes appear to have been cut by a thin, sharp device to convert them into microbeads. A simple device to serve this purpose is a horse hair. Harappans had horses (Marshall 1931: 653-54; Joshi 1972: 135). The fact that they could melt copper at 1080°C, clearly shows that they had suitable kilns or open fires with a forced draught to raise the temperature of the fire to 1200°C so as to bake the beads at 1000°C.

It appears probable therefore, that the Harappan microbead makers produced these beautiful, tiny beads by means of a simple process. But it was, nevertheless, a laborious, painstaking, unhurried job. Like the other ancient Indian craftsmen who produced good quality metal objects or ceramics (Hegde 1973: 416-21; 1975: 187-90; 1979: 141-55), the Harappan microbead makers also spared no pains in their efforts to achieve a high level of excellence in their work.

ACKNOWLEDGMENT

The authors wish to thank Professor R.N. Mehta and Professor S.S. Merh for useful discussions.

BIBLIOGRAPHY

Ghosh, A., editor, 1967
 Ajanta Murals. Delhi: Archaeological Survey of India.
Hegde, K.T.M., 1973
 A model for Understanding Ancient Indian Iron Metallurgy. *Man* 8: 416-21.
Hegde, K.T.M., 1975
 The Painted Grey Ware of India. *Antiquity* 49: 187-90.
Hegde, K.T.M., 1979
 Analysis of Ancient Indian Delux Wares. *Archaeo-Physika* 10: 141-55.
Heron, A.M., 1953
 Geology of Central Rajasthan. Geological Survey of India Memoir 79 (1). Calcutta: Government of India.
Insley, H. and Frechette van Derck, 1955
 Microscopy of Ceramics and Cements. New York: Academic Press.
Joshi, J.P., 1972
 Exploration in Kutch and Excavations at Surkotada and New Light on Harappan Migration. *Journal of the Oriental Institute, Baroda University,* 12: 98-144.
Mackay, E.J.H., 1937
 Bead Making in Ancient Sind. *Journal of the American Oriental Society* 57: 1-15.
Mackay, E.J.H., 1938
 Further Excavations at Mohenjodaro. 2 vols. Delhi: Government of India.
Marshall, Sir John, editor, 1931
 Mohenjodaro and the Indus Civilization. 3 vols. London: Arthur Probsthain.
Parikh, R.T., 1978
 Archaeology of Banaskantha District. Ph.D. dissertation, Department of Archaeology and Ancient History, M.S. University of Baroda.
Rao, S.R., 1973
 Lothal and the Indus Civilization. Bombay: Asia Publishing House.

MARCIA FENTRESS

22. From Jhelum to Yamuna: City and Settlement in the Second and Third Millennium B.C.

SETTLEMENT patterns around Harappa are unique in the ancient Near East and Indus Valley. On maps of Harappa's greater hinterland showing site distribution from the Pre-Harappan to the Painted Gray Ware Period, the northern Indus City appears to exist in a near vacuum. In an area which has been subjected to much field work and archaeological attention, this is a very unusual settlement situation. Other early urban cities, Mohenjodaro, Kish, Nippur, and Susa all have closely connected networks of towns and villages around them. The questions I explore here are: Why does this settlement pattern exist and what does it tell about the interaction and support networks necessary for the existence of a major city? Further, what can it tell about Harappa's function in the greater Indus Civilization?

Harappa is central to a large, well-watered plain surrounded on three sides by mountain ranges bearing varied and fabulous resources (Figs. 22.1 to 22.3). At a distance of only 300 to 400 kilometers to the west, north and east lie the Sulaiman Range and the Himalayas. The great plains which stretch from the Jhelum to the Yamuna are of one piece, environmentally speaking. Endowed with six major rivers—the Jhelum, the Chenab, the Ravi, the Sutlej, the Beas and the Yamuna—the plains also have predictable rainfall ranging between 20 and 70 centimeters per year. To the west of the Jhelum rise the Potwar Plateau, the Salt Range and the Thal desert—very different areas from Harappa's immediate hinterland. To the east of the Yamuna, begins the Gangetic Basin, subtly but clearly different from the Great Punjab Plain, which is heavily influenced by the desert and the dry and bare Aravalli rock ridges to the south.

The only two sites in the immediate vicinity of Harappa which can be thought of as contemporary to it are the Mature Indus site of Chak Purbane Syal (Vats 1940), 15 miles to the southeast and Jalilpur (Mughal 1972), an Early Harappan site 30 miles to the southwest. Far away to the west and northwest beyond the Indus are a few Harappan and Early Harappan sites in the Gomal and Taxila areas. Settlements well to the east of Harappa number about 50 Harappan and 36 Pre-Harappan.[1] These appear to be concentrated in three areas (Fig. 22.1): along the Ghaggar River system through Ganganagar, Hissar, Sangrur, Karnal and Patiala Districts, as well as up the Drishadvati River Valley through Hissar, Jind and Karnal Districts, and along the upper Sutlej River through Amritsar, Jullundur, Ludhiana and Ropar Districts (Bisht 1976, 1978, in press; Dikshit 1968, 1977, 1979; Ghosh 1952; Pande 1977). About 200 kilometers south and west of Harappa along the old Hakra River on the Pakistan side are 32 Pre-Harappan, 41 Early Harappan and 166 Mature Harappan sites between Fort Abbas and Derawar (Mughal 1980).

Late Harappan sites in the east number about 90 (Fig. 22.2) concentrated along the upper Sutlej, Drishadvati and Ghaggar-Sarasvati. In no case are they found further south or west of Hissar District in Haryana, and some are found in the direction of the upper Beas in Amritsar and Gurdaspur Districts. On the Hakra side, Late Harappan sites—defined as Cemetery H—are concentrated to the southwest of

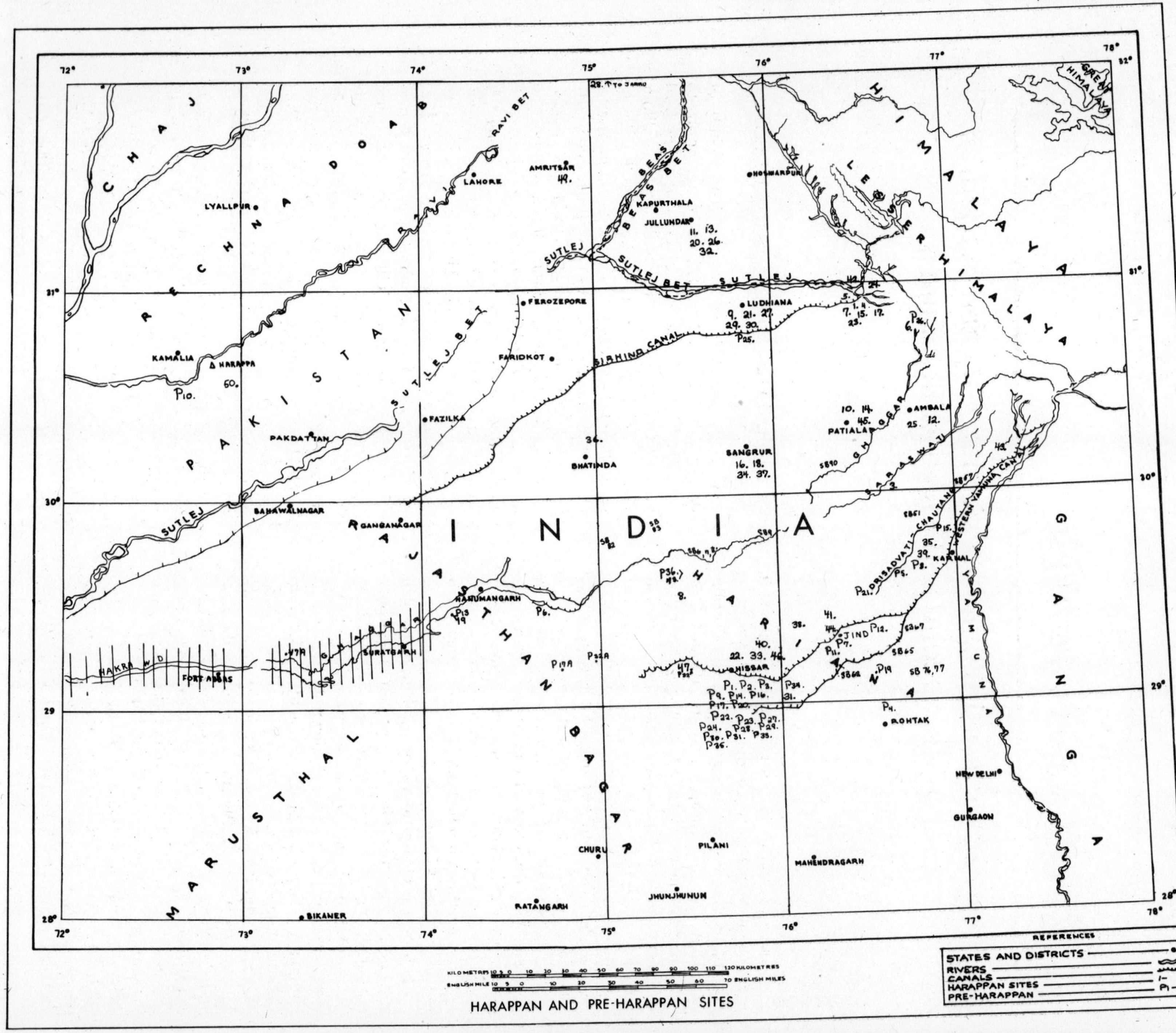

Fig. 22.1. Harappan and Pre-Harappan sites.

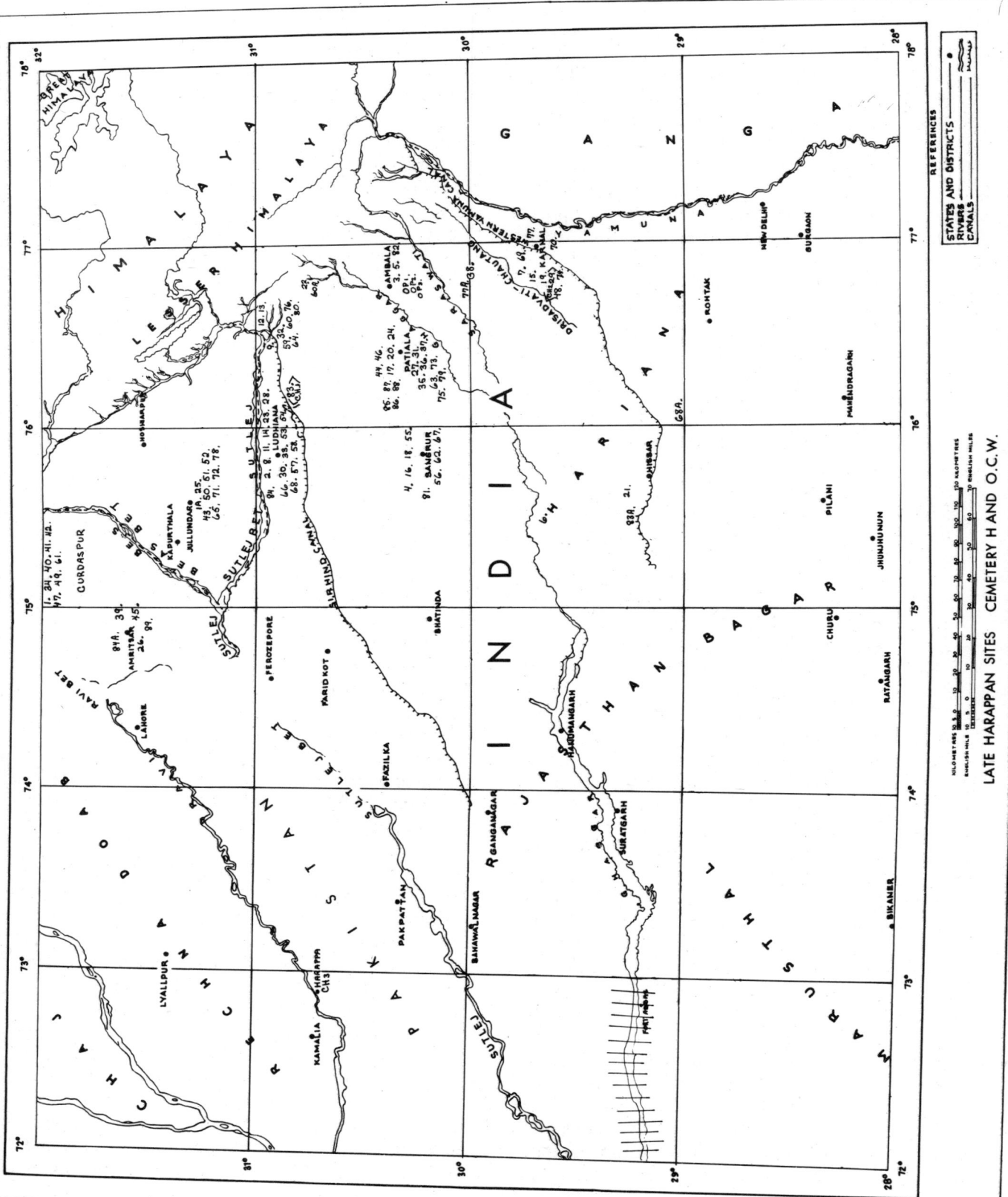

Fig. 22.2. Late Harappan, Cemetery H and OCP sites.

Harappa in the Derawar area, and number about 72 (Sharma 1973, 1976, in press; Suraj Bhan 1969, 1973, 1976, in press).

Painted Gray Ware is most numerous in the east (Fig. 22.3) with about 180 sites, heavily concentrated along the upper reaches of the Sarasvati-Drishadvati in Patiala, Ambala and Kurukshetra districts. Some are found in Ludhiana-Jullundur along the upper Sutlej and some in the lower Ghaggar from Hanumangarh to Anupgarh. Only 10 are found in the Hakra region and these west of Fort Abbas. Altogether some 650 sites have been found between the Jhelum and Yamuna spanning some two millenia (Stein 1942; Tripathi 1975; Joshi 1977).

Outside the plains area, on the upper Chenab in Jammu, a Late Harappan site—Manda has been found which also has Gray Ware of the kind associated elsewhere with PGW. Because of yet another Gray Ware (thick burnished) found at this site, it has been suggested that there were links with the Swat and Kashmir Valleys. Ties to the Gandhara Grave Culture and Burzahom II may be confirmed with further field work (Khazanchi and Dikshit 1980).[2]

Prime agricultural land around Harappa is found immediately northeast of the site between an old bed of the Ravi and the present Ravi. The area is lowlying land and could have been irrigated by flow irrigation through old *bundhs* of the river. The Kamalia Plain immediately across the Ravi is well watered by a large hill *nai* flowing down from the high ground of the Rechna *doab* and by lowlying *jhils* or *dhands* which retain water much of the year. These two areas taken together provide almost 6600 square kilometers of immediately available farm land for Harappa thus precluding any necessity for dependence on a wide ranging network of agricultural villages for its food needs (Fentress 1976).

That the two major cities had distinctly different access to stone, mineral and exotic resources is clear. Elsewhere I have put forth a dynamic model for internal and external trade based on resource access and exchange systems in the central Indus (Fentress 1978). Harappa's natural hinterland, comprising the Sulaiman Range, the outer Himalayas, the eastern *Doab* and northern Rajasthan was a much richer and more diverse area than the hinterland to which Mohenjodaro was central. Mohenjodaro had to extend its procurement systems well beyond its own region for metal and mineral resources. But Harappa had access to diverse and rich resources almost within its own geographic region. On the other hand, Mohenjodaro could take advantage of three major trade routes to the west: the Arabian Sea, southern Baluchistan and the Bolan Pass. Thus it seems very possible that Harappa functioned primarily as a trade center for the collection of hard-to-get resources from its diverse hinterland and for transhipment of these resources down the river to the capital and premier foreign trade center of Mohenjodaro.

A further observation bearing on an explanation for the settlement patterns around Harappa concerns the greater diversity in type, motif, and style of artifacts at Harappa as compared to Mohenjodaro. Previous work describes in detail these differences (Fentress 1976, 1978) so several significant traits are only summarized here:

Harappa does not conform to the pattern of the two mounds, with the high mound or citadel isolated on the west and totally separated from the lower city. On the contrary, its layout is in a rough "L" shape with the small F mound at the top of the "L," the high AB mound in the middle and the G mound forming the base. In looking at its artifacts, much more internal variation is apparent in several ways at Harappa than at Mohenjodaro. For instance, among the human figurines the percentage of male to female is much more balanced at Harappa, while at Mohenjodaro the figurines are predominantly female. The seals of Harappa include types not found at Mohenjodaro and the variety of motifs and designs is also greater. Harappa, on the seal impressions and miniatures, shows many diverse small animals which do not appear at Mohenjodaro at all. Vats, the excavator, states quite clearly that Harappa has all of the pottery types found at Mohenjodaro in addition to several other unique types and shapes. Two types of animal figurines not present at Mohenjodaro but found at Harappa are the crude humped bull, and the seated elongated figures having Gomal Valley parallels. Further, burial practices seem to be quite different between the two sites. Leaving aside the cemetery evidence which has not been found at Mohenjodaro, the post-cremation urns are quite interesting. Only twelve of these have been found at Mohenjodaro. At Harappa some 238 were found in all excavated areas of the site in many contexts and depths and *in situ*. In addition, different cemeteries were found at Harappa. These minor but significant variations may reflect the diversity of the regions, ethnic groups and cultures with which Harappa was interacting for its

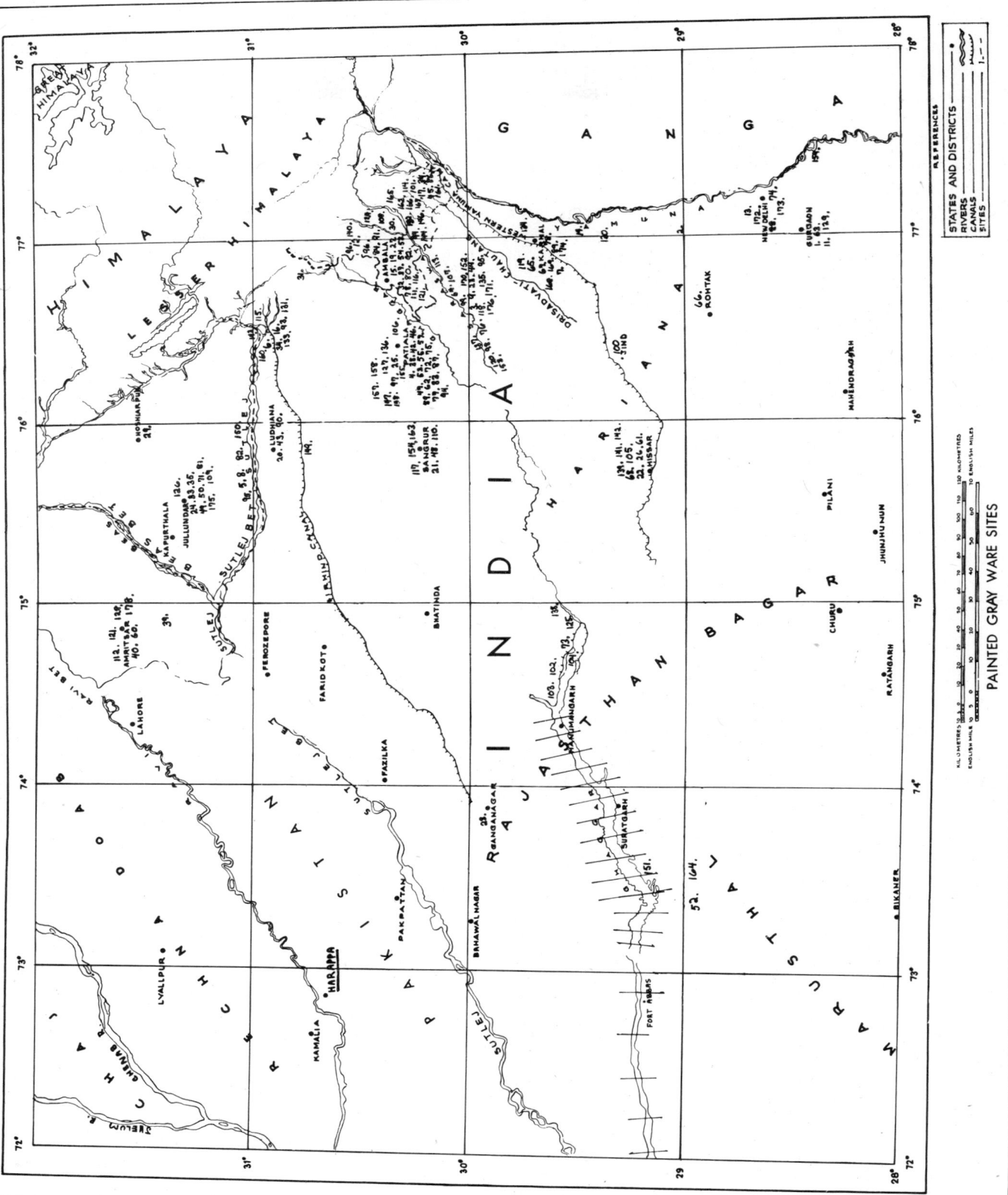

Fig. 22.3. Painted Gray Ware sites.

nonagricultural resources. These include the Jammu foothills, possibly Kashmir, northern Rajasthan, the eastern *Doab* and other areas of the outer Himalayas where the six rivers have their headwaters. Moreover it is very probable that the northern part of the Jhelum-Yamuna Plain which today receives 50 to 70 centimeters of dependable annual rainfall was under thick forest cover in Harappan times, and could only have been inhabited by mobile pastoral groups. These may have provided a link between the rich mountain areas, and Harappan and southern Indus areas.

To summarize the points regarding Harappa and the settlement patterns of its hinterland:

1) The presence of prime agricultural land immediately adjoining Harappa.

2) Presumed thick forest cover between Harappa and essential resource areas.

3) A multi-river system fanning out north and east and west of Harappa, leading into resource areas and to the south converging into one large river leading to market areas.

4) Presence in Harappa's greater hinterland of unique and diverse essential raw materials.

Given these points, what kind of settlement pattern would one expect to find? What one actually does find is a dendritic type of pattern which follows the rivers, without much settlement in between. There is evidence of some contact with different cultures in the highlands and resource areas. If additional field work confirms and maintains this pattern, Harappa is best viewed in the Indus urban network as the main northern supply center to Mohenjodaro. It was a city essentially isolated in a large plain without permanent settlement except along the rivers. As such it presents a rather unique early urban network pattern. This fragile settlement pattern spread thin along river valleys is very different from the widespread, interlocking support systems of other early urban settlement patterns. Clues for understanding the decline of the Indus Civilization will lie in further exploration and confirmation of this settlement pattern.

APPENDIX

List of sites on maps[3]

PAINTED GRAY WARE SITES

No.	Site name	District	Source
1.	Aharwan	Gurgaon	IAR 1966-67
2.	Akarpur-Baroth	Karnal-Rohtak	IAR 1960-61
3.	Amin	Karnal	AI, no. 10
4.	Alipur	Patiala	Madhu Bala
5.	Apra	Jullundur	IAR 1963-64
6.	Arnauli	Ropar	IAR 1962-63, 1964-65 (H, LH)
7.	Asandh	Karnal	IAR 1960-61
8.	Ashaur	Jullundur	IAR 1963-64
9.	Astipur	Thanesar	IAR 1964-65
10.	Astipur	Gurgaon	Tripathi
11.	Autha	Gurgaon	IAR 1964-65
12.	Badhauli	Ambala	IAR 1963-64
13.	Badli-ki-sarai	Delhi	Tripathi
14.	Bahola	Karnal	IAR 1960-61
15.	Balana	Ambala	IAR 1963-64 (LH)
16.	Bara	Ropar	IAR 1963-64
17.	Basantaur	Ambala	IAR 1963-64

No.	Site name	District	Source
18.	Basrai	Gurdaspur	Madhu Bala
19.	Baterla	Ambala	IAR 1964-65
20.	Baundal	Ludhiana	Madhu Bala
21.	Bhasaur	Sangrur	Madhu Bala
22.	Bhiwani Khera	Hissar	IAR 1966-67
23.	Bibipur-Kalan	Karnal	IAR 1964-65
24.	Bir Basiem	Jullundur	Tripathi
25.	Brass	Patiala	Madhu Bala
26.	Burj	Hissar	IAR 1966-67
27.	Chadiala Khanpur	Ambala	IAR 1962-63
28.	Chak	Ganganagar	Tripathi
29.	Chajja	Hoshiarpur	Tripathi
30.	Chamkaur	Ambala	Tripathi
31.	Chandigarh	Chandigarh	IAR 1970-71 (H, KLB, B)
32.	Chandpur	Ambala	Tripathi
33.	Charan	Jullundur	Tripathi
34.	Chaunkair	Ropar	IAR 1953-54
35.	Chini-Kanjri-da-Theh	Jullundur	Madhu Bala
36.	Chitorgarh	Gurdaspur	Tripathi
37.	Chudiala	Ambala	IAR 1964-65
38.	Chhai	Patiala	Tripathi
39.	Chhichhariwal	Amritsar	IAR 1966-67
40.	Chhina	Amritsar	Madhu Bala
41.	Damla	Ambala	IAR 1963-64
42.	Dadhera	Patiala	Madhu Bala
43.	Dadheri	Ludhiana	Madhu Bala
44.	Daulatpur	Karnal	IAR 1960-61, 68, 69 (LH)
45.	Deen	Ambala	IAR 1963-64
46.	Dhammo Majra	Patiala	Madhu Bala
47.	Dhangeri	Patiala	Madhu Bala
48.	Dher Majra	Sangrur	Madhu Bala
49.	Dhuleta	Jullundur	IAR 1963-64
50.	Dhuderi	Jullundur	Madhu Bala
51.	Dodwan	Gurdaspur	Tripathi
52.	Dotheri	Bikaner	Tripathi
53.	Dudhan	Patiala	Madhu Bala
54.	Dugri	Ambala	Tripathi
55.	Durd	Patiala	Madhu Bala
56.	Fattupur Dher	Gurdaspur	Tripathi
57.	Gajju-Khera	Patiala	Madhu Bala
58.	Ghanauli	Ambala	AI, no. 10
59.	Gharan	Patiala	Madhu Bala
60.	Gharinda	Amritsar	Madhu Bala
61.	Ghaswa 2	Hissar	IAR 1966-67
62.	Gheoria	Patiala	IAR 1966-67
63.	Gohana	Gurgaon	Tripathi
64.	Gudana	Karnal	IAR 1964-65
65.	Gumad	Karnal	Tripathi
66.	Gumad	Rohtak	Tripathi

No.	Site name	District	Source
67.	Hamirpur	Karnal	Tripathi
68.	Hansi	Hissar	IAR 1963-64
69.	Hardo-Rawal-Khurd	Gurdaspur	Tripathi
70.	Haripur	Gurdaspur	Tripathi
71.	Haripur	Jullundur	IAR 1961-62
72.	Hasali	Patiala	Madhu Bala
73.	Humayan Khera	Hissar	IAR 1967-68
74.	Indrapat	Delhi	Tripathi
75.	Isar Hol	Patiala	Madhu Bala
76.	Jalkhedi	Karnal	IAR 1964-65
77.	Jhansla	Patiala	Madhu Bala
78.	Jorasi Khurd	Karnal	Tripathi
79.	Kalon	Ambala	IAR 1963-64
80.	Kardhan	Ambala	IAR 1963-64
81.	Kartarpur	Jullundur	Madhu Bala
82.	Katpalon	Jullundur	IAR 1963-64
83.	Kauli	Patiala	Madhu Bala
84.	Khanpur	Ambala	IAR 1964-65
85.	Khannwala	Gurdaspur	Tripathi
86.	Khera	Ambala	IAR 1964-65
87.	Khijrabad	Patiala	Madhu Bala
88.	Khera-Kalan	Delhi	Tripathi
89.	Kheri	Karnal	Tripathi
90.	Kheri Nand Singh	Ludhiana	Madhu Bala
91.	Kotla Nihang	Ropar	Tripathi
92.	Kumbra	Patiala	Madhu Bala
93.	Kurukshetra	Karnal	Tripathi
94.	Ladhora	Ambala	IAR 1964-65
95.	Lataur	Patiala	Madhu Bala
96.	Lukhi	Karnal	IAR 1964-65
97.	Jorasi Khurd	Karnal	IAR 1960-61
98.	Kalayat	Jind	IAR 1966-67 (Pre-H, H)
99.	Kal Khera	Ambala	IAR 1963-64
100.	Kariwali 1 (Dharampur)	Hissar	IAR 1967-68
101.	Kariwali 2 (Majjal Ther)	Hissar	IAR 1967-68
102.	Kariwali 3	Hissar	IAR 1967-68
103.	Kaulgarh	Hissar	IAR 1966-67
104.	Kauli	Patiala	IAR 1968-69
105.	Kheri	Karnal	IAR 1960-61
106.	Lakhnaur Sahib	Ambala	IAR 1963-64
107.	Madhopur	Jullundur	IAR 1956-57
108.	Mahorana	Sangrur	Madhu Bala
109.	Mallaur	Ambala	IAR 1963-64
110.	Marari Khuro	Amritsar	IAR 1962-63
111.	Mehawa Kheri	Karnal	IAR 1964-65
112.	Mehbubpur	Ambala	IAR 1964-65
113.	Merhanwal	Ropar	Madhu Bala
114.	Mirzapur	Ambala	IAR 1963-64
115.	Moonak	Sangrur	IAR 1968-69

No.	Site name	District	Source
116.	Morthali	Karnal	IAR 1960-61
117.	Monhali	Karnal	Tripathi
118.	Murthala	Karnal	IAR 1964-65
119.	Murarikhurd	Amritsar	Madhu Bala
120.	Mustafabad	Ambala	IAR 1966-67
121.	Nagar	Jullundur	IAR 1963-64
122.	Nagiari	Ambala	IAR 1962-63, 64-65
123.	Nakora	Hissar	IAR 1967-68
124.	Nao	Jullundur	Tripathi
125.	Nandpur-Kesho	Patiala	Madhu Bala
126.	Natthurpur Toda	Amritsar	IAR 1965-66
127.	Palwal	Gurgaon	Tripathi
128.	Panirt	Karnal	Tripathi
129.	Panjola	Ropar	Madhu Bala
130.	Pathorheri	Ambala	Tripathi
131.	Patharheri Choti	Ropar	IAR 1962-63, 64-65
132.	Pehowa	Karnal	Tripathi
133.	Raja Karna-ka-Qila	Karnal	IAR 1970-71
134.	Rajgarh	Patiala	Madhu Bala
135.	Ramsaran Majra	Karnal	IAR 1964-65
136.	Raniya (Lahoronwali Theri)	Hissar	IAR 1967-68
137.	Ratta Tibba	Hissar	IAR 1966-67
138.	Rohan	Ambala	IAR 1964-65
139.	Rupan Wali	Hissar	IAR 1966-67
140.	Rupan Wali 2	Hissar	IAR 1966-67
141.	Rupar	Ropar	Tripathi
142.	Sadhaura	Ambala	IAR 1963-64
143.	Sakala	Gurdaspur	Tripathi
144.	Salaura	Ambala	Tripathi
145.	Salaha	Patiala	Madhu Bala
146.	Samdu	Patiala	Madhu Bala
147.	Sanghol 3	Ludhiana	IAR 1969-70, 70-71
148.	Saprota	Jullundur	IAR 1963-64
149.	Sardargarh	Ganganagar	Tripathi
150.	Sarsa Bhor	Karnal	?
151.	Sasa Talhedi	Karnal	IAR 1964-65
152.	Satanj	Sangrur	Madhu Bala
153.	Seal	Patiala	IAR 1964-65
154.	Secta	Ambala	IAR 1963-64
155.	Shebbupura	Patiala	Madhu Bala
156.	Sialu	Patiala	Madhu Bala
157.	Sihi	Gurgaon	IAR 1969-70
158.	Singh	Ropar	IAR 1962-63, 64-65
159.	Suga	Ambala	IAR 1963-64
160.	Such	Ambala	IAR 1965-66
161.	Sunam	Sangrur	Madhu Bala
162.	Surawalli	Bikaner	Tripathi
163.	Talapur	Ambala	Tripathi
164.	Tandiwal	Ambala	IAR 1963-64

No.	Site name	District	Source
165.	Tandiwal	Ambala	IAR 1964-65
166.	Teora	Karnal	Tripathi
167.	Thal	Karnal	IAR 1968-69
168.	Thanesar City Mound	Karnal	IAR 1964-65
169.	Theh Polar	Karnal	IAR 1963-64
170.	Tilpat	Delhi	Tripathi
171.	Timarpur	Delhi	Tripathi
172.	Topra Kala	Karnal	IAR 1968-69
173.	Uehha-Lutera	Jullundur	Madhu Bala
174.	Urnai	Karnal	IAR 1960-61
175.	Vedala Garanthian Sahar	Gurdaspur	Tripathi
176.	Vadala (Granthian)	Amritsar	Madhu Bala

LATE HARAPPAN

No.	Site name	District	Source
1.	Aechal Sahib	Gurudaspur	
2.	Apara	Jullundur	Joshi 1977
3.	Badala (2)	Ludhiana	Madhu Bala
4.	Badhauli	Ambala	IAR 1963-64
5.	Bahwa	Sangrur	Madhu Bala
6.	Balana	Ambala	IAR 1963-64
7.	Banawali	Hissar	ME
8.	Banehra	Karnal	IAR 1966-67
9.	Banrai	Ludhiana	Madhu Bala
10.	Bara	Ropar	Madhu Bala
11.	Barwali	Ludhiana	Madhu Bala
12.	Bassigujaran	Ropar	Madhu Bala
13.	Bathlana	Ropar	Madhu Bala
14.	Baundal	Ludhiana	Madhu Bala
15.	Bhagwanpura	Kurukshetra	PT
16.	Bhasaur	Sangrur	Madhu Bala
17.	Bhasmara (Burj)	Patiala	Madhu Bala
18.	Bhudan	Sangrur	Madhu Bala
19.	Bodha	Karnal	IAR 1966-67
20.	Brass	Patiala	Madhu Bala
21.	Burj	Hissar	IAR 1966-67
22.	Chandigarh	Chandigarh	Madhu Bala
23.	Chandiala	Ludhiana	Madhu Bala
24.	Chever-thal-Kalal	Patiala	Madhu Bala
25.	Chini-Kanjri-da-Theh	Jullundur	Madhu Bala
26.	Chaina	Amritsar	Madhu Bala
27.	Dadhera	Patiala	Madhu Bala
28.	Dadheri	Ludhiana	Madhu Bala
29.	Daulatpur	Karnal	IAR 1968-69
30.	Daheru	Ludhiana	Madhu Bala
31.	Dhammo Majra	Patiala	Prufer 1951

From Jhelum to Yamuna

No.	Site name	District	Source
32.	Dher Majra	Ropar	Prufer 1952
33.	Doraha	Ludhiana	Prufer 1952
34.	Dodwan	Gurudaspur	Madhu Bala
35.	Dure	Patiala	Madhu Bala
36.	Gajju-Khera	Patiala	Madhu Bala
37.	Galoraddi	Patiala	Madhu Bala
38.	Garhi Radan	Kurukshetra	Joshi 1977
39.	Gharinda	Amritsar	Joshi 1977
40.	Gurdasnangal-da-Theh	Gurdaspur	Joshi 1977
41.	Hardo-Rawal-Khurd	Gurdaspur	Joshi 1977
42.	Haripur	Gurdaspur	Joshi 1977
43.	Haripur	Jullundur	Joshi 1977
44.	Hasali	Patiala	Joshi 1977
45.	Her	Amritsar	Joshi 1977
46.	Isar Hol	Patiala	Joshi 1977
47.	Jagvia	Gurdaspur	Madhu Bala
48.	Jatheri	Karnal	IAR 1966-67
49.	Kanwa	Gurdaspur	Madhu Bala
50.	Karalan	Jullundur	Madhu Bala
51.	Kartarpur	Jullundur	Madhu Bala
52.	Katpalon	Jullundur	Madhu Bala
53.	Khera	Ludhiana	Madhu Bala
54.	Kheri Nand Singh	Ludhiana	Madhu Bala
55.	Khokari 1	Sangrur	IAR 1966-67
56.	Khokari 2	Sangrur	IAR 1966-67
57.	Kohada	Ludhiana	Madhu Bala
58.	Kotmandial	Ludhiana	Madhu Bala
59.	Kubhrai	Ropar	Madhu Bala
60.	Kurari	Ropar	Madhu Bala
60A.	Kurdi	Chandigarh	Suraj Bhan 1973
61.	Lohgarh	Gurdaspur	Madhu Bala
62.	Mahorana	Sangrur	Madhu Bala
63.	Majiri	Patiala	Madhu Bala
64.	Manala	Ropar	Madhu Bala
65.	Malsian	Jullundur	Madhu Bala
66.	Manupur	Ludhiana	Madhu Bala
67.	Manoharpur	Sangrur	IAR 1966-67
68.	Mathan	Ludhiana	IAr 1965-66
68A.	Mitathal IIB	Hissar	Suraj Bhan 1969
69.	Mohanpur	Karnal	IAR 1966-67
70.	Mohna	Karnal	IAR 1977-67
71.	Nagar	Jullundur	Madhu Bala
72.	Nauli	Jullundur	Madhu Bala
73.	Nagwan	Patiala	Madhu Bala
74.	Neesamg 2	Karnal	IAR 1966-67
75.	Panandian	Patiala	Madhu Bala
76.	Pallanpur	Ropar	Madhu Bala
77.	Pilana	Karnal	IAR 1966-67

No.	Site name	District	Source
77A.	Pipli	Kurukshetra	Joshi 1977
78.	Rahon	Jullundur	Madhu Bala
78A.	Raja-Karna-ka-Qila		
79.	Rajgarh	Patiala	Madhu Bala
80.	Rampur	Ropar	Madhu Bala
81.	Rohira	Sangrur	Madhu Bala
82.	Sandhai	Ambala	IAR 1965-66
83.	Sanghol	Ludhiana	IAR 1966-67, 70-71
83A.	Siswal II B		
84.	Somavi	Ludhiana	Madhu Bala
84A.	Sosan	Amritsar	Joshi 1977
85.	Seel	Patiala	Madhu Bala
86.	Suni Arkheri	Patiala	Madhu Bala
87.	Uccha-Gaon	Patiala	Madhu Bala
88.	Uchcha-Khera	Patiala	Madhu Bala
89.	Vadlan	Amritsar	Madhu Bala

HARAPPAN

No.	Site name	District	Source
1.	Arnauli	Ropar	IAR 1962-63, 64-65 (LH)
2.	Baola	Karnal	IAR 1966-67
3.	Bara-Samana	Ropar	IAR 1962-63, 64-65 (LH)
4.	Bikkun	Ropar	IAR 1953-54
5.	Chandigarh	Chandigarh	IAR 1970-71 (Pre-H, KLB, B)
6.	Chaunkair	Ropar	IAR 1953-54
7.	Chimur	Hissar	IAR 1966-67
8.	Daheru	Ludhiana	IAR 1961-62
9.	Dharmheri	Patiala	IAR 1966-67
10.	Dhogri	Jullundur	IAR 1956-57
11.	Dukheri	Ambala	IAR 1963-64 (LH)
12.	Fategarh-Neuan	Ludhiana	IAR 1963-64
13.	Gheora	Patiala	IAR 1966-67
14.	Hawara	Ropar	IAR 1953-54
15.	Jind Bir Bada Ban	Sangrur	IAR 1966-67 (Pre-H)
16.	Ka-inor	Ropar	IAR 1962-63, 64-65 (LH)
17.	Kalayat	Sangrur	IAR 1966-67 (Pre-H, PGW)
18.	Kalibangan	Ganganagar	IAR 1967-68 (Pre-H, KLB)
19	Katpalon	Jullundur	IAR 1963-64 (PGW)
20.	Kheri Nand Singh	Ludhiana	IAR 1961-62
21.	Khirka	Hissar	IAR 1966-67 (Pre-H)
22.	Kotli	Ropar	IAR 1953-54
23.	Kotla Nihang Khan	Ropar	Madhu Bala
24.	Kurrara-Kurrari	Ambala	IAR 1962-63, 64-65 (LH)
25.	Madhopur	Jullundur	IAR 1956-57
26.	Madiala-Kalan	Ludhiana	IAR 1965-66
27.	Manda	J & K	

From Jhelum to Yamuna

No.	Site name	District	Source
28.	Manikpur-Sharif	Ludhiana	IAR 1962-63 (LH)
29.	Manupur	Ludhiana	IAR 1961-62
30.	Mitathal	Hissar	Suraj Bhan 1973
31.	Nagar	Jullundur	IAR 1963-64 (PGW)
32.	Pali 2	Hissar	IAR 1966-67 (Pre-H)
33.	Pauli	Sangrur (Jind)	IAR 1968-69
34.	Pujam	Karnal	IAR 1966-67
35.	Raja Sirkap	Bhatinda	IAR 1958-59
36.	Rahina	Sangrur	Madhu Bala
37.	Rakhigarhi	Hissar	IAR 1966-67 (Pre-H)
38.	Ratta Khera	Karnal	IAR 1966-67
39.	Ratta Theh	Hissar	IAR 1966-67 (Pre-H)
40.	Ritoli	Jind	IAR 1966-67
41.	Rupar	Ropar	LK (LH)
42.	Sandeh	Jagadhari	IAR 1963-64
43.	Sangat Pura	Jind	IAR 1966-67
44.	Sasi	Patiala	IAR 1966-67
45.	Sisai	Hissar	IAR 1966-67 (Pre-H)
46.	Siswal	Hissar	IAR 1966-67 (Pre-H)
47.	Tar Khanwala Dera	Ganganagar	Ghosh 1952
48.	Vanawali (Banswali)	Hissar	IAR 1966-67 (Pre-H)
49.	Wazir Bhullar	Amritsar	IAR 1964-65
50.	Chak Purbane Syal	Sahiwal	Vats 1940

PRE-HARAPPAN SITES

No.	Site name	District	Source
1.	Alipur Kharar, 1	Hissar	IAR 1966-67
2.	Alipur Kharar, 2	Hissar	IAR 1966-67
3.	Alipur Kharar, 3	Hissar	IAR 1966-67
4.	Balian	Rohtak	Suraj Bhan 1973
5.	Bani	Hissar	Suraj Bhan 1973
6.	Barsana, 2	Jind	IAR 1966-67
7.	Farmana	Karnal	Suraj Bhan 1973
8.	Dachar	Karnal	IAR 1966-67
9.	Ghaswa 1	Hissar	IAR 1966-67
10.	Jalilpur	Sahiwal	PA 1967
11.	Jind Bir Badaban	Jind	IAR 1966-67
12.	Kalayat	Jind	IAR 1966-67
13.	Kalibangan	Ganganagar	IAR 1966-67
14.	Kirka	Hissar	IAR 1966-67
15.	Manak Majra	Karnal	Suraj Bhan 1973
16.	Mata Shyam	Hissar	IAR 1966-67
17.	Milakpur 3	Hissar	IAR 1966-67
18.	Pali 2	Hissar	IAR 1966-67
19.	Paoli	Hissar	Suraj Bhan 1973
20.	A. Nohar	Ganganagar	Pande 1977

No.	Site name	District	Source
21.	Patan 1	Hissar	IAR 1966-67
22.	Rakhigarhi	Hissar	IAR 1966-67
23.	Rakhi Shahpur	Hissar	IAR 1966-67
24.	Rattan Theh	Hissar	IAR 1966-67
25.	Saleem Garh	Hissar	IAR 1966-67
26.	Sanghol	Ludhiana	IAR 1966-67
27.	Sarangpur	Chandigarh	Suraj Bhan 1973
28.	Satrod Khurd 1	Hissar	IAR 1966-67
29.	Satrod Khurd 2	Hissar	IAR 1966-67
30.	Shahpur	Hissar	IAR 1966-67
31.	Sisai 1	Hissar	IAR 1966-67
32.	Sisai 3	Hissar	IAR 1966-67
33.	Siswal	Hissar	IAR 1966-67
34.	Sothi	Ganganagar	Pande 1977
35.	Talwara	Hissar	IAR 1966-67
36.	Tigrana	Hissar	Suraj Bhan 1973
37.	Theraj (Chakko)	Hissar	IAR 1966-67
38.	Vanawali	Hissar	IAR 1966-67

NOTES

[1] A word about the preparation of the distribution maps is necessary. The site lists attached as the Appendix were compiled from *Indian Archaeology: A review*—1953 to 1972, Ancient India, Pakistan Archaeology, Ancient Pakistan, various site reports mentioned in the bibliography and numerous journal articles also cited in the bibliography. No new field work was conducted to prepare the lists, nor was any field checking done for the published sites. Two publications which were very useful for the Painted Gray Ware and Late Harappan sites were Tripathi (1975) and Madhu Bala (1978).

A very real difficulty lies in terminology. The publications consulted spread over almost 30 years, and definitions have changed during this time. Thus what one excavator may call Late Harappan may not be what another excavator calls Late Harappan. Bara sites have been included in Late Harappan because of the available ^{14}C dates, although the excavator has proposed earlier dating. New evidence will give us a clearer picture. Mature Harappan sites are listed as about 50, but they may in fact be much less if carefully looked at, with some of these falling into the Late Harappan category. Only a small percentage of the sites were published with exact locational data, either geo-coordinates or direction and distance from a town site (estimated 10 percent of the list). Therefore the sites whose location is given only by district have been placed in linear order under the district town name. This of course causes considerable distortion to the true picture, and limits the map and its interpretation to certain general uses. Still, it was felt that preparation of the map was worthwhile for some purposes, and it may inspire the publication of greater locational detail for the listed sites.

[2] Painted Gray Ware has been reported from a site near Srinagar by Converse (1978).

As yet this find has not been confirmed either by an archaeologist or the Archaeological Survey.

[3] Abbreviations used in the Appendix:

Sources:

IAR	Indian Archaeology: A review (by year)
AI	Ancient India (by number)
Madhu Bala	Madhu Bala, 1978
Tripathi	Tripathi, 1975
ME	Man and Environment, Vol. 2
PT	Puratattva, no. 8
LK	Lalit Kala 1-2, 1955
PA	Pakistan Archaeology, 1967

Abbreviations following the source:

Pre-H	Pre-Harappan
H	Harappan
LH	Late Harappan
KLB	Kalibangan
B	Bara
PGW	Painted Gray Ware

These abbreviations are used to indicate that the site is a multiperiod site and includes pottery from other periods.

Indian Archaeology: A review was used as a source for all the published issues from 1953 on. Other journals cited above were searched for sites from the beginning of publication.

BIBLIOGRAPHY

Bisht, R.S., 1976
 Transformation of the Harappa Culture in Punjab with Special Reference to the Excavations at Sanghol and Chandigarh. In *Archaeological Congress and Seminar 1972*. U.V. Singh, ed. Pp. 16-22. Kurukshetra: Kurukshetra University.

Bisht, R.S., 1978
 Banawali: A new Harappan site in Haryana. *Man and Environment* 2: 86-88.

Bisht, R.S., in press
 Harappa Culture in Punjab: A study in perspective. In *Indus Civilization: Problems and issues*. B.B. Lal and S.C. Malik, eds. Simla: Indian Institute of Advanced Study.

Converse, Hyla Stuntz, 1978
 Similarities in Certain Pottery Fabrics Found at Hastinapura, an Unexcavated Site in Kashmir, and Shahi Tump. *Journal of the American Oriental Society* 98 (4): 478-82.

Dales, George, 1973
 Recent Pre- and Protohistoric Researches in Pakistan and Afghanistan. In *Radiocarbon and Indian Archaeology*. D.P. Agrawal and A. Ghosh, eds. Pp. 118-30. Bombay: Tata Institute of Fundamental Research.

Dikshit, K.N., 1968
 Nature of Harappan Wares in Sutlej Valley. In *Potteries in Ancient India*. B.P. Sinha, ed. Pp. 56-66. Patna: Patna University.

Dikshit, K.N., 1977
 Distribution and Relationship of Protohistoric Sites along Old River Channels of the Ghaggar system. In *Ecology and Environment in Western India*. D.P. Agrawal and B.M. Pande, eds. Pp. 61-66, Delhi: Concept Publishing.

Dikshit, K.N., 1979
 Late Harappan Cultures in India. In *Essays in Indian Protohistory*. D.P. Agrawal and D.K. Chakrabarti, eds. Pp. 123-33. Delhi: B.R. Publishing Corp.

Fentress, Marcia, 1976
 Resource Access, Exchange Systems, and Regional Interaction in the Indus Valley: A study of archaeological variability at Harappa and Mohenjodaro. Ph.D. dissertation, Department of Oriental Studies, University of Pennsylvania.

Fentress, Marcia, 1978
 Regional Interaction in Indus Valley Urbanization: The key factors of resource access and exchange. In *American Studies in the Anthropology of India*. Sylvia Vatuk, ed. Pp. 399-424. Delhi: Manohar.

Ghosh, A., 1952
 The Rajputana Desert: Its archaeological aspect. *Bulletin of the National Institute of Sciences in India*. 1: 37-42.

Joshi, J.P., 1977
 Excavations at Bhagwanpura. *Puratattva* 8: 178-79.

Khazanchi, T.N. and K.N. Dikshit, 1980
 The Grey Ware Cultures of Northern Pakistan, Jammu and Kashmir, and Punjab. *Puratattva* 9: 47-51.

Madhu Bala, 1978
 A Survey of the Protohistoric Investigation in Punjab and the Emergent Picture. *Indian Anthropology* 8: 89-118.

Mughal, M.R., 1972
 A Summary of Excavations and Explorations in Pakistan. *Pakistan Archaeology* 8: 113-58.

Mughal, M.R., 1980
 New Archaeological Evidence from Bahawalpur. *Man and Environment* Vol. 4: 93-98.

Pande, B.M., 1977
 Archaeological Remains on the Ancient Saraswati. In *Ecology and Archaeology of Western*

India. B.M. Pande and D.P. Agrawal, eds. Pp. 55-59. Delhi: Concept Publishers.

Prufer, Olaf, 1952
Nalagarh 1951: Interim report on the excavations carried out at Dher Majra. Calcutta: Jamia Millia Islamia Historical Research Foundation.

Sharma, G.B., 1978
Excavations at Sanghol. *Times of India*. October 23: 11.

Sharma, Y.D., 1973
Value of Common Painted Ceramics from Different Sites as a Guide to Chronology with Special Reference to Bara. In *Radiocarbon and Indian Archaeology*. D.P. Agrawal and B.M. Pande, eds. Pp. 222-30. Bombay: Tata Institute of Fundamental Research.

Sharma, Y.D., 1976
Transformation of Harappa Culture in the Punjab. In *Archaeological Congress and Seminar 1972*. U.V. Singh, ed. Pp. 5-15. Kurukshetra: Kurukshetra University.

Sharma, Y.D., in press
Bara and the so-called Late Harappa cultures of the Punjab. In *Indus Civilization: Problems and issues*. B.B. Lal and S.C. Malik, eds. Simla: Indian Institute of Advanced Study.

Singh, U.V., in press
Late Harappan Culture as Revealed by the Excavations at Mirzapur and Aulatpur, District Kurukshetra. In *Indus Civilization: Problems and issues*. B.B. Lal and S.C. Malik, eds. Simla: Indian Institute of Advanced Study.

Suraj Bhan, 1969
Excavations at Mitathal (Hissar), 1968. *Journal of Haryana Studies* 1 (1): 1-15.

Suraj Bhan, 1973
The sequence and spread of prehistoric cultures in the upper Saraswati Basin. In *Radiocarbon and Indian Archaeology*. D.P. Agrawal and A. Ghosh, eds. Pp. 252-63. Bombay: Tata Institute for Fundamental Research.

Suraj Bhan, 1976
Transformation of Harappa Culture in Haryana. In *Archaeological Congress and Seminar 1972*. U.V. Singh, ed. Pp. 23-30. Kurukshetra: Kurukshetra University.

Suraj Bhan, in press
Protohistoric settlement pattern in Haryana. In *Indus Civilization: Problems and issues*. B.B. Lal and S.C. Malik, eds. Simla: Indian Institute of Advanced Study.

Stein, Sir A., 1942
A Survey of Ancient Sites Along the 'Lost' Saraswati River. *Geographical Journal* 99 (4): 174-82.

Thapar, B.K., 1978
The Mosaic of Indus Civilization beyond the Indus Valley. Unpublished paper presented at the International Symposium on the Indus Valley Civilization. Karachi, December 30. Cyclostyled Copy.

Tripathi, Vibha, 1975
The Painted Grey Ware: An Iron Age culture of northern India. Delhi: Concept Publishers.

Vats, M.S., 1940
Excavations at Harappa. 2 vols. Delhi: Government of India.

SHEREEN RATNAGAR

23. The Location of Harappa

Mohenjodaro and Harappa (Fig. 23.1) are the largest known Harappan settlements. The artifactual remains at these sites indicate that a significant proportion of their inhabitants were engaged in activities other than food production: that, in fact, they were truly urban in character. Reference here is to the public buildings including public stores, the evidence for manufacturing, the exceptionally large number of seals, and the wide range of materials excavated at the two sites.

These two cities seem to have been headquarters for administration, collection points for tax or tribute, production centers for particular goods and the loci of exchanges. They are also located in river valleys with a fairly uniform distribution of resources and where there are no barriers to communication. Given these situations one would expect both cities to be located within easy access to rural Harappan settlements; in other words, to be centrally located with smaller settlements surrounding them on all sides. But this is not so, especially in the case of Harappa.

Data on Harappan site location in the greater Indus Valley reveal two regions with relatively dense settlements: the lower Sarasvati Valley, and lower Sind. Mohenjodaro is not located at the center of a polygonal or circular field. There are few sites to its north or west. Jhukar does lie on the Larkana plains but Judeirjodaro, near Jacobabad, and Pathiani Kot at the mouth of the Mula Pass, appear to be outposts rather than satellites of Mohenjodaro. Mohenjodaro was located in the northern part of the Harappan-occupied area of Sind. Historically, Larkana has been the most productive region of Sind. Thus local fertility, as well as access to trade routes over the Bolan and other more southerly passes, were major factors in the location of Mohenjodaro.[1]

Where Harappa is concerned, the eccentricity of location appears to be even more marked. Aside from Chak Purbane Syal and Vainiwal, the nearest known cluster of settlements lies in Cholistan, some 150 kilometers to the south.

Vats (1940: 1) believed that in the Harappan times Montgomery District was watered by several streams: two branches of the Ravi, an old course of the Beas, two minor streams, as well as the Sutlej. There is no evidence, of course, for necessarily dating these old channels to the third millennium. But there is no reason to doubt that, at the regional level, land utilization in Sind during the third millennium would have presented a contrast to that in southwestern Punjab, just as it does today. The Indus in Sind is aggrading its bed and flows on a ridge higher than the surrounding plain. Thus, flood waters flow out to an appreciable distance from both banks of the river. In the lower Punjab, however, the rivers are entrenched and the strip of new alluvium available along their banks for farming is significantly narrower than in Sind. Nineteenth century reports on Montgomery District describe vast tracts of land between the annually flooded tracts of the Ravi and Sutlej. These could not be cultivated but only put to seasonal pasture (Gazetteer of the Montgomery District 1884). Thus village communities, as such, did not exist in the arid "bars" of the southern Punjab until the introduction of canal irrigation during the British rule. Compact villages with joint claims over land only developed in the fertile riverine tracts which benefited from annual flooding. Nomadic herding was the dominant occupation in the harsh environment of the "bars"

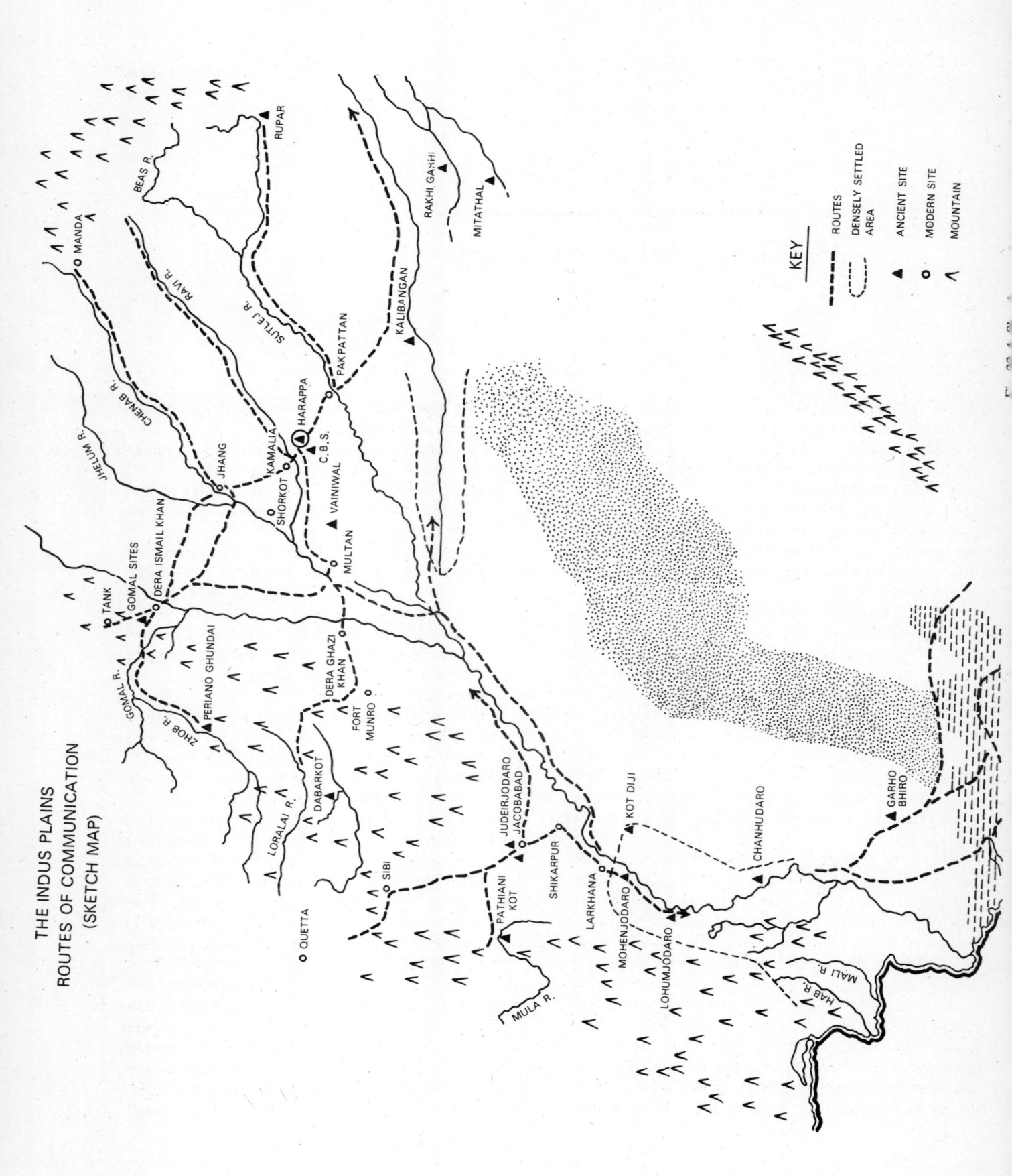

The Location of Harappa

(Bharadwaj 1961: 157).[2] Harappa appears to have been located to the north of the zone of high agricultural productivity, and near the southern limits of the pastoral region.[3]

What could have been the factors which influenced the location of Harappa? It is not surprising that the central place theory does not explain spatial relationships in the Harappan Period since it is predicated on the predominance of rural marketing in situations where demand is diffused uniformly over the region and where perfect competition is assumed. An alternative model is the "gateway city." This is a part of a settlement system characterized not by centrality and the interstitial placing of sites, but by dendritic networks where lower level centers are tributary to only one higher level center—not to more than one as in central place systems. With primate cities functioning as "gateways" the networks connecting the settlement points are like elongated fans radiating from the primate city. The points are linked to the latter, rather than to each other except along routes. Such systems are connected with long distance trade and bulk shipment rather than with local exchange or retail networks. This is especially true in regions where the economy has a strong external orientation. The primate city sees the convergence of commodity flows, and functions as a redistributive or wholesaling center as the case may be. In such a system the primate city is located at a point where it can control the movements of goods: at a break of bulk point, at an important river crossing, or at the junction of several natural routes. It forms the major link between the core territory and the peripheral region or external world. (See Burghardt 1971; Smith 1976; Kelley 1976; Hirth 1978.)

If Harappa functioned as a gateway city, rather than as a central place, one would expect that transportation functions and facilities would outweigh the importance of manufactures there. It is very difficult to glean information from the excavation report regarding manufacturing at Harappa—other than the presence of sixteen furnaces on Mound F. In contrast, Mohenjodaro has evidence for the manufacture of pottery, copper/bronze, gold ornaments, and agate beads. Ivory carving, shell working and possibly textile dyeing are also attested.

It is significant that several routes of historical importance converge on Harappa. The rivers of the Indus system provide natural waterways and routes of communication from the Himalayan region to the plains. Traffic between the mountains to the west and the upper plains has traditionally flowed through Dera Ismail Khan and Dera Ghazi Khan. Multan, a frontier city of the medieval period, is connected to both places by good routes; the Chenab being fordable in its vicinity. Routes move up the Ravi from Multan to Harappa, and thence some 60 kilometers southeast to Pakpattan. This has been the traditional ferry point on the Sutlej for centuries, and is an important stage on routes connecting the Punjab with the Sarasvati Valley. Alternately, a winter caravan route has traditionally moved from Dera Ismail Khan to Jhang, Kamalia, Harappa, Pakpattan and thence to Delhi (Gazetteer of Montgomery District 1884: 147-48, 184-85).

Thus, Harappa is in a situation of maximum advantage for procuring goods from the mountain zones west, northwest and northeast of the upper Indus plains. Consider also the existence of Harappan settlements in the Gomal Valley, at Manda near Akhnoor, where the Chenab becomes navigable, and at Ropar (Rupar) on the Sutlej at the foot of the Siwaliks, just a few miles below the point where that river becomes navigable. One may thus imagine a dendritic fan with its apex at Harappa. This fan spreads out from northwest to northeast, and in turn feeds the core Harappan regions in the lower Sarasvati and Sind.

The materials known at the Harappan sites that could have been procured along this network would include lapis lazuli from Badakhshan (via the Gomal Valley), deodar wood from the Himalayan temperate forests, pine wood from the Himalayan ranges east of Kashmir, elm wood from the subtropical Himalayas east of Dehra Dun, copper and steatite from the Zhob Valley (Mughal 1970: 194), placer gold from the upper reaches of the Chenab, and perhaps copper from scattered deposits in the Simla and Kangra regions.

More detailed work is necessary for the substantiation of this hypothesis, and it should be noted that the paucity of sites in the vicinity of Harappa may be a factor of chance survival or discovery. If, however, this hypothesis is correct it will indicate that at least at Harappa, the processes of urban growth were related less to increasing rural productivity and the proliferation of local exchange systems than to redistributional mechanisms and an external trade orientation. That the Harappans exported several kinds of goods to Mesopotamia is well known. What needs greater emphasis is the fact that many of these goods were not local products in the strictest sense, but were procured from regions outside the Indus plains.

Harappa is an obvious case, but if this hypothesis is to stand one will need to consider the possibility that Judeirjodaro and Rakhigarhi, relatively large Harappan settlements located near the peripheries of the settled plains, also functioned as "gateway cities" though on a smaller scale.

NOTES

[1] The location of Shikarpur, an important town of Sind in the historical period, perhaps provides an analogy to the location of Mohenjodaro.

[2] To the best of my knowledge southwestern Punjab to the west of the Sutlej was not settled by the Painted Gray Ware producing people either.

[3] Harappa lies near the 25 centimeter isohyet (Naqvi and Rahamatullah 1962; Almad 1963) which crosses lower Punjab approximately west to east. It would be useful to know what that isohyet signifies in terms of the original forest cover and the problems of land clearance. I am grateful to Marcia Fentress for bringing this fact to my attention.

BIBLIOGRAPHY

Ahmad, K.S., 1963
   Land Use in the Semi-arid Zone of West Pakistan. *Pakistan Geographical Review* 18: 1-18.
Bharadwaj, O.P., 1961
   The Arid Zone of India and Pakistan. In *A History of Land Use in Arid Regions*. L. Dudley Stamp, ed. Pp. 143-74. Paris: UNESCO.
Burdhardt, A.F., 1971
   A Hypothesis about Gateway Cities. *Annals of the Association of American Geographers*. 61: 269-85.
Gazetteer of the Montgomery District, 1884
   Punjab Government Gazetteer of the Montgomery District 1883/84. Lahore: Government of India.
Hirth, K., 1978
   Interregional Trade and the Formation of Prehistoric Gateway Communities. *American Antiquity* 43: 35-45.
Kelley, L., 1976
   Dendritic Central-Place Systems and the Regional Organization of Navajo Trading-Posts. In *Regional Analysis*. C. Smith, ed. pp. 214-19. New York: Academic Press.
Mughal, M.R., 1970
   The Early Harappan Period in the Greater Indus Valley and Northern Baluchistan (3000-2400 B.C.). Ph.D. dissertation. Anthropology Department, University of Pennsylvania.
Naqvi, S.N. and M. Rahamatullah, 1962
   Weather and Climate of Pakistan. *Pakistan Geographical Review* 17: 1-18.
Smith, C., 1976
   Regional Economic Systems: Linking Geographical Models and Socioeconomic Problems. In *Regional Analysis*. C. Smith, ed. Pp. 3-61. New York: Academic Press.
Vats, M.S., 1940
   Excavations at Harappa. 2 vols. Delhi: Government of India.

DILIP K. CHAKRABARTI

24. 'Long Barrel-Cylinder' Beads and the Issue of Pre-Sargonic Contact between the Harappan Civilization and Mesopotamia

ERNEST MACKAY has discussed and illustrated long barrel-cylinder beads from both Mohenjodaro and Chanhudaro (see Table 24.1, Fig. 24.1 and Pl. 24.2). There is also a mention of these beads in H.C. Beck's report (1940) on selected beads from Harappa. Because of the lack of suitable publications it is difficult to locate this bead type at other excavated Harappan sites. But even on the basis of its occurrence at Mohenjodaro, Chanhudaro and Harappa it may be said that this is a distinct Indus bead type, as distinctive in its own way as the etched carnelian beads. And unlike the latter, which are also known to occur in later Indian historic contexts, this bead type died with the Indus Civilization.

This type has been found in various stages of manufacture at Chanhudaro. Apart from carnelian it is also known in pottery, often with a red slip. The specimens in pottery are obviously poor men's imitation of the carnelian variety. There is also at least one specimen from Mohenjodaro in a dark green chalcedony called plasma. Similar specimens have not been reported from Chanhudaro or Harappa.

Table 24.1. Long barrel-cylinder beads at Harappan sites

Mohenjodaro		
Mackay 1931: 511-12	Pl. CXLV, 24-32	
	Pl. CLI, b	
Mackay 1938: 512-13	Pl. LXXXII, 9-10	
	Pl. CXI, 32, 40	
	Pl. CXXXVI, 9, 17	
	Pl. CXXXIX, 65, 72, 78 (see Fig. 24.1)	
	Pl. CXXXVIII, 20	
	Pl. CXXXVII, 47 (see Fig. 24.1)	
Chanhudaro		
Mackay 1943: 203-204	Pl. XCIII, 14	
Boston Museum of Fine Arts	36.1507 and 36.1564 (see Pl. 24.1)	
Harappa		
Beck 1940: 400	Pl. CXXXI, 2a, b	

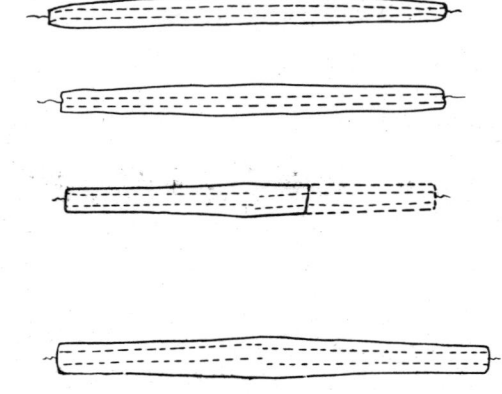

Fig. 24.1. Long barrel-cylinder beads from Mohenjodaro. From top to bottom: Mackay 1938: Pl. CXXXIX, nos. 65. 72, 78 and Pl. CXXXVII, no. 47. Scale: ca. 1:1.

The carnelian variety is discussed in the present context. These beads are long, being anything from about two to three inches. Ernest Mackay aptly christened the type as "long barrel-cylinder." The distinctive feature is a barrel-like swelling in the middle. The west Asiatic significance of this bead-type was first noticed by Mackay himself.

> This type of bead is of unusual interest, as similar beads found at Kish have been dated to the pre-Sargonic period. As, however, beads of this type were uncommon in early Mesopotamia and fairly plentiful at Mohenjodaro, in both the Late and Intermediate periods, there is reason to think that they were made in India and exported to Mesopotamia. They have apparently not been found in Elam (Mackay 1931: 511-12).

It was Beck (1940: 400) who drew attention to this after Mackay. In the Harappa collection he noticed two "very interesting" exceptionally long barrel beads of carnelian. He wrote:

> These beads are exactly similar in shape to some from Mesopotamia; but the latter are shorter, rarely exceeding two inches in length, whilst no. 129 from Harappa must have been over three-and-a-half inches long and some from Mohenjodaro are over five inches long. Sir Leonard Woolley, however, states that a very few similar beads from Ur are nearly four inches long.

It is somewhat curious that the significance of this bead-type as a possible item in the Indus-West Asia contact has been subsequently ignored.

The Kish analogies of this bead-type suggested by Mackay were reported in his own report in 1929.

> A favourite shape for carnelian beads is the long one shown on either side of the decorated bead in Pl. XLIII, no. 9. These beads, 5.50 and 4.90 cm in length, are beautifully made and finished. The boring of their holes, which was performed from both ends, is extremely well done. Similar beads were found in burial 51.... They also occur in necklaces from other burials, but the longer ones are on the whole rather rare, and are only to be found in the more important graves (Mackay 1929: 184).

At Kish the same bead form was also found made of lapis lazuli.

Regarding this type in carnelian, Mackay went to the extent of asserting that he regarded these carnelian beads as important from the point of view of dating Mohenjodaro. "They seem not to have been worn in Babylonia later than ca. 2700 B.C. and are also unknown in India, as far as one can ascertain, except in the Indus Valley Civilization" (Mackay 1931: 511, note 2).

It may be noted that this carnelian bead type occurs along with etched carnelian beads at Kish. Regarding these etched beads a recent researcher is of the opinion that they are found in Cemetery A and do not seem to have been imported after Early Dynastic IIIB (During Caspers 1971: 88).[1] Obviously this chronological range should apply as well to the long barrel-cylinder carnelian beads at this site and there is seemingly no doubt about Mackay's Pre-Sargonic dating of this bead type there.

The Pre-Sargonic chronology for this Indus bead type is also confirmed by its presence in the Royal Graves at Ur. It is clear from Beck's statement cited earlier that Woolley found "a very few similar beads from Ur." It has not been possible to locate them in Woolley's publications on Ur, but a study of the Beck collection in the Haddon Museum, Cambridge leaves no doubt of their occurrence in the Royal Graves. There are four unmistakably Indus long barrel-cylinder carnelian beads in that collection. The museum record on them is not detailed but is clear enough for one's purpose:

No. 47.2215 B: one specimen. There is no detailed record except that it is from the Royal Graves at Ur. 1933-34 is noted as the excavation season.

No. 47.2116: two specimens. There is no specific record except that they are from Ur. The year mentioned is 1927-28.

No. 48.2411: one specimen. It is supposed to be from the "Early Sumerian" Period at Ur. The year noted is 1928-29.

In the University Museum, Philadelphia, there are at least four carnelian beads of this type, apart from three more similar beads of an unidentified material (Pl. 24.2).

Museum no. 30-12-566: three specimens. The author could not identify the very dark green stone used for these beads (Pl. 24.2a).

Museum no. 30-12-567: one specimen. Carnelian (Pl. 24.2b).

Museum no. 32-40-227: two specimens; one complete, one broken. Carnelian (Pl. 24.2c).

Expedition no. U 17745: one specimen. Carnelian.

The Museum records for these beads indicate that they belong to the Akkadian graves at Ur. Those with museum numbers 30-12-566 and 30-12-567 are from private grave 1422 which has been dated by Buchanan

(1954) to the Post-Akkadian Period. Maxwell-Hyslop (1974: 67, Pl. 48a, c) in her study of West Asian jewelry has illustrated four of these specimens (University Museum nos. 30-12-566, 567) and she has put them under "the Guti-Gudea period, Third Dynasty of Ur to the Isin-Larsa Dynasties, 2250-1894 B.C." (Maxwell-Hyslop 1974: 67). In any case, if our study is correct, the carnelian long barrel-cylinder beads were known at Ur from the Pre-Sargonic Period to the Akkadian or even the Isin-Larsa Period.

There are two additional sites of interest outside Mesopotamia: Susa and Jalalabad. The occurrence of long barrel-cylinder carnelian beads at these sites has been reported (Chakrabarti and Moghadam 1977). The specimens are housed in the Tehran Museum. There is only one specimen from Susa (Tehran Museum necklace no. 11726). There are three complete specimens and two broken ones from Jalalabad (Tehran Museum necklace nos. 26040 and 26036). The museum record only mentions the sites from where these specimens came. The material from Jalalabad, which also contains etched carnelian beads, is a part of the surface collection. As far as one could ascertain, there is only one published reference to a site called Jalalabad in Iran. It is near Persepolis and is shown as number 32 on Paul Gotch's survey of Bakun A5 sites on the Fars Plain (Gotch 1971: Fig. 1). Bakun A5 Ware is supposed to continue up to the middle of the third millennium B.C., and thus the Harappan contact at the site is not surprising. Incidentally, this evidence of interaction, in the form of two types of Indus beads (etched carnelian and long barrel-cylinder carnelian) at Jalalabad is particularly significant because the route between Tepe Yahya and Susa, two well-known points of Indus contact in southern Iran, must have passed along the Fars Plain. It would be well worth a visit for those interested in the Indus-West Asia relationships to explore this site.

There are thus four sites in West Asia with Indus long barrel-cylinder carnelian beads: Kish, Ur, Jalalabad and Susa. Each of these sites has also produced etched carnelian beads. At both Ur and Kish the earliest occurrence of this bead type is Pre-Sargonic which is the earliest context for etched carnelian beads. The long barrel-cylinder carnelian beads are thus one of the earliest pieces of evidence for Indus-Mesopotamia contact, and Mackay's original postulate seems to be amply vindicated.

At this point I want to recount the basic evidence for Pre-Sargonic contact between the Harappan Civilization and Mesopotamia. The purpose of this exercise will be directed toward corroborating the evidence furnished by the etched and long barrel-cylinder carnelian beads for Pre-Sargonic interaction. A piece of evidence which immediately comes to mind is the steatite/chlorite vessel-fragment from the lower levels of Mohenjodaro. This belongs to an intercultural style of vessels which, as P. Kohl has demonstrated, are "best dated to the end of Early Dynastic II-Early Dynastic IIIA" (Kohl 1974: 271). There are two more steatite/chlorite pieces which were reported from Tell Agrab in the Diyala region Mesopotamia by Henry Frankfort in 1936 and 1937 (Frankfort 1936, 1937). These have been generally ignored in the recent literature on the subject. For instance, none of the three recent bibliographies of the Indus Civilization even mentions these publications by Frankfort (Pande and Ramachandran 1971; Brunswig 1973; Possehl 1979). In his first report on Tell Agrab in 1936 Frankfort published two fragments of a steatite vase belonging to the Early Dynastic Period. Frankfort writes:

> While the human figure on the one fragment is purely Mesopotamian, the scene on the other hand is as certainly alien to Sumerian art and religion. This shows the building in front of which the figure is seated. The facade is mostly lost, but just connects the two sherds. Inside the building we see a large humped bull standing in front of a manger. Now, the wild ox and the water buffalo were indigenous to Mesopotamia: the humped bull was not. Moreover, no scene which could be interpreted as a rendering of animal worship is known in Mesopotamia. We find in an entirely Mesopotamian setting the rendering of an Indian cult.

Gordon Childe (1964: 170) subsequently wrote that the style of the vase could be used to date it to Early Dynastic III. He also accepted the Indus significance suggested by Frankfort. Another authority who agrees with Frankfort's conclusion on this point is Max Mallowan (1965: 22).

In 1937 Frankfort reported a painted pot from Tell Agrab which also belonged to the Early Dynastic period and confirmed, according to him, the evidence of the stone vase found in the previous season. The painted frieze on the pot shows:

> A bull tethered inside a building, and it is difficult not to connect the three female figures, who seem to be beating cymbals or tambourines with some ceremony of worship, the central feature of which

is the bull.... Neither the texts nor other monuments have so far supplied us with evidence about this curious feature, which is shown, by the seals from Mohenjodaro and Harappa, to have been quite usual in India.

It is possible to argue that the evidence cited by Frankfort is not conclusive; but when viewed in the total context of the Pre-Sargonic occurrence of etched and long barrel-cylinder carnelian beads and the intercultural style vessel fragment from the lower levels of Mohenjodaro, this evidence from Tell Agrab makes good sense. Incidentally, the design of a bull seated in front of a temple facade is a common enough motif on ritual metal vessels sold in Hindu pilgrim centers even today.

Another piece of evidence may be interesting in the present context. This was published by Charles Fabri (1937). He reported a short (only three signs) inscription on a vessel from Mohenjodaro. These signs do not obviously resemble any of the signs of the Indus script. Fabri did, however, find them in Mercer's *Sumero-Babylonian Sign List*. The identifications (and Fabri's translation) were sent to, and endorsed by, Franz M. Th. Bohl who is mentioned by Fabri as "the world-famous Assyriologist of Lyden University." Fabri's translation need not concern one here, but what is significant in the present context is Fabri's suggestion that the shape of characters indicates that they "cannot be older than 2800 (B.C.) by any means, and that it is much more likely that it belongs to a period not far removed from 2500 B.C." As far as one can determine, this publication and opinion of Fabri have not been subject to close scrutiny.[2]

Finally, in view of all this evidence the so-called Pre-Sargonic rectangular seal with a bull and an inscription in three or four signs, found virtually on the surface at Ur (Gadd 1932: 3) merits some attention. According to Gadd the signs "are in any case pre-Sargonic" (Gadd 1932: 4). There is, however, nothing specifically Indus about the seal except the bull and the distinctive rectangular shape. It is possible to agree with Gadd that this may be an adaptation from the Harappan type either at Ur or at a place "under the influence both of the Indus and of the Sumerian civilization" (Gadd 1932: 5). The point to note is the Pre-Sargonic character of the signs along with the rectangular shape of the seal which is alien to the Mesopotamian repertoire. There is another rectangular seal (bearing only a scorpion and a sign of writing) from Private Grave no. 791 in the Royal Cemetery at Ur (Woolley 1934: 568, Pl. 192). This grave, according to Woolley, is "clearly dated by external evidence to the time of Shub-ad" (1934: 568).

To sum up, with the long barrel-cylinder carnelian beads as a starting point the present paper has tried to underline different pieces of the evidence for Pre-Sargonic Indus-Mesopotamia contact. The primary data, as noted, belong to three categories: long barrel-cylinder and etched carnelian beads and the steatite/chlorite vessel fragment with mat or basket weave from the lower levels of Mohenjodaro. Attention has also been drawn to Frankfort's, Childe's and Mallowan's opinions on the Indus character of the Early Dynastic vase from Agrab. This vase has however been treated by Kohl as a part of the intercultural style vessels with "figure" motifs. He is doubtful of the Indian characterization of the humped bull: "Today the bulls of the Soghun valley are humped, and it may be possible to prove that they existed at Tepe Yahya as early as its initial occupation" (Kohl 1974: 168). However, as has been emphasized, what makes this vase (and the Tell Agrab painted pot) interesting is not merely the humped bull but also the general composition with the suggestion of a religious association which recalls India.

No inference can yet be made from Fabri's "Sumero-Babylonian" inscription from the Mohenjodaro jar; but surely this publication deserves far more careful scrutiny than it has been accorded so far. Finally, two rectangular seals in Pre-Sargonic context have been discussed for the simple reason that the rectangular shape in itself suggests the Harappan Civilization.

One may note in conclusion that the basic theoretical significance of Pre-Sargonic contact between the Harappan Civilization and Mesopotamia is that it makes it possible to visualize the growth of urbanization in India at virtually the same time as Sumer.

NOTES

[1] During Caspers' comparison of a small stone head from a presumably Harappan level of Dabar Kot with an Early Dynastic Sumerian sculpture from the Diyala Valley (During Caspers 1963) is suggestive of a Pre-Sargonic contact between the Indus Valley and Mesopotamia. This stylistic argument is interesting, but cannot be treated as conclusive given the nature of the evidence from Dabar Kot and our general knowledge of Baluchistan at this time.

[2] The present author sought the opinion of J.V. Kinnier-Wilson in this matter. He disagreed with Fabri's suggestion of "Sumero-Babylonian" affinity for these signs. But, the signs do not seem to be purely Harappan and considering that Fabri had the backing of a professional Assyriologist the issue is perhaps deserving of a review from both sides at this time.

BIBLIOGRAPHY

Beck, H.C., 1940
 Report on Selected Beads from Harappa. In *Excavations at Harappa.* M.S. Vats, Vol. 1. Pp. 392-412. Delhi: Government of India.

Brunswig, Robert H., 1973
 A Comprehensive Bibliography of the Indus Civilization. *Asian Perspectives* 16: 75-111.

Buchanan, B. 1954
 The date of the so-called "Second dynasty" graves of the Royal Cemetry at Ur. *Journal of the American Oriental Society* 74.

Chakrabarti, Dilip K. and Parveen Moghadm, 1977
 Some Unpublished Indus Beads from Iran. *Iran* 15: 166-68.

Childe, V.G., 1964
 New Light on the Most Ancient East. Revised edition. New York: Praeger.

During Caspers, E.C.L., 1963
 A Male Head Found at Dabar Kot. *Antiquity* 37: 294.

During Caspers, E.C.L., 1971
 Etched Carnelian Beads. *Bulletin of the Institute of Archaeology* 10. London: London University.

Fabri, C.L., 1937
 A Sumero-Babylonian Inscription Discovered at Mohenjodaro. *Indian Culture* 3: 662-73.

Frankfort, H., 1936
 A New Site in Mesopotamia: Tell Agrab, temples deserted 5000 years ago and a wealth of art relics, including fresh proof of Indo-Sumerian cultural associations. *Illustrated London News.* September 12: 432-36.

Frankfort, H., 1937
 Revelations of Early Mesopotamian Culture. New Discoveries at Tell Agrab: An ass-drawn chariot and art relics from an Early Dynastic temple with indications of bull worship and communications with ancient India. *Illustrated London News.* November 6: 792-95.

Gadd, C.J., 1932
 Seals of Ancient Indian Style Found at Ur. *Proceedings of the British Academy* 18: 1-22.

Gotch, P., 1971
 Bakun A5 Pottery. *Bulletin of the Asia Institute of Pahlavi University*, Shiraz 2: 73-90.

Kohl, P., 1974
 Seeds of Upheaval: The production of chlorite at Tepe Yahya and an analysis of commodity production and trade in southwest Asia in the third millennium. Ph.D. dissertation, Anthropology Department, Harvard University.

Mackay, E.J.H., 1929
 A Sumerian Palace and the 'A' Cemetery at Kish, Mesopotamia. Anthropology Memoirs, I (2). Chicago: Field Museum of Natural History.

Mackay, E.J.H., 1931
 Personal Ornaments. In *Mohenjodaro and the Indus Civilization.* J. Marshall, ed. Vol. 2, Pp. 509-48. London: Arthur Probsthain.

Mackay, E.J.H., 1938
 Further Excavations at Mohenjodaro. 2 vols. Delhi: Government of India.

Mackay, E.J.H., 1943
 Chanhudaro Excavations, 1935-36. American Oriental Series 20. New Haven: American Oriental Society.

Mallowan, M., 1965
 Early Mesopotamia and Iran. London: Thames and Hudson.

Maxwell-Hyslop, K.R., 1974
> *Western Asiatic Jewellery*. Reprinted edition. London: Metheun.

Pande, B.M. and K.S. Ramchandran, 1971
> *Bibliography of the Harappan Culture*. Florida: Field Research Projects.

Possehl, G.L., 1979
> An Extensive Bibliography of the Indus Civilization. In *Ancient Cities of the Indus*. G.L. Possehl, ed. Pp. 363-422. Delhi: Vikas.

Woolley, L., 1934
> *Ur Excavations II. The Royal Cemetery*. London and Philadelphia: The British Museum and the University Museum.

SHASHI ASTHANA

25. Harappan Trade in Metals and Minerals: A Regional Approach

THE Harappans, like the Sumerians, made many articles fashioned from a variety of metals and minerals including semiprecious stones. The area most closely identified with the Harappan Civilization is, however, nearly devoid of these products which seem to have been so essential to the functioning of this urban system. Thus the Harappans, once again like the Sumerians, were involved in a complex trading system which allowed them access to these metals and minerals and the means for their internal distribution. The primary sources for the products under discussion appear to have been Baluchistan, Afghanistan, Iran, Soviet Central Asia, the lands bordering the Persian Gulf as well as interior, peninsular India (Fig. 25.1). Products such as lapis lazuli, chlorite/steatite and turquoise have already been discussed in detail as individual components of this commerce (e.g., Herrmann 1966, 1968; Kohl 1975, 1976; Tosi 1974). But to the best of my knowledge no integrated picture of the Harappan exploitation and trade in metals and minerals has yet been attempted. It is hoped that this paper will make some progress in this direction by highlighting two important aspects: (1) the extent to which the Harappans exploited these resources directly and/or indirectly, and (2) the extent to which archaeological remains outside the Harappan Culture area help in visualizing the pattern of natural resource exploitation and trade.

These aspects are dealt with in the framework developed elsewhere (Asthana 1979a: 31-47). There it has been shown that two major units of trade[1]—production and distribution—were used by the Harappans to strengthen their commerce. The production unit, which procured raw materials from neighboring areas or distant places, worked for the distribution unit which serviced outside markets.

There is a frustrating paucity of published geological and mineralogical information on Iran, Afghanistan, Pakistan, and neighboring countries. Nevertheless, the known source areas for the metals and semiprecious stones which have been found at Harappan sites, (e.g., lapis lazuli, turquoise, steatite/chlorite, carnelian, gold, silver, lead, copper and tin) have been plotted. In the process it has been shown that the exploitation pattern was essentially regional. The distribution pattern of rare minerals and metals was centralized, however, since their procurement could not be diffused.

SEMIPRECIOUS STONE

Lapis Lazuli

Lapis lazuli was in great demand in Mesopotamia where it was used for personal adornment and for the decoration of temples. It was also prized by the Harappans. This stone is first documented during the Pre- and Early Harappan times and it continued to be used through the Late Harappan Period. Beads of lapis lazuli have been found in Baluchistan at Nal (Hargraves 1929: 34, 43), Kulli (Stein 1931: 123), Mehi (Stein 1931: 158) and Shahi Tump (Stein 1931: 96). In the greater Indus Valley, Rahman Dheri (Durrani 1977), Sarai Khola (Halim 1972a, 1972b), Jalilpur (Mughal 1974: 112), Gumla (Dani 1970-71: 86), Amri (Casal 1964: 154-55), Pandi Wahi (Majumdar 1934: 13), Jhukar (Majumdar 1934: 13),

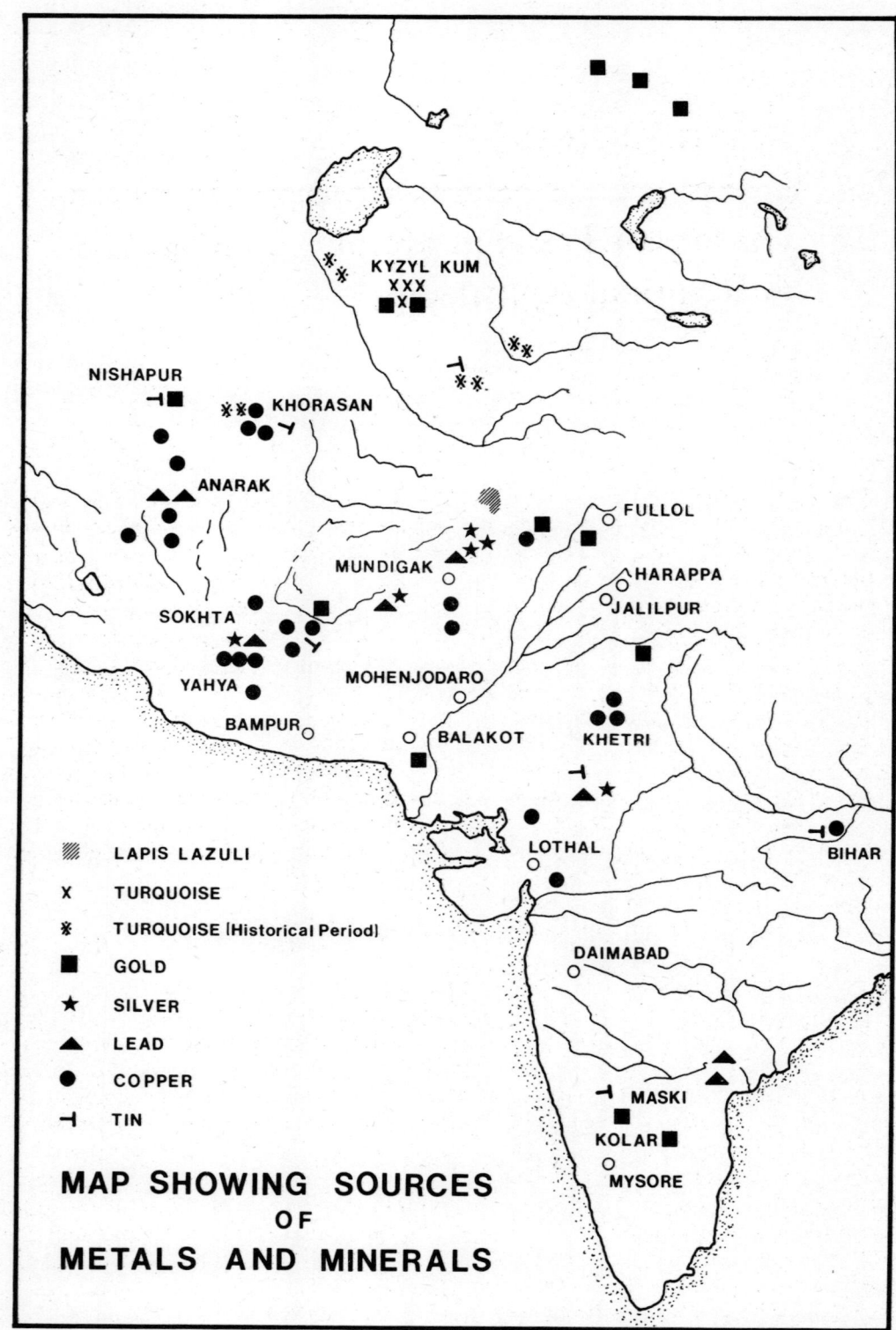

Fig. 25. 1. Harappan sources of metals and minerals.

Mohenjodaro (Marshall 1931: 542-43, 571), Chanhudaro (Mackay 1943: 203, 207, 209; Majumdar, 1934: 40), Harappa (Vats 1940: 59, 403, 413, 441) and Balakot (Dales 1979b: 50) have yielded the lapis lazuli beads. Lapis beads and pendants were found in limited quantities at Kalibangan (Chakrabarti 1978: 53) in Rajasthan, Lothal in Gujarat (Rao 1973: 102), Surkotada in Kutch (Joshi unpublished) and Banawali (Bisht 1978: 88) in Haryana. The trading importance of lapis lazuli cannot be denied since it has been found on all the important excavated Harappan sites, beginning from the Pre-Harappan times.

The source areas for this semiprecious stone are eastern Siberia—the Pamirs and an area near Lake Baikal (Webster, 1975: 219-22); Afghanistan—Badakshan (Herrmann 1968) and a few hypothetical Iranian and Indian sources (Chakrabarti 1978). The eastern Siberian sources do not produce as fine a quality of stone as the one used by the Harappans. Further, these sources were probably beyond the practical reach of the Harappans due to the great distances. The Iranian and Indian sources are known to us only from literary documents and have not been confirmed by geological survey. Thus, while the Iranian literary sources locate lapis mines in Mazanderan and Dizmar in Azerbaijan as well as Kirman (Hamd-Allah Mustawfi of Qazvin 1919: 197), the geological survey reports are absolutely silent on the subject. The well-known mines of Afghanistan are thus the most likely sources. These are located in the Kerano Munjan District of Badakshan Province in the Hindu Kush (Herrmann 1968: 21-57). This is an inhospitable country of bare mountains and deep ravines. A group of four mines is situated in the Kerano Munjan Valley, altitudes ranging between 2000 and 5500 meters (Herrmann 1968: 22):

1) Chilmak
2) Shaga-Darra-i-Robat-i-Paskaran
3) Stormy
4) Sar-i-Sang

In 1964 an Oxford University expedition examined these ancient works (Herrmann 1968: 24) and found that Sar-i-Sang is the only mine which is in use today. Unfortunately no remains of the Protohistoric Period were found during this visit. These settlements were perhaps washed away by the eroding river just as happened to a recently abandoned village called Lajvar Shui. In any case the lapis from these mines could easily have been taken on tracks to the north or south, following the course of the Kokcha River.

It is a reasonably established fact that Badakshan was supplying lapis lazuli to the whole of West and South Asia. Discovery of the Harappan trading posts at Shortugai, near Ai-Khanum in Afghanistan (Lyonnet 1977) indicates that the Harappans were present in this region and were familiar with this source. Still, the limited quantity of lapis objects at Harappan settlements poses a peculiar problem. If the Harappans were exploiting this source why aren't there more lapis objects at their settlements? It appears that during the Pre-Harappan times the lapis trade was in other hands, possibly the people of Shahr-i Sokhta, and when the Harappans came, they took over (Gupta 1979). Archaeological evidence at Sokhta also shows that by 2300 B.C. the trade in lapis had declined considerably there. This is possibly a reflection of Harappan activity. Cuneiform texts from Mesopotamia (Leemans 1960), which list lapis as one of the commodities coming from Meluhha, further affirm the contention that the Harappans were fully involved in the lapis trade. They may even have been the main suppliers. They probably brought this material up the Makran Coast to Sutkagendor and shipped it from there to Mesopotamia, and places like Shahdad in Kirman (Asthana 1979b). To reach Shahdad they may have used the Bampur Valley and the Kirman gap. Thus, the Harappans appear to have been the primary exporters, and not the consumers, of lapis and lapis objects, and this is the reason that Harappan towns have yielded the stone, but not in an appreciable quantity. This view is somewhat at variance with that held by Chakrabarti (1978) and others.

Turquoise

Only a few Harappan sites have yielded turquoise, and it does not appear to have been a very popular item with them. It is not found in India though there are literary sources of the historical period which state that it could be found in the Ajmer Hills of Rajputana. Mohenjodaro (Marshall 1931: 523, 525) Rahman Dheri (Durrani 1977) and Mehrgarh (Jarrige and Lechevallier 1979) are so far the only sites to have yielded turquoise and these were just a few in the form of beads. This may indicate that the Harappans obtained the finished beads and not the raw material. In other words, turquoise may not have figured as an item in organized trade.

Turquoise comes from the mountainous territory of the inner Kyzyl Kum and the mountains of Ilak (Karamazar) in ancient Khodjent (Leninabad), located along the upper reaches of the Syr Darya in Soviet Central Asia (Tosi 1974). According to Hole and Flannery (1968: 179) and Wright (1969: 55) during prehistoric times turquoise came from the well-known sources near Nishapur in Iran. Several deposits have also been reported between Kirman and Yazd and there is evidence of early working at these sites (Pogue 1915: 40). Literary sources also attest this. According to Pliny (Book XXXVII, Chap. 33) Carmania was a source of callaina (turquoise). Marco Polo also mentions the presence of turquoise in Kirman (Sykes 1902: 265). It is thus somewhat puzzling that with turquoise so amply available in Iran the Harappan towns did not make more extensive use of it.

As the evidence stands to date Mehrgarh VI has yielded a few turquoise beads (Jarrige and Lechevallier 1979) along with those of lapis lazuli. The beads appear to have come to the site in finished form. Shahr-i Sokhta II (Tosi 1974: 147-62) has evidence for a workshop for lapis and turquoise as does Mundigak III (Jarrige and Lechevallier 1979). It is thus possible that Mehrgarh got its turquoise beads from Shahr-i Sokhta or Mundigak. The turquoise beads at Mohenjodaro could have come from either of these sources, but Mundigak is possibly the more likely since it was in regular contact with the Harappans as is evident from several objects of Harappan type that were found there. Sokhta may also have been the source for at least some of the turquoise beads but unfortunately nothing tangible has yet come from this site which could establish Sokhta-Harappan interaction.

Steatite/Chlorite

Alabaster, carnelian and steatite/chlorite are not very useful commodities for the study of trade because they are relatively widely found in Iran, Pakistan, India and Saudi Arabia. The extensive use of steatite for making vases, seals, beads, figurines and decorative objects found on almost all Indus sites suggests that there was a regular supply of this material to Harappan cities. It also indicates that the stone was readily available in the neighboring regions. A number of sources have been reported in North Gujarat (Rao 1973: 116) at Devni Mori, Kundol, Lokha and Mora; although there is no proof of their being in use during prehistoric times. Marshall (1931: 678) reported a number of sources in Rajasthan, such as at Dogetha, Gisgarh and Morra and he suggested that these were the Harappan sources. Rao (1973: 116) however, suggests that Karnataka might have supplied this material to the Indus people via the contemporary Neolithic people of the Deccan. In return they may have obtained copper tools and steatite disc beads. To support his theory he uses two points: (1) the disc beads of burnt steatite found at the Chalcolithic/Neolithic sites of the Karnataka/Andhra region are identical to Harappan wafer beads, and (2) the occurrence of parallel-sided stone blades and evolved Harappan ceramic types in a form of Black and Red Ware at Singanapalli, Pusalapadu, etc., in Kurnool District may indicate interaction.

Another promising steatite source is in northern Baluchistan and the adjoining areas. The Zhob District has two localities, the largest of which occurs about 50 kilometers north of Fort Sandeman (Pithawala 1952: 202). There is evidence that these were mined in the ancient past. Chlorite is available in the Kirman region of Iran, near the Soghun Valley (Kohl 1976: 74) and also in western Saudi Arabia (Goldsmith 1971: 54).

The most important objects made of steatite/chlorite are stone vases like those found from Mari to the Indus. The exact places of production of these objects and the sources of raw material are imperfectly known; however there is at least one major workshop at Tepe Yahya in the Soghun Valley which is very rich in this raw material. From this evidence it is clear that some chlorite was mined in the southern part of Iran and vases of this material were made at Yahya and supplied to areas both east and west. But the typological studies of these vases and scientific analysis of the raw material made by Philip Kohl (1975: 30) indicate the existence of workshops other than Yahya and sources other than the Kirman mines. The two fragments of four-compartmented vessels showing a zigzag pattern, which were found at Mohenjodaro (Marshall 1931: 36-37, Pl. CXXXI) have no parallels at Yahya but they do have at Shahdad (Hakemi 1972: Pl. XIVa, b). The latter site may have been the workshop which can only be confirmed by further excavation there. Scientific analysis (Kohl 1975: 30) further shows that the stone was obtained from several sources and not from Kirman alone. It has been proved beyond doubt that the Sumerian chlorite is different from that at Yahya. The former is closer to the material coming from farther east and there is some possibility that the Sumerians obtained their steatite/chlorite via trade from the sources in Baluchistan. But at the same time the Harappans appear to have been very much aware of the Kirman sources and the workshops at Yahya and Shahdad. This is evident from the two compartmented vessels at Mohenjodaro and etched carnelian beads at Shahdad (Kohl, personal examination) and Yahya as well as the Harappan characters on a potsherd from Yahya (Lamberg-Karlovsky 1970; Lamberg-Karlovsky and Tosi 1973; Asthana 1979b).

Carnelian

The use of carnelian for beads and pendants was fairly common amongst the Harappans. Almost all Indus sites have yielded carnelian beads in a variety of forms. Of them, those of etched carnelian are worth particular note since they crossed the borders of India to reach Mesopotamia and Iran (Susa, Shahdad, Yahya). This stone is widely available in India. There are a number of sources in Madhya Pradesh, Rajasthan, etc., but the main deposit for the Harappans appears to be in Kathiawad at Rajpipla near the village of Ratanpur (Marshall 1931: 681). There are also Harappan sites near this place. The only well-known Iranian carnelian source is in the dry branches of the Helmand River in Seistan near Shahr-i Sokhta (Tosi 1969: 374). The absence of any Harappan remains in the Seistan area (of course only at the present showing) makes it difficult to assess the possible Harappan knowledge of this source.

A cylinder seal of Gudea of Lagash refers to bright carnelian, copper, tin and lapis lazuli coming from Meluhha (Leemans 1960). If Meluhha can be taken as the area of the Harappan Civilization, then it was exporting carnelian, probably by exploiting Indian sources. But other mines may have been involved as well. The discovery of etched carnelian beads at Mesopotamian and Iranian sites (Susa, Shahdad and Tepe Yahya) demonstrates, however, that carnelian beads were in demand in the West Asian markets (During Caspers 1971: 205-76; Asthana 1979a, 1979b).

METALS

By Harappan times metallurgy was a refined technique. Gold, silver, copper, tin and lead were all available to Harappan smiths.

Gold

Gold objects and ornaments have been found at Mohenjodaro, Harappa, Lothal, Kalibangan, Banawali, Rahman Dheri, etc. Gold is widely distributed in India. A majority of Indian rivers have gold in their sands, although only in very small amounts when washed (Marshall 1931: 674). South India is, however, very rich in gold with mines located in Anantpur, Coimbatore, (Hadabanatta, Kavudahalli and near Porsegaundanpalayan) and Wynaad (Marshall 1931: 674). In Karnataka old mining areas are numerous and the Kolar mines are still famous for their gold. According to Marshall, the Kolar mines may have supplied gold to the Harappans (Marshall, 1931: 674). This view is also held by Rao (1973: 116).

Iran, Afghanistan and Soviet Central Asia also have several important gold sources which may have supplied Harappan demand. Literary sources give some clues to these ancient deposits. Strabo refers to the River Hyktanis in Carmania as a source of gold and an Assyrian inscription indicates the presence of gold in Kawend (Media) (Forbes 1971: 165). The other important deposits which do not have reference in the texts (Forbes 1971: 166), are the one near Damghan; another between Nishapur and Meshad; a third, about three kilometers east of Meshad in the Tiran mountains; a fourth, west of Isphan near Hamadan; a fifth, in the region of southeast of Tehran; and finally, the one in the northwest of the Takht-i Suleiman. But Afghanistan may also have provided some gold to the Harappans. It is found in small quantities near Kandahar. So also does it come from the north side of the Hindu Kush. The other sources are the streams draining the Kuh-i-Baba, the streams in Kohistan and above Laghman and Kunar (Marshall 1931: 674). However, the richer sources lie in Soviet Central Asia. South of the Caucasus, in Armenia, the famous metal workers, the Chalybes, are credited with rich mines. This probably means the deposits near the Taldjen River, close to Artwin. Other traditional gold bearing areas are the Urals, Siberia and the Far East. Gold is washed in many places in the Karakoram and in the beds of a number of rivers of Central Asia. The Muruntau mountains in the Kyzyl Kum desert has the largest deposit of gold (Forbes 1971: 166; Kalesnik and Pavlenko 1976: 202).

Today the Soviet Union is a major supplier of gold to the world market and it probably played the same role in the remote past. The discovery of the famous Fullol Hoard in the Hindu Kush of northern Afghanistan (Tosi and Waradak 1972: 9-17) contained a number of gold objects with Mesopotamian and South Turkmenian motifs. This proves that the region (the Oxus basin—northern Hindu Kush) was as important to the Middle East for gold as it was for lapis lazuli. Incidentally, the Harappan trading posts at Shortugai are also in the same region (Francfort and Potter 1978: 29). Harappan contacts with Central Asia are now beyond doubt especially after the discovery of: (1) a few Harappan pottery types in Namazga V sites, (2) a Harappan inscribed seal at Altin Depe, (3) comparable ivory objects at Altin Depe, and (4) a close similarity in a few copper artifacts (Gupta 1979: Vol. 2). Thus, the role of Shortugai as transit camp is made self evident. The Harappans were evidently supplying ivory to Central Asians, either as raw material or in the form of finished goods. What is important to infer is what the Harappans got in return. It may have been gold.

Silver and Lead

Silver was another important metal known to the Harappans. It was apparently quite popular with the Harappans living at Mohenjodaro and Harappa, but those at Lothal and Kalibangan rarely used it. Silver was used for making vases and ornaments, such as bracelets, bangles and beads. The source of this metal is difficult to ascertain as far as the Harappans were concerned; however small quantities of silver are frequently found in conjunction with lead at a few places in India. Lead is plentiful at Mohenjodaro (Marshall 1931: 524) and it is to be noted that traces of lead have been found in a sample of silver from the site (Marshall 1931: 524). This makes it probable that it was extracted from lead ores. Rajasthan (Rao 1973: 116), Bihar and Orissa (Marshall 1931: 675) contain several silver-bearing lead deposits; but these are small. Since Bihar and Orissa are so far from the Indus, the Ajmer and Jawar mines in Rajasthan are likely sources for these metals as far as the Harappans are concerned. But the case is not proved. Gold mines at Kolar and Anantpur also yield silver with gold, but not in quantity enough for commercial purposes.

Another silver source, possibly the most promising for Mohenjodaro and Harappa, is in Afghanistan and Iran (Marshall 1931: 675-77). Lead mines, which could have been a source for silver as well, are situated in Faranjal in the Ghorband Valley of Afghanistan and are common in southern Afghanistan, especially at Hazara Jat. Well-known silver mines are also known to have existed near the head of the Panjsher Valley in the southeastern Hindu Kush and in the vicinity of Herat.

The Persian sources are located in the southeast at Khu-i Nugre and between Fasa and Zahedan. Armenia also had silver mines at Gumush Khaneh. These were exceptionally rich and known in ancient times. Indus-Caucasus interaction, however, has still not been proved. The finds of silver in appreciable quantities at Mohenjodaro and Harappa coupled with the fact that there is little at either Lothal or Kalibangan indicates that the source was probably on the western borderlands. Afghanistan is the most likely source area at this time.

The source of lead may also be investigated. As noted above, lead ores were mined during the Harappan period. This metal was added to copper to increase the feasibility of molding and has been extensively reported in Harappan artifacts (Agrawal 1971: 156). It was rarely used for making utensils and ornaments. Large finds of lead at Harappa (Vats 1940: 58) and Mohenjodaro include only a lead vase and a lead dish (Mackay 1938: 450). Besides the dish, Mohenjodaro has produced the following lead objects: a small lead ornament with faience disc, a hook (Mackay 1938: 472) a round lead ball with a copper or bronze staple attached to it (Mackay 1938: 476) and a lump which may be the net sinker (Marshall 1931: 30). Balakot had produced a flat, semicircular piece of native lead (Dales 1979a).

Lead might have been used mainly as a smelting flux. This is evident because of the discovery of copper ore together with a small piece of lead in a bricklined pit in a house at Mohenjodaro (Mackay 1938: 41). That lead was available in India has been noted above. Afghanistani and Irani sources were, however, also quite important for the Indus, as has also been mentioned. Along the road, between the mines at Nakhlak and Bayazeh one can see numerous heaps of lead slag (Wertime 1968: 930-31). The mines of Nakhlak represent the easternmost extension of the Anarak Zone of ores. Kazakhstan is also very rich in lead, especially the western part of the Altai mountains and the Karatau range (Kalesnik and Pavlenko 1976: 199). The best mines, however, occur around Ispahan, Kirman and in the Elburz mountains. Conclusively, it seems very likely that the Harappans obtained their lead from the same place they procured their silver—Afghanistan.

Copper

Copper is not too useful for the study of trade as it

is widely distributed in both Iran and India. It was very popular with the Harappans and they used it for many purposes. In fact, there is not a single site which has not yielded copper objects. This indicates that it was readily available and abundant, and, therefore, was not a precious or rare item.

The wide distribution of copper ores in India, Baluchistan, Afghanistan, Central Asia, Iran and Oman poses a serious archaeological problem: which area(s) were actually used by the Harappans? It is obvious that the whole Harappan area is not likely to have obtained copper from a single source, and the pattern of impurities in copper attests this. For example, the copper at Mohenjodaro and Harappa contained nickel and arsenic (Agrawal 1971) while Lothal copper is arsenic free (Rao 1973: 80). Several copper sources are known in India: Rajasthan, Bihar, Andhra and Kumaon. The Rajasthan mines are at Khetri, Singhana, Kho-Dariba (Alwar), Delwara Kirovli (Udaipur) and Debari (Udaipur) (Seth 1956). Of these, Khetri is the most important for two reasons. First, a close comparison of the impurity patterns derived from the spectroscopic analysis of the Harappan artifacts and various ores shows that there is a close correspondence with the Khetri mines (Agrawal 1971: 175). Second, there are copper celts, Indus arrowheads and pottery of the third millennium B.C. (Agrawala 1978, 1979) from Ganeshwar (Sikar District). This suggests that Khetri-Ganeshwar copper mines were exploited as the source for this metal since Khetri is only 60 kilometers from Ganeshwar. The copper at Mohenjodaro and Harappa may also have come from the Khetri area (or from Afghanistan as discussed later) while Lothal copper probably came from another source, possibly Oman in Saudi Arabia (Rao 1973: 80).

It is almost impossible to believe that the Khetri mines were supplying copper to all Harappan sites. Alternate sources, probably exploited by the Harappans, are on the western frontiers in Baluchistan, Afghanistan and Iran. There are copper deposits in Zhob District (Mughal 1970: 194), Robat (Hunting Survey Corporation 1961) and Shah Bellaul (Forbes 1972) area of Baluchistan. This metal has also been located between Ziarat (Quetta District) and Sohan (Sarawan Subdistrict) but it is not known that they were mined during Harappan times (Mughal 1970: 194). Huan Tsang mentions copper mines in Afghanistan and ancient workings have been located near the Safed-Kuh between Kabul and Kurram (Forbes 1972: 13). Shah Maqsud also contains rich veins of copper ore and it is said that Nadir Shah exploited them (Forbes 1972: 13). Rich ores are also said to occur at Nesh, 100 kilometers from Kandahar. Other localities are Tezin, east of Kabul, Musai in the Shadkani Pass and the Silwatu Pass (Forbes 1972: 13).

Iran is rich in copper, and metallurgy has a long tradition there going back to the fifth millennium B.C. at Tal-i Iblis in Kirman (Caldwell 1967). The best mines are in Kirman as well as Kal-seb Zarre, Sabzwar and Cahr Daud near Meshad, Kaleh near Astrabad and in the Elburz mountain districts of Kashan Kohund and Isfahan and Anarak (Wertime 1968).

There are also rich deposits with signs of ancient working in the Altai mountains at Ridder and other places. In Kazakhstan there are rich ore deposits in Makain, Boschtschekul, Kounrad and Dscheskagan. It is only certain that these were worked in recent times. Kyzyl Kum desert has a copper industry at Temba Bulach but this is of uncertain antiquity (Kalesnik and Pavlenko 1976). The eastern Iranian border also has a long belt of copper deposits.

It is difficult to say which of these deposits were definitely exploited by the Harappans. It should not be difficult to comprehend, however, that people as adventurous as the Harappans, who crossed the seas to Mesopotamia and ventured to Soviet Central Asia for trade, could have exploited several of them, some possibly indirectly through intermediaries. In short, it can be said that both Indian sources and those on the western borderlands are most likely to have been directly exploited by the Harappans. Those in the more remote areas of Iran or Central Asia may have served as "markets" from which Harappans obtained this metal in return for finished goods or raw materials. Oman may have played an especially important role in this context; but nothing precise can be said about this at the present stage of knowledge.

Tin

Copper was in extensive use during Harappan times. But tin was also known and they used it to make tin-based bronze. Nothing definite is known about tin in the Pre-Harappan tool assemblage; however Stein's findings in Baluchistan throw some light on it (Marshall 1931: 488). He collected a few bronzes from Shahi Tump, Mehi, Siah Damb and Segak Mound, all of which have a high tin percentage. This suggests an awareness during the Pre-Harappan times regarding the hardening property of tin. During the Harappan Period tin was frequently used; but even at this time it was a precious commodity as is evident from the finding of bronze scraps, stored along with other valuables in copper vessels at both Harappa and Mohenjodaro (Vats 1940: 381). According to Agrawal (1971: 168) only 14 percent of Harappan tools were alloyed in the optimum range of 8-12 percent tin. Furthermore tin bronze is more abundant (23 percent of the tools) in the upper levels of Mohenjodaro than in the lower levels (6 percent). It shows quite clearly that the availability of good quality bronze was somewhat slow to come to this site. It is possible that the same was true of other places as well.

Since the data on bronze are very limited, few conclusions can be drawn. Still one more observation can be made. The Harappans used tin-based bronzes in preference to those of arsenic or other compounds. In this respect their preference differed from that of their successors, the Copper Hoard people. These folk used arsenic when they produced the few bronze tools known of from their sites. In fact, in Post-Harappan contexts tin is very scarce for more than a millennium.

Does the scarcity of tin-based bronze objects even in Harappan contexts indicate that it was not readily available? The tin deposits known in India are located in the Palampur region of Maharashtra, Dharwar District in Karnataka and Hazari Bagh District of Bihar (Marshall 1931: 682). Bhilwara in Rajasthan and Hosainpura in Gujarat are also known to have a limited quantity of tin (Chakrabarti 1979: 70). Outside India, on the western frontier, tin is known to occur in Kuh Banan, Karadagh and Khorasan (Marshall 1931: 483-84; Vats 1940: 378-82) between Astrabad and Shah Rud in Iran (Gowland 1912) and between Bukhara and Samarkand in Soviet Central Asia (Crawford 1974; Masson and Sarianidi 1972: 128).

Of the Indian sources, those in Rajasthan and Gujarat are the most significant, though the quantity of tin is very small in these areas. The main supply of tin, may therefore, have come from the western regions: Khorasan and the area between Bukhara and Samarkand (Chakrabarti 1979: 70) through sites like Shortugai.

Here again a passing reference to Sumerian import of tin is essential. This metal was one of the commodities which the Sumerians got from Meluhha (Leemans 1970; Muhly 1976: 306-307). The scarcity of this metal in India has led some scholars to doubt that Meluhha, if it was Indus, was exporting tin (Chakrabarti 1979: 70-71). The identification of Meluhha as the Harappan Culture area has also been doubted (Chakrabarti 1979: 70-71). However, it is possible that tin was basically a trading item which the Harappans were obtaining from Khorasan and Central Asia for export to Mesopotamia, just as they obtained lapis lazuli from Badakshan for export there.

TRADE MECHANISMS

The procurement of raw materials is the first stage in trade. This may involve long distance travel as seems to have been the case during the Harappan Period when traders used to undertake substantial journeys to obtain the raw materials as well as to carry the finished goods to local and foreign markets. However, the controlling authority of the Harappan trade is still not fully known. Whether the trade was state organized or private enterprise has yet to be ascertained. But one thing is clear: a number of groups must have been actively engaged in the business operations. This may have been a very complex affair involving not only the procurement of raw materials from distant areas but also large-scale production and distribution of manufactured goods. These are operations which must have involved a number of different commercial towns doing different things.

1) *Towns connected with production.* A few Harappan groups specialized in the procurement of raw materials while others produced various goods at specialized centers. Harappa may have specialized in making metal tools while Mohenjodaro took on other metal objects, textiles, and the like. Chanhudaro specialized in bead making and seal engraving, while Lothal was also involved in bead making (Gupta in press).

2) *Towns connected with distribution.* Ports like Sutkagendor, Sotka Koh, Balakot and Lothal came under this category. They were mainly established to send consignments in various directions, particularly to West Asia.

Raw materials would have been the main concern of production centers if trade was to be carried out only in finished items. However, this was not the case with the Harappans since they are likely to have been involved in exporting both raw materials, including timber for boat making, as well as finished goods, such as etched carnelian beads. After obtaining materials from their source areas they may have taken them directly to the port for shipment to foreign markets. For example, lapis lazuli from Badakshan may have been taken to Sutkagendor in its raw form. This appears to have been the case because on the one hand finished items of lapis are very rare at Harappan sites, and on the other, there is circumstantial evidence from the location of Shortugai sites (near Badakshan) and the absence of lapis lazuli working at Shahr-i Sokhta from about 2000 B.C.

SUMMARY AND CONCLUSIONS

The purpose of this paper is twofold: first, to attempt to locate the source areas which the Harappans are likely to have exploited, either directly or indirectly, for metals and minerals; and second, to search for a pattern in the exploitation of natural resources.

These points have been raised here because many statements made in these areas, even those by very senior authors, are often vague and very general (e.g., "the Harappans got their copper from the Khetri and Debari mines of Rajasthan" or "the Harappans got their supply of gold from the Kolar mines in Mysore" or "the Harappans got the much needed steatite from either Rajasthan or Baluchistan"). But when one uses the term "Harappans" and does not specify which Harappans, those living in the Punjab or those living in Rajasthan or those living in Gujarat, one lacks essential precision. Such general usage takes the entire Harappan area as a single unit, both culturally and commercially. That is why while authors like Marshall (1931) and Rao (1973: 115) talk in terms of the total Harappan economy as though it was based largely on western borderlands trade, scholars like Shaffer (in press) can question the credibility of this formulation. In fact Shaffer (in press) offers an alternate model in which the Indus industrial economy was based primarily on its internal resources.

I disagree with both views. A culture area of a half million square miles, covering a vast variety of environmental zones, could not develop a "unilinear" economy, save under a unified empire administered by a supreme ruler, for which there is no definite archaeological proof. On the other hand, there are reasons to believe that there was a variety of Harappan socioeconomic groups. Those living in Sind must have been significantly different from those living in the Punjab as they are even today. These differences are mainly due to environmental factors like the presence of the Arabian Sea and near-desert conditions in southeastern and southwestern Sind. These features still play a major role in the socioeconomic pattern of the people of Sind, while these factors were totally absent around Harappa and other cities of the Punjab. Similarly, those living in Gujarat and those living in Rajasthan must have had their own socioeconomic characteristics. There were also marked cultural differences. For example, Black and Red Ware, Micaceous Red Ware and stud-handled bowls characterize only the Gujarati Harappan complex, while the Baluchi painted pottery finds its way only into Sind and the Punjab. It is therefore a viable working hypothesis to suggest that each regional group exploited its own metal and mineral resources. Studies also show that the sources for the metals and minerals used by the Harappans were located not only in India (Mysore, Gujarat, Kathiawad and Rajasthan) but also in Baluchistan, Afghanistan, Iran and Soviet Central Asia.

Looking at these resource areas in terms of locational proximity to the Harappan Culture area it can be suggested that the Harappans living in Sind were exploiting sources on the southwestern frontiers (Baluchistan and southern Afghanistan). Northern Iran and Soviet Central Asia were then exploited mainly by the Harappans of the Punjab. Those in Gujarat and Saurashtra were apparently getting their raw materials from the more than adequate sources in their own area, as well as from the South, including Mysore. Northern Rajasthan and Haryana must have taken most of their raw materials from central and southern Rajasthan.

For certain materials, like lapis lazuli or turquoise, there was no other choice except to go to Afghanistan (Badakshan), Iran (Nishapur) or Soviet Central Asia (Kyzyl Kum area). These resources must have been the monopoly of a few selected groups, either privately sponsored or sponsored by the state.

Since only a few sites have yielded turquoise it appears that it was not a very popular item with the Harappans. Whatever may have been the reasons for this, one thing is certain, the Harappans did get the turquoise from their western frontier regions. They had no source of their own. The mountain territory of the inner Kyzyl Kum and the mountains of Ilak

(Karamazar) in ancient Khodjent (Leninabad), and along the upper reaches of the Syr Darya in Central Asia all had good turquoise deposits. Deposits with the evidence of early work are also located near Nishapur and between Kirman and Yazd. The Harappans may have obtained this stone from Soviet Central Asia but the Iranian sources cannot be ruled out completely. But there is another likely possibility. There are very few turquoise items in the Indus: a few beads from Mohenjodaro, Rahman Dheri and Mehrgarh. Since Mundigak and Shahr-i Sokhta had turquoise production centers, these places may have been the sources for the sites, particularly when there is definite archaeological evidence of Harappan contact, at least with Mundigak.

The sources of minerals and metals in Afghanistan, Iran and Soviet Central Asia may have been more or less monopolized by one or another of the Harappan groups: those in the West Punjab. The other groups may have been getting their items through them.

The seven Harappan settlements at Shortugai on the confluence of the Oxus and Kokcha in the Hindu Kush area is evidence which seems to indicate that the Harappans of the northern region established trading posts to monopolize trade in raw materials from northeast Iran and Soviet Central Asia. In the absence of detailed reports on the Shortugai excavation one is unsure about the raw materials traded by the people of these sites. But the location to the north of the lapis mines, and at a crucial point on the trade route connecting northern Iran and Central Asia with India, suggests that they were controlling items other than lapis. Gold and tin, which also came from Central Asia and northern Iran, may have been involved as well. If these items were not under state monopoly, the people living in Gujarat and Rajasthan must have taken their lapis lazuli from the Harappans of the Punjab and not directly from the Badakshan region. Gold and tin were also coming to the Punjab from Central Asia but Gujarat and Sind may have been getting their supply of gold from Mysore. The Mysore fields, and the possible ties between the Harappans and the Southern Neolithic, have already been discussed. Two further points need to be added. First, the gold at Neolithic sites like Piklihal, Kodekal and Maski almost has to come from the Mysore sources which were thus worked during the third millennium. Second, some gold from Mohenjodaro has silver as a trace element and this is what would be expected if Mysore was the source. This is, of course, excepting those objects which are made of electrum, an alloy of gold and silver. A valid objection to this hypothesis may lie in the absence of Harappan sites between Gujarat and the Andhra/Mysore region. By and large it is true, but the discovery at Daimabad of a terracotta seal with a Harappan sign, and a sherd with three signs, as discussed in S.A. Sali's contribution to this volume, speaks for links between the Harappan and Neolithic-Calcolithic culture zones. There is also some force to Rao's argument for Indus-Neolithic trade based on the occurrence of thin paste "Harappan" beads in the Neolithic sites. Unfortunately, silver is also present in Soviet Central Asian gold (Kalesnike and Pavlenko 1976: 202). One of the largest mother lodes of gold has been discovered in the Murunatau Mountains, in the Kyzyl Kum desert. (It may be recalled that turquoise is also found in Kyzyl Kum.) It is, therefore, quite possible that this gold came to the Indus; but there is no way of ascertaining which objects were made of the Mysore-Maski metal and which of the Kyzyl Kum.

Tin in western India is reported from Bhilwara (Rajasthan) and Hosainpura (Gujarat); however there is very little of it. The other sources for tin are Khorasan, Kara Dagh and the area between Bukhara and Samarkand. It thus appears that this scarce metal could only be obtained and used in some significant quantity when regular trade was established between the Indus and Central Asia. This is precisely why tin-based bronze objects at Mohenjodaro came in larger numbers from the upper levels (Agrawal 1969-70: 16). The tin that went from Meluhha to Mesopotamia also probably originated in Central Asia (including northern Iran and northern Afghanistan). The same may be true of silver and lead. As noted earlier, only Iran and Afghanistan could supply silver and lead to the Indus. This is also evident from the frequent use of silver at Mohenjodaro and Harappa. However, Rajasthan and Gujarat may have obtained their silver from the Ajmer and Zawar mines of Rajasthan. The quantities may have been limited as the people there used it sparingly.

Copper has a very wide distribution in India, Baluchistan, Afghanistan, Central Asia, Iran and Oman. It thus poses a serious problem to the archaeologists who want to know which areas were actually used by the Harappans.

A number of scholars, including Desch (1931), Ullah (1940: 378-79), Ray (1956) and Agrawal (1971) have tried to establish the sources of copper exploited by the Harappans. Their approach has been a comparative study of the nature of impurities present in artifacts and copper ores from different areas. On the basis of the presence of lead in the Harappan tools (Agrawal 1971: Table 13-14) Desch proposed that the Baluchi ores were exploited by the Harappans. But the Baluchistan copper ores do not show any lead.

Based on the presence of arsenic, nickel and lead in artifacts from Mohenjodaro and Harappa, Ullah (1940) determined the sources of their copper to have been Khetri, Alwar, Singhbhum and Afghanistan mines where nickel and arsenic both are supposed to be present in the copper ores. He held that the Sumerian ores could be distinguished from Indian ores since the former are virtually free from arsenic (Ullah 1940).

Agrawal (1971) has made spectrographic analyses of Harappan artifacts and of various ores. He took twenty elements into consideration and found that the metallic composition of Harappan artifacts is close to the composition of the Khetri ores. He thus holds that Khetri is the area which the Harappans of the Punjab and Sind exploited. He further observes that the Khetri sources alone could justify the Mesopotamian imports of copper from Meluhha. The discovery of several copper celts, an Indus arrowhead and the Ochre Colored Pottery of the late third millennium B.C. by R.C. Agrawala (1978) at Ganeshwar also gives weight to this theory. Khetri is only 60 kilometers from Ganeshwar.*

All these analyses show that Harappan copper objects have arsenic, nickel and lead. The Khetri belt was very well situated for the Harappans to get copper; but did it provide everything? Possibly not. As one knows, the Afghanistan sources also contain arsenic, nickel and lead and, therefore, it may be possible that these sources were used. After all Indus-Afghan contacts were regular. The Harappans of Sind and Punjab, therefore, are likely to have exploited the mines of Afghanistan in addition to the Khetri source. The Baluchistan ores—Robat and Shah Bellual—should be analyzed more carefully. But there were certainly more sources than those of the Khetri belt and Afghanistan. The Lothal and Rangpur copper tends to prove it beyond doubt, since it is arsenic free (Rao 1973). This fact points to Oman as a source since copper there is supposed to be arsenic free. Rao supports this hypothesis by further observing that Oman was apparently supplying copper to the Sumerian cities since their copper tools were also free of arsenic. But this does not appear to be the case. Agrawal's Table 11 (1971) shows that at Khafaje and Ur, 88 percent of the artifacts contain arsenic. So this difference is ruled out. One is not sure about the Oman sources and their pattern of impurities or any correspondence to the Lothal/Rangpur copper. More data are needed before one can arrive at a sound conclusion.

The frequent use of steatite for making various objects leads one to believe that there was a regular flow of this mineral to the Harappan cities. A number of steatite sources are reported in North Gujarat (Devni Mori, Kundol, Lokha and Mora) and in Rajasthan (at Dogetha, Gisgarh and Morra). Marshall thought that Rajasthan was giving steatite to the Harappans while Rao suggests that Mysore might have supplied this material to the Indus people through the contemporary Neolithic folk of the Deccan. But with steatite locally available in Gujarat and Rajasthan why would the Harappans have gone all the way to Mysore?

The most promising source for steatite is northern Baluchistan and the area around Fort Sandeman. This zone might have supplied steatite to the Sind-Punjab area. Another piece of evidence which adds to the credibility of the Baluchi sources is the scientific analysis of the stone vases from sites in Syria, Mesopotamia, Iran and the Indus (Kohl 1975, 1976). It shows that the stone for these objects came from several different sources. It has also been proved beyond doubt that the Sumerian chlorite is different from the Yahya chlorite and that the former is much more like that coming from the east of Yahya. Baluchi sources might thus have been exploited by the traders to fulfill Mesopotamian demand.

The sources for chlorite in Kirman, were also known to the Sind Harappans. They exploited these for raw material and/or finished steatite vases.

As far as carnelian is concerned, its use was fairly common amongst the Harappans. Etched carnelian beads are important because they crossed the Indus borders to reach Iran and Mesopotamia. This stone was readily available over a vast area of India. A number of sources are located in Madhya Pradesh, Rajasthan and Gujarat. It was probably supplied to

---

*Editor's note: See R.C. Agrawala's paper in this volume for a discussion of recent copper finds in Rajasthan.

the Harappans of Kathiawad, Kutch and other southern areas from the Rajpipla mines of Ratanpur. The Harappans, themselves, then traded this stone to other parts of the civilization.

The Iranian source for carnelian lies in the dried up branches of the river Helmand in Seistan near Shahr-i Sokhta. But in the absence of archaeological remains one cannot be sure that the Harappans knew of this source. Carnelian is also on the list of Mesopotamian imports from Meluhha. If Meluhha can be equated with the area of Harappan Culture it was then exporting carnelian, probably from Indian sources.

If the above analysis is correct, even approximately, one then has every reason to believe that the exploitation of different metal and mineral sources was more a matter of regional organization than a business of centralized agencies like the state. This observation is applicable even to those items (e.g., lapis lazuli) which may have been the monopoly of one regional group or the other. The Indus area covers too much territory and could not be traversed without a large network of well-maintained roads and fast-moving vehicles, for which, so far, there is no definitive proof.

If the pattern of exploitation of natural resources was regional, and not centralized, can this be seen in the archaeological records? I have already mentioned the evidence of copper-bronze tools (in Gujarat sites the copper is arsenic free while in the Punjab and Rajasthan it has arsenic). Obviously, two different copper sources were exploited by two different groups of people. There is also the evidence of steatite and chlorite which shows that while Baluchi sources were exploited by those in the Punjab and Sind, the Rajasthan and Gujarati sources were exploited by the Rajasthani and Gujarati Harappans. There is also similar evidence for tin, silver and lead. The case for gold is not as clear since gold from both Mysore and Central Asia contains a small percentage of silver. On grounds of geographical proximity and the location of Shortugai it is suggested that while Gujarat may have taken this precious metal from South India, the Punjab sites may have obtained it from Soviet Central Asia. Lapis was certainly a monopoly item with one of the North Harappan groups. The Gujarati Harappans monopolized trade in etched carnelian beads. Turquoise at Indus sites is extremely limited, (only to a few beads at Mohenjodaro, Rahman Dheri and Mehrgarh), therefore, it may have come to the Indus in its finished form from sites like Mundigak.

The situation can be summed up by reiterating the basic stand: the natural resources used by the Harappans were widespread, with enormous choice in source areas. These facts determined the exploitation pattern which was, by and large, regional.

NOTE

[1]These two major units were further subdivided into smaller organizations as well. For the moment I will only focus on the production and distribution units.

BIBLIOGRAPHY

Agrawal, D.P., 1969-70
    The Metal Technology of the Indian Protohistoric Culture: Its archaeological implications. *Puratattva* 3: 15-22.
Agrawal, D.P., 1971
    The Copper Bronze Age in India. Delhi: Munshiram Manoharlal.
Agrawal, D.P., 1976
    Problems of Protohistoric Copper Artifacts and Their Ore Correlation. In *Archaeological Congress and Seminar, 1972*. U.V. Singh, ed. Pp. 85-89. Kurukshetra: Kurukshetra University.
Agrawal, D.P., *et al.*, 1976
    Ancient Copper Working: Some new C^{14} dates. *Indian Journal of the History of Science* 11 (2): 133-36.
Agrawal, D.P., *et al.*, in press
    Arsenical Copper in the Indian Bronze Age. To

appear in the M.N. Deshpande Felicitation Volume.

Agrawala, R.C., 1978
Copper Celts and an Indus Arrow Head from Khulhade-ka-Johad, District Sikar, Rajasthan. *Man and Environment* 2: 123-24.

Agrawala, R.C., 1979
More Copper Finds from Rajasthan. *Man and Environment* 3: 91-92.

Asthana, S., 1979a
Indus-Mesopotamian Trade: Nature of the trade and a structural analysis of the operative system. In *Essays in Indian Protohistory*. D.P. Agrawal and D.K. Chakrabarti, eds. Pp. 31-47. Delhi: B.R. Publishing Corp.

Asthana, S., 1979b
Harappan's Interest in Kirman. *Man and Environment* 3: 55-60.

Bisht, R.S., 1978
Banawali: A new Harappan site in Haryana. *Man and Environment* 2: 86-88.

British Association for the Advancement of Science, 1931
Reports. London: British Association for the Advancement of Science.

Caldwell, Joseph, 1967
Investigations at Tal-i Iblis. Illinois State Museum Preliminary Report No. 9: Springfield.

Casal, Jean-Marie, 1964
Fouilles d'Amri. Paris: Librarie C. Klincksieck.

Chakrabarti, D.K., 1978
Lapis Lazuli in Early India. *Man and Environment* 2: 51-58.

Chakrabarti, D.K., 1979
The Problem of Tin in Early India: A preliminary survey. *Man and Environment* 3: 61-74.

Crawford, H.E.W., 1974
The Problem of Tin in Mesopotamian Bronzes. *World Archaeology* 6: 242-47.

Dales, G.F., 1979a
The Bala Kot Project: A summary of four years excavations in Pakistan. In *South Asian Archaeology, 1977*. Maurizio Taddei ed. Pp. 241-47. Instituto Universitario Orientale, Seminario di Studi Asiatici, Series Minor VI: Naples.

Dales, G.F., 1979b
The Bala Kot Project: A summary of four years of excavation in Pakistan. *Man and Environment* 3: 45-53.

Dani, A.H., 1970-71
Excavations in the Gomal Valley. *Ancient Pakistan* 5: 1-177.

Desch, C.M., 1931
Sumerian Copper. *British Association for the Advancement of Science, Reports*. London: British Association for the Advancement of Science: 269-72.

During Caspers, E.C.L., 1971
Trucal Oman in the Third Millennium B.C.: New evidence for contacts with Sumer, Baluchistan and the Indus Valley. *Origini* 4: 205-76.

Durrani, F.A., 1977
Excavations at Rahman Dheri. Paper read at the IV Conference on South Asian Archaeology, Naples.

Forbes, R.J., 1971
Studies in Ancient Technology. Vol. VIII. Leiden: E.J. Brill.

Forbes, R.J., 1972
Studies in Ancient Technology. Vol. IX. Leiden: E.J. Brill.

Francfort, H.P. and M.H. Potter, 1978
Sondage Preliminair Sur L'Etablissement Protohistorique Harappan et Post-Harappan de Shortugai (Afghanistan du N.E.). *Arts Asiatiques* 34: 29-79.

Goldsmith, R., 1971
Mineral Resources of the Southern Hijazqudrangle Kingdom of Saudi Arabia. Mineral Resources Bulletin 5: Jiddah.

Gowland, H., 1912
Metals in Antiquity. *Journal of the Royal Anthropological Institute* 42: 235-87.

Gupta, S.P., 1979
The Archaeology of Soviet Central Asia and the Indian Borderlands. 2 vols. Delhi: B.R. Publishing Corp.

Gupta, S.P., in press
Internal Trade Patterns of the Harappans. In *Indus Civilization: Problems and Issues*. B.B. Lal and S.C. Malik eds. Simla: Indian Institute of Advanced Study.

Hakemi, A., 1972
Catalogue de L'Exposition Lut Xabis (Shahdad). Tehran: Premier Symposium Annuel de la Researche Archaeologique en Iran.

Halim, M.A., 1972a
Excavations at Sarai Khola, Pt. I. *Pakistan Archaeology* 7: 23-89.

Halim, M.A., 1972b
Excavations at Sarai Khola, Pt. II. *Pakistan Archaeology* 8: 1-112.

Hamd-Allah Mustawfi of Qazwin, 1919
The Geographical Part of the Nuzhat-al-Qulub. Guy Le Strange, trans. Leyden: E.J. Brill.

Hargreaves, H., 1929
Excavations in Baluchistan, 1925. Memoirs of the Archaeological Survey of India No. 35: Calcutta.

Herrmann, G., 1966
The Source, Distribution and Use of Lapis Lazuli in Western Asia from the Earliest times to the end of the Selucid Era. Ph.D. dissertation, Oxford University.

Herrmann, G., 1968
Lapis Lazuli: The early phases of its trade. *Iraq* 30 (1): 21-57.

Hole, F. and K.V. Flannery, 1968
The Prehistory of South Western Iran: A preliminary report. *Proceedings of the Prehistoric Society* 33: 147-206.

Hunting Survey Corporation Ltd., 1961
Reconnaissance Geology of Part of West Pakistan. A Colombo Plan Cooperative Project. Toronto: Government of Canada.

Jarrige, J.F. and M. Lechevallier, 1979
Excavations at Mehrgarh, Baluchistan: Their significance in the prehistorical context of the Indo-Iranian borderlands. In *South Asian Archaeology, 1977.* Maurizio Taddei, ed. Pp. 463-536. Instituto Universitario Orientale, Seminario di Studi Asiatici, Series Minor VI: Naples.

Joshi, J.P., 1976
Transformation of Harappan Culture in Kutch: Examination of the evidence from Surkotada. In *Archaeological Congress and Seminar 1972,* U.V. Singh, ed. Kurukshetra: B.N. Chakravarty University: 38-45.

Kalesnik, S.V. and V.F. Pavlenko, eds., 1976
Soviet Union: A geography. Moscow.

Kohl, Philip L., 1975
Carved Chlorite Vessels: A trade in finished commodities in the third millennium. *Expedition* 18 (1): 18-31.

Kohl, Philip L., 1976
Steatite Carvings of the Early Third Millennium B.C. An archaeological seminar given at Columbia University, 1973-74. *Amercian Journal of Archaeology* 80 (1): 73-75.

Lamberg-Karlovsky, C.C., 1970
Excavations at Tepe Yahya, Iran 1967-69. American School of Prehistoric Research Bulletin No. 27: Cambridge.

Lamberg-Karlovsky, C.C. and M. Tosi, 1973
Shahr-i-Sokhta and Tepe Yahya: Tracks on the earliest history of the Iranian plateau. *East and West* 23 (1-2): 21-53.

Leemans, W.F., 1960
Foreign Trade in the Old Babylonian Period. Leiden: E.J. Brill.

Le Strange, G., 1905
The Lands of the Eastern Caliphate. Cambridge: Cambridge University Press.

Lyonnet, B., 1977
Decouverte de Sites L'Age du Bronze dans le N.E. L'Afghanistan: Leurs repports avec la Civilization de L'Indus. *Annali dell'Instituto Orientale de Napoli* 37 (N.S. XXVIII): 19-35.

Mackay, E.J.H., 1938
Further Excavations at Mohenjodaro. 2 vols. Delhi: Government of India.

Mackay, E.J.H., 1943
Chanhudaro Excavations 1935-36. American Oriental Series 20. New Haven: American Oriental Society.

Majumdar, N.G., 1934
Explorations in Sind. Memoirs of the Archaeological Survey of India No. 48. Delhi: Government of India.

Marshall, Sir John, editor, 1931
Mohenjodaro and the Indus Civilization. 3 vols. London: Arthur Probsthain.

Masson, V.N. and V. Sarianidi, 1972
Central Asia before the Achaemenids. London: Thames and Hudson.

Mughal, M.R., 1970
The Early Harappan Period in the Greater Indus Valley and Northern Baluchistan (c. 3000-2400 B.C.). Ph.D. dissertation, Department of Anthropology, University of Pennsylvania.

Mughal, M.R., 1974
New Evidence of the Early Harappan Culture from Jalilpur, Pakistan. *Archaeology* 27 (2): 106-13.

Muhly, J., 1976
Copper and Tin. Hamden: Archon Books.

Pakistan Department of Archaeology, 1968
Pakistan Archaeology 5: Karachi.

Pithawala, M.B., 1952
The Problem of Baluchistan: Development and conservation of water resources, soils and natural vegetation. Karachi: Ministry of Economic Affairs.

Pogue, J.E., 1915
Turquoise. Memoirs of the National Academy of Science 12 (2): 1-154.

Rao, S.R., 1973
Lothal and the Indus Civilization. Bombay: Asia Publishing.

Ray, P.C., 1956
History of Chemistry in Ancient and Medieval India. Calcutta: Indian Chemical Society.

Seth, M.L., 1956
Mineral Resources of Rajasthan. Jaipur: Government of Rajasthan.

Shaffer, J., in press
Harappan External Trade: A critical assessment. In *Indus Civilization: Problems and issues.* B.B. Lal and S.C. Malik, eds. Simla: Indian Institute of Advanced Study.

Stein, M.A., 1931
An Archaeological Tour in Gedrosia. Memoirs of the Archaeological Survey of India 43. Delhi: Government of India.

Sykes, P.M., 1902
Ten Thousand Miles in Persia or Eight Years in Iran. New York: John Murray.

Tosi, M., 1969
Excavations at Shahr-i-Sokhta: Preliminary report on the second campaign, September-December 1968. *East and West* 19 (3-4): 283-386.

Tosi, M., 1974
The Problem of Turquoise in Protohistoric Trade on the Iranian Plateau. *Memoire dell'Institute di Palaeontologie Umana* II: 147-62.

Tosi, M. and R. Waradak, 1972
The Fullol Hoard: A new find from Bronze-Age Afghanistan. *East and West* 22 (1-2): 9-17.

Ullah, M.S., 1940
The Sources, Composition and Technique of Copper and its Alloys. In *Excavations at Harappa.* M.S. Vats. Pp. 378-82. Delhi: Government of India.

Vats, M.S., 1940
Excavations at Harappa. 2 vols. Delhi: Government of India.

Webster, R., 1975
Gems: Their sources, description and identification. Hamden, Connecticut: Archon Books.

Wertime, T.A., 1968
A Metallurgical Expedition Through the Persian Desert. *Science* 159: 927-35.

Wright, G.A., 1969
Obsidian Analysis and Prehistoric Near Eastern Trade: 7500-3500 B.C. Anthropological Papers of the Museum of Anthropology 35. Ann Arbor: University of Michigan.

PART IV

BIOLOGICAL ANTHROPOLOGY

KENNETH A.R. KENNEDY

26. Skulls, Aryans and Flowing Drains: The Interface of Archaeology and Skeletal Biology in the Study of the Harappan Civilization

As an archaeologist, most of what one reads about the skeletons from Mohenjodaro, Harappa, Chanhudaro and Lothal leads back to the same question: To what ancient race of mankind did the Harappans belong? This is a reasonable question but it seems a rather moribund issue for those seeking to reconstruct the lifeway of an extinct population. As it is, interpretations of the archaeological record have often been overthrown when a physical anthropologist has announced that the bodies of the builders of the Harappan cities supported skulls typed as Proto-Nordic, Irano-Afghan, Veddoid, Proto-Australoid, Pre-Dravidian, Pseudo-Alpine, Negritoid, Proto-Mediterranean, Dravidian, Mongoloid, Scytho-Dravidian, Turko-Iranian, Irano-Caspian, Dinaric, Aryan, or Paleo-Mongolid. Archaeologists are also often disturbed upon recalling that the crania may belong to a mysterious race of hyperleptoprosopic brisoids with a dash of Nilotic prognathism.

Admittedly these racial curries add a certain zest to otherwise dry bones, but in this paper I should like to turn to some aspects of on-going research concerned with the skeletal biology of earlier populations which are directly relevant to current problems of archaeological import in the reconstruction of the lifeways of the Harappans.[1]

For the skeletal biologist examining the remains of the ancient dead, an important key is the study of stress, or more specifically, the interpretation of markers of stress which are preserved in the hard tissues of bones and teeth. Stress is a medical term for the body's responses to a wide variety of irritating agents ranging from invasion of parasites to psychological pressures. An individual continues to survive so long as his mind and body can mobilize their forces and develop a general response pattern to threats to the integrity of his system. Aware of the role played by both natural and cultural environmental forces in human groups, anthropologists have been turning to problems of cold stress, high temperature stress, altitude stress, overcrowding, atmospheric and water pollution, noise pollution and pathology. These studies take into account human responses with respect to the species' genetic endowments and degrees of phenotypic plasticity as well as attempt to interpret accurately the ways that cultural practices are adaptive in buffering human minds and bodies from stress (Alland 1970). Stress is imposed upon human populations adapted at any given moment to particular ecological settings, by demographic events such as foreign invasion or migration, and by internal social changes. Stress may be imposed gradually or abruptly, be of brief duration, persist, confer an evolutionary advantage upon the population or be deleterious. Some stresses are constants in all human populations.

Take a look at some situations pertaining to the Harappan Civilization where archaeological interpretations are supported by mortuary data for which markers of stress are discerned by the skeletal biologist. Most archaeologists would agree that the basic components of Harappan Culture find their roots in earlier urban centers in western Asia. Few would take the stand today that the origins of the Harappan achievement were to be traced to indigenous cultures from peninsular India or from Southeast Asia whose influence diffused northwards to the Indian Plain. The former thesis finds confirmation in the skeletal record with respect to measures of stress in the dentition.

Tooth size reductions have occurred in a predictable fashion during the past five millennia over the geographic landmass extending from China, Melanesia, Polynesia and Australia to Eurasia and parts of Africa. Brace (1975) attributes this trend towards smaller tooth size to relaxation of selective forces. In earlier periods of prehistoric time, human evolution had favored larger teeth and as such were adaptive for the maximization of masticatory stress. Brace writes, "The longer the period of time a population has enjoyed the benefits of technology, particularly where that concerns food preparation, the smaller are its teeth." In charting the distribution of relative tooth size before the Age of Discovery, Brace observes that in South Asia the smallest teeth appear in the north and northwestern sectors of the Subcontinent. Teeth become larger in the western and central Deccan, the largest teeth being found in southeastern India and Sri Lanka (Brace and Montagu 1977). These observations, confirmed by studies of ancient human dentitions from South Asia, correlate with the archaeological thesis that higher technologies, including those relating to food production and preparation, are of greatest antiquity in northern India and Pakistan, as attested by the emergence of the Harappan Culture by 3000 B.C. To be sure, megadonty (large teeth) appears sporadically in skeletal specimens from Harappan sites, but it is in much higher frequency among non-Harappan skeletal specimens recovered from Neolithic, Chalcolithic and Iron Age sites to the south of the Harappan realm.

The important message for archaeologists from this example is that whatever the racial origins of the Harappans may have been, they were a relatively stable population inhabiting the northern and northwestern sectors of the Subcontinent for several millennia prior to their climactic moment of urbanization and commercial influence. That is to say, the skeletal evidence relating to megadonty as one adaptation to masticatory stress does not support an hypothesis that would derive the Harappan population from peninsular sectors of the Subcontinent nor suggest any abrupt demographic transitions within the region of the Indus Plain. Absolute tooth size is a dental trait under genetic control, not a physical variable attributable to short-term environmental modeling. If the high incidence of micro- and mesodonty in the Harappan population is due to the phenomenon of relaxed selection, then a temporal continuum of some duration and embracing many generations is implicit in these observations. Furthermore, this dental character is expressed as a spatial continuum as well, since it is a part of a clinal distribution of reduced dental size that appears in the early urban peoples of western Asia and survives there today.[2]

There has been much eulogizing of the straight streets, uniform measures, building materials of brick, and flowing drains of Harappan cities, accomplishments which one is assured, could be maintained only by rigorous enforcement of a finely structured system of social controls and, by inference, marked social stratification of the citizenry. In some parts of the world, as in dynastic Egypt, Mesopotamia, Meso-America and the Woodland-Mississippian Cultures of the Illinois Valley, the skeletal biologist is able to document some biological manifestations of social organization by observing differential frequencies of growth patterns and diseases in mortuary series. High ranking individuals enjoy a greater potential to attain their full ontogenetic development, hence are taller in stature, and tend to suffer less from abnormalities of nutritional stress than do individuals of subordinate social status within the same society. However, observations of Harappan skeletal series from five major sites, which comprise about 350 individuals, have not revealed significant differences in patterns of growth and development as would be recognized by lines of arrested growth in long bones and hyperplasia or dental enamel. Osseous malformations suggestive of nutritional stress are absent as well. Nor are there any striking differences in incidences of dental attrition and common dental pathologies such as caries, abscess, malocclusion and ante-mortem tooth loss in Harappan skeletons. In short, the Harappan skeletal series is aberrant when compared with series from other archaeological sites for which archaeological data suggest a significant development of social stratification. This negative evidence from the Harappan sample should not be interpreted to mean that a social hierarchy was absent in Harappan culture.

Rather, biological observations suggest that social control may have been exercised by the Harappan elite in a way that did not evoke the usual dietary stressers so often imposed elsewhere upon an urban proletariat. The absence of royal tombs in Harappan centers may be significant in this connection. Confirmation of this interpretation of the skeletal record awaits further archaeological investigation and, perhaps, analysis of a deciphered Indus script.

Finally, what might the student of ancient bones and teeth add to the interpretations which seek to account for the decline of Harappan Culture? Surely one encounters here the quintessence of any documentation of stress! And what can one conceive as being more obviously fraught with stress than the grisly incident of the so-called massacres at Mohenjodaro? Chatterjee and Kumar (1973) ascribe certain incomplete and distorted burials found in the ruins to the aggressive acts of invading Aryans, a view proposed earlier by Wheeler (1952). Indeed, an unnamed European antiquarian has proposed that the abundance of pottery sherds at Mohenjodaro testifies to the energy of these energetic Aryans who were as bent on shattering pots as they were on severing heads! Be that as it may, skeletons associated with this tragedy have been attributed more often to the hapless Harappans than to their foreign aggressors. Actually two problems exist here: (1) the skeletal evidence for actual victims who expired traumatically, hence the demonstration that a massacre had taken place, and (2) the determination of the ethnic identity of the skeletal remains as native Harappans, as Aryans or as members of some other foreign population. Dales (1964) argues on archaeological grounds that actual dates for the Harappan Civilization and the arrival of Aryans cannot be established. He goes on to note that armed invasion is not indicated by the presence of extensive destructive levels at the site, that there is no evidence that the skeletons belong to a single period of time and therefore no proof of a single tragedy, and that only two of the skeletons bear evidence that a massacre had occurred at their place of deposition. Finally, weapons and armor are not associated with any of the skeletons. Observations of 1964 of the Mohenjodaro skeletons go far to support Dales' conclusions, but only indisputable evidence of injuries can establish the cause of death by slaughter in cases where bone is affected. Such physical evidence is not apparent in the majority of skeletons assigned the status of massacre victims.

In short, the establishment of direct evidence of traumatic stress has priority over nonbiological theories of a Mohenjodaro massacre. I was able to observe two traumatic lesions on cranial bones from this series, but in both cases some resorption of bone had taken place along the margins of the wound, thus indicating that the unfortunate recipients of thumps on the head had survived this outrage by several months, their death being attributable perhaps to other causes.

It is not discernible that any of the so-called massacre victims were phenotypically distinct from other denizens of Mohenjodaro whose remains are uncovered in circumstances of casual or irreverent burial. Even if a foreign ethnic element was present at Mohenjodaro—which does not appear to be the case—how would it be identified as Aryan? Whatever future archaeological and linguistic research may bring to light about the Aryan presence, the skeletal record is mute. But one is on surer ground with respect to the Harappans themselves, for which there is in evidence a relatively large skeletal sample. One recognizes a biological continuum of many of their morphometric variables in the modern populations of Punjab and Sind.

Disease as a factor contributing to the Harappan decline has been suggested by some investigators. A study has been recently initiated which explores the question of malaria and thalassemia as endemic diseases in the region of Harappan activity. These conditions were endemic in the Aegean region since Neolithic times, as Angel (1971) has demonstrated for a number of mortuary series from the eastern Mediterranean, and historic records for South Asia confirm the presence of malaria over many centuries. In the course of human evolution, populations have adapted to the *Plasmodia* parasites borne by the *Anopheles* hosts by genetic means whereby recessive variants of normal human hemoglobin (S. sicklemia) and alpha and beta chain variants of thalassemic hemoglobin occur in high frequencies in malarial areas. Children who are homozygous for sicklemia and thalassemia usually die before reaching reproductive maturity after the onset of hemolytic anemia. Children who are heterozygous for these inherited diseases are more likely to attain reproductive age since they are genetically protected from extreme ravages of both pathological conditions. A population pays a high cost for this kind of balanced polymorphism resistant to malaria with respect to high infant mortality and shortened maternal life span, a price measurable in paleodemographic data when large and representative mortuary series are available for analysis. As with other anemias, such as are caused by hookworm, rickets and certain iron deficiency diseases, there may be a physiological affect resulting from decreased oxygen transport. The consequence is the enlargement of blood-forming marrow in long bones which leads to extensive bone remodeling and widening of osseous spaces, vertebral depression, and thinning and porosity of cortical bone of the cranial vault and face. Porotic hyperostosis is the most striking diagnostic feature of these anemias whereby aseptic necrosis of bone tissue leads to the "hair-on-end" or "crew-cut" pattern of diploic tissue between the internal and external tables of cranial flat bones. It has been possible to distinguish in bone tissue the effects of the anemias caused by sicklemia and thalassemia from one another and from manifestations of some of the other diseases which affect transport of oxygen, largely on the basis of localized concentrations of porotic hyperostosis. For example, the occipital region of the skull is most commonly affected by conditions of iron deficiency. For sicklemia the frontal and parietal bones are most often those portions of the vault which are altered. Our research indicates the presence of porotic hyperostosis of the frontal and parietal bones in the Harappan skeletal series, certainly one indication that the Harappan population possessed an adaptive polymorphism with the capacity to act as a malarial prophylaxis. It would be unwarranted to suggest that malaria or genetic pathologies were fundamental causes for the Harappan decline. But this question of endemic malaria in the Indus Valley of 5,000 years ago is one aspect of the broader question concerning the health status of this population, the issue of the percentage of manpower available for labor and the bearing of arms at any given period of time. Certainly the ponding effect of water trapped by intermittent flooding, as described by Raikes (1965) in connection with a theory of coastal tectonic uplift, would have been conducive to the formation of breeding places for malarial mosquitoes, although the same result might ensue from irrigation practices. It is interesting that human skeletal remains from South Asia which date to Late Stone Age (Mesolithic) cultural horizons exhibit porotic hyperostosis and related distortions of long bones in very low frequencies. Endemic malaria in human populations may have commenced with Neolithic technologies of food production in South Asia, as in the lands to the west of the Indus.

In closing this summary of some current researches into the paleodemographic problems of the ancient Harappans, I do not wish to create the impression that the more venerable studies of ethnic identification and biological affinities are irrelevant. This is not the case. However, skeletal biologists have become much less concerned in recent years with racial typologies based upon morphometric sorting criteria for which the effects of stress are unknown or unappreciated. Furthermore, the decline of the traditional race concept in systematic biology and physical anthropology has forced many to question the validity of the old racial taxa. For these reasons, most skeletal biologists today approach questions of population identity and biological distance from a fresh point of view, with a sensitivity to phenotypic variables of the skeleton for which both genetic and environmental causes are identifiable. For instance, one now knows that the more significant anatomical differences between populations are signaled by variations in the breadth of the cranial base, in the protrusion of the subnasal region, in the prominence of the interorbital region and of the orbital rim as well as in the zygomatic height and biauricular height (Howells 1969). Less reliable data for multivariate analysis measurements of biological distance would be the traditional observations of cranial length and breadth or the cranial circumference as these features are especially responsive to environmental stressers whatever their polygenic bases may be. Therefore, the reexamination of mortuary data from South Asia with respect to more reliable anatomical criteria for establishing biological distance and with attention to the role of stress is the task ahead.[3]

In conclusion, some cases of ongoing research have been discussed, in which data of skeletal biology may contribute to archaeological investigations of Harappan studies. This summary is focused upon paleodemographic questions pertaining to the recognition and evaluation of biological markers of stress exhibited in Harappan skeletons. Human responses to stress imposed by the natural and social environments are manifested by physiological adaptations and cultural strategies. In the first instance this documentation may be contained in the residua of bones and teeth; in the second instance the behavioral record is preserved in aspects of archaeological inquiry. It is suggested that appreciation of this interface of biology and behavior will generate new and exciting questions regarding the lifeways of the ancient Harappans and other prehistoric populations of the Indian Subcontinent.

NOTES

[1] It has been my privilege to examine all of the human skeletal remains recovered from the Harappan sites of Mohenjodaro, Harappa, Chanhudaro and Lothal in 1964. While in Pakistan in 1977, I was given leave to examine skeletal remains recovered from Mohenjodaro and Harappa since partition in 1947. I am grateful to the persons and institutions who made this survey possible, particular thanks going to the Anthropological Survey of India at Calcutta and the Department of Archaeology at Karachi. My research has been supported by grants from the National Science Foundation, American Institute of Pakistan Studies, Smithsonian Institution, Howard Foundation, South Asia Program of Cornell University and the Faculty Research Grants Committee of Cornell University.

[2] Megadonty is one adaptation to attritional stress in populations practicing simple technologies and methods of food preparation. Other dental adaptations to stress include increase in enamel thickness, development of effective interstitial occlusal surfaces, molarization or premolars, higher incidence of normal eruption of all teeth including the third molars, and modifications in the rate and order of dental eruption. Such adaptations are predictable when the rate of dental wear is high, as in circumstances where gritty particles are incorporated with the nutrients through the use of stone grinders. However, abrasion of the teeth may be a consequence of dust-laden air, as in arid regions, or it may be attributable to cultural practices which employ the mouth as a tool for habitually holding objects, chewing hides to soften them, stripping bark, etc. Unconscious tooth grinding, as often occurs in sleep as a tension releaser, and excessive damage of teeth due to trauma and pathology are additional agents of dental stress which the skeletal biologist can recognize and the paleo-demographer can assess within the context of a population.

Until recently, dental anthropology has been neglected by skeletal biologists working in South Asia. Metress and Conway (1974) include only 13 entries for Indians in their *Guide to the Literature on the Dental Anthropology of Post Pleistocene Man*, and none of their bibliographic citations refers to prehistoric skeletal data. Some attention is given to dentition in the reports describing skeletons from Langhnaj, Piklihal, Nagarjunakonda, Nevasa, Inamgaon, Brahmagiri, Maski, Bagor, Yeleswaram and Harappan centers (Kennedy 1980). Sarkar (1972) included some morphometric data of prehistoric dentitions in this posthumous book *Ancient Races of the Deccan*. There is some dental analysis of Sri Lankan skeletal series as well (Kennedy 1965, Lukacs 1976, Begley, Kennedy and Lukacs 1979). The most current summary of dental anthropology for South Asia has been prepared by Lukacs (1977) who had examined dentitions of both prehistoric and contemporary populations of North India and Pakistan. Lukacs (1978) has reported also upon problems of sampling of dental series for Late Stone Age and Neolithic/Chalcolithic populations.

[3] A classic example of how misinterpretation of morphometric data can lead to incorrect conclusions is Guha's (1935) attempt to account for the low incidence of mesocrany and brachycrany in Harappan cranial series by hypothesizing the intrusion of foreign racial elements. Although there has been an awareness for some three-quarters of a century that changes in cranial form are reflective of environmental shifts of which nutritional stressers are perhaps most important in affecting growth (Boas 1912), the use of the cranial index as a guide to population identity continues to be used by some writers up to the present time. One is also aware that brachycranialization had continued as an evolutionary trend in world populations during the past 10,000 years. While specific causes for this phenomenon continue to be elusive, the fact of brachycranialization is established by the prehistoric skeletal record. It is a response to some stresser yet to be identified. Brachycrany which is evidence in low frequency in cranial specimens from Harappa and Lothal cannot be cited as a hallmark of racial identity for segments of those

populations once one understands the demographic distribution of meso- and brachycrany beyond the Himalayas. Cappieri (1970) has given considerable attention to this problem and it would be hazardous to dispute his conclusions in the light of what one knows about the phenotypic plasticity of cranial form in world populations. Cappieri writes:

> (1) there is no evidence of brachycephalic populations in the period covered by my study (the Harappan period) which might have influenced the local fundamental dolichocephally; and (2) there is no element proving migration of population from one region to another in the period mentioned. I calculated for the 11 essential characters 469 differences of mean between each local series of crania and all the others, mutually and inversely. Most differences—83.4—were 'not significant' and such a high value proves the genetic and somatic homogeneity of all these (specimens) as a single population.

Recognition of the evolutionary fact of brachycranialization bears upon the question of the biological identity of the ancient Harappans whom, it now appears from multivariate analysis, were a relatively homogeneous population (Dutta 1972). The so-called foreign elements are better attributed to immigration of rural peoples or possible nomadic groups coming from outlying Harappan townships, hamlets and grazing areas. In Bronze Age times, as today, South Asia peasant agriculturalists contained in their communities varying numbers of low or outcast groups which are constituted, in part, of acculturated tribal elements. Once defined into the social category as low ranking people, many individuals of tribal ancestry leave singly or with their families as migrant enclaves to urban centers (Kennedy 1977). This is an ancient demographic process, one which seems to be a biological and cultural universal. But this phenomenon of regional one-way gene flow of isolated tribal populations into the relatively more heterogeneous gene pools of villages and towns is of a completely different order of evolutionary change than that conceived by writers who would assign brachycranic crania of Harappan centers to foreign "invaders."

BIBLIOGRAPHY

Alland, A., 1970
 Adaptation in Cultural Evolution: an Approach to Medical Anthropology. New York: Columbia University.

Angel, H.L., 1971
 The People of Lerna: Analysis of a Prehistoric Aegean Population. Washington D.C.: Smithsonian Institution Press. Princeton: American School of Classical Studies at Athens.

Begley, V., K.A.R. Kennedy and J.R. Lukacs, 1979
 Excavations of Iron Age Burials at Pomparippu (Sri Lanka). *Ancient Ceylon* 4.

Boas, F., 1912
 Changing Bodily Form of Descendants of Immigrants. *American Anthropologist* 14: 530-62.

Brace, C.L., 1975
 Technology versus tooth size in Australasia. *Abstracts of the 74th Annual Meeting of the American Anthropological Association* 1975: 214.

Brace, C.L. and A. Montagu, 1977
 Human Evolution: An Introduction to Biological Anthropology. 2nd ed. New York: Macmillan.

Cappieri, M., 1970
 The Population of the Indus Civilization. *Field Research Projects, Occasional Papers* 11 Miami.

Chatterjee, B.K. and G.D. Kumar, 1973
 The Racial Affinities of the Builders of the Harappan Culture. Paper Read at the 9th International Congress of Anthropological and Ethnological Sciences, August-September, 1973. Chicago.

Dales, G.F., 1964
 The Mythical Massacre at Mohenjodaro. *Expedition* 6: 36-43.

Dutta, P.C., 1972
 The Bronze-Age Harappans: A Re-Examination of the Skulls in the Context of the Population Concept. *American Journal of Physical Anthropology* 36: 391-96.

Guha, B.S., 1935
 The Racial Affinities of the Peoples of India. *Census of India 1931:* III-A: 2-22. Simla: Government of India.

Howells, W.W., 1969
 Criteria for Selection of Osteometric Dimensions. *American Journal of Physical Anthropology* 30: 451-57.

Kennedy, K.A.R., 1965
: Human Skeletal Material from Ceylon, with an Analysis of the Island's Prehistoric and Contemporary Populations. *Bulletin of the British Museum (Natural History).* Geology II, 4: 135-213.

Kennedy, K.A.R., 1977
: *A Reassessment of the Theories of Racial Origins of the People of the Indus Valley Civilization from Recent Anthropological and Archaeological Data.* Paper read at the 6th Wisconsin Conference on South Asia, November 4-6, 1977. Madison.

Kennedy, K.A.R., 1980
: The Prehistoric Skeletal Record of Man in South Asia. *Annual Review of Anthropology* 9: 391-432.

Lukacs, J.R., 1976
: Dental Anthropology and the Biological Affinities of an Iron Age Population from Pomparippu, Sri Lanka. In *Ecological Backgrounds of South Asian Prehistory.* K.A.R. Kennedy and G.L. Possehl, eds. Pp. 197-215. Occasional Papers and Theses of the South Asia Program of Cornell University 4. Ithaca: Cornell University.

Lukacs, J.R., 1977
: *Morphological Aspects of Dental Variation in North India: a Morphometric Analysis.* Ph.D. dissertation, Anthropology Department, Cornell University.

Lukacs, J.R., 1978
: Bio-Cultural Interaction in Prehistoric India: Culture, Ecology and the Pattern of Dental Disease in Neolithic-Chalcolithic Populations. In *American Studies in the Anthropology of India.* S. Vatuk, ed. Pp. 425-44. New Delhi: Manohar.

Metress, J.F. and T. Conway, 1974
: A Guide to the Literature on the Dental Anthropology of Post Pleistocene Man. *Bulletin of the Toledo Area Aboriginal Research Club* 1.

Raikes, R.L., 1965
: The Mohenjo-Daro Floods. *Antiquity* 39: 196-203.

Sarkar, S.S., 1972
: *Ancient Races of the Deccan.* New Delhi: Munshiram Manoharlal.

Wheeler, Sir Mortimer, 1952
: Archaeology and the Transmission of Ideas. *Antiquity* 26: 180-92.

A.K. SHARMA

27. The Harappan Cemetery at Kalibangan: A Study

The well-known Harappan town of Kalibangan (long. 29° 25′ north; lat. 74° 05′ east), situated on the left bank of the Ghaggar (ancient Sarasvati), has one of the well-planned cemeteries (IAR 1962-63: 20) of Harappan times.

The Harappans at Kalibangan meticulously planned the location and maintenance of the ground for the disposal of their dead and rituals connected with it. They chose flat open land on the river flood plain west-southwest of the habitational area. This is a respectable distance from the settlement: nearly 300 meters (Pl. 27.1). The reasons to prefer this area were perhaps the following:

Wind Direction

At Kalibangan the wind blows from southwest to northeast for most of the year. Thus, wind blowing through the cemetery would not pass through the habitational area—an important point for hygienic considerations.

Flow of the River

The cemetery is situated on the downstream flood plains. Water first passes by the side of the habitation mound and then touches the fringes of the cemetery. The chance that flood waters from the cemetery could ever reach the habitation were thus remote.

Slope of the Ground

The ground they selected had a slope of two to three degrees to the north. In the *Satapatha Brahmana* (Kane 1953) one of the ideal conditions for a burial ground is that it should slope in this direction.

From the location of the graves it is evident that the Harappans at Kalibangan tried to maintain a well-defined facility and hardly any grave was noticed outside the area.

THE BURIALS

The cemetery (IAR 1964-65: 38-39) has yielded three types of burials:

1) Typical Harappan extended inhumation in rectangular or oval pits (Pl. 27.2).
2) Pot burials in circular pits (Pl. 27.3).
3) Pottery deposits in rectangular or oval pits, devoid of any skeletal remains (Pl. 27.4).

A demographic survey (Sharma 1972) of the cemetery gave some interesting results. While the first two burial types were predominant, the third type occurred infrequently.

The first and second burial types occurred in distinctly demarcated areas of their own. Circular pit pot burials were located on the northern end of the cemetery. The extended burials were found in groups of six to ten graves.

The third type (Thapar 1978), the large rectangular or oval pit, was found in the grave area with skeletons. Each group of extended burials associated with at least one rectangular pot burial of this type. These pits were left open as shown by the presence of uniformly laid bands of fine sand, clay and water marks on the bottom and sections of the pit. These pits were probably only filled to the extent that the earth covered the pots. The rest of the pit was then filled in course of time.

The definite groups of extended burials are probably indicative of families. It appears that each family group was allotted a specific area for the disposal of its dead. The occurrence of at least one pit of the third type with each group of extended burials, infers that these were probably meant for some sort of inhumation ritual. The pots in these pits were those that might have been deposited after rituals from time to time (Stacul 1975).

A remarkable feature of the cemetery at Kalibangan is that the large and spacious area was neatly divided into two sections for the extended inhumation, and pot burial types. As stated earlier, the area of extended burials had subareas demarcated for family groups. The grave pits were neatly dug to a safe depth. Except for a few cases of overlapping in case of pot burials, there was hardly any case of one burial cutting across or overlapping the other burials in the area with the extended type. This is in sharp contrast to the burials at Lothal.

At Lothal the cemetery was on slightly raised ground, adjacent to the habitation. The area was very small and congested. This is probably due to the fact that enough flat, open, dry ground was not available. There was no specified area for family groups. Since there was so little space, graves were found overlapping one another and later burials cut earlier ones.

SOME SOCIOLOGICAL ASPECTS

A close examination of the different types of burial shows that sociological norms were followed when disposing of the dead, selecting funerary goods and practicing the burial ritual.

The grave pits were neatly dug and bottoms were invariably covered with a thin carpet of hard speckled brownish clay. Normally the skeletons were kept in the center of the pit, in a supine position, with the head towards the north. The funerary goods, which included earthen pots, shell bangles, beads, bone points and in one case, a copper mirror, were deposited in the area around the head.

As indicated below, some departures from normal practice were also noticed. These appear to be instances of the burial of unusual persons or unnatural deaths. There was also one case of an extraordinarily rich burial.

1) In case of an important man's burial, the rectangular grave pit, four by two meters on plan, was lined on all four sides with typical Harappan mud bricks (40 by 20 by 10 centimeters). The inner sides of the walls were plastered with mud, *chunam* plaster. The walls were sloped, with the inner space gradually widening toward the bottom. The pit contained more than 70 pots of various shapes and sizes.

The skeleton of the old man was placed over carefully arranged layers of platters in such a manner that no part of his body touched the ground below.

2) In another case the skeleton was found carelessly dumped upside down in a crouching position, with the head toward the south. The funerary goods consisted of only three pots (Pl. 27.5). The position of the limbs and torso indicate that the man was probably a paralytic case. Rigor mortis had also set in before the body was deposited in the grave.

3) The third was a case of a crippled man (Sharma 1969) about 30 years of age. The bones of the left hand, radius and ulna show marked pathological deformities. The carpals and metacarpals were badly twisted to left, outwards (Pl. 27.6). The left radius and ulna were smaller than their right hand counterpart. The phlanges of the left foot were represented by only rudimentary bones, riding over each other.

4) One grave pit yielded three disarticulated skulls, along with several other fragmentary bones. It appears that the occupants of this grave probably died in an accident, in which different parts of the body were dismembered and it was difficult to identify and separate them. Thus, it might have been thought proper to give them a combined burial.

The grave also yielded an earthen casket with a lid. It contained the deciduous molar of a child. The rim of the casket and lid had four equidistant perforations to be used to secure the contents of the casket.

5) There was an interesting burial containing the skeleton of an adult male, with the skull, a part of the pectoral girdle and the right humerus missing. These portions were chopped off by another grave pit.

On the inner side of the left knee, in the medial condylar region of left femur and tibia, sharp vertical cut marks were noticed. The cut was three centimeters deep and 9.5 centimeters long. The wound did not show any signs of healing. It appears that the man was hit by a sharp instrument (probably a copper celt) and did not survive the injury due to excessive bleeding (Pl. 27.7).

The occurrence of a very large number of circular pits with only pots points out that the Harappans at Kalibangan probably practiced another mode, or modes, apart from extended inhumation. The question then arises as to which people were buried and who were disposed of by other methods. Except in one case, all the extended burials exposed so far have yielded very poor burial furnishings. Does this point to the fact that these burials belonged to a particular section of the society, with the other section or sections practicing some other mode of disposal of the dead or even had a separate cemetery?

The data available so far are insufficient to answer these questions. In order to understand and reconstruct a complete sequence of probable customs more data are necessary, and this requires further field work.

ACKNOWLEDGMENTS

I am grateful to Shri B.K. Thapar, Director General, Archaeological Survey of India for allowing me to utilize the material and photographs; to Shri Jagat Pati Joshi, Director (Exploration), Archaeological Survey of India, for extending all assistance in preparing this paper and the slides in a very short time; and to Shri Dhan Pal for the final typescript.

NOTE

[1] Similar evidence has been referred by Giorgio Stacul in case of burials at Loebaur, Katelai and Butkara II in the Swat Valley. He states that the widespread existence of graves that are empty or which contain only some vases and totally lack any skeletal remains, may have been used as temporary graves, to house the corpses awaiting burial or cremation. He also states that these empty graves might have also been used for performing a special ceremony connected with burials as same types of vases found in cremation graves were found in these graves.

BIBLIOGRAPHY

Indian Archaeology: A review (IAR), 1962-63
   Excavation at Kalibangan, District Ganganagar. Pp. 20-31. Delhi: Archaeological Survey of India.
Indian Archaeology: A review (IAR), 1964-65
   Excavation at Kalibangan, District Ganganagar. Pp. 35-39. Delhi: Archaeological Survey of India.
Kane, P.V., 1953
   History of Dharmashastra. Vol. 4. Poona.
Sharma, A.K., 1969
   Kalibangan Human Skeletal Remains: An osteo-archaeological approach. *Journal of the Oriental Institute, Baroda* 19: 109-14.
Sharma, A.K., 1972
   Harappan Cemetery at Kalibangan-Archaeological Approach. In *Archaeological Congress and Seminar Papers.* S.B. Deo ed. Pp. 113-16. Nagpur: Nagpur University.
Stacul, G., 1975
   The Fractional Burial Custom in the Swat Valley and Some Connected Problems. *East and West* 25 (3-4): 323.
Thapar, B.K., 1978
   The Mosaic of the Indus Civilization Beyond the Indus Valley. Unpublished paper presented at the International Seminar on the Indus Civilization, Karachi, December 30. Cyclostyled copy.

JOHN R. LUKACS

28. Dental Disease, Dietary Patterns and Subsistence at Harappa and Mohenjodaro

DENTAL DISEASE AND DIETARY PATTERNS: A MODEL

THIS analysis of Harappan dental disease, dietary patterns and subsistence is based on a model of biocultural interaction. The first assumption of this model is that a change in the subsistence strategy of a population results in an alteration in the groups' dietary pattern. The adoption of new and different kinds of food and the implementation of different food preparation techniques produces a change in the magnitude and type of stress on man's masticatory apparatus: his teeth and jaws. Changing dietary patterns and the associated dental stresses leave visible marks on the teeth and jaws in the form of distinct patterns of attrition and shifts in the incidence of dental pathology.

One might reasonably expect the highly varied, eclectic diet and coarse foodstuffs of the hunter-gatherer to result in a limited variety of dental attrition patterns and suite of dental diseases. These would differ in kind and/or frequency from the attrition patterns and dental pathologies characteristic of sedentary agricultural populations. One might predict that nomadic pastoralists largely dependent on one, or a few, animal species (sheep, goat, cattle, reindeer, etc.) would differ in their dental disease and attrition patterns from both hunter-gatherer and agricultural populations.

The problem of establishing a positive correlation between subsistence or dietary pattern on one hand, and dental disease and attrition on the other, is a new and fertile area of inquiry in physical anthropology. Preliminary investigations into this problem have been conducted on Amerindian populations from the Ohio River Valley and the American southwest. These studies, which will be briefly discussed below, and others currently in progress on prehistoric South Asian populations, provide basic empirical data that confirm specific aspects of this theoretical model.[1]

Molnar (1971) for example, has shown a higher range of variation in dental attrition patterns in hunting and gathering populations than in sedentary agricultural groups. Also, variation in the nature, degree and plane of attrition exhibits strong sexual dimorphism among hunter-gatherer groups, but not among agricultural populations. This phenomenon is best explained by the more highly varied diet and the sex-based foraging strategy commonly found in nomadic hunters and gatherers. Agriculturalists, increasingly dependent on mono-crop agricultural systems, rely heavily on one or a few staple crops. Consequently, these groups exhibit far less variation in their dental attrition patterns.

Furthermore, an association between subsistence techniques, collecting versus farming, and the incidence of dental pathology was demonstrated by Addington (1973) for the prehistoric inhabitants of the Ohio River Valley. He found that hunting and gathering populations exhibited a higher frequency of dental abscesses, periodontal disease (alveolar resorption) and ante-mortem tooth loss than sedentary agricultural groups. Alternatively, incipient and full time agriculturalists show a different pattern of dental pathology characterized by high frequencies of dental caries and calculus formation, and a reduction in the frequency of dental abscesses. The incidence of ante-mortem tooth loss may be high in both hunting and gathering and early farming communities. Investigations of dental pathology among early farming populations of the Deccan Plateau and the research presented here for Harappan populations suggests that very different etiological factors may be responsible for this superficial similarity in the frequent and often premature loss of teeth.

Before turning to the dental diseases of ancient Harappans a note of caution is in order. That all human populations, past and present, are omnivorous in their dietary intake must be emphasized for this fact has obvious implications for what one can and cannot expect to learn from the data on dental pathology and attrition. Since human populations are omnivorous, it is unrealistic and naive to expect two groups to be dramatically different and show no overlap in their dental disease and attrition patterns. Most populations, regardless of cultural, technological or dietary differences will be found to share many of the same kinds of pathological conditions, but the *incidence* or frequency with which specific diseases occur and the etiological factors behind the diseases will be found to vary with diet and ultimately subsistence strategy.

METHODOLOGY

This analysis and interpretation of dental pathology among the ancient Harappans is based upon several lines of evidence, all of which are ultimately derived from published sources.[2] The conceptual and methodological framework within which the initial description and analysis of these important skeletal collections was conducted must be reviewed.

Metrical dimensions of the dentition were widely regarded as a biological variable that would shed light on racial affinities. The dimensions of the teeth of "Proto-Australoid" skulls from Mohenjodaro (Skulls 2, 11 and M) were compared with Melanesian and Australian aborigine populations by Sewell and Guha (1931) in their osteological report. Difficulties arose in the comparative study of the skeletal biology of these prehistoric populations due to the absence of rigorous standards for osteometric analysis. Consequently, while tooth size was recorded by most investigators, there was great variation in the method of measurement and even in which teeth were selected for analysis. Gupta, Dutta and Basu (1962) in their description of the skeletal series from Harappa recorded length and breadth of the molar teeth only, while Sewell and Guha (1931) in their analysis of the skeletons from Mohenjodaro measured all preserved teeth.

These early osteological reports demonstrate an awareness of the interaction between diet, dental health and attrition, though the level of understanding may strike one as being very fundamental.

> As in the other skulls from Mohenjo-daro, the teeth are very much worn and the dentine freely exposed. The marked wear of the teeth associated with the most ancient skulls is probably due, as pointed out by Keith and noticed by us also, to the admixture of dirt in the food (Guha and Basu 1938).

Nevertheless, osteological reports on the human skeletal remains from Harappa and Mohenjodaro include individual specimen descriptions which contain specific remarks regarding: (1) the nature and degree of dental attrition, (2) the presence or absence of certain dental pathologies, and (3) variations in dental occlusion. These observations have not previously been scrutinized or interpreted from the perspective of modern paleopathology. When analyzed in the proper framework these data provide significant insights into the dietary stresses and subsistence strategies of the ancient Harappans.

The inconsistency evident in the metric analyses of the Harappan dentition appears to be less prevalent in comments on dental attrition, pathology and occlusion. The investigators whose reports were consulted recognized and recorded three types of dental pathology: (1) caries, (2) alveolar resorption, and (3) ante-mortem tooth loss. The first line of evidence on which this study is based is the published record of dental diseases observed by the initial describers of the human skeletal remains from Harappa and Mohenjodaro.

While there is obvious consistency between observers regarding the kinds of dental pathology noted, a serious methodological problem is the apparent inconsistency in recording the same observations from specimen to specimen within a single skeletal series. The osteological studies by Guha and Basu (1938) and Sewell and Guha (1931) on the skeletal remains from Mohenjodaro and the monograph by Gupta, Dutta and Basu (1962) on the material from Harappa were read with specific attention to remarks regarding the dentition, especially dental pathology. Several instances occur where no mention is made of the dentition of a particular specimen, but photographic plates and/or dioptrographic drawings of the specimen show that well-preserved dental structures were indeed present. Such irregularities in the description and recording of dental pathologies results in an underestimation of the incidence of dental disease among Harappans.

A second line of evidence was employed in an attempt to offset this inherent bias in the specimen descriptions. The abundant photographic plates and dioptrographic drawings which accompany each of these reports were studied in an attempt to gain additional information regarding dental disease. In numerous instances reference to photographs and drawings simply confirmed statements made in the text description of the specimen. In several cases where no mention of the dentition was made in the text, clear and unequivocal evidence of dental disease could be discerned in photographs and drawings. This line of evidence permitted inferences regarding the type of dental pathology, its location and extensiveness, often in greater detail than the authors' descriptions of the disease.

A final note on method concerns the nature, composition and size of the skeletal sample on which this study is based. The provenience and size of the skeletal samples employed in this study are given in Table 28.1. These specimens constitute only a portion of the total collection of human skeletal remains recovered from these archaeological sites. Study samples were selectively chosen for the primary purpose of shedding light on the racial relationships of the populations, and therefore only well-preserved adult crania were utilized. The cranial remains of children, and the fragmentary jaws and isolated teeth which could provide additional valuable data regarding dental pathology were not studied by most investigators.

Consequently, this study is actually an analysis of the pattern of dental disease among the adult segment of the ancient Harappan population. This fact also results in the tabulated incidence of dental disease among Harappans being an underestimation. Throughout this paper I rely on the demographic parameters of age and sex as assigned to each specimen by the initial describers of these skeletal collections.

DENTAL DISEASE AT HARAPPA AND MOHENJODARO

Disease, as every anthropologist knows, is a culture-bound term and the recognition, diagnosis and treatment of disease varies widely from culture to culture. By referring to the conditions described below as diseases one simply implies that they either caused the individual in which they occurred some discomfort, or hindered normal bodily functions in some way. The term *disease* as used here is not meant to convey uniqueness, abnormality or aberrancy of the conditions to be discussed.

Four dental diseases occur in some frequency at Harappa and Mohenjodaro. They include alveolar resorption (also referred to as periodontal disease), ante-mortem tooth loss, dental caries and dental abscesses. For the benefit of those unfamiliar with these pathological conditions a brief description of the symptoms and associated skeletal lesions of each are outlined:

1) *Alveolar Resorption.* This condition is characterized by the degeneration of bony tissue which supports the teeth. The alveolar bone, covered in life by the gums (gingival tissue), may reduce or resorb for a variety of different reasons including pyorrhea (inflammation of the gingival tissue), abscess formation or excessive and prolonged masticatory pressure on the tooth. The ultimate result of advanced alveolar resorption is exposure of the roots of the tooth, tooth evulsion and finally, obliteration of the tooth sockets.

2) *Ante-mortem Tooth Loss.* A condition in which the tooth is shed prior to the individuals' death. This pathology may result from cultural practices, as in some African tribes where lower central incisors are intentionally removed for aesthetic reasons. More frequently though, ante-mortem tooth loss occurs because severe dental attrition exposes the pulp cavity, infection ensues and the tooth is prematurely shed. Alternatively, severe and untreated dental caries may

Table 28.1. Provenience and sample size of human skeletal remains from Harappa and Mohenjodaro

	n
HARAPPA	
Square (Cemetery) R-37	33
Area G 289	10
Area (Mound) AB	3
Cemetery H (Stratum II) Open Burials	9
Cemetery H (Stratum I) Jar Burials	15
Sub-total: Harappa	70
MOHENJODARO	
Guha and Basu (1938)	15
Sewell and Guha (1931)	13
Sub-total: Mohenjodaro	28
Grand total: Harappa and Mohenjodaro	98

effectively destroy the bulk of the tooth crown and penetrate the pulp cavity, thereby causing infection and premature tooth evulsion. While the ultimate result is the same, early loss of teeth, the etiological causation may be very different.

3) *Dental Caries.* This more widely known dental affliction, caused by a variety of bacterial microorganisms including *Lactobacillus,* results in the decay of both enamel and dentine tissues of the tooth. Food particles that become entrapped in the intercuspal fissures of the tooth crown provide ideal microenvironments for the reproduction and destructive activity of these acidogenic microorganisms.

4) *Dental Abscesses.* A condition characterized by the necrosis of cancellous bone and the creation of circular puss-filled cavities in the maxilla or mandible. These cysts are most frequently located at or near the apex of the tooth roots. The occurrence of dental abscesses is positively associated with alveolar resorption and/or caries formation, but may occur independently of either of these afflictions. In cases where dental abscesses appear alone, the cause may be excessive and prolonged tooth wear.

The occurrence of these dental pathologies in the human skeletal remains from Harappa and Mohenjodaro is recorded by specimen in Tables 28.2 and 28.3.

Table 28.2. Dental pathology at Harappa by specimen

Specimen number	Sex	Age	Type of dental pathology
H 791/A	F	adult	alveolar resorption
H 798/A1	F	30 yrs	ante-mortem tooth loss
H 801/A	F	adult	alveolar resorption, ante-mortem tooth loss
H 804	F	adult	alveolar resorption, ante-mortem tooth loss
H 806	M	adult	caries
H 806/A	F	adult	caries
Skl. 1	M	adult	alveolar resorption, ante-mortem tooth loss
II S 18	M	adult	caries
Mound AB (Rec)	F	25 yrs	caries
H 488	F	30 yrs	alveolar resorption
H 344	M	adult	alveolar resorption, ante-mortem tooth loss
H 206 (d)	F	30 yrs	alveolar resorption
Pot No. 12(a)	F	25 yrs	abscesses

While most specimens exhibit only a single pathological condition several individuals from both Harappa (H 801/A, H 804, Skl. 1, H 344) and Mohen-

Table 28.3. Dental pathology at Mohenjodaro by specimen

Specimen number	Sex	Age	Type of dental pathology
DK 7411F	M	adult	caries
DK 7773	?	child	caries
DK 7829A	?	child	caries
Skull 6	M	adult	caries
Skull 8	M	adult	alveolar resorption, ante-mortem tooth loss
Skull 11	M	adult	alveolar resorption, ante-mortem tooth loss

jodaro (Skull Nos. 8 and 11) were afflicted by more than one dental disease. The distribution of dental diseases across the sexes, is quite uneven at Harappa, with nine of the thirteen afflicted individuals being female (69.24 percent). Only four males were suffering from dental pathologies. Unfortunately, the number of individuals exhibiting dental diseases at Mohenjodaro is too few to permit analysis by sex.

The incidence of dental pathology at Harappa and Mohenjodaro is summarized in Table 28.4. This table indicates the frequency of occurrence of each dental pathology in the total skeletal sample. For example, four individuals from Harappa ($n=70$) were affected by dental caries, resulting in a total incidence of 5.71 percent. However these figures do not show the extent of caries formation in a given individual. Some may have only one small carious tooth, while others may have three or four teeth affected by extreme carious decay.

The relative incidence of specific dental diseases is consistently higher at Harappa than at Mohenjodaro with the single exception of ante-mortem tooth loss which occurs with equal frequency at both sites. This pattern of a higher incidence of disease at Harappa is best attributed to sampling problems rather than to real ecological, dietary or subsistence differences between the two sites. The number of specimens described from Mohenjodaro is significantly fewer than the number recovered from Harappa. Further, reports on the human skeletal remains from Mohenjodaro include immature and pre-adolescent individuals, while young specimens were excluded from the study sample at Harappa. Since many dental diseases appear to be positively correlated with age, the age bias of these skeletal series would result in a lower estimated incidence of dental pathology at Mohenjodaro than at Harappa.

Table 28.4. Incidence of dental pathology at Harappa and Mohenjodaro

Dental pathology	Harappa		Mohenjodaro		Sites combined	
	n	%	n	%	n	%
Abscesses	1	(1.43)	0	(0)	1	(1.02)
Alveolar resorption	7	(10.00)	2	(7.14)	9	(9.13)
Caries	4	(5.71)	3	(10.71)	7	(7.14)
Ante-mortem tooth loss	5	(7.41)	2	(7.14)	7	(7.14)
Number of individuals affected	13	(18.57)	6	(21.43)	19	(19.39)
Total skeletal sample	70		28		98	

DISCUSSION AND CONCLUSIONS

The kinds of dental diseases that affected the ancient inhabitants of Harappa and Mohenjodaro and the frequency and pattern of distribution of these diseases by site and by sex has been reviewed. Now the question of interpreting these data must be considered. How do the inhabitants of these Indus Valley sites compare with the theoretical model briefly described above in terms of the frequency and distribution of specific dental diseases? How do these data for the Harappans compare with the patterns of dental disease exhibited by the more recent Chalcolithic populations of the Deccan Plateau?

When data on dental disease for Harappa and Mohenjodaro are combined the most frequently occurring pathology is alveolar resorption. Dental caries and ante-mortem tooth loss occur with equal frequency, but are somewhat less common than alveolar resorption. The least frequent dental disease is the isolated case of dental abscesses present in a specimen from Harappa [Pot No. 12(a)].

The types and relative frequencies of dental pathology for the ancient Harappans are compatible with expectations based on the theoretical model for sedentary agricultural populations. Dental abscesses, a condition associated with increased masticatory stresses imposed by a tough, fibrous and poorly prepared diets of the hunter-gatherer, are very infrequent among Harappans. The moderate frequency of dental caries and ante-mortem tooth loss is also typical for agricultural populations. The softer foods resulting from dependency on milled grains and the high carbohydrate intake of agriculturalists causes a reduction in the degree of dental attrition and an increase in the frequency of dental caries formation (in contrast to hunter-gatherer groups). Reduced dental attrition permits food particles to become lodged in the inter-cuspal fissures of the tooth crown, providing an ideal environment suitable for the bacterial agents responsible for tooth decay.

That the frequency of ante-mortem tooth loss and dental caries is similar among the two Harappan populations may not be simply coincidental. As cariogenic decay proceeds to destroy the tooth crown and exposes the dental pulp cavity, the tooth is ultimately and prematurely shed. The corresponding incidence of tooth decay due to caries and the frequency of ante-mortem tooth loss is clearly suggestive of a causal relationship. In hunting and gathering populations ante-mortem tooth loss may reach high frequencies, similar to or higher than those found in agricultural groups, but the etiology is distinctly different. In hunters and gatherers dental caries are very infrequent, but dental attrition is usually quite severe, often exposing the pulp cavity at an early age. This permits infection of the tooth and rapidly results in tooth loss. The superficial similarities in the frequency of a specific dental disease may actually have very different etiologies.

Alveolar resorption, the most commonly occurring dental disease among the ancient Harappans, may also be caused by a variety of factors. While the possible causes of this dental affliction can be listed here, the data at hand are insufficient to determine with certainty the primary causal factor involved. One widely recognized cause of alveolar resorption is *pyorrhea alveolaris,* a disease involving an infection of the gums (gingival tissue) and tooth sockets. The occurrence of pyorrhea is facilitated by the absence of dental hygiene and is often transmitted by communal use of kitchen eating utensils. A second cause of alveolar resorption is heavy masticatory stresses associated with either prolonged chewing of tough dietary items or stress due to the inclusion of foreign items (sand, grit, flecks from the millstone, etc.) that become incorporated in the food. Alveolar resorption also regularly accompanies ante-mortem tooth loss. Once a tooth is shed, osteoclasts (specialized cells that resorb bone) destroy the unoccupied tooth socket(s) and restructure the jawbone through resorption. Most of the cases of alveolar resorption recorded in the Harappan populations are probably due to tooth loss. However, both alternative explanations may be in part responsible for cases of alveolar resorption prior to tooth loss.

The dental pathology of Chalcolithic populations of the Deccan Plateau has been described by various authors. Human skeletal remains from Apegaon, Inamgaon and Nevasa have been examined by Lukacs (1977, 1978, in press; Lukacs and Badam 1977) with particular attention to the dentition. Kennedy and Malhotra (1966) conducted a very thorough osteometric analysis of the human skeletal remains from Chalcolithic and Indo-Roman levels at Nevasa. These populations represent early farming communities of the Deccan Plateau, most are situated in central and western Maharashtra. Archaeological evidence indicates that these Jorwe people had only recently adopted large-scale agricultural subsistence strategies (Dhavalikar 1977; Deo, Dhavalikar and Ansari 1979; Sankalia, Ansari and Dhavalikar 1971).

The pattern and incidence of dental pathology among these early farming populations is highly variable because of the variation in demographic structure of each group. For example, the young mean age at time of death for the Nevasa skeletal series accounts for the very low incidence of dental disease in this population. Adult specimens from Inamgaon, whose mean age at time of death is between 30 and 40 years, all exhibit ante-mortem tooth loss due to the combined causes of severe dental attrition and dental caries. Young adults from Inamgaon have very healthy, disease-free teeth, suggesting that the stresses of heavy mastication begin to leave their mark on the dentition during the third decade of life. This contrasts vividly with the data reported here for Mohenjodaro which show two pre-adolescent children affected by carious formation. The frequency of dental caries among the Chalcolithic populations of the Deccan Plateau is low, again a contrast to the moderately high incidence of caries reported here for the Harappans. The etiological cause of ante-mortem tooth loss among the Deccan populations appears to be severe dental attrition, in some instances combined with dental caries. Among the Harappans the primary cause of ante-mortem tooth loss seems to be carious formation.

The overall impression derived from this comparative evaluation of the evidence of dental pathology is that the Harappans exhibit a dental disease pattern that indicates a longer period of dependency of agricultural subsistence strategies. The dental disease profile of the Harappans suggests a reduction in masticatory stresses and associated dental diseases, but an increase in dental caries in conjunction with soft foodstuffs and increased carbohydrate intake. By contrast, the Chalcolithic people of the Deccan Plateau exhibit a dental disease pattern indicative of a more recent shift to sedentary agricultural subsistence patterns. The low incidence of dental caries and the heavy dental attrition evident among these Chalcolithic populations suggests that the shift to agricultural pursuits may not have been complete or total. Farming activities may well have been periodically supplemented by hunting and gathering subsistence activities. Faunal remains from these sites add further support to this hypothesis since the osteological remains of non-domestic animal species are often recovered from Chalcolithic kitchen middens (Badam 1979).

The ancient Harappans appear to have paid a price in dental discomfort for their soft and easily masticated foods. Technological advancement frequently alters established patterns of natural selection often resulting in an adjustment in the adaptiveness of the population. The integral interrelationship shown to exist between subsistence, dietary pattern and dental disease is a clear indication of the direct manner in which biology and culture are intertwined in the course of human evolution.

ACKNOWLEDGMENTS

Special thanks are due Dr. Kenneth A.R. Kennedy for discussions and comments of the many problems considered in this paper.

Mr. Donald C. Dunbar read and offered useful comments on the manuscript during the final stages of its preparation.

The author is deeply indebted to the Indo-American Fellowship Program and the Council for International Exchange of Scholars for supporting this research and for travel funds that permitted his participation in the American Institute of Indian Studies Seminar on the Harappan Civilization.

NOTES

[1] The author has studied the pattern of dental disease among Chalcolithic populations of the Deccan Plateau in some detail and although sample sizes are small, a characteristic pattern is beginning to emerge (Lukacs 1977, 1978, in press).

[2] Access to the prehistoric human skeletal remains curated at the Anthropological Survey of India (Calcutta), which includes the remains from Harappa and Mohenjodaro is difficult to secure. The author hopes to obtain permission to examine the dental structures of these skeletal series during a future research visit to India.

BIBLIOGRAPHY

Addington, J.E., 1973
  Collectors or Farmers: Dental attrition and pathology as related to subsistence in the Ohio Valley. Paper read at the 72nd annual meeting of the American Anthropological Association, New Orleans.

Badam, G.L., 1979
  Faunal Remains from Apegaon. In *Apegaon Excavations—1979.* S.B. Deo, M.K. Dhavalikar and Z.D. Ansari. Pp. 40-49. Pune: Deccan College.

Deo, S.B., M.K. Dhavalikar and Z.D. Ansari, 1979
  Apegaon Excavations—1979. Pune: Deccan College.

Dhavalikar, M.K., 1977
  Inamgaon: The pattern of settlement, *Man and Environment* 1: 46-51.

Guha, B.S. and P.C. Basu, 1938
  Report on the Human Remains Excavated at Mohenjodaro in 1928-29. In *Further Excavations at Mohenjodaro.* E.J.H. Mackay, Vol. 1. Pp. 613-38. New Delhi: Government of India.

Gupta, P., P.C. Dutta and A. Basu, 1962
  Human Skeletal Remains from Harappa. Anthropological Survey of India, Memoir No. 9. Pp. 3-186. Calcutta.

Kennedy, K.A.R. and K.C. Malhotra, 1966
  Human Skeletal Remains from Chalcolithic and Indo-Roman Levels from Nevasa. Deccan College Building Centenary and Silver Jubilee Series, No. 55.

Lukacs, John R., 1977
  Anthropological Aspects of Dental Variation in North India: A Morphometric Analysis. Ph.D. dissertation, Anthropology Department, Cornell University.

Lukacs, John R., 1978
  Biocultural Interaction in Prehistoric India: culture, ecology and the pattern of dental disease in Neolithic-Chalcolithic populations. In *American Studies in the Anthropology of India.* S. Vatuk, ed. Pp. 425-44. Delhi: Manohar.

Lukacs, John, R., in press
  The Apegaon Mandible: Morphology and pathology. *Deccan College Research Institute Bulletin.*

Lukacs, J.R. and G.L. Badam, 1977
  Biological Anthropology of Human Skeletal Remains from Chalcolithic Inamgaon, Western India. *Deccan College Research Institute, Bulletin* 36: 73-83.

Molnar, S., 1971
  Human Tooth Wear, Tooth Function and Cultural Variability. *American Journal of Physical Anthropology* 34: 27-42.

Sankalia, H.D., Z.D. Ansari and M.K. Dhavalikar, 1971
  Inamgaon: A chalcolithic settlement in western India. *Asian Perspectives* 14: 139-46.

Sankalia, H.D., Z.D. Ansari and M.K. Dhavalikar, 1975
  An Early Farmer's Village in Central India. *Expedition* 17: 2-11.

Sewell, R.B.S. and B.S. Guha, 1931
  Human Remains. In *Mohenjodaro and the Indus Civilization.* Sir John Marshall, ed. Vol. 2. Pp. 599-648. London: Arthur Probsthain.

PART V

THE INDUS SCRIPT

IRAVATHAM MAHADEVAN

29. Terminal Ideograms in the Indus Script

The study of the Indus script has come of age with the publication of two comprehensive, computerized concordances which cover between them the entire known inscriptional material of the Harappan Civilization (Parpola *et al.*, 1973, 1979; Mahadevan 1977). These concordances present the texts and the relevant background data in a systematic manner, enabling scholars without direct access to the original material to undertake analytical studies of the inscriptions and to formulate or verify hypotheses regarding the nature of the script and the typology of the underlying language.

Some positive results have already emerged or been confirmed by analytical studies based on the concordances. The determination of the direction of writing (from right to left) and the segmentation of the texts into probable "words" and "phrases" through simple word-division techniques are among the more secure results obtained so far (Mahadevan 1977, in press a).

It is, however, significant that most of the initial results flowing from a careful study of the concordances are negative in character:

1) The Indus script is *not* alphabetic or quasi-alphabetic, judging from the number of individual signs and their functional and distributional characteristics.

2) The Indus script is *not* closely related to any of the contemporary pictographic scripts of the third and the second millennia B.C., even though the Harappans were in contact with the West Asian cultures and there could have been diffusion of ideas regarding writing systems. The presence of a few common pictograms or ideograms (e.g., man, fish, mountain, river, rain, city, crossroads, house, plough, etc.) may be traced to such diffusion of ideas rather than to direct borrowing or common descent. Pictograms and ideograms, by their very nature, are bound to have resemblances even if they belong to different and independent writing systems. Sign sequences in the Indus script are unique, bearing no relation to any of the West Asian scripts.

3) The Indus script is *not* related to the later Indian scripts, namely, the Brāhmī and the Khorashṭhi. The attempts to link features like conjunct-consonants or medial vowel signs of the later Indian scripts with the supposedly similar features of the Indus script have not been successful.

4) The most common supposition that the frequent terminal signs of the Indus script represent grammatical suffixes, especially case endings, has *not* been confirmed by the concordances. A careful study of the concordances shows that the most frequent terminal signs are too closely related to their antecedent signs and sign groups with which they occur in terminal positions in all contexts, to be variable case endings. The relationship appears to be semantic rather than grammatical.

5) The Harappan language is *not* related to the Indo-European family of languages, as there is no evidence for prefixing or inflectional endings in the Indus script.

6) The Harappan language is *not* related to Sumerian or other West Asian languages which place the attribute after the substantive. The reverse word order of the Harappan language is proved by the occurrence of the numerals before the enumerated objects in the Indus script.

7) A major negative conclusion emerging from an analytical study of the concordances is that none of the published claims of decipherment of the Indus script is valid. Most of the attempts (especially those

which assign alphabetic or quasi-alphabetic values to the signs) can be easily disproved by a simple comparison of the frequency and distribution characteristics of the signs with those of the corresponding values in the assumed models. The more sophisticated attempts remain, at best, not proven.

Shall one conclude therefore that the Indus script cannot be deciphered at all and that all further attempts are bound to be futile and a waste of time? There are two good reasons why such a wholly pessimistic attitude should not be adopted. Firstly, it is an axiom of cryptology that, given adequate material, no code or cipher can successfully resist decipherment for all time. This is all the more true of ancient undeciphered scripts whose unintelligibility is a matter of accident rather than design. The corpus of Harappan inscriptions is growing steadily as new sites are being discovered and the known sites are taken up again for more intensive excavation. It is, therefore, reasonable to hope that in the near future the number of inscriptions in the Indus script will be large enough to lend itself to normal cryptanalytical procedures. The possibility that the Harappan language is totally lost without any surviving descendants in the Subcontinent is also too remote, considering the vast extent and the long duration of the Harappan Civilization. Secondly, it is quite likely that the Indian historical tradition, with its astonishing continuity and vitality, has managed to preserve at least some facets of the Indus Civilization, thus providing valuable clues for an understanding of the contents of the inscriptions in the Indus script. Since the pictorial motifs associated with these inscriptions, like the depiction of *Paśupati,* phallic symbolism, veneration of the *pipal* tree and the serpent are clearly seen to be connected with later Indian tradition, there is no good reason to deny the possibility of such interconnection between the contents of the Harappan inscriptions and the later tradition.

Any serious study of the Indus script must begin with a formal or structural analysis of the texts. Such a study will include compilation of a sign list and a concordance, tabulation of sign frequencies and statistical-positional analyses to determine the nature of the script and the language. It is also necessary to carry out a context-analysis of the inscriptions with reference to their background viz., sites of occurrence, stratigraphy, types of inscribed objects and the pictorial motifs associated with the inscriptions. It is at this level that the use of the computer has been most productive (Knorozov *et al.,* 1965, 1968; Parpola *et al.,* 1969, 1973, 1979; Mahadevan 1977, in press a; Mahadevan and Visvanathan 1973). It is also at this level that some measurable progress has been achieved in matters like determination of the direction of writing, word division and delineation of the broad syntactical features of the texts. These studies seem to indicate that the typology of the Harappan language is non-Indo-European and resembles the Dravidian languages closely. One has however to leave the computer behind at this stage when one proceeds further to look for clues to find the meaning of the texts or phonetic values of the signs.

Emil Forrer (1932) pointed out that it was possible to acquire an objective comprehension of the contents of an inscription in an undeciphered script by the observance of parallel phenomena. Parallels can occur between a symbolic representation and a text associated with it, between the written object and its designation, or between the written symbol itself and its meaning. Parallels can also be set up by observing the similarities in the standard formulae employed in ancient inscriptions. Forrer was able to show that such comparisons revealed the basic grammatical features of the writing system even before its linguistic decipherment.

As I mentioned earlier, the method of parallels is particularly apt for a study of the Indus script on account of the continuity of the Indian historical tradition. It is probable that even when the Indus script ceased to be a writing system, some of the more important ideograms survived and evolved into traditional symbols of various kinds. Such survivals may consist of iconographic elements and other religious symbols, royal insignia, emblems on coins and seals, heraldic signs of the nobility, corporate symbols, totem signs of clans and tribes and the like. Pictograms and ideograms of contemporary pictographic scripts may also furnish valuable clues to the recognition of the probable objects or meanings (but not of course the sounds) depicted by similar signs in the Indus script. The comparisons should not be inconsistent with the results obtained from the formal textual analysis of the inscriptions.

In one of my earlier papers (Mahadevan 1972) I suggested the possibility that parallels drawn from the Harappan substratum might occur in both the Indo-Aryan and the Dravidian languages. To recapitulate briefly, the method of bilingual parallels is based on the following assumptions:

1) The Harappan seals, in accordance with universal usage, give the names and titles of the owners. It is likely that due to prolonged bilingualism and racial fusion in the Subcontinent, the more important Harappan names and titles passed into the later Indo-Aryan languages as loan words or loan translations.

2) It is possible that the later symbols, derived from the Indus ideograms were continued to be associated, even though in a conventional manner, with the later forms of the older names and titles represented originally by the Indus ideograms.

3) It should be possible to undertake a comparison of such traditional symbols resembling the signs of the Indus script and names and concepts associated with them in the Indian historical tradition, in an attempt to establish the original ideographic meanings of the signs.

Before I proceed to illustrate the method of bilingual parallels, I must mention two important changes in my line of thinking in the light of the new evidence available from the concordances:

1) I now consider that, in the present state of our knowledge of the Indus script, it would be more productive to search for ideographic parallels from the later bilingual Indian traditions, rather than look for homophones or rebus writing. The method of bilingual parallels enables one to extend the search for Harappan survivals to the historical, literary and religious traditions available in the Indo-Aryan and the Dravidian languages, without having to make any *a priori* assumptions about the nature of the Harappan language or the actual phonetic values of the signs, which would be implicit in a search for homophones. I am not suggesting that the method of homophones or rebus is inapplicable to the Indus script; but I now believe that one should first exhaust the possibilities of finding ideographic parallels to acquire a greater comprehension of the likely contents of the inscriptions, before proceeding to the stage of linguistic decipherment.

2) In my earlier papers (1970, 1972, 1973) I had proceeded on the assumption that the frequent terminal signs of the Indus script probably represented grammatical suffixes and that their values could be ascertained through the method of homophones. As I have mentioned earlier in this paper, the concordances do not bear out this theory. I am presently inclined to the view that the frequent terminal signs were most probably employed in an ideographic sense to indicate the class of persons to whose names they are found suffixed.

It is also necessary to emphasize here the limitations of the method I propose. The tentative linguistic parallels suggested in this paper are not to be regarded as a decipherment of the Indus script. The very diversity of the later Indian parallels would preclude us from assigning any specific phonetic values to the ideograms of the Indus script. However I do claim that the parallels suggested from later Indian historical traditions would enable one to broadly comprehend the probable original meanings of the ideograms and the general contents of the texts. I readily concede that the results are tentative, even speculative, and will require much further study before they can be confirmed.

THE 'JAR' SIGN: ⋃

This is the most frequent sign of the Indus script. It accounts for about 10 percent of the total sign occurrences. It can be established from formal analysis that the sign occurs as a post-fix, suffix or determinative at the end of the seal texts which probably give the names and titles of the owners (Hunter 1934). The sign seems to depict a vessel with ears or handles (?) and a tapering bottom. The vessel form of the sign is clearly indicated in the naturalistic representations found in two graffiti on potsherds excavated from an early level at Kalibangan (Lal 1974, 1978).

The symbolism of the JAR is closely associated in the later Indian religious tradition with priestly ritual. The legend of the "jar-born" sages is very ancient and is even found in the *Rigveda* (VII: 33) where it is said that Vasishtha and Agastya were born in a sacred pitcher. The Tamil tradition (*Puṟam*: 201) also refers to Agastya, who led the southern migration of the Vēḷir clans from Dwārakā, as having "arisen from a vessel." In Vedic literature and ritual treatises, (*Śatapatha Brāhmaṇa*: XII 7, 2, 13, etc.), *sata* is mentioned as some kind of a sacrificial vessel used in ritual. A later commentator (Śabaraswāmin in *Mīmāṁsa Sūtra Bhāshya*, 1:3:10) described *sata* as a wooden vessel, round in shape and perforated with a hundred holes. He has also cited this term as an example of words of *mlechha* origin without an etymology in Sanskrit. There have been numerous finds of perforated pottery jars from the Harappan sites. It is not unlikely that these perforated jars had some ritual purpose.

It thus appears that the JAR sign of the Indus script

is a pictogram depicting a sacrificial vessel used in priestly ritual and probably employed as an ideogram suffixed to names to denote the concept of a priest. In later times, the jar symbolism continued to be associated with priestly and ruling classes and gave rise to the myth of miraculous birth from a jar. I now believe that since the JAR sign was probably used ideographically to denote a priest, it is not necessary that the words for "priest" and "jar" were homophones in the Harappan language.

THE 'LANCE' SIGN:

This is a terminal sign and it functions like the JAR sign. Both signs function as terminals not only at the end of texts but also in medial positions. The preceding sequences in either case can be shown to be complete "words" or "phrases" by themselves, most probably names and titles (Hunter 1934). There is therefore reason to believe that the LANCE sign, like its functional twin, the JAR sign is an ideogram suffixed to name formations. It is easy to recognize the pictogram as an arrowhead or a lance. I suggest that the LANCE sign was employed as an ideogram denoting the meaning of "warrior" when suffixed at the end of names and titles.

THE 'BEARER' SIGN:

The pictogram depicts a person carrying a yoke across his shoulders with loads suspended from either end. The positional and functional characteristics of this sign are very similar to those of the JAR sign. Thus the BEARER sign also appears to be an ideogram occurring as a suffixed element in name formation.

It appears possible to interpret the ideographic meaning of this sign with reference to the "bearer" motif occurring in later Indian tradition. The term "bearer" is applied idiomatically in Indian languages to a person who "shoulders" any responsibility or "bears" the "burden" of any office. Thus the Sanskrit word for husband *bhartṛ* (literally one who sustains or maintains) is from the root *bhṛ*, "to bear." There are similar expressions derived from the root *vah*, "to bear," as in *kārya-vāhaka* "office bearer." One may also refer to the "yoke" words like *dhuraṁdhara* or *yugaṁdhara* (literally "yoke bearer") used as honorifics or names. It is interesting that in ancient Tamil tradition, ministers and senior officers of the king were given the title *kāviti* (literally "yoke bearer")

probably from *kā*, "yoke" (DED: 1193). On the basis of this evidence, one can interpret the "bearer" sign in the Indus script when suffixed to names as an ideogram with the approximate meaning of "officer" or "functionary."

A common tendency in the Indian tradition is for honorifics and titles to lose their original significance and become proper names. If a similar development had taken place in respect of the "bearer" symbolism, such names should be found among the princely or priestly families in later times. This reasoning leads one straight to the earliest and the most famous of the "bearer" clans in ancient India, the Bharatas (literally "bearers"). It is significant that the Bharatas were both priests and rulers and occupied the Indus region during the Vedic Period. The Andhras were another famous dynasty with royal names derived from the "bearer" motif, viz., Sātavāhana and Sālivāhana. In the Tamil country, the Cheras were also known as Poṛaiyar, literally "bearers" from *poṛu* "to bear" (DED: 3729). Important evidence to corroborate this association comes from a series of late medieval copper coins of the rulers of Travancore (inheriting the tradition of the Cheras), which portray the "bearer" motif which is pictorially practically identical with the BEARER ideogram of the Indus script. (Cf. Elliot 1886: no. 197.)

It is interesting to observe the connection between the JAR and BEARER signs in the Indus script as well as in the later Indian tradition. The two signs occur in a similar environment in the inscriptions indicating that they belong to the same category. Another interesting feature is that these two signs are often found ligatured. In fact the compound JAR-BEARER sign occurs more often than the BEARER sign. When one turns to later Indian tradition one finds that names or myths connected with the "jar" and "bearer" motifs tend to occur in the same groups. The Kurus were generated in jars (*Mahabharata, Ādiparvan Gāndhārīputrotpatti*) and were also called the Bhāratas ("bearers"). The Andhras had "jar" names (*Sāta*) as well as "bearer" names (Sātavāhana, Sālivāhana). The names of the Cheras, Ātaṉ (probably to be derived from *Sāta*), and Poṛai also show both the associations. The Pallavas who claimed descent from a vessel (cf. *pāttraskhalitavṛttīnām* occurring on the seal of the Pallamkoyil Plates of Rājasimha; Subramanian 1959) belonged to the Bhāradvāja gotra, another name with the "bearer" motif.

I have published earlier (Mahadevan 1972) what I consider to be the most interesting evidence connecting the ideograms of the Indus script with later Indian historical names. A search for royal names based on the "bearer" motif led me to the famous Andhra dynasty whose kings called themselves Sātavāhanas or Sālivāhanas. The suffix *vāhana* is connected with the "bearer" theme (*vahana*: bearing, carrying). However since the second element *vāhana* never occurs separately in these names, it struck me as probable that the preceding elements *sāta* and *sāli* might also be derived from the Harappan substratum. The BEARER ideogram in the Indus script often appears ligatured or compounded with one of two other signs—the JAR sign or the LANCE sign. In an earlier paper (1972) I proposed reading these ligatures from bottom to top on the ground that the JAR and LANCE signs were grammatical suffixes. I no longer hold this view and now believe that the ligatures may be read from top to bottom in the normal manner. These compound ideograms can be considered in the light of the interesting parallelisms shown in figure 29.1. The very close parallelisms between the compound ideograms of the Indus script and the compound names in the later Indian historical tradition provide good confirmation of the approach I have suggested.

The two compound ideograms can be interpreted on the basis of the ideographic values of their components. Thus the ligature JAR-BEARER ("priest plus officer") may indicate an officer or functionary with priestly duties. Similarly the ligature LANCE-BEARER ("warrior plus officer") may stand for an officer or functionary with military duties.

THE 'MAN' SIGN:

This is a simple pictogram almost universally interpreted as representing a human figure. As a final sign it forms a frequent pair with the JAR sign, but never with the LANCE sign. It is to be contrasted with the ideogram of a "horned person," the latter obviously depicting a chieftain or a divine personage. Thus the plain MAN sign can be interpreted as depicting a servant or an attendant. The pair JAR-MAN occurring in terminal positions can be interpreted as ideograms for a lower order of priestly functionaries.

THE 'HARROW' SIGN:

Kosambi (1956, 1965) made the suggestion that this sign is a pictogram representing the toothed harrow. Internal evidence for this identification is provided by the following compound signs:

- Note the position of the harrow shown in front of the human figure and with the teeth facing the ground.

- Harrow in conjunction with a sheaf or bundle of grain stalks.

I interpret the sign as depicting a harrow and ideographically representing a farmer or tiller of the land. The characteristic position of the sign is terminal, frequently occurring in conjunction with the JAR, LANCE or BEARER signs. Such terminal clusters can be provisionally interpreted to indicate that the persons named in the inscriptions were perhaps farmers or tenants, serving under either priests, warriors or

Sign	Pictorial value	Equivalents in Sanskrit	Meaning
∪	JAR	*Sata*	A kind of sacrificial vessel
↑	LANCE	*Śalya*	Lance, spear
大	BEARER	*Vahana*	Bearing, carrying
	JAR + BEARER	*Sata-vahana* > Sātavāhana	lit., jar-bearing n. pr. of Andhra dynasty
	LANCE + BEARER	*Śalya-vahana* > Sālivāhana	lit., lance-bearing n. pr. of Andhra dynasty

Fig. 29.1. Indus ideograms in Indian historical tradition.

Sign	Pictorial value	Ideographic meaning
⋃	JAR (sacrificial vessel)	Priest
↑	LANCE	Warrior
𓀂	BEARER	Officer or functionary
𓀂	JAR + BEARER	Officer or functionary with priestly duties
𓀂	LANCE + BEARER	Officer or functionary with military duties
𐀀	MAN	Servant, attendant or lower functionary
E	HARROW	Farmer, tiller, tenant.

Fig. 29.2. Terminal ideograms of the Indus script.

officers (as the case may be) or, alternatively, themselves belonging to these categories. It is interesting to recall here the ancient classification of the Veḷḷāḷar (the predominant agricultural population among the Tamils) into those who earned their livelihood by ploughing the land themselves or by having the land ploughed by others (Naccinarkkiniyar on *Tolkāppiyam, Poruḷ*, 34).

To sum up, it appears likely that the frequent terminal signs in the Indus script are probably ideograms indicating the occupations and social status of the persons to whose names these signs are suffixed. The tentative interpretations of these ideograms are summarized in figure 29.2. It is not yet clear whether these ideograms were actually pronounced as part of names and titles, as in later Indian caste names, or merely served as mute determinatives, as in the Egyptian script.

BIBLIOGRAPHY

Burrow, T. and M.B. Emeneau, 1961
 Dravidian Etymological Dictionary. Oxford: The University Press.
Elliot, W., 1886
 Coins of Southern India. London: Macmillan.
Forrer, Emil, 1932
 The Hittite Idiographic Writing. Chicago: University of Chicago Press.
Hunter, G.R., 1934
 The Script of Harappa and Mohenjodaro and its Connection With Other Scripts. London: Kegan Paul.
Knorozov, Yu.V. *et al.*, 1965
 Preliminary Report on the Investigation of the Proto-Indian Texts. Moscow: Soviet Institute of Scientific and Technical Information, Institute of Ethnography. Translated by Arlene R.K. Zide and Kamil V. Zvelebil as *The Soviet Decipherment of the Indus Valley Script*. 1976. The Hague: Mouton.
Knorozov, Yu.V. *et al.*, 1968
 Proto-Indica: Brief report on the Investigation of Proto-Indian Texts. Moscow.
Kosambi, D.D., 1956
 An Introduction to the Study of Indian History. Bombay: Popular Book Depot.
Kosambi, D.D., 1965
 The Culture and Civilization of Ancient India in Historical Outline. London: Routledge and Kegan Paul.
Lal, B.B., 1974
 Some Aspects of the Archaeological Evidence

Relating to the Indus Script. *Puratattava* 7: 20-24.

Lal, B.B., in press
On the Most Frequently Used Sign in the Indus Script. Paper read at the Xth International Congress of Anthropological Ethnological Sciences, December 1978, New Delhi.

Mahadevan, Iravatham, 1970
Dravidian Parallels in Proto-Indian Script. *Journal of Tamil Studies* 2 (1): 157-276.

Mahadevan, Iravatham, 1972
Study of the Indus Script Through Bi-lingual Parallels. *Proceedings of the Second All-India Conference of Dravidian Linguists.* Tirupati: Sri Venkateswara University. Reprinted in *Ancient Cities of the Indus.* G.L. Possehl, ed. Pp. 261-67. Delhi: Vikas.

Mahadevan, Iravatham, 1973
Method of Parallelisms in the Interpretation of the Proto-Indian Script. *Proceedings of the IIIrd International Conference-Seminar on Tamil Studies.* Paris: Institut Francais d'Indologie.

Mahadevan, Iravatham, 1977
The Indus Script: Texts, Concordance and Tables. Memoirs of the Archaeological Survey of India 77. Delhi: Government of India.

Mahadevan, Iravatham, in press a
Recent Advances in the Study of the Indus Script. Paper read at the Xth International Congress of Anthropological and Ethnological Sciences, December 1978, New Delhi.

Mahadevan, Iravatham, in press b
Indus Script in the Indian Historical Tradition. Paper read at the Seminar on Astronomical Data from History, 1979, Madras.

Mahadevan, I. and K. Visvanathan, 1973
Computer Concordance of Proto-Indian Signs. In *Radiocarbon and Indian Archaeology.* D.P. Agrawal and A. Ghosh, eds. Pp. 291-304. Bombay: Tata Institute of Fundamental Research.

Parpola, A. *et al.*, 1969
Decipherment of the Proto-Indian Inscriptions of the Indus Civilization: A first announcement. Copenhagen: Scandinavian Institute of Asian Studies.

Parpola, A., *et al.*, 1973
Materials for the Study of the Indus Script: I. A Concordance to the Indus Inscriptions. Helsinki: Helsinki University.

Parpola, A. *et al.*, 1979
Corpus of Texts in the Indus Script. Helsinki: Helsinki University.

Subramanian, T. N., 1959
Pallaṉkōvil Jaina Copper Plate Grant of the Early Pallava Period. *Transactions of the Archaeological Society of South India:* 41.

PART VI

THE LATER PHASES OF THE
HARAPPAN TRADITION

A. GHOSH

30. Deurbanization of the Harappan Civilization

WHILE many definitions of preindustrial urbanization are available, I am inclined to think that the list of the ten abstract criteria laid down by Childe (1950) still holds good. It is true that the list is "a mixed bag of characteristics" and that all the criteria are not primary ones, some being derived from others (Adams 1966: 45-47); nevertheless, in their practical application they are not devoid of relevance.

Deurbanization of a civilization would involve the reversal of all the criteria. Thus, the settlements, extensive and densely populated, would become smaller with a thinned population. The non-food-producing people such as full-time specialist craftsmen, transport workers, merchants and officials would dwindle in number and the food-producing people would be left with little incentive to produce surplus. Monumental buildings—the symbol of social surplus—would no longer dominate a settlement. The use of a script would be a thing of the past, unless it is adapted by some other urbanized community. Long-distance trade to meet the requirements of specialized craftsmen and to supply luxury goods would not be required, though imports of essential items, prevalent even in Neolithic times, would continue. With all this there would be a fall in the material prosperity of a deurbanized population and the need for central enforcement would be reduced.

As Childe's criteria for urbanization are abstract, so too are the signs of deurbanization and their character varies from civilization to civilization. While applying them to the deurbanized Harappan Civilization, I shall have to say a few words on the character of the urban Harappan to understand the process of Harappan deurbanization. I think Fairservis has unduly emphasized the religious character of the civilization by holding that Mohenjodaro was almost a purely ceremonial center and that trade had not much influence on its location and upkeep (Fairservis 1967: 1-35). While his remarks primarily apply to Mohenjodaro, it is clear from what he says that they are intended to apply to the totality of the civilization, since his main theme is the progressive "Indianization" of the cultures of the Indo-Iranian borderlands. This is a process in which the bull, appearing on the seals and pottery and represented in terracotta, plays a prominent role. I do not think that this hypothesis is plausible. It is now generally accepted that the Harappan seals were used for commercial purposes, viz., to authenticate merchandise. Further, the bull is certainly not the most recurring "field symbol" on the seals. The unicorn, which has no place in later Indian religious belief, heads the list with a frequency of 1159, while the bull, in all its forms, is a poor second, with only 156 (Mahadevan 1977: 793) and it is altogether absent at Lothal (Rao 1973: 139). Ritual bathing, another piece of evidence for Indianization cited by Fairservis can be deduced at Mohenjodaro, and to a lesser extent at Kalibangan, but is absent at other important sites of the civilization such as Harappa and Lothal. It is also difficult to generalize on the form of the Harappan religion: the fire altars of Lothal (Rao 1973: 139) and Kalibangan (Lal 1979: 77) are unreported from Mohenjodaro and Harappa. A uniform set of Harappan religious beliefs and practices is therefore difficult to envisage. Equally so, therefore, is the 'Indianization' of the Indus Cultures. A religion-based Harappan Civilization is far from established, though religion had no doubt its share in the life of the people. In which prehistoric and historical society did it not?

On the other hand, trade seems to be the *leitmotiv*

of the Harappan Civilization. The Indus-Mesopotamian trade relations have been extensively discussed in many works on the civilization. The nature of this long-distance trade is now fairly well known and new facets have been added to it by the discoveries at Lothal, as well as the now identified trading centers on the Oxus, in Afghanistan (Gupta 1979: I, 133-220) and on the Makran Coast. The generally accepted identification of Meluhha with the Indus world is also of relevance. This long-distance trade was both direct and indirect (Asthana 1979: 31-43). It is also known that it declined at the end of the Third Dynasty of Ur and virtually stopped with the Isin-Larsa Period, when the Mesopotamians turned to Arabia and Egypt for their commodities (Asthana 1979: 31-43). The cessation of this trade at about 1900 B.C. must have had an adverse effect on the prosperity of the Harappan Civilization and must therefore have been one of the factors leading to the decay of the cities, to the deurbanization of the civilization and to the dispersal of its population.

But perhaps physical variables were more potent in this matter than the loss of trade. Guesses on the cause of the decay of the civilization have been many and need not be recounted here, but it seems certain that each of the different regions had its own particular problems. Desiccation may have been a difficulty at Kalibangan, but too much moisture, waterlogging, may have been a problem for the Sind sites. However, the theory put forward by Raikes (1964) on the presence of a great lake in the Indus Valley formed by tectonic movements has been, to my mind, successfully refuted by Lambrick (1967). Man-made factors, such as the wearing out of the landscape, deforestation and foreign invasions have sometimes been alleged to be the culprits.

It is irrelevant for the present purpose to evaluate the different propositions. It would suffice to point out that in all the regions—Sind, Gujarat and Rajasthan—the catastrophe took place in the early centuries of the second millennium B.C., and it is not insignificant that Harappan foreign trade ceased at about the same time. The people were evidently so overwhelmed by their own troubles that they could no longer pursue the luxury of foreign trade.

Even before the final catastrophes, the civilization was on its decline. A possible reason for this may have been the natural fatigue of an overgrown culture. Thus, the latest levels of Mohenjodaro show a marked decadence and loss of civic control—clear signs of deurbanization. It is only after the final Harappan abandonment of the sites that squatter populations move in. There is the Cemetery H occupation at Harappa and the Jhukar occupation at Chanhudaro. The recent theory that these cultures were continuations and derivations of the Mature Harappan (Possehl 1977) requires further investigation. They will not be called 'late Harappan' in this paper. Lothal Period II and Rangpur Period II B (Period I of Lothal and Period II A of Rangpur being Mature Harappan) show signs of degeneration. There is also a spread of sites into the interior of Saurashtra at this time, and it is interesting to find that the people chose elevated grounds and rocky outcrops to settle upon. as if they had learnt the lesson of the dangers of living on flood plains (Chitalwala 1979: 116). This naturally restricted the size of the settlements.

On the mainland coast of Gujarat, S.A. Sali has discovered some fifty sites in the Tapti Valley of Dhule District. Two of them have only late Harappan material, while the rest have late Harappan mixed with the Savalda and Jorwe Wares (Sali in press). At Hingoni Budrukh, a site in the latter category, a sherd with two Indus characters was found. At the other sites the Red Ware is the only criterion for Harappan occupation. Sali says that this Red Ware has a thicker, sturdier and finer fabric than any other Red Ware in the region and includes typical Harappan shapes such as the dish-on-stand and perforated vase. But the painting consists of only monotonous geometric designs and lacks the varied designs of the 'Indus' and 'provincial' styles. Sali has emphasized the absence of the urban discipline of the Mature Harappa at these sites.

Further south, in the Dogavari Valley, Sali's re-excavation of Daimabad on the Pravara has revealed a late Harappan Culture overlying the Salvada Culture. This is followed successively by the buff-and-cream, Malwa and Jorwe Cultures. The late Harappan occupies a respectable area of about 20 hectares, though this may not entitle it to be called "the capital of the Harappans in this region," for it can be doubted that the decentralized and scattered late Harappan population formed a sufficiently organized society to need a capital. Mud walls give place to mud-brick walls, and an excavated grave is lined with mud-bricks of two sizes, the dimensions of both of which have the ratio of 1:2:4—a continuity of the Harappan tradition. The late Harappan pottery shows a marked degeneration over that of the Tapti Valley, but the painting continues to be monotonous geometric designs. In spite of the occurrence of three Indus signs on the rim-fragment of a pot, the process of deurbanization is complete. I refrain from commenting on the Harappan affinity of the four controversial bronze figures from Daimabad.

What contacts, if any, the Harappans had with the contemporary Neolithic people of South India, is difficult to say. The tradition of painting red pottery with black pigment and the occurrence of long blades, copper tools and microbeads in the Neolithic have been ascribed to trade contacts with the Harappans and the Neolithic folk are proposed to have supplied the Harappans with gold and steatite (Rao 1973: 116). But such trade could have taken place only in the mature stage of the Harappan Civilization. The late Harappans of the Deccan were far too impoverished to have engaged in long-distance trade. It is also not explainable as to why the Neolithic folk having adopted the fashion of painting their vessels from the Harappans, refrained from accepting things of greater utility, such as the potter's wheel.

I now turn to Sind. After adversity had overtaken them, the Sind Harappans seem to have largely moved up the tributaries of the Indus, carefully avoiding the already desiccated lower valleys of the Sarasvati-Drishadvati. They were not traversing lands entirely unknown to them. They had already settled at places such as Kotla Nihang Khan and Ropar (Rupar, now named Roopnagar) in the Sutlej basin. Lower down, at Rakhigarhi in Hissar District in the upper Sarasvati Valley, they had established themselves during the Mature (if late Mature) stage of their civilization. With the cultural center of the civilization in disarray, the process of degeneration started and the urban character of the Ropar and Rakhigarhi settlements disappeared. This region had already been settled by the Barans, whose culture was a cognate of the Pre-Harappan Sothi/Kalibangan I Culture of the Sarasvati-Drishadvati Valleys that provided important elements to the make-up of the Harappan Civilization. It can indeed be called "proto-Harappan" (Ghosh 1965: 116; Lal 1979: 94).

In fact there are not many late Harappan settlements in Haryana where the Sothi/Kalibangan I/Bara element is not present. In Haryana these later settlements are located outside the flood plains of the seasonal streams (Dikshit 1979: 125), as if the people were intentionally avoiding the floods. The pottery shows a general decadence in fabric, potting and surface treatment (Dikshit 1979: 125). Incised designs, a Sothi characteristic, occur on the exterior of the pots.

Recent discoveries have shown that at some sites in Jammu, Punjab and Haryana the late Harappans even lived with the totally different Painted Gray Ware people (J.P. Joshi, personal communication). This phase is of great significance to the study of both the late Harappan and the Painted Gray Ware and requires further investigation. Further east, in western Uttar Pradesh, at sites like Bargaon and Ambkheri the admixture of the late Harappan with the so-called Ochre Colored Ware is also found (Dikshit 1979: 127), though at many other Ochre Colored Ware sites Harappan traits are absent (Gaur 1971-72: 10).

Thus, late Harappan took different hues in different parts of its diffusion and it cannot be regarded as homogenous. (That is why I have refrained from using a capital initial in the word "late.") All, however, share the common features of deurbanization—the relative smallness of the settlements, lack of monumental buildings and the absence of long-distance trade. While typical Harappan seals occur at some sites, they seem to be more survivals of the past than objects of effective use. No doubt, graffiti on some pottery bear a resemblance to the Harappan alphabet, but their scriptal value remains to be established.

In conclusion, I would like to say that it seems to have become a habit to dub cultures "late Harappan" without defining and pinpointing the differences. I admit that I have myself used the term loosely in the preceding paragraphs. I feel that the time has come to organize a seminar on the late Harappan cultures themselves, in which our colleagues from Pakistan should participate, as without them no consensus can be reached.

BIBLIOGRAPHY

Adams, Robert McC., 1966
The Evolution of Urban Society. Chicago: Aldine.

Asthana, Shashi, 1979
Indus-Mesopotamian Trade: Nature of Trade and Structural Analysis of Operative System. In *Essays in Indian Protohistory*. D.P. Agrawal and D.K. Chakrabarti, eds. Pp. 31-47. Delhi: B.R. Publishing Corp.

Childe, V. Gordon, 1950
The Urban Revolution. *The Town Planning Review* 21 (1): 13-17.

Chitalwala, Y.M., 1979
Harappan and Post-Harappan Settlement Patterns in the Rajkot District of Saurashtra. *Essays in Indian Protohistory*. D.P. Agrawal and D.K. Chakrabarti, eds. Pp. 113-21. Delhi: B.R. Publishing Corp.

Dikshit, K.N., 1979
The Late Harappan Cultures in India. *Essays in Indian Protohistory*. D.P. Agrawal and D.K. Chakrabarti, eds. Pp. 123-33. Delhi: B.R. Publishing Corp.

Fairservis, Walter A., Jr., 1967
The Origin, Character and Decline of an Early Civilization. *Novitates* 2032. New York: American Museum of Natural History.

Gaur, R.C., 1971-72
Contribution to the Seminar on OCP. *Puratattva* 5: 10-12.

Ghosh, A., 1965
The Indus Civilization: Its origins, authors, extent and chronology. *Indian Prehistory: 1964*. V.N. Misra and M.S. Mate, eds. Pp. 113-36. Poona: Deccan College.

Gupta, S.P., 1979
Archaeology of Soviet Central Asia and the Indian Borderlands. 2 vols., Delhi: B.R. Publishing corp.

Lal, B.B., 1979
Kalibangan and the Indus Civilization. In *Essays in Indian Protohistory*. D.P. Agrawal and D.K. Chakrabarti, eds. Pp. 65-97. Delhi: B.R. Publishing Corp.

Lambrick, H.T., 1967
The Indus Flood Plain and the 'Indus' Civilization, *Geographical Journal* 133 (4): 483-94.

Mahadevan, I., 1977
The Indus Script: Texts, concordance and tables. Memoirs of the Archaeological Survey of India 77. Delhi: Government of India.

Possehl, G.L., 1977
The End of A State and the Continuity of a Tradition. In *Realm and Region in Traditional India*. R. Fox, ed. Durham: Duke University Press: 234-54.

Raikes, Robert L., 1964
The End of the Ancient Cities of the Indus. *American Anthropologist* 66 (2): 284-99.

Rao, S.R., 1973
Lothal and the Indus Civilization. Bombay: Asia Publishing.

Sali, S.A., in press
The Harappan Contacts in the Deccan. In *Indus Civilization: Problems and issues*. B.B. Lal and S.C. Malik, eds. Simla: Indian Institute of Advanced Study.

Suraj Bhan, 1973
The Sequence and Spread of Prehistoric Cultures in the Upper Sarasvati Basin. In *Radiocarbon and Indian Archaeology*. D.P. Agrawal and A. Ghosh, eds. Pp. 252-63. Bombay: Tata Institute of Fundamental Research.

Suraj Bhan, 1976
Excavation at Mitathal and Exploration in the Sutlej-Yamuna Divide. Kurukshetra: Kurukshetra University.

Yadav, K.C., editor, 1968
Haryana Studies in History and Culture. Kurukshetra: Kurukshetra University.

F.R. ALLCHIN

31. The Legacy of the Indus Civilization

THIS paper was originally written in the spring of 1974. It was planned as the first of a series of essays in which I intended to put forward my personal ideas on certain topics with the aim of inviting discussion and criticism. For this reason I have thought fit to leave aside the usual apparatus of references and footnotes. My doing so is in no way intended to detract from the many scholars whose work and ideas have contributed to my own. Nor is it to deny or minimize the importance of the many different, often conflicting, views which others, often better placed than myself, have published on many matters. But to do justice to all such views would have necessitated a book rather than an essay, and would have defeated my own aim. In presenting the paper several years after its composition I have made a small number of editorial changes and introduced some new matter where new discoveries made this possible or desirable. A second essay, dealing with the Indo-Aryan languages in relation to archaeological evidence, was read in Dushanbe in 1977, and as the proceedings of that meeting appear as though they will be long delayed it is now in press elsewhere.

One thing is beyond a peradventure: that the cultural-historical phenomenon known as the Indus Civilization was, from the moment of its first inception through to its final stages, a unique event, the like of which the Indian Subcontinent had not seen before, and the like of which it was not to see again for almost a thousand years thereafter. The same cannot be said for the second civilization, which developed in North India during the first millennium B.C., and which has justly been spoken of as the Ganges Civilization; although it spread far more widely than the valley of that river. As the successor to an earlier civilization the question must arise of what, if any, links of culture or tradition survived through the intervening centuries, and of what, if any, awareness there was on the part of the founders of the new cities that they followed in the footsteps of those earlier city builders. Was there, indeed, a Harappan legacy, and if so what form or forms did it take? How far did it contribute to the tradition of the later Indian Civilization? This present essay is an attempt to examine these questions at the level of hypothesis.

The discoveries of the first twenty-five years of Harappan studies, massive and valuable as they were, left many questions unanswered. Those of the second quarter century have been more varied, and as a whole on a more restricted scale. If they have answered some questions, they have also posed many more. As more and more data accumulate I have become increasingly aware of the need for a conceptual framework within which discussion may fruitfully develop. Similarly one needs a set of general hypotheses relating to the several aspects of the civilization. There is reason to be grateful to Dr. Malik for drawing attention to the comparative backwardness of this aspect of Indian archaeology, in his *Indian Civilization: The formative period* (1968). With the growing up of a younger generation of Indian archaeologists the subject may be said to be coming of age, and the spate and quality of publications, particularly by younger workers is, in my view, most encouraging. But not much has yet appeared which relates to the broader aspects of the subject under review, and one should like to commend one of the most senior of Indian archaeologists, Professor Sankalia, who has recently suggested the need for the interpretative disciplines implicit in the 'new archaeology' in this context (1977).

While considering this question one became

aware that any such general hypothesis must be prepared to treat the rise and fall of the Indus Civilization as an organic process, for it seemed difficult to discuss the legacy until one knew who had made the bequest and how he had acquired the things he had to bequeath. In consequence this paper is divided into two parts. In the first part the origin of the civilization and its relations with neighboring regions are discussed; it touches on two tendencies, towards cultural convergence and cultural divergence, and on the spread of the civilization. The second part begins with a discussion of the "end" of the civilization and what it entailed, and goes on to ask what was lost and what remained. This leads one to think of the different status of a "great" tradition and folk traditions in the context of the Indus Civilization. Finally, India in the Post-Harappan Period is discussed, speculating on the media through which a legacy might have been transmitted to the new cities of North India.

PART ONE

Perhaps the most significant discoveries of the past two decades have been those relating to the spread of peasant settlements in the Indus Valley in Pre-Harappan (or as one should prefer to call them, Early Indus) and even earlier Neolithic times. Among the excavated sites of this group are Amri, Kot Diji, Gumla, Harappa and Kalibangan. In the north an extension to the foothills is indicated by the discovery of Sarai Khola near Taxila. The development must have resulted from the initial exploitation of the rich flood plain of the Indus and its tributaries, and must have spread outward with the expansion of the population this produced. It seems to have been accompanied throughout by a tendency toward cultural convergence, and it provides the unequivocal basis in terms of human, technical and cultural resources on which the succeeding Mature stage of Indus Civilization is based. From the present point of view the maturity of the civilization must be seen as the climax of an organic developmental process starting in the early Indus times, if not yet earlier. Acceptance of this model suggests profoundly important analogies between it and the luminous words of Robert Redfield (1956: 77 ff.) respecting the special character of Indian Civilization as indigenous, having "developed out of the precivilized people of that very culture, converting them into the peasant half of the same culture-civilization," so that "the continuity with their own native civilization has persisted," peasant tradition affects the doctrine of the learned, and there is continuing interaction between the learned and folk levels. In short, while there is no reason to neglect the possibility that the Indus Civilization arose as a partial result of stimuli applied from outside, either from the uplands to the west, or more distantly from the Persian Gulf or Mesopotamia in the Early Dynastic or Sargonid times, or from Central Asia, and that these stimuli may have involved the arrival of men as well as ideas, its actual emergence must be seen primarily as a dynamic socioeconomic process, taking place on Indian soil, and not as something implanted from outside. This is profoundly significant for subsequent developments, since it implies that the legacy of the Indus Civilization may be sought in the life style of the common people of India and Pakistan, as much as in the learned tradition. This is exemplified by such things as the identity of ploughing patterns in the fields of Pre-Harappan Kalibangan and of the modern peasant population of the region; or by the direct analogy of one of the distinctive types of terracotta model carts from Mohenjodaro to a type which today survives only in upper Sind. These things can only mean that there is a direct and unbroken craft tradition or tradition of agricultural practice linking the two periods, and this in turn implies a continuum of population and a direct and unbroken rural life style from the Early Indus times forward.

Another important set of discoveries has provided evidence that the hunter-gatherers, using a stone technology and generally spoken of as Mesolithic, or Late Stone Age, had spread widely across the Subcontinent long before the emergence of the Indus Civilization. The current excavations of the French Archaeological Mission at Mehrgarh near Sibi have added a new perspective to the knowledge of the antecedents of the Indus Civilization, and may be expected in particular to throw very important light on the earliest stages of the development of settled agriculture in the Indian Subcontinent. This in turn is likely to contribute to the understanding of relations of the first agricultural communities to such groups of hunter-gatherers. Further, it is beginning to emerge that, at least in those places where evidence is available, groups of these people continued to live predominantly as stone-using hunter-gatherers, sometimes driven into areas of relative isolation, long after the use of metals had become common in the more advanced communities. It is now apparent that even before the emergence of the Indus Civilization in many regions of South Asia peasant or pastoral communities had appeared, and that in some cases these groups may have enjoyed social, economic or political relations of one kind or another with the Pre-Harappan settlements. How far both these and the settled communities arose as the result of the age-old tendency of peoples to move into the Subcontinent from the less hospitable lands to the west or north, and how far they arose by a process of local evolution from among the existing tribal populations has yet to be established. Probably both tendencies played their parts. But it is in such early settlements that the first localized cultural characters of some of the regions can be distinguished. The coexistence of groups at different socioeconomic and cultural levels, in close association with each other, often over long periods of time, may already at this stage be clearly distinguished. Both these tendencies were to play a significant role in the subsequent lifestyle of the regions of the Subcontinent. Thus they deserve to be borne in mind while considering the transmission of the legacy of the Indus Civilization.

It has been suggested that already during the Early Indus stage there was a period of rapid expansion of settled population throughout the Indus Valley and that it was accompanied by an outward spread towards less densely settled but attractive areas. This process may have involved both the establishment of new settlements in regions hitherto largely unsettled (i.e., populated by groups of hunters and collectors, or by primarily nomadic or seminomadic pastoralists); and the conquest or colonization of areas which already had a settled agricultural population. In some cases it may have involved the establishment of new settlements among the settlements of the already existing regional culture. Such variations in the pattern of culture contact are likely to be recognizable in the archaeological record, once their hypothetical existence is admitted. At a certain point this process triggered off changes resulting in the formation of cities, and the development of a new set of socioeconomic relations—the Indus Civilization. One must expect the same processes of growth and spread to have continued thereafter, and hence one would expect to find an outward spread of the Mature Urban Culture into areas hitherto peopled by tribal and/or peasant communities. Evidence to support this hypothesis appears to be forthcoming in several regions. In Saurashtra and Gujarat, Harappan settlements seem to be dispersed among those of a regional peasant culture, and this must be presumed to have led to contacts between the two at various levels. In East Punjab, in the Drishadvati and Sarasvati Valleys, and even further east in the Ganga/Yamuna *Doab,* there are somewhat similar indications. Dr. Suraj Bhan has reported sites related to the Early Indus stage at Kalibangan, and their continued occupation alongside sites which may more properly be called Harappan. This suggests the sort of culture contact situations to be found in the areas in which this spread was taking place. It is interesting to notice how the Rajasthan desert seems to have acted as a barrier to expansion, even though there was already a population of tribal people of mixed economy (as at Bagor) and perhaps also of agricultural settlements in parts of the region, and finds of Mesolithic tools suggest that such people were widely distributed there. One may expect that they enjoyed some sort of contacts with the Harappans prospecting for ores or raw materials and trading with them in such things as metal tools.

Within the area embraced by the Early and Mature Indus Civilization two opposing tendencies may be noticed: one convergent and the other divergent. The first is the more prominent: It has long been apparent that one of the concomitants of the change from the Early to Mature Indus Cultures was the establishment of an extraordinary degree of cultural uniformity over a vast area. This convergent tendency is indeed already clearly visible during the Early Indus Period, and as this fact becomes more apparent it makes the change of style from Early to Mature Indus times all the more remarkable. Sir John Marshall discussed this aspect at length, and others have generally agreed with him. What was involved in terms of the population as a whole can only be partly guessed at, but it seems that the convergent tendency reached a new height with the growth of Mohenjo-daro as a city, and therefore that the tendency may well go back to the foundation of that city whenever it may have been, perhaps towards the end of the second quarter of the third millennium. Presumably it would have more or less coincided with the first development of a full system of writing and the manufacture of inscribed seals. This seems to have been the signal for a rapid and wholesale diffusion of traits recognizable in the archaeological record, suggesting the spread or imposition of a common lifestyle which in time extended throughout the entire Harappan Culture region. The means for this spread remain unclear. That it was assisted by an unprecedented extension of internal trade in all manner of raw materials and commodities may be safely inferred, and that it witnessed a distribution of the specialist craft products of the cities is probable. Among trade goods one may cite the stone blades which appear to have been obtained and manufactured at such centers as the vast factories at Rohri, the similar indications of centralized manufacture of various classes of metal objects, of shell bangles and carnelian beads. An aspect of the mechanism by which this trade was carried on has been discussed by my wife (B. Allchin 1979). It seems certain that the emergence of urbanism must have also involved the extension of a single unifying socioeconomic pattern, including government and administration, and of a common pattern of beliefs and ideology. In sum it must have witnessed the promulgation of what one may call the Indus lifestyle, with all that went with it. The fact that the geographical confines of this culture region embraced an area far greater than that of any other of the great civilizations of the third millennium makes the process all the more remarkable. It may also be stated with certainty that the lifestyle incorporated not only popular matters but also the learned or 'great' tradition of the Indus Civilization. It is from among these things that scholars have found, or at least believed that they found, all manner of traits ancestral to those of later, even of modern, Indian civilization.

However, while recognizing the convergent tendency in the Indus Civilization, one must not neglect to notice the indications of regionalism or cultural divergence within the greater Indus system, leading to what may even be seen as separate culture provinces. One would expect there to be several kinds of divergence. First, the very real differences which already begin to emerge during the Neolithic stage, and later within the provinces of the early Indus Culture regions between such sites as Amri, Kot Diji, Gumla or Kalibangan, evidently continued to a certain extent, even after the imposition of the Indus style, reflecting no doubt these earlier differences. Second, even during the comparatively short life of the Mature Indus Civilization one may expect that there would have been a further general tendency towards separate development in certain respects in the different provinces, due to all sorts of possible causes. The divergences could in part reflect local reactions against the convergent tendency. A third possible cause could be the arrival in a given region of new groups who established some sort of power over, or relationship with, the existing population and proceeded in one way or another to influence the final stages of the Indus Culture therein. This aspect is crucially important in terms of legacy, and it must be considered further. A fairly circumscribed regional development appears to be represented by the Cemetery H Phase at Harappa and probably at related sites (at Bara and sites of East Punjab, in Bahawalpur, etc.). One is inclined to follow Vats in seeing this phase as a final stage in the Indus Culture representing the arrival of some sort of "Aryan" invaders in the region and their interaction with the existing population, leading to a degree of cultural synthesis. Another set of data which suggests something of the same kind is provided by the apparent contrast between certain sites at which stone or terracotta *linga* are reported, notably at Mohenjodaro, at Harappa, and at Surkotada, and other sites (or perhaps a phase at some sites) at which "ritual" fire altars are reported. Such altars are expressly absent at Surkotada, and also apparently at Mohenjodaro and Harappa, but are reported at Kalibangan from the beginning of the Harappan Period. Here several types of hearth are found; among them one is distinguished from the normal domestic types by the excavators. The "ritual" hearth, with a brick or clay "pillar" in its center occurs in three locations: on the top of a brick platform in the walled brick "Citadel" enclosure a row of seven were found, associated with a brick pit containing animal bones and with a well; single examples of the same type occur in small rooms in domestic houses, perhaps used for domestic rituals; and several more were found in a square brick enclosure (KLB 3) outside the east wall of the lower city (Thapar 1973: 101). These three contexts suggest that fire rituals formed a part of the religious life of the town, at a civic, domestic and popular level. They are also highly suggestive of an Indo-Iranian, if not more specifically Indo-Aryan, element in the culture of the period covered by these excavations.

Thus, if enough evidence of this sort were forthcoming, the regional divergences might in some instances be associated with the meeting of indigenous Indus populations and intrusive Indo-Iranian or Aryan elements, and with some sort of resulting cultural synthesis. This would clearly be of great significance for any discussion of legacy. It is of course wholly possible that similar intrusive groups may also have moved into the southern Indus provinces, but if

The Legacy of the Indus Civilization

they did so they seem to have coincided with a more or less complete extinction of the centralized urban authority rather than with its late stages, and their contribution to the legacy may be expected to have been therefore mainly at the village level. Thus there is likely to have been a major difference between the situation in the northern and southern parts of the Harappan Culture region.

One must now consider certain aspects of the civilization which resulted from this transformation of existing peasant and tribal social elements. The access of new data has already revealed much and doubtless much more awaits both discovery and analysis, but some aspects remain, and are long likely to, elusive for the archaeologist. Thus while one is learning more about the town planning, and such things as house plans, plant and animal foods, technology and crafts, one still has only rudimentary indications as to the meaning of all these in terms of social and economic relations. Similarly, while there are seals and art objects which reveal a clearly defined body of symbols and myths, there is still surprisingly little definite knowledge of the religious beliefs or ideology of their makers, although here one is beginning to gain an important new dimension from finds in the Early Indus Cultures. The reading of the script will almost certainly throw new light on trade and economics, and perhaps marginally on ideology, but even so the absence of longer inscriptions must mean that many topics will remain essentially speculative. This point is made mainly because it is just in these fields, in economic and social relations, in religious beliefs and ideology, that an important part of the Harappan legacy is likely to be most strongly evident in later Indian culture, and if one cannot positively identify such things at their source, how far is one entitled to speak of the legacy at all? This prompts one again to stress the importance of the framing of general hypotheses, as without them the contexts of individual facts, or groups of data, may be difficult to establish.

PART TWO

There is still much room for divergent views about the end of the Indus Civilization, but as this event provides, in a sense, with a terminus for consideration of the legacy, as opposed to the nature of the civilization itself, one must try to establish a satisfactory general hypothesis. The civilization has been thought of as a social, economic and cultural phenomenon produced as a consequence of the build up of population on the fertile plains of the Indus and the Punjab. It involved a delicate balance of internal relations between cities, towns and villages, and of external relations with neighboring peasant societies and with more distant urban societies. The end of the civilization probably arose from some major upsetting of this balance. This could have been produced by a variety of causes, acting either singly or in combination. It is possible, although there is as yet little supporting evidence, that there was a deterioration of climate; but as the main food production depended upon exploiting the Indus river's flood plain inundation this is unlikely to have been sufficient cause. It is possible too that there was a "wearing out" of the land, due to overcultivation; but in the light of the enduring fertility of the soils of the Indian Subcontinent over subsequent millennia of intensive cultivation this too seems unlikely. One accepts Lambrick's 1967 demonstration of the implausibility of the theory that Mohenjodaro was engulfed in a vast flood, and one is inclined to agree with his well-argued case that there may have been disastrous changes in the course of the Indus, resulting in the desiccation of areas which were essential for the feeding of the city's population, as a more likely cause of the end of that city. Such an event would lead to depredations by tribesmen from the nearby hills, and might well have brought about the desertion of the city and of outlying settlements. But would it have been a sufficient shock to upset the whole balance? This is a more difficult question, even if it is assumed, as it is more and more, that Mohenjodaro was in some way the "epicenter" around which the whole structure was held in balance. Would the attackers have been Aryan? This one cannot tell, but both in terms of the probable date of the event, and of the history of the dispersal of the Indo-European language family, there is no inherent impossibility in such a thing. If this was the state in Sind, what of the Punjab? Here too there are suggestions that there may have been major changes in the channels of rivers, due in part no doubt to tectonic events; but there is no very clear evidence that any of these coincided with the end of Harappa or Kalibangan. Moreover as has been seen at both sites there are suggestions that there may have been a period of coexistence of the population with conquering "Aryan" elements. Nevertheless, whatever may have been the cause or causes of the end of the civilization, what is of primary concern is that at a certain point in time it came to an end.

One must now proceed to consider "what was lost" and "what survived." Clearly the postulated central power and authority, together with whatever administrative machinery it possessed, must have been the first to go; and with them the economic organization and the highly organized trade or exchange of goods. All of these would seem to have followed upon the abandonment of the urban nucleus at Mohenjodaro, if this were the primary cause of the breakdown. But there need not, indeed there is most unlikely to have been, a comparable or simultaneous abandonment at all the other centers. Even if there is a marked and abrupt break in the material culture, this need not indicate desertion of a site, followed by reoccupation, but it may indicate no more than a withdrawal of the centrally imposed "urban" uniformity, and a return to (even reemergence of) the regional peasant styles. In some cases the break may indicate the arrival of conquerors, and the imposition of new elements upon the existing style. The uniformity of the Indus period is replaced by a whole series of local culture patterns; and at the socio-economic level the breakdown of the centrally imposed authority must have been marked.

These things one may expect to have disappeared in their entirety. But what was retained or at least partly retained? First, many of the crafts and technical skills which were flourishing also at village level, and for which there would have been a continuing demand, would have persisted; while certain specialized urban or luxury crafts, including seal making, would have disappeared. Some parts of the urban lifestyle may have partly survived. For example, writing and the uniform system of weights and measures would almost certainly have gone as coherent systems, but must surely have left certain signs or convenient units of weight or measure in use. Many domestic aspects of the Indus lifestyle, the house plans, disposition of water supply, hearth and kitchen types, attention to bathing, etc. would survive in the settlements, and much could have been absorbed by newly arrived barbarian conquerors. There would be a very wide survival of traits pertaining to ideology and religious belief, particularly of those which were in common acceptance and which involved domestic practice.

The religious beliefs of the Indus Civilization would have been maintained in several ways: first, in the cities there must have been a class of specialist exponents or priests (who may also have constituted, or been closely associated with, the administrative group). Such people would be among those more likely to intermarry with a new ruling class, or in other ways to win for themselves positions of power or influence in a new order. Such a pattern was often witnessed much later, during the centuries of early Muslim conquest. Thus they would find themselves in a position to maintain an important body of their own beliefs, and to pass it on to their children, if not to their conquerors. At the popular level, tradition must also have been passed on within the family, in much the way as it has continued to be in India down to modern times. Through these two channels the cult of sacred places, rivers or trees, of sacred animals, and of symbols or myths would have survived; as too might a large part of the cosmology, philosophy and other parts of the learned tradition, even after the end of the cities. The strength and maintenance of the tradition would be greatly enhanced if, as one is inclined to believe, the initial period of "Aryan" settlement in the north coincided with the survival, at least for a time, of more or less full urban life under foreign rule, and with a situation such as that which one has surmised the Cemetery H Phase to have witnessed. This period of coexistence would have provided an opportunity for the priests or administrators to acquire the language of the conquerors and to have begun integrating the ideologies of the two groups. Here too the rapid acquisition first of Persian, later of English, by higher castes may suggest an appropriate model from recent times. Thus from the meeting of the two a new amalgam, an *Indian or Indo-Aryan cultural tradition was born*. This hypothesis does not demand "armies" of invaders. One would expect rather small bands, whose horses made them relatively mobile, and who may often have achieved whatever power they acquired by means other than open warfare. It is still not possible to decide at what precise stage groups ancestral to the authors of the *Rigveda* arrived, but one believes that there was a period during which there was a general restlessness, and it may well be that a whole series of waves drifted into the Indus Valley and the Punjab over succeeding centuries. This, after all, has been a pattern which continued through the historical period also. It is not even necessary that all the groups should have been Indo-Aryan speaking, or even Indo-Iranian. But it may be imagined that the closer were the ties of language and ancestry between such groups, the more marked would have been their own solidarity, and the polarity between them and the indigenous population.

Thus one can see that the survival and onward transmission of the Harappan legacy must have been at several different levels and of several different kinds. First, a widespread survival of the way of life among the common people particularly in the villages, in each of the main areas of settlement; and associated with this there would have been the survival of a series of little traditions in the several culture regions into which the peasant societies of Post-Harappan times devolved. With the removal of the urban authority the difference between the structure of village societies within and without the confines of the civilization would have been considerably reduced, and roughly similar structures would appear throughout. At the same time there would be a tendency for older, distinctive, culture traits to reemerge regionally. Hence, in all these regions one may expect the Harappan legacy to be passed down at the folk level, and to spread with the continuing expansion of the peasant society. Indeed this was probably the time when the village assumed the dominant role in Indian society which it has continued to occupy henceforward; so that while cities may have come and gone, the villages have survived with their own special Indian lifestyle. But at this level the surviving elements would be mainly those appropriate for the folk or village society, and many others of distinctly urban character would tend to disappear.

A second kind of transmission of the legacy must have been at the level of the great or learned tradition and would presumably have been much more restricted geographically, being mainly confined to those areas in which there was already a synthesis of Indus urban and "Aryan" ruling elements, during the later stages of the civilization. This sort of transmission probably developed in the Punjab and spread eastwards with the expansion of population and settlements into the *Doab* and Ganges Valley. Already by the time of a compilation of the Vedic *Samhitas* the process must have been providing an increasingly distinct element of the ideology, which one may now begin to call Indian, or culturally Indo-Aryan, as distinct from either Indus or Aryan. This is not the place to discuss the interesting and important question of which among the several groups of possible Aryans constituted the first arrivals in the Indus culture region; whether they were "Pre-Vedic" or "Non-Sanskritic," or "Proto-Rigvedic." This matter has recently been discussed by Dr. Parpola (1977a, 1977b) and I have touched on it in another paper (F. Allchin in press). But one has long been of the view that they must be regarded as culturally at least the direct ancestors of the Vedic Aryans. In these areas of course the transmission at the folk or village level also took place, and this in turn would have facilitated at a later date the secondary spread of the great tradition to other regions sharing the legacy at those levels. This hypothesis does not altogether preclude a similar survival of elements of the great tradition in other regions, notably in the South, in Sind or Saurashtra and beyond, but one believes that there it would be relatively much less powerful than in the North.

If the legacy thus transmitted was partly at the level of the great tradition, it is unlikely that it was done without considerable attenuation. The use of writing seems to have vanished, indeed one does not know how far it was used in Harappan times for purposes other than narrowly commercial, and probably much else with it. But the newly emerging Indian tradition must have received continuing enrichment from the folk level, and much may have survived at that level, to be later reabsorbed into the learned tradition.

The period following the end of the Harappan cities was one of continuing eastward expansion of Indo-Aryan Culture, now associated with the cultivation of rice and with an unprecedented growth of population. One may expect that already in the East (and for that matter the South) there were distinctive peasant societies in existence, each with its own cultural tradition, and thus the spread of the Indo-Aryan great tradition would have coincided with its encountering them. These factors led to the rapid expansion of settlements in the upper, middle and lower Ganges Valley and paved the way to the reemergence of cities there. These, like their Indus predecessors, were the products of their social and economic bases. But it is important to note that they were not the centers for the emergence of the early Indian tradition. This tradition was there before the cities, in the shape of the Vedic *Samhitas*, the accompanying schools of exegesis, and all that went with them; and also at the level of a more or less related series of little traditions, transmitted at the folk level. The new cities produced, however, a profound, even traumatic, reformulation of received tradition and ideology, and witnessed the development of Buddhism, Jainism and the other new "city" religious movements, notably Vaishnavism. But throughout this reformulation the prior existence of a tradition, from which to borrow and against which to react, can be clearly recognized. Thus while the life style of the Gangetic cities is also in many ways new, it embodies an incalculably large element which is very old, and which survived in one way or another from the earlier cities of the Indus.

The hypothesis advanced must be tested against the available data. For example, the presence of *lingas* or of an iconographic type suggestive of Śiva-Paśupati in the Indus cities, has often been seen as anticipating the later "emergence" of Rudra-Śiva in the Vedic-late Vedic literature. One may now postulate that Śiva-Mahādeva was a central concept of the Indus religion, which survived in both the great and folk traditions and developed as the process of the Indianization advanced. A problematic gulf appears to separate the narrow Indo-Iranian, polytheistic ideology postulated by philologists as that of the early Vedic hymns, from both the mature "Indian" character of the "late" hymns of the first and tenth *Mandalas* of the *Rigveda*, and their remarkably constant interpretation in Indian tradition thereafter. Although the gulf may be partly illusory, it undoubtedly exists. Just how early this shift began would depend, in terms of this hypothesis, upon the date at which the cultural synthesis of the two groups began. It is also worth considering whether the decline of the *Asuras* and the rise to eminence of the *Devas*, which seems to be happening in the body of the *Rigveda*, and to be looked back on as something already complete in such hymns as X.124, may indicate not so much a divergence of beliefs among separated Indo-Iranian groups, but rather—by this time—the process of Indianization in action.

One does not propose to anticipate objections to this hypothesis, but one is well aware that at more than one point the data are not available from which even a probable conclusion may be drawn, and where therefore it is possible to propose various alternative hypotheses. One such point concerns the moment when "Aryan" influence first began to exert itself on the Indus Civilization. For instance, one possible version would be that it was the arrival of Indo-Aryan speakers which provided the initial stimulus needed to tip the scales towards city life, and thus that the whole Indus Civilization from the start may have had a dominant Aryan strain. This hypothesis, attractive as in some ways it is, can only be sustained in the face of formidable objections, but it must not be too lightly dismissed. At the other extreme it is possible to argue that there was a final and irrevocable gap between the end of the cities and the arrival of the ancestors of the authors of the *Rigveda*. This, raises almost insuperable problems of interpretation, not least in terms of the transmission of the Harappan legacy. Thus one is led to prefer a hypothesis which lies somewhere between the two extremes, that is, bringing the first Aryans into contact with the still flourishing Mature Indus society.

To sum up the main points of this essay—The Indus Civilization arose on Indian soil as an organic process: it was not primarily superimposed from outside, even if external stimuli may have contributed. Because of this there was already the necessary basis of continuity between the peasant and urban communities to permit the sort of persistence of the lifestyle which Robert Redfield remarked. An outward spread of peasant cultures from the Indus system had already begun in Pre-Harappan times, and the lifestyle spread with the continuation of that process both during the Mature Indus Civilization and after. Within the Early Indus and Mature Indus Civilization the tendency towards cultural convergence implies the emergence of a central ideology and learned tradition, and this one may call the Indus great tradition. In the north of the region there was an appearance of Indo-Aryan speaking people even during the life of the civilization, and this permits one to postulate a degree of synthesis between the exponents of the Indus great tradition and those of the arriving conquerors. This process is of enormous significance in terms of the onward transmission of the legacy, and of the translation of the Indus tradition into a unified Indian or culturally Indo-Aryan tradition. The end of the Indus Civilization appears to have been brought about by an upsetting of the delicate balance which maintained its social and economic life, and was probably linked with the abandonment at Mohenjodaro. The Indus legacy survived and was passed on most widely at the folk or village level, in almost all regions, while the learned tradition mainly survived in the Punjab, whence it spread eastwards with the spread of settlements in Post-Harappan times. The surviving tradition, an amalgam of Indus and Aryan elements was already active before the reemergence of cities in the Ganges Valley and in North India more generally during the first millennium B.C., and served as the ideological basis upon which the cities produced their own distinctive ideology. Therefore, to paraphrase an old saying: "if you seek a legacy, look about you."

BIBLIOGRAPHY

Allchin, B., 1979
Stone Blade Industries of Early Settlements in Sind as Indicators of Geographic and Socio-Economic Change. In *South Asian Archaeology, 1977*. Maurizio Taddei, ed. Pp. 173-211. Instituto Universitario Orientale, Seminario di Studi Asiatici, Series Minor VI: Naples.

Allchin, F.R., in press
Archaeological and Language Historical Evidence for the Movement of Indo-Aryan Speaking Peoples into South Asia. Paper read at the International Symposium on Ethnic Problems of the Early History of Central Asia, Dushanbe, 1977.

Lambrick, H.T., 1967
The Indus Flood-plain and the 'Indus' Civilization. *The Geographical Journal* 133: 483-94.

Malik, S.C., 1968
Indian Civilization: The formative period. Simla: Indian Institute for Advanced Study.

Parpola, A., 1974a
On the Protohistory of the Indian Languages in the Light of Archaeological, Linguistic and Religious Evidence: An attempt at integration. In *South Asian Archaeology, 1973*. J.E. van Lohuizen-de Leeuw and J.M. Ubaghs, eds. Pp. 90-100. Leiden: E.J. Brill.

Parpola, A., 1974b
Review of *Die Saṃhitā der Maitrāyaṇīyaśākhā*. Leopold von Schroeder, trans. Wiesbaden: Franz Steiner Verlag GmbH and *Die Saṃhitā der Kaṭha-śākhā*. Leopold von Schroeder, trans. Wiesbaden: Franz Steiner Verlag GmbH. *Acta Orientalia*, Vol. 36: 491-96.

Redfield, R., 1956
Peasant Society and Culture. Chicago: University of Chicago Press.

Sankalia, H.D., 1977
New Archaeology: Its scope and application to India. Lucknow: Ethnographic and Folk Culture Society.

Thapar, B.K., 1973
New Traits of the Indus Civilization at Kalibangan: An appraisal. In *South Asian Archaeology*. N. Hammond, ed. Pp. 85-104. Park Ridge: Noyes Press.

B.B. LAL

32. West was West and East was East, but When and How Did the Twain Meet? The Role of Bhagwanpura as a Bridge between Certain Stages of the Indus and Ganges Civilizations

When in 1952 the report on the excavations at Hastinapura was written there was no evidence to show that the Painted Gray Ware (PGW) Culture overlapped with the Indus Civilization or even with any of its devolutionary phases. The present writer, therefore, placed the PGW occupation at Hastinapura broadly between the end of the Indus Civilization on the one hand and the beginning of the Northern Black Polished Ware (NBPW) Period on the other, adding that although there was no overlap between the PGW and NBPW at Hastinapura, such an overlap at other sites could not be ruled out (Lal 1955: 150).

Subsequent excavations have shown that toward the end of the PGW Period, the NBPW does emerge and that there is a *continuous* story from the PGW Period onwards, as at Atranjikhera for example (Gaur and Hasan 1964). Indeed, it is the PGW Culture that provided the real base to what was to happen in Madhyadesh (a term used in ancient literature to denote broadly the area comprising the upper Ganges Valley) for centuries to come. And it is possibly this aspect that led Wheeler to use the term "Ganges Civilization" (1960: 127-28). But the question of an overlap between the Indus and the Ganges Civilization, here symbolically called West and East, remained an open one.

During the course of his excavations at Kausambi, G.R. Sharma discovered that the fortification wall around the site had a mud core but was provided with a battered burnt brick revetment on the exterior (Sharma 1960). He also discovered a corbelled drain, again of burnt bricks (Sharma 1960). The burnt brick revetment reminded him of a similar revetment at Harappa, and the corbelled drain (called an "underground passage" by Sharma) brought to his mind the drain associated with the Great Bath at Mohenjodaro. All this led him to stipulate that the architecture of the fortifications and drain at Kausambi was borrowed from that of the Indus Civilization. He stated:

> The early defences at Kausambi closely recall the Harappan citadel. The mud-packed rampart revetted externally with baked bricks in the so-called English bond in alternate courses of headers and stretchers, battered back to angles of 20° to 40°, bastions at intervals, rectangular towers and underground passage built on corbelled arch, are significant features of architecture at Kausambi with prototypes for each one of them in Harappan architecture. The very idea of town life was so far unknown in the Gangetic Valley. The defences show that in the first centuries of the first millennium B.C. Kausambi developed as a town fully equipped for its protection by the magnificent defences built on the Harappan pattern. Evidently, this was not an achievement of the P.G. Ware culture which shows a distinct aversion

to the very concept of urban life in its earlier settlements in the Ghaggar Valley, the Punjab and Western U.P. Nor can it be associated with the Red Ochre-washed Ware. It is equally significant that P.G. Ware occurs at Kausambi two structural periods after the original construction of the defences. The recent discovery at Alamgirpura (District Meerut, U.P.) has established definite evidence of the penetration of the Harappan culture in the Ganga-Yamuna Doab. If the Harappans could reach the banks of the Hindon, a tributary of the Yamuna, the percolation and the survival of the Harappan influences at Kausambi, only 300 miles down the Yamuna, *is more than likely* (Sharma 1960: 6) (emphasis mine).

According to Sharma, the Kausambi fortifications went back to 1025 B.C. (1960: 22).

To strengthen his stand, Sharma even drew attention to some pottery which he thought was comparable to that from Navdatoli and other western Indian sites and may have been produced under Harappan influence (1960: 6-7).

Sharma's dating of the Kausambi fortifications has been challenged by K.K. Sinha (1973) and A. Ghosh (1973: 81). The grounds they have adduced against such an early chronology are quite valid and one would have expected the excavator of Kausambi to rethink the matter. Instead, he has come out with renewed vigor about the Harappan influence on Kausambi, saying:

> The available evidence, particularly the pottery obtained from the lowest levels of the Defences and the Palace-areas suggest that the earliest settlement at the site can be pushed back to the mid of IInd millennium B.C. The recent physical comparison of the material of Bhagwanpura (Haryana) has revealed the existence of the late Harappan material in the Central Ganga Valley at the following sites. (Note of Sri J.P. Joshi enclosed herewith): Kausambi, Onaur, Unchadih and Kakoria. The chalcolithic cultures of the Central Ganga Valley show a fusion of the late Harappan and the Chalcolithic elements of the Vindhyas, the latter being preponderant (Sharma 1979).

In view of the foregoing, it is imperative to examine the matter once again.

While the positions Sinha and Ghosh stated in their comments still hold good, there are many more grounds to challenge the Harappan influence at Kausambi. For example, the Harappans are known to have used two brick sizes: 30 by 15 by 7.5 centimeters and 40 by 20 by 10 centimeters; but in both cases the length, breadth and thickness ratio was invariably 4:2:1. On the other hand, the average size of the bricks used in the Kausambi fortifications is 49.5 by 30.5 by 7 centimeters (Sharma 1960: 27). Quite clearly this size concept has nothing to do with Harappan bricks. If anything, the Kausambi bricks may have something to do with the measurement concept indicated by *angula, hasta, pada,* etc., enunciated in the literature of the Early Historic Period in northern India. Second, and this is a point which cannot be overemphasized, no site around Kausambi—be it Sravasti, Ayodhya or Sringaverpura to the north, or Rajghat to the east, or Atranjikhera or Ahichchhatra to the northwest—has yielded a burnt brick structure prior to the NBPW Period. In fact, very closely observed excavations in 1979 at Sringaverpura have revealed the possibility of dividing the NBPW Period into three subperiods. The earliest of these proposed subperiods is characterized by the absence of such distinctive pottery types as the pear-shaped vase (popularly known as Ahichchhatra type 10 A) and small incurved bowl, loosely called the "miniature bowl." It was also *devoid* of any kiln-burnt brick structure. This is not the place to go into the dating of the NBPW, but it can safely be said that the beginning of burnt brick structures is unlikely to go very much earlier than about the middle of the first millennium B.C. Now, if this is the case at all the other sites in the middle Ganges Valley, how can Kausambi be expected to stand in sheer isolation?

The so-called Late Harappan pottery at sites like Kausambi, Kakoria, etc., referred to in Sharma's 1979 publication was jointly examined by B.K. Thapar, K.N. Dikshit and myself in March 1979. It was observed that most of the specimens of the so-called "button-based goblets" were incomplete. Thus, the "button"-like part could easily have been mistaken for a base, while the flaired out portion could give the impression of the goblet shape. However, we were lucky to notice a complete specimen in the collection displayed at the Allahabad University Museum itself. This turned out to be a lid, the "button-base" being in fact a knob. Likewise, the so-called "beakers," which were again incomplete, were found to be the lower parts of a particular type of elongated vessel which was sometimes cylindrical and sometimes partly conical, with a flat or somewhat conical base. Many of the specimens had a slightly faceted exterior. These did not remind us of the typical Harappan beakers. As regards the dish-on-stand, it must be stated that this shape is not confined exclusively to the Harappan Culture, having been found in both the Ahar as well as the Malwa Cultures. In fact, the corrugated stem in the PGW Culture shows that a kind of dish-on-stand was available in that culture as well. Basically, therefore, there was nothing in the pottery from Kausambi, Kakoria, etc., which could really lay claim to being Harappan in the true sense of the term. Under the circumstances, it would not carry much weight to argue that if the Harappan Culture could reach Alamgirpur on the bank of the Hindon, a tributary of the Yamuna, why could it not reach Kausambi on the Yamuna itself? (Cf. Sharma's remarks as quoted above.)

But, one must put aside these personal assessments of certain disputed pottery types, and architectural features, which in themselves are not disputed, but whose ancestry is, and look at the problem as a whole. To sharpen the focus, one asks pointedly: Did Indus *urbanism* really reach the heart of the Ganges Valley? Even for the moment, if the Kausambi fortifications and drain are accepted to have been derived from their counterparts at Harappa and Mohenjodaro, one would still have to answer the question: How is it that only these two isolated features reached Kausambi, without the brick sizes about which the Harappans were so meticulous all over their area of thousands and thousands of square kilometers? And even if one would wish to overlook this point, there are much more important issues that stand out: What about grid patterned town planning? And if one ignores even this, what about the other elements which gave the Indus Civilization its urban character; like the seals and sealings, and weights and measures? None of these have been found at Kausambi—nor at any of the other sites excavated in that region (e.g., Sravasti, Ayodhya, Sringaverpura, Rajghat, etc.). To say that all these items have eluded the spade would be placing too much credence on chance. To be precise, whatever the future might have to reveal, let it be plainly admitted that in the present state of knowledge, *Indus urbanism did not reach the heart of the Ganges Valley.*

In fact, while Alamgirpur, Hulas (recently excavated by K.N. Dikshit) and a few of the other sites, do indicate an "infiltration" of Harappan Culture into the uppermost part of the Ganges-Yamuna *Doab*, even this infiltration is not of the Mature Phase, and certainly the sites concerned do not represent urban settlements like Mohenjodaro or Harappa or even Kalibangan. The situation would then seem to be that it was only toward the end of its life, in any case *after* the eclipse of its urbanism, that the Indus Civilization entered the Ganges-Yamuna portals. Thus, it could not have provided the urban base for the civilization of the Ganges-Yamuna Valley, which in fact witnessed that phenomenon only a millennium later.

But then did the West and the East, standing, as already mentioned, for the Indus and Ganges Civilizations respectively, never meet? The answer would be: As mature civilizations they never met. But there did exist a meeting point between the two. This was at a time when the Indus had *completely* lost its urban character and had been diluted, with the amalgamation of other cousin cultures, to a stage almost beyond recognition, and the Ganges Civilization was only in its infancy, much before it acquired its urbanism. This meeting is typified at sites like Bhagwanpura, Dadheri, etc. recently excavated by J.P. Joshi (1978). Bhagwanpura, Period IA yielded a few pottery types which had a Harappan affiliation, (e.g., the goblet) but most others were either only remotely derivable from the Harappan complex, or were influenced by the Pre-Harappan Culture. Indeed, even in this region the Pre-Harappan formed the base on which the Mature Harappan appeared like bubbles on a vast lake, only to disappear and merge into the waters of the lake itself. To quote Joshi:

> The pottery of this Sub-Period (IA) is comparable to late Harappan ceramic types available at Bara, Bahadarabad, Atranjikhera, Siswal LLB, Mitathal I IB, Daulatpur and Raja Karan-Ka-Kila. Goblets are available but no beakers or perforated jars are found. Painted and incised pottery is also available. The technique in incised red ware is reminiscent of fabric D of Kalibangan pre-Harappan ceramic industry. Pottery with Harappan graffiti marks is yet another important find (Joshi 1978: 98).

I have some reservations about the use of the term "Late Harappan," for the pottery from either Bahadarabad or Atranjikhera. Neither ceramic corpus could be called "Late Harappan," since this term would apply only to the stage ensuing immediately from the Mature Harappan. Anyway, as a whole the pottery of Bhagwanpura IA is an amalgam in which trends derivable from various sources can be discerned.

While one may also take note of the "Harappan graffiti" from this subperiod, let it be added that it is of such a kind that it does not establish the regular use of a script. At the most it implies a "hangover" of some symbols. But the more important point is the total absence of seals and sealings. Likewise, there are no weights or measures, nor are there the typical Harappan bricks, much less town planning. The faience beads and bangles do, of course, remind one of a Harappan survival. However, the point to be emphasized is that the Bhagwanpura culture complex, composed of what can be termed an amalgam of the nth generation of Harappans; the $n+x$th generation of Pre-Harappans and the yth generation of Harappan cousins, *was in no way urban*. It was in this essentially rural setting that the meeting with the PGW Culture took place, the period of overlap being termed IB at Bhagwanpura, and likewise at Dadheri.

In this context one point deserves to be highlighted: whereas the PGW Culture at sites like Hastinapura. Atranjikhera, etc., is known to be associated with iron, that at Bhagwanpura and Dadheri has been reported to be *without* that metal; although objects of copper were duly found (Joshi 1978: 98-100). This would place the PGW Culture at the latter sites at a stage earlier than that at Hastinapura, Atranjikhera, etc. This would also explain why there was no overlap between the Late Harappan Culture and the PGW Culture at, for example, Alamgirpur or Hulas. To elucidate, the Late Harappan Culture at Alamgirpur was earlier than the IA Culture of Bhagwanpura and the PGW Culture at the former site was later than the PGW Culture met with in Subperiod IB of Bhagwanpura. Thus, while there remained a gap at Alamgirpur, the same was bridged at Bhagwanpura.

Another aspect of this "standing apart" in the former case and the "shaking of hands" in the latter may now be emphasized. Since the meeting did not take place at the time of Indus urbanism, the same was lost forever. But, as the co-mingling took place at a time when there was a relapse into the rural stage, the rural traits of the Harappa Culture, and of its ancestor and cousins, survived. This is seen for example, in the crisscross ploughing pattern of the fields, and *tandurs* of the Pre-Harappan levels at Kalibangan (Lal 1971 and 1979).

BIBLIOGRAPHY

Gaur, R.C. and S. Nurul Hasan, 1964
Excavations at Atranjikhera, 1964. Cyclostyled preliminary report, informally circulated.

Ghosh, A., 1973
The City in Early Historical India. Simla: Indian Institute of Advanced Study.

Joshi, J.P., 1978
Interlock of Late Harappa Culture and the Painted Grey Ware Culture in the Light of Recent Excavations. *Man and Environment* 2: 98-101.

Lal, B.B., 1955
Excavations at Hastinapura and Other Explorations in the Upper Ganga and Sutlej Basins, 1950-52. *Ancient India* 10-11: 4-151.

Lal, B.B., 1971
Perhaps the Earliest Ploughed Field so far Excavated Anywhere in the World. *Puratattva* 4: 1-3.

Lal, B.B., 1979
Kalibangan and the Indus Civilization. In *Essays in Indian Protohistory*. D.P. Agrawal and D.K. Chakrabarti, eds. Pp. 65-97. Delhi: B.R. Publishing Corp.

Sharma, G.R., 1960
The Excavations at Kausambi (1957-59). Allahabad: Allahabad University.

Sharma, G.R., 1979
Performance, Programme: A synopsis. Cyclostyled document issued by the Center of Advanced Study, Department of Ancient History, Culture and Archaeology, University of Allahabad.

Sinha, K.K., 1973
Stratigraphy and Chronology of Early Kausambi: A reappraisal. In *Radiocarbon and Indian Archaeology*. D.P. Agrawal and A. Ghosh, eds. Pp. 231-38. Bombay: Tata Institute of Fundamental Research.

Wheeler, Sir Mortimer, 1960
Early India and Pakistan. London: Thames and Hudson.

K.N. DIKSHIT

33. Hulas and the Late Harappan Complex in Western Uttar Pradesh

INTRODUCTION

IN 1959, with the discovery of the remains of the Harappan Culture at Alamgirpur, on the River Hindon, a tributary of the Yamuna, a new possibility was opened: the Harappan Culture could have extended through the Ganges-Yamuna *Doab* (Indian Archaeology: A review 1958-59) (Fig. 33.1). From 1962 to 1965 systematic exploration was conducted by the Archaeological Survey of India along the River Budhi Ganga from Hastinapur to Hardwar as a follow-up to this discovery. Exploration in nearby Saharanpur District was also carried out by the Survey for the same purpose at about this time. This was directed by Shankar Nath (Indian Archaeology: A review 1963-64a and 1966-67). Thereafter Bargaon was selected for limited excavation (Indian Archaeology: A review 1963-64b).

In recent years, a few more sites with Harappan pottery have been found; but all of them are badly disturbed. The mounds at Krishni, Chilhera, Nayabans and Hulas were recently checked as candidates for proper excavation, since all of them have yielded Harappan animal figurines, terracotta cakes and typical pottery, including incised ware of the Bara Complex. In 1978-79 the site of Hulas (lat. 28°43′ north; long. 77°22′ east), located in Saharanpur District along the Eastern Yamuna Canal, was selected and subjected to a large-scale excavation by the Archaeological Survey of India. This operation has been undertaken to further understand the character of the Harappan Civilization in a peripheral region, the State of Uttar Pradesh.

HULAS EVIDENCE

The mound at Hulas, which measures approximately 330 by 172 meters (Fig. 33.2), has about five meters of occupation. This is divisible into five cultural periods (Fig. 33.3). Period I, the lowest, has yielded Harappan Ware; Period II Painted Gray Ware; Period III Northern Black Polished Ware; Period IV Sunga-Kushan Ware and Period V Gupta Molded Ware. Only Period I will be discussed here as the others are beyond the scope of this paper.

Period I, represented by 1.4 meters of deposit, rests on natural soil. It yielded Harappan Red Ware as well as associated non-Harappan Red and Thick Gray Wares. The other finds include terracotta beads, bangles, animal figurines and cartwheels with raised central hub, faience beads and bangles, agate and carnelian beads, a copper bangle, bone point and stone querns and pestles. The terracotta cakes from this site are generally oval in shape but have pointed ends. Other cake varieties, such as round ones with a deep finger impression in the center, are also available.

Fragmentary kiln-burnt bricks with husks as degraissant were found with a complete dish-on-stand in an oval hearth with a constricted mouth. This hearth is on the southern edge of the habitation. A few brickbats in the ratio of 1:2 were also found in the Harappan layers. The limited occurrence of these bricks rules out for the moment the possibility that they were used for house construction. The use of burnt brick was also very limited at Ropar, Bhagwanpura and Alamgirpur, where houses were generally

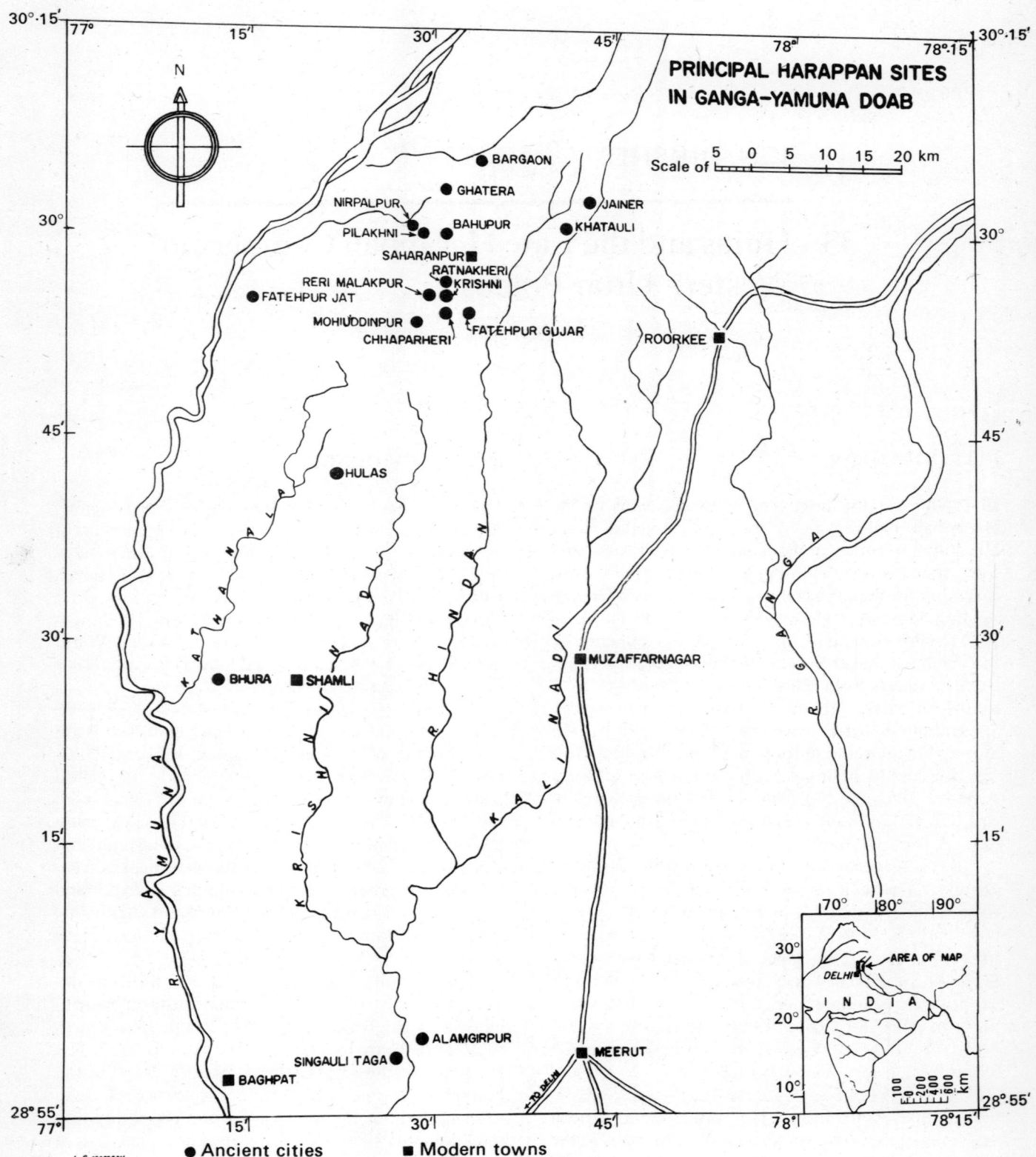

Fig. 33.1. Principal Harappan sites in the Ganga-Yamuna *Doab*.

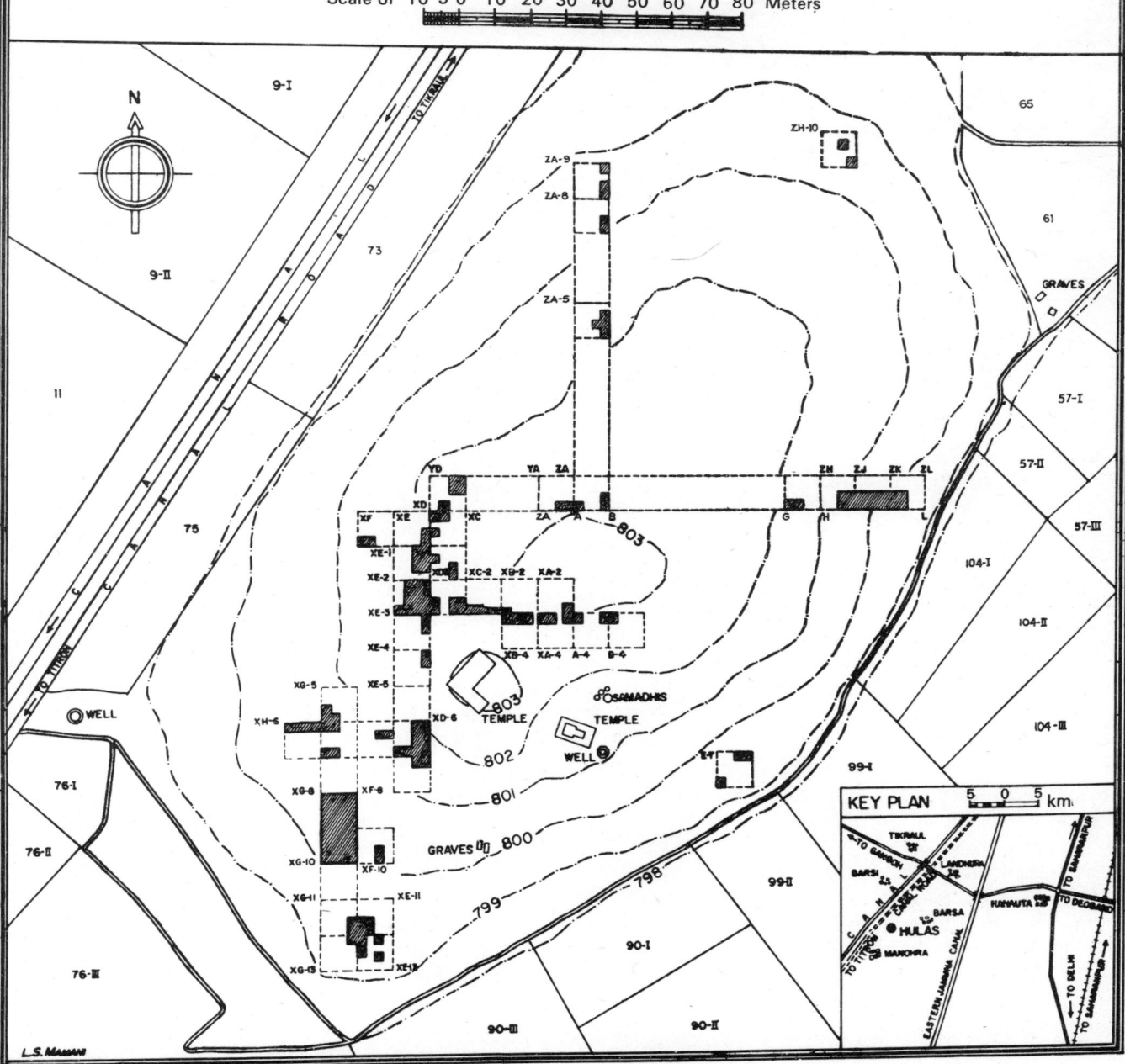

Fig. 33.2. Site plan of Hulas 1978–79.

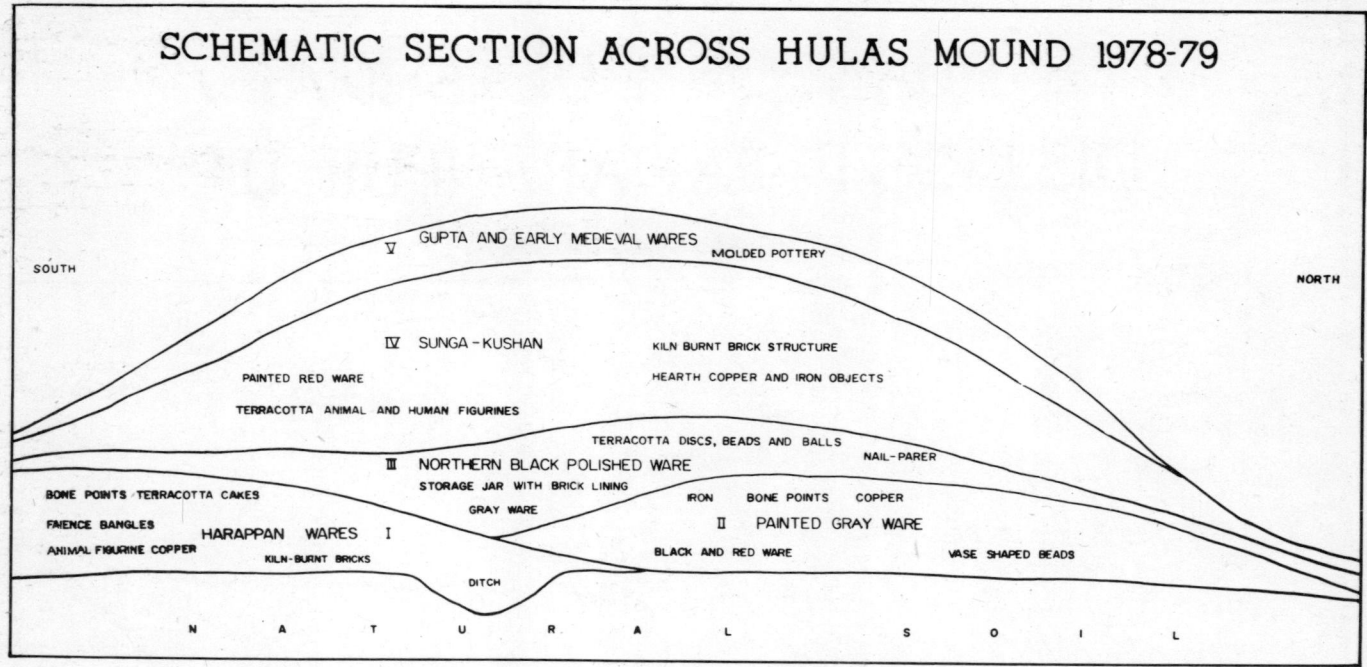

Fig. 33.3. Schematic section across Hulas mound, 1978–79.

built with mud walls.

Characteristic Harappan pottery forms like the dish with a projected rim and carinated shoulder, or the globular vessel with a flange round the neck, or the shallow dish with an incurved rim or the jarstand with a concave profile (Wheeler 1947: types I, XIII, XXX, SLV) are rare at Hulas. Alamgirpur types 15, 16, 21, 22 and 23 are absent (Indian Archaeology: A review 1958-59: Fig. 4). Other characteristic types occur in profusion: dish-on-stand with a drooping rim, jar with a horizontally splayed rim, medium sized jar with an everted rim, bowl-like lid with a central knob, and miniature pots with a ring or pedestaled base (Fig. 33.4). A few flasks with a very thin fabric and a red slip were also encountered. Similar potsherds were noticed at Bargaon (Indian Archaeological Society 1971-72: Fig. 4, type 11) although are perhaps unknown elsewhere. A few sherds with a paring technique were also found. The painted motifs, which are executed in black pigment, are all simple bands, triangles, mat designs, rows of hatched diamonds within horizontal bands, chains within bands, leaf patterns and a dancing peacock with a hatched body. A few painted motifs placed on the neck and shoulder seem to have been derived from the Pre-Harappan tradition. Still, a majority of painted motifs are Harappan (Figs. 33.5 and 33.6). There is also incised decoration on the exterior of some pots: sets of wavy lines, sigmas, chevrons, cord impressions, compartmented designs, and the like. One of the sherds had deep conspicuous compartmented designs on the inner side. This is definitely a Pre-Harappan feature. Sherds with raised horizontal bands in a restricted area were also noticed. However, there are only ten incised sherds from the site at this time and these would not account for even one percent of the total collection.

The types of thick Gray Ware are limited. Only basins with out-turned rims, thick jars with under-cut rims and bowls with everted rims were found.

The Harappan settlers of Hulas originally occupied a natural hill or hillock. Later, they constructed a solid mud platform running northeast/southwest. This was apparently a protective measure against the floods. A major portion of this platform, which was damaged at one stage by floods, was also cut by the Painted Gray Ware (hereafter PGW) people of a later period. However, the full extent of this mud platform, and its phases of construction will require further work. Damage to the site has been done in recent years by villagers who have completely removed a large portion of the southernmost part of

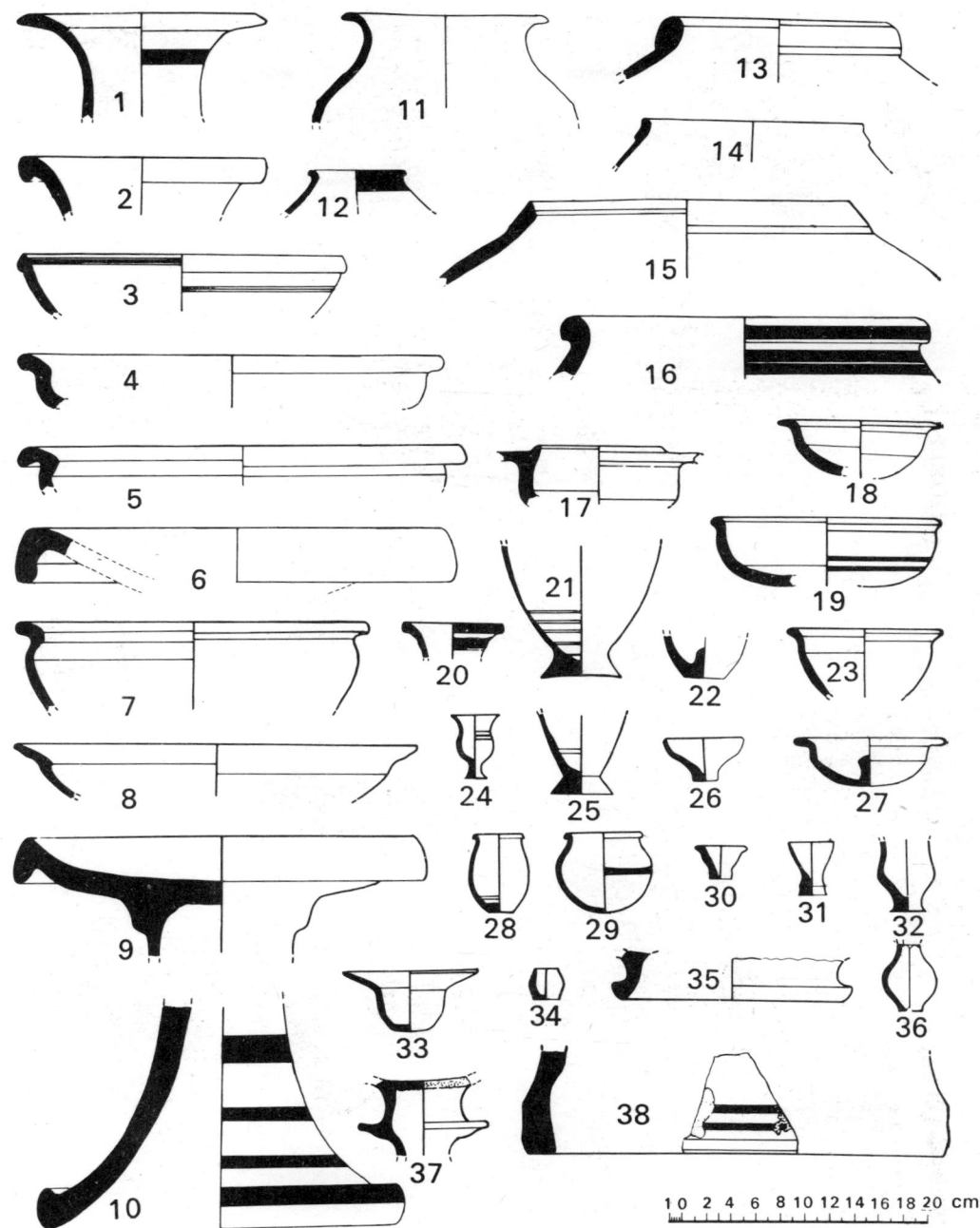

Fig. 33.4. Pottery types from Hulas.

the mound for agricultural operations.

In the following period, the PGW people did not settle on the area once occupied by the Harappans. They instead settled on virgin soil to the north and east of the Harappan settlement. There is also a ditch or ancient rain gully, encountered at the depth of 4.3 meters from the surface of the trench lying somewhere in the middle of the mound and demarcating the two settlements. The NBP settlers expanded the area used by the PGW settlement but it was only in the Kushan times that the people occupied the area covered by both Harappans and makers of PGW.

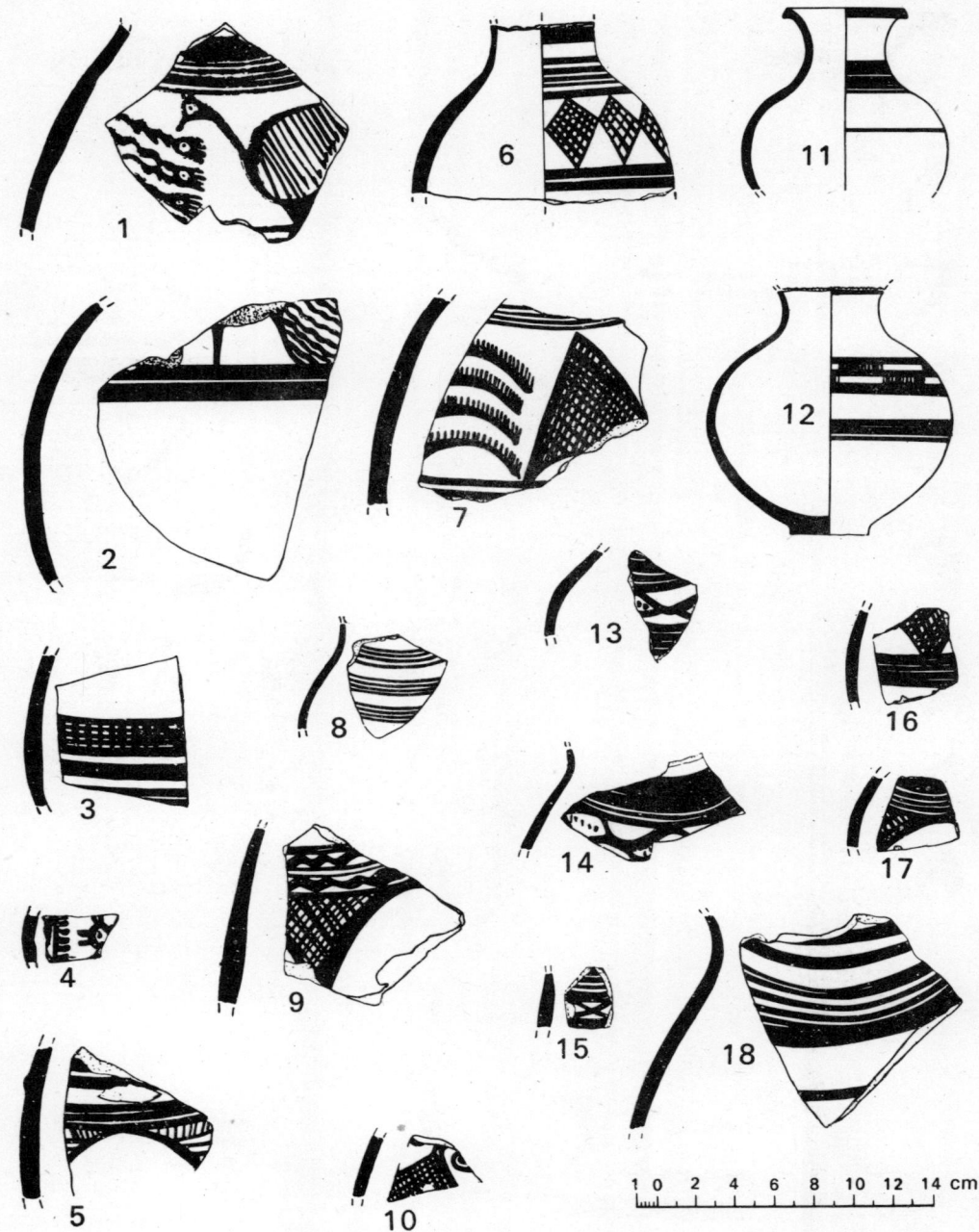

Fig. 33.5. Painted designs from Hulas.

This feature of the Harappan and PGW settlements at this site conforms to the situation observed in the Ghaggar Valley in northern Rajasthan and Haryana but differs from the Hindon River area (type site: Alamgirpur) and Sutlej Valley (type site: Ropar).

There is a ditch, or ancient rain gully, at a depth of 4.3 meters from the surface. This feature lies toward the middle of the mound and separates the Harappan and PGW areas. At approximately 90 centimeters deep it was possibly a significant barrier to the northward expansion of the Harappan settlement; but much more needs to be known about it. For example,

Hulas and the Late Harappan Complex in Western Uttar Pradesh

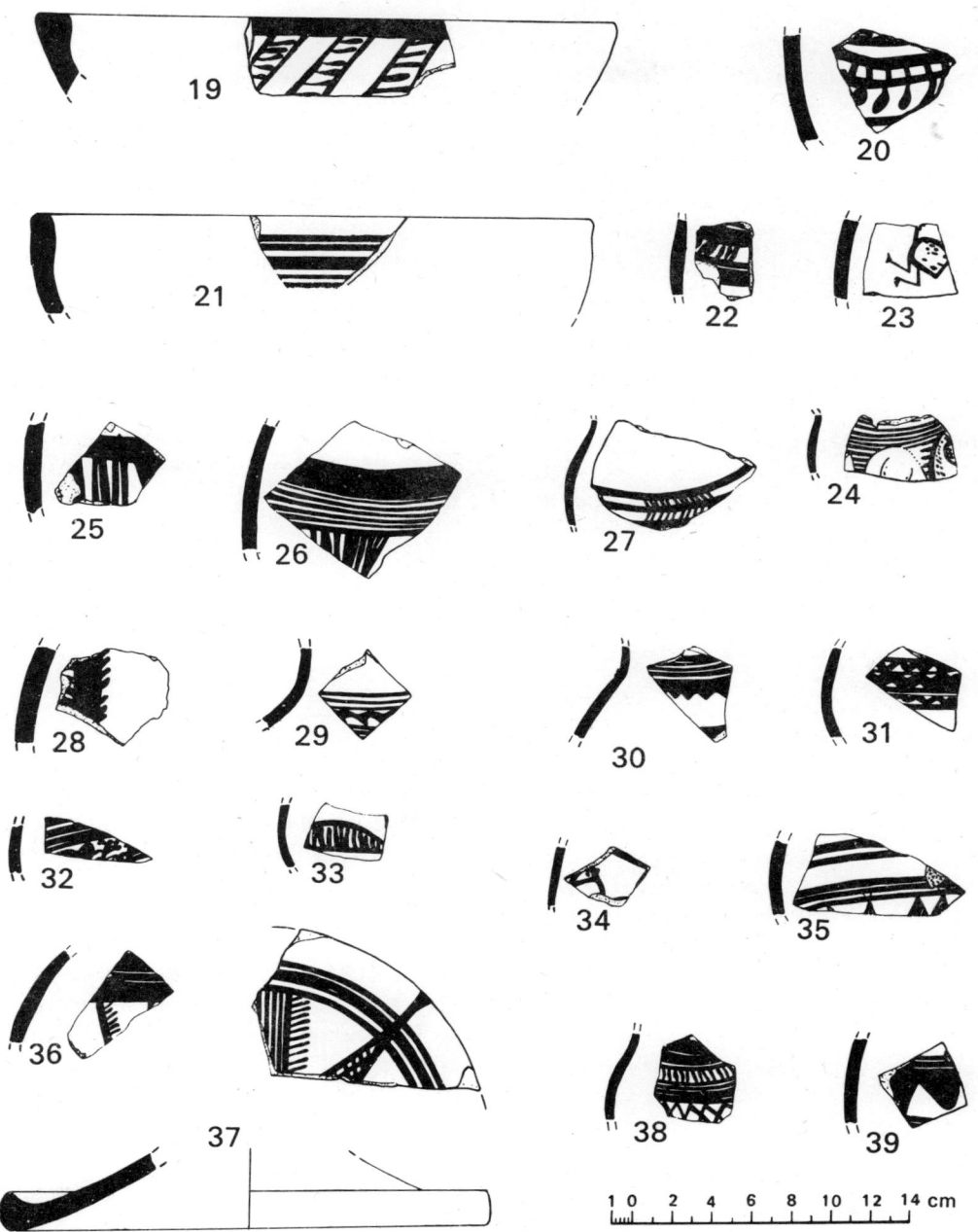

Fig. 33.6. Painted designs from Hulas.

the exact width of the ditch could not be ascertained this year; although it was observed in cross-section running for about five meters. The Harappan potsherds which were found in the bottom of the feature show a waterlogging effect and are like the Ochre Colored Ware encountered at other sites in the *Doab*.

The slip is usually separated from the surface of these sherds. Dishes-on-stand, jars with splayed rims and miniature pots were found in the ditch. The sherds of successive periods, to NBP at a depth of 2.2 meters from the surface are very small, rolled and weathered. It thus appears that the area was unoccupied and that the ditch was partly filled up by the Harappans and altered by the PGW people. This area was further leveled by washed material of NBP times.

DATA FROM OTHER EXCAVATED SITES

Alamgirpur, District Meerut and Bargaon, District Saharanpur, are the only excavated Chalcolithic sites in the *Doab*.

Alamgirpur: The earliest period at Alamgirpur, represented by a thickness of 1.8 meters has typical Harappan pottery, notably the dish-on-stand, goblet with pointed base, cylindrical jar, beaker and perforated jar. Cloth impressions on a trough are also extremely interesting. A variety of objects made of terracotta, faience, steatite, semiprecious stone, bone, and copper or bronze were recovered from this level. Two groups of kiln-burnt brick were found. A short incised inscription, consisting of two characters on a trough, was found. Alamgirpur also yielded triangular terracotta cakes. The site was occupied by PGW makers after a break. They used plain black and red and black slipped wares.

Bargaon: This is a single culture site. Two trenches measuring five meters on a side were laid there to investigate the details of the Harappan occupation as well as the nature of its pottery with an unslipped red ware which looks like OCP. From top to bottom, the pottery recovered from an occupational thickness of about 1.2 meters was Harappan plain, painted and incised wares. An unslipped Ochre Colored Ware was noticed. Terracotta cakes, a bull headed toy cart, wheels with central hubs, beads, chert blades, bone points, a copper ring, stone weights and faience bangles were also found.

The excavations have not yielded some typical Harappan types, such as a jar, the Indus goblet, the beaker and a few other characteristic types found at Alamgirpur. There is no evidence for kiln-burnt brick.

DATA FROM EXPLORED SITES

There is a concentration of Harappan sites in District Saharanpur. These are confined to the tributaries of the Yamuna found in the districts of Saharanpur, Muzaffarnagar and Meerut (Dikshit 1970). But, there is not one site with all of the typical Harappan pottery in this area which is within the Ganges Valley proper. A few of the more important sites of this type have been discussed elsewhere (Dikshit *in* Deshpande in press: Appendix I).

The average thickness of Harappan strata in this region varies between one-half and 1.8 meters. These people had a preference for settling on steep river banks with the insecure silts of the flood plain below them. This was a source of constant catastrophe. The habitations, which cover areas about 200 meters in diameter, suggest that they were used by a small number of families whose basic subsistence was derived by farming the land around them. The spacing of these sites at about one every eight to 12 kilometers conforms to the Chalcolithic pattern in Haryana, Punjab, and even Gujarat. In Saurashtra, as in Sind, sites range from tiny hamlets to villages and towns and are also located close to banks of rivers and streams (Chitalwala 1978). Since there is neither a city nor town dating to the Harappan period in this region, it may be inferred that one is dealing with a deurbanized phase of the Harappan Culture. This is what has been called the Late Harappan.

CHRONOLOGY

The beginning of the Mature Phase of the Harappan Culture can be put at ca. 2350 B.C. on the basis of a critical evaluation of Harappan artifacts found in datable contexts in West Asia. Radiocarbon dates indicate that the time bracket of Harappan Culture nuclear regions was ca. 2300 to 2000 B.C. and in peripheral areas was 2200 to 1700 B.C. These dates are without MASCA correction. However, Surkotada in Gujarat dates to ca. 2100 to 1650 B.C., and Banawali in Haryana extends to 1400 or 1300 B.C. (Agrawal 1978).

The number of characteristic Harappan pottery types found in the nuclear and adjoining peripheral regions of this civilization are certainly limited at Hulas. The site chronology discussed here is based on typology. An evaluation of the latest types at Hulas, in the amalgam of late Mature Harappan, Late (or transformed) Harappan and forms of unknown origin with a legacy of Pre-, or Post-Harappan Cultures (e.g. Cemetery H) of the Indus proper, indicates that the date of this culture complex, including that found at Bargaon, can be suggested to have been ca. 1700 to 1000 B.C. The Harappans migrated to the Yamuna Valley through that of the Sutlej. This route was also possibly followed by the Post-Harappan Cultures of the Indus Valley, such as Cemetery H (Dikshit 1967). New pottery forms started appearing at Ropar, Bara,

Bargaon, Alamgirpur and Hulas, while the traditional characteristic types lost their use, as the Harappan Culture in this region underwent a substantial transformation.

Y.D. Sharma once suggested a culture sequence for the Punjab that began with Kotla Nihang Khan, moved to Ropar and ended with Bara (Sharma 1964). He has recently suggested* that Ropar I (Harappan Period) has a predominance of Pre-Harappan, Harappan and cognate elements in different levels or areas. It can be divided into two phases (A and B) which combined date to ca. 2100-1400 B.C. The earliest settlers at Ropar lived on the northern edge of the mound. They were either Pre-Harappans, with contacts with the Harappans, or were a mixed community. A few pottery types are clearly of the Pre-Harappan Kalibangan type, or even exhibit an affinity with the Pre-Harappan pottery from Pre-defense Harappa, Amri, Kot Diji, Sarai Khola or Siswal. In Phase B, the Bara people occupied the eastern slope of the mound. They cohabited the place with Harappans (Sharma in press). Since no stratigraphic correlation has been made between the northern, eastern and center portions of the mound this sequence is difficult to deal with. But, Sharma's earlier treatment of Bara Ware, a late contemporary of the Harappan, appears to be valid. In fact, some pottery of unknown connections was always present in the Harappan complex; although its independent status always lacked recognition.

Since there is no overlap between the Harappan and PGW Cultures at Ropar the end date of ca. 1400 B.C. has been used. This was done because it would be difficult to push back the antiquity of PGW at Bhagwanpura to a date earlier than ca. 1200 B.C. since this would also be the date of the survival of the Bara Culture. At Nagar and Katpalon the pure Bara Phase is absent since even in the lowest levels there is an overlap between Bara and PGW Wares (Sharma in press). The excavation at Mitathal in Haryana is worth mentioning in this connection. This site has a cultural sequence from the late Pre-Harappan to the Late Harappan. Mitathal IIA is a Mature Harappan settlement with some Pre-Harappan pottery. Period II B is marked by a gradual decline in the material culture and is comparable to Daulatpur, Mirzapur, Bhagwanpura IA, Alamgirpur and Hulas. This period is dated to ca. 1700 to 1500 B.C. (Suraj Bhan 1973).

This sequence is also found at Banawali which starts with Kalibangan I. The upper phase is predominantly Bara Ware recovered from pits cut through Harappan levels. The primary Bara habitation was to the east of the Mature Harappan settlement (Bisht in press). No Bara Ware was found in the early levels of the Harappan occupation at Banawali; although some Pre-Harappan (Kalibangan I or Sothi Complex) elements persisted throughout the period. It is not clear that the habitation area of the Bara Culture, as designated by the excavator, existed along with the Mature Harappan. If this is the case then Bara's history will begin much earlier than what is supposed when it is called Late Harappan.

The deurbanized Harappan Culture continued for some time on a few sites in Haryana and Punjab. Here it came into contact with the complexes of a Pre-Harappan (Kalibangan I) genre which had lingered in comparative isolation for several centuries. This gave rise to an amalgam of culture with distant Harappan and Pre-Harappan traditions (Thapar 1978). The influence of Cemetery H in the Late Harappan complex has recently been suggested to have been more of an echo than something substantial in terms of cultural traits.

THE THEORY OF OVERLAP

This hypothesis suggests three substages of the Harappan Culture within its Late Phase. These are: (1) Harappan pottery without PGW, (2) Harappan pottery with PGW, and (3) Harappan pottery with Gray Ware. The following sites are associated with each substage:

1) Ropar, Daulatpur, Kurukshetra, Alamgirpur and Hulas.

2) Bhagwanpura, Dadheri and Katpalon (Joshi in press).

3) Manda (Dikshit 1978; Joshi in press).

If PGW is earlier in Haryana and the Punjab, then it is not clear why the composite culture (Harappa and PGW) did not penetrate the Yamuna Valley. In western Uttar Pradesh and eastern Rajasthan there is a clear antecedent stage to PGW (i.e., the Black and Red Ware stage) but there is no such phase in Haryana and Punjab. At Dadheri and Katpalon, Harappan Ware has been reported to occur with Black and Red and Painted Gray Ware. It can therefore be

---

*Editor's note: See Dr. Sharma's paper in this volume for a full discussion of this issue.

argued that this kind of overlap between the Late Harappan and PGW was: (1) a localized phenomenon at a few sites in Haryana and Punjab, and (2) that it never penetrated the Yamuna Valley. If the chronology of Ropar is accepted then most of the sites in western Uttar Pradesh should be placed in the middle phase of Ropar (the Harappan of Bara tradition) which Sharma has designated Phase IB. Again, he feels that it is the Bara Culture which overlapped PGW.

I have developed two phases for the Harappan complex in western Uttar Pradesh: Phase I between ca. 1700 and 1300 B.C., and Phase II between 1300 and 1000 B.C. (Dikshit 1970). This scheme is based on the presence or absence of certain Harappan traits and is a tentative suggestion. Phase I is represented by sites like Alamgirpur, Bhura, Kalaheti, Tatarpur Kalan and Hulas. It is made up of typical Harappan pottery, carnelian beads, terracotta animal figurines, triangular cakes, stone objects and burnt bricks. The presence of inscribed pottery at Alamgirpur clearly proves that this phase is near the Urban Phase of the Harappan Culture. Phase II consists of the following sites: Bargaon, Pilkhani, Bahpur, Hardakheri, Bakarka, Gathera and Budha Khera. They have an unslipped red ware which looks like the so-called Ochre Colored Pottery (OCP) which clearly dominates the assemblage. The density of population in the second phase may have been comparatively high since there is an increase in the number of sites; however they appear to be on the average smaller than the earlier ones. Bargaon has some characteristic Harappan pottery, but there are no inscriptions. The assemblage also lacks triangular terracotta cakes and kiln-burnt bricks.

The Allchins have also suggested a two-phase scheme. The first of these is contemporary with a Late Harappan and the second is Post-Harappan (Allchin and Allchin 1968). But Possehl (1977) has equated Bargaon and Ambkheri with Alamgirpur and suggested the date of ca. 1900-1000 B.C. As outlined above, the cultural elements noticed at Alamgirpur are much closer to the Mature Harappan complex than to the Bargaon complex. Further, signs of contact with Ambkheri, essentially an OCP site in the Ganges Valley, suggests only typological affinity of certain ceramic types. It would be hasty to put OCP sites in the Post-Harappan times. The distribution of this ware in the upper and central Ganges Valley, eastern Rajasthan has revealed a different sequence (Dikshit 1978b). However, a fuller understanding of the material culture of this period will be known only when more sites have undergone horizontal excavations.

The evidence for the interrelationship between sites in Haryana, Punjab and Uttar Pradesh reveals the stages in which the Harappan Culture appeared in this homogenous belt. The cross current in the period immediately following the Mature Harappan in the area is still not clear in terms of a unilinear sequence; although the chronology proposed here appears to be substantially correct as far as major stages are concerned. No attempt has been made to correlate this picture with that for Gujarat and Saurashtra since the latter region is in a different environmental setting.

RADIOCARBON DATES

The Late Harappan sites in the Yamuna and Sutlej Valleys have not yet been dated by ^{14}C; although four dates ranging between ca. 1890 ± 95 and 1645 ± 90 B.C. have come from Bara (Sharma 1973). The earliest date (1890 ± 95 B.C.) is from midlevel (layer 9), at a depth of 2.2 meters. Surprisingly enough the other date (1280 ± 100 B.C.) is from layer 10 of the same trench at a depth of 2.5 meters below surface. These dates have obviously not helped in developing an accurate chronology.

DISCUSSION

The Pre-Harappan cultural horizon found in northern Rajasthan and Haryana is absent in western Uttar Pradesh; although Hulas has yielded a few painted and incised pots which may be from the Pre-Harappan tradition. Similar painted sherds have also been picked up from Tatarpur Kalan.

The Mature Harappan sites which are found in southern Sind, the Punjab (Pakistan), Bahawalpur, northern Rajasthan, Gujarat and Saurashtra are also not found in this peripheral region. Alamgirpur and Hulas represent a late Mature stage of Harappan Culture in western Uttar Pradesh. In fact it is the amalgamated tradition of Harappa-Bara which forms the base cultural stratum in the *Doab*. No influence of Cemetery H is noticed in this region. The next phase of this composite culture is again not found in Uttar Pradesh but it is present in Haryana and Punjab where sites with predominantly Bara Ware dominate the scene.

It may be pointed out that full impact of the Bara Culture was never felt in Uttar Pradesh. A legitimate question may be posed about the personality of the Bara Culture. Save for a few shapes and the decoration of pots with horizontal or wavy incised lines, the antecedents of this culture are not clear. There is, however, a diversity in slips and painting. Terracotta cakes and pointed goblets are rare in this complex (Indian Archaeology: A review 1954-55). In western Uttar Pradesh the incised elements or typical Bara designs are there, but always in very restricted number. It has been said that the end of Harappan settlements in the *Doab* created a cultural vacuum for a time (Fairservis 1971). But the present survey did not reveal this. In western Uttar Pradesh the Harappans gradually merged into the local culture identified as the Ochre Colored Pottery assemblage. The Unslipped Ware of the Yamuna Valley differs from the OCP of the Ganges Valley in texture. The latter is more powdery and the color sticks to the hand when a sherd is rubbed. The sites at Nahli and Malhera in District Meerut, and Manpur, Bhatpur and Lal Qila in District Bulandshahr belong to the Ganges Valley. The Ganges Valley OCP sherds are generally gray in the core although sherds with red core are also available.

The OCP sites in the Ganges Valley have a typological affinity with the Harappan in the Yamuna and Sutlej Valleys. The complex at Ambkheri consists of a variety of utilitarian pottery types, terracotta and carnelian beads, animal figurines and stone objects. The painted and incised sherds of Bara type noticed in the OCP complex of the central *Doab* are not present on any of the sites in the upper *Doab*. In the central *Doab*, at Atranjikhera and Saipai, a few incised designs, painted sherds and other pottery types occurring in small numbers (e.g., channel-like spout and handled pots) were noticed in the OCP complex. No Harappan type (e.g., dish-on-stand, jar stand, etc.) was encountered in this complex (Dikshit 1978b). The excavations at Noh, Jodhpura and Ganeshwar in eastern Rajasthan revealed an extension of the OCP Complex of the Central *Doab* through the tributaries of the Yamuna. The study of this material is important (Agrawala 1978). Work is in progress at Ganeshwar.

CONCLUSION

The archaeological evidence at Hulas has confirmed the diffusionary processes of the Harappan Culture which spread these people into the region where they developed local variation. The widespread degeneration or decay in this cultural traits or elements, noticed at Alamgirpur in Uttar Pradesh, Ropar and Sanghol in the Punjab and Mitathal and Banawali in Haryana, bear ample testimony to this fact. Contact with the parent culture in the Indus Valley seen in a few ceramic forms and designs and perhaps in the stray finds of stone weights, faience objects, terracotta cakes and animal figurines, suggests a close identity in terms of the spread and expansion of common systems and ideas. The absence of inscribed seals, and the general scarcity of copper, bronze and other raw materials, such as chert, lapis lazuli and gold, shows that there was a severe setback to internal and external trade. The presence of some Bara Ware in the Harappan complex provides evidence for inter-regional contacts between the Punjab and Uttar Pradesh; although the vigorous and vivid impact of the Bara Culture was never felt in the *Doab*.

ACKNOWLEDGMENTS

I am extremely grateful to Shri B.K. Thapar, Dr. (Mrs.) D. Mitra and Shri H. Sarkar who have kindly visited Hulas and offered their valuable guidance. Professor B.B. Lal and Dr. Y.D. Sharma, who are fully aware of the problems in the region, also visited the site. My thanks are due to my colleagues in the Archaeological Survey of India: Sarvashri B.P. Saxena, B.R. Meena, V.C. Sharma, Dharam Vir Sharma, R.S. Sharma, Lal Singh Mamani and D.K. Malik who actively assisted me in the field and also helped in the classification of material for the preparation of this paper. I also feel obliged to Sarvashri S.S. Saar and J.N. Ghandi for the preparation of drawings and to Shri T.R. Kakar for typing the manuscript.

The line drawings in the paper are by courtesy of the Archaeological Survey of India.

BIBLIOGRAPHY

Agrawal, D.P. *et al.*, 1978
Chronology of Indian Prehistory from the Mesolithic Period to the Iron Age. *Journal of Human Evolution* 7: 37-44.

Agrawala, R.C., 1978
Personal communication.

Allchin, B. and F.R. Allchin, 1968
The Birth of Indian Civilization. Baltimore: Penguin Books.

Bisht, R.S., in press
Harappan Culture in the Punjab: A study in perspective. In *Indus Civilization: Problems and issues*. B.B. Lal and S.C. Malik, eds. Simla: Indian Institute of Advanced Study.

Chitalwala, Y.M., 1978
Harappan and Post-Harappan Settlement Patterns in the Rajkot District of Saurashtra. In *Essays in Indian Protohistory*. D.P. Agrawal and D.K. Chakrabarti, eds. Pp. 113-21. Delhi: B.R. Publishing Corp.

Deshpande, M.N., in press
The Harappan Settlements in the Ganga/Yamuna Doab. In *Indus Civilization: Problems and issues*. B.B. Lal and S.C. Malik, eds. Simla: Indian Institute of Advanced Study.

Dikshit, K.N., 1967
Harappa Culture and its Aftermath. *Archaeo-Civilization* 3-4 (NS): 27-36.

Dikshit, K.N., 1970
Harappan Culture in Western Uttar Pradesh. *Bulletin of the National Museum* 2: 21-28.

Dikshit, K.N., 1978a
The Late Harappan Cultures in India. In *Essays in Indian Protohistory*. D.P. Agrawal and D.K. Chakrabarti, eds. Pp. 123-33. Delhi: B.R. Publishing Corp.

Dikshit, K.N., 1978b
The Ochre Colored Ware Settlements in the Ganga/Yamuna Doab. In *Essays in Indian Protohistory*. D.P. Agrawal and D.K. Chakrabarti eds. Pp. 285-99. Delhi: B.R. Publishing Corp.

Dikshit, K.N., in press
The Chronological Problem of the Late Harappans with Special Reference to Western Uttar Pradesh. In *Indus Civilization: Problems and issues*. B.B. Lal and S.C. Malik, eds. Simla: Indian Institute of Advanced Study.

Fairservis, W.A., 1971
The Roots of Ancient India. New York: Macmillan.

Indian Archaeological Society, 1971-72
Proceedings of the Seminar on OCP and NBP. *Puratattva* 5: 1-104.

Indian Archaeology: A review (IAR), 1954-55
Bara and Salaura, District Ambala. Pp. 9-10. Delhi: Archaeological Survey of India.

Indian Archaeology: A review (IAR), 1958-59
Alamgirpur Excavations. Pp. 50-55. Delhi: Archaeological Survey of India.

Indian Archaeology: A review (IAR), 1963-64a
Exploration in Districts Muzaffarnagar and Saharanpur. Pp. 53-56. Delhi: Archaeological Survey of India.

Indian Archaeology: A review (IAR), 1963-64b
Excavations at Bargaon, District Saharanpur. Pp. 56-57. Delhi: Archaeological Survey of India.

Indian Archaeology: A review (IAR), 1966-67
Exploration in District Saharanpur. P. 43. Delhi: Archaeological Survey of India.

Joshi, J.P., in press
Overlap of Late Harappan Culture and Painted Grey Ware Culture in Light of Recent Excavations in Haryana, Punjab and Jammu. In *Indus Civilization: Problems and issues*. B.B. Lal and S.C. Malik, eds. Simla: Indian Institute of Advanced Study.

Possehl, G.L., 1977
The End of a State and the Continuity of a Tradition. In *Realm and Region in Traditional India*. R. Fox, ed. Pp. 234-54. Delhi: Vikas.

Sharma, Y.D., 1964
Protohistoric Remains. *Archaeological Remains, Monuments and Museums*. Pp. 7-10. Delhi: Archaeological Survey of India.

Sharma, Y.D., 1973
Value of Common Painted Ceramic Designs from Different Sites as a Guide to Chronology with Special Reference to Pottery from Bara (Punjab). In *Radiocarbon and Indian Archaeology*. D.P. Agrawal and A. Ghosh, eds. Pp. 222-30. Bombay: Tata Institute of Fundamental Research.

Sharma, Y.D., in press
The Harappans and the Painted Grey Ware

People in the Punjab. *XIII Annual Session of the Punjab History Conference*. Patiala.

Suraj Bhan, 1973
The Sequence and Spread of Prehistoric Cultures in the Upper Sarasvati Basin. In *Radiocarbon and Indian Archaeology*. D.P. Agrawal and A. Ghosh, eds. Pp. 252-63. Bombay: Tata Institute of Fundamental Research.

Thapar, B.K., 1978
The Mosaic of the Indus Civilization Beyond the Indus Valley. Unpublished paper presented at the International Seminar on the Indus Civilization, Karachi, December 30. Cyclostyled Copy.

Wheeler, Sir Mortimer, 1947
Harappa 1946: The Defenses and Cemetery R-37. *Ancient India* 3: 58-130.

S.R. RAO

34. New Light on the Post-Urban (Late Harappan) Phase of the Indus Civilization in India

It is now generally agreed that the Indus Civilization did not die a sudden death with the destruction of Harappa and Mohenjodaro in ca. 1900 B.C., but survived for three centuries more outside the Indus Valley.

The causes for the destruction and consequent abandonment of most of the Mature Harappan settlements, both urban and rural, in Kutch, Saurashtra and South Gujarat have been discussed in *Lothal and the Indus Civilization* (Rao 1973). Subsequent to the publication of this work a few more Mature Harappan sites and a large number of degenerate, or Late Harappan sites were discovered in Gujarat, Rajasthan, Punjab, Haryana and Maharashtra. Some of them have been excavated.

This paper is based on a region by region study of the archaeological evidence from: (1) Kutch, (2) Saurashtra, (3) Gujarat, (4) northern Deccan, (5) Haryana and Punjab, (6) Rajasthan, (7) Jammu and Kashmir, and (8) western Uttar Pradesh. Late Harappan settlements chosen for study are classified into two groups:

Group I: Mature Harappan settlements which continued to be occupied in the Post-Urban, (i.e, Late Harappan) Phase:

Lothal, Rangpur, Atkot (Adkot), Bhela in Saurashtra; Desalpur, Pabumath, Dhola Vira (Kotada), Netra Khirsara, and Surkotada (Surkotda) in Kutch; Bhagatrav in South Gujarat; Siswal, Mitathal, Banawali, Hulas, Ropar (Rupar), Katpalon and Dadheri in Haryana-Punjab and Manda near Jammu.

Group II: Late Harappan settlements without an antecedent Mature Harappan phase:

Prabhas, Kindarkhera (Kinnarkheda), Rojdi, Devaliyo, Babarkot, Gop, Beyt Dwarka, Amra and Lakhabawal in Saurashtra; Kana Sutaria, Zekda, Kanewal and Mehgam in North Gujarat; Luna, Kotada-Bhadli and Todio in Kutch; Bhyana, Hingoni Bhudruk and Daimabad in the Tapti-Godavari Valleys; Alamgirpur in Uttar Pradesh; Mirzapur, Bara and Katpalon in Haryana-Punjab and Kayatha in Malwa.

In order to follow the process of the deurbanization of the Harappan Civilization, it is necessary to examine, in the first instance, whether it was an urban civilization at all. Trade, planning, literacy and established civic administration are some of the distinguishing features of urbanization. The Harappan cities show a capacity to have a wide habitational spectrum. Lothal had a population of 15,000 (Rao 1973: 53),[1] Mohenjodaro 33,469 (Datta 1962), and Harappa 37,155 (Datta 1962) and in each city the municipal administration was efficient, and civil discipline was firmly established. The cities were well planned as can be seen from the neatly laid streets; although all of them may not be to a gridiron plan. In one respect Lothal appears to be better planned than Mohenjodaro. The streets at Lothal are straight and are consistently run in cardinal directions: Street 2, Street 3, Steet 4, Street 6 and Street 9 run east-west; while Street 1, Street 5, and Street 8 and some lanes which lie in the north-south direction join the former at right angles. All the Harappan cities, and quite a few towns and villages, were fortified against flood. Some difference is noticed in the plans of granaries and in the location of cemeteries, but the overall picture is one of regimentation to some degree.

Another feature of urbanization is organized

trade. If the number of seals/sealings found in Harappan settlements is taken as an index to the volume of trade, Mohenjodaro, Harappa, Lothal and Kalibangan can be placed in a descending order in this matter.

Lothal has yielded 213 seals/sealings and Kalibangan 65. While Mohenjodaro and Lothal reveal special skills like bead making, shell working, ivory carving, metallurgy, no such specialization is seen at Kalibangan. Though smaller in size than Kalibangan, Chanhudaro developed a bead making industry. The importance of Harappa lies in the volume of trade and not in developing any particular industry.

Extensive trade, internal as well as external, necessitated the introduction of uniform weights and production of goods to a uniform standard throughout the Indus Empire. The enforcement of trade regulations resulted in the extension of political control over the provinces and villages. With a centralized administration the distribution of goods and planning of towns and cities conforming to a general pattern became easy.

TERMINOLOGY

The decline in the material prosperity of the people as a result of a sudden stop in long-distance trade and a steep fall in internal trade cutting off the supply of essential raw materials required by specialized craftsmen is conspicuous in the Post-Urban Phase of the Harappan Civilization to which the name "Late Harappan" was first given (Rao 1963: 15; 1973: 60). This term has gained currency and is widely used in almost all publications by archaeologists in India and abroad. The diagnostic features of the "Late Harappan Culture" highlighted at Lothal and Rangpur, can be traced in similar situations at nearly 200 sites in Gujarat, 152 sites in Haryana-Punjab (India) and 25 sites in the Bahawalpur district of Pakistan. The term "Late Harappan Culture" or "Late Harappan Phase," as modified by some writers, is used in a cultural, not a chronological sense. It implies the phase immediately following the destruction of the urban centers of the Harappan Civilization when the process of deurbanization had begun in the regions east and south of the Indus Valley, to which the Harappan refugees came to occupy in large numbers. The connotation of the term "Late Harappan" encompasses the entire gamut of the decadent culture and not merely its ceramic wares. With this explanation in mind one may examine what deurbanization meant to the Late Harappans.

Deurbanization is often taken to mean the total reversal of the forces operating in urban life. True, there would be a smaller population, fewer civic amenities, a diminished volume of trade, although not a total stoppage of transactions, and fewer industries; but this need not imply a total reversal of cultural values, and much less a sinking into illiteracy and complete backwardness. To deserve the term "Late Harappan" it is essential that the inhabitants of the deurbanized phase must have retained the core of Harappan achievements such as writing, use of the Harappan standard of weights and Harappan religious beliefs including the method of the disposal of the dead. A particular craft or industry might die or decline and there would be fewer material comforts, but certain old values would be retained. After the initial decline there would be a slow rate of growth or recovery which can be further accelerated. The stage of decline is identified as "Late Harappan" at Rangpur and Lothal. The stage of slow recovery is called the "Transition Phase." Accelerated change in the context of the Harappan Culture, resulting in a new culture, is designed the "Lustrous Red Ware Culture," in Gujarat. It was a failure to distinguish these stages at Rangpur that had led earlier excavators to confuse the Harappan Civilization with an evolved culture. That part of the Rangpur mound where the Mature Harappans lived for a long time was not uncovered prior to 1953. When excavated, four structural phases of the Mature Harappan Culture (Rangpur IIA), which is distinguishable from the degenerate and immediately succeeding phase (Rangpur IIB), came to light.

In summarizing the distinguishing features of the Late Harappan Culture of Rangpur (Period IIB) the following observations made in 1963 should hold good in other cases too.

> The fabric of the ceramic wares of Period IIB is found to be coarse. In some cases the surface of the vessels is not rendered smooth and the paintings are indifferent. But it must be noted that there is no major change in the forms of the vessels themselves except in the convex-sided bowl. Certain types of vessels such as the beaker and goblet which were scarce in the preceding period were almost completely discarded. Only a couple of sherds of each type are found in Period IIB levels. The small jar and basin become less popular, but the heavy rimmed jar, dish-on-stand and bowl continue to be in demand.

The bowl with straight sides and a thick rim also came into use in Period IIB. Besides the poorer fabric of the earthenware as a whole and the discarding of certain types of vessels, there are other indications of the decline in the prosperity of the Harappans. The utter scarcity of steatite ornaments, cylindrical carnelian beads, cubical (hexahedron) stone weights and chert flakes, all of which used to be imported in Period IIA, shows that the inhabitants could not do so in Period IIB. Owing to their adverse economic conditions the inhabitants could not build comfortable houses—not even the mud-bricks were used for building houses. No drains and baths were built. This decadent phase of the Harappa Culture lasting for about 200 years (revised date—1900-1700 B.C.) after the destruction of the first township of the Harappan settlers at Rangpur is represented by a deposit of more than 3 metres in RGP 2 and RGP 5 (Rao 1963: 15-16).

At Lothal two ^{14}C dates for the early and middle levels of Period B are available. The ^{14}C samples TF-19 and TF-23 from Structural Phase VA are dated 1865 ± 110 B.C. and 1800 ± 145 B.C. respectively, but none are available for the upper levels of VA and VB. The lower limit of Phase VA is fixed at 1700 B.C. and that of Phase VB at 1600 B.C. when further changes in ceramic forms and the decoration of the vessel surface by painting wavy lines, fronds and loops took place. Lothal Period B is equated to Rangpur IIB and IIC. Strictly speaking, the presence of a number of evolved pottery types should be distinguished as a subphase in Lothal B.

During the Late Harappan Phase at Lothal the continuity of Harappan traditions such as bathing (as indicated by jerry-built baths and drains), fire worship and burying the dead can be seen. The Harappan tools and ornaments (i.e., copper celts and bangles) continued to be in use, although in very limited numbers. The quality of ceramic production suffered, but most of the Harappan pot shapes survived. Even the Harappan standard of weight, in very limited use in the Mature Phase, continued to be used, although the cubical, hexahedron, was replaced. The technique of producing beads and blades did not change, but the locally available chalcedony was substituted for imported chert. The extended burials of Phase V at Lothal, and those of Daimabad, confirm that the Late Harappans continued to follow the Harappan practice in disposing of the dead. The decline in trade drastically reduced the utility of seals; but writing did continue.

WEIGHTS

Recent investigations into the weight standard of Late Harappan sites has thrown welcome light on the continuity of Harappan traditions. The hexahedron (cubical) chert weights of the Urban Phase run in the ratio $1:2:4:6:8:16:32:64$ etc. This Indus standard was used in almost all Harappan towns, including Lothal and Rangpur; but it was confined to the Mature Phase. There was, however, another type of weight, here called the "truncated spheroid." These were generally of agate, chert or dolerite in the Mature Harappan Phase at Lothal. This type continued to be used in the Late Harappan levels of Lothal, as well as Rangpur, but only in dolerite or sandstone.

It would be of interest to know whether the weight standard indicated by truncated spheroids of the Late Harappan Phase corresponds to the standard of hexahedrons in the Mature Harappan Phase. The smallest weight in one group of hexahedrons weighs 4.337 grams. The one next to it weighs 8.5733 grams, corresponding to the shekel (8.37 grams) in the Babylonian system, which was in vogue at Susa. The truncated spheroids of Lothal weigh 98.2 grams; 156 grams; 229.5 grams; 271.2 grams; 275.2 grams; 280 grams; and 300 grams. To find the standard underlying this series one has to turn to the hexahedrons weighing 8.5753 grams. Taking into account all the hexahedrons of the Late Harappan and Transition Phases, along with those of Rangpur, the following ratios are arrived at:

$$
\begin{aligned}
\text{Unit:} \quad 8.5753 \times 3/2 &= 12.8629 \text{ gm} = 12.767 \text{ gm} \quad \text{(RGP III)} \\
8.5753 \times 3 &= 25.7259 \text{ gm} = 26.611 \text{ gm} \quad \text{(RGP IIC)} \\
8.5753 \times 6 &= 50.4518 \text{ gm} = 48.766 \text{ gm} \quad \text{(RGP IIC)} \\
8.5753 \times 7 &= 60.0271 \text{ gm} = 58.126 \text{ gm} \quad \text{(RGP IIC)} \\
8.5753 \times 12 &= 102.9036 \text{ gm} = 98.2 \text{ gm} \quad \text{(Lothal B)} \\
8.5753 \times 18 &= 154.3554 \text{ gm} = 156.0 \text{ gm} \quad \text{(Lothal B)} \\
8.5753 \times 32 &= 274.4096 \text{ gm} = \frac{271.2 + 275.2}{2} \quad \text{(Lothal B)} \\
&= 273.2
\end{aligned}
$$

The ratio 1 : 3/2 : 3 : 6 : 12 : 18 : 32 is thus obtained. There is one example which is seven times the unit. It is thus evident that the truncated spheroid weights which were in use in the Mature Harappan Phase continued to be used in the deurbanized phase and later. Truncated spheroids found in other sites might not have been recognized as weights and not reported. It is worth examining all such stone objects from the point of view of ascertaining the weight standard of the Late Harappan Phase outside Gujarat.

RELIGION

Continuity of Harappan religious practices in the Late Harappan Phase is indicated by certain altars built in Lothal B, Rangpur IIC and Daimabad.

METALLURGY

One of the distinguishing features of the Mature Phase of the Harappan Civilization is the plentiful use of copper and bronze. Even in a small village like Allahdino copper was used in plenty. In the Late Harappan Phase copper became scarce; but the technology did not suffer. The tool types remained the same. A glance at some of the copper objects from Rangpur IIB, IIC and Lothal B gives a clue to the continuity of the Harappan tradition.

Rangpur IIB
1. Copper pin with a rolled head 96.6 percent copper; 0.8 percent nickel, 1.86 percent iron.

Rangpur IIC
1. Copper celt: 91.2 percent copper, 2.6 percent tin, 2.1 percent nickel
2. Bronze knife: 59 percent copper, 5.28 percent tin
3. Copper knife: 94.8 percent copper, 0.7 percent tin, 0.4 percent nickel
4. Bronze bangle: 86.4 percent copper, 11.07 percent tin, 1.8 percent nickel

Lothal B
1. Shaft balance: 88.27 percent copper, 0.19 percent nickel; no tin
2. Transverse axe: 94.33 percent copper, nickel traces; no tin
3. Axe with a short broad blade: 70 percent copper; no tin
4. Lunate shaped blade (not analyzed)
5. Awl with a round section (not analyzed)
6. Nail with a square section (not analyzed)
7. Hook with a round section (perhaps a fish hook) of which barb loop and shank are damaged (not analyzed)
8. Bangle with overlapping ends (not analyzed)
9. Ring: 63.58 percent copper, iron traces
10. Ring coiled in three spirals made from a flat strap
11. Figurine of a fowl (cock) with a prominent crown and a short pointed beak (not analyzed)

Lothal Period B yielded a total of 102 copper objects or its alloy. Most of them are too fragmentary to be identified as tools or ornaments. Of particular significance is a smithy of Period B situated at the northern end of the town, where a number of copper smiths worked under a single roof. Five brick-skirted pavements, each with a pot furnace associated with it, were built in the smithy for cooling the metal. Among new tools produced by the smith mention may be made of the shaft balance, transverse axe and awl. Flat celts of Harappan type continued to be produced by the Late Harappans at Lothal, Rangpur, Somnath and Rojdi. On the whole it can be said that metal technology did not suffer in quality, though the number of tools and ornaments produced declined steeply.

TRADE AND INDUSTRY IN THE LATE HARAPPAN PHASE

Two major industries, namely bead making which catered to the foreign market and metal working which catered to the domestic market, were organized on a fairly large scale in the last days of the Mature Harappan Phase. For example, several lapidaries lived and worked under a single roof in Phase IV (Lothal A). They seem to have depended on the merchant/manager for a supply of raw material and the marketing of the finished product. In Phase V (Lothal B) the coppersmiths depended on a middleman for the supply of metals and marketing of goods. The initiative which lay with the individual craftsman to sell goods was lost in the Late Harappan Phase, as long-distance trade declined.

Owing to deurbanization the craftsmen had to move to distant places where their skill was in demand or where raw material could be easily obtained. A wider dispersal of industries is thus the hallmark of the Late Harappan Period, in contrast to the concentration of several industries (e.g., ivory and shell working, bead making, seal cutting, copper working and blade making) at Lothal and Mohenjo-daro in earlier days. The shell workers moved to Amra and Lakhabawal at the northern tip of the Kathiawad peninsula and the copper workers moved towards the Debari mines near Ahar and perhaps to the Godavari Valley. The bead makers moved to Mehgam and Bhagatrav which are near agate beds, though some might have gone to Kayatha in Madhya Pradesh.

When the supply of fine grained chert needed for making long blades was stopped, the craftsmen used the chalcedony available in Kathiawad. The blades produced from this material were necessarily shorter in size; but the production technique remained the same as in the Mature Harappan Phase. It is only in Maski that one finds the use of long chert blades by the Chalcolithic folk who had contact with the Late Harappan craftsmen. It is not unlikely that some steatite bead makers moved in the Late Harappan Phase to Zekda in North Gujarat and as far south as the Ramavaram in Kurnool district. The wafer steatite beads of Harappan origin are found in large numbers here. The copper deposits of Tintini and Koppal in Raichur District of Karnataka appear to have been worked during the Late Harappan Phase (Rao 1978a; 1978b). Harappan chert blades and steatite beads occur at the nearby Chalcolithic site at Maski.

With the cessation of long-distance trade, seals served no real purpose. A few continued to be in use for a very short time at Lothal in Period B. Two specimens found at Daimabad seem to be curios only; but writing did continue.

CERAMIC INDUSTRY

As far as the ceramic industry is concerned the Red Ware of the Late Phase is of inferior fabric with an indifferently painted surface. The painting consists of elementary forms like horizontal bands, wavy lines, etc. But two Late Harappan sites deserve special mention. Venivadar (Vaniavadar) in Amreli District of Saurashtra was a small village producing a great deal of painted pottery in the coarser ware. Atkot in Central Saurashtra was a larger settlement of the last days of Mature Harappan Culture which continued to produce painted pottery in the Late Harappan and Transition Phases; but the painting was executed on a very limited surface of the vessels. A few Harappan motifs such as fish and bird did survive.

The contention that the Late Harappan Culture hardly touched Kutch (Soundara Rajan in press) is not correct. Six Late Harappan sites have been identified so far in Kutch. Quite a few are in the interior.

In the Sutlej Valley, out of 81 Harappan sites, only four or five belong to the Mature Harappan and the rest to the Late Harappan; but it is necessary to distinguish a subphase of evolved Harappan ceramic forms within the Late Harappan Phase. Harappan settlements at Manda and Ropar (Rupar) continued to survive into Late Harappan times also. Neither the Cemetery H Ware nor the Bara Ware is found at Manda, but both are said to occur at Bhagwanpura. There is, however, no substantial Late Harappan ceramic ware at all there. Owing to the disturbed condition of the site the so-called overlap of the Late Harappan Ware and Painted Gray Ware is not beyond doubt. A fresh excavation is, therefore, essential to confirm an overlap.

In Haryana the position is slightly different. Suraj Bhan (in press) has used the term "Late Harappan" for a culture complex resulting from the synthesis of Harappan and Late Siswal, since the evolved ceramic types of both the cultures occur together.

The Late Harappan Culture of Gujarat denotes the dominance of Harappan elements minus the urban discipline, architecture and sophistication in decorating earthenwares; but more than 75 per cent of the ceramic types in these sites is Harappan. The fabric is, however, poor. At Lothal, Rangpur and Rojdi, Micaceous Red Ware types occur in small quantities in the Late Harappan context. On the contrary, in a majority of the sites designated as "Late Harappan" in Haryana, the Siswal element is dominant and the Late Harappan Ware is meager. Hence it is desirable to distinguish those sites in which elements of other cultures (e.g., Mitathal IIB) are dominant and the Late Harappan element is much less, from sites in which the Late Harappan ceramic ware is dominant. The latter may be designated "Late Harappan" and the former as those "having Late Harappan contact." The reason for much of the Harappan tradition disappearing early in the Sutlej Valley and upper Yamuna may be that the Late Harappans encountered a strong non-Harappan folk in the Siswal culture; unlike Gujarat where their immediate ancestors had lived for a long time. The indigenous folk in Gujarat had themselves taken much that was Harappan.

The rate of degeneration and subsequent resurgence varied from region to region. In the relatively isolated regions like Saurashtra and Kutch, the Late Harappans retained the Harappan tradition for long; but in Haryana and Punjab they had to compromise with the Siswal tradition, and as they moved further east and north, they retained hardly anything that could be called Harappan or Late Harappan, as seen at Bahadarabad, Bhagwanpura, to name two places.

CONCLUSION

In the final analysis one finds that the administrative machinery and civic amenities of the Mature Harappan were lost, but some architectural features like building drains and platforms survived in the Late Harappan Phase. Highly organized trade suffered heavily; but the more important trade mechanism, namely weights, did survive. Although seals had a short life the more essential feature of an enlightened society, that is writing, not only survived but was also improved upon. Metallurgy suffered in quantity, but not in quality. Figurines were cast as before and a better tool type, such as the shaft hole axe, was added to the tool kit. Harappan social customs and religious beliefs also survived. The dead were buried as before and altars for fire worship were constructed. As the "Śiva-Mahadeva concept" and "Linga worship" are only imaginary (Dales in press) they do not find any place in the Late Harappan Phase. The worship of the Mother Goddess, which was limited to the Indus Valley even during the Urban Phase, ceased to be of any significance in the Late Harappan Phase everywhere. As far as ornaments were concerned, steatite beads were replaced by faience beads and terracotta bangles by shell bangles; but the love of personal ornaments did not diminish in the Late Harappan Phase. Precious metal was not, however, available in adequate quantity.

Finally, it must be admitted that the decline was not uniform in different regions. If the Late Harappan sites in Rajasthan, Haryana, Punjab, Jammu and Kashmir and Western Uttar Pradesh are classified on the lines of the Subperiods IIB-IIC of Rangpur it would be easier to follow the diffusionary process of the Late Harappan Culture. The duration of the Late Harappan Phase in Kutch, Rajasthan, Haryana, Punjab, Jammu and Kashmir was shorter than in Saurashtra and North Gujarat. In the northern and northwestern zones there is a mixture with other indigenous cultures, such as the Siswal or Gray Ware (Plain), which were more virile than those in Saurashtra. This accounts for the Late Harappans losing their identity sooner in the north than in the south.

NOTE

[1] In assessing the Lothal population at 10,000 Dilip K. Chakrabarti has not taken into account the full habitation area of 1100 by 1000 feet, nor the per house population at five (Chakrabarti 1979: 210).

BIBLIOGRAPHY

Chakrabarti, D.K., 1979
    Size of Harappan Settlements. In *Essays in Indian Protohistory*. D.P. Agrawal and D.K. Chakrabarti, eds. Pp. 205-15. Delhi: B.R. Publishing Corp.

Dales, George F., in press
    Mohenjodaro: Some new data and interpretations.

Datta, J.M., 1962
    Demographic Notes on Harappan Skeletons. In *Human Skeletal Remains from Harappa* P. Gupta, P.C. Datta and A. Basu. Anthropological Survey of India Memoir 9. Pp. 6-12. Calcutta.

Rao, S.R., 1963
    Excavations at Rangpur and Other Explorations in Gujarat. *Ancient India* 18-19: 5-207.

Rao, S.R., 1973
    Lothal and the Indus Civilization. Bombay: Asia Publishers.

Rao, S.R., 1978a
    Bronzes from the Indus Valley. *Illustrated London News* March: 62-63.

Rao, S.R., 1978b
    Late Harappan Daimabad. *Illustrated London News* April: 74-75.

Soundara Rajan, K.V., in press
    Kutch Harappan. In *Indus Civilization: Problems and issues*. B.B. Lal and S.C. Malik eds. Simla: Indian Institute of Advanced Study.

Suraj Bhan, in press
    The Protohistoric Settlement Pattern in Haryana. In *Indus Civilization: Problems and issues*. B.B. Lal and S.C. Malik, eds. Simla: Indian Institute of Advanced Study.

M.K. DHAVALIKAR

35. Daimabad Bronzes

THE discovery of the Daimabad bronzes (Pls. 35.1 to 35.5) though momentous has caused considerable controversy among archaeologists. They were the subject of heated debate during the seminar on the "Indus Civilization: Problems and Issues," organized by the Indian Institute of Advanced Study, Simla, November 1977. M.N. Deshpande then Director General of the Archaeological Survey of India, referred to these objects in his inaugural address and S.A. Sali, the excavator of Daimabad, also discussed them in the course of the deliberations of the seminar (Sali in press). S.R. Rao, who preceded Sali at the renewed Daimabad excavations, has also published his views (Rao 1978). All these authorities are of the view that the bronzes belong to the Late Harappan times, but this opinion appears to be based on the circumstantial evidence. At the Simla seminar this dating was questioned. Some scholars feel that the bronzes are tribal in origin, and as such may be as late as the 18th century A.D. Recently, D.P. Agrawal and his team have analyzed the elemental composition of the bronzes using atomic absorption spectrophotometry and have concluded that "We would not be surprised if these images turned out to be of the historical period" (Agrawal, Krishnamurthy and Kusumgar 1978: 45). His argument is based on the negative evidence that "no arsenical alloying has been reported from the Chalcolithic Cultures so far, but these Daimabad bronzes show greater than 1 percent arsenic.... It may also be pointed out that the Chalcolithic Cultures are very poor in copper and such massive figures appear completely out of place in the Chalcolithic context" (Agrawal, Krishnamurthy and Kusumgar 1978: 45). The exquisite hoard is thus hanging in a sort of chronological vacuum between the 18th century B.C. and the 18th century A.D. I therefore propose to examine the stylistic and technological aspects of the bronzes, as well as investigate their probable function, in order to establish their antiquity and authorship.

Before beginning the discussion of the authorship and the antiquity of bronzes some note of the objects in the hoard and the circumstances of their discovery is called for. The bronzes were found at Daimabad (District Ahmednagar, Maharashtra), an extensive Chalcolithic site located on the left bank of Pravara River, a tributary to the Godavari. The site was first excavated on a small scale in 1959 by M.N. Deshpande (Indian Archaeology: A review 1958-59; Dhavalikar 1969-70) and has been worked on a large scale since 1974 by S.A. Sali (Sali in press). It is a purely Chalcolithic site which, as the recent excavations show, was first occupied about 2000 B.C. and was finally deserted by 1000 B.C. after which it was never reoccupied.

The hoard consists of four bronzes: an exquisite chariot pulled by a pair of bulls, an elephant, a rhinoceros and a buffalo. They are all in an excellent state of preservation and have not lost their pristine features.

CHARIOT AND BULLS (Pls. 35.1 and 35.2)

The chariot and bulls are the most remarkable pieces in the hoard. Its total length is 45 centimeters and the width is 16 centimeters. The complete bronze consists of an elaborate chariot yoked to two bulls and driven by a man standing within it. Two solid wheels rest

---

*Editor's note: See S. A. Sali's paper in this volume for a review of Daimabad.

over the light body of the chariot. The wheels have a projecting hub on the inner side in which the axle is fixed so that it moves along with the wheels. This is an extremely interesting feature which will be discussed later.

The vehicle, because of its light construction, looks more like a Roman *biga* than a cart and justifies its classification as a chariot. It has a front guard composed of two vertical curved bars with out-turned upper ends, whereas the lower ends are attached to a horizontal bar which, in its turn, has two ring loops for the axle. The guard also has two horizontal bars fixed to it. Of these, the upper one is straight while the lower one is angular. The guard is further strengthened by two oblique bars, the upper ends of which are attached to the top of the vertical bars with the lower ends joined. They are soldered together in a dog on the central pole, just in front of the guard.

The platform on which the guard rises is a truncated oval, on either side of which is a bird which merges with the chariot body. The two birds do, however, face in opposite directions. They are related to Harappan terracotta bird whistles.

The man driving the chariot is 16 centimeters high and stands on the platform. His left hand rests over the upper horizontal bar of the guard while the right hand holds a long stick curved at its upper end. The man is portrayed realistically. His physiognomy indicates that he is probably a Proto-Australoid (Pl. 35.2). To a great extent he resembles stylistically the terracotta head of a man from Kalibangan which, according to B.B. Lal, resembles the head of the famous limestone priest from Mohenjodaro (Lal 1979: 89, Pl. XXIV). He has a broad, snubbed nose with wide nostrils. His lower lip is thick and protruding. The curly hair, indicated by incised lines, is parted in the middle and is gathered at the back in an elongated roll. His body is neither muscular nor proportionate. The chest and the belly are somewhat elongated and the hips appear rather steatopygous. This latter feature is a physical trait which is also noticed on the man painted on a Malwa jar from Daimabad (Indian Archaeology: A review 1958-59: Fig. 8) (Fig. 35.1). The chariot rider does not appear to be wearing a lower garment but a vertical projection on the abdomen, resembling a hooded cobra, may be some part of the clothing. This projection is broken at the lower end and is difficult to identify with certainty.

The chariot has an inordinately long (32 centimeters) central pole which rises in a curve from the

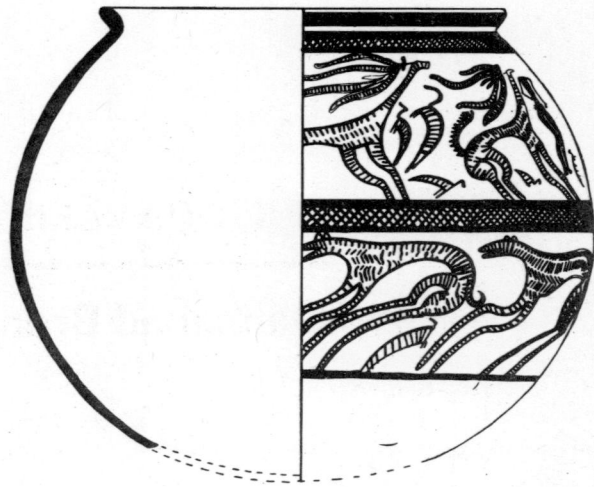

Fig. 35.1. Malwa Ware jar from Daimabad.

bottom of the chariot. The pole has curved vertical bars near its far end in which the necks of the bulls are accommodated. The bulls are not fixed to the yoking pole but can be removed. It may be noted that modern carts in Sind also have an inordinately long pole, but high bent poles seem to be a peculiarity of Sumerian chariots (Mackay 1929; 28, Figs. 1 and 2).

The pair of bulls yoked to the chariot are extremely interesting with regard to the modeling of their hind parts which gives them the appearance of a horse rather than a bull. In fact their tails cannot by any stretch of imagination be likened to those of bulls. They look distinctly more horse-like, as do their mouths. This bull-horse combination of the body is strikingly similar to that of the "unicorn" which is so commonly depicted on Indus seals. It is equally noteworthy that a "unicorn" with two horns has been found on a seal from Kalibangan (Lal 1979: 91). The Daimabad bulls stand together on two separate metal strips, one for the front and the other for the hind legs. Their humps are quite massive. But another remarkable feature of these bulls is the prominence of their projecting horns. This is also a feature which is characteristic of the terracotta bulls from Chanhudaro and apparently they are also seen on animals in Sind today (Mackay 1943: 164, Pl. LVIII, 1, 1a). Such bulls, however, are not represented in the Chalcolithic art of the Deccan.

The chariot has many Harappan features. It should be made clear, however, that such an elaborate vehicle has so far not been reported from any

Harappan site. There are a few toy cart models of copper (Piggott 1970). But they too share some elements with the Daimabad chariot. The copper carts all have projecting ring loops through which the axle is passed. The most noteworthy feature of the axle is that it is fixed to the wheels so that it moves along with them: the same feature is also a part of the modern chariot. The toy carts, presumably of bronze, from Chanhudaro were apparently built the same way. "The wheels are now immovable, but they must originally have revolved in two axle-brackets cast in one with the frame" (Mackay 1943: 164). This feature may have facilitated the dismantling of the vehicle since the chasis could just be lifted off the axle much as they do today in Sind (Mackay 1929: 26-28). It is pertinent to quote Childe in this connection: "Sumerian and other early vehicles were probably just as easily taken to pieces, and this point must be remembered in considering the possibility of using them for long distance transport" (Childe 1951: 183). This would be possible because of the manner in which the axle was fixed to the wheels. One is told that this mechanism actually marks an early stage in the evolution of wheeled vehicles (Singer et al., 1956: 72). And what is more, even the village carts of modern Sind "preserve the main outline of the ancient Harappan vehicles, the wheels turn in one piece with the axle as do those of many other recent carts with solid wheels" (Mackay 1929). The joined wheel and axle is thus a distinguishing feature of Harappan vehicles and same is to be seen in the Daimabad chariot.

ELEPHANT (Pl. 35.3)

The elephant is the largest of the three animals in the hoard. The beast stands on a platform 27 centimeters long and 14 centimeters broad. There are four ring loops which once held the wheels, all of which are unfortunately missing. The total height, including the platform, is 25 centimeters. The large trunk is curved at the lower tip but the tusks appear to be broken or not completely indicated. A short tail is almost hidden in the rump. This animal recalls another bronze elephant from the southeast Deccan (Barret 1958) which is dated to about the third century A.D. Barret's specimen is a female, standing, or rather running, on a platform with raised edges and ring loops for wheels (all of which are missing). There is a small bell tied around its body.

There is some superficial resemblance between Barret's pachyderm and the Daimabad specimen. Technologically, however, they are far removed from one another. The former was hollow cast. The Daimabad elephant is solid. There are sufficient stylistic and technological differences between these two specimens which show that the Daimabad elephant cannot be dated to the early historical period.

RHINOCEROS (Pl. 35.4)

The rhino stands not on a platform as in the case with the elephant, but on two horizontal bars over two sets of wheels; the bars are bent at both the ends with the axle passing through them. The wheels, which are solid with a projecting hub on the inside, are fixed to the axle and move along with it. The rhino is 25 centimeters long and 19 centimeters high with a distance of 13 centimeters between the two sets of wheels. Skin folds on the animal's body are rather stylistically depicted with those on the back and the belly forming a sort of rectangle. This resembles the treatment on some of the Indus rhino seals (Marshall 1931: III, Pl. CXV, No. 342-46). Short ears are pointed upwards. The mouth is too long and resembles the snout of a bear. A short horn on the tip of the snout is also indicated. Rhinos probably inhabited the northern Deccan in prehistoric times and the beast has been tentatively identified at Inamgaon (Classon 1977: 255).

The presence of the rhinoceros in the hoard is extremely important because the animal was never portrayed in Indian art save the Harappan,[1] and they delineated the beast with considerable sympathy. Thus its presence in the Daimabad hoard points to its Indus origin. The Daimabad example can also be favorably compared with a terracotta specimen from Lothal (Rao 1978: 62).

WATER BUFFALO (Pl. 35.5)

The buffalo also is modeled in a naturalistic manner. Its height, including that of the wheels, is 31 centimeters and the length is 25 centimeters. It resembles a bison somewhat, but on close observation it is clearly a water buffalo with characteristic transverse ribbing on its horns. The animal stands on a platform similar to that of the elephant, but the corner near the right foreleg is broken. The axles attach to the platform through vertical bars which are provided with holes. The front wheels are smaller (eight centimeters in diameter) than those on the rear (10 centimeters).

DISCUSSION

The bronzes described above are no doubt the handiwork of an extremely skilled sculptor. They are in fact the finest of their kind in the whole range of Indian prehistoric art. But they were not recovered from sealed deposits in a controlled dig. This fact, in addition to the excellence of the workmanship, has caused doubts to be expressed regarding their age.

The four pieces were actually found by some Bhils who were digging on the site for a large tree root they had cut for firewood. When the bronzes came to light they were reported to the police authorities since they came from an ancient site protected by the Archaeological Survey of India. The press learned of it the next day and we lost no time in visiting the spot since we were closely associated with the earlier excavation at the site. The pit dug by the Bhils in which the objects were found was located. The tree they had cut was not very large so the pit was correspondingly small: about a meter in diameter and a meter deep. We scraped the section and the bottom of this pit to ascertain whether a later pit had been cut into the earlier layers. If traces of a later pit had been present it would then definitely have proved that the bronzes were interred after the Chalcolithic occupation at the site. We did not, however, come across evidence for a later pit. On the contrary, there were regular horizontal layers undisturbed by any later activity. This has now been confirmed by the recent excavations by S.A. Sali (in press) who has encountered a distinct cultural strata, about a meter thick, with Late Harappan material. Stratigraphically, therefore, the bronzes have to be ascribed to the Late Harappan Period—Phase II of Sali—which can be dated to the first quarter of the second millennium B.C. This is also confirmed by S.R. Rao (1978: 62) who states: "I examined the place where they (the bronzes) were found and after sinking an exploratory trench at the site, confirmed on the basis of stratigraphic and ceramic evidence that the bronzes belonged to the Late Harappan (circa 1800-1600 B.C.) phase." Stuart Piggot has also suggested a Late Harappan date for the bronze toy carts from Harappan sites. He is of the opinion that "they are (not) stratified in meaningful terms and we are free in fact to assign them either to the Indus Civilization...or to some later period within the second millennium B.C." (Piggott 1970: 202).

The next problem to be examined relates to the authorship of the bronzes. Agrawal, Krishnamurthy and Kusumgar (1978: 45) have questioned their antiquity on the basis of the presence of arsenic, which according to them, is absent in artifacts from Chalcolithic sites in the Deccan. It should also be noted that the Deccan has no known copper ore deposits and the poor Chalcolithic farmers could not have afforded the luxury of these bronzes. But now that it is seen that they can be assigned to the Late Harappan Period at the site, the possibility that they were imported into the Deccan should be discussed. In this connection it must be pointed out that of all the Indus centers, the bronze artifacts from Harappa have a considerable proportion of arsenic. It has been observed that "The hardness of most of the copper objects found at Harappa has been shown on analysis to be due to a high arsenic content. The presence of this arsenic is believed to be accidental, being indigenous to the copper deposits from which the ores were extracted rather than secondarily introduced" (Coghlan 1951: 44-56). Lamberg-Karlovsky (1967: 151) therefore rightly argues that "We must not disregard the possibility, however, that the smiths recognized the advantages of an ore with arsenic in it for producing a harder, less brittle tool." In the light of evidence from Harappan artifacts, one is of the opinion that the Daimabad bronzes may originally have been Harappan, that is, from Harappa proper, and that they were probably imported into the Deccan.

Arsenical alloying is also significant in the Copper Hoard from the Ganges-Yamuna *Doab* (Agrawal, Krishnamurthy and Kusumgar in press). But there was no contact between them and the Chalcolithic Cultures of the Deccan. The present hoard, therefore, cannot be attributed to the Copper Hoard Culture. Incidentally it may be mentioned that copper was plentifully available to the Harappans if judged by the quantity of copper artifacts from Indus sites. And if the identification of Meluhha with the Indus empire is accepted, they were even exporting copper to West Asia (Rao 1968).

Now, a few words on the function of the bronzes. All the objects in the hoard are too big and heavy to play with and therefore cannot be classed as toys as is the case with the bronze elephant from the southern Deccan (Barret 1958). Second, copper was an extremely scarce commodity in the Deccan. The bronzes may then have been created on the order of the ruling chief/priest of Daimabad. It is also possible that the entire community contributed towards the

Daimabad Bronzes

cost. This is especially likely if the bronzes were required for community religious purposes. Recall that all the bronzes were provided with wheels; although those on the elephant were lost. Thus it is not unlikely that they were meant to be used in procession, possibly as seen on a seal from Mohenjodaro with four animals (an elephant, a rhino, a tiger and one unidentified animal) in a file facing right (Marshall 1931: II, 365; III, Pl. CXVI, 14 & CXVIII, 10). Again from Mohenjodaro comes a seal amulet on one side of which is an animal in the center, a *gharial* according to Marshall, on either side of which is a bull. Below the central animal is an elephant on the left and a tiger on the right (Mackay 1938: Vol. I, 357; Vol. II XCI, 13, 19a; XC, 2a, 10). It is thus clear that these animals (viz. the elephant, rhino, bull, buffalo, tiger, etc.) played an important role in the religious life of the Harappans. The same tradition, in some form or other, seems to have continued to some extent in the succeeding Chalcolithic cultures of the Deccan. A Malwa Ware jar, again from Daimabad, is profusely painted with a jungle scene in two horizontal registers (Fig. 35.1). The upper one shows a muscular human male figure with two deer approaching, as if enchanted, and peacocks in between. The lower register has three tigers springing away in the opposite direction. The human figure is solid while the bodies of the animals are hatched. These scenes have a narrative quality, and one feels that the animals are paying obeisance to their Lord (Indian Archaeology: A review 1958-59: Fig. 8). Similar animals are depicted on a Malwa Ware vase fragment from Prakash (Thapar 1967: Fig. 12; and Fig. 35.2).

It is tempting to identify the person in the chariot as *Paśupati*, "The Lord of Beasts," for the simple reason that all the animals, save the tiger, which appear on the famous *Paśupati* seal from Mohenjodaro, are present in the Daimabad hoard. Marshall's identification of *Paśupati* on the seal was based on comparisons with medieval representations of Śiva

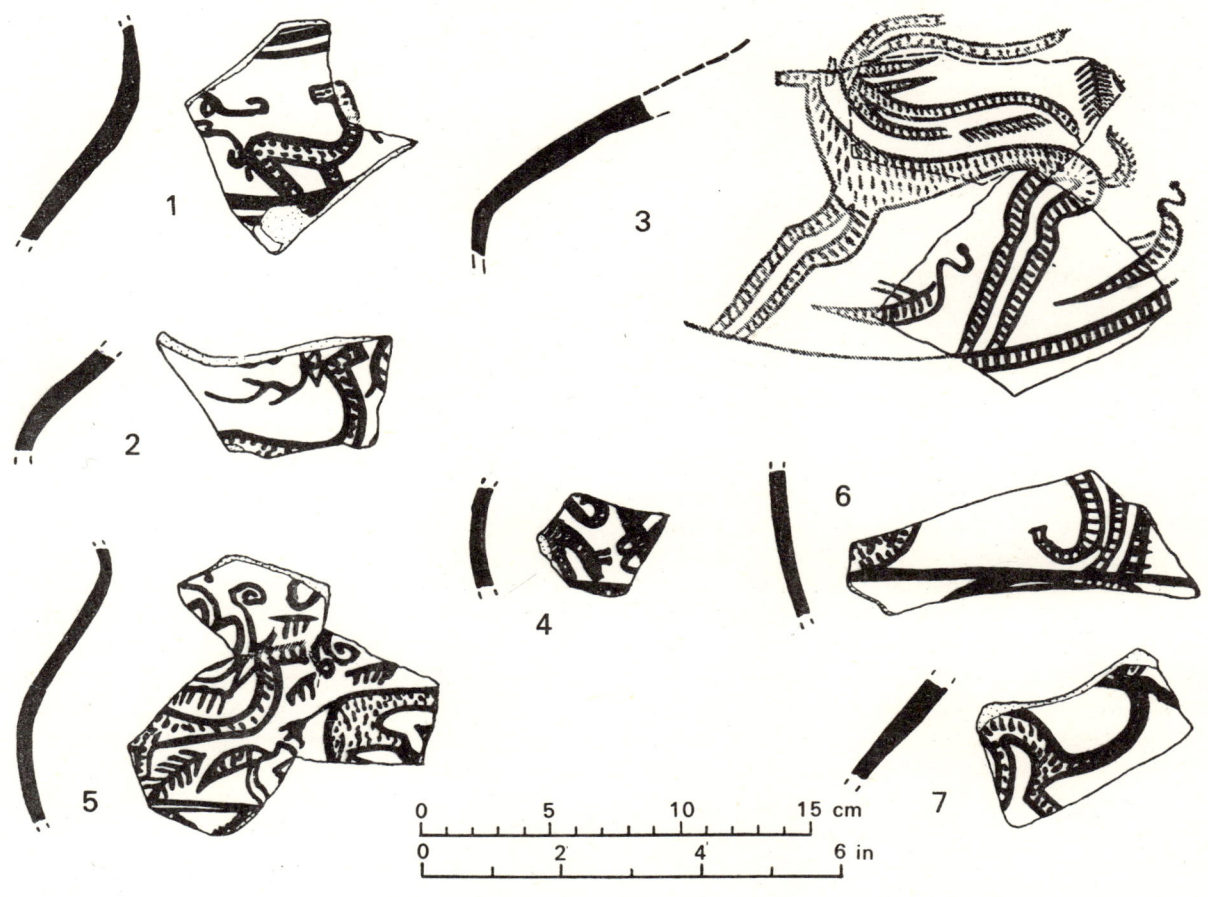

Fig. 35.2. Malwa Ware jar from Prakash.

(Marshall 1931: I, 52-56; Pl. VII, 4). Presently, however, one is not concerned with the identification and the iconography of the figure. One can only conclude that the evidence discussed in the foregoing pages amply demonstrates that in all probability the bronzes in the hoard belong to the Late Harappan period at Daimabad, and that they were probably imported from Harappa, or some smith from Harappa made them locally.

NOTE

[1] The rhinoceros is depicted on the coins of Chandragupta II (A.D. 380-415) where it signifies the conquest of eastern India.

BIBLIOGRAPHY

Agrawal, D.P., R.V. Krishnamurthy and S. Kusumgar, 1978
    New Data on the Copper Hoards and the Daimabad Bronzes. *Man and Environment* 2: 41-46.

Agrawal, D.P., R.V. Krishnamurthy and S. Kusumgar, in press
    Arsenical Coppers in the Bronze Age. To appear in the M.N. Deshpande Felicitation Volume.

Barret, Douglas, 1958
    An Early Indian Toy. *Oriental Art* 4 (N.S.): 118-19.

Childe, V. Gordon, 1951
    First Wagons and Carts—From the Tigris to the Severn. *Proceedings of the Prehistoric Society*. 17 (N.S.): 177-94.

Classon, A.T., 1977
    Wild and Domestic Animals in Prehistoric and Early Historic India. *The Eastern Anthropologist* 30: 241-89.

Coghlan, H.H., 1951
    Notes on the Prehistoric Metallurgy of Copper and Bronze in the Old World. *Occasional Papers on Technology* 4. Pitt-Rivers Museum, Oxford.

Dhavalikar, M.D., 1969-70
    Daimabad: A rediscovery. *Puratattva* 3: 34-43.

Indian Archaeology: A review (IAR), 1958-59
    Excavation at Daimabad, District Ahmednagar. Pp. 15-18. Delhi: Archaeological Survey of India.

Lal, B.B., 1979
    Kalibangan and Indus Civilization. In *Essays in Indian Protohistory*. D.P. Agrawal and Dilip K. Chakrabarti, eds. Pp. 65-97. Delhi: B.R. Publishing Corp.

Lamberg-Karlovsky, C.C., 1967
    Archaeology and Metallurgical Technology in Prehistoric Afghanistan, India and Pakistan. *American Anthropologist* 69: 145-62.

Mackay, E.J.H., 1929
    Note on a bas-relief found at Ur. *The Antiquaries Journal* 9: 26-29.

Mackay, E.J.H., 1938
    Further Excavations at Mohenjodaro. 2 vols. Delhi: Government of India.

Mackay, E.J.H., 1943
    Chanhudaro Excavations, 1935-36. American Oriental Series 20. New Haven: American Oriental Society.

Marshall, Sir John, editor, 1931
    Mohenjodaro and the Indus Civilization. 3 vols. London: Arthur Probsthain.

Piggott, Stuart, 1970
    Copper Vehicle Models in the Indus Civilization. *Journal of the Royal Asiatic Society*: 200-202.

Rao, S.R., 1968
    Contacts between Lothal and Susa. *26th International Congress of Orientalists, New Delhi*. Vol. 2: 10-11.

Rao, S.R., 1978
    Bronzes from the Indus Valley. *Illustrated London News* March: 62-63.

Sali, S.A., in press
    Harappan contacts in the Deccan. In *Indus Civilization: Problems and issues*. B.B. Lal and S.C. Malik, eds. Simla: Indian Institute of Advanced Study.

Singer, Charles, *et al.*, 1956
    A History of Technology. Vol. 2. Oxford: Clarendon Press.

Thapar, B.K., 1967
    Prakash—1955: A Chalcolithic site in the Tapti Valley. *Ancient India* 20-21: 5-167.

ROBERT SHARER

36. Did the Maya Collapse? A New World Perspective on the Demise of the Harappan Civilization

"Once this whole area teemed with life. Mayans, with an ancient culture far advanced for their times, had lived here, died here, and when they were unable to cope with the steady approach of the jungle, they left—before they starved to death. They had no equipment strong enough to fight the advance of the jungle so that most of them finally had to give up."

Dorothy Daniels

THIS paper considers a question of general interest to most archaeologists and prehistorians, the nature of the demise of complex, preindustrial societies. It does so from the perspective afforded by a single example from the New World, that of the collapse of the Classic Maya Civilization. Over the years a number of theories have been proposed to account for this collapse, recognized from the archaeological record by the abandonment of the largest and most sophisticated Maya centers in the lowland rainforests of Guatemala, Belize and Mexico. It must be borne in mind that, unlike the demise of civilizations known from the historical record, the Maya, like Harappan society, represents an example of collapse identified solely from archaeological evidence. While historical records of the Maya Civilization are being recognized as the result of recent advances in the decipherment of hieroglyphic texts, these sources thus far are mute as to the events surrounding the collapse. Events of this kind, therefore, pose a problem in which explanations for the demise of civilization must be sought from the available archaeological record, aided by analogies drawn from appropriate documented cases in the historical, ethnohistorical and ethnographic record.

With these thoughts in mind, it is hoped that an inquiry into the theories advanced to account for the collapse of Classic Maya Civilization may provide a useful perspective for scholars concerned with similar issues arising from the investigation of Harappan Civilization.

CULTURE HISTORICAL BACKGROUND

Maya Civilization developed in an extremely differentiated environment, within an area defined by the extent of known archaeological sites and the present (or ethnohistoric) distribution of Maya-speaking peoples. This corresponds to southeastern Mexico, including the entire Yucatan peninsula, Guatemala, Belize and the western portions of Honduras and El Salvador. This area has been described as comprising two basic ecological zones, the highlands to the south and the lowlands to the north. According to this view, the highland zone was characterized as ecologically diverse and rich in a variety of resources, while the lowlands were viewed as ecologically uniform and poor in resources. Based upon these purported environmental contrasts, a distinction was often made between the cultural developments in these zones; that is, between highland and lowland Maya Civilization. Because the lowlands were viewed as a less advantageous zone, the ancient lowland Maya were seen as an enigma, an exception to the rule that brilliant civilizations could not develop in marginal tropical environments (Meggers 1954). Alternatively, the same environmental assumptions have been used more recently to "explain" the rise of lowland civilization by positing the development of organizational complexity as a consequence of the need to maintain long distance trade networks that supplied the "deficient" lowlands with imported necessities (Rathje 1971).

Recent ecological studies have overthrown the notions implicit in the simple highland-lowland environmental contrast. It is now recognized, for example, that the Maya lowlands are not deficient in resources, and that instead of being ecologically uniform, they are characterized by a considerable diversity in soil types, vegetation, hydrology and climate. As a result, recent ecological and archaeological research demonstrate that both the environment of the Maya area, and the cultural developments it fostered, are too varied to be subsumed under a simple highland-lowland dichotomy.

An obvious, but often ignored, geographical fact is that the ancient Maya as a whole occupied an extremely strategic position, both because of their wealth of resources (jade, chert, obsidian and cacao being among the most prized commodities) and because of their location between the heavily populated urban states of Central Mexico to the northwest and Central America to the southeast (Fig. 36.1). The Maya Civilization reached its zenith during the Classic Period (ca. A.D. 250-900) in the central and southern lowlands. The Maya Classic is traditionally defined by the appearance of hieroglyphic texts carved on stone monuments, wooden lintels or other artifacts, as well as painted on pottery and occasionally preserved on wall frescos, along with the advent of polychrome decorated pottery, and certain architectural traits such as the use of corbelled masonry vaults. However, it is recognized that many of these characteristics, along with the more significant development of complex social, economic and political organizations, arose in the Maya area during the pre-

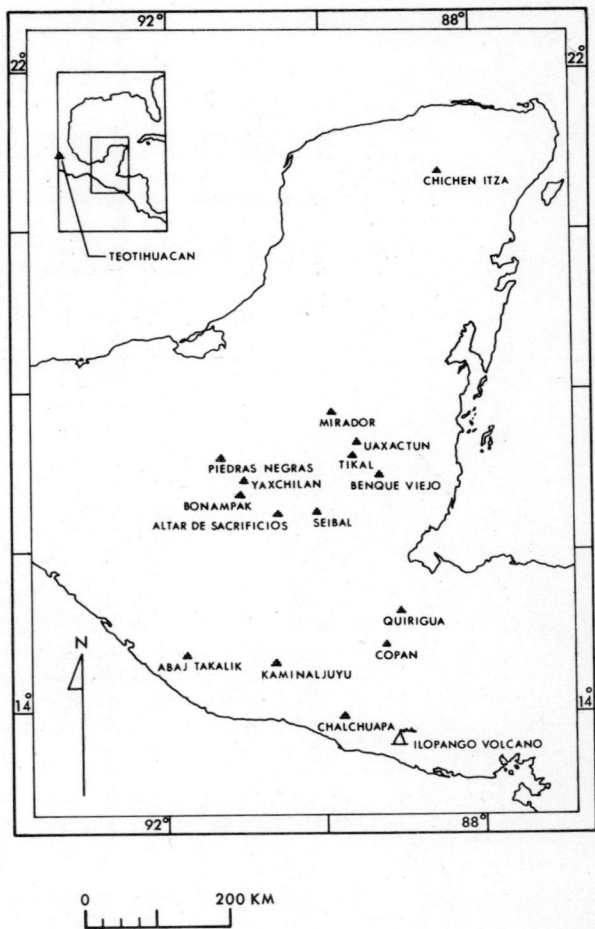

Fig. 36.1. Archaeological sites mentioned in the text.

ceding Preclassic Era (ca. 2000 B.C.-A.D. 250). While occupation in the Maya lowlands is believed to begin at least by ca. 2000 B.C. (Hammond et al. 1979), it is likely that the direct antecedents to the Classic Maya Civilization lie to the south, in the Highlands and the adjacent Pacific coastal region.

THE RISE AND FALL OF THE SOUTHERN MAYA

The Pacific plain provided the earliest and most direct trade routes between Central Mexico and Central America. This coastal area was also one of the prime regions of Precolumbian cacao cultivation. The adjacent highlands provided both jade and obsidian, as well as other valuable commodities such as hematite, volcanic grinding stones and quetzal feathers (prized for use in elite headdresses). The Olmec of the Mexican Gulf coast appear to have been the first power in Mesoamerica to control these resources and the Pacific coastal route during the Middle Preclassic Period (ca. 1200-400 B.C.).

After the decline of the Olmec, a series of centers along the coastal plain, many probably founded by the Olmec, seem to have gained control over local resources, such as cacao production, and at least portions of the coastal trade route. The earliest examples of Maya hieroglyphic texts and Maya sculptural style are found at several of these sites, such as Abaj Takalik (Graham 1976), and Chalchuapa (Sharer 1974, 1978). In addition, the primary southern Maya highland site of Kaminaljuyu, located near both jade and obsidian sources, also rose to prominence during this period (Shook and Kidder 1952). Archaeological investigations at these southern sites indicate rapid growth in population and the development of stratified, theocratic organizations, including evidence of ceremonial structures and ritual activities recognized as typically Maya. In other words, these coastal and highland centers represent the first florescene of the Maya Civilization several centuries before the beginning of the Lowland Classic Period.

The precocious development of the southern Maya fell into a sudden decline at the end of the Preclassic Period. This setback seems due to two related causes, the first being a major volcanic event, the eruption of Ilopango in Central El Salvador (Sheets 1971) that cut agricultural production, depopulated a wide area and severed the coastal trade connections between Mexico and Central America (Sharer 1974, 1975). The timing of this disaster (third century A.D.) and its consequences, including the rendering of a vast area within a 100 kilometer radius of Ilopango uninhabitable because of massive ash falls, for up to 200 years, has been documented by Sheets (1976, 1979) and his colleagues. Depopulation due to death and migration of survivors was immediate. Investigators have long noted an apparent population decline at some southern sites (Parsons 1969: 27) and even abandonment of others (Shook and Proskouriakoff 1956) during this period. While the bulk of the Pacific coastal agricultural region appears to have escaped heavy damage, ashfalls probably reduced soil fertility and production. It has been proposed that disastrous flooding from torrential rainfalls spawned by Ilopango's ash cloud affected much of the Maya area, and that even light ashfalls could have reduced food resources such as the aquatic life harvested from rivers and coastal areas (Dahlin 1979). Dahlin (1979) has hypothesized that it was the refugees from Ilopango who introduced cacao production and an era of prosperity into new areas, most notably the Maya lowlands. The coastal trade network on the other hand, certainly could not be maintained without the population that sustained it. The subsequent loss of trade connections through the area produced a final economic disaster for the southern Maya.

The second factor in the decline of this region followed closely on the heels of the first: the colonization by Teotihuacan and the consequent loss of independence for the southern Maya. Teotihuacan was the first true urban state in Mesoamerica, and rose to power in Central Mexico during the last few centuries of the Preclassic Period. Perhaps taking advantage of the disruption and chaos in the wake of the Ilopango eruption, Teotihuacan appears to have seized control of the south coast. Eventually, as the area's population and cacao production recovered, Teotihuacan established a colonial capital at Kaminaljuyu in an attempt to monopolize the acquisition and distribution of jade and obsidian throughout Mesoamerica.

As the southern Maya lost their control over cacao production and the trade routes, several centers located to the north in the central lowlands began an era of prosperity and growth that endured throughout the Classic Period.

THE RISE OF THE LOWLAND MAYA

The best known and seemingly dominant center of the Maya Classic was Tikal, extensively investigated from 1956 to 1970 (Coe 1967). Many other lowland sites are known, and a dozen or so have been subjected to detailed archaeological study, including Uaxactun (Ricketson and Ricketson 1937; Smith 1950), Altar de Sacrificios (Willey 1973), Seibal (Willey 1978), Lubaantun (Hammond 1975), Quirigua (Sharer 1978; Ashmore 1979) and Copan (Willey and Leventhal 1979; Baudez 1979). Most of the sites known from the central lowlands were founded by the Middle Preclassic Era (ca. 1200-400 B.C.), although several from peripheral areas appear to have been established as colonies as late as the Early Classic Period (ca. A.D. 250-600).

For the most part these lowland centers served a variety of functions. During the Preclassic Period these certainly included ritual events, agricultural production, as well as the manufacture and trade of products from local resources such as chert, wood, clay and animal pelts. The larger lowland centers appear to have included ceremonial structures and the residences and administrative headquarters for an emerging theocratic ruling elite, as well as the workshops, storerooms, markets and homes for the non-elite classes. The growth of long distance trade certainly played a role in the development of the lowland Maya society. For example, sites located along major river systems such as Altar de Sacrificios and Seibal, were intermediaries in trade between the highlands and the Gulf Coast. Tikal, however, is not located on a river; instead it is centered between the headwaters of the river systems that drain both to the east (Caribbean) and to the west (Gulf of Mexico). It was, therefore, along the route across the base of the Yucatan peninsula and in a prime position to monitor and control the portage of goods transported by canoe over both river systems (Jones 1977a). For this reason Tikal appears to have become a dominant economic power. However, the yet-to-be excavated site of Mirador, situated in a similar position to the northwest of Tikal, promises to have been a rival power, at least during the critical Preclassic-Classic transitional period.

The trans-lowland routes would have been of only minor importance as a long distance trade connection between Mexico and Central America as long as the more direct southcoast route prospered. However, with the breakdown in the latter route due to Ilopango, the best alternative connection would be to the north, bypassing the difficult highlands, and utilizing the already developed canoe transport system of the lowlands. It is postulated that Tikal was in the best position to profit from the expansion of the trans-lowland route, and thus its rapid rise to dominance may have been due in no small measure to its strategic economic and geographic position (Sharer 1975).

Present understanding of the lowland Maya sees a society of evolving complexity that was quite different in many respects in its final form (Late Classic) from that of the Preclassic or even the Early Classic. The present view relies heavily upon the Tikal evidence, the most comprehensive lowland data base. In fact, it appears that the socio-cultural development of Tikal was accelerated, compared to other lowland sites, by the Early Classic. Tikal's precocious size, importance and vigor clearly indicates that it held a dominant position in the southern Maya lowlands (Willey 1974: 426), and it seems to have eclipsed other centers that had enjoyed prominent positions during the Late Postclassic such as Mirador, or the smaller site of Cerros (Freidel 1979). Tikal's dominant position probably stems from a central position that allowed it to control trade across the base of the Yucatan peninsula, and offered a natural defense against attack. By Early Classic times Tikal's natural defenses were strengthened by earthworks (Puleston and Callender 1967).

The Tikal ruling elite seem to have achieved hereditary status before other centers in the lowlands, recording dynastic succession at that site by the Early Classic (Coggins 1975) or possibly before (Haviland 1967, 1977). The elite of Tikal, perhaps in the role of merchant princes, amassed considerable power and wealth by controlling the internal overland and river trade routes, monopolizing raw-material acquisition and distribution of goods within the lowlands. Early Classic Tikal and its lowland domain were incorporated into a much larger Mesoamerican economic network managed ultimately by Teotihuacan (Ball 1974). Tikal's role was probably that of the major lowland transhipment center (Rathje 1973: 441) principally for highland obsidian (Sanders 1973: 353) and lowland resources destined for manufacturing centers via both the Gulf Coast and the Teotihuacan-controlled center of Kaminaljuyu in the highlands. Political alliance with Teotihuacan appears likely, and Tikal's elite may have legitimatized their power and authority in both practical and supernatural terms. Coggins (1975) has proposed that the Early Classic ruler known as "Stormy Sky" was the child of a marriage between families representing the indigenous ruling lineage of Tikal (his mother) and an elite lineage from Kaminaljuyu (his father, a member of the Teotihuacan-derived "Sky" dynasty). As ruler, "Stormy Sky" brought the aggressive mercantile orientation of Teotihuacan into power at Tikal, founding a new dynasty made legitimate by his descent, via his mother, from the traditional ruling lineage (Coggins 1979).

Outside of Tikal, the Maya lowland society in the Early Classic seems to have been less stratified, characterized by considerable social mobility (Rathje 1970, 1973). In other lowland centers, individuals appear to have achieved elite status by amassing power and wealth through successfully controlling the access and distribution of lowland resources (Rathje 1973: 416-17). However, these local merchant-elites were probably economically dependent upon the Tikal rulers, because of Tikal's role as the central redistribution center for lowland resources. Furthermore, it now appears that Tikal may have sponsored the founding of colonial centers in peripheral regions of the lowlands in order to gain control of resources as well as to monopolize trade routes that passed through these areas. A case in point appears to be Quirigua, located in the southeastern periphery and within the rich Motagua valley, commanding a position, along with Copan, to control trade between the lowlands and Central America (Sharer 1979).

The mid-Classic decline and eventual destruction of Teotihuacan resulted in the collapse of its long-distance trade network. These events must have been a profound setback for the elite of Tikal, and for the entire lowland economic system. This disruption appears to have produced a perceptible lag in the archaeological record known as the lowland hiatus (Willey 1974). It has been suggested (Coggins 1979) that the hiatus at Tikal was marked by a struggle and, perhaps, a compromise sharing of power, between the traditional ruling lineage and the mercantile "Sky" dynasty founded by "Stormy Sky." Regardless, although the power of Teotihuacan was gone, its efficient political and economic management was not forgotten by the Maya. The new order that emerged in the lowlands in the wake of Teotihuacan was probably modeled in some ways after the Mexican state system. However, Late Classic lowland society was less centralized, with numerous elite centers, free from the control of both Teotihuacan and Tikal, vying for domination (Willey 1974: 426). It is likely that this renewed system was forged by a few aggressive leaders in various elite centers. Jones (1977b) has identified the first dominant ruler of Late Classic Tikal ("Ruler A"), and this individual probably both led the rebirth of that center and reasserted the power of the Early Classic "Sky" dynasty symbolizing his supernatural and lineage ties to the dynasty founder, "Stormy Sky" (Coggins 1975, 1979).

Tikal, representing the traditional lowland dynastic power (Haviland 1967, 1977) appears to have played a key role in the development of ruling lineages at other lowland sites. The dynasties at these other sites probably derived and periodically reinforced their legitimacy by intermarriage with the ancient Tikal ruling families (Molloy and Rathje 1974). Dynastic intermarriage between various elite families seems also to have been a common means of establishing political alliances (Molloy and Rathje 1974). The "Jaguar" lineage at Yaxchilan, especially its most aggressive ruling member, "Bird Jaguar," exemplifies this process (Proskouriakoff 1963, 1964). At Quirigua the ruling dynasty may have come from Tikal, using the same name ("Sky") and symbols of authority such as the so-called manikin scepter, that Coggins (1979) sees at Tikal as deriving from the mercantile heritage of Teotihuacan.

In the economic sphere, it appears that the lowland centers gained control of the local trade networks, with Maya elite managers reaping the wealth and power that were formerly siphoned-off to Teotihuacan. Instead of being a resource area and market for Teotihuacan, the lowland Maya developed their own economic organization. Tikal may have used marriage alliances with the newly emerging lowland powers in order to re-open and control the old long-distance trade routes extending through the Maya area (Jones 1977b). Once re-established, external trade provided an important source of the material wealth that characterizes Late Classic Maya society. Internally, Tikal and the other lowland centers increased their potential for manufacturing as regional networks supplied raw materials, and a variety of craft specialists produced goods for the internal market. For example, about one-third of the pottery used by the average Tikal household in Late Classic times was elaborately decorated polychrome, the product of specialized local manufacture (Culbert 1974: 52-53). Distribution, in turn, was handled by an expanding group of specialized merchants (Adams 1970). This is exemplified at Tikal by the large Late Classic constructions (Structures 5E-32 through 36), identified as the central market complex (Coe 1967). Significantly, as population increased throughout the lowlands, the distrubution of food probably became increasingly dependent upon the same trade and exchange mechanisms.

To summarize, Late Classic Maya society can be viewed as a series of independent secondary state systems (Webb 1964) each modeled after Teotihuacan. Throughout the lowlands absolute power was vested in dynastic rulers assisted by hereditary elites. Late Classic lowland society became politically fragmented and culturally diversified as competing dynasties maneuvered to secure or increase their power and wealth (see Willey 1974: 426). This trend is reflected in the diversity of Late Classic material culture, especially pottery (Willey, Culbert and Adams

1967). At the same time, the alliances between ruling families are reflected in the uniformity of elite-related culture such as regalia, writing and calendrical systems, and so forth. Overall, society tended to be more rigid; social mobility was reduced as status, at least for the elite class, came to be based more on birth than ability (Rathje 1970). Most significantly, the emergence of a state system was accompanied by expansive growth among the lowland Maya. State control over the economy and labor allocations resulted in more efficient production and distribution of food, as well as other goods and services. And until the environment became exploited to its limits, increases in food supplies and efficiency of distribution allowed further population rise throughout the lowlands. The larger populations then required more structured managerial control, and both the size and complexity of society began an upward growth spiral.

THE MAYA COLLAPSE

It was this rich and complex Maya lowland society that suffered a seemingly dramatic demise at the close of the Classic Period. Over a relatively short period of time, roughly corresponding to the ninth century (A.D. 790 to 889, or 9.18.0.0.0 to 10.3.0.0.0 in the Maya calendar) the archaeological record indicates a slowdown and even a cessation in activities over most of the central lowlands, an area of some 150,000 square kilometers (Adams 1973). At most sites in this area the construction of administrative, residential and ceremonial structures declined. No further dynastic monuments were erected, hieroglyphic texts and calendrical dates were no longer recorded. The manufacture and distribution of traditional luxury and ritual goods made of pottery, jade, wood, bone and shell ended. From this kind of evidence, it can be inferred that the failure of the lowland Maya involved primarily the ruling elite, the class that sponsored and directed the majority of the activities that disappear from the archaeological record. Furthermore, the spatial pattern of the cessation of these activities indicates that the failure was more complete in the central lowlands than it was towards the peripheries to the north (Yucatan) and east. Occupation is continuous in these regions, albeit on a presumably less complex scale. But, in the case of Yucatan the population appears to increase. In fact, even in the great central lowland sites such as Tikal, the archaeological record reflects a continuity of occupation, in ever diminishing numbers, for several centuries after the end of the old elite-associated activity (Coe 1968: 175). At some point several hundred years before the arrival of the Spanish, all of the central lowlands was abandoned to the rainforest, except for small settlements around the lakes of the central Peten.

It should be noted that Maya Civilization does not terminate with the end of the Classic Period. However, developments from the ninth century until the Spanish Conquest in the sixteenth century, corresponding to the Postclassic Period, are devoid of many characteristics that define Classic Maya lowland culture, especially in those traits that distinguish the elite segment of society. Furthermore, Postclassic Maya society is centered in two distinct regions, the northern half of the Yucatan peninsula and the southern highlands of Guatemala.

The question as to what caused this demise appeared as soon as many of the great centers of the Classic Maya were rediscovered in the lowland rainforests during the 18th and 19th centuries (Stephens 1841, 1843). The early answers to this question all stressed sudden catastrophe, an obvious conclusion given the dramatic contrast between the empty and silent jungle-covered ruins and what was recognized as once being a populous and highly developed civilization. To the European mind, a great civilization set in the depths of an inhospitable rainforest seemed like a contradiction in terms. Thus it seemed only logical to assume that the Maya would fail due to the hardships of their environment. That they succeeded so brilliantly for a time was viewed, often even unto this day, as something of a "mystery." To early scholars, however, the question of why the Mayans failed was often not as important as the question of origins; where did they come from? And, of course, this question was initially answered by recourse to migrations from a host of known civilizations in the Old World (Willey and Sabloff 1974: 21-40).

With the general acceptance of the idea that the Maya represented an indigenous New World development, attention turned to the reasons for the mysterious abandonment of the lowland cities. Since the turn of the century dozens of theories have been advanced, and two general trends can be discerned. In the first place, there has been a shift away from theories that propose a single cause, towards theories that advance multiple factors as responsible for the Maya demise. Secondly, there has been a shift away from sudden and dramatic catastrophes, towards more subtle, longer-acting processes. Both of these trends reach a culmination in the results of a symposium held in 1970 to consider the collapse question and to re-evaluate the problem in light of the rapidly accumulating new evidence about Maya Civilization resulting from an unprecedented amount of archaeological research available at that time (Adams 1969).

The results of this conference have been published (Culbert 1973) and provide the most comprehensive treatment of the subject to date. Significantly, one conclusion from the conference was the realization that a better understanding of the Maya demise could only be achieved by a better understanding of the cultural processes operating in ancient Maya Civilization (Culbert 1974: 113). Given the additional progress made in the knowledge of the ancient Maya since the collapse conference was held, it is obvious that one should be in a better position to understand the Maya demise today than one was only ten years ago. In other words, as traditional concepts of the ancient Maya are modified or replaced by new information, understanding of the collapse will be altered, and any evaluation of the Maya collapse issue must be considered with this perspective in mind. For example, results of research completed during the last twenty years have challenged and overthrown traditional concepts about ancient Maya social and political organization (Becker 1979). The view of Maya sites as "ceremonial centers" and the "priest-peasant" organizational model (Thompson 1954, 1966) have been replaced by far more complex reconstructions of ancient Maya society. The belief that swidden agriculture provided the subsistence base (Morley 1946) has been the latest casualty of more thorough, problem-oriented research. Although a fundamental change in concepts of ancient Maya subsistence was on the verge of being recognized at the time of the collapse conference, the full realization that the lowland Maya relied upon a complex intensive agricultural system has come about *since* the conference (Harrison and Turner 1978).

Old ideas die hard, in this case one reason being that Maya archaeology (like the archaeology of many complex societies) has long been dominated by "the pyramid syndrome." Investigations have traditionally been directed towards the largest sites and, within sites, the most elaborate or impressive buildings. As a result, knowledge of Maya society is heavily biased towards the elite segment that occupied palaces, temples and tombs. One reason why the remains of intensive agriculture in the Maya lowlands were unrecognized until recently was simply because few scholars bothered to investigate the fields and terraces of the ancient farmer.

While it is obvious that a more balanced sampling of archaeological data should produce a better picture of all aspects of ancient Maya society, excavation and funding priorities have tended to preserve this traditional research bias even to the present day. Until recently the only exception to the traditional approach was Willey's 1954 investigation of rural Maya settlement in the Belize River Valley (Willey *et al.*, 1965). Future work, including more studies based upon probabilistic sampling strategies and regional rather than site-oriented research problems, should produce a more representative picture of ancient Maya society. If this be true, it can be expected that the present assessment of the Maya collapse question will need to be modified in only a few years time.

THEORIES CONCERNED WITH THE DEMISE OF THE MAYA

Following Sabloff (1973), it is convenient to consider the theories of the Maya collapse according to those that stress internal factors and those that stress external factors. The former category includes theories that view the Maya collapse as generally isolated from developments occurring in the wider context of Mesoamerica. The latter category includes theories that propose that the collapse was *due to* developments originating outside the immediate Maya area.

Internal Theories

Most of the earliest attempts to explain the end of Maya Civilization were in this category, but several recent proposals have also emphasized internal factors involved in the collapse. The most useful internal theories can be considered according to three themes: natural catastrophes, ecological disaster and sociopolitical disintegration (Sabloff 1973).

Several kinds of natural catastrophes have been advanced as possibly triggering the demise of Maya Civilization. The hypothesis concerning the role vulcanism played in causing the decline of Preclassic society in the southern Maya area has already been mentioned (Sharer 1969, 1974; Sheets 1971, 1979). While most of the Maya lowlands are not geologically active, earthquakes do occur. The southern fringes of the lowlands are especially vulnerable to tectonic activity. Based upon the evidence of unrepaired structural damage to a major palace at the site of Xunantunich (Benque Viejo) in the central lowlands, MacKie (1961) proposed that one or more catastrophic earthquakes may have contributed to the downfall and abandonment of lowland sites.

While earthquake damage at Xunantunich remains possible, recent excavations at Quirigua leave no doubt that major earthquakes plagued the Maya inhabitants of the southeastern Maya lowlands. Quirigua was built directly on the Motagua fault, the same one that ruptured in 1976, causing a disastrous earthquake in Guatemala and clearly revealing the fault trace. At Quirigua evidence of ancient damaged and collapsed construction as well as massive secondary buttressing of masonry buildings, testifies to ancient tectonic activity (Sharer and Bevan, in press).

While earthquakes may have affected specific areas including Quirigua and perhaps Xunantunich, there is no evidence and little likelihood that tectonic catastrophes could have devastated the entire Maya lowlands.

Other natural disasters have been proposed as culprits for the Maya downfall. The Maya lowlands are frequently visited by Caribbean hurricanes. A major storm of this kind could easily destroy agricultural production over a wide area. However, as in the case with earthquakes, it is difficult to accept that the relatively localized destructive effects of hurricanes could trigger the failure of the entire Maya Civilization. Furthermore, as several scholars have suggested the destruction of forests in a hurricane's path may have benefited the lowland Maya by clearing new lands for agricultural exploitation.

Epidemic diseases could have produced catastrophic depopulation of the Maya lowlands. Shimkin (1973) provides a good summary of the recent evidence bearing upon this possible cause. Among the first to mention this factor, Spinden (1928: 148) proposed yellow fever epidemics as a possibility. The disastrous effects of epidemic disease among New World populations is tragically documented by the consequences of the introduction of Old World diseases such as malaria and smallpox after the Spanish Conquest. Yellow fever is also usually considered an Old World disease, but its discovery among New World primates (especially howler monkeys) indicates that it may also be indigenous to Central and South America (Shimkin 1973: 283). Recently, Adams and Smith (1977) have suggested that the historically documented Black Plague that ravaged late Medieval Europe provides a possible analog for the Classic Maya, especially for the social consequences of its sudden and severe depopulation. That the ancient Maya were vulnerable to epidemic disease is indicated by skeletal studies from both Tikal (Haviland 1967) and Altar de Sacrificios (Saul 1973). Both cases demonstrate progressive nutritional deficiencies and increasing disease potentials in lowland populations towards the end of the Classic Period.

A variety of proposals involving ecological disaster have been advanced to explain the Maya demise. The earliest of these were concerned with harmful consequences derived from swidden agriculture, once believed to have been the basis of lowland subsistence. The assumed destructive effects on soil fertility caused by swiddening were used by Cook (1921) to explain the failure of the Maya Civilization. Morley (1946: 71-72) proposed that swidden agriculture gradually converted forested areas into savanna grasslands. Since the Maya had no tools to cultivate the grasslands, they were eventually forced to abandon the central lowlands. Another effect of swidden cultivation in combination with the heavy tropical rainfall, according to Cooke (1931), was severe erosion and deposition of soil into what were formerly shallow lakes, but are now the swampy depressions (*bajos*) found in many areas of the lowlands. Yet a study of one lowland *bajo* (Cowgill and Hutchinson 1963) fails to indicate that these depressions were shallow lakes, at least within the span of the Maya Civilization.

Perhaps the first to explicitly propose that the Maya collapsed because of their failure to successfully adapt to the lowland environment was Meggers (1954), although her thesis is flawed by grossly underestimating the subsistence potential of the Maya lowlands. Subsequent examinations of subsistence capabilities, assuming swidden cultivation, have resulted in the same verdict, that is, over-exploitation of the environment would lead to agricultural failure and this produced the Classic Maya collapse (Sanders 1962, 1963). More recently, Sanders (1973) proposed that the Maya began to intensify their agricultural base to meet growing population pressures, but the means used, grassland swiddening, proved to be ecologically disastrous.

Obviously the ecological disaster theories based upon swidden cultivation can no longer be supported given recent evidence of diversified and intensive agriculture practiced by the ancient Maya (Harrison and Turner 1978). However, over forty years ago, Ricketson and Ricketson (1937: 12) rejected the idea that the ancient Maya relied upon swiddening, and proposed that intensive agriculture would have been required to support peak populations in the lowlands. The recognition and acceptance of ancient Maya intensive agriculture does not rule out ecological disaster as a cause for the collapse. Harrison (1977) has re-introduced the *bajo* hypothesis, proposing that these features were indeed shallow lakes and could have supported intensive cultivation using a raised field (*chinampa*) system. The failure to properly manage this system, according to Harrison, resulted in the silting of the *bajos*, although more recently (Turner and Harrison 1978: 370-71) it has been suggested that environmental or climatic changes could have altered the *bajos* to produce their present condition. Most Maya scholars now agree that the documented intensification of Maya agriculture was a response to increasing population and ecological pressures. From this, it follows that the collapse may have been due, at least in part, to Maya populations overwhelming the environmental limits of the lowlands (Culbert 1974: 115-17; Sharer 1977: 544-48). Although no longer based upon the false premise of swidden and an underestimation of the lowland potential, this conclusion nonetheless strongly echoes the original ecological failure thesis of Meggers (1954).

The socio-political disintegration theories are all based, either implicitly or explicitly, upon postulated weaknesses inherent in Classic Maya society. That is, they assume that the prestige and authority of the ruling elite was destroyed, often via violent confrontations, and as a result, classic society fell apart and the lowland centers were abandoned. Over forty years ago Satterthwaite (1937: 20) had raised the possibility of revolt against the rulers, based upon the evidence of broken thrones at Piedras Negras. Later research uncovered smashed or mutilated monuments at Tikal that were cautiously taken as the result of acts of violence (Satterthwaite 1958). More recent interpretations of the Tikal evidence indicate that monument mutilation was a custom practiced throughout the Classic Period, and thus need not indicate revolution (Coe 1962: 484-97).

But the revolt idea became extremely popular. A.V. Kidder (in Smith 1950) proposed that the increasing size of the ruling class, combined with their abuses of power, led to a revolution. The best known advocate of the revolution theory was Sir Eric Thompson (1954, 1966). As Becker (1979) has pointed out however, the idea, together with the complementary two-class ("priest-peasant") model of Maya society, was associated with Thompson's popular writings and seldom appeared in his scholarly publications. Nonetheless, Thompson's "peasant revolt" theory received wide acknowledgement and even acceptance among Maya scholars (Brainerd, *revision of* Morley 1956; Altschuler 1958; Culbert 1973). The thesis holds that a combination of factors, including agricultural difficulties, malnutrition or disease, and perhaps even natural disasters, culminated in widespread disillusionment as the Maya peasant class lost confidence in their rulers. The situation was made worse by an increasing disassociation from the everyday concerns of the populace by the elite, as theocratic rulers turned increasingly to esoteric matters instead of the practical solutions for a mounting crisis. The inevitable result was a violent revolt by the peasants who then destroyed the ruling class.

An economic variation on this theme has been proposed by Rathje (1971, 1973). In this view, the elite-controlled trade network of the central lowlands (the "core area") was eventually cut off from access to critical commodities by the rise of trading centers on the peripheries (the "buffer zone"). As a result, the core area collapsed, followed thereafter by the buffer zone, which was left with no trading customers. Yet, the archaeological evidence indicates that many sites located in the buffer zone collapsed long before those in the core area, quite the opposite of what one would expect from this theory.

While based upon external conditions, a theory advanced by Webb (1964, 1973) postulates that the failure of the Maya elite to adapt their society to a changing economic and political environment, specifically, competition from rival Mexican states, led to the collapse of the lowland Maya. The conclusions of the Maya collapse symposium also point to specific failures by the ruling elite that led to the demise of their civilization, for "the Maya of the Late Classic period apparently made no technological or social adaptive innovations which might have mitigated these difficulties" (Willey and Shimkin 1973: 491). Yet others have indicated that several changes seen in the archaeological record during the Late Classic might be interpreted as attempts by the ruling elite to adapt to crisis conditions (Culbert 1977: 526-28;

Sharer 1977: 544-48).

The Maya concept of cyclical history is of relevance to the collapse issue, especially their emphasis upon fatalistic prophecies associated with the Katun cycle (an approximately 256-year span composed of 13 Katuns, each a 7,200-day time period). Each Katun in the cycle was numbered and had a distinctive set of prophecies; the Maya believed that the reoccurrence of a particular numbered Katun every 256 years brought with it the recurrence of the corresponding events and conditions from the past. Elite invocation of this cyclical concept of history at Late Classic Tikal and deliberate public association of individual rulers with Katuns linked with earlier periods of prosperity have been proposed by Coggins (1975) and Jones (1977b). This in turn has led to the hypothesis that the Late Classic Maya rulers at Tikal were leaders of a cultural revitalization process (Ashmore and Sharer 1975), and that these processes culminated in unsuccessful revitalization at the time of the collapse (Sharer 1977: 548-49).

Recently, Puleston (1979) advocated that the Maya concept of cyclical history contributed actively to the collapse. Prophecies of fundamental political and religious change associated with specific Katuns are known from the ethnohistoric record. For example, the Spanish Conquest of the last bastion of Maya independence at the site of Tayasal in 1697 was probably hastened by the approach of a new Katun cycle that augured momentous changes. Noting that the earliest signs of trouble in the Maya lowlands begin with the onset of a new Katun cycle in A.D. 790, Puleston points out that the beginning of the previous cycle (A.D. 534) corresponds with the so-called Middle Classic hiatus (Willey 1974), a time of depressed activity in the lowlands. Counting back an additional Katun cycle brings one to A.D. 278, a time eerily close to the eruption of Ilopango and the demise of the southern Maya's prosperity. The conclusion drawn from these regularities is that as the Late Classic Katun cycle approached its end, the fatalistic Maya failed to resist the forces of change that were sweeping the old order away because of prophecies that foretold fundamental changes in their society.

The final internal theory considered here calls for accelerating civil warfare as a contributing factor leading to socio-political disintegration and collapse (Cowgill 1979). This thesis sees attempts to conquer and consolidate the lowland area by one or more of the major centers in a situation analogous to the Peloponnesian wars that debilitated Greece in the fifth century B.C. Evidence for warfare among the Classic Maya exists, as in the battle and judgment scenes on the Bonampak murals (Ruppert, Thompson and Proskouriakoff 1955), and in the captive motifs frequently found in Maya sculpture. The inscriptions at the site of Quirigua frequently mention the "capture" of the ruler of Copan, a larger and presumably rival center located some 50 kilometers to the south (Proskouriakoff 1973: 168; Marcus 1976: 135). This event, apparently occurring in A.D. 737, corresponds to archaeological evidence that heralds the beginning of an era of independent prosperity for Quirigua (Jones 1977c; Sharer 1978), while possibly contributing to a decline at Copan. However, most scholars interpret evidence of this kind as depicting small-scale raiding or even ritualized conflict between centers, the result of increasing competition for land, labor, trade routes and other economic resources. It is more difficult to find support for the idea of wars of conquest on a scale sufficient to bring ruin upon the lowland Maya. Of course, mutilated sculpture, the same evidence used to support the idea of a popular revolution, could also be interpreted as the consequence of warfare.

External Theories

Explanations for the demise of the Maya that call for external causes have gained increased favor in recent years. Sabloff (1973: 37) notes that this might be due to a reaction against the isolationism inherent in the internal theories, or to the recent renewal of cultural evolutionary theory that has refocused attention on wider areas of cultural development (Erasmus 1968). Regardless of the reasons, it is obvious that the question of the Maya downfall must be viewed in the context of larger issues throughout Mesoamerica.

Foreign invasion of the Maya lowlands has been proposed by several scholars. Cowgill (1964) hypothesized that militaristic Mexican invaders conquered the lowlands and forcibly resettled the survivors in northern Yucatan, nearer the "Toltec" capital of Chichen Itza. Adams (1973) has reviewed the evidence from Altar de Sacrificios, provided primarily by a rather complete shift in the pottery inventory, and concludes that the site was invaded and conquered at the close of the Classic Period. A similar event has been advanced by Sabloff and Willey (1967) at the site of Seibal, but is based upon changes seen in the architectural and sculptural records as well as pottery. From this there would seem to be little doubt that Seibal was not only conquered but occupied by a new ruling group at the end of the Classic. The homeland for these invaders remains in doubt, but stylistic evidence and the portraits of individual rulers on the post-conquest monuments of Seibal suggest that they were foreigners sharing at least some cultural traditions with the lowland Maya. Thompson (1970) suggested that they were the Putun Maya, an ethnohistorically identified Gulf Coast group peripheral to the Classic Maya Civilization that rose to power as sea traders in the Postclassic Period. Adams (1973) rejects Thompson's Putun Maya identification, although he sees the takeover of Altar de Sacrificios as originating from the Gulf Coast. However, Adams (1973) sees the Seibal occupation as occurring slightly earlier in time by a group originating from the north (Yucatan) that is ultimately swept away by the same Gulf Coast group that later invades Altar de Sacrificios. Apart from these disagreements, all proponents of the foreign invasion thesis propose that the resultant disruptions in lowland Maya society were sufficient to bring about its demise. However, the lack of evidence for invasion or conflict at centers other than Seibal and Altar de Sacrificios, casts doubt on the cause and effect relationship between invasion and collapse. It can be argued that rather than being a cause for the collapse, the invasion was more of an effect, an event made possible by the already weakened condition of Maya society (Culbert 1974: 111). At Tikal, for instance, Culbert (1973) sees no indication of invasion or any disruption originating outside the Maya area.

The last theory to be treated involves the economic relationships between the lowland Maya and other peoples of Mesoamerica. Webb (1973) has traced the changes in Mesoamerican long-distance trade networks that mark the Classic/Postclassic transition, and concludes that the Maya became isolated from the reoriented economic and political powers that came to dominate the Postclassic. Thompson (1970) advanced a more specific scenario for this period, involving the rise of a new mercantile group, the Putun Maya, who monopolized sea coast trade routes that emerged at the end of the Classic Period. Sabloff and Rathje (1975), using data from their investigation of a Postclassic port-of-trade, on Cozumel Island, related these events to the failure of the traditional lowland elite to adapt to the new sea trade routes around the Yucatan peninsula, and thus they became economically cut off as the old land routes became obsolete. A specific case for the rise and fall of Tikal has been made by Jones (1977a), based upon that site's position controlling the trans-lowland canoe routes. When these routes diminish in importance, the site of Tikal falls on hard times and is eventually abandoned. Culbert's (1974: 108) reconstruction of terminal occupation at Tikal as being "so impoverished that it became almost a parody of what had been" suggests the consequences of a failure in the economic system. Willey (1974) proposes a variation on this theme that is of special significance since it provides an opportunity to test ideas about the collapse against data from the Middle Classic hiatus. He hypothesizes that the long recognized pause in building and monumental activity that occurs between the Early and Late Classic (ca. A.D. 530-600) represents a "little collapse," or a pre-enactment of events due to the same causes that ultimately led to the complete collapse some 300 years later. Willey postulates that the cause of both events was severance of the symbiotic economic relationships between the lowland Maya and other Mesoamerican civilizations. In the Early Classic the dominant relationship was with Teotihuacan. Willey, following Blanton's (1972) model for the Valley of Mexico, suggests that economic control of the lowlands in the Early Classic was centralized under the domain of Tikal, the principal lowland intermediary for long-distance trade with Teotihuacan. The termination of this interaction after Teotihuacan's destruction was the cause of the hiatus in the Maya lowlands. After the disruption of the hiatus, a reorganized Late Classic society became engaged in more diverse external economic relationships, that, following Webb's hypothesis, ultimately were bypassed and superseded by adjacent societies, spawning a lowland collapse. The question remains, why did the Maya recover from one breakdown in their external economic networks but fail to recover from a similar situation later on? The answer appears to be that by the end of the Classic Period the long distance trade routes were firmly under the control of new mercantile powers based on sea commerce.

Summary

One may summarize the Maya collapse theories according to a model based upon the conclusions of the Maya collapse symposium with additions based upon data made available since 1970:

1) The complexity and growth of Classic lowland Maya society were stimulated by interaction with Teotihuacan, especially at Tikal (Coggins 1975, 1979). Withdrawal of Teotihuacan power from the lowlands precipitated the hiatus (Willey 1974), but also provided the opportunity for independent

development and competition between the Maya centers of the Late Classic. Tikal, for instance, undergoes a revitalization under its Ruler A and his successors (Jones 1977b; Ashmore and Sharer 1975).

2) The lowland elite promoted common training, beliefs, symbols of prestige and authority among themselves, reinforced by increasingly elaborate ceremonialism, to foster cooperation in controlling trade and warfare, and to promote the expansion of their power. These factors also served to increase the social distance between the elite and the various non-elite classes. Fatalistic beliefs in prophecies of change coinciding with the Katun cycle may have contributed to the elite's loss of morale and eventual downfall (Puleston 1979).

3) Continued population growth resulted in increasing pressures upon an already complex and vulnerable subsistence system, as the incidence of malnutrition and disease expanded and productivity decreased. Certain elite responses to the crises, such as accelerated construction of ceremonial structures, may have exacerbated the situation by placing heavier labor demands upon the populace, thus increasing the problems of adequate food production.

4) The traditional long distance trade networks (overland and via river canoe) diminished in importance with the advent of seacoast trade around the Yucatan peninsula. Failure of the established elite to adapt to the changing economic situation led to loss of wealth, prestige and power (Sabloff and Rathje 1975). Several centers, such as Altar de Sacrificios and Seibal were occupied by the new mercantile elite, but were eventually abandoned when these sites lost their importance as trade centers.

The combination of these factors produced a change in the centers of political and economic power, and the lowland populations, including those members of the elite class able to adapt to new conditions, moved to the new power centers located in areas controlled by the Mexican states, or by the new Maya mercantile elite situated in northern Yucatan and along the Gulf and Caribbean Coasts.

A MAYA PERSPECTIVE FOR THE HARAPPAN DEMISE

This paper is based upon the premise that, while the developmental career of each human society is unique, the underlying processes that result in cultural change are often similar. Examples of similar cultural processes invite examination and comparison to thereby increase our understanding of the past. In this way an examination of the demise of the Classic Period Maya Civilization may offer useful insights for scholars concerned with the fate of Harappan Civilization. That is, the analysis of the archaeological evidence from the Indus Valley will undoubtedly reveal examples of factors analogous to those that have been identified as important in the cultural processes of the ancient Maya. This could lead to the formulation and testing of specific hypotheses using the Harappan data.

For example, economic factors such as shifts in ancient trade routes might have played a key role in changes within Harappan society, just as they did among the ancient Maya. Given adequate temporal control, the reconstruction of the ancient Indus economic system, including sources and distribution patterns of resources, along with routes and methods of transport, could reveal changes that correspond to the weakening and abandonment of Harappan sites. Research leading to the delineation of the ancient Indus economic system is already underway, as attested by the recent contributions of several Harappan scholars (Agrawal 1971; Fentress 1976; Possehl 1976; Ratnagar 1977; etc.).

Of course, it may also be beneficial to apply hypotheses based upon factors identified in the Indus Valley to the ancient Maya. For example, Harappan sites were obviously affected by changes in the floodplain environment of the Indus Valley. Flooding and sudden shifts in river channels, albeit on a smaller scale, may have had similar consequences for Maya centers situated in alluvial valleys. A prime case in point would be the site of Quirigua. As a hypothesis it may be proposed that the abandonment of this riverine center was caused, at least in part, by a shift in the course of the Motagua River that left Quirigua isolated from access to its communication and commercial lifeline.

On a very different level, by examining the themes and development of theories concerned with the demise of the Classic Maya, this paper has sought to illustrate a trend visible within all of prehistoric archaeology. That is, the emergence of increasingly sophisticated reconstructions of past cultural processes, including the derivation of testable hypotheses. The issue of the Maya demise began with the assumption that this civilization had suddenly collapsed. The initial search was for a single cause dramatic enough to have triggered such a widespread and sudden failure. After this, the issue was met by proposals of multiple causes, often working in combination, but still sufficient to produce a dramatic collapse. More recent theories have been based upon multiple and subtle, rather than dramatic causes, that produced a more gradual transformation of ancient Maya society. In other words, the basic assumption that Classic Maya Civilization suddenly collapsed has been challenged. The issue, therefore, has shifted from finding causes to the examination of the concept of "collapse" itself.

Erasmus (1968) questioned the appropriateness of the term "collapse" for the Classic Maya over a decade ago, and his insight has been validated by the new archaeological evidence made available during the intervening years. With far more archaeological data in hand, it is now apparent that the abandonment of Classic Maya centers was not sudden, but occurred over one or two hundred years of population decline. Not all these sites declined at the same time, and most significantly, some sites were never abandoned, but continued to prosper through the Postclassic Period. The great regional variations within Classic Maya Culture are also becoming apparent so that the concept of a rise and fall of a uniform civilization has been laid to rest. A more reasonable view would see each Maya center pursuing its own career, so that the causes and timing for its rise and fall were probably unique.

In sum, the Classic Maya appear not to have suddenly fallen apart. Instead, both internal and external processes combined to transform the social, political, economic and even ideological foundations of that society until a reoriented culture, based in areas outside the central lowlands, emerged and prospered during the Postclassic Era. It is hoped that this brief epistomological summary of the development of Maya "collapse" theories may be used as a mirror to reveal similar trends within Harappan archaeology.

BIBLIOGRAPHY

Adams, R.E.W., 1969
 Maya Archaeology 1958-1968, a review. *Latin American Research Review* 4 (2): 3-45.

Adams, R.E.W., 1970
 Suggested Classic Period Occupational Specialization in the Southern Maya Lowlands. In *Monographs and Papers in Maya Archaeology*. W.R. Bullard, Jr., ed. Pp. 487-502. Papers of the Peabody Museum 61. Cambridge: Peabody Museum.

Adams, R.E.W., 1973
 Maya Collapse: Transformation and termination in the ceramic sequence at Altar de Sacrificios. In *The Classic Maya Collapse*. T.P. Culbert, ed. Pp. 133-63. Albuquerque: University of New Mexico Press.

Adams, R.E.W. and W.D. Smith, 1977
 Apocalyptic Visions: The Maya Collapse and Mediaeval Europe. *Archaeology* 30 (5): 292-301.

Agrawal, D.P., 1971
 The Copper Bronze Age in India. Delhi: Munshiram Manoharlal.

Altschuler, M., 1958
 On the Environmental Limitations of Maya Cultural Development. *Southwestern Journal of Anthropology* 14 (2): 189-98.

Ashmore, W.A., editor, 1979
 Quirigua Reports, I. Museum Monographs 37. Philadelphia: University Museum.

Ashmore, W.A. and R.J. Sharer, 1975
 A Revitalization Movement at Late Classic Tikal. Paper presented at Area Seminars in Ongoing Research, West Chester State College.

Ball, J.W., 1974
 A Teotihuacan-style Cache from the Maya Lowlands. *Archaeology* 27 (1): 2-9.

Baudez, C.F., 1979
 Cuarto Informe Sobre las Actividades del Proyecto. Proyecto Arqueologico Copan.

Becker, M.J., 1979
 Priests, Peasants and Ceremonial Centers: The intellectual history of a model. In *Maya Archaeology and Ethnohistory*. N. Hammond and G.R. Willey, eds. Pp. 3-20. Austin: University of Texas Press.

Blanton, R.E., 1972
 Prehispanic Adaptation in the Ixtapalapa Region, Mexico. *Science* 175: 1317-26.

Brainerd, G.W., 1956
 Revision of: *The Ancient Maya* by S.G. Morley. Palo Alto: Stanford University Press.

Coe, W.R., 1962
 A Summary of Excavation and Research at Tikal, Guatemala: 1956-61. *American Antiquity* 27 (4): 479-507.

Coe, W.R., 1967
Tikal: A Handbook of the Ancient Maya Ruins. Philadelphia: University Museum.

Coe, W.R., 1968
Tikal: In search of the Mayan past. *The Worldbook Year Book.* Field Educational Enterprises: 160-90.

Coggins, C.C., 1975
Painting and Drawing Styles at Tikal: An historical and iconographic reconstruction. Ph.D. dissertation, Department of Fine Arts, Harvard University.

Coggins, C.C., 1979
A New Order and the Role of the Calendar: Some characteristics of the Middle Classic Period at Tikal. In *Maya Archaeology and Ethnohistory.* N. Hammond and G.R. Willey, eds. Pp. 38-50. Austin: University of Texas Press.

Cook, O.F., 1921
Milpa Agriculture: A Primitive Tropical System. *Annual Report of the Smithsonian Institution, 1919.* Pp. 307-26. Washington D.C.: Smithsonian Institution.

Cooke, C.W., 1931
Why the Mayan Cities of the Peten District, Guatemala, were Abandoned. *Journal of the Washington Academy of Sciences* 21 (13): 283-87.

Cowgill, G.L., 1964
The End of Classic Maya Culture: A review of recent evidence. *Southwestern Journal of Anthropology* 20 (2): 145-59.

Cowgill, G.L., 1979
Teotihuacan, Internal Militaristic Competition, and the Fall of the Classic Maya. In *Maya Archaeology and Ethnohistory.* N. Hammond and G.R. Willey, eds. Pp. 51-62. Austin: University of Texas Press.

Cowgill, U.M. and G.E. Hutchinson, 1963
El Bajo de Santa Fe. *Transactions of the American Philosophical Society* 53 (7). Philadelphia: American Philosophical Society.

Culbert, T.P., editor, 1973
The Classic Maya Collapse. Albuquerque: University of New Mexico Press.

Culbert, T.P., editor, 1974
The Lost Civilization: The Story of the Classic Maya. New York: Harper and Row.

Culbert, T.P., editor, 1977
Maya Development and Collapse: An economic perspective. In *Social Process in Maya Prehistory*. N. Hammond, ed. Pp. 509-30. London and New York: Academic Press.

Dahlin, B.H., 1979
Cropping Cash in the Protoclassic: A cultural impact statement. In *Maya Archaeology and Ethnohistory.* N. Hammond and G.R. Willey, eds. Pp. 21-37. Austin: University of Texas Press.

Daniels, D. 1972
The Maya Temple. New York: Warner Books. P. 15.

Erasmus, C.J., 1968
Thoughts on Opward Collapse: An essay on explanation in Anthropology. *Southwestern Journal of Anthropology* 24: 170-94.

Fentress, M., 1976
Resource Access, Exchange Systems and Regional Interaction in the Indus Valley: An investigation of archaeological variability at Harappa and Mohenjodaro. Ph.D. dissertation, Department of Oriental Studies, University of Pennsylvania.

Friedel, D.A., 1979
Culture Areas and Interaction Spheres: Contrasting approaches to the emergence of civilization in the Maya lowlands. *American Antiquity* 44 (1): 36-54.

Graham, J.A., 1976
Maya, Olmec and Izapans at Abaj Takalik. Paper presented at the 42nd International Congress of Americanists, Paris.

Hammond, N., 1975
Lubaantun: A classic Maya realm. Monographs of the Peabody Museum 2. Cambridge: Peabody Museum.

Hammond, N., D. Pring, R. Wilk, S. Donaghey, F. Saul, E.S. Wing, A.V. Miller and L.H. Feldman, 1979
The Earliest Lowland Maya: Definition of the Swasey Phase. *American Antiquity* 44 (1): 92-110.

Harrison, P.D., 1977
The Rise of the *Bajos* and Fall of the Maya. In *Social Process in Maya Prehistory*. N. Hammond, ed. Pp. 469-508. London and New York: Academic Press.

Harrison, P.D. and B.L. Turner II, editors, 1978
Pre-Hispanic Maya Agriculture. Albuquerque: University of New Mexico Press.

Haviland, W.A., 1967
Stature at Tikal, Guatemala: Implications for ancient Maya demography and social organization. *American Antiquity* 32 (3): 316-25.

Haviland, W.A., 1977
  Dynastic Genealogies from Tikal, Guatemala: Implications for descent and political organization. *American Antiquity* 42 (1): 61-67.

Jones, C., 1977a
  Tikal and the Mexican trade. Paper presented at the 2nd Area Seminar in Ongoing Research, West Chester State College, West Chester.

Jones, C., 1977b
  Inauguration Dates of Three Late Classic Rulers of Tikal, Guatemala. *American Antiquity* 42 (1): 28-60.

Jones, C., 1977c
  Research at Quirigua, Guatemala: The site-core program. Paper presented at the 42nd annual meeting of the Society for American Archaeology, New Orleans.

MacKie, E.W., 1961
  New Light on the End of Classic Maya Culture at Benque Viejo, British Honduras. *American Antiquity* 27 (2): 216-24.

Marcus, J., 1976
  Emblem and State in the Classic Maya Lowlands: An epigraphic approach to territorial organization. Washington D.C.: Dumbarton Oaks.

Meggers, B.J., 1954
  Environmental Limitation on the Development of Culture. *American Anthropologist* 56 (5): 801-24.

Molloy, J.P. and W.L. Rathje, 1974
  Sexploitation Among the Late Classic Maya. In *Meso-american Archaeology: New Approaches.* N. Hammond, ed. Pp. 431-44. Austin: University of Texas Press.

Morley, S.G., 1946
  The Ancient Maya. Palo Alto: Stanford University Press.

Parsons, L.A., 1969
  Bilbao, Guatemala: An archaeological study of the Pacific Coast Cotzumalhuapa region, II. Milwaukee Public Museum Publications in Anthropology 12, Milwaukee: Milwaukee Public Museum.

Possehl, G.L., 1976
  Lothal, A gateway settlement of the Indus Civilization. In *Ecological Backgrounds of South Asian Prehistory.* K.A.R. Kennedy and G.L. Possehl, eds. Pp. 118-31. Occasional Papers and Theses of the South Asia Program of Cornell University 4. Ithaca: Cornell University.

Proskouriakoff, T., 1963
  Historical Data in the Inscriptions of Yaxchilan, I. *Estudios de Cultura Maya* 3: 149-66.

Proskouriakoff, T., 1964
  Historical Data in the Inscriptions of Yaxchilan, II, *Estudios de Cultura Maya* 4: 177-201.

Proskouriakoff, T., 1973
  The Hand-grasping-fish and Associated Glyphs on Classic Maya Monuments. In *Mesoamerican Writing Systems.* E.P. Benson, ed. Pp. 165-73. Washington D.C.: Dumbarton Oaks.

Puleston, D.E., 1979
  An Epistemological Pathology and the Collapse, or Why the Maya Kept the Short Count. In *Maya Archaeology and Ethnohistory.* N. Hammond and G.R. Willey, eds. Pp. 63-74. Austin: University of Texas Press.

Puleston, D.E. and D.W. Callender, Jr., 1967
  Defensive Earthworks at Tikal. *Expedition* 9 (3): 40-48.

Rathje, W.L., 1970
  Socio-political Implications of Lowland Maya Burials: Methodology and tentative hypotheses. *World Archaeology* 1 (3): 359-74.

Rathje, W.L., 1971
  The Origin and Development of Lowland Classic Maya Civilization. *American Antiquity* 36 (2): 275-85.

Rathje, W.L., 1973
  Classic Maya Development and Denouement: A research design. In *The Classic Maya Collapse.* T.P. Culbert, ed. Pp. 405-56. Albuquerque: University of New Mexico Press.

Ratnagar, S., 1977
  Trading Contacts between India and Western Asia in the Third and Second Millennia B.C. Ph.D. dissertation, Center for Historical Studies, Jawaharlal Nehru University.

Ricketson, O.G. and E.B. Ricketson, 1937
  Uaxactun, Guatemala, Group E 1926-1937, Carnegie Institution of Washington Publication No. 477. Washington D.C.: Carnegie Institution.

Ruppert, K.J., J.E.S. Thompson and T. Proskouriakoff, 1955
  Bonampak, Chiapas, Mexico. Carnegie Institution of Washington Publication No. 602. Washington D.C.: Carnegie Institution.

Sabloff, J.A., 1973
  Major Themes in the Past Hypotheses of the Maya Collapse. In *The Classic Maya Collapse.*

T.P. Culbert, ed. Pp. 35-40. Albuquerque: University of New Mexico Press.

Sabloff, J.A. and W.L. Rathje, 1975
The Rise of a Maya Merchant Class. *Scientific American* 233 (4): 72-82.

Sabloff, J.A. and G.R. Willey, 1967
The Collapse of Maya Civilization in the Southern Lowlands: A consideration of history and process. *Southwestern Journal of Anthropology* 23: 311-36.

Sanders W.T., 1962
Cultural Ecology of the Maya Lowlands, I. *Estudios de Cultura Maya* 2: 79-121.

Sanders, W.T., 1963
Cultural Ecology of the Maya Lowlands, II. *Estudios de Cultura Maya* 3: 203-41.

Sanders, W.T., 1973
The Cultural Ecology of the Lowland Maya: A reevaluation. In *The Classic Maya Collapse*. T.P. Culbert, ed. Pp. 325-65. Albuquerque: University of New Mexico Press.

Satterthwaite, L., 1937
Thrones at Piedras Negras. *University Museum Bulletin* 7 (1): 18-23.

Satterthwaite, L., 1958
The Problem of Abnormal Stela Placements at Tikal and Elsewhere. Tikal Reports 3, Museum Monographs. Philadelphia: University Museum.

Saul, F.P., 1973
Disease in the Maya Area: The Pre-Columbian evidence. In *The Classic Maya Collapse*. T.P. Culbert, ed. Pp. 301-24. Albuquerque: University of New Mexico Press.

Sharer, R.J., 1969
Chalchuapa: Investigations at a highland Maya ceremonial center. *Expedition* 11: 36-38.

Sharer, R.J., 1974
The Prehistory of the Southeastern Maya periphery. *Current Anthropology* 15: 165-87.

Sharer, R.J., 1975
The southeast periphery of the Maya area: A prehistoric perspective. Paper presented at the 74th annual meetings of the American Anthropological Association, San Francisco.

Sharer, R.J., 1977
The Maya collapse revisited: Internal and external perspectives. In *Social Process in Maya Prehistory*. N. Hammond, ed. Pp. 531-52. London and New York: Academic Press.

Sharer, R.J., 1978
Archaeology and History at Quirigua, Guatemala. *Journal of Field Archaeology* 5(1): 1-70.

Sharer, R.J., 1979
Classic Maya Elite Occupation in the lower Montagua Valley, Guatemala: A preliminary formulation. Paper presented at the Ethnohistory Workshop, University of Pennsylvania.

Sharer, R.J. and B. Bevan, in press
Quirigua and the Earthquake of February 4, 1976. *Quirigua Reports, II.* Museum Monographs. Philadelphia: University Museum.

Sheets, P.D. 1971
An Ancient Natural Disaster. *Expedition* 14 (1): 24-31.

Sheets, P.D., 1976
Ilopango Volcano and the Maya Protoclassic: A report of the 1975 field season of the protoclassic project in El Salvador. Carbondale: University of Southern Illinois Museum of Anthropology.

Sheets, P.D., 1979
Maya Recovery from Volcanic Disasters: Ilopango and Ceren. *Archaeology* 32 (3): 32-42.

Shimkin, D.B., 1973
Models for the Downfall: Some ecological and culture-historical considerations. In *The Classic Maya Collapse*. T.P. Culbert, ed. Pp. 269-99. Albuquerque: University of New Mexico Press.

Shook, E.M. and A.V. Kidder, 1952
Mound E-III-3, Kaminaljuyu, Guatemala. Carnegie Institution of Washington Publication No. 596. Washington D.C.: Carnegie Institution.

Shook, E.M. and T. Proskouriakoff, 1956
Settlement Patterns in Mesoamerica and the Sequence in the Guatemalan Highlands. In *Prehistoric Settlement Patterns in the New World*. G.R. Willey, ed. Pp. 93-100. Viking Fund Publication 23. New York: Wenner-Grenn Foundation.

Smith, A.L., 1950
Uaxactun, Guatemala: Excavations of 1931-1937. Carnegie Institution of Washington Publication No. 588. Washington D.C.: Carnegie Institution.

Spinden, H.J., 1928
The Ancient Civilizations of Mexico and Central America. American Museum of Natural History, Handbook Series No. 3. New York: American Museum of Natural History.

Stephens, J.L., 1841
Incidents of Travel in Central America, Chiapas

and Yucatan. 2 vols. New York: Harper and Brothers.

Stephens, J.L., 1843
Incidents of travel in Yucatan. 2 vols. New York: Harper and Brothers.

Thompson, J.E.S., 1954
The Rise and Fall of Maya Civilization. Norman: University of Oklahoma Press.

Thompson, J.E.S., 1966
The Rise and Fall of Maya Civilization, 2nd Edition (Revised). Norman: University of Oklahoma Press.

Thompson, J.E.S., 1970
Maya History and Religion. Norman: University of Oklahoma Press.

Turner, B.L. and P.D. Harrison, 1978
Implications from Agriculture for Maya Prehistory. In *Pre-Hispanic Maya Agriculture*. B.L. Turner and P.D. Harrison, eds. Pp. 337-73. Albuquerque: University of New Mexico Press.

Webb, M.C., 1964
The Postclassic Decline of the Peten Maya: An interpretation in the light of a general theory of state society. Ph.D. dissertation, University of Michigan.

Webb, M.C., 1973
The Maya Peten Decline Viewed in the Perspective of State Formation. In *The Classic Maya Collapse*. T.P. Culbert, ed. Pp. 367-404. Albuquerque: University of New Mexico Press.

Willey, G.R., 1973
The Altar de Sacrificios Excavation: General summary. Papers of the Peabody Museum 64 (3). Cambridge: Peabody Museum.

Willey, G.R., 1974
The Classic Maya Hiatus: A rehearsal for the collapse? In *Mesoamerican Archaeology: New Approaches*. N. Hammond, ed. Pp. 417-44. Austin: University of Texas Press.

Willey, G.R., editor, 1978
Excavations at Seibal. Memoirs of the Peabody Museum 14 (1-3). Cambridge: Peabody Museum.

Willey, G.R., W.R. Bullard, Jr., J.B. Glass and J.C. Gifford, 1965
Prehistoric Maya Settlements in the Belize Valley. Papers of the Peabody Museum 54. Cambridge: Peabody Museum.

Willey, G.R., T.P. Culbert and R.E.W. Adams, 1967
Maya Lowland Ceramics: A report from the 1965 Guatemala City Conference. *American Antiquity* 32 (3): 289-315.

Willey, G.R. and R.M. Leventhal, 1979
Prehistoric Settlement at Copan. In *Maya Archaeology and Ethnohistory*. N. Hammond and G.R. Willey, eds. Pp. 75-102. Austin: University of Texas Press.

Willey, G.R. and J.A. Sabloff, 1974
A History of American Archaeology. San Francisco: W.H. Freeman.

Willey, G.R. and D.B. Shimkin, 1973
The Maya Collapse: A summary view. In *The Classic Maya Collapse*. T.P. Culbert, ed. Pp. 457-502. Albuquerque: University of New Mexico Press.

PART VII

HISTORY OF RESEARCH

KRISHNA DEVA

37. Contributions of Aurel Stein and N.G. Majumdar to Research into the Harappan Civilization with Special Reference to Their Methodology

CONTRIBUTION OF N. G. MAJUMDAR

N. G. MAJUMDAR was one of the brilliant alumni of Calcutta University and combined a command of Sanskrit and Prakrits, epigraphy and numismatics, history and iconography with an incisive critical faculty. A reputed epigraphist and a keen explorer, he combined a flair for antiquarian research and museum work with a penchant for field excavation and exploration.

He started his professional life in 1924 as a curator in the Rajshahi Museum and within a short time revealed his scholarship and epigraphical talents by critically editing the Sena and contemporary epigraphs from eastern India in a book entitled *Inscriptions of Bengal*, which was published in Calcutta during 1929. His interests and talents, however, merited a wider outlet and he did not have long to wait. From 1925 to 1927 he participated in the excavation at Mohenjodaro under Sir John Marshall, Daya Ram Sahni and E. J. H. Mackay. He gained familiarity with whatever remains were then exposed of the Indus Civilization together with the technique of excavation (bench-level method) then practiced by archaeologists in India. Impressed with his ability, Sir John Marshall appointed N. G. Majumdar an Assistant Superintendent in the Archaeological Survey of India (A.S.I.) in June 1927—an association which was to last till the end of his brief but brilliant life.

Soon after the initial excavations at Mohenjodaro and Harappa had established the antiquity and wide extent of the so-called Indus Civilization, a plan was launched by the Archaeological Survey of India for a systematic survey of the Chalcolithic sites in the Indus Valley and the contiguous Indo-Iranian borderlands. In 1925-26, H. Hargreaves explored Nal and adjoining sites in the Jhalawan tract of Baluchistan. Almost simultaneously K. N. Dikshit examined two sites in Sind proper. One, Luhumjodaro on the Indus and the other, Limo Junejo, to the north in the Upper Sind Frontier District. Shortly after his appointment to the Survey in 1927, Majumdar was entrusted with an excavation at the site of Jhukar, near Larkana on the Indus, in pursuance of the same plan. In spite of the limitations of the bench-level method of excavation, Majumdar was sufficiently perceptive to be able to demarcate three distinct cultures at the site. Jhukar I, which was confined to the lowest levels (18 to 25 feet below surface), belonged to the Mohenjodaro phase and yielded typical Harappan painted pottery, an inscribed seal, chert blades, terracotta cakes, bull figures, and the like. Jhukar II, the middle layers, represented a later Chalcolithic Culture, characterized by a coarse Bichrome Ware with limited types and poor decoration, both painted and incised. The painted designs were executed in black on a light red or pink wash with chocolate lines or minor registers on the shoulders. Jhukar III, the top layers, belonged to the Indo-Sassanian Period and yielded pottery, both plain and decorated, datable coins and sealings, besides plans of houses and a large lofty platform built of mud bricks. The latter was designed for protection against flood.

The period from 1927 to 1931 was one of considerable achievement for the A.S.I. While excavations were at their peak at the twin city sites of Mohenjodaro and Harappa, exploratory surveys were being pursued with great forethought and zeal in Baluchistan by Sir Aurel Stein and in Sind itself by N. G. Majumdar. Following the excavation of Nal in Baluchistan by Hargreaves in 1925-26, Aurel Stein made a rapid survey of Northern and Southern Baluchistan between 1927 and 1928 and discovered more than 120 protohistoric sites with links to Mohenjodaro and Harappa on the one hand and with Nal on the other. Majumdar, who had conducted an excavation at Jhukar on the Indus in 1927, continued his explorations in the Indus Valley and in the hill tracts of Johi, Sehwan and Kohistan in Sind between 1929 and 1931. He succeeded in discovering some 62 sites, of which half the number were protohistoric or Chalcolithic in age.

The publication of the results of these operations by Majumdar in his monograph *Explorations in Sind* (1934) added new dimensions to Indian archaeology. This monograph is a model of exploratory report writing which probes and assesses the archaeological character and potential of each site against the background of regional topography and ecology, history and tradition, natural resources and mechanics of trade/communication through the ages. One outstanding contribution made by this work was the discovery of the type site at Amri where Period I, with its distinctive pale Bichrome Ware, was confined to the lower strata and was clearly Pre-Harappan. Period II, with its typical sturdy ware including black on red painted pottery belonging to the Harappan Culture, came from the upper horizon. The Pre-Harappan layers were demarcated from the Harappan by a substantial deposit of dark cultural soil. To quote the words of the explorer:

> In this trench, at a depth of 6′, we lighted upon a darker soil, unlike that of the upper levels, in which was found painted pottery of an altogether different fabric, hitherto unknown in Sind. The pots had generally thin walls having a plain reddish brown band at the neck, a chocolate band on the inner side of the lip and geometric patterns on the body, in black or chocolate on pink, and in some cases on cream wash. The general effect of the decoration is not so striking as that of the rich Mohenjo-daro pottery recovered from the upper stratum of the trench.... Considering that in trench I 'geometric pottery' occupies a lower level than the 'black-on-red,' it would be reasonable to assume that the former belongs to an *earlier period*. Moreover, the fundamental difference, both in technique and decoration, between the two wares, would suggest not merely a difference in age but also one in culture between the two strata. The later pottery of Amri, on account of its affinities to that of Mohenjodaro, should be regarded as a typical product of the Indus civilization. The earlier pot-fabrics of Amri, which will henceforth be called the 'Amri pottery,' should be looked upon as representing an earlier phase of the chalcolithic civilization than that represented by Harappa and Mohenjo-daro (1934: 26-27).

Explaining why he used the sobriquet "bichrome" for Amri and expatiating on its contrast to Harappa, Majumdar observes in his concluding chapter:

> First of all, there is a class of thin ware of buff or light red clay with purely geometric patterns. In Sind, this pale ware, which shows a three-colour scheme, was found for the first time at Amri on the Indus, and subsequently at Lohri near Lake Manchhar and at a number of sites in the hills of Western Sind, e.g., at Pandi Wahi, Bandhni, Damb Buthi and Chauro. The designs are painted in black or chocolate on a matt surface which bears either a thin slip or merely a wash, of buff or light red colour. Frequently, a reddish brown band is introduced, side by side with black or chocolate, which produces a polychrome effect. This ware, however, has not been called 'polychrome' in the present Memoir. In order to distinguish it from the more developed multi-coloured specimens of Nal, on which three or more paints are sometimes used, it may be described as 'bichrome', the paints used on it being two only, leaving the ground colour out of consideration (1934: 148). A noteworthy feature of the decoration is the evanescent character of some of the colours which must have been applied after firing. The vessels of this class of pottery are mostly 'rimless,' the predominant types being beakers and bowls. They reveal two distinct tendencies: They are either steepsided and have slightly everted lip, or have a straight shoulder and bulged out body with a straight lip. From the number of specimens recovered from each of the respective sites, painted pottery of this class appears to have been produced in very large quantities.

> Then we have a well-baked thick ware of bright terracotta colour with decorations in black on polished red slip, which varies between Indian red and vermilion. The red colour was produced, as analysis has shown, by oxide of iron contained in a kind of ochrous earth. The ornaments were evolved by combining geometric devices with plant and animal forms; but on this pottery there is a distinct paucity of purely geometric patterns. The principal site of the black-on-red as well as the plain pottery of the aforesaid types is, of course, Mohenjo-daro. What is particularly noteworthy at this site is that rimmed vessels and

vessels with splayed out neck are quite common, beakers of the Amri type are extremely rare, and straight-shoulder pots are practically nonexistent. From all points of view, therefore, the pale pot-fabrics of the Amri family are to be regarded as quite of a different class from the black-on-red and its undecorated companions from Mohenjo-daro (1934: 149).

Majumdar's exploration methodology was to first send his trained exploration Jamadar to pick up potsherds and other significant objects, like chert flakes, beads and terracotta figurines, from the surface of the reported mounds. If the surface finds convinced him of the potentiality of a site he would visit and closely examine it and would decide whether it deserved to be excavated. If it did, he would normally sink three trenches if the site was small: one at the top, a second at the slope and a third at the lowest level of the mound. But where a site was large, or comprised more than one mound, he would sink a larger number of trenches of large or small size. The latter, generally square, he designated "pits." If he came across a structure on the surface, or in a trench, he would follow it and if it proved significant, generally expose its full plan and probe it to the foundation. In the case of a structure encountered in a trench he would take care to differentiate the respective cultural deposits alongside it and beneath it as he did at Amri. On sites with deep cultural deposits, like Pandi Wahi and Ghazi Shah, Majumdar took care to distinguish the varying proportions of the Harappan and the Amri wares in the upper, middle and the lower levels; thus clearly revealing the antecedence of the former over the latter with an overlap of the two wares in the middle layers. But generally he did not dig deep trenches, since he aimed at achieving the maximum result in a minimum time, and with minimum effort.

It will be seen that while this method yielded quick results which were by and large correct and rewarding, it suffered from two principal shortcomings: (1) while the composition of selected, significant layers were described, the detailed soil sections or the stratification of the cultural deposits of the trenches, were neither drawn nor documented, and (2) virgin soil was seldom reached. It must, however, be said to Majumdar's credit that in spite of all the problems with his method he could determine the relative chronology and stratigraphy of the Indus Cultures and placed Amri, Harappa, Jhukar and Jhangar in their proper sequence.

Among the places he explored were two burial sites at Bandhni and Damb Buthi. There were also two fortified sites, namely, Kohtras and Ali Murad, belonging respectivly to the Amri and Harappan Cultures. He also identified quite a number of flint knapping stations, which formed handy sources for the supply of the flint and chert tools. Majumdar thus presented as comprehensive a picture of Chalcolithic Sind as was possible with the evidence he collected and interpreted, certainly with keen observation and a highly analytical mind. That he realized the far reaching implications of his discovery of Amri and its bearing on the wider question of the relationship between the Chalcolithic Cultures of Iran, Seistan, Baluchistan and the Indus Valley is borne out by this observation:

> The sequence of the two classes of Sind pottery is a matter of great importance, as with it is indirectly linked up the question of the dating of the Nal culture which appears to have been essentially different from that of Mohenjodaro, that is to say, from Indus. The ceramic remains of Nal, Nundara and kindred sites in Baluchistan, which show a 'geometric style,' form a distinct group by themselves, related more or less to the pale wares of Sistan and of areas farther afield. On the other hand, fabrics of a typical black-on-red class, representing a mixture of geometric, zoomorphic and plant forms, from sites in Northern Baluchistan like Dabarkot, form another group intruding into this zone of pale pottery. This group can be affiliated directly to the cultural zone of Indus. Likewise, the pale wares of Sind, which bear a family likeness to the potteries of Kulli and Mehi, and also to some extent to those of Nal and Nundara, in Baluchistan, must be reckoned as an intrusive element in the Indus valley (Majumdar 1934: 150).

Majumdar resumed his explorations in Sind after a lapse of seven years, in 1938 and surveyed the foothills of the Kirthar Range and the adjoining highlands and plains. That he exercised great forethought in planning his survey is indicated by the fact that he discovered in the short space of three weeks some half dozen Chalcolithic sites (Deva and McCown 1949) including the site of Rohel-jo-kund where he was killed by bandits.

Rohel-jo-kund is unique among the Sind sites as a settlement predominantly of the Nal Culture with some Amri contacts. This is not surprising in view of the fact that the site is situated on the bank of the Nai Gaj, a perennial hill stream along which people traveled in antiquity, as now, between Baluchistan and Sind. Three neighboring sites surveyed by

Majumdar also yielded typical Nal motifs mixed largely with Amrian pottery. These observations show that during the last days of his life, N. G. Majumdar was on the trail of important discoveries which should have helped elucidate, if not clinch, the problems of the relationship between the Chalcolithic Cultures of Sind and Baluchistan.

THE CONTRIBUTION OF AUREL STEIN

Sir Aurel Stein (1862-1943), the great explorer and archaeologist, became a legend even in his own life time. An eminent orientalist, linguist and educator, Aurel Stein started his distinguished career in India as a member of the Indian Educational Service and worked first as a Principal of the Oriental College, Lahore. He rose subsequently to the position of Inspector General of Education in the Punjab. From 1888 to 1898 he utilized his leisure and vacations in editing the text of the *Rājataraṅgiṇī*, an eleventh century Sanskrit classic dealing with the history and traditions of Kashmir. He was also preparing a critical historical and geographical introduction to the work which entailed a thorough exploration, partly geographical and partly archaeological, of the hills and the valley of Kashmir. During this period he also traveled widely in the Punjab, the Northwest Frontier Province and Baluchistan and closely studied the geography, history and monumental remains of these regions.

From the beginning, Stein believed in the close relationship and interdependence of history and geography and was of the firm view that geophysical features and climate molded a peoples character, outlook and way of life. He loved to view history and archaeology from a geographical perspective. The more he traveled and explored, the more he felt convinced that the land conditions that sustained and preserved a culture, in some form or another were essential for understanding history. This was the precise crux of his thinking that ran as a golden thread through all of his exploration and reports.

In 1899 Aurel Stein was transferred to Calcutta as a Principal of the Calcutta Madrasa, a post once held by the well-known orientalist and epigraphist, Rudolf Hoernle. Since 1891, when the so-called Bower manuscript was discovered in Central Asia, manuscripts and art treasures from this region kept trickling into museums in Europe. They literally flooded the Calcutta market between 1897 and 1899. Hoernle and Stein were greatly exercised over these and the latter felt an inner urge to ascertain their provenance and archaeological context and to stop the treasure hunting which involved the destruction of valuable historical evidence. This inner urge ultimately launched Stein on the most remarkable archaeological explorations of this century in Central Asia where he led three expeditions with the active support of the Archaeological Survey of India, the Survey of India and, to some extent, the British Museum. In the words of the explorer:

> Those expeditions were started as long ago as 1900-1 and were continued from 1906 to 1908 and again from 1913 to 1916. They lasted altogether for close on seven years and allowed me by marches on horseback and on foot to cover distances aggregating to a total of some 25,000 miles.
>
> Journeys carried out by such quasi-archaic methods of locomotion and over so great distances, so protracted in time and accompanied by systematic surveys, provided the right means of acquiring familiarity with a region vast in extent and presenting exceptional interest alike by its physical features and by the remains of its human history. It comprises Chinese Turkistan with its border-lands towards the Oxus in the west and China proper in the east. Though composed for the most part of desert ground, whether in the mountains or in its drainageless sand-covered plains, it has yet played a very important part in the records of the past. For centuries it served as the channel for that interchange of the early civilizations of India, China and the Hellenized west of Asia which forms such a fascinating chapter in cultural history. These civilizations have left behind there abundant traces in the shape of remains of all kinds, which the aridity of the land has helped to preserve for us. The search for these remains of ancient civilization, together with the problems raised by the present physical conditions of the region, provided the strongest incentive for my explorations (Stein 1933: 1-2).

From 1903 onwards he formally joined the Archaeological Survey of India as the Archaeological Surveyor for the Northwest Frontier Province and Baluchistan; though he generally took on special assignments for distant explorations in the Survey. By 1906 he completed a preliminary as well as a detailed report on his first expedition in Central Asia which appeared under the title *Ancient Khotan* (Stein 1907). The decade from 1917 to 1926, following his return from the last Central Asian expedition, was largely devoted to writing his travelog and detailed accounts of his second and third Central Asian expeditions. In all he published his reports of these explorations in eleven monumental, sumptuously illustrated volumes, which opened a flood gate of information on the art, architecture, religion, history, literature and scripts, etc., of the civic and cultural centers which flourished in and around the waterless deserts of Taklamakan in Central Asia from about the second to tenth centuries A.D. As noted above, these explorations involved a travel of about 25,000 miles through an area occupied largely by snowclad mountains, glaciers and sandy deserts, a good part of which had not been mapped. Alongside his archaeological exploration, Stein also conducted a geographical and trigonometrical survey of the unmapped area with the assistance of two trained surveyors from the Survey of India. He prepared 47 topographical map sheets of Central Asia covering 28 degrees of longitude and eight degrees of latitude.

These achievements earned Aurel Stein well-merited fame and recognition. By 1926, when he had reached the age of 64 years, he could well have retired to a quiet life full of contentment for having contributed so gloriously to human knowledge. But Stein knew no rest. Being consumed by a passion for travel and exploration he persisted in exploratory surveys of difficult and inhospitable regions under the auspices of the Archaeological Survey of India till 1930, and thereafter mainly on his own.

He surveyed the Swat Valley (Stein 1930) and the adjacent hill tracts in 1926 and having traced there only historic remains of mainly Buddhist affiliation, Stein turned his attention in 1927 to Waziristan and Northern Baluchistan (Stein 1929). There he discovered a number of Chalcolithic sites of which Periano Ghundai and Moghal Ghundai in the Zhob Valley and Rana Ghundai, Dabar Kot and Sur Jangal in the Loralai area are noteworthy. The southwest monsoon does not affect Baluchistan which consequently gets scanty rainfall. Poor irrigation facilities coupled with low rainfall renders cultivation in these tracts precarious and they are able to support only a sparse population. This is in contrast to the large size and deep cultural deposits at these sites: 75 feet at Periano Ghundai, 113 feet at Dabar Kot and more than 50 feet at the much denuded site of Rana Ghundai. This attests to their prolonged occupation in the Chalcolithic age. Stein's trial trenches were confined to the upper layers of the sites and revealed the so-called "Zhob mother-goddess" and bull figurines of terracotta, together with painted Black on Red Ware recalling the Mature Harappan. In the house floors at Periano Ghundai Stein uncovered an interesting inhumation practice in the form of cinerary pot burials with disarticulated remains and signs of cremation. The structures were made of mud brick resting on stone foundations. His trench at Dabar Kot yielded pottery of undoubted Harappan vintage as well as a mud-brick building with well finished drains made of kiln-burnt bricks, typical of the Harappan.

During 1927-28, after surveying Northern Baluchistan, Stein took up the exploration of Southern Baluchistan, ancient Gedrosia (1931), covering the arid regions of Kharan, Sarawan, Jhalawan and Makran. Here he succeeded in locating more than a hundred Chalcolithic sites of which more significant are Kulli, Mehi and Nundara in Jhalawan and Shahi Tump and Sutkagendor in Makran. Stein carefully surveyed these sites and drove trenches in them. He found Siah Damb Nundara (measuring 220 yards by 180 yards by 40 feet high) to be a habitation site with many well-built structures of dressed shale, associated with the polychrome pottery typical of Nal. He noted the absence at Nal and Nundara of terracotta bull and female figurines which are found at a large number of Baluchi sites. The important mounds of Kulli (400 yards by 330 yards by 30 feet) and Mehi (360 yards by 330 yards by 50 feet) were extensively trenched. These sites, belonging to a cognate culture, yielded a distinctive type of painted Black on Red Ware with an abundance of terracotta bull and pedestaled female figurines which bear some affinity to the "Zhob mother-goddess" figurines. While Kulli rendered numerous well-built structures of dressed stone, one of them had steps indicating the presence of an upper story, Mehi had a few indifferent structures of only undressed stone and mud. Stein brought out the nature of Mehi as essentially a burial site, full of cinerary urns with a few inhumations. But all were post-exposure or post-cremation remains associated with smaller pots and sometimes accompanied by copper bangles, mirrors or beads. Shahi Tump in the Kej Valley of the Makran is a small, (about 85 yards square) but crucial site. Stein's excavation there showed that the inhabitants used a Red Ware pottery. A later cemetery, with flexed inhumations, was dug into this mound. These burials were associated with groups of pottery vessels, some of which contained remains of animal bones or food offerings, bead necklaces and copper objects and implements including a spearhead and a shaft-hole axe. The pottery was of fine fabric with open bowls and cups painted in black on gray or grayish buff with distinctive geometrical designs. Stein's excavation at Shahi Tump, however, was confusing and did not elucidate the identification of the original dwellers. Stein also discovered Stukagenodor in Makran, the westernmost output of the Harappan Civilization and its massive defences with a gate flanked by bastion towers; but he missed the lower habitation site nearby.

In 1932 Stein explored the southeastern tracts of Iran (Stein 1937) which adjoin Baluchistan. Here he was able to discover the significant Chalcolithic sites of Bampur, Khurab, Katukan, Damin, Chah Husaini, Tal-i Pir (Haraj) and Tal-i Iblis.

During 1933 and 1934 Stein pushed his archaeological investigation in the province of Fars (Stein 1936) in Iran and was able to survey the important Chalcolithic sites of Firuzabad, Fasa, Sarvistan, Darab, Bavanat, Madavan, Tal-i Skau, Tal-i Regi, Khusu, Chir, Deh-Bid and Do-Tulan. The surveys in Iran from 1932 to 1934 were largely financed by grants from Harvard University and the British Museum.

A survey of the ancient settlements along the "lost" Sarasvati was Stein's next project (Stein 1942). This now dry river is today represented by the Ghaggar-Hakra which issues from the Siwaliks and passes across the eastern Punjab (now Haryana) through the tracks of Bikaner and Bahawalpur, going as far south as Sind. Stein worked in this area from December 1940 to March 1941. With his vast experience with geophysical features he could plot and map the ridges of sand dunes marking the banks of the river bed for a length of more than 250 miles from Hanumangarh in Bikaner to the deltaic terminations beyond Derawar in Bahawalpur. He also identified two old beds of the Sutlej, lately utilized for channeling the Hakra Branch Canal and the Desert Branch Canal. The former meets the Hakra below the border of Bikaner and Bahawalpur and the latter near the site of Kudwala deep inside Bahawalpur. Stein located a large number of Chalcolithic sites along the river bed in Bahawalpur, but failed to locate any in Bikaner territory. Since then A. Ghosh (1952) identified a number of Harappan and Pre-Harappan sites in Bikaner including the well-known site of Kalibangan (Lal and Thapar 1967) where the Archaeological Survey of India carried on systematic excavation for about a decade under the direction of B. K. Thapar and B. B. Lal. Suraj Bhan (1973) has greatly augmented the number of sites in the region, including those of Late Harappan date, and traced them all along the upper courses of the ancient Sarasvati and its tributary, the Drishadvati, now represented by the Chautang.

Stein undertook the last survey of his eventful life in Las Bela and the southern part of Gedrosia, just eight months before his death in October 1943 at the ripe age of eighty-one. The objective of this survey was twofold: 1) to test the archaeological potential of Las Bela, and 2) to determine the route which Alexander took for the retreat of his legions through Gedrosia. That he was attracted by the second objective more than the first is clear from the title of his write up on this survey: "On Alexander's Route to Gedrosia: An Archaeological Tour in Las Bela" (Stein 1943). He explored Las Bela, but located only one important Chalcolithic site; Niai Buthi near the town of Bela. He laid two shallow trenches at Niai Buthi and found it to be a site of mixed Nal and Harappan Cultures. Later research (Fairservis 1971: 189–94) however, has confirmed and amplified Stein's findings and differentiated two periods (Niai Buthi I and II) which represent an earlier and later phase of the Kulli Culture at the site.

Stein completed the survey of Las Bela in March 1943 and was in Kabul in October of the same year. He was there to explore "Ariana Antiqua" which he had wanted to do since his boyhood. He actually died in the saddle, traveling almost to the last day of his life.

Stein was essentially a geographer and an explorer and is to be admired for his indomitable courage and spirit of adventure in undertaking hazardous journeys through difficult terrain. He discovered a large number of Chalcolithic and related sites in the Great Indian Desert and the entire reach of the Indo-Iranian borderlands, covering Northern and Southern Baluchistan and a good part of Iran. He was a pioneer and a pathfinder and was to Indian protohistoric archaeology what Alexander Cunningham was to Indian historical archaeology.

Stein was proud of his association with the Archaeological Survey of India and having no family, was literally wedded to field exploration. He loved Kashmir and settled there in the secluded Mohand Marg with its Alpine climate and scenery but used to leave Kashmir every winter when he occupied himself with field survey in warmer regions.

His *modus operandi* was to use a geographical approach on a historical or archaeological problem. He would study in depth the geophysical environment and the ecological and other related features to investigate changes, if any, brought about to these features in a given region through the ages. He was also fond of studying the problem of desiccation which he often encountered in course of his exploration in Central Asia. He would carefully note the extent, height and surface indications of each site he surveyed and for the important ones he would prepare detailed contour maps. If a site looked promising, or yielded interesting pottery or other surface indications of structures or burials, etc., he would take on trial excavation. Normally his trenches were shallow and would not exceed three meters in depth and four meters in width. He generally collected only painted pottery from the trenches or complete plain pots and other interesting finds. He cared more for stone or burnt brick structures than for those of mud brick or mud. Since he had no training in archaeology and did not observe even the basic principles of stratification, his excavations were insensitive and the data and observations he collected are not useful in scientific analysis or for the identification of cultural traits. That Stein knew this shortcoming, and did not claim any competence in archaeological observation and interpretation, is borne out from his own admission:

> It has been my endeavour to give a full account of all I was able to observe and note at each surveyed site and by description and illustrations adequately to represent the general character of the archaeological materials secured there. But neither the range of my competence nor the time available to me for the preparation of this report will permit of my attempting here a systematic analysis of these abundant materials (1931: 4).

BIBLIOGRAPHY

Deva, Krishna and D. McCown, 1949
 Further Explorations in Sind, 1938. *Ancient India* 5: 12-30.
Fairservis, W.A., 1971
 The Roots of Ancient India. New York: Macmillan.
Ghosh, A., 1952
 The Rajputana Desert: Its archaeological aspect. *Bulletin of the National Institute of Sciences of India* 1: 37-42.
Lal, B.B. and B.K. Thapar, 1967
 Excavations at Kalibangan: New light on the Indus Civilization. *Cultural Forum* 9 (4): 78-88.
Majumdar, N.G., 1934
 Explorations in Sind. Memoirs of the Archaeological Survey of India 48: Delhi.
Stein, Sir Aurel, 1907
 Ancient Khotan: Detailed report of archaeological explorations in Chinese Turkestan. 2 vols. Oxford: The Clarendon Press.
Stein, Sir Aurel, 1929
 An Archaeological Tour in Waziristan and Northern Baluchistan. Memoirs of the Archaeological Survey of India 37: Calcutta.
Stein, Sir Aurel, 1930
 An Archaeological Tour in Upper Swat and Adjacent Hill Tracts. Memoirs of the Archaeological Survey of India 42: Calcutta.
Stein, Sir Aurel, 1931
 An Archaeological Tour in Gedrosia. Memoirs of the Archaeological Survey of India 43: Calcutta.
Stein, Sir Aurel, 1933
 On Central-Asian tracts: Brief narrative of three expeditions in innermost Asia and northwestern Kansu. London: Macmillan.
Stein, Sir Aurel, 1936
 An Archaeological Tour in the Ancient Persis. *Iraq* 3 (2): 111-225.
Stein, Sir Aurel, 1937
 Archaeological Reconnaissances in Northwestern India and Southeastern Iran. London: Macmillan.
Stein, Sir Aurel, 1942
 A Survey of Sites Along the 'Lost' Sarasvati River. *Geographical Journal* 99 (4): 174-82.
Stein, Sir Aurel, 1943
 On Alexander's Route to Gedrosia: An archaeological tour in Las Bela. *Geographical Journal* 102 (5-6): 193-227.
Suraj Bhan, 1973
 The Sequence and Spread of Prehistoric Cultures in the Upper Sarasvati Basin. In *Radiocarbon and Indian Archaeology*. D.P. Agrawal and A. Ghosh eds. Pp. 252-63. Bombay: Tata Institute of Fundamental Research.

B.M. PANDE

38. History of Research on the Harappan Culture

In his preface to the *Mohenjodaro and the Indus Civilization,* summarizing the evidence about the Indus Civilization from the excavations at Harappa and Mohenjodaro, John Marshall stated "the civilization hitherto revealed at these two places is not an incipient civilization, but one already age-old and stereotyped on Indian soil, with many millennia of human endeavour behind it" (Marshall 1931: viii). Writing almost a generation later, Wheeler wrote: "much that is essential to an understanding of this ancient Indian Civilization, both in detail and in general context, still eludes us" (Wheeler 1968: 1). The situation regarding the understanding of the Harappa Culture is today the same as when Wheeler wrote.

A survey of research beginning with the discovery of the Indus Civilization from the excavations at Harappa and Mohenjodaro, to date, shows that despite a steady stream of writings (Pande and Ramachandran 1971; Possehl 1979: 368–420), by and large the basic questions remain unanswered. In this survey of the work on the Harappan Culture I will try to broadly delineate the course and nature of work on this civilization and to indicate how preconceptions influenced the interpretation of the Indus Culture and its sites. In this survey I have drawn upon the excellent summary by Mughal (1973) and other writing on the subject by Mackay (1935), Wheeler (1953, 1960, 1968), Allchin and Allchin (1968), etc.

The earliest recorded reference to an Indus Civilization site—though not recognized then as such—is by C. Masson (1842) who, in 1826 during the course of his travels, saw at Harappa: "a ruinous brick castle" having "remarkably high" walls and towers spoiled by "the ravages of time and decay" (Masson 1842, Vol. I: 452). In 1931, A. Burnes saw there " a ruined citadel on the river-side of the town" (1834, Vol. III: 137).

During the course of archaeological survey, A. Cunningham visited Harappa, first in 1853 and again in 1856. In the account he published (Cunningham 1875), Cunningham found that: "the ruins of Harappa are the most extensive of all the old sites along the banks of the Ravi" represented by "a continuous line of mounds about 3500 feet in length" with "a complete gap of 800 feet" between the mounds "on the east side, which is only 2000 feet in length." He also conducted an excavation at Harappa and published (Cunningham 1875: Pl. XXXIII) some of the objects which are recognizably Harappan. He also published a plan of the site which, (Cunningham 1875: Pl. XXXII) if compared with the site-plan published by Vats (1940: Vol. 2, Pl. I) would show interesting differences. In consonance with his aims, Cunningham identified Harappa with *po-fa-to* or *po-fa-to-lo* where the Chinese pilgrim Huan-Tsang halted for two months. The seal he discovered at Harappa was initially taken to be foreign to India as the bull device was without a hump and the six characters were considered to be certainly not Indian letters. However, in his work on Asokan inscriptions, he read the word *Lachhmiva* in "archaic Indian letters of as early an age as Buddha himself" (Cunningham 1877: 61).

Cunningham's reading of the seal, and his identification of the site, are synoptic of the state of research into India's past in his time, and so is the description of Harappa in the travelogs of Masson and Burnes. In 1886 more seals from Harappa were published (Dames 1886) and in 1912 J.F. Fleet published two others (Fleet 1912: 669–70).

The Indus Civilization was recognized as a distinct

cultural entity only after the excavations conducted by Vats at Harappa (Vats 1940) between the years 1920–21 and 1933–34 and by Marshall at Mohenjodaro (Marshall 1931) between 1922 and 1927. Summarizing the results of the excavations Marshall wrote:

> Hitherto it has commonly been supposed that the pre-Aryan peoples of India were on an altogether lower plane of civilization than their Aryan conquerors; that to the latter they were much what the Helots were to the Spartans, or the Slavs to their Byzantine overlords—a race so servile and degraded, that they were commonly known as *Dasas* or slaves. The picture of them gleaned from the Hymns of the Rigveda was that of black skinned, flat-nosed barbarians, as different from the fair Aryans in physical aspect as they were in speech and religion, though at the same time it was evident that they must have been rich in cattle, good fighters, and possessed of many forts in which they defended themselves against the invaders. These "forts", however, were explained by Vedic scholars as being no more than occasional places of refuge—simple earthworks, that is to say, surrounded, may be, by palisades or rough stone walls; for, seeing that the Aryans themselves were still in the village state and that their society was in other respects correspondingly primitive, it was deemed impossible that the older races of India—the contemptible, outcast *Dasas*—could already have been living in well-built cities or fortresses, or in other respects have attained to a higher state of culture. Mentally, physically, socially, and religiously, their inferiority to their conquerors was taken for granted, and little or no credit was given them for the achievements of Indian civilization. Never for a moment was it imagined that five thousand years ago, before ever the Aryans were heard of, the Punjab and Sind, if not other parts of India as well, were enjoying an advanced and singularly uniform civilization of their own, closely akin but in some respects even superior to that of contemporary Mesopotamia and Egypt. Yet this is what the discoveries at Harappa and Mohenjodaro have now placed beyond question. They exhibit the Indus peoples of the fourth and third millennia B.C., in possession of a highly developed culture in which no vestige of Indo-Aryan influence is to be found. Like the rest of Western Asia, the Indus country is still in the Chalcolithic Age—that age in which arms and utensils of stone continue to be used side by side with those of copper or bronze. Their society is organized in cities; their wealth derived mainly from agriculture and trade, which appears to have extended far and wide in all directions. They cultivate wheat and barley as well as the date palm. They have domesticated the humped zebu, buffalo, and short horned bull, besides the sheep, pig, dog, elephant, and camel; but the cat and probably the horse are unknown to them. For transport they have wheeled vehicles, to which oxen doubtless were yoked. They are skilful metal workers, with a plentiful supply of gold, silver, and copper. Lead, too, and tin are in use, but the latter only as an alloy in the making of bronze. With spinning and weaving they are thoroughly conversant. Their weapons of war and of the chase are the bow and arrow, spear, axe, dagger, and mace. The sword they have not yet evolved; nor is there any evidence of defensive body armour. Among their other implements, hatchets, sickles, saws, chisels, and razors are made of both copper and bronze; knives and celts sometimes of these metals, sometimes of chert or other hard stones. For the crushing of grain they have the muller and saddlequern but not the circular grindstone. Their domestic vessels are commonly of earthenware turned on the wheel and not infrequently painted with encaustic designs; more rarely they are of copper, bronze, or silver. The ornaments of the rich are made of the precious metals or of copper, sometimes overlaid with gold, of faience, ivory, carnelian, and other stones; for the poor, they are usually of shell or terra-cotta. Figurines and toys, for which there is a wide vogue, are of terra-cotta, and shell and faience are freely used, as they are in Sumer and the West generally, not only for personal ornaments but for inlay work and other purposes. With the invention of writing the Indus peoples are also familiar, and employ for this purpose a form of script which, though peculiar to India, is evidently analogous to other contemporary scripts of Western Asia and the Nearer East (Marshall 1931: v-vi).

Apart from looking for identities or differences with contemporary civilizations elsewhere, Marshall recognized in its general homogeneity many widely differing branches and found the religion characteristically Indian. One can, however, discern the influence of West Asian discoveries, and the ideas about early India based on linguistic-cultural theories, in Marshall's interpretation of the Indus Culture.

In 1938 Ernest Mackay published the report on his excavations at Mohenjodaro. These had been conducted between the years 1927 and 1931. He concentrated mainly in the DK Area, with a small amount of work in the SD Area. He carried out deep digging at the site, not attempted in the earlier excavations. He wanted to: "understand the growth of the city, and at the same time ... to examine the different levels with their associated objects, so that each might properly be compared with those below and above" (Mackay 1938: xi). He also undertook "further and more detailed examination of the immediate surroundings" of the site which added considerably to "the knowledge on the conditions in which its citizens lived, their avocations and mode of life" (Mackay 1938: 1). Marked by comprehensive details, the report could be considered a forerunner of "settlement archaeology" in India, notwithstanding Wheeler's polemics about the techniques employed by the excavators of Mohenjodaro and Harappa.

Mohenjodaro was subjected to limited excavations in 1950 by Wheeler which indicated that "the building of the citadel corresponded with no break in the cultural sequence and, if the work of foreigners, can be ascribed only to dynastic domination" (Wheeler 1968: 38). In 1964, George Dales drilled beneath the surface of the floodplain in the vicinity of the HR Mound at Mohenjodaro and found that the total accumulation of cultural deposits at the site was nearly 70 feet (Dales 1965a, 1965b, 1965c; also see Possehl 1979: 192-95) and "the highest recognizable flood deposits at Mohenjodaro are thirty-one feet above the present level of the plain!" (Dales 1965b). Dales' aim was "to study and re-evaluate the ancient geography and ecology of the lower Indus valley" for which he, in association with Raikes undertook geological and archaeohydrological studies. He tentatively suggested that "Mohenjo-daro and much of the lower Indus Valley suffered from a series of severe and extensive floods which eventually forced most of the population to abandon the area possibly around 1800 or 1700 B.C." (Dales 1965b; also see Dales in Possehl 1979: 194). The studies show close cooperation between the archaeologist and natural scientist and were followed by intensive work of Raikes (1964, 1965, 1967a, 1967b) who also made similar studies at Kalibangan (Raikes 1968).

The result of excavations conducted between the years 1920-21 and 1933-34 at Harappa were embodied in the report by Vats (1940), which largely supplemented the evidence from Mohenjodaro. In 1946, Wheeler excavated the mud-brick fortifications at the site and thus added new dimensions to one's knowledge of the defensive aspect of the Indus Civilization. Wheeler's excavations also established Cemetery H as Post-Harappan (Wheeler 1968: 69).

As a sequel to the results obtained from the excavations at Mohenjodaro and Harappa, explorations were undertaken in Sind and Baluchistan. During the course of a survey of ancient sites in Sind, N. G. Majumdar located a number of settlements which were either contemporary with, or earlier than the Indus Civilization. He also discovered the mounds at Chanhudaro in 1931 which he excavated on a limited scale (Majumdar 1934) and established the nature of the remains there. Chanhudaro was subjected to excavation by Mackay (1943) in 1935-36. He found the remains of the Jhukar Culture, which was to some extent found overlapping the earlier Harappan remains as well as the Jhangar Culture. It may be incidentally mentioned that Mackay had proposed the sobriquet Harappan Culture instead of Indus Valley Culture in his report on Chanhudaro excavations (Mackay 1943: viii-ix).

The site of Amri, also discovered by Majumdar, was subjected to excavation by Casal from 1959 to 1961 (Casal 1964, 1979: 99-112) where he found remains of the Amri Culture preceding the Harappan. Following the Harappan were the Jhukar and Jhangar Cultures. Majumdar, in the course of his explorations in Sind, and in the hill tracts of Johi, Sehwan and Kohistan, also excavated Jhukar in the earliest levels of which typical Harappan material was found.

Between 1927 and 1928 Sir Aurel Stein (Stein 1929) surveyed northern and southern Baluchistan and brought to light a number of Harappan and affiliated sites. In 1942, he took up explorations along the dried bed of the Ghaggar Hakra River in the central Indus Valley near Bahawalpur. He discovered a number of Harappan settlements here (Stein 1942). His work was followed by A. Ghosh. Between 1950 and 1952, during his explorations (Ghosh 1952) of the valleys of the dried up Sarasvati and its tributary, the Drishadvati in Ganganagar district, north Rajasthan, he discovered about two dozen Harappan sites. One of them, Kalibangan, is a major Indus site which was intensively excavated between 1961 and 1969 by B. B. Lal and B. K. Thapar (Lal 1962, 1979; Lal and Thapar 1967; Thapar 1975 also reprinted in Possehl 1979: 196-202; see also annual reports in Indian Archaeology: A review for the years 1961-62 through 1968-69). Kalibangan has added "substantially to our knowledge of the cultural style of the Indus Civilization beyond the Indus Valley" (Thapar 1975) in the form of typical remains of the Harappan Period in a twin settlement, a cemetery with three varieties of burials and, like Amri, Harappa and Kot Diji, it has yielded evidence of a Pre-Harappan settlement. In the course of explorations during the sixties in the upper Sarasvati basin, Suraj Bhan (1973) noticed a number of Harappan sites, among which the more important are Banawali, Rakhigarhi and Mitathal. In the Punjab and Haryana exploratory work was done between 1953 and 1957 by Y. D. Sharma (IAR 1953-54: 39, 1954-55: 59, 1956-57: 79) and from 1966 to 1973 by Suraj Bhan (IAR 1966-67: 11-14). There was also more sporadic exploration in the area by others.

The results of excavations carried out at Banawali by R. S. Bisht indicate that this site can be ranked among the major sites of the Indus Culture (Bisht 1978: 86-88, in press). In the upper Sarasvati basin, Ropar, a Harappan site, was excavated by Y. D. Sharma in 1954-55. This was followed by excavation at Alamgirpur near Meerut, which is the easternmost Indus site known so far. The place of Ropar as the northernmost Indus site has now been taken by Manda on the right bank of the Chenab near Jammu (Thapar 1978). Explorations during the past two decades in the Punjab, Haryana, Jammu and Kashmir and western Uttar Pradesh have led to the discovery of many Harappan sites in addition to the Early and Late Harappan sites.

Lothal, discovered by S. R. Rao in 1954 and excavated by him between 1954 and 1958 "brought to light the existence of a flourishing port-city of the Indus Civilization with an excellent brick-built dock" (Rao 1973: 2). The site, one of the most significant Indus sites in Gujarat, did not contain the usual twin mounds, though there were three areas: the citadel, the lower town and the dockyard. In Rao's view, "a section of the cosmopolitan Harappan population" could be identified "with the pre-Rigvedic Aryans" (Rao 1973: 160). Rao had earlier excavated Rangpur (Rao 1963) between 1953 and 1956. This site was discovered by Vats in 1934 and excavated in a limited manner in 1935 (Government of India 1934-35: 34-38). This was followed by small-scale excavations by Ghurye in 1936, and M. G. Dikshit in 1947. On the basis of the ceramics, Vats had considered Rangpur to be an outpost of the Indus Culture. The excavations by Rao revealed remains of a Prepottery Microlithic Culture, the Harappa Culture and the Post-Harappan Lustrous Red Ware Culture (Rao 1963: 13). Rao demonstrated the transition from Harappan to Post-Harappan at the site and utilized the evidence of graffiti from this site for his "decipherment" of the Indus script.

In the Kutch area, J. P. Joshi's explorations revealed the existence of a large number of Harappan settlements. Based on the distribution of these sites he postulated overland movement into Kutch by the Harappans. In 1964 he discovered the mound at Surkotada which he excavated in 1970-71 and 1971-72 (Joshi 1973; IAR: A review 1970-71: 13-15, 1971-72: 13-21) and found remains of the Harappan, its antecedent and succeeding culture. The remains of the latter showed "the residual Harappans ... to be still living with a people using a white-painted black-and-red ware akin to that of Ahar in southeastern Rajasthan" (Joshi 1973: 175). Between 1964 and 1968, J. P. Joshi undertook explorations in Kutch with a view to locating Harappan sites in the area between the already known Harappan sites like Surkotada and Desalpur in Kutch and discovered (IAR 1964-65: 10-11, 1965-66: 12-18, 1966-67: 8-10, 1967-68: 13-17) more than a score of Harappan, Pre-Harappan and Late Harappan sites. Systematic explorations in Gujarat by P. P. Pandya (IAR 1955-56: 7-8) S. R. Rao, J. M. Navavati, Gregory Possehl and teams of the Gujarat State Department of Archaeology and M. S. University of Baroda have further added to the list of Harappan and affiliated sites in the area.

The discovery of four solid bronze objects, three Indus characters incised on the rim of a vase and a terracotta circular seal bearing an Indus character, and other evidence from Daimabad, on the banks of the Pravara, a tributary of the Godavari, have extended the area of the Indus Culture. The site has also provided continuous evidence for succeeding cultures which "ties up the site with the flourishing chalcolithic cultures of central India and provides the Indus civilization with a rational sequel" (Thapar 1978).

About twenty Harappan and affiliated sites have been excavated in India during the last 25 years. While in Pakistan, of the large number of Harappan sites discovered, (Mughal 1973, 1980; Shaffer 1979) excavations have been conducted at Kot Diji (Khan 1964, 1965), Amri (Casal 1964), Gumla (Dani 1970-71), Jalilpur (Mughal 1973, 1974), Allahdino (Shaffer 1979) and Balakot (Dales 1979). A number of sites have also been reported indicating connections with the Harappan Culture in Afghanistan and the southern Soviet Union (Gupta 1979). At Altin Depe a rectangular stone seal with two Indus characters has been found (Gupta 1979: 168). A metal seal with a three-headed animal from this site is also reminiscent of Mohenjodaro examples.

DISCUSSION

The first synthesis of Indus material was made by V. G. Childe. In his view this thoroughly individual and independent civilization was technically the peer of the rest and deeply rooted in Indian soil. It "represents a very perfect adjustment of human life to a specific environment, that can only have resulted from years of patient effort. And it has endured; it is already specifically Indian and forms the basis of modern Indian culture. In architecture and industry, still more in dress and religion, Mohenjodaro reveals features that have always been characteristic of historical India" (Childe 1958: 183-84). Piggott examined the Indus material along with that of the other communities in Sind, Baluchistan and the Punjab and emphasized its static character marked by uniformity both spatially and temporally (Piggott 1950: 132-213). Gordon considered the Indus Culture to be the work of immigrant people who brought with them the knowledge which was exploited and adopted to suit the environment (Gordon 1958: 57-76). Wheeler's chapter on the Indus culture was first published as a supplementary volume to the *Cambridge History of India* in 1953, with two more editions in 1960 and 1968. It is the most detailed account of Indus Culture. He examined it by evaluating "... three factors: the contribution of the earlier civilization of Mesopotamia, the initiative of the constituent Indus population, and the debt of both to a pre-existing or underlying continuum of ideas" (Wheeler 1968: 134). He also summarized the results in two other works (Wheeler 1959: 93-117; 1966). Bridget and Raymond Allchin (1968: 126-44) studied its growth and extent and showed that there is a direct cultural continuity between the pre-Harappan and the Harappan Periods and that during its mature period there was a general cultural evolution and internal development. In their view, not only the end of the Indus cities, but even their initial impetus may have been due to Indo-European speaking peoples (Allchin and Allchin 1968: 144).

In his two papers, Fairservis (1961, 1967), reprinted in Possehl 1979) analyzed the evidence with a cultural ecological orientation and suggested their interaction in the origin, growth and decline of the Indus Culture. In his second paper (Fairservis 1967; Possehl 1979: 66-89), which is "particularly significant since it is nowhere paralleled in other literature on the Indus Civilization" (Possehl 1979: 48), Fairservis gave a developmental model and population estimates of various sites. He further elaborated his synthesized studies in *The Roots of Ancient India* published in 1971 (Fairservis 1971: 217-311) and concluded that "it is a civilization still emerging out of an essentially village ethos" (Fairservis 1971: 299).

Apart from these, the evidence has been summarized by Casal (1969), Kosambi (1956, 1965) Subbarao (1958), Sankalia (1974), Lal (1964a, 1964b), Struve and Bongard-Levin (1964), Agrawal (1971), Thapar (1978), etc., in addition to a number of survey articles (Pande and Ramachandran, 1971; Possehl, 1979) detailing the results of excavation at Harappan sites.

It is not possible to mention individual books and articles which have been published in recent years on different aspects of the Indus Culture. From the published summaries (Anderson 1967; Pande and Ramachandran 1971; Brunswig 1974; Possehl 1979) it is obvious that the largest concern is for the script, followed by the chronology and end of the Indus Culture. These are also the issues which are the most controversial.

Marshall's report on the Indus Script (1931) was done by Gadd, Sidney Smith and Langdon. They organized the material and drew some conclusions. Pran Nath's proposed decipherment was published soon thereafter. Hunter's (1934) analysis of the script is a model of sound work. Thereafter followed a spate of writings on the subject (Zide 1970) and the language of the Indus inscriptions has been variously claimed to be Sanskrit or archaic Vedic, symbols of the Tantric code, Hittite, Sumerian, Dravidian and even Bundelkhandi. The script has also been compared to the Etruscan, Egyptian and Easter Island scripts. None of these attempts has stood the test of objective scrutiny and claims of decipherment are considered invalid. A tangible outcome of the efforts has been the publication of two computer-aided concordances of the Indus inscriptions prepared by a Finnish team (Koskenniemi, Parpola and Parpola 1973) and Mahadevan (1977) and settling the issue about the direction of writing of the script (Lal 1966). The latest attempt to read the Indus inscriptions, assuming Proto-Dravidian as the language of the inscriptions, is by Fairservis. This has yet to be put on the anvil.

The problem of Harappan chronology has been

discussed by a large number of scholars and one finds much polemical writing on the subject. After Marshall's initial chronology many schemes were proposed and it has now been suggested that the calibrated ^{14}C dates fit the "artifact-association" chronology (Brunswig 1975).

Scholars from different disciplines have contributed to the solution of the problem of the end of the Indus Culture. From their writing one now finds increasingly a multidisciplinary approach to this problem. The same is true in the study of Harappan technology. It has been variously suggested that the end of the Indus cities was due to internal decay, onslaught of the Aryans, floods, climatic change, etc. In the writing on the problem of the end of the Indus Culture, like those on the origin and authors, one can discern the influence of thinking in terms of Aryan and Dravidian which has also influenced the writings on the Indus script.

Equally debated is the problem of Harappan interconnections or interrelations, with which are connected the issues relating to trade and sources of raw materials. The studies in recent years (Chakrabarti 1978, 1979; Asthana 1979a, 1979b) are no longer based on artifact associations alone and indicate an increasing reliance on multiple data sources. One can now see a blend of the humanities and natural sciences in these writings.

Studies of the technology, environment and ecology of the Indus Culture have in recent years attained a new orientation. A large body of specialized literature dealing with these aspects has been published.

We have outlined in very broad and general terms the course of progress of the study of the Indus Culture and indicated in a few examples how the West Asian archaeological discoveries influenced the interpretations about and researches into the Indus Culture. It is also true that linguistic-cultural-historical considerations have been the *leitmotiv*. While F. R. Allchin in his preliminary study of Indian archaeological thought and practice (Allchin 1961) discussed broadly the writing and course of Indian archaeological research, and Malik made a critical appraisal of Indian archaeological writings "in terms of the explicit or implicit concepts underlying them" (Malik 1968: 25 ff.), it seems to us that the writing and research into the Indus Culture could form a rich subject for a historiographical study.

BIBLIOGRAPHY

Agrawal, D.P., 1971
 The Copper Bronze Age in India. Delhi: Munshiram Manoharlal.

Agrawal, D.P. and D.K. Chakrabarti, 1979
 Essays in Indian Protohistory. Delhi: B.R. Publishing Corp.

Allchin, B. and F.R. Allchin, 1968
 The Birth of Indian Civilization. Harmondsworth: Penguin Books.

Allchin, F.R., 1961
 Ideas of History in Indian Archaeological Writing: A preliminary study. In *Historians of India, Pakistan and Ceylon*. C.H. Phillips, ed. Pp. 241-59. London: Oxford University Press.

Anderson, B., 1967
 Indus Valley Civilization: A bibliography, 1954/66. *Indica* 4 (2): 107-24.

Asthana, Shashi, 1979a
 Harappan's Interest in Kirman. *Man and Environment* 3: 55-60.

Asthana, Shashi, 1979b
 Indus-Mesopotamian Trade: Nature of trade and a structural analysis of the operative system. In *Essays in Indian Protohistory*. D.P. Agrawal and D.K. Chakrabarti, eds. Pp. 31-47. Delhi: B.R. Publishing Corp.

Bisht, R.S., 1978
 Banawali: A new Harappan site in Haryana. *Man and Environment* 2: 86-88.

Bisht, R.S., in press
 Harappan Culture in the Punjab: A study in perspective. In *Indus Civilization: Problems and issues*. B.B. Lal and S.C. Malik, eds. Simla: Indian Institute of Advanced Study.

Brunswig, R., 1974
 A Comprehensive Bibliography of the Indus Civilization and Related Subjects and Areas. *Asian Perspectives* 16 (1): 75-111.

Brunswig, R., 1975
 Radiocarbon Dating and the Indus Civilization:

Calibration and chronology. *East and West* 25 (1-2): 111-45.

Burnes, Alexander, 1834
Travels into Bokhara. 3 vols. London: John Murray.

Casal, J.M., 1964
Fouilles d'Amri. 2 vols. Paris: Librarie C. Klincksieck.

Casal, J.M., 1969
La Civilization de l'Indus et ses Énigmes. Paris: Fayard.

Casal, J.M., 1979
Amri: An introduction to the study of the Indus civilization. In *Essays in Indian Protohistory*. D. P. Agrawal and D.K. Chakrabarti eds. Pp. 99-112. Delhi: B.R. Publishing Corp.

Chakrabarti, D.K., 1978
Lapis Lazuli in Early India. *Man and Environment* 2: 51-58.

Chakrabarti, D.K., 1979
The Problem of Tin in Early India: A preliminary survey. *Man and Environment* 3: 61-74.

Childe, V.G., 1958
New Light on the Most Ancient East. Revised ed. New York: Praeger.

Cunningham, Sir Alexander, 1875
Harappa. *Archaeological Survey of India, Report for the Year* 1872-73. Pp. 105-108. Calcutta.

Cunningham, Sir Alexander, 1877
Inscriptions of Aśoka. Corpus Inscriptionum Indicarium, Vol. 1. Calcutta: Office of the Superintendent of Government Printing.

Dales, G.F., 1965a
New Investigations at Mohenjodaro. *Archaeology* 18: 145-50.

Dales, G.F., 1965b
Re-opening the Mohenjodaro. Excavation *Illustrated London News* May 29: 25-27.

Dales, G.F., 1965c
Civilization and Floods in the Indus Valley. *Expedition* 7 (2): 10-19.

Dales, G.F., 1979
The Balakot Project: Summary of four years of excavation in Pakistan. *Man and Environment* 3: 45-53.

Dames, M.L., 1886
Old Seals Found at Harappa. *Indian Antiquary* 15: 1.

Dani, A.H., 1970-71
Excavations in the Gomal Valley. *Ancient Pakistan* 5: 1-177.

Fairservis, W.A., 1961
The Harappan Civilization: New evidence and more theory. *Novitates* 2055. New York: American Museum of Natural History.

Fairservis, W.A., 1967
The Origin, Character and Decline of an Early Civilization. *Novitates* 2302. New York: American Museum of Natural History.

Fairservis, W.A., 1971
The Roots of Ancient India. New York: Macmillan.

Fleet, J.F., 1912
Seals From Harappa. *Journal of the Royal Asiatic Society*: 698-701.

Ghosh, A., 1952
The Rajputana Desert: Its archaeological aspect. *Bulletin of the National Institute of Sciences in India* 1: 37-42.

Gordon, D.H., 1958
The Prehistoric Background of Indian Culture. Bombay: Bhulabhai Memorial Institute.

Government of India, 1934-35
Rangpur. *Annual Report of the Archaeological Survey of India, 1934-35*. Pp. 34-38. Delhi.

Gupta, S.P., 1979
Archaeology of Soviet Central Asia and the Indian Borderlands. 2 vols. Delhi: B.R. Publishing Corp.

Hunter, G.R., 1934
The Script of Harappa and Mohenjodaro and its Connection with Other Scripts. London: Kegan Paul.

Indian Archaeology: A review (IAR), 1953-54
Harappa and Other Early Settlements on the Upper Sutlej. P. 38. Delhi: Archaeological Survey of India.

Indian Archaeology: A review (IAR), 1954-55
Harappa and Other Early Settlements in Gujarat. P. 59. Delhi: Archaeological Survey of India.

Indian Archaeology: A review (IAR), 1955-56
Excavations of Other Harappa Sites in Saurashtra. Pp. 7-8. Delhi: Archaeological Survey of India.

Indian Archaeology: A review (IAR), 1956-57
Harappa and Painted Grey Ware Sites in Punjab. P. 79. Delhi: Archaeological Survey of India.

Indian Archaeology: A review (IAR), 1964-65
Exploration in Districts Banas-Kantha, Mehsana and Surendranagar. Pp. 10-11. Delhi: Archaeological Survey of India.

Indian Archaeology: A review (IAR), 1965-66
    Gujarat. Pp. 12-18. Delhi: Archaeological Survey of India.
Indian Archaeology: A review (IAR), 1966-67
    Gujarat and Haryana. Pp. 8-14. Delhi: Archaeological Survey of India.
Indian Archaeology: A review (IAR), 1967-68
    Exploration in District Kutch. Pp. 13-17. Delhi: Archaeological Survey of India.
Indian Archaeology: A review (IAR), 1970-71
    Excavation at Surkotada, District Kutch. Pp. 13-15. Delhi: Archaeological Survey of India.
Indian Archaeology: A review (IAR), 1971-72
    Excavation at Surkotada, District Kutch. Pp. 13-21. Delhi: Archaeological Survey of India.
Joshi, J.P., 1973
    Excavation at Surkotada. In *Radiocarbon and Indian Archaeology*. D.P. Agrawal and A. Ghosh, eds. Pp. 173-81. Bombay: Tata Institute of Fundamental Research.
Khan, F.A., 1964
    Kot Diji. Karachi: Government of Pakistan.
Khan, F.A., 1965
    Excavations at Kot Diji. *Pakistan Archaeology* 2: 13-85.
Kosambi, D.D., 1956
    An Introduction to the Study of Indian History. Bombay: Popular Book Depot.
Kosambi, D.D., 1965
    The Culture and Civilization of Ancient India. London: Routledge and Kegan Paul.
Koskenniemi, S.A., A. Parpola and S. Parpola, 1973
    Materials for the Study of the Indus Script I: A Concordance to the Indus Inscriptions. Helsinki: Suomalainien. Tiedeakatemia.
Lal, B.B., 1962
    A New Indus Provincial Capital Discovered: Excavation at Kalibangan in northern Rajasthan. *Illustrated London News* March 24: 454-57.
Lal, B.B., 1964a
    Archaeological Excavations and Expeditions. *International Congress of Orientalists* 26th Session, New Delhi: 171-94.
Lal, B.B., 1964b
    India. *Asian Perspectives* 8: 76-86.
Lal, B.B., 1966
    The Direction of Writing in the Harappan Script. *Antiquity* 40: 52-55.
Lal, B.B., 1979
    Kalibangan and the Indus Civilization. In *Essays in Indian Protohistory*. D. P. Agrawal and D. K. Chakrabarti, eds. Pp. 65-97. Delhi: B. R. Publishing Corp.
Lal, B.B. and B.K. Thapar, 1967
    Excavation at Kalibangan: New light on the Indus Civilization. *Cultural Forum* 9 (4): 78-88.
Mackay, E.J.H., 1935
    Early Indus Civilization. London: Clay and Sons Ltd.
Mackay, E.J.H., 1938
    Further Excavations at Mohenjodaro. 2 vols. Delhi: Government of India.
Mackay, E.J.H., 1943
    Chanhudaro Excavations, 1935-36. American Oriental Series 20. New Haven: American Oriental Society.
Mahadeven, I., 1977
    The Indus Script: Texts, Concordance and Tables. Memoirs of the Archaeological Survey of India No. 77. Delhi.
Majumdar, N.G., 1934
    Exploration in Sind. Memoirs of the Archaeological Survey of India No. 48. Delhi.
Malik, S.C., 1968
    Indian Civilization: The formative period. Simla: Indian Institute of Advanced Study.
Marshall, Sir John, editor, 1931
    Mohenjodaro and the Indus Civilization. 3 vols. London: Arthur Probsthain.
Masson, C., 1842
    A Narrative of Various Journeys in Baluchistan, Afghanistan and the Punjab. 3 vols. London: Richard Bently.
Mughal, M.R., 1973
    The Present State of Research on the Indus Valley Civilization. International Symposium on Mohenjodaro: 1-28.
Mughal, M.R., 1974
    New Evidence of the Early Harappan Culture From Jalilpur, Pakistan. *Archaeology* 27 (2): 106-13.
Mughal, M.R., 1980
    New Archaeological Evidence From Bhawalpur. *Man and Environment,* Vol. 4: 93-98.
Pande, B.M. and K.S. Ramachandran, 1971
    Bibliography of the Harappan Culture. Florida:

Field Research Projects.

Piggott, S., 1950
Prehistoric India. Baltimore: Penguin Books.

Possehl, G.L., 1979
Ancient Cities of the Indus. Durham: Carolina Academic Press.

Raikes, R.L., 1964
The End of the Ancient Cities of the Indus. *American Anthropologist* 66: 284-99.

Raikes, R.L., 1965
The Mohenjodaro Floods. *Antiquity* 39: 196-203.

Raikes, R.L., 1967a
The Mohenjodaro Floods: Further notes. *Antiquity* 41: 64-66.

Raikes, R.L., 1967b
The Mohenjodaro Floods: Riposte. *Antiquity* 41: 309-10.

Raikes, R.L., 1968
Kalibangan: Death from Natural Causes. *Antiquity* 42: 286-91.

Rao, S.R., 1963
Excavations at Rangpur and other Explorations in Gujarat. *Ancient India* 18-19: 5-207.

Rao, S.R., 1973
Lothal and the Indus Civilization. Bombay: Asia Publishing.

Sankalia, H.D., 1974
The Prehistory and Protohistory of India and Pakistan. 2nd ed. Poona: Deccan College Postgraduate and Research Institute.

Shaffer, J., 1979
The Indus Civilization: New evidence from Pakistan. In *Essays in Indian Protohistory.* D.P. Agrawal and D.K. Chakrabarti, eds. Pp. 17-29. Delhi: B.R. Publishing Corp.

Stein, Sir Aurel, 1929
An Archaeological Tour in Waziristan and Northern Baluchistan. Memoirs of the Archaeological Survey of India 37. Calcutta.

Stein, Sir Aurel, 1942
A Survey of Ancient Sites Along the 'lost' Sarasvati River. *Geographical Journal* 99(4): 174-82.

Struve, V.V. and G.M. Bongard-Levin, editors, 1964
Ancient India Moscow: Akademiia Nauk SSR, Institut Narodov Azii (In Russian).

Subbarao, B., 1958
The Personality of India. 2nd ed. M.S. University of Baroda. Archaeology Series 3. Baroda.

Suraj Bhan, 1973
The Sequence and Spread of Prehistoric Cultures in the Upper Sarasvati Basin. In *Radiocarbon and Indian Archaeology.* D.P. Agrawal and A. Ghosh, eds. Pp. 252-63. Bombay: Tata Institute of Fundamental Research.

Thapar, B.K., 1975
Kalibangan: A Harappan metropolis beyond the Indus Valley. *Expedition* 17 (2): 19-32.

Thapar, B.K., 1978
The Mosaic of the Indus Civilization Beyond the Indus Valley. Unpublished paper presented at the International Symposium on the Indus Civilization, Karachi, December 30. Cyclostyled copy.

Vats, M.S., 1940
Excavations at Harappa. 2 vols. Delhi: Government of India.

Wheeler, Sir Mortimer, 1953
The Indus Civilization. 1st ed. Supplementary Volume to the Cambridge History of India. Cambridge: The University Press.

Wheeler, Sir Mortimer, 1959
Early India and Pakistan: To Ashoka. London: Thames and Hudson.

Wheeler, Sir Mortimer, 1960
The Indus Civilization. 2nd ed. Supplementary Volume to The Cambridge History of India. Cambridge: The University Press.

Wheeler, Sir Mortimer, 1966
Civilizations of the Indus Valley and Beyond. London: Thames and Hudson.

Wheeler, Sir Mortimer, 1968
The Indus Civilization. 3rd ed. Supplementary Volume to The Cambridge History of India. Cambridge: The University Press.

Zide, Arlene, 1970
A Brief Survey of the Work to Date on the Indus Valley Script. *Journal of Tamil Studies* 2 (1): 1-12.

GREGORY L. POSSEHL

39. Discovering Ancient India's Earliest Cities: The First Phase of Research

IN THE winter of 1911-12 D.R. Bhandarkar, Superintending Archaeologist of the Western Circle of the Archaeological Survey of India, visited a site in Sind Province known to the local inhabitants of Larkana District as Mohenjodaro—Mound of the Dead Men (Bhandarkar 1912). Bhandarkar was engaged in a broadly conceived survey of ancient sites and monuments within his Circle which had been ordered by John Marshall, the Director General of the Survey. Bhandarkar has left the following description of the site:

> I also visited what is called Mohen-jo-daro, seven miles southeast of Dokri in Larkhana district. We had received glowing accounts of this spot, and I had great hopes of finding it to be as interesting as the ruins of the Mirpur Khas stupa before they were dug out. But on visiting the place I was greatly disappointed. Here are spread the remains of an old place for about three-fourths of a mile. Near the western edge is a tower on a mound nearly seventy feet high from the ground-level, from which the mound gradually rises. Of the top portion only the inner core has remained, consisting of sun-dried brick work. The bottom of it appears to have been reached most probably by treasure hunters, who, I was told, frequently excavated the most promising sites here. Close by towards the west and south are six mounds, but of far less height, and there seems to have been a river once running between the tower mound and the other heaps. On the north side of the tower again are vestiges of an old brick road running up. The bricks as a rule are of modern type and not of large dimension like the old. There are no doubt some here which look old, but they are few and far between. Not a single carved moulded brick was I able to discover here. What a contrast to the Mirpur Khas stupa, where cart loads of such bricks were found before it was excavated! The probabilities, therefore, are that the Mohen-jo-daro does not represent the remains of a Buddhist stupa or of any ancient monument. According to the local tradition, these are the ruins of a town only two hundred years old, and the daro or tower itself a part of the bastion guarding its west side. This seems to be not incorrect, because the bricks here found, as just said, are of the modern type, and there is a total lack of carved terra-cottas amidst the whole ruins (Bhandarkar 1912: 4-5).

That Bhandarkar completely missed the mark as to the significance of Mohenjodaro is best accounted for by the fact that at that time nothing was known of the eras predating the Buddhist period in the early centuries before Christ. Moreover, the discovery of the Harappan, or Indus Civilization is set apart from that of the other great ancient urban systems of Asia. In the South Asian case there was no hint, even in the earliest written texts, that the Harappan Civilization had once flourished on the fertile plains of Sind, Gujarat and the greater Punjab, extending even as far west as the Dasht River on the modern border between Pakistan and Iran. That the remains of this urban complex would be found buried within the mounds of what was then western India was therefore not suspected by Marshall and his colleagues, or anyone else for that matter. This is a significantly different historical context from that which led to the discovery of the other ancient states where historical documents clearly pointed to the Sumerians, Dynastic Egyptians and those who once inhabited the Shang settlements of northern China. It is therefore not surprising that Bhandarkar failed to realize that he had inadvertently visited one of ancient India's earliest cities.¹ But others before him had made the same mistake.

As early as 1826 a person known as Charles Masson visited the huge mound adjacent to the village of Harappa.² Masson had just entered the Punjab and left this impression of the place:

> A long march preceded our arrival at Haripah (Harappa) through jangal of the closest description. East of the village was an abundance of luxuriant grass, where, along with many others, I went to allow my nag to graze. When I joined the camp I found it in front of the village and ruinous brick castle. Behind us was a large circular mound, or eminence, and to the west was an irregular rocky height, crowned with remains of buildings, in fragments of walls, with niches, after the eastern manner. The latter elevation was undoubtedly a natural object; the former being of earth only, was obviously an artificial one. I examined the remains on the height, and found two circular perforated stones, affirmed to have been used as bangles, or armrings, by a faquir of renown. He has also credit for having subsisted on earth, and other unusual substances, and his depreved appetite is instanced in testimony of his sanctity. The entire neighborhood is embellished with numerous pipal trees, some of them in the last stage of lingering existence, bespeaking a great antiquity, when we remember their longevity. The walls and towers of the castle are remarkably high, though, from having been long deserted, they exhibit in some parts the ravages of time and decay. Between our camp and it extended a deep trench, now overgrown with grass and plants. Tradition affirms the existence here of a city, so considerable that it extended to Chicha Watni, thirteen cosses distant, and that it was destroyed by a particular visitation of Providence, brought down by the lust and crimes of the sovereign.
>
> We were cautioned by the inhabitants, that on the plain we were likely to be assailed by Makkahs, or stinging-gnats, and in the evening we ascended the circular mound behind us. There was ample room on the summit to receive the party and the horses belonging to it. It was impossible to survey the scene before us, and to look upon the ground on which we stood, without perceiving that every condition of Arrian's Sangala was here fulfilled,—the brick fortress, with a lake, or rather swamp, at the north-eastern angle; the mound, protected by a triple row of chariots, and defended by the Kathi before they suffered themselves to be shut up within their walls; and the trench between the mound and fortress, by which the circumvallation of the place was completed, and whence engines were directed against it. The data of Arrian are very minute, and can scarcely be misapplied to Haripah, the position of which also perfectly coincides with what, from inference, we must assign to Sangala. I have made public my convictions on this point, but repeat them, as I doubt not they are just; and the identification of Sangala gives a point from which we may safely calculate upon the site of the celebrated altars of Alexander, which in all probability, were in the neighborhood of Pak Pattan, on the Satlaj, two marches from Haripah, Alexander having there gained the high road into India, which was afterwards followed by Timur (Masson 1844, Vol. 1: 452-54).

Thus, Charles Masson, too, missed the mark by a relatively wide margin; but he is undoubtedly one of the most fascinating characters in the history of Indian archaeology.³ According to Frank E. Ross (1933), documents in the India Office Library enable us to know that he was not Charles Masson, late of Kentucky, U.S.A. but rather James Lewis late of Captain Hyde's First Brigade of Horse Artillery. Masson (né Lewis) had enlisted as a private soldier in the British Army and sailed for Bengal in January of 1822 on board the *Dutchess of Athol*. While in service he fought in the siege of Bharatpur, but more importantly, I think, was employed by Major-General Hardwicke, commandant of Bengal Artillery, to catalog the General's collection of zoological specimens. Shortly thereafter, in the summer of 1826, Masson deserted the army and headed west to the Punjab. Over the next twenty years he traveled widely on the western borderlands of the British Empire, reaching the most remote areas of Central Asia, Afghanistan and Baluchistan. Apparently a gifted polyglot he was also keenly interested in geography, customs and political conditions. As Ross has noted:

> Masson's work was peculiarly distinctive and valuable. A shrewd observer of all matters political, economic, scientific, and social, he took the role of an Afghan traveller, clad in native garments. He lived and travelled not with the chiefs but with the people, a manner never since duplicated in Afghanistan and a method which gives 'a peculiar value' to his works. There is scarcely a place in the Kabul area which he did not visit and describe. Many of the names and events he mentioned were so unfamiliar to his contemporaries that he was called 'fanciful' (*Calcutta Review* August 1844: 449). For many years his work remained unchecked, but was finally proven to be 'marvellously accurate in geographical detail' (Holdich 1910: 348). Half a century later, after twice invading and occupying Afghanistan, the British authorities possessed no knowledge of the country that they could not have obtained from Masson (Holdich 1910: 362). For fifteen years

Masson was 'an irreclaimable nomadic vagabond.' His life was constantly in danger. Often he fell among thieves. Once he was stripped of clothes and money and left 'destitute, a stranger in the center of Asia ... exposed ... to notice, inquiry, ridicule, and insult' (Masson 1844, Vol. 1: 309-10). But if there was hardship, there were also consolations: occasionally Masson paused in his travels to comfort a lonely female in some far away corner of Asia (Masson 1844, Vol. 1: 375) (Ross 1933: 222).

Masson was a man of intense antiquarian interests and he recorded ancient sites wherever he found them. Begram, the ancient Kapisa, summer capital of the Kushans, attracted his interest and he was one of the first to excavate there. By 1834 he had acquired a substantial collection of coins, from this and other exploratory digging, which were donated to the Government of India and transferred to the East India Company Museum in London. It was this collection, and other inscriptional materials from the northwest of Pakistan and Afghanistan, which allowed James Prinsep to outline the Kushan Dynasty. Masson was also an early visitor to Bamiyan where he left the following penciled inscription in a small cave to the west of the larger of the two colossal Buddhas:

> If any fool this high samootch explore
> Know Charles Masson has been here before
> (Hakin 1933)

This bit of doggerel was even signed and dated 1833, as seen in Plate 39.1.

To return to the problem at hand—the location of Sangala remains an elusive problem; but it is clearly not the site at Harappa. Still, given the times and knowledge then available, Masson's speculation would have to be considered a good guess.

Five years later, in 1831, Alexander Burnes visited Harappa while in the course of delivering a gift of five horses from the King of Great Britain to Ranjit Singh, and incidently exploring the Indus River and its tributaries. His observations, not at significant variance from Masson's, are:

> About fifty miles eastward of Toolumba, I passed inland for four miles to examine the ruins of an ancient city, called Harappa. The remains are extensive, and the place, which has been built of brick, is about three miles in circumference. There is a ruined citadel on the river side of the town; but otherwise Harappa is a perfect chaos, and has not an entire building: the bricks have been removed to build a small place of the old name hard by. Tradition fixes the fall of Harappa at the same period as Shorkote (1300 years ago), and the people ascribe its ruin to the vengeance of God on Harappa; its governor, who claimed certain privileges on the marriage of every couple in his city, and in the course of his sensualities, was guilty of incest. At a later period, Harappa became a Mahommedan town; and there is a tomb of a Saint of the 'faithful,' eighteen feet in length, the assigned, but fabulous, stature of the deceased. A large stone of annular form, and a huge black slab of an oval shape, which lie near the grave, are said to represent the ring and its gem of this departed giant, and to have been converted from more valuable to their present base materials. Where such fables are believed, we must cease to hope for even reasonable fiction. I found some coins in these ruins, both Persian and Hindoo, but I cannot fix its era from any of them (Burnes 1834, Vol. III: 137-38).

These two early notices of Harappa seem to have had an historical importance only because they came to the notice of Sir Alexander Cunningham, the first Director General of the Archaeological Survey. In 1875 he reported (Cunningham 1875) that he visited Harappa on three occasions (1853, 1856, and 1872-73). It is at this point that something more than casual observation about the site comes to light. Cunningham noted its size (2.5 miles in circuit) and the height of the mounds (40 to 60 feet). He also corrected some of the inaccuracies found in the Masson and Burnes accounts; but more importantly he stated that: "In 1853, and again in 1856, I traced the remains of flights of steps on both the eastern and western faces of the high mound to the northwest, as well as the basement of a large square building" (1875: 106). Concerning these remains and others, particularly a large building with rooms on four sides, he went on to say: "... but the whole have now been removed to form ballast for the Railway. Perhaps the best idea of the extent of the ruined brick mounds of Harapa [sic] may be formed from the fact that they have more than sufficed to furnish brick ballast for about 100 miles of Lahor [sic] and Multan Railway" (1875: 106-107).

The complete details of this abominable act seem to be obscure. In a curious little book Mr. John Brunton describes his direction of the construction of the Sind Railway in the later half of the 1850s (Brunton 1939). His work was faced with the same peril as that in the Punjab—where to find ballast. He described the situation, and his solution to it:

> My own servants and tent-pitchers amounted in number to 35—for whom tents and provisions had to be collected with a supply of camels to carry them. Then there were my horses for riding the

marches, so altogether when we collected at Hyderabad it formed a rather imposing procession. Before leaving I had learnt the position of an old ruined city, called Brahminabad in the "Great Desert" of Scinde—it lay about 15 or 16 miles from the selected course of the left bank line, away in the Desert of rolling banks of sand. I had been much exercised in my mind how we were to get ballast for the line of Railway. If all I heard were true, this ruined city, built of brick, would form a grand quarry for ballast, so I determined to visit it and judge for myself, for we cannot in India any more than in England, trust to hearsay (Brunton 1939: 121).

He did visit the city and found it an acceptable quarry. At another point in this book Mr. Brunton mentions that his brother Robert was supervising the construction of the Lahore to Multan section of the Western Railway (1939: 83). It seems reasonable to presume, then, that it was Robert Brunton who ordered the dismantling of Harappa, just as John Brunton had at Brahminabad.

The railroad's plunder of the site seems to have motivated Alexander Cunningham to carry out several modest excavations which were apparently quite unsuccessful because of the total disruption of the site. But he did acquire a seal which today can be identified as a reasonably typical Harappan type (Fig. 39.1). This object was the property of one Major Clark and Cunningham had the following to say of it:

> The seal is a smooth black stone without polish. On it is engraved very deeply a bull, without hump, looking to the right, with two stars under the neck. Above the bull there is an inscription in six characters, which are quite unknown to me. They are certainly not Indian letters; and as the bull which accompanies them is without a hump, I conclude that the seal is foreign to India (Cunningham 1875: 108).

Cunningham's conclusion concerning this seal is at least something more than a bold assertion, and that he was wrong about its identification, and that of the site as well, cannot be counted against his favor.[4]

The report on Harappa by Sir Alexander was clearly not forgotten. M. Longworth Dames (1886) published a second seal from the site which had been acquired by a Mr. J. Harvey, Inspector of Schools. In this one page note he discusses and illustrates Cunningham's (or more precisely, Major Clark's) seal and the new find, as well as some interesting, but obscure bibliography.[5] Still later, a third seal from Harappa was published by J. F. Fleet (1912). This

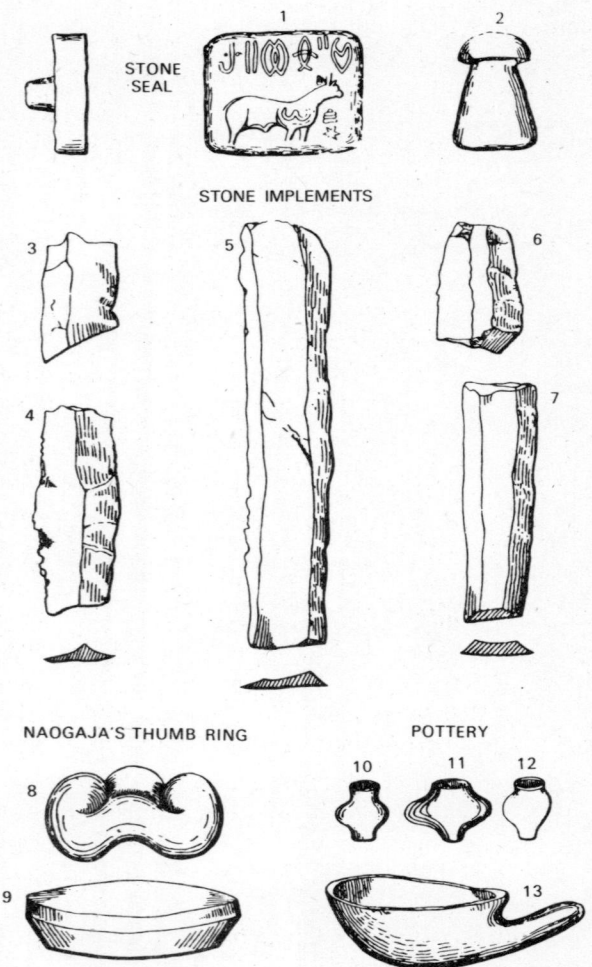

Fig. 39.1. Cunningham's figure of objects from Harappa.

had been recovered from the site in 1886 by T. A. O'Connor the District Superintendent of Police. Fleet's paper is interesting for two reasons. First, he informs that all three seals could then be found in the British Museum and second, the seal illustrated by Sir Alexander Cunningham is for the first time published as a photograph of the impression (Pl. 39.2) and not as Cunningham's drawing.

This short recapitulation of the early notices of Harappa, and the Bhandarkar visit to Mohenjodaro, are sufficient to know that these sites, especially Harappa, were known entities among professionals in Indian archaeology. Sir John Marshall even went so far as to send Henry Hargreaves on an inspection of Harappa in 1914 to determine its potential for excavation (Majumdar 1939: 99) since as Sir John

Discovering Ancient India's Earliest Cities

noted later: "The desirability of continuing the exploration of the remains begun on so small a scale many years ago by Cunningham was of course obvious from the first" (Marshall 1926: 51). It seems clear that this site, at least, was a place of great interest, deserving the thorough attention of an intensive investigation. Harappa never slipped back into obscurity once Cunningham brought the seal to the attention of a scholarly community. But what follows this, the earliest period of discovery, is in part a story of the Survey's orderly approach to mounting an excavation at Harappa and an unanticipated coincidence.

Marshall set in motion a process which would end in the acquisition of the mounds at Harappa "... which seem to have suffered least, namely those marked (A) and (B) on Cunningham's plan and a third (F on the plan of recent excavations) which is shown without a letter to the east of mound A and B on Cunningham's plan...." (Marshall 1923: 16). Once this was completed (1920-21) Rai Bahadur Daya Ram Sahni went to the site to begin an excavation. Starting with Mound F he laid a trench nearly 500 feet long and 16 feet wide across the mound (Marshall 1923: 16). In the course of this work he found two more seals similar to the one published by Cunningham. Sahni also did some digging on Mound A-B where architecture assigned to the Mauryan and Kushan Periods was found. By the end of the season Marshall felt confident to state: "Thus, although the results attained so far are undoubtedly meagre, they are important in that, according to Mr. Sahni, they prove that the Harappa seals and their curious pictographic legends belong to the pre-Mauryan epoch; and it is to be remembered that the digging to date has pierced only the topmost levels" (1923: 17). This was, of course, a somewhat conjectural conclusion at that time, but it was to be proved correct. It was also of extraordinary importance since it was the first indication that the history of South Asia might be pushed back into the pre-Buddhist, even pre-Vedic era. Lack of funds prevented the Survey from moving vigorously ahead with this work until 1923-24 (Marshall 1926: 47). At this time Sahni expanded his long trench on Mound F and opened new exposures on the A-B Mound. Many significant finds came to light during this excavation, including several more seals. But, the excavation at Harappa was soon to be almost completely, and unexpectedly, overshadowed by Mohenjodaro.

During the field season of 1919-20, one year prior to Mr. Sahni's initial probing of Harappa, the new superintendent of the Western Circle, Mr. R. D. Banerji, visited Mohenjodaro. There is insufficient historical information available to know what it was that brought him there, but he did leave the following paragraphs in his "Progress Report for the year Ending 31 March 1920."

> The ruins at Muhen-jo-daro lie at a distance of 6 miles from the Railway Station at Dokri on the Rohri-Kotri Section of the N.W. Railway. The locality does not seem to have attracted notice before though the height of the mound and the extensity of the ruins is well known in the neighbourhood. The ruins cover an area of about 2 square miles and are visible from a distance. They are not mentioned in the revised list of ancient monuments in the Bombay Presidency, but were visited by my Predecessor in 1913.[6]
>
> The ruins consist of vast mounds of burnt bricks surrounded by smaller ones. In the centre of this area is a very high mound about 80 or 90 feet above the level of the surrounding country. This is called Muhen-jo-daro. The top of the entire mound consists of debris and brick bats but here and there loose debris has slipped away exposing straight walls of burnt bricks. This mound is about 600 feet in length and 200 in breadth. In one place on this mound there is the drum of a stupa made of sun-dried bricks. Only the shell of the drum remains as the core has been excavated to a depth of some 30 to 40 feet by treasure seekers. The inhabitants of the surrounding village have dug out and removed bricks from this mound from time immemorial and do so even now. Some of these people who do not acknowledge to have excavated this mound for bricks within the last ten or twelve years, state that when they dug for bricks previously, they found the entire mound to consist of a huge platform, of burnt bricks on which were built numerous round hemispherical objects of burnt as well as sun-dried bricks (?votive stupas).
>
> Close to this platform of stupas there is another high mound which is the second largest in this place. This appears to have been a temple or monastery as the old villagers state that they found rows of small square chambers arranged around a square courtyard in this mound. Search among the ruins led to the discovery of numbers of carved bricks but no human figures or images were found. The villagers are unanimous in stating that no coins have ever been found in any of these mounds.
>
> These two mounds are surrounded by numerous small mounds which represent the ruins of the village or township which had grown around this stupa and temple in the height of their glory. The stupa at this place is much higher than the stupas

at Depar Ghangro or Mirpur-Khas and appears to have been the largest and highest Buddhist stupa in the country of Sindh. The stupas and the surrounding ground is full of saltpetre or some other salt which is carried away and sold as a manure. The digging for bricks and the removal of this sort of manure constitute a serious danger to the structures that may lie under the covering of loose brick bats and debris and therefore steps ought to be taken to stop excavation in this area immediately (Banerji 1921) (Pls. 39.3 and 39.4).

Other details of what he observed at the site in terms of pottery, artifacts or seals (?) are not known. Nor is there any positive evidence of what Mr. Banerji knew of Harappa generally or Marshall's plans for excavation there. It is reasonable speculation, however, to presume that he was acquainted with the Cunningham report and those articles on the seals which followed it, and it is likely that his position as superintendent would have made him aware of the Survey's research and excavation program in a general way. Thus, the lack of real information in this regard notwithstanding, I would presume that it is prudent for us to think of Banerji as a knowledgeable person as regards these matters. Further to the point, it must therefore be within these contexts that his excavation at Mohenjodaro is placed.

In 1921-22 (Marshall 1926: 48)[7] Banerji returned to Mohenjodaro and opened a trench in the stupa area. His finds there (summarized in Banerji 1922-23), indicated that there were buildings of four periods. The uppermost level, with coins of the Kushan king Vasudeva I were taken to indicate that the stupa itself was built and maintained during the second century A.D. Beneath this level, however, he recovered three seals. He describes these finds in this way:

> The most important discovery of the season was a seal of soapstone, found on the staircase on the riverside, at the bottom of the eastern retaining wall of the tower. This seal bears in the centre the figure of a one-horned quadruped, which has been identified by Dr. D. B. Spooner as the unicorn. The fragment of a similar seal was discovered in a drain at the same place and a third specimen was discovered on a small shrine to the north-east of site No. 1. These seals bear ideograms or pictograms like the seals discovered at Harappa (Banerji 1922-23: 103).

Banerji went on to suggest that there were "affinities" between these, and other finds from Mohenjodaro and Minoan antiquities. This suggestion has, of course, proved incorrect; but his discrimination of several strata below the stupa and the tie between Mohenjodaro and Harappa was a very significant contribution to the archaeology of the day. Equally to the point is the incredible coincidence between the timing of Banerji's excavation and the work at Harappa. Of course, it is possible that this is all happenstance. Banerji could have gone to Mohenjodaro in 1919-20 as a routine part of his duties and he could have selected the site for excavation because of the brick robbing and other damage being done there as indicated in his yearly report quoted above. But the fact remains that between 1919-20 and 1923-24 there was a great flurry of serious archaeological activity around two sites which had heretofore been largely ignored. It is almost as if R. D. Banerji knew that there was a relationship between Mohenjodaro and Harappa; at least after his initial visit to the site. I am not raising this issue to reflect in any way upon the reputation or character of any individual. There is, however, room for further research on the matter and it is in an effort to clarify the history of research into the discovery of the Indus Civilization that my attention is directed.

Unfortunately Mr. Banerji's health seems not to have been good at this time and consequently there was some delay in publication and dissemination of his important material (Marshall 1926: 48). But in the summer of 1924 Marshall arranged for the finds from Mohenjodaro to be brought to his headquarters where they could be compared directly with those from Harappa (Marshall 1926: 48).

> That the finds from the two sites belonged to the same stage of culture and approximately to the same age, and that they were totally distinct from anything previously known to us in India was at once evident. So impressed indeed was I by their novel character that I lost no time in publishing an account of them in the *Illustrated London News*, my hope being that through the medium of that widely read journal I might succeed in getting some light thrown on their age and character by archaeologists in other countries. This hope, I am glad to say, was at once fulfilled. In the following issue of the *Illustrated London News* appeared a letter from Professor Sayce pointing out the close resemblance between these objects from the Indus Valley and certain Sumerian antiquities from Southern Mesopotamia, and a week later there appeared in the same journal a longer article from the pens of Messrs. Gadd and Sidney Smith giving a more detailed comparison of the pictographic scripts and other antiquities found in the two

countries. Some of the analogies suggested by these two writers are fanciful, but most of them are undoubtedly correct and there can now no longer be any doubt that the Punjab and Sind antiquities are closely connected and roughly contemporary with the Sumerian antiquities of Mesopotamia dating from the 3rd or 4th millennium before Christ. Simultaneously also the same conclusion was reached by Dr. E. Mackay, Director of the American Expedition at Kish, who in an unpublished letter to me pointed out the similarity between the ceramic wares found at Mohenjodaro and at Kish, and also brought to my notice that a seal identical with those found at Harappa and Mohenjodaro had been discovered in the debris beneath a temple at Hammurabi's time (Marshall 1926: 48).

From this point on the situation was clear. Marshall interrupted his excavation at Taxila to direct the work at Mohenjodaro. He brought Mr. Mackay into the Survey on an *ad hoc* basis and eventually relinquished the direction of the field operation at the site to him. M. S. Vats went off to Harappa to do what he could with that very disturbed site. The Indus Civilization had been discovered and these men began the task of revealing it to the world.

NOTES

[1] A truism in science is probably applicable here as well. Those engaged in research tend to find what they are looking for, and this is not necessarily due to misrepresentation or overt preconception. It is theory which shapes what we come to call facts and a fact is not such without being somehow lodged within a larger order of intellectual structure. As Julian Steward noted when he was grappling with the problem of early urbanization: "Fact collecting of itself is insufficient scientific procedure; facts exist only as they are related to theories and theories are not destroyed by facts—they are replaced by new theories which better explain the facts. Therefore, criticisms of this paper which concern facts alone and which fail to offer better formulations are of no interest" (1955: 209).

[2] This is a modern place name. We have absolutely no idea of what the city was originally called. Sir Mortimer Wheeler (1947: 78-82) has suggested that the name can be found in the *Rigveda*, but this is more or less pure conjecture.

[3] Masson eventually received a pension from the East India Company and retired to complete his books. I am certain there is much to this man's life which has a direct bearing on the history of research on the archaeology of India, Pakistan and Afghanistan and he is therefore someone deserving of complete biographical research.

[4] Cunningham identified Harappa as the *Po-fa-to* or *Po-fa-to-lo* (1875: 107) mentioned by the Chinese traveler Huan Tsang, whose journey through India provided him with an ancient geography which he was attempting to reconstruct. It is therefore not so curious that Cunningham's identification of Harappa was tied to some aspect of the Monk's travels. We really do tend to find what we look for, and not necessarily because of *malice* of forethought.

[5] The Dames article may provide a solution to a small mystery which has appeared in the early discourse on Harappan seals. On September 27, 1924, A.H. Sayce published a letter to the editor of the *Illustrated London News* commenting on Sir John Marshall's first general article on the Indus Civilization (Marshall 1924) which had been published there the week before. In this note Sayce drew attention to the similarities between the seals from Mohenjodaro and others from Mesopotamia, of which more will be said later. However, the last sentence of this letter reads: "An inscribed 'seal' from Harappa was published by Terrien de la Couperie in an early number of the 'Proceedings of the Society of Biblical Archaeology'" (Sayce 1924). My search for this reference has failed to produce such a paper and I might add that C.J. Gadd apparently also tried to locate it with the same lack of success (Gadd 1932: 14). But in Mr. Dames' paper we come to know that:

> In the Academy for May 2nd, 1885, M. Terrien de la Couperie, in an article on the meaning of the word Tin-Yut, refers to "the stone seal of Setchuen or Shuh writing which was found a few years ago in the ruins of Harappa, near Lahor." 'This' he adds, "is attributed by General Cunningham on archaeological evidence to the fourth century B.C., and is the oldest fragment of writing found in India" (Dames 1886).

To add a footnote to a footnote: the editor of that

issue of *The Indian Antiquary* properly notes that in neither the 1875 report nor in his *Ancient Geography of India* does Cunningham attribute Major Clark's seal to the fourth century B.C. More to the point, however, is the fact that the La Couperie paper referred to here can be found in *The Academy* (la Couperie 1885), and it does indeed mention the seal from Harappa. It seems reasonable to at least tentatively conclude that this is the reference that Sayce had intended to make in his letter to the editor and later in another article (Sayce 1927: 206, fn. 3).

[6]This date should read 1911-12.

[7]There seems to be a bit of confusion on this date.

Whereas Marshall clearly indicates in the *Annual Report of the Archaeological Survey of India,* 1923-24, page 48 that Banerji first excavated at Mohenjo-daro in the field season 1921-22, Banerji's report for this work is found in the Report for 1922-23 without an indication that it is out of chronological order (see Banerji 1922-23). Other experts (e.g. Majumdar 1939: 100) agree that Banerji worked at Mohenjo-daro in 1922 but given the fact that excavation in India was at that time confined to the winter months it is impossible to remove this discrepancy using these sources.

BIBLIOGRAPHY

Banerji, R.D., 1921
Muhen-jo-daro. *Progress Report of the Archaeological Survey of India: Western Circle, For the Year Ending 31 March 1920,* Pp. 79-80. Calcutta: Government of India.

Banerji, R.D., 1922-23
Mohen-jo-daro. *In Annual Report of the Archaeological Survey of India, 1922-23.* D. B. Spooner ed. Pp. 102-104. Calcutta: Government of India.

Bhandarkar, D.R., 1912
Excavation. *Progress Report of the Archaeological Survey of India: Western Circle, for the year ending 31 March 1912,* Pp. 4-5. Calcutta: Government of India.

Burnes, Alexander, 1834
Travels into Bokhara. 3 vols. London: John Murray.

Brunton, John, 1939
John Brunton's Book: Being the memoirs of John Brunton, engineer, from a manuscript in his own handwriting for his grandchildren and now first printed. Cambridge: Cambridge University Press.

Cunningham, Sir Alexander, 1875
Harappa. *Archaeological Survey of India, Report 1872-73.* Pp. 105-108, Calcutta: Government of India.

Dames, M.L., 1886
Old Seals from Harappa. *Indian Antiquary* 15: 1.

de la Couperie, Terrien, 1885
'Tin-Yut' Not India. *The Academy: A Weekly review of literature, science and art,* No. 678. May 2: 315.

Fleet, J.F., 1912
Seals From Harappa. *Journal of the Royal Asiatic Society:* 698-701.

Gadd, C.J., 1932
Seals of Ancient Indian Style Found at Ur. *Proceeding of the British Academy* 18: 1-22.

Hackin, J., 1933
Nouvelles Researches Archaeologiques a Bamiyan. *Memoires de la Delegation Archaeologique Francaise en Afghanistan.* Vol. 3, P. 2. Paris: Les Editions G. Van Oest.

Holdich, Thomas H., 1910
The Gates of India. London: Macmillan.

Majumdar, N.G., 1939
Prehistoric and Protohistoric Civilization. In *Revealing India's Past,* Sir John Cumming, ed. Pp. 91-116. London: The India Society.

Marshall, Sir John, 1923
Harappa. *Annual Report of the Director General of the Archaeological Survey of India: 1920-21.* Pp. 15-17. Calcutta: Government of India.

Marshall, Sir John, 1924
First Light on a Long Forgotten Civilization. *Illustrated London News.* September 20: 528-32, 548.

Marshall, Sir John, 1926
Mohenjo-daro and Harappa, Introductory. *Annual Report of the Archaeological Survey of India: 1923-24.* Pp. 47-51. Calcutta: Government of India.

Masson, Charles, 1844
A Narrative of Various Journeys in Baluchistan,

Afghanistan and the Punjab. 3 vols. London: Richard Bently.

Ross, Frank, 1933
New Light on Charles Masson. *Indian Antiquary* 63: 221-22.

Sayce, A.H., 1924
Remarkable Discoveries in India. *Illustrated London News.* September 27: 566.

Sayce, A.H., 1927
The Aryan Problem—fifty years later. *Antiquity* 1: 204-15.

Steward, Julian, 1955
A Theory of Culture Change. Urbana: University of Illinois Press.

Wheeler, Sir Mortimer, 1947
Harappa 1946: The defenses and cemetery R-37. *Ancient India* 3: 58-130.

PART VIII

CONCLUSION

ROBERT H. DYSON, Jr.

40. Paradigm Changes in the Study of the Indus Civilization

THE papers included in this volume, and the extended discussions which surrounded them at the seminar, provided a rich and rewarding experience to a scholar of Iranian archaeology looking in from the perspective of that distant country. As an outsider, it may, then, be of some use to record here some impressions drawn from the papers presented and from notes on the conference relating to major changes taking place in the paradigms governing the subject. I hope I may be excused for the brevity of my remarks, but I also hope that they may serve to focus further discussion on the issues raised.

The foregoing papers point to four major conclusions:

1) That until recently progress in the interpretation of new data and the formulation of research strategies has been seriously handicapped by the persistence of certain traditional paradigms of thought which can and must now be set aside;

2) That the entire process surrounding the rise and decline of the Indus Civilization involves vastly more complex cultural dynamics than anyone suspected even a short while ago;

3) That the lack of agreed-upon criteria for basic terminology in this area has led to considerable confusion in the use of terms due to the fact that the same term is sometimes employed as a cultural or ethnic label and at other times as a period designation; and

4) That there is great need for coordinated research employing new methods and standardized concepts over larger geographic areas with the cooperation of a variety of disciplines in the natural sciences. Let us examine these points further.

I. THE STATE OF TRADITIONAL PARADIGMS

The specific paradigms which defined the study of Indus Civilization in the earlier years, and which must now be abandoned, include the concepts of: (a) a sudden and late origin, (b) a long period of widespread and static cultural uniformity, (c) a sudden and uniform collapse (Piggott 1950) caused by (d) an invasion of the Indo-Aryans (with an assumed 2nd millennium date). These paradigms were built initially on a limited data base which lacked a detailed stratigraphic or quantitative analysis of material at key sites. Little information on the variation in ecological setting was available and almost no data on the Pre- and Post-Harappan occupations were in hand. Furthermore, the geographic area explored was then limited largely to Sind and the Punjab and chronological control was lacking for much of the material in the border area (e.g. Dales 1965). Thus the superstructure of interpretation was necessarily one which was largely speculative.

Recent field work and new laboratory studies as reflected in the papers show a vast chronological and geographic expansion of the available data base. This new work and the shift in paradigms which it entails must be seen also in the light of a larger intellectual shift (J.G. Shaffer in this volume) which has taken place at mid-century. The philosophical approach based on the type-fossil classificatory concepts of the seventeenth-through-nineteenth centuries as applied in archaeology (as *type* artifacts, *type* sites, *type* cultures, etc.) and which used qualitative presence/

absence measurements as a primary methodological approach has largely been replaced by concepts evolved in the first half of the present century based on population genetics (biology) and statistical probability (physics). In particular, these fields have introduced the concept of ranges of variability and the application of quantitative methods to the analysis of data and the description of cultural dynamics (Adams 1968). This major shift, greatly facilitated by the institutionalization of archaeology in universities, has led to an interest in variability in site content and artifact classification, systems of settlements and the variability in their ecological setting, and degree, direction and rate of change in cultural phenomena. The members of the conference represented a wide range of generations and experience and found themselves on different sides of these larger and smaller paradigms. Given the rich mix of personal backgrounds combined with the wide range of problem orientation, the complexity of the data, and the range of methods of excavation and recording, the participants showed a remarkable tolerance for divergent views with their sometimes pointed exchanges, which were nevertheless, marked by a sense of humor. Their papers, as presented in this volume, represent an extraordinary documentation for this transitional stage of changing paradigms.

a) A Sudden and Late Origin

One of the first of the older paradigms to disintegrate under the impact of recent research is the concept of a relatively late introduction of agriculture into the Indus Valley and hence of a rather short period for the development of the autochthonous cultures from which the classic Harappan arose. M.R. Mughal (1970) had already proposed that in the "Early Harappan" that "widespread cultural phenomena had already set a permanent and uniform pattern of essential elements." Shaffer, however, points out that even so, the exact relation of the Amri, Kot Diji, and Sothi Cultures to the crystalization of the classic Harappan remains to be explained.

Jean-Francois Jarrige's presentation of the discoveries at Mehrgarh, which document the introduction of a subsistence economy to the valley well before 5000 B.C., dramatically lengthens the time involved in this process and casts the whole problem of Indus origins in a new light. Jarrige suggests that the foundations of the later development go back to the Neolithic and the appearance of cereal cultivation. Kenneth Kennedy points out that the available human skeletal evidence suggests a stable population in the northwest continent for several millennia prior to the Harappan period. Already in the sixth and fifth millennia craft specialization and the beginnings of long distance trade are indicated (turquoise, lapis, sea shells). The needs of agriculture are seen as causing the movement of people as their numbers increased into alluvial areas where a base of wealth (surplus grain) was gradually built up leading to exchange networks reaching out to people in neighboring areas and beyond. By the fourth millennium at Mehrgarh mass production already is in evidence for pottery and objects of lapis, turquoise, steatite, shell, and copper. By about 3300 B.C. mass production of terracotta figurines was underway. Thus the basic pattern of craft specialization precedes the "Harappan" periods. The future focus of attention, therefore, must shift from the concept of sudden origins to a study of a long and complex background and to an examination of the degree of regional variation evidenced in the process of cultural adaptation to new environments as these cultural patterns spread through the area.

b) A Long Period of Widespread and Static Cultural Uniformity in the Mature Harappan

Although the majority of the papers deal with the problems of the Post-Urban Phase of the Harappan Culture, these discussions repeatedly underline the difficulty of discussing the nature of the devolution and adaptations of the "Late Harappan" in the absence of a fundamental agreement on, and adequate analytical description of, the Mature Harappan of the Urban Phase itself. Here we run first into basic problems of description and, thereafter, into problems of inference and interpretation. In this respect another paradigm of earlier thinking is clearly seen to be in a state of collapse: the concept of cultural uniformity through the Mature Harappan Period.

The introduction of quantitative data gives different weight to evidence formerly described only on a present/absent basis in support of the assumed unchanging nature of the Harappan Culture. Within Mohenjodaro itself G. F. Dales has re-examined the ceramic sequence in the light of the stratified sample produced by his recent field work and the proposition of a static culture does not stand up. Similarly, quantitative differences between the ceramics of different sites suggest the inadequacy of the homogeneous mode. This is particularly true, as pointed out by Shaffer, when the total ceramic inventory is examined as opposed to the painted pottery only. Shaffer points out at Allahdino that the distinctive Harappan Black-on-Red Ware was restricted to specific vessel shapes and sizes and constituted less than one percent of all pottery found. He suggests that factors governing the use of such pottery and its distribution were distinct from those affecting other types. A study of regional patterns of this kind would no doubt be most instructive in ways not yet considered. That similar results might be obtained for other artifact categories has already been indicated by Marcia Fentress's (1976) comparative study of Mohenjodaro and Harappa. Shaffer hypothesizes that the similarities were maintained by an internal trading network. Some testing of these aspects of trading activities through the use of trace element analysis would be most valuable. Y. D. Sharma, working with pottery at Ropar and Kotla Nihang also argues that the Mature Harappan has different forms representing regional groupings.

The geographical location of sites of the Mature Period in terms of key ecological factors is also undermining this paradigm, as reflected by changes in agricultural crops and subsistence patterns. As the limits of known Harappan settlements have been defined over an ever wider area, very distinctive environments have been included. The significance of this variation is now beginning to be intensively studied in terms of cereal crops (Vishnu-Mittre and R. Savithri) which reflect basic differences in the subsistence patterns between the major sites: wheat and barley at Mohenjodaro, Chanhudaro and Harappa; barley at Kalibangan; and rice and millet at Rangpur, and Surkotada.

That these crops played a major role in cultural dynamics is indicated by the fact that the number of sites in Saurashtra increased from 18 to 120 in the early second millennium B.C. during Rangpur II B and C times and the subsistence base changed from *rabi* to *kharif* crops; although for some reason this increase in the number of settlements did not continue into the Rangpur III period.

A second key factor influenced by geographical location which undermines the paradigm of homogenity is the nature of trading activities which are reflected primarily by imported raw materials and occasionally by exported items such as the long-barrel cylindrical carnelian beads found in Mesopotamia (D.K. Chakrabarti). This long-distance commerce now appears to be quite different for areas involved in sea trade (southwest Sind and the western Gulf) and overland trade (Baluchistan, Punjab, etc.) as discussed by B.K. Thapar and Shashi Asthana. It is also reflected in detail in the differences between material present at Harappa and Mohenjodaro as discussed by Fentress at the conference and in 1976. Shereen Ratnagar suggests that woods such as deodar, pine and elm may well have been important trade items at Harappa which, in view of its relative isolation from any adjacent clustering of village sites, may have functioned as a "gateway city" in relation to trade.

The non-homogeneous nature of the Mature Harappan Period is indicated by cultural elements other than ceramics. Fentress' study of artifact groups at Mohenjodaro and Harappa indicate important differences as do the major architectural elements. For example, altars appear to be absent at these two sites while present at Lothal (S. R. Rao) and Kalibangan (B. B. Lal). The ritual bathing evidenced at Mohenjodaro and to a lesser extent at Lothal may well be absent at Harappa and Kalibangan. In A. Ghosh's opinion "a uniform set of Harappan religious beliefs and practices is, therefore, difficult to envisage." It is noted that even the way in which baked bricks were used varied from site to site, a fact which indicates the need to look beneath the simple presence or absence of traits to their functional context.

Variations within and between sites of the Mature Harappan is also indicated by some of the available evidence on funerary practices. Kennedy points out that the Harappan skeletal series is aberrant when compared with other such series for which archaeological data suggest a significant development of social stratification. He raises the question of whether or not social control was exercised by the Harappan elite in such a way so as not to evoke the usual dietary stress on ordinary people often imposed elsewhere. In respect to this question it is interesting to recall the fact that metal tools, which were mainly utilized for daily activities, were found widely distributed in both the large urban centers and the small sites like Allahdino (Shaffer) and were not concentrated in special situations and rarely occurred in graves. This distribution pattern indicates that metal was widely available to the inhabitants and was not a monopoly of any one group or institution, a fact which Shaffer points out and which indicates that we are dealing with a qualitatively different social organization when compared to the Mesopotamian urban centers of the same period.

At Kalibangan the cemetery yields abundant evidence for heterogeneous funerary practices with mutually exclusive areas devoted to extended inhumation burials (with very poor furnishings) and pot burials in circular pits (A. K. Sharma). In both cases the burial may have been associated with offering pits containing pottery which were gradually filled with silt. Social differentiation or even ethnic differences may be indicated by this evidence. The variance in funerary practice is compounded further through the presence of a plaster-lined brick tomb containing over 70 pots and a body placed on a layer of platters. Elsewhere in the cemetery a grave with a lidded earthen casket containing the deciduous molars of a child was accompanied by three skulls and finger bones. The contrast between the Kalibangan evidence, indicating as it does important status differences within the community, and the dietary evidence reflected in the skeletons at Harappa, which suggest just the opposite insofar as food consumption is concerned, opens up a whole field for future study and analysis.

With increasing survey activity, the overall geographic extent of the Mature Harappan has been expanded. This has important implications for the paradigm of homogeneity. It is now recognized that several types of sites exist which include a hierarchy of size as well as differential functions in relation to social organization, trade and colonization. It has, at long last, also been recognized that these sites form systems and subsystems which must be understood as such, rather than being studied in isolation.

The types of sites clearly differ—some are indigenous metropolitan centers with a surrounding hinterland of smaller towns and villages, some have specialized functions as port towns or trading outposts, and still others represent colonial settlements in new areas. Most of these specialized sites seem to have a commercial orientation and lie along trade routes. Ratnagar, as already mentioned, has suggested that Harappa functioned as a gateway city for trade from the northeast, while Asthana points out that some towns seem to be production centers and others are distribution points. Y. D. Sharma believes that many of the smaller sites were villages which supported the urban Harappan centers while other groups formed separate rural areas. Agrawal takes a different view when he argues that most of the sites were probably towns rather than villages and did not produce their own food. He points out that agriculture was based largely on cover and meander flood plains of the Indus. These shifted frequently, making fixed village life difficult. The full discussion of this question suffers from the general lack of horizontal excavation at small sites; an exception is Allahdino which sheds important light on one such smaller settlement. Shaffer points out that almost every major artifact category of the Mature Harappan is present at this small site but there is virtually no evidence for their manufacture there. This situation indicates the importance of working out distribution networks by plotting out controlled isotopic or other spatial distribution analyses of items with identifiable characteristics. Quantitative data on their occurrence can do much to demonstrate centers of manufacturing and related trading zones.

At the core of the discussion of the homogeneous nature of the settlements is the speculation and argument over the nature and role of Mohenjodaro itself. Since the site may be five times larger than Harappa and has its own unique features, it is not representative of more numerous small sites. The very size of Mohenjodaro demonstrates its power of attraction for the population while the scale of the structures there reflects the availability of sufficient wealth for investment in the labor and materials to build them. It is the presence of such wealth, and its management, which essentially sets off the major cities from the small towns and villages. S.P. Gupta argues that such urbanism "is the product of material prosperity regulated by political authority through its control over economic channels and organs of corporate life, such as guilds of professionals and municipalities." W. A. Fairservis suggests that Mohenjodaro was almost purely a ceremonial center without trade as an important influence in its location and upkeep. Ghosh disagrees. D. V. Soundara Rajan argues that the organization of the city with a citadel reflects the presence not of a civic or community administration of the people, but rather the presence of a center of management and control (the "Citadel") for the benefit of the "Citadel people". The latter are described as "a stringent centralized oligarchy; which had invented a disciplined civil model, with a consumer policy for drawing the agricultural surplus of the villages. The so-called standardization of the structures, pottery, and antiquities of the Harappan culture may essentially be an index of the *vogues* created by craft guilds of the city states." Shaffer argues that the functional division of the city, including its walled citadel, is probably a key to understanding its organization. Both he and Jansen (1979) question the degree of reality of the so-called "grid system" of streets although they accept the fact that the streets which existed in this period were broad and open, which was not the case during later phases of the city's occupation.

Thus, although the study and analysis of the hinterland with its many small sites is essential to a full clarification of how Harappan civilization functioned, by itself it is not sufficient to that explanation. Mohenjodaro is so unique that it cannot be ignored in any real explanation of the mechanism that created and maintained that degree of cultural homogeneity which did exist in Harappan sites, any more than the existence of Delhi can be ignored in understanding modern India.

Two additional elements have now been made visible, and they change the traditional concept of a static and homogeneous mature phase. The first is the addition of an exceptionally large and previously unknown settlement area on the Hakra River, as revealed by Mughal's survey. The second is the identification of colonial sites where Mature Harappan control was superimposed over a variety of local indigenous, non-Harappan cultures (as at Kalibangan, Kot Diji, Gumla, Bala Kot, etc.). Two fortified sites, Surkotada and Sutkagendor appear to be military outposts. If this identification is correct, they imply (1) The existence of a military organization of some kind, and (2) that expansion into the border areas was not necessarily peaceful. B. Allchin, senses something like this when she notes the sudden control of other sites, and the presence of walled compounds; she argues that the extent of the area and the degree of homogeneity present in the Mature Harappan Period required effective administrative political control with military authority to maintain and defend it. Sankalia (1977) has already questioned the implications of the presence of quantities of baked clay sling pellets in the large and small sites of the Mature Harappan in comparison to their rare occurrence in earlier or later contexts. It would appear that the careful study of the border areas may provide more useful data on the question of military practices than the nuclear area. Certainly the colonial expansion already underway in the later stages of the Mature Harappan, combined with the abandonment of the Hakra River settlement system, had a profound impact on the whole Harappan world. The understanding of the resulting changes in the balance of the whole system, the chronology of these events, and the rate and nature of the cultural changes induced, present a major challenge to future scholarship.

c) A Sudden and Uniform Collapse

Another major paradigm that has been destroyed is the theory of an abrupt and catastrophic destruction of the civilization. The field evidence now shows that the decline was irregular, covered a long period of time, and was caused by different factors in different areas. These factors included changes in coastlines, the drying up of river beds, the mismanagement of resources (salinity of fields, deforestation, etc.), and possibly malaria and disease (Vishnu-Mittre, Fairservis, Kennedy). Thus the causes can be seen as due to climate, tectonics, and man (D. P. Agrawal). Climatic shifts were probably important as major factors only in the local, marginal areas. The major shift of population due to the drying of the Hakra (Mughal) is certainly of crucial importance.

To these explanations may be added evidence for the decay of administrative structures (R. N. Mehta) or the appearance of social disunity (Gupta). It was generally agreed that if the administrative structure was disrupted for whatever reason—social or ecological—the surplus wealth supporting the network of long distance trade would have declined, and esoteric imported materials would have disappeared. This effect would also have occurred if effective police safety along the trade routes had ended due to administrative failure. The rate of such change could have been very rapid—easily within two generations (50 years) as may be seen historically in the abandonment of many capital cities (Mehta). When such events occur (as Gupta points out) oral traditions are apt to carry through the following "dark age."

The general thesis expressed by the papers appears to endorse the concept that the basic subsistence skills and crafts, which had been present all along at the village level and in both central and peripheral areas, simply once again became the norm while luxury items, civic amenities and administrative structures gradually disappeared. B. Allchin suggested that religious practitioners probably survived along with popular traditions involving sacred places, myths, and symbols much like Europe in the Middle Ages. In some areas these surviving patterns are the peasant aspect of former urban systems; in others they are the coexisting non-urban and non-Harappan cultures some of which began in the Pre-Harappan Period and which persisted well into the Post-Harappan Period.

Although it is true, as Dales has noted, that in the final levels of Mohenjodaro that city had become an urban slum, it is now apparent that a process of cultural transformation or readjustment was taking place which involved the shifting of the settlement areas and adaptation to new ecological conditions. In general this movement seems to have been toward the east and south. Border sites which flourished in Baluchistan and Afghanistan ceased to exist. In the Punjab-Haryana area there was a gradual resettlement toward the east (J.P. Joshi and Madhu Bala; K.N. Dikshit). Rao discovered new Harappan sites without antecedents in western central India east of the nuclear area, indicating a population shift. Y.M. Chitawala (1977) has pointed out that with the degeneration of the cultural pattern in Lothal II and Rangpur II B people seem to have moved into Saurashtra to smaller sites, some on higher ground. This population was small in numbers and may be refugee settlers rather than colonial conquerors since there is no evidence that they imposed themselves on other local people. This situation is thus different from that described by Lamberg-Karlovsky for Central Iran. Ghosh refers to an "impoverished" Harappan in the Godavari Valley. In the Punjab, Haryana and western Uttar Pradesh some old settlements continued but there were also new sites and shifts in settlement areas (Bhan and Shaffer 1978).

A significant population may have moved east from the Hakra area into Haryana and Uttar Pradesh since the number of sites in this region goes up from two or three in the Mature Harappan to sixty or more afterwards. While Harappa and Kalibangan were abandoned (Gupta suggests perhaps due to overgrazing in the area), some sites in the lower Indus continued in spite of the so-called floods (e.g., Chanhudaro, Amri).

In all these areas regional assemblages arise combining some cultural continuity with considerable change (Dikshit). Each peripheral region had a distinctive pattern of change due to different factors and different rates of change. This was clearly a *process* and not a *single* event. Ghosh pointed out that the diffusion going on in this period "cannot be regarded as a homogeneous one." Vishnu-Mittre agrees that the decline was neither uniform nor simultaneous. Some traditions were retained, some modified, and many abandoned owing to their non-utility in new contexts. Many things lost were replaced by new features related to new needs. The question arose as to why the urban aspect of the civilization declined so quickly—a fact which again raised the possibility of elite control rather than basic civic organization. Gupta points out the radical effect of the population shifts on the urban centers with Mohenjodaro dropping from 850,000 m^2 to 30,000 m^2 or so, Lothal from 47,500 m^2 to 20,000 m^2 or so. Soundara Rajan believes that "economic disintegration" was one of the vital reasons for the disappearance of what could be termed the "high life style" of the Mature Harappan Culture. In this process oral tradition and crafts persisted (e.g., in stone, wood, clay, some metalurgy and *faience* making). The basic subsistence techniques present in the hinterland continued. In all probability the Harappan Culture declined without any outside *political* or *military* influence as a devolution related to a variety of causes both social and ecological. Gupta summed up the new processual paradigm by stating that this was "not an haphazard process." There was a conscious effort on the part of people to re-adjust their life to the changed hydrological and socio-economic conditions which the second millennium presented. In the end the "Harappan" gradually merged into the existing local cultures. In many instances this meant true cultural regression as illustrated by the burning of Surkotada at the end of Period IB and its occupation by food gatherer newcomers (as evidenced by thousands of wild seeds) and the introduction of the Black and Red Ware related to the Ahar Culture (Vishnu-Mittre and Savithri).

d) An Invasion of Indo-Aryans as the Major Cause of Collapse

The abandonment of the catastrophe paradigm for the demise of Harappan Civilization has led to the realization that we are dealing with a complex process of cultural change which took place over a prolonged period of time, and which manifested itself in different ways in different areas. Thus, the invasion thesis also becomes a paradigm of limited usefulness. By freeing themselves from this hypothesis drawn from earlier linguistic studies, archaeologists may now focus their attention on the archaeological evidence in its own terms. There is a continuing lack of agreement over the criteria by which the presence of the

Indo-Aryans can be demonstrated and, even more surprisingly, an absence of a rigorous analysis of available archaeological evidence against the cultural content of traditional Vedic literature. Thus, there must be a change of concern from trying to identify the date and direction of movement of an "event" like an invasion to the complexities of the processes of cultural change and adaptation.

Even so, the subject of the history of the Indo-Aryans cannot help but continue to haunt the study of this period of subcontinent archaeology and sooner or later it must be better understood. It is interesting in this regard to note the tendency among Iranian and Central Asian scholars to accept the growing evidence for the continuity of population in the Turanian area from Neolithic times onward—from the painted pottery through the gray pottery of the Bronze Age (e.g. Deshayes 1969) and probably onward through the Iron Age and Parthian Periods (Hlopina 1972: 213-14). The suggestion of an indigenous Indo-Aryan population going far back into pre-history in Northeastern Iran and nearby Turkmenia is now taken quite seriously. With this trend in mind it is interesting that the discussion between present contributors indicated a parallel trend. Both Lal and B.P. Sinha commented on the need to trace the continuity of elements back through the Harappan into the Pre-Harappan and to relate these elements to the Vedic literature. Carl Lamberg-Karlovsky also suggested that Indo-Aryan elements were already present in the Harappan Culture. I. Mahadevan suggested that Indo-Aryan priests married into the local population and that a long period of bilingualism and racial fusion ensued. The hearth at Kalibangan identified as a fire altar was suggested by B. Allchin as indicating the presence of the Indo-Aryans. Thapar (1973: 101) describes this as a ritual hearth with a clay or brick pillar at the center. This feature immediately brings to mind a hearth of this type in room seven of the Burned Building at Tepe Hissar (not indicated in the plan in the site report) and a group of three other such hearths on the Main Mound dated by radiocarbon to the mid-third millennium B.C. (Schmidt 1937; Fig. 162, Fig. 84 square DG 20; Dyson and Remsen, in press). If these were ritual hearths then B.B. Lal's point that Aryans were present at the very beginning of the site is a good one. This is so because there is a close association between such features and Indo-Aryans in India. F.R. Allchin agrees with this correlation; however Lal notes that it is not a feature of later Indian culture.

In relation to the so-called "massacre" at Mohenjodaro, traditionally cited to demonstrate the invasion thesis, Kennedy points out that there is no evidence of injury to the bones of the so-called victims at the time of death. In some cases, however, there are partially healed cranial lesions which indicate wounds several months old. He argues on the basis of the available skeletal evidence that a biological continuum exists with many of the Harappan morphometric variables continuing in the modern population of the Sind and Punjab, thus supporting a concept of population continuity rather than displacement.

The disagreements as to the attributes suitable to the identification of Indo-Aryans spilled over to a discussion of Cemetery H at Harappa. Allchin felt that the birds on the jars represented the sun and fire combined, but Gupta objected that the manner of disposing of the dead in Cemetery H was wrong for the Vedic literature. Deo agreed that basic concepts drawn from the Indo-Aryans were already present in the Indus Civilization. Fairservis expressed his opinion that Indo-Aryans could have been in the Indus Valley a thousand years before we traditionally think so. Jarrige's discoveries at Mehrgarh of direct linkages between the site and Namazga V and VI in Turkmenia in Pre-Harappan times provides an important piece of new evidence for culture contact between these regions which will have to be taken into consideration in any further speculation on this subject

II. CULTURAL DYNAMICS WERE MORE COMPLEX THAN EXPECTED

The major problem for those seeking a deeper understanding of Harappan Civilization is to construct interpretative models for their data. First in this process must be an effort to provide close chronological control for the data, clear definitions of the terms used, and the application of methods consistent in both their qualitative and quantitative aspects. Interpretation must then begin with some defined guiding concept—in this instance the central concept of a functional archaeological "culture" or a "cultural system" including its ecological setting, could provide an integrating device for the description of all the available material in a meaningful functional context. The comparison of isolated artifacts or patterned groups of artifacts in terms of style or function, or selected ceramic wares does not suffice for this task. Thus, a major problem underlying this set of papers is that there is as yet no agreed upon definition of what constitutes such an integrating mechanism, so that comparative statements are not presently based on comparable criteria from paper to paper. Instead, the discussion proceeds piecemeal, based now on isolated artifacts, now on pottery types, now on radiocarbon dates. What is called for is an approach stressing elements such as overall settlement organization, subsistence activities and architectural traditions (as opposed to simple brick size for example. Masonry represents, after all, a craft tradition in its own right involving far more than brick sizes). An holistic approach to internal patterns of social behavior as indicated by the arrangement of houses and settlements, features and artifacts, burial customs and the like is essential to a full understanding of the process under study. It is the totality of the evidence that speaks to the life style of the Harappan—and it is that style, reflecting their cultural values, that is the subject of the kind of comparisons we must use to understand the nature of the culture and the changes it underwent. We must take the total urban pattern of the Mature Harappan Period as the descriptive base (i.e., including the urban center and its satellite towns and villages). This should be studied as a cultural system in its own terms. The pattern of organization changes, but the population is probably essentially continuous, even if resettled in new locations. As Deshpande pointed out, cultures do not as a rule die abruptly, more usually they are transformed into new forms. As our knowledge grows it is necessary to continually reassess the published and unpublished evidence in terms of changed paradigms and perspectives. This is especially true as previously unassociated materials come to be identified with newly defined cultural units (e.g. floating material in Baluchistan which can now be seen to be Namazga V–VI material). In this process there is also a need to distinguish clearly those aspects of culture and culture change most dependent on environmental determinants from those dependent on cultural and social traditions.

The vast array of new data shows the need for the use of broad concepts of cultural process in understanding the Harappan culture. These concepts must be applicable to a variety of dynamic processes rather than to the simple biological analogy implied by the birth, maturity and death (Early, Middle and Late) sequence.

Much of the work done over the past 10 years has been site specific, but spread over large areas. Since these sites were not isolated, and since it is now clear that a variety of mechanisms were at work at different times—trade networks, colonization, acculturation, cultural regression, etc.—the need for a broader conceptualization of cultural contact is apparent. Ghosh encouraged us to look at parallel processes in search of historic causes. Lamberg-Karlovsky agreed that we could not deny historical models and also pointed out that the whole subject of population growth as a factor in social change was absent from the discussions. Robert Sharer, another non-Indus observer, pointed out the complexity of cultural change in a whole region using the Maya area as an example and emphasizing the importance of studying differential rates in types of change, and the rates of change at different sites, in order to identify the variation in causal factors. He concluded that the term "Indus Civilization" is an artificial concept masking the reality of great variation and that the whole approach to the area to date had been too simplistic to deal with the reality of the phenomena involved.

Much theoretical discussion centered on the role of agriculture as a causal factor in change. Mehta suggested that the early settlement pattern was based on agricultural needs but that in the last stage it was the water supply and sources of raw materials which became major factors in determining locations of sites. He also suggested that agricultural practice leads to conflict which in turn induces control structures which create favorable conditions and support urban populations. Such centers decline when conditions become unfavorable, but are capable of regeneration if conditions change. Lamberg-Karlovsky suggested another model drawn from Sumer and Elam and sites in Iran which include major centers and colonized locations. Yahya and Sialk in the Proto-Elamite levels suggest, he said, direct colonization of a foreign area probably for resource control and to facilitate trade into the primary area. Beyond these sites lay a more distant "secondary area" in which isolated finds indicate only limited contact. This was a pattern which lasted only two to three centuries and then collapsed abruptly with the reemergence of indigenous cultures. He suggested that the concept of primary and secondary areas could apply to the Indus area with Shortugai and Lothal representing colonies and Turkmenistan a secondary area (with isolated "Indus seals." etc.). Jarrige's presentation dealing with Namazga V-VI artifacts and burials at Mehrgarh however, shows that such a model is incomplete and dramatically underlines the true complexity of what is taking place in the Harappan area.

III. TERMINOLOGICAL CONFUSION

A principle cause for the terminological confusion in the scholarship on Harappan Civilization arises from the use of the same term to designate three different concepts: a chronological period, a cultural stage, and an ethnic group.

The basic chronological terminology of Pre-Harappan, Early, Middle and Late Harappan rests primarily on the stratigraphic evidence from Mohenjodaro, Harappa, and neighboring sites in the nuclear area. In this scheme "Pre-Harappan" means those assemblages of varying character which lie stratigraphically below the Harappan; "Late Harappan" is defined by materials in the impoverished terminal levels of Mohenjodaro itself. "Post-Harappan" should logically be what follows but in most papers the term "Late Harappan" is extended to cover this next time period as well. Thus, the term "Late Harappan" as presently used is especially confusing in that it sometimes stands for the time period between the abandonment of Harappa and Mohenjodaro and the appearance of the Painted Gray Ware and sometimes only for the period of the terminal manifestations of the major Mature Harappan sites in the nuclear area.

A confusion is introduced by the shift to a cultural frame of reference in which "Harappan" is equated with "urban." Later assemblages are then called "Post-Urban." The reason for this double usage is the need which has arisen to describe the non-urban settlements in non-nuclear areas which represent a different organizational system following upon the demise of the classic centers. This usage introduces an internal contradiction in that "Late Harappan" at Mohenjodaro is still "urban" while elsewhere it is "post-urban." Such treatment warps any attempt at the interpretation of cultural dynamics since by definition it logically precludes any prosperous settlement with "urban" characteristics from being classified as "Late Harappan," though such centers could well have existed. Fentress pointed out how such terminology affects the plotting of sites since excavators using differing terms make different chronological assessments based on the assumptions underlying the terms. Lal argued for "Late Harappan" as a chronological term applying to a general stage ensuing immediately from the Mature Harappan.

Much of the difficulty in developing separate terms for cultural interpretation arises from the lack of horizontal excavation at sites chronologically of the Late Harappan Period in each geographic region. Such work would establish definitive, full descriptions of the cultural patterns involved. F.R. Allchin also commented on this lack. "Late Harappan" as used by a majority of speakers simply meant the presence of some combination of "Harappan" artifact types (whether 1, 10 or 100) sites in various areas with no weighing of the evidence, and without consideration of the overall functional aspects of each site as an operative community. Possehl stressed the need to add aspects like ecological setting, subsistence pattern, etc., for a reliable system of cultural classification. Instead, at present any sites containing artifacts already known in the classic Harappan are automatically classified "Harappan" when found in a later period. Dikshit used the term "Post-Harappan" for Cemetery H since it is later than the main site, and stated that later but contemporary non-Harappan cultures should not be called "Late Harappan." This suggestion, however, would leave us without a period designation.

The third usage as pointed out by Vishnu-Mittre, links the terminology to ethnic groups by assuming that each pottery ware represents a separate ethnic group. In this situation, by definition, every individual site with two or more pottery traditions automatically becomes a mixed community of separate ethnic groups living together. Y.D. Sharma pointed out that three types of pottery ("Pre-Harappan," "Mature Harappan" and "Baran") may occur at "Mature Harappan" sites but in varying percentages. He suggests that "Late Harappan" is a misused term (thinking of Harappan as a certain type of pottery) since it is applied to several pottery traditions. In the absence of extensive data on the distribution of shapes and functions among such wares, and loci of their discovery in the context of the settlement, the validity of this ethnic approach remains undemonstrated.

Another extremely confusing practice involves the use of "Pre-Harappan" as an identifying cultural term for the later stage of a non-Harappan pottery tradition in the chronological context of the Late Harappan Period! To make matters worse the usage sometimes indicates an ethnic identity as well. Thus artifacts become people, and "Pre-Harappans" live side by side with "Late Harappans" as Mehta pointed out. As an alternative to this approach cultural overlap within single communities has been indicated in some cases by the use of the percentages of wares present as shown by Joshi in his treatment of ceramics. To add further confusion the term "Pre-Late Harappan" has also been introduced (Rao).

Clearly a major task for archaeologists in this part of the world is to agree on some general system of chronological period names, and then to select some specific criteria for naming cultural complexes as an independent exercise. Until this effort is made the organization of the data and the construction of interpretive models will be seriously handicapped.

IV. THE PROSPECTS FOR COORDINATED RESEARCH

A number of papers show a significant trend toward interdisciplinary research through the inclusion of natural scientists. Encouraging progress has been made in mineral analysis, geology, paleobotany and paleozoology. A wider use of flotation techniques for the elaboration of data on the ecological setting and agricultural production of sites promised to add a significant dimension to the data available for analysis. Possehl argued for the use of team research to study all aspects of cultural life and to collect comparable data from place to place. Progress in such research requires an agreed upon problem orientation and methodology. A good beginning has been made along those lines in the trade studies of Fentress and Asthana and the botanical and ecological studies of Vishnu-Mittre and Savithri as well as Agrawal and Sood.

One area where immediate and much needed progress could be made by a cooperative effort is in the construction of an absolute chronology through the systematic collection and evaluation of Carbon-14 (^{14}C) samples for each area. Only through such a chronological structure can a controlled pattern of the rate and direction of cultural change be established (as pointed out by Vishnu-Mittre).

The comparative study of artifact assemblages needs to move from a presence/absence approach to the inclusion of quantitative information which is essential in dealing with slow transitions across geographical zones and vertical change in continuous sequential deposits. At the same time, a greater emphasis is needed not on artifacts as individual types but as groups with functional meaning in relation to one another and to associated features and structures.

A cooperative strategy for sampling several sites for the purpose of comparative settlement study could yield dramatic results. Shaffer points out that two key sites were the sole basis for the reconstruction of a civilization with several hundred known settlements. The most common site, the small settlement, is understood virtually not at all and yet certainly represents the common basis of ancient life. The enlargement of the number of accurately described and studied sites to create an adequate sample for interpretation is thus an important task. Deshpande pointed out in discussion that horizontal excavation aimed at understanding all aspects of the structure and function of the communities in question, rather than a focus on the origin and diffusion of single items, is greatly needed. Thapar made the important point that regional generalizations must rest on an adequate understanding of local material. Local settlement patterns should thus be studied on their own terms as the nuclear Indus Sequence cannot be assumed to be useful over long distances. Within the local studies, concepts of locational geography such as central place theory, site size hierarchies and distances may provide new perceptions of cultural organization (Thapar).

Finally, a cooperative effort for the systematic study of the Indus symbol systems—not just the "script" but also the iconography of seals, figurines and other items—would almost certainly be a rewarding venture.

The foregoing comments perhaps sound overcritical. In fact they reflect a situation brought about by colleagues. The net effect of this work is to vastly enrich the data base available for study. It is an inevitable effect of progress that paradigms which were once useful should be replaced and that the generation of new knowledge should cause conceptual confusion until it has been reviewed systematically and thus synthesized. That is a challenge and the next step. I have no doubt whatsoever of the ability of Indus scholars to deal with this challenge effectively and imaginatively. Clearly the problems of the Harappan Civilization will continue to be one of the most exciting subjects of current archaeology and all of us will be watching for further developments with great interest.

BIBLIOGRAPHY

Adams, Robert McC., 1968
"Archaeological Research Strategies: Past and Present." *Science 160:* 1187-92.

Allchin, Bridgett and Raymond Allchin, 1968
The Birth of Indian Civilization. Baltimore: Penguin Books.

Bhan, Suraj and Jim G. Shaffer, 1978
New Discoveries in Northern Haryana. *Man and Environment* 2: 59-68.

Dales, George F., 1965
"A Suggested Chronology for Afghanistan, Baluchistan, and the Indus Valley." In *Chronologies in Old World Archaeology,* Robert W. Ehrich, ed. Chicago: Pp. 257-84. University of Chicago Press.

Deshayes, Jean, 1969
"New Evidence for the Indo-Europeans from Tureng Tepe, Iran," *Archaeology* 22 (1): 10-17.

Dyson, Robert H. Jr. and William C.S. Remsen (in press)
"Observations on Stratigraphy and Architecture at Tappeh Hesār." In Dyson, Robert H., Jr. and Susan M. Howard, eds. *Preliminary Reports of the Tappeh Hesar Restudy Project, 1976.* Mesopotamia Supplementary Volume, University of Torino.

Fentress, Marcia, 1976
Resource Access, Exchange Systems, and Regional Interaction in the Indus Valley. Ph.D. dissertation, University of Pennsylvania

Hlopina, L.I., 1972
"Southern Turkmenia in the Late Bronze Age." *East and West* 22 (3-4): 199-214.

Jansen, Michael, 1979
"Architectural Problems of the Harappan Culture." 4th International Conference of South Asian Archaeology; Naples 1977.

Mughal, M. Rafique, 1970
The Early Harappan Period in the Greater Indus Valley and Northern Baluchistan. Ph.D. dissertation, University of Pennsylvania.

Piggott, Stuart, 1950
Prehistoric India. Baltimore: Penguin Books.

Sankalia, H.D., 1977
New Archaeology: Its Scope and Application to India. Lucknow: Ethnographic and Folklore Cultural Society.

Schmidt, Erich F., 1937
Excavations at Tepe Hissar. Philadelphia: University Museum.

Thapar, B.K., 1973
New Traits of the Indus Civilization at Kalibangan: An appraisal. *South Asian Archaeology.* Normal Hammond, ed. Pp. 85-104. Park Ridge: Noyes Press.

Thapar, B.K., 1977
Harappan and Post-Harappan Settlement Patterns in Saurashtra. *Ecology and Archaeology of Western India.* D.P. Agrawal and B.M. Pande, eds. Pp. 93-98. Delhi: Concept Publishing Company.

Index

Abaj, 369
Abbas, Fort, 5, 85, 91, 94, 245, 248
Addington, J.E., 301
Adi Badri, 114
Afghan/Baluch area, 199
Afghanistan, 9, 11, 17, 48, 54, 56, 113, 271, 273, 275, 276, 277, 279, 280, 322, 398, 406, 407, 422; south, 116
Africa, 290; southern, 234
Agastya, 313
Agate, 111, 150, 154, 178, 181, 239; beads, 138, 263, 339
Agra, 35
Agrawal, D.P., 46, 278, 361
Ahar, 129, 130, 136, 171, 357; Culture, 214, 218, 337, 422; ware, 240
Ahichchhatra, 336
Ahirwala, 128
Ahmednagar District, 175, 214
Ajmer, 36: hill, 273; mines, 276, 280; District, 127, 131, 241
Akhnoor, 185, 263
Akkadian grave, 266; writing, 62
Alamgirpur, 23, 135, 136, 138, 163, 337, 338, 339, 346, 347, 348, 349, 353, 398
Alamgirpur I, 121
Alamgirpura, 336
Alcock, Professor Leslie, 101
Alexander, 7, 392, 406
Ali Murad, 11, 12, 389
Alibandar, 35
Allaha Bund, 197
Allahdino, 11, 12, 44, 45, 46, 47, 107, 108, 109, 110, 111, 112, 200, 235, 356, 398, 419, 420; architecture, 109–110; artifacts, 111; excavations, 47; irrigation, 110–111; lithics, 47; trade, 111-112
Allchin, B., 225
Allchin, F.R., 400
Alor, 129
Altai mountains, 276, 277
Alter de Sacrificios, 369, 370, 374, 376, 377, 378
Altin Culture cycle, 51
Altin Depe, 51, 61, 63, 65, 66, 276, 398
Altin people, 52

Alveolar resorption, 303, 305
Ambaji, 241
Ambakhedi, 53, 56
Ambala District, 248
Ambika River, 9
Ambkheri, 26, 135, 136, 323, 348
America, Central, 368, 369, 370, 371, 374; South, 374
Amerindian population, 301
Amiet, Pierre, 62
Amiliano, 107, 108, 109
Amra, 170, 353, 357
Amreli District, 357
Amri, 33, 42, 43, 46, 53, 65, 70, 90, 102, 116, 136, 151, 271, 326, 328, 347, 388, 389, 397, 398, 422; Culture, 418
Amritsar, 190; District, 158, 245
Anantpur, 275, 276
Anarak, 277
Andhra, 277
Andropogon, 214
Angel, H.L., 291
Anopheles 291
Ante-mortem tooth loss, 303–304, 305
Anupgarh, 90, 226, 248
Apaya, 114
Apegaon, 306
Arabia, 322
Arabian Sea, 9, 12, 17, 107, 113, 199, 248, 279; Coast, 92, 111
Aravalli Hills, 11, 241
Aravallis, 9, 19, 113, 114, 120
Ariana Antiqua, 392
Armenia, 275, 276
Arrian, 406
Arrow Heads, 126; Banawali, 132; bone, 189; copper, 132; Indus, 281
Artemisia, 34
Arthashastra, 167
Arvavat Sea, 130
Aryan Skull, 289
Aryans, 37, 52, 102, 291, 329, 331, 332, 396, 400, 423; Vedic, 57, 331
Aryavarta, 69
Asia, 405, 407; Central, 22, 56, 57, 61, 63, 65, 79, 275, 276, 277, 278, 280, 282, 326, 390, 391, 392; Hellenized west of, 390;

South, 42, 82, 215, 273, 290, 291, 292, 294, 327, 409; Southeast, 290; West, 72, 79, 267, 273, 278, 346, 364; Western, 218, 234, 290, 396
Astrabad, 277, 278
Atkot, 198, 201, 353, 357
Atranjikhera, 26, 125, 136, 138, 191, 218, 335, 336, 337, 338, 349
Australia, 290
Avanti, 57
Ayodhya, 336
Azerbaijan, 273

Babarkot, 353
Babylonia, 266
Bactria, 56, 57
Bactrian pottery, 57
Badkshan, 11, 263, 273, 278
Bagor, 24, 126, 128, 131
Bahadar, 9
Bahadarabad, 53, 56, 136, 191, 337, 358
Bahar, 114
Bahawalnagar District, 90
Bahawalpur, 5, 51, 53, 92, 93, 94, 392, 397; District, 96, 354; Domain, 20
Bahpur, 348
Baikal Lake, 273
Bairat, 125
Bajos, 374, 375
Bajra, 199, 215, 219
Bakun, A5 site, 267; ware, 267
Balakot, 65, 102, 273, 276, 398, 421
Baleshwar, 128
Baleshwar-Dariba copper hills, 128
Balu, 12, 24, 53, 161
Balu II, 24
Baluch Hills, 92, 114
Baluchistan, 9, 11, 19, 54, 57, 79, 82, 83, 109, 116, 205, 206, 215, 216, 271, 277, 279, 280, 387, 388, 389, 391, 397, 399, 422; dry plateau of, 3; North, 66; northern, 17, 161, 274, 281, 389, 391, 392, 397; southern, 248, 391, 392, 397
Bamiyan, 407
Bampur, 392; Valley, 273
Banas, 7, 9
Banaskantha. II; District, 240

Banawali, 12, 33, 52, 53, 91, 113, 114, 115, 117, 118, 119, 120, 121, 126, 161, 205, 206, 215, 273, 275, 346, 347, 349, 353, 398
Banawali-Bara Culture, 115, 121; Post-Indus, 120–122; Ware, 121, 122
Bandhni, 388, 389
Banerjee, R.D., 409, 410, 412
Banerjee, S., 223
Bannister, F.A., 242
Bannu, 17, 234
Bannu Basin, sites in, 91
Banswara, 36
Banti Sama, 174
Bara, 23, 25, 33, 54, 122, 130, 135, 136, 143, 191, 337, 346, 347, 353; pottery of, 143, 191; Culture, 157, 158, 161, 162, 163, 347, 349; Ware, 23, 25, 118, 141, 150, 154, 157, 158, 161, 162, 163, 188, 349, 357
Baragaon, 136, 163, 323
Barasingha, 173
Bargaon, 342, 346, 347, 348
Barley, 82, 83, 111, 178, 183, 206, 207, 208, 209, 211, 213, 215, 216, 217, 218, 419; cultivated, 210; hulled, 82, 211; Indian, 211; modern cultivated, 211; naked, 211
Barley grain, carbonized, 212; hulled, 212; naked, 213
Barli River, 131
Barmer, 36
Bars, 17
Basalt, 9
Basu, A., 302
Baudhayana Dharma Sutra, 114
Bavanat, 392
Bay of Bengal, 113
Bayazeh, 276
Bazaar Nadi, 107, 108
BEARER sign. 314–315
Beas, 7, 141, 245, 261
Beck, H.C., 265, 266
Begram, 407
Behar, 128
Belize, 367
Belize River Valley, 373
Bengal *see* West Bengal
Beriwala, 226
Bespura, 131
Beyt Dwarka, 353
Bhadar, 198
Bhadar Valley, 201
Bhadra, 125
Bhagalpur District, 137
Bhagatrav, 353, 357
Bhagwanpura, 37, 55, 56, 93, 114, 122, 158, 162, 163, 185, 189, 190, 191, 193, 336, 337, 339, 347, 357, 358
Bhagwanpura IA, 121, 337, 347

Bhagwanpura IB, 190, 192, 338
Bhagwanpura Culture complex, 338
Bhalbaru, 168
Bhan, Suraj, 26, 52, 114, 128, 158, 327, 357, 392, 398
Bhandarkar, D.R., 405
Bharatas, 314
Bharatpur, 218, 226, 406
Bharuch, 170
Bhatpur, 349
Bhedi, 198
Bhela, 353
Bhilwara, 11, 278, 280; District, 131
Bhiwani, 129
Bhoj Raja, 174
Bhudan, 158
Bhudan IB, 161
Bhuj, 35, 198
Bhura, 348
Bhyana, 353
Bihar, 11, 56, 135, 137, 218, 276, 277, 278
Bikaner, 34, 36, 217, 392; District, 131
Bird Jaguar, 371
Bisht, R.S., 154, 398
Bitumen, 9
Black Plague, 374
Black Wares, 93, 125, 136, 171
Bolan Passes, 3, 11, 79, 248, 261
Bolan River, 5, 57
Bopardikar, B.P., 175
Boschtschekul, 277
Brace, C.L., 290
Brachiaria, 214
Brahmagiri I, 175
Brahmavarta, 69
Brāhmī, 311
Brahminabad, 408
Brassica juncea, 208
Bread Wheat, 82
Bronze, 150, 277, 278, 356, 361, 363, 364, 365, 396
Bronze Age, 423; sites, 47
Brunton, John, 407, 408
Buddhism, 70, 331
Buddhist stupa, 410
Budha Pushkar, 127, 131
Budhi Ganga, 339
Budki Madi, 143
Buff and Cream Ware Culture, 177, 178, 180, 322
Buff Ware, 171
Buffalo, 173, 181, 396
Bukhara, 278, 280
Bukkur gap, 7
Bulandshahr District, 349
Bulsar, 7
Burnes, Alexander, 407
Burnished Gray Ware, 176, 177, 178, 180
Burnished Thick Gray Ware, 189, 190
Burzahom, 3

Burzahom II, 248
Burzhom, 189
Byzantine overlords, 396

Cahr Daud, 277
Calico printing, 34
Cambay, 7, 9, 35
Camel, 396
Cappieri, M., 294
Cardi, B. de, 79
Caribbean Coasts, 378
Carmania, 274, 275
Carnelian, 83, 111, 142, 150, 178, 181, 193, 266, 271, 274, 275, 282, 396; beads, 265, 266, 267, 268, 281, 282, 339
Caucasus, 275
Celts, 128
Cemetery A, 136, 266
Cemetery H, 33, 245, 346, 347, 348, 397, 423, 425; Culture, 92, 142; materials 93; people, 51; Phase, 328, 330; potteries, 54, 121, 122, 191; sites, 53; Ware, 154, 188, 357
Ceramophiles, 233
Cerros, 370
Chabbuwala Ther, 12
Chah Husaini, 392
Chak Purbane Syal, 245, 261
Chakar nais, 5
Chakrabarti, Dalip K., 237
Chakrabarti, S., 223, 229
Chalcedony, 239
Chalchuapa, 369
Chalcolithic Cultures, 9, 69, 121, 135, 137, 177, 182, 336, 361, 364, 365, 387, 398; population, 305, 306, 307; settlement, 168, 226, 237; sites, 47, 114, 182, 290, 357, 361, 364, 387, 389, 391, 392
Chambal, 226
Champa, 137
Champaner, 172
Chandaravati, 171
Chandigarh, 54, 118, 121, 151, 157, 162
Chandrashila, 178
Chanhudaro, 32, 33, 51, 53, 83, 101, 127, 137, 205, 207, 208, 215, 218, 239, 241, 242, 265, 273, 278, 289, 293, 322, 354, 362, 363, 397, 419, 422
Charr-Marr-da Theh, 190
Chatterjee, B.K., 291
Chauro, 388
Chautang, 5, 91, 226, 227, 392
Cheetah, 173
Chenab, 7, 141, 185, 245, 248, 263, 398
Cheno-amaranths, 214
Cheras, 314
Chert, 9, 11
Chicha Watni, 406
Chichen Itza, 376
Childe, V. Gordon, 41, 267, 321, 363, 399

Index

Chilhera, 339
Chilmak, 273
China, 290, 390, 405
Chinese Turkistan, 390
Chiplata, 128
Chir, 392
Chirand, 135, 136, 137, 138, 218
Chirawa, 129
Chital, 173
Chittor District, 130
Chlorite, 274–275, 281
Cholistan, 53, 90, 91, 92, 93, 94, 261; greater, 90; lesser, 90
Cholistan Desert, 85
Chomu Tehsil, 34
Chong Depe, 63
Chowdhury, K.A., 223
Churu, 36
Cicer arietinum (chickpea), 213
Citadel Mound, 97, 103
Claringbull, G.F., 242
Classic Maya, 369, 372, 374, 378, 379
Classic Maya Civilization, 377, 378, 379; Culture, 379
Cleland, J., 46
Coarse Bichrome Ware, 387
Coimbatore, 275
Common pea, 183
Copan, 369, 371
Copper, 9, 17, 92, 111, 114, 116, 121, 129, 135, 163, 171, 235, 239, 243, 263, 271, 275, 276–277, 280, 356, 364, 396; coins, 189; mines, 128; objects, 126, 128, 130, 192, 193, 200
Copper-bronze, 46, 178; tool, 282
Copper Hoard Culture, 130, 132, 218
Costantini, L., 82
Cotton, 216
Cozumel Island, 377
Cream Slipped Ware, 177
Cretaceous-Eocene Age, 175
Culbert, T.P., 377
Cunningham, Sir Alexander, 395, 407, 408, 409
Cylinder seals, 22

Dabar Kot, 54, 389, 391
Dadheri, 37, 54, 55, 93, 122, 158, 163, 185, 189, 192, 337, 338, 347, 353
Dadheri IA, 121
Dahars, 90
Daheda, 169
Daimabad, 9, 175, 177, 178, 179, 180, 181, 182, 183, 205, 214, 280, 322, 323, 353, 355, 356, 357, 361, 362, 364, 365, 366, 398
Dales, George F., 291, 397, 418
Damb Bhuti, 11, 12, 388, 389
Damb Sadaat I, 83
Damb Sadaat II, 33, 84

Damb Sadaat II–III, 64
Damb Sadaat III, 84
Damghan, 275
Damin, 392
Damlotti, 107, 110
Dani, A.H., 15, 17
Darab, 392
Dariba, 128
Dasas, 396
Dasht River, 405
Daulatpur, 163, 191, 215, 337, 347
Dailatpur I, 121
Debari, 277; mines; 357
Deccan, 19, 70, 122, 175, 182, 274, 290, 323, 362, 364, 365; lower, 72; northern, 353, 363; southeast, 363
Deccan Plateau, 302, 305, 306, 307
Deccan Trap, 197
Degenerate Siswal Wares, 26
Deh Morasi Ghaundai, 48
Deh-Bid, 392
Dehra Dun, 263
Delhi, 263, 421
Delwara Kirovli, 277
Dental abscesses, 304, 305
Dental caries, 304, 305
Deodar (*Cedrus deodar*), 11
Depar Ghangro, 410
Dera Ghazi Khan, 263
Dera Ismail Khan, 263
Derawar, 12, 53, 91, 93, 94, 245, 248, 392; Fort, 85, 91, 92
Desalpar, 198, 201
Desalpur, 72, 353, 398
Desch, C.M., 281
Desert Branch Canal, 392
Deshpande, M.N., 175
Devaliyo, 353
Devni Mori, 274
Dhalewan, 12
Dharwar District, 278
Dhatva, 168, 169, 170, 171, 172
Dher Majra, 141, 142
Dhola Vira, 353
Dhule District, 175, 322
Digitaria, 214
Dikshit, K.N., 85, 336
Dinaric skull, 289
Dish-on-stand, 135, 136, 137, 143, 150, 171, 180, 187, 191, 218, 336, 337, 342, 345
Dizmar, 273
Doab, 25, 53, 331, 345, 348, 349; Central, 26, 130, 349; Eastern, 248, 250; Ganga-Yamuna, 131, 132, 327, 336, 339, 364; Northern, 26; Ravi-Beas, 141; Rechna, 248; Sabarmati-Mahi, 9; Sind-Sagar, 114; Sutlej and the Yamuna between, 141; Sutlej-Ghaggar, 141

Dog, 173, 396
Dogavari Valley, 322
Dogetha, 274
Dohan River, 128, 130
Dokri, 409
Dolichos lablab, 216
Do-Tulan, 392
Dravidian language, 312, 313
Dravidian skull, 289
Drishadvati, 5, 9, 12, 37, 114, 128, 130, 392, 397
Drshaduati valley, 52, 218, 245, 327
Dronamukhas, 167
Dscheskagan, 277
Durganivesa, 167
Dutta, P.C., 302
Dvaitvana Lake, 130
Dwarka, 34, 174
Dynastic Egyptians, 405
Dyson, R.H., 223

Early Baran Culture, 158, 161–162, 163
Early Classic Period, 369, 377
Early Dynastic Period, 267
Early Dynastic II, 267
Early Dyanstic III, 267
Early Harappan, 23; cultural development, 42; elements, 25, 65; Period, 91–92, 94; Phase, 37; settlement, 53, 93; sites, 66, 91, 109 245, 398
Early Harappans, 24
Early Indus Civilization, 332
Early Iron Age, cities, 56; sites, 114
Early Iron Age Urban Cultures, 69
Early Iron Phase, 56
Early (Kot Diji/Sothi) Harappan pottery, 25
East Bein, 141, 158
Eastern Domain, 20, 25
Echinochola, 214
Egypt, 66, 290, 322, 396
Egyptian Civilization, 3
Einocorn Wheat, 82
Ekalasingha, 131
El Salvador, 367; Central, 269
Elam, 61, 62, 63, 64, 65, 66, 67, 266, 424
Elamites, 62
Elana, 131
Elbreez mountains, 276
Electrum, 46
Elephant, 363, 396
Eleusine coracana, 214, 215, 216, 217
Elm, 11
Emerald, 142
Emmer Wheat, 82
Equus Cabalius linn, 192
Eragrostis, 214
Etawah, 34
Etched beads, 22

Euphorbia pycnostegia, 214
Euphorbia spp., 214
Euphrates, 22, 64
Eurasia, 290
Europe, southern, 218

Faience, 142, 150, 154, 163, 396; bangles, 191, 192; beads, 191, 192, 339, 358
Fairservis, W.A., 79, 83, 102, 116, 223, 236, 321, 399
Far East, 275
Faranjal, 276
Farghana, 11
Fars plain, 267
Fasa, 276, 392
Fatehbad, 91
Fentress, Marcia, 44
Field, Henry, 85
Figurines, 248, 358, 396, 426; animal, 119, 143, 193, 248, 339; anthropomorphic, 191; anathrophomorphic ceramic, 44; human, 119, 143; Indus, 119; male, 44; terracotta, 119, 162, 163, 239, 388; zoomorphic, 44
Fine Deep Red Ware, 180
Finger millet, 214
Firuzabad, 392
Fish hooks, 127
Fleet, J.F., 408
Flint, 11, 111
Forrer, Emil, 312
Frankfort, Henry, 267
Fullol Hoard, 66, 275

Gabarbands, 223
Gamanwala, 91
Gandhara Grave Culture, 57, 248
Gandhara Grave Culture I, 192
Ganeshwar, 9, 19, 24, 125, 126, 127, 128, 129, 130, 132, 349
Ganeshwar-Jodhpura Culture, 130; routes of communications, 128–129
Ganeshwar-Khetri Region, 130
Ganagangar, 36, 161; District, 125, 131, 245, 397
Ganga system *see* Gangetic system
Ganga Valley *see* Gangetic Valley
Ganges, 23, 25, 137, 138, 226
Ganges Civilization, 335, 337
Ganges Valley, 69, 70, 72, 113, 114, 122, 331, 332, 337, 346, 348, 349; middle, 336
Ganges-Yamuna Valley, 337
Gangetic Basin, 245; system, 5, 12, 54; Valley, 135, 335, 336
Ganweriwala, 19, 92
Gara Depe, 63
Garden Reg, 9
Gaur, R.C., 136
Gaya District, 137
Gedrosia, 391, 392

Gedrosia Domain, 20
Geoksyur I, 63
Geokshurian Culture complexes, 63
Ghaggar, 5, 7, 52, 85, 94, 114, 158, 161, 226, 248, 297
Ghaggar-Hakra Basin, 52; river, 397
Ghaggar/Hakra (Sarasvati), 24
Ghaggar-Hakra system, 52
Ghaggar (Hakra) Valley, 129
Ghaggar-Hakra-Wahinda system, 12
Ghaggar-Nara flow channel, 12
Ghaggar Valley, 29, 336, 344
Ghaligai, 57
Ghazi Shah, 389
Ghorband Valley, 276
Ghosh, A., 23, 85, 226, 336, 392
Ghosh, S.S., 223
Ghotaru, 129
Gisgarh, 274
Goat, 173, 174
Godavari, 7, 175, 361, 398
Godavari Basin, 175, 182
Godavari Valley, 177, 178, 357, 422
Godin Tepe, 62
Gold, 46, 119, 239, 263, 271, 275–276, 280, 282, 323, 396; leaf, 182; ornament, 263
Gomal, area, 245; Passes, 11; Plain, 17; River, 5; Valley, 263
Gomti River, 131
Gop, 353
Goudie, A., 225
Gram, 216, 218, 219
Granary, 216, 218, 219
Granary, 45, 83
Granite, 9
Gray Slipped Ware, 177
Gray Ware, 185, 187, 188, 189, 190, 192, 193; Harappan variety of, 187; thick coarse, 175
Great Bath, 99, 100, 335
Great Desert of Scinde, 408
Great Indian Desert, 392
Great Rann, 34, 198
Green millet, 214
Guatemala, 367, 372, 374
Gudea, 275
Guha, B.S., 302
Gujarat, 7, 9, 11, 12, 34, 36, 52, 53, 56, 70, 92, 122, 168, 170, 171, 173, 174, 175, 177, 183, 199, 200, 206, 207, 217, 223, 229, 235, 237, 273, 278, 279, 280, 322, 327, 346, 348, 353, 354, 357, 398, 405; central, 168; coastal southern, 174; north, 168, 170, 274, 281, 353, 357; northern, 34; south, 168, 169, 170, 353
Gulf of Cambay, 7, 9
Gulf of Kutch, 198, 200, 201
Gumla, 11, 12, 46, 54, 65, 271, 326, 328, 398, 421

Gumla I, 90
Gumla II, 64
Gumush Kaneh, 276
Gupta Molded Ware, 339
Gupta, P., 302
Gupta, S.K., 200
Gurdaspur, 190; District, 158
Gurnikalan, 12
Guti-Gudea Period, 267
Gypsum, 217, 218

Hab Chauki, 107, 109
Hab River, 5, 11, 107, 109
Hab River Valley, 111
Habuba Kabira, 62, 64
Hajnali, 198, 200, 201
Hakra, 5, 12, 37, 85, 90, 91, 93, 94, 245, 248, 392, 421
Hakra Ban, 114
Hakra Branch Canal, 392
Hakra Ghaggar system, 7
Hakra-Wahinda, 5
Hakra Ware sites, 94
Hakra Wares, 90, 91
Hamadan, 275
Hanumangarh, 248, 392
Harappa, 12, 15, 17, 19, 20, 22, 32, 43, 44, 45, 46, 47, 51, 52, 61, 65, 71, 72, 91, 93, 100, 115, 127, 129, 136, 137, 141, 162, 182, 183, 187, 198, 205, 206, 215, 223, 229, 239, 245, 248, 250, 261, 263, 264, 265, 268, 273, 275, 276, 277, 278, 279, 280, 281, 289, 293, 302, 304, 305, 321, 322, 326, 328, 329, 335, 337, 353, 354, 364, 366, 387, 388, 395, 396, 397, 406, 407, 408, 409, 410, 411, 419, 420, 422, 423, 425
Harappa/Ghaggar/Mohenjodaro axis, 24
"Harappan", 425
Harappan, architectural feature, 45; Black-on-Red Ware, 419; burials, 49, 157, 297–298; Civilization, 70, 71, 79, 197, 200, 218, 223, 225, 229, 239, 267, 268, 289, 291, 312, 321, 322, 323, 356, 378, 392, 405, 421, 422, 423; communication, 199–201; Cultural Complex, 37, 38; Culture, 31, 32, 33, 35, 41, 42, 43, 45, 49, 70, 71, 135, 136, 199, 205, 209, 279, 290, 291, 336, 337, 339, 346, 347, 349, 388, 389, 392, 418, 422, 423, 426; Culture Cycle, 51; Empire, 37, 38, 41, 201, 205, 215, 217, 218, 237; food economy, 206–214; language, 311, 312, 313, 314; Phase, 33, 209; plus Early Baran Culture, 158, 162, 163; Red Ware, 187, 188, 339; script, 47, 158; settlements, 198, 201, 229, 240, 261, 263, 273, 280, 323, 327, 343, 344, 349, 354, 357, 397, 398, 419; sites, 7, 37, 46, 54, 107, 108, 136, 141, 198, 201, 208, 217,

239, 240, 245, 256–257, 263, 273, 275, 277, 290, 293, 346, 357, 378, 392, 397, 398, 421, 422; skeletal series, 290; technological period, 168; trading network, 45; Urbanization, 22, 72, 73; Ware, 33, 189, 339, 347, 357
Harappans, 33, 36, 37, 102, 136, 154, 162, 170, 175, 180, 182, 183, 187, 189, 276, 277, 279, 280, 281, 282, 289, 291, 292, 297, 298, 301, 303, 305, 306, 311, 322, 323, 336, 337, 338, 343, 346, 349, 398; cemetary of, 154; plant economy of, 32
Hardakheri, 348
Hardwar, 339
Hari Rud, 11
Harike, 7
Harrison, P.D., 375
HARROW sign, 315-316
Haryana, 5, 12, 20, 23, 25, 26, 51, 52, 53, 56, 93, 113, 114, 118, 128, 129, 130, 135, 158, 161, 188, 189, 191, 206, 215, 216, 218, 273, 279, 323, 344, 346, 347, 348, 349, 353, 354, 357, 358, 398, 422; central, 114; eastern, 53; north, 114; southern, 24
Hasan Wali, 107, 109, 111
Hasan Wali II, 109
Hastinapur, 335, 338, 339
Hastinapura, 23, 25
Hazara, 5
Hazara Jat, 276
Hazari Bagh District, 278
Hegde, K.T.M., 225
Helmand River, 93, 275, 282
Helots, 396
Hemmy's Indus Weight Unit, 119
Hilmand Civilization, 66
Himalayas, 37, 113, 120, 245, 248, 250, 263, 294
Hindon, 336, 337, 339
Hindu Kush, 5, 11, 17, 19, 273, 275
Hingoni Budrukh, 322, 353
Hisham Dheri, 11, 237
Hissar, 63, 91, 129
Hissar District, 113, 114, 245, 323
Hog deer, 173
Honduras, 367
Hordeum, agriocrithon, 210
Hordeum agriocrithon Aberg, 210
Hordeum distichon, 215
Hordeum distichon Limm, 210
Hordeum spontancum, 210, 215
Hordeum spontancum Koch, 209
Hordeum vulgare, 206, 210, 215
Hordeum vulgare, L., 209
Horsegram, 183, 215
Hosainpura, 278, 280
Hoshiarpur, 190
Huan-Tsang, 395, 411
Hulas, 135, 136, 163, 191, 337, 338, 339, 342, 346, 347, 348, 349, 353
Humped Zebu, 396
Hyktanis River, 275
Hyrcania, 57
Hystera, 34

Ice Age, 224
Ilak, mountains of, 273, 279
Illinois Valley, 290
Ilopango, 369
Inamgaon, 180, 306, 363
Incised Ware, 171, 191
India, 51, 53, 56, 57, 72, 93, 197, 206, 234, 266, 268, 274, 275, 276, 277, 279, 280, 290, 326, 390, 396, 398, 406, 412, 423; central, 70, 114, 122, 182, 216, 398; north, 218, 219, 293, 325, 326, 332; northern, 336; north-western, 216, 219; south, 182, 275, 323; southeastern, 290; western, 79, 201, 223
Indian script, 311
Indigo, 35
Indo- Aryan Cultural tradition, 330, 332
Indo-Aryan Culture, 331
Indo-Aryan language, 312, 313
Indo-Aryans, 417, 423
Indo-Sassanian period, 387
Indus, 5, 7, 12, 22, 66, 67, 141, 162, 197, 217, 228, 229, 261, 274, 280, 281, 282, 292, 326, 329, 346, 387, 388, 389, 407, 417, 422; Basin, 11, 12, 54, 183; lower, 52; City, 399; northern, 245; Civilization, 4, 6, 7, 8, 9, 10, 11, 12, 65, 70, 79, 85, 92, 113, 233–236, 250, 265, 268, 312, 325, 326, 327, 328, 329, 330, 332, 335, 337, 353, 364, 387, 395, 397, 398, 399, 405, 423, 424; Culture, 70, 115, 120, 168, 237, 321, 328, 389, 398, 399, 400; Delta, 7; Plain, 5, 64, 234, 237, 262, 263, 264, 290; Red Ware, 118; script, 174, 177, 178, 181, 182, 291, 311, 312, 313, 314, 315, 398, 399; seals, 65; system, 5, 229, 328; Central, 12; Valley, 3, 17, 22, 41, 42, 43, 48, 49, 54, 79, 92, 113, 114, 130, 177, 182, 199, 229, 245, 292, 322, 326, 327, 330, 346, 353, 354, 358, 378, 387, 388, 389, 410, 418, 423; Central, 397; Greater, 91, 92, 93, 261, 271; lower, 397; upper, 92; Wares, 118; weight system, 119
Intaglio stamp seals, 44
Iran, 9, 11, 52, 113, 267, 271, 274, 275, 276, 277, 278, 279, 280, 281, 389, 391, 392, 405, 424; Central, 422; dry plateau of, 3; eastern, 22, 84; northeastern, 423; northern, 279; southern, 61, 62
Iranian highlands, 3
Iranian Plateau, 3, 48, 62, 63
Irano-Afghan skull, 289
Irano-Caspian skull, 289

Iron, 114, 135
Iron Age, 423; Empire of, 168
Iron Age Urbanization, 73
Isfahan *see* Ispahan
Isin-Larsa Dynasties, 267
Isin-Larsa Period, 267, 322
Ispahan, 276, 277
Italian millet, 214, 215, 218

Jacobabad, 261
Jade, 9, 11
Jafarabad, 168, 169, 170
Jagdusha, 199
Jaguar lineage, 371
Jainism, 70, 331
Jaipur District, 34, 125, 131, 241
Jaisalmer, 35, 36, 129
Jalalabad, 267
Jalilpur, 65, 90, 245, 271, 398
Jalilpur I, 90
Jalilpur II, 90
Jalore, 36, District, 131
Jalwali, 91
Jammu, 168, 185, 189, 190, 248, 323, 398; foothill, 250
Jammu and Kashmir, 23, 353, 358, 398
Jamnagar District, 35, 168, 174
Janapadanivesa, 167
Jansen, Dr. Michael, 15, 100
JAR sign, 313-314
JAR-BEARER sign, 314, 315
Jarrige, Jean-François, 418
Jasper, 111, 138
Jatakas, 56
Jawai River, 131
Jawar mines, 276
Jhadol, 131
Jhalawan, 391
Jhalawar, 36
Jhang, 17, 263
Jhangar, 389
Jhangar Culture, 33, 397
Jhelum, 7, 245, 248
Jhelum-Yamuna Plain, 250
Jhukar, 53, 55, 101, 102, 261, 271, 322, 387, 388, 389; Culture, 33, 92, 102, 122, 397; people, 51; pottery, 102; settlements, 53; sites, 53
Jhunjhunu, 36, 92; District, 130
Jind, 52; District of, 114, 161, 245
Jodhpur, 34, 35, 36
Jodhpura, 24, 125, 129, 349; Culture, 125; mound, 125
Johi, 388, 397
Jokha, 168, 169, 170, 172
Jorwe, 135, 179; Culture, 177, 178, 322; Occupation, 176; Ware, 176, 178, 179, 322
Joshi, J.P., 158, 398
Jowar, 215, 216

Judverjodaro, 12, 261, 264
Jujube, 206
Jullundur, 190, 248; District, 158, 193, 245

Kabul, 392
Kabul River, 5
Kachi, 5, 57
Kachi Plain, 5, 12, 79, 80, 82, 84
Kahpuz Depe, 63
Kakadbhit, 198
Kakoria, 336, 337
Kalaheti, 348
Kaleh, 277
Kalepar, 12
Kal-Seb Zarre, 277
Kalibangan, 12, 20, 23, 32, 33, 37, 43, 45, 51, 52, 65, 66, 70, 72, 85, 91, 115, 120, 125, 127, 128, 130, 131, 136, 161, 182, 183, 189, 205, 206, 208, 211, 213, 215, 216, 217, 223, 229, 235, 237, 239, 273, 275, 276, 297, 298, 321 322, 326, 327, 328, 329, 337, 338, 354, 362, 392, 397, 419, 420, 421, 422, 423; cemetary at, 298; Culture, 115–116; Fabric D, 158; Ware, 118
Kalibangan I, 24, 52, 115, 130, 136, 151, 154, 163, 187, 347; Fabric B, 187; Fabric D, 187; Pre-Harappan, 136
Kalibangan II Ware, 26
Kamalia, 263
Kamalia Plain, 248
Kaminabjuju, 369, 370
Kama Sutaria, 353
Kanahan Nadi, 142
Kandahar, 11, 275, 277
Kandla, 200
Kanewal, 169, 170, 171, 172, 174, 353
Kangra, 263
Kanakaria vago, 169
Kantali River, 128, 130
Kapalmochan, 114
Kapisa, 407
Kara Depe, 63
Karachi, 107, 108, 109, 200
Karadagh 278, 280
Karakoram, 275
Karatau range, 276
Karnal District, 245
Karnataka, 11, 274, 275, 278, 357
Karbatika, 167
Kasaunti, 128, 130
Kashan Kohund, 277
Kashmir, 168, 189, 218, 250, 263, 390, 392
Kashmir Valley, 189, 248
Kasi, 57
Kathi, 406
Kathiawad, 7, 9, 282, 357; plateaus of, 7
Kathiawar, 275
Katpalon, 54, 158, 163, 185, 193, 347, 353

Katukan, 392
Katun, 376
Katun Cycle, 376, 378
Kausambi, 138, 335, 336, 337
Kausambi IA, 136
Kautilya, 167
Kawend, 275
Kayatha, 128, 353, 357
Kazakhstan, 11, 276, 277
Keji Valley, 391
Kennedy, Kenneth, 418
Kerano Munjan Valley, 273
Kerasi, 201
Kesarising's Khetar mound, 170
Khadir, 198, 199, 200, 201
Khafaje, 281
Khairpur, 129
Khandesh, 174
Khaparda, 170
Kharan, 391
Khari, 131
Khetri, 9, 129, 277, 281
Khetri Belt, 24, 129, 130, 281
Khetri-Singhana source, 92
Khira District, 169
Khirasara, 198, 201
Khlopin, I.N., 63
Kho-Dariba, 277
Khodjent, 273, 280
Khorasan, 11, 278, 280
Khorashthi, 311
Khu-i Nugre, 276
Khurab, 392
Khusu, 392
Khuzistan, 62
Kidder, A.V., 375
Kili Ghul Mohammad II Style, 83
Kili Ghul Mohammad III Style, 83
Kim, 7
Kinderkhera, 353
Kindred, 389
Kirnan, 273, 274, 276, 277, 280, 281
Kirthar, 3, 11
Kirthar Range, 5, 20, 113, 389
Kish, 136, 245, 266, 267, 411
Knobbed Ware, 138
Kodekal, 280
Kohistan, 5, 7, 11, 107, 111, 275, 388, 397
Kohtras, 389
Kokcha River, 273, 280
Kolar mines, 275, 276
Koldihwa, 219
Kopet Dagh mountains, 63
Kopet Dagh rivers, 56
Koppal, 357
Kori Creek, 35, 197
Kosal, 57
Kosala, 57
Kot Diji, 23, 32, 33, 42, 43, 46, 65, 66, 70, 91, 116, 129, 136, 158, 161, 171, 326,

328, 347, 397, 421; Pre-Harappan, 136
Kot Diji Culture, 418
Kot Diji I, 151
Kot Dijian Ware, 90
Kot Dijians, 234
Kota-Maholi, 131
Kotada-Bhadli, 353
Kotada Dholavira, 198, 199, 200, 201
Kothara, 198
Kotla Nihang, 24, 141, 162, 419
Kotla Nihang Khan, 23, 141, 190, 323, 347
Kotputli, Tehsil, 125
Kotri, 7
Kounrad, 277
Krishni, 339
Kuba, 171
Kundwala, 12, 93, 94, 392
Kuh Banan, 278
Kuh-i-Baba, 275
Kulhade-Ka-Johad, 128
Kulli, 271, 389, 391
Kulli Culture, 392
Kulli-Harappan symbiosis, 102
Kumaon, 277
Kumar, G.D., 291
Kumar, 275
Kundol, 274
Kurada, 129, 131
Kurnool District, 357
Kurram River, 5
Kurukshetra, 163, 347; District, 158, 191, 215, 248
Kurus, 314
Kushan, Dynasty, 407; Period, 185, 189, 409; pottery, 189; Ware, 185
Kutch, 7, 9, 35, 36, 168, 174, 197, 198, 199, 200, 201, 229, 273, 282, 353, 357, 358, 398; Central, 198; District of, 34
Kutch-Kathiawad coasts, 12
Kyzyl Kum, 273, 275, 277, 279, 280
Kyzyl Kum desert, 280

Ladakh, 5, 34
Ladgaon, 175
Lagash, 275
Laghman, 275
Lahor and Multan Railway, 407
Lak Phusi, 11
Lakhabaval, 170, 353, 357
Lakhapar, 201
Lakhmirwala, 12
Lakhpat, 35, 217
Lal, B.B., 25, 85, 392, 397
Lal Qila, 394
Lamberg-Karlovsky, C.C., 364
Lambrick, H.T., 217, 228, 322
LANCE sign, 314
LANCE-BEARER sign, 315
Langhanaj, 171
Lapis lazuli, 9, 11, 22, 48, 82, 83, 119, 142,

Index

174, 193, 263, 266, 271–273, 275, 276, 278, 279, 280
Larkana, 19, 261, 387; District, 405
Las, plain of, 5
Las Bela, 107, 392
Late Baran Culture, 158, 162–163
Late Baran plus Painted Gray Ware Culture, 158, 163
Late Bronze Age Cities, 56
Late Chalcolithic Culture, 63
Late Classic Maya Society, 371
Late Classic Period, 375, 377
Late Harappan, 23, 163, 425; ceramics, 49; Civilization, 354; cultural development 42; Culture, 9, 49, 56, 177, 182, 193, 194, 322, 338, 354, 357, 358; Degenerate, 92; Period, 92–93, 94, 199, 366, 425, 426; Phase, 37, 38, 49, 93, 180, 181, 185, 205, 354, 355, 356, 357, 358; Red Ware, 180, 185, 189, 193; settlements, 53, 93, 175, 353; sites, 52, 53, 93, 190, 198, 227, 245, 254–256, 348, 355, 357, 358, 398; Ware, 190, 193, 357
Late Harappans, 51, 52, 189, 190, 191, 192, 217, 323, 355, 357, 358, 426; food economy of, 214–215
Late Pleistocene Period, 175
Late Siswal Ware, 118
Late Stone Age, 292; Culture, 172; Microlithic Culture, 70; site, 171
Later Chalcolithic Culture, 135
Lathyrus odoratus, 135
Latin America, 234
Latyayana Srauta Sutra, 114
Lead, 46, 271, 275, 276, 281, 396
Lecromina croix, 174
Leiah, 17
Lentil, 183, 215
Lewis, James, 406
Limboli, Taluka, 168
Limo Junejo, 387
Lingas, 235
Lithic artifacts, 46
Lithophiles, 233
Little Ice Age, 244
Little Rann, 9, 34, 200, 201
Lohri, 388
Lokha, 274
Long barrel-cylinder beads, 265, 266, 267, 268
Loralai, 391
Lothal, 7, 11, 12, 19, 32, 33, 36, 43, 51, 53, 71, 72, 117, 127, 136, 168, 171, 172, 182, 183, 198, 200, 201, 205, 206, 207, 215, 217, 227, 229, 239, 273, 275, 276, 277, 278, 289, 293, 298, 321, 322, 353, 354, 355, 357, 398, 419, 422, 424
Lothal B., 55, 122, 355, 356, 357
Lothal Domain, 20
Lothal II, 422

Lower Town, 100, 103
Lowland Classic Period, 369
Lubaantum, 369
Ludhiana, 190, 248; District, 154, 158, 192, 245
Luhumjodaro, 387
Lukacs, J.R., 293, 306
Luna, 353
Luni, 7, 131, 200
Lurewala, 93
Lustrous Red Ware, 56
Lustrous Red Ware Culture, 354
Lyari hills, 111

Mackay, Ernest, 97, 236, 239, 242, 265, 266, 396, 411
Madhya Pradesh, 168, 275, 281, 357
Madhyadesh, 57, 335
Magadha, 57
Mahabharata, 56, 114, 226
Mahadevan, I., 99
Mahajanapadas, 56, 57, 69
Maharashtra, 168, 175, 180, 199, 219, 278, 306
Maheswere, 172
Mahi, 7, 9
Maize, 215
Majumdar, N.G., 387, 388, 389, 390, 397
Makain, 277
Makran, 9, 12, 391, 392
Makran Baluchistan, 11
Makran coast, 199, 200, 273, 322
Malaria, 374
Maler Kotla, 158
Malhar Rann, 225
Malhera, 349
Malir Basin, 111
Malir River, 5, 107, 110
Malir system, 110
Mallinath, 199
Malvan, 169, 170, 174
Malwa, 179; Culture, 177, 322, 337; Ware, 176, 177, 178, 365
MAN sign, 315
Manava Dharma Sastra, 114
Manchar Lake, 5, 7, 12, 388
Manda, 11, 23, 24, 34, 141, 185, 189, 190, 248, 263, 347, 353, 357, 398
Maner, 137
Mangalasutra, 239
Manjhi, 137
Manot, 12
Manpur, 349
Margiana, 57
Mari, 274
Markanda, 7
Marot, 226
Marshall, Sir John, 97, 129, 235, 236, 237, 281, 327, 365, 395, 396, 408, 409, 411
Marwar, 171

Mashkai-Jhalwan area, 223
Maski, 280, 357
Masson Charles, 31, 395, 406, 407
Mathooka, 128
Matsya Desa, 125
Matsyanyaya, 174
"Mature Harappan", 425
Mature Harappan, ceramics, 44; cultural development, 42; cultural complex, 42, 43; culture, 235, 354, 422; gridiron layout, 45; material, 24; material culture, 43, 44, 45, 46; period, 92, 93, 94, 189, 237, 418, 419, 421, 424; phase, 38, 49, 355, 356, 357; settlements, 45, 201, 235, 347, 353; sites, 7, 15, 43, 44, 46, 48, 53, 54, 84, 93, 198, 235, 236, 245, 348, 357, 419, 425; urban sites, 43
Mature Harappans, 24, 354
Mature Indus, Civilization, 65, 332; Culture, 116–120, 235, 237; site, 245
Mature Urban Culture, 327
Mauryan Empire, 167
Mauryan Period, 409
Maya, 368, 371, 372, 373, 375, 376, 378, 379, 424; low land, 368, 369, 370, 372, 373, 374, 376, 377, 378; southern, 369
Maya Civilization, 367, 368, 369, 372, 373, 374
Maya Classic, 368
Mazanderan, 273
Meadow, Richard, 82
Medieval Historic site, 49
Mediterranean, eastern, 291
Mediterranean Region, 72
Meerut, 398; District, 136, 346, 349
Meggers, B.J., 375
Mehgam, 168, 353, 357
Mehi, 271, 277, 389, 391
Mehrgarh, 57, 79, 81, 82, 83, 84, 273, 274, 280, 418, 423, 425
Mehrgarh Mound Three, 82, 83
Mehrgarh VI, 274
Mehta, R.N., 236, 237
Melanesia, 290, 302
Melechha, 17, 65, 273, 275, 278, 280, 281, 282, 322, 364
Meshad, 275, 277
Meso-America, 290, 369, 373, 376, 377
Mesolithic Culture, 233
Mesopotamia, 3, 22, 23, 41, 43, 48, 61, 62, 65, 66, 67, 79, 263, 266, 267, 268, 271, 273, 277, 278, 280, 281, 290, 326, 396, 399, 411, 419; southern, 62, 410
Mesopotamian seal, 65
Mesopotamians, 322
Mexican Gulf Coast, 369, 370
Mexico, 367, 369, 370; Central, 368
Micaceous Red Ware, 201, 279, 357
Middle Classic hiatus, 376, 377
Middle Harappan Phase, 37

Middle Pre-Classic Period, 369
Mihran of Sind, 5
Millet, 419
Minoan antiquities, 410
Mirador, 370
Mirpur Khas Stupa, 405, 410
Mirzapur, 118, 163, 347, 353
Mitathal, 12, 25, 33, 52, 115, 116, 122, 129, 135, 347, 349, 353, 398
Mitathal I, 24
Mitathal IIA, 347
Mitathal IIB, 26, 52, 54, 121, 162, 337, 347
Mithankot, 5
Mithrau, 129
Moghal Ghundai, 391
Moh Scale, 239, 241, 242
Mohammad of Gazni, 35
Mohenjodaro, 12, 15, 17, 19, 22, 32, 33, 43, 44, 45, 46, 47, 51, 53, 54, 71, 72, 92, 97, 100, 102, 104, 111, 115, 127, 129, 136, 137, 141, 162, 171, 182, 198, 205, 207, 208, 215, 218, 223, 228, 229, 235, 236, 245, 248, 250, 261, 263, 265, 266, 268, 273, 274, 275, 276, 277, 278, 280, 281, 289, 291, 293, 302, 304, 305, 321, 322, 327, 328, 329, 330, 332, 335, 337, 353, 354, 357, 362, 365, 387, 388, 395, 396, 397, 399, 405, 409, 410, 411, 412, 418, 419, 420, 421, 422, 423, 425; DK Area of, 44, 100, 103, 396; DK-B Area of, 99; DK-I Area of, 99; HR Area of, 99, 100, 102, 103; SD Area, 396; VS Area of, 99, 103
Mohenjodaro Domain, 20
Mohenjodaro excavation, 46
Molnar, S. 301
Moneer, Q.M., 97
Moneer site, 15, 97, 99, 100
Mongoloid skull, 289
Montogomery District, 206, 261
Mora, 35, 217, 274
Mohra, 274
Motagua fault, 374
Motagua, River, 378; Valley, 371
Mount Abu, 37
Mughal, M. Rafique, 15, 20, 65, 102, 119, 418
Mula, 3
Mula Pass, 11, 261
Multan, 7, 263
Mundan, 35
Mundhan, 217
Mundigak, 48, 54, 63, 84, 206, 215, 280, 282
Mundigak II, 205
Mundigak III, 274
Mundore Fort, 35
Mundra, 198, 200
Mung, 215
Murgab Valley, 52

Muruntau mountains, 275, 280
Musa Khel, 17
Musai, 277
Mushkat, 3
Muzaffarnagar, 53; District, 346
Mysore, 279, 280, 281, 282

Nadi, 114
Nagar, 54, 158, 163, 185, 193, 347; District, 225
Nagara, 172
Nagaur, 129; District, 131
Nahli, 349
Nai, 114, 130
Nai Gaj, 389
Naitandava, 37
Naiwal, 5
Najafgarh Lake, 130
Nakhatrana Taluka, 198
Nakhlak, 276
Nal, 271, 387, 388, 389, 391
Nal Culture, 392
Namazga Depem, 51, 63
Namazga III, 63
Namazga III/Geoksyurian Cultural Complex, 64
Namazga V, 63, 276, 423
Namazga V–VI, 425
Namazga VI, 56, 423
Namazga VI pottery, 57
Namazga VI times, 52
Nandlalpura, 131
Nar, 168
Nara, 228; eastern, 226
Nari, 5
Narmada, 7, 9, 10
Narmini, 37
Narnaul, 129
Narwana, 52
Navadatoli, 57, 128, 135, 136, 336
Navinal, 198, 201
Nayabans, 339
Neem-ka-Thana, 129; Sub Treasury at, 125; Tehsil, 128
Negritoid skull, 289
Neolithic Brzahomians, 218
Neolithic Chirand, 138; culture, 135, 218; deposits, 82, 83; food economy, 218; people, 189, 219, 274, 323; Period I, 90
Nesh, 277
Netra Khirsara, 353
Nevasa, 306
Niai Buthi, 392
Nickel, 9, 281
Nilgai, 173, 174
Nindowari, 102
Nippur, 245
Nisanta Pranadhih, 167
Nishapur, 274, 275, 279, 280
Noh, 125, 349

Northern Black Polished Ware, 335, 336, 339; period, 336
Northern Tropical Thorn Forest, 34
North West Frontier Province (NWFP), 234
Northwest Frontier, 17, 19
Nowsharo, 11, 12, 84
Nundara, 389, 391

Ochre Colored Pottery (OCP), 25, 26, 33, 125, 129–130, 281, 348, 349; complex, 56; food economy of, 218; sites, 53, 136, 218; Ware culture, 218, 219
Ochre Colored Ware, 191, 323, 345, 346
Ohio River Valley, 301
Okhamandel, 35
Olinec, 369
Oman, 9, 277, 281
Onaur, 336
Orangi, 109
Orissa, 276
Oxus Basin, 11
Oxus River, 48, 65, 280, 322, 390
Oxus system, 56

Pabumath, 198, 200, 201, 353
Padhegaon, 175
Painted Black on Red Ware, 391
Painted Gray Ware (PGW), 25, 33, 93, 122, 125, 130, 163, 188, 189, 190, 192, 193, 248, 336, 339, 347, 357, 425; complex, 56; culture, 38, 157, 158, 163, 194, 335, 337, 338, 347; people, 191, 323, 342, 343, 346; phase, 185; settlements, 94, 344; sites, 130, 190, 249, 250–254
Painted Gray Ware/NBP occupations, 26
Pakistan, 79, 85, 92, 93, 94, 101, 128, 162, 192, 197, 206, 223, 226, 237, 245, 271, 274, 290, 293, 326, 354, 398, 405, 407
Pasepattan, 263, 406
Palampur, 278
Pale Bichrome Ware, 388
Paleo-Mongolid skull, 289
Pallavas, 314
Pamirs, 273
Panchavisma Brahman, 114
Panchinad, 5, 17, 19
Pandi Wahi, 11, 12, 54, 388, 389
Pandu Rajar Dhibi, 137
Panicum, 214
Panicum miliaceum, 215
Panicum sumatrense, 215
Panipat, 52
Panjsher Valley, 276
Par River, 9
Parbatsar-Kurada, 129
Parpola A., 99
Parthia, 57
Parthian Period, 423

Index

Paspalum serobiculatum, 215
Pathiani Kot, 261
Patiala, 190, 226; District, 245, 248
Patialvi, 7
Pea (*Pisum arvense* L.), 206, 215
Pehoa, 114
Peloponnesian Wars, 376
Pennisetum typhoides, 216
Periano, A. 90
Periano Ghundai, 90, 391
Persepolis, 267
Persian Gulf, 17, 113, 200, 201, 271, 326
Peten Central, 372
Phalodi, 36, 129
Phragmites Karka, 214
Pidaria, 170
Piedras Negras, 375
Pig, 173, 174, 396
Piggott, Stuart, 135, 223, 364, 399
Pikhami, 348
Piklihal, 280
Pind Padliya, 130
Pindi Wahi, 271
Pine (*Pinus roxburghii*), 11
Pir Panjal Range, 185
Pir Shah Jurio, 107, 109
Pisum, 218
Pisum arvense, 208, 213
Plain Gray Ware, 192
Plasmodia, 291
Pokaran, 129
Pokurna, 35
Polygonum spp., 214
Polynesia, 290
Porabander, 9
Porali Basin, 111
Porali River, 5
Possehl, G.L., 228, 348
Post-Akkadian Period, 267
"Post-Harappan", 425
Post-Harappan, Chalcolithic Culture, 136; Chalcolithic sites, 57; Culture, 33, 34, 70, 135, 183, 240, 346; Lustrous Red Ware Culture, 398; Period, 93, 326, 422; technological period, 168
Post-Indus culture, 115
"Post-Urban", 425
Post-Urban Phase, 25
Potwar Plateau, 245
Prabhas, 198, 353
Prabhas Ware, 33, 56
Prakash, 215
Pravara, 175, 177, 322, 361, 398
Pre-Classic Period, 368, 369
Pre-Dravidian skull, 289
Pre-Defense Harappa, 151, 154, 161, 187, 347; Ware, 121
"Pre-Harappan", 425
Pre-Harappan Bara pottery, 54
Pre-Harappan, Culture, 33, 71, 79, 130, 158, 161, 163, 337, 346; food economy, 206; genre, sites of, 12; phase, 38, 209; pottery, 158, 187, 189; Red Ware, 187; settlements, 32, 327, 397; sites, 7, 12, 51, 129, 245, 257-258, 392, 398; technological period, 168; Ware, 190
Pre-Harappans, 33, 189, 205, 338, 426
Pre-historic sites, 17
Pre-Indus Culture, 115-116
"Pre-Late Harappan", 426
Pre-pottery Microlithic Culture, 398
Pre-Sargonic Period, 267
Pre-Urban Harappan phenomenon, 24
Proto-Australoid skull, 289, 302
Proto-Elamite material inventory, 62
Proto-Elamites, 64
Proto-historic Culture, Chalcolithic stage of, 70
Proto-Mediterranean skull, 289
Proto-Nordic skull, 289
Pseudo-Alpine skull, 289
Pugal, 131
Punjab, 5, 7, 11, 12, 15, 17, 23, 25, 52, 54, 56, 57, 70, 92, 93, 113, 118, 128, 129, 130, 135, 158, 162, 168, 185, 188, 189, 190, 192, 208, 215, 216, 218, 223, 236, 241, 263, 279, 282, 291, 323, 329, 330, 331, 332, 336, 346, 347, 348, 349, 353, 354, 358, 392, 396, 398, 399, 405, 412, 422, 423; East, 20, 92, 327; lowlands, 17; rural, 118; southern, 216; south-western; 261; West, 17, 20, 280
Puran, 35
Pranas, 56
Puras, 37
Puri, K.N., 97
Purna River, 9
Pusalapadu, 274
Pushkar, 225
Putun Maya, 377
Pyorrhea alveolaris, 305

Quetta, 161
Quetta Valley, 84
Quirigua, 369, 371, 374, 376, 378

Ragi, 215, 216, 218
Rahimar Khan District, 90
Rahman Dheri, 11, 12, 54, 66, 84, 90, 91, 237, 271, 273, 275, 280
Raichur District, 357
Raikes, Robert L., 104, 223, 226, 292, 322
Raja Karam-ka-Qila, 141, 337
Raja Sirkap, 158, 161
Rajasthan, 5, 11, 19, 24, 26, 35, 36, 52, 70, 92, 122, 128, 130, 132, 168, 171, 200, 208, 216, 223, 224, 225, 226, 241, 273, 274, 275, 276, 277, 278, 280, 281, 322, 353, 358, 397; eastern, 219, 347; northern, 23, 24, 25, 93, 114, 120, 218, 227, 248, 250, 279, 244; southern, 214; West, 34; Western, 227
Rajasthan desert, 35, 37, 215, 216, 218, 327
Rajgarh, 129
Rajghat, 336
Rajkot district, 53, 56
Rajpipla, 275, 282
Rakhigarhi, 35, 115, 161, 264, 323, 398
Ramavaram, 357
Ramayana, 56
Rana Ghundai, 391
Rang Mahal People, 53
Rangoi, 114
Rangpur, 32, 33, 36, 72, 135, 136, 168, 183, 198, 201, 207, 215, 217, 353, 354, 355, 356, 357, 398, 419
Rangpur IIA, 199
Rangpur IIB, 355, 356, 419, 422
Rangpur IIB-C, 55, 199
Rangpur IIC, 122, 199, 355, 356, 419
Rangpur III, 122, 419
Rangpur Period IIA *see* Rangpur IIA
Rangpur Period II C *see* Rangpur IIC
Rann of Kutch, 7, 113, 131, 197, 198, 199, 200, 226
Rao, S.R., 177, 288, 364, 398
Ratanpur, 282
Rathji, W.L., 375, 377
Ratnagar, Dr. S., 19
Ravi, 7, 17, 52, 141, 158, 245, 245, 248, 261, 263, 395
Red Ochrewashed Ware, 336
Red Ware, 93, 125, 136, 171, 189, 191, 192, 193, 322, 357, 391; dull, 177; handmade, 121; non-Harappan, 339; site, 130
Redfied, Robert, 326
Reed, C.A., 79
Reserved Slip Ware, 171
Rewari, 129
Rhinoceros, 173, 174, 363
Ribbed Bichrome Ware, 180
Rice, 207, 208, 215, 216, 217, 218, 219, 419
Ridder, 277
Rigveda, 37, 114, 313, 330, 332, 396, 411
Robat, 281
Rohel-jo-Kund, 389
Rohri, 7, 11, 328
Rohtak, 91
Rojadi, 9
Rojdi, 198, 201, 239, 353, 356, 357
Roopnagar, 115, 121
Roopnagar I, 118
Ropar, 7, 11, 23, 54, 118, 141, 142, 143, 151, 158, 161, 162, 190, 226, 245, 263, 323, 339, 346, 347, 348, 353, 357, 398, 419
Ropar I, 151, 347

Ropar IA, 24, 151, 161
Ropar IB, 24, 151, 162
Ross, Frank E., 406
Royal Grave, 266
Rudra-Siva, 332
Rupen, 9

Sabania, 131
Sabarkanta District, 241
Sabarmati, 7, 9
Sabi River, 125, 130
Sabi Valley, 52
Sabloff, J.A., 377
Sabzwar, 277
Sahara, 35
Saharanpur, 138; District, 53, 136, 339, 346
Sahera, 217
Sahni, Rai Bahadur Daya Ram, 409
Said Qala Tepe, 48, 64
Sai-no-tekro, 170, 172
Saipai, 26, 349
Sali, S.A., 322
Sālivāhana, 314, 315
Salt Range, 245
Samarangana Sutradhara, 174
Samarkand, 278, 280
Sambhar Lake, 37, 52
Sanduman, Fort, 274, 281
Sandhanawala, 12
Sandstone, 9
Sangala, 406, 407
Sanghol, 24, 54, 122, 151, 154, 161, 163, 349
Sanghol IA, 118, 121
Sanghol IB, 54, 120, 121
Sangrahamis, 167
Sangramikam, 167
Sangrar, 129, 190
Sangrur, 245
Sankalia, Prof. H.D., 57, 236
Sappali-Dashly, pottery, 57; sites, 56
Sarai Khola, 12, 17, 46, 65, 90, 271, 326, 347
Sarai Khola II, 151, 154
Saran District, 135
Sarangpur, 158, 161
Sarasvati, 5, 7, 9, 23, 24, 25, 37, 93, 94, 113, 114, 158, 163, 191, 226, 263, 392, 397; Basin, upper, 72, 397, 398; Valley, 12, 52, 114, 218, 261, 263, 323, 327
Sarasvati-Drishadvati, 248; Valley, 323
Sarawan, 391
Sari-i-Sang, 273
Sarvistan, 392
Satapatha Brahmana, 130, 297, 313
Sātavāhana, 314, 315
Satterthwaite, L., 375
Saudi Arabia, 274, 277; Western, 274
Saurashtra, 9, 35, 122, 170, 171, 174, 197, 198, 200, 201, 279, 322, 327, 346, 348, 353, 357, 358, 419, 422; Central, 168, 357
Savalda, 9; Culture, 177; Ware, 177, 322
Sawai Madhopur, District, 131
Seytho-Dravidian skull, 289
Sea shells, 83
Sedges, 214
Segak Mound, 277
Sehore, 241
Sehwan, 388, 397
Seibal, 369, 370, 377, 378
Seistan, 11, 64, 93, 275, 282, 389
Serahs, 63
Sesame (*Sesamum indicum*), 206, 216
Setaria, 214, 215, 217
Setaria italica, 214, 216
Setaria glauca, 216
Sewell, R.B.S., 302
Shaffer, Jim, 111, 279, 419
Shaga-Darra-i-Robat-i-Paskaran, 273
Shah Bellual, 281
Shah Maqsud, 277
Shah Rud, 278
Shahdad, 83, 274, 275
Shahi Tump, 271, 277, 391
Shahiwala, 93
Shahr-i-Sokhta, 48, 51, 52, 63, 64, 83, 84, 273, 274, 275, 279, 280, 282
Shahr-i-Sokhta II, 274
Shamlaji, 172
Shang settlements, 405
Sharer, Robert, 424
Sharma, G.B., 163
Sharma, G.R., 335, 336
Sharma, Y.D., 54, 120, 347, 398, 419
Shatrana, 226
Sheep, 173, 396
Shorkote, 407
Shortugai, 11, 48, 65, 66, 273, 276, 278, 424; sites, 17
Shri Ganganagar, 34
Shrirampur Taluka, 175
Siah Damb, 277
Siah Damb Nundara, 391
Sialk *see* Tepe Silk
Siberia, 275; eastern, 273
Siddhuwala Ther, 92
Sikar-Jhunjhunu, area, 129; District, 130
Silver, 46, 239, 271, 276, 396
Simashki, 62
Simla, 263
Sind, 5, 7, 9, 11, 12, 35, 49, 52, 92, 109, 122, 136, 174, 197, 198, 199, 200, 201, 206, 207, 208, 215, 216, 237, 261, 279, 280, 282, 291, 322, 323, 326, 346, 362, 363, 387, 388, 389, 392, 396, 397, 399, 405, 417, 423
Sind Kohistan, 3

Sindri, 35
Singanapalli, 274
Singhana, 277
Sinha, K.K., 336
Sirhind Nadi, 7
Sirhind, 226
Sirsa, 142; District of, 114
Siswal, 12, 24, 25, 52, 116, 130, 135, 154, 347, 353; Complex, 23, 26; Ware, 26
Siswal A, 24,
Siswal B, 24, 158
Siswal IIB, 191
Siswal LLB, 337
Śiva-Mahadeva, 332, 358
Śiva-Pasupati, 332
Sivirights, Robert, 199
Siwaliks, 5, 7, 114, 263, 392
Skandhavaras, 167
Slavs, 396
Smallpox, 374
Smriti code, 72
Soghun Valley, 274
Somnath, 33, 168, 356
Sonari-Jodhpur, 130
Sonepur, 137
Sorghum, 216, 219
Sota River, 128, 130
Sothi, 23, 42, 43, 52, 130, 161; Culture, 418
Sothi-Bhadra, 129
Sotkakoh, 201, 278
Sottar, 5
Sottar Valley, 114
South Asian population, 301
Soviet Central Asia, 51, 52, 53, 56, 63, 271, 274, 275, 277, 278, 279, 280
Soviet Union *see* USSR
Spartans, 396
Spear heads, 127
Spiral-headed Pins, 128
Sravasti, 336
Sri Lanka, 290
Sringaverpura, 336
Stacul, Georgio, 299
Steatite, 11, 142, 159, 174, 239, 241, 242, 263, 271, 274, 275, 279, 323; beads, 138, 358; seals, 118; source, 281; telcose, 241, 243
Stein, Aurel, 15, 85, 92, 223, 388, 390, 391, 392, 397
Steward, Julian, 411
Stupa Mound, 103; SD Area of, 100
Sthaniya, 167
Suasti, 239
Sukhar Rohri, 129
Sukkur, 7, 11
Sukkur Barrage, 52
Sulaiman ranges, 3, 5, 19, 113, 245, 248
Sulaiman-Kirthar ranges, 111
Sulemanki Weir, 5

Index

Sumer, 61, 63, 64, 65, 66, 67, 268, 424
Sumerian, antiquities, 410, 411; Civilization, 268; economic documents, 17; groups, 23; language, 311
Sumerians, 62, 64, 271, 274, 278, 405
Sunga-Kushan Ware, 339
Sur, Sher Shah, 114
Sur Jangal, 391
Suratgarh, 226
Surkotada, 32, 33, 37, 44, 71, 72, 172, 198, 199, 201, 205, 214, 215, 217, 218, 273, 328, 346, 353, 398, 419, 421, 422
Susa, 61, 62, 63, 245, 267, 355
Susiana, 62, 79
Sutkagendor, 11, 12, 72, 201, 273, 278, 391, 392, 421
Sutlej, 5, 7, 23, 24, 25, 85, 94, 141, 142, 154, 158, 161, 163, 226, 229, 245, 248, 261, 263, 392,
Sutlej Basin, 54, 323
Sutlej Valley, 129, 344, 346, 348, 349, 357
Sutlej-Harappan Complex, 158
Sutluj *see* Sutlej
Swat Valley, 248, 299, 391
Syr Darya, 274, 280
Syria, 281

Tadjikistan, 57
Taittiriya Brahmana, 37
Takalik 369
Takht-i-Suleiman, 275
Taklamakan, 391
Tal-i Ghazir, 62
Tal-i Iblis, 277, 392
Tal-i Malyan, 62
Tal-i Pir, 392
Tal-i Regi, 392
Tal-i Skau, 392
Taldjen River, 275
Tamarindus indicus, 35
Tapi, River, 169, 170, 174; Basin, 175, 183
Tapti, 7, 9; Valley, 175, 176, 182, 322, 323; lower, 9
Tapti-Godavari Valley, 353
Tatarpur Kalan, 348
Taxila, 57, 245, 326, 411
Taxila Valley, 91
Tedzen Delta, 63, 64
Tel Asmar seals, 65
Tell Agrale, 267, 268
Telod, 168
Temba Bulach, 277
Teotihuacan, 369, 370, 371, 377
Tepe Hissar, 423
Tepe Sialk, 62, 63, 424
Tepe Yahya, 22, 48, 62, 64, 65, 66, 267, 268, 274, 275, 424
Tezin, 277
Thal Desert, 245
Thanesar-Kurukshetra, 114

Thano Bulla Khan Road, 107
Thapar, B.K., 85, 223, 336, 392, 397
Thar Desert, 3, 5, 20, 24, 94, 113
Thar Parker, 174
Thatta, 7
Thick Burnished Gray Ware, 188, 248
Thick Coarse Red Ware, 177
Thick Coarse Ware, 180, 181
Thick Gray Ware, 339, 342
Thompson, Sir Eric, 375, 377
Tidi, 131
Tigris, 22, 64
Tikal, 369, 370, 371, 372, 374, 375, 376, 377, 378
Tikrial, 17
Timur, 406
Tin, 9, 11, 48, 271, 275, 277–278, 280, 396
Tintini, 357
Tiran mountains, 275
Tiz-Lasbela, 11
Tochi River, 5
Todio, 353
Togau style, 83
Togau B style, 83
Togau D style, 83
Toltec, 376
Toolumba, 407
Traghda, 198
Transition Phase, 354, 355, 357
Trench RPR-1, 151, 154
Tripathi, Dr. K.K., 127
Tripuri, 172
Triticum aestivum, 206, 208, 215
Triticum aestivum L., 207
Triticum compactum, 206, 207
Triticum compactum Host, 207
Triticum sphaerococcum, 206, 207, 208, 213, 215, 216, 217
Triticum sphaerococcum Perc., 208
Triticum vulgare, 206, 207
Turan, 66, 67
Turkistan 22; eastern, 11
Turkmenia, 51, 57, 423; South, 56, 57, 63, 64
Turquoise, 9, 11, 82, 83, 271, 273–274, 282
Turkmenistan, 424
Turko-Iranian skull, 289

USSR, 113, 275; southern, 398
Uaxactum, 369
Udaipur, 11; District, 130, 131
Ulug Depe, 63
Unchadih, 336
Unchravritti, 174
Unslipped Ware, 349
Ur, 65, 66, 266, 267, 268, 281; Third Dynasty of, 267, 322
Ural, 275
"Urban", 425

Urban Harappan society, 162
Urban Harappans, 24
Urd, 215
Uruk, 61, 62
Utpuria, 131
Uttar Pradesh 12, 20, 26, 34, 53, 56, 57, 129, 135, 163, 168, 216, 218; Western, 23, 25, 53, 93, 125, 128, 130, 215, 218, 323, 336, 347, 348, 349, 353, 358, 398, 422

Vadgam, 168
Vaged, 198
Vainiwal, 261
Vaishnavism, 331
Vanprasthas, 174
Varanus, 173
Vasishtha, 313
Vasudeva I, 410
Vats, Pandit Madho Swarup, 15, 55, 141, 168, 396, 411
Vatsa, 57
Veddoid skull, 289
Vellālar, 316
Venivadar, 357
Verstappan, H.T., 225
Vigna mungo, 215
Vinayadhikarana, 167
Vindhyas, 113
Vrijii, 57
Vyarna, 37

Wahinda, 5,
Water buffalo, 363
Waziristan, 391
Webb, M.C., 375
West Asian language, 311
West Bengal, 137, 237
Western Ghats, 20
Western highlands, 3
Wheat, 111, 183, 206, 207, 213, 215, 216, 217, 218, 419
Wheat grain, modern, 207
Wheeler, Sir Mortiner, 22, 64, 79, 97, 101, 223, 236, 291, 397, 411
White microbeads, 239, 241, 242
White Painted Black and Red Ware, 214, 218, 240, 398
Wild Grass, 214
Willey, G.R., 377
Woodland-Mississippian Culture, 290
Wolley, Sir Leonard, 266
Wynaad, 275

Xunantunich, 374

Yaha *see* Tepe Yaha
Yamuna, 5, 12, 92, 114, 130, 226, 229, 245, 248, 337, 357
Yamuna Nagar, 52

Yamuna Valley, 52, 346, 347, 348, 349
Yaxchilan, 371
Yazd, 274, 280
Yazman, 91, 94
Yellow Fever, 374
Yucatan, 372, 376

Yucatan Peninsula, 367, 370, 372, 377

Zahedan, 276
Zawar mines, 280
Zekda, 168, 170, 171, 172, 174, 239, 240, 241, 353, 357

Zhob, District, 274; River, 5; Valley, 90, 161, 263, 391
Zupadi parnakuti, 170
Zyzyphus jujuba Mill, 206
Zyzyphus mauritiana Lam., 206
Zyzyphus nummularia, 206